CRISIS, ABSOLUTISM, REVOLUTION

EUROPE 1648–1789

About the Cover   Engraving by Noël Lemire, "The Cake of Kings." This contemporary print is an allegorical representation of the First Partition of Poland in 1772. (See pp. 330–333.) The outer figures demanding their share are Catherine II of Russia and Frederick II of Prussia. The inner figure on the right is the Hapsburg Emperor Joseph II, who appears ashamed of his action. On his left is the beleaguered Polish king, Stanislaus Poniatowski, who is experiencing difficulty keeping his crown on his head. Above the scene the angel of peace trumpets the news that civilized eighteenth-century sovereigns have accomplished their mission while avoiding war. Courtesy of the Staatsbibliothek Preussischer Kulturbesitz, Berlin.

CRISIS, ABSOLUTISM, REVOLUTION

EUROPE 1648–1789

Second Edition

Raymond Birn

University of Oregon

HARCOURT BRACE JOVANOVICH COLLEGE PUBLISHERS

Fort Worth   Philadelphia   San Diego   New York   Orlando   Austin   San Antonio
Toronto   Montreal   London   Sydney   Tokyo

Publisher	Ted Buchholz
Acquisitions Editor	David Tatom
Developmental Editor	Martin Lewis
Senior Project Editor	Charlie Dierker
Production Manager	Annette Dudley Wiggins
Art & Design Supervisor	John Ritland
Text and Cover Design	Pat Sloan

Library of Congress Cataloging-in-Publication Data
Birn, Raymond.
    Crisis, absolutism, revolution : Europe, 1648–1789 / Raymond Birn.
—2nd ed.
      p.   cm.
    Includes bibliographical references and index.
    1. Europe—History—1648–1789.   2. Europe—History—1789–1815.
I. Title.
    D273.B55 1992
    940.2′5—dc20   91-32048
                                                  CIP
ISBN: 0-03-053328-7

Address for Editorial Correspondence
Harcourt Brace Jovanovich College Publishers,
301 Commerce Street, Suite 3700, Fort Worth, TX 76102

Address for Orders
Harcourt Brace Jovanovich College Publishers,
6277 Sea Harbor Drive, Orlando, FL 32887
1-800-782-4479, or 1-800-433-0001 (in Florida)

Printed in the United States of America

2 3 4 5   090   9 8 7 6 5 4 3 2

PREFACE

Published in 1977, the first edition of this book expressed its indebtedness to a generation of historians whose imaginative interpretations had emphasized the social bases of early-modern Europe's political, economic, and cultural achievements. Their work, and my synthesis, sought to link familiar themes such as the development of absolutism, decline of religious authority, and even international rivalries, to the lives of groups hitherto treated condescendingly or ignored altogether.

Today, as the perceived certainties of contemporary life are challenged from all sides, familiar approaches to interpreting the past no longer are as dominant as they once were. New political and cultural histories inform our understanding in ways but dimly perceived only a few years ago. For example, late seventeenth-century European absolute monarchy—long thought to be a splendidly repressive institution born of deep social crisis—is increasingly seen in terms of day-to-day government negotiation with potentially rambunctious elites. Furthermore, looking ahead, much recent scholarship identifies precisely these aristocratic elites as unwitting inventors of the late eighteenth century's revolutionary political language.

None of this means that any one significant interpretation must necessarily cancel out another. This edition of *Crisis, Absolutism, Revolution: Europe, 1648–1789* remains sensitive to the interplay among "the people, the land, and the state" and therefore has retained the social flavor of the first edition's introductory chapters. However, I now have deepened my appreciation of early-modern political culture and perceive the supposedly placid eighteenth century as a time of unprecedented confrontation and conflict, with governments' timeworn catch-as-catch-can solutions to domestic and international problems breaking apart. In this edition I emphasize more than I did previously the impact of Europeans on the non-European world, and I underscore the communications revolution and development of print culture. As in the first edition, I try to strike a balance between chronological narrative and comparative analysis. Because the book is primarily an introduction to the period, I have kept footnotes and traditional scholarly apparatus to a minimum.

The 1977 edition stated my indebtedness to colleagues at the University of Oregon and to my friends Robert and Pat Patterson. I wish to

repeat that earlier acknowledgment and specifically mention a newer one—
to Matthew Dennis, Joseph Fracchia, Robert Haskett, Elizabeth Reis,
George Sheridan, and John Theibault. They are perceptive readers, firm
critics, wonderful colleagues. My sincere thanks also go to Richard Golden
of Clemson University, James D. Hardy, Jr., of Louisiana State University,
and Philip Hoffman of the California Institute of Technology for their
helpful and constructive review of the text. At Harcourt Brace Jovanovich,
David Tatom, Martin Lewis, and Charlie Dierker have provided me with as
much editorial compassion as professional skill, for which I am grateful.
Most important of all is an acknowledgment of another kind. I hope that
Joyce Hatch realizes how completely heartfelt one's thanks can be.

Raymond Birn   Eugene, Oregon, May 1991

CONTENTS

PART
TWO

AN AGE OF HOPE AND REVOLUTION (1715–1789) 201

MAPS

ILLUSTRATIONS

P A R T

AN AGE OF CRISIS AND DISCOVERY (1648–1715)

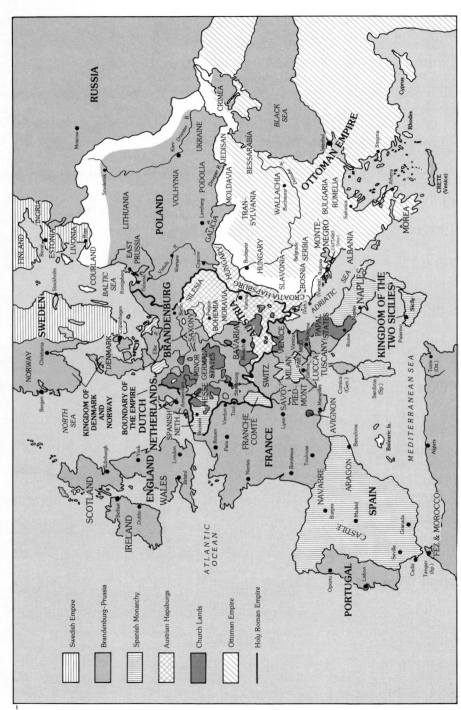

Map 1.1—Europe in 1648

Legend

- Swedish Empire
- Brandenburg-Prussia
- Spanish Monarchy
- Austrian Hapsburgs
- Church Lands
- Ottoman Empire
- Holy Roman Empire

RUSSIA

FINLAND

INGRIA

ESTONIA

LIVONIA

COURLAND

LITHUANIA

POLAND

VOLHYNIA

PODOLIA

UKRAINE

CRIMEA

BLACK SEA

OTTOMAN EMPIRE

NORWAY

SWEDEN

BALTIC SEA

EAST PRUSSIA

GALICIA

BESSARABIA

MOLDAVIA

TRAN-SYLVANIA

WALLACHIA

BULGARIA

RUMELIA

KINGDOM OF DENMARK AND NORWAY

BOUNDARY OF THE EMPIRE

DENMARK

BRANDENBURG

SILESIA

BOHEMIA

MORAVIA

HUNGARY

HUNGARY

CROATIA

SLAVONIA

BOSNIA

SERBIA

MONTE-NEGRO

ALBANIA

MOREA

CRETE (Venice)

NORTH SEA

DUTCH NETHERLANDS

SPANISH NETH.

SAXONY

MINOR GERMAN STATES

HESSE

AUSTRIA

BAVARIA

VENICE

PAPAL STATES

TUSCANY

LUCCA

KINGDOM OF THE TWO SICILIES

ADRIATIC SEA

SCOTLAND

IRELAND

ENGLAND

WALES

FRANCE

FRANCHE COMTE

SWITZ.

SAVOY

PIED-MONT

MILAN

PARMA

MOD.

AVIGNON

Corsica (Gen.)

Sardinia (Sp.)

NAPLES

Sicily

MEDITERRANEAN SEA

ATLANTIC OCEAN

NAVARRE

ARAGON

SPAIN

CASTILE

PORTUGAL

FEZ & MOROCCO

Baleanic Is.

Cyprus

Rhodes

Moscow

Smolensk

Kiev

Dnieper R.

Dniester R.

Revel

Riga

Stockholm

Christiania

Bergen

Edinburgh

York

Belfast

Dublin

London

Bristol

Rouen

Paris

Nantes

Bordeaux

Toulouse

Barcelona

Madrid

Seville

Cadiz

Tangier (Sp.)

Granada

Lisbon

Oporto

Algiers

Tunis (Ott.)

Athens

Smyrna

Salonica

Istanbul

Danube R.

Bucharest

Belgrade

Ragusa

Venice

Genoa

Rome

Naples

Palermo

Cattaro (Ven.)

Budapest

Cracow

Warsaw

Danzig

Königsberg

Copenhagen

Vistula R.

Elbe R.

Berlin

Prague

Vienna

Munich

Strasbourg

Verdun

Toul

Marseilles

Lyon

Amsterdam

Brussels

Lemberg

JEDISAN

1

THE PEOPLE, THE LAND, AND THE STATE

POPULATION

The "Long" Seventeenth Century

Between 1620 and 1720 the population of the world rose from about 460 million to about 600 million. During this same period, Europe's share of humanity rose from about 95 million to nearly 105 million. To a modern observer, painfully aware of contemporary overpopulation crises, Europe's increase of approximately 3 percent per generation seems like a model of demographic restraint. To the historian, however, aware that Europe's population had doubled in the sixteenth century and that from 1750 to 1850 it would double again, the interim period of 1620 to 1720 looks exceedingly strange. This is because the reproductive habits of people in preindustrial societies did not necessarily counsel restraint.

It is doubly surprising that during this hundred-year period, when Europeans exercised an unprecedented dominion over nature, thanks to their scientific and technological achievements, and over the non-European world, thanks to their military and commercial prowess, their demographic vigor failed to keep pace with what had gone before and with what came later. Around 1620 the dramatic population increase of the sixteenth century abruptly halted, and for the next three generations the traditionally high birthrate was accompanied by an exceptionally high death rate. Italy, Germany, the Southern Netherlands, and Spain suffered severe population losses; economically advanced England and the Northern Netherlands barely held their own. In 1620, France, Europe's most populous country, had approximately 20 million inhabitants. A century later its population hovered between 18 and 19 million. Around 1720 the European pattern started shifting again, and by 1750 births would outstrip deaths dramatically. Twice as many infants would survive their first year than had been the case only two generations earlier. Those reaching adolescence would live ten years longer than their parents had.

Food Production, Famine, and Epidemic

The nagging question remains: Why was there such an upsurge in mortality between 1620 and 1720? War and epidemic were the causes most apparent to contemporaries. Yet these were secondary factors. The primary one was Europe's extremely fragile level of agricultural productivity. For example, even Europe's great sixteenth-century population increase was halting and irregular, its cap determined by the availability of arable land and what could be produced from it. By 1620 most of Europe had reached technological limits in terms of food production, and new breakthroughs would have to await two to four generations. The harvest brutally determined population growth, and consecutive poor harvests spelled famine. Scotland knew four terrible harvests between 1695 and 1699, and it took two generations to make up a 15 percent population loss during these years. At the least, without famine, war, and epidemic, Europe's population would have stagnated during the seventeenth century. The sudden shocks provoked by these calamities propelled the longer term decline. One fact is apparent. What used to be called the splendid century, an age dazzled by the achievements of Louis XIV, Peter the Great, Descartes, and Newton, is now seen as a difficult time punctuated by brutal warfare, economic stagnation, and political instability. The consequences can be measured in sheer human losses.

For the overwhelming number of Europeans, the consequences of famine, war, and epidemic overshadowed the intellectual and material achievements of the period. The condition of the harvest wielded absolute power over the rhythm of life. In preindustrial Europe, where two-fifths of the land under cultivation had to lie fallow each year and where three-fourths of the population lived on the soil, two consecutive poor harvests, a paucity of available cereals, and the conversion of producers into purchasers, could create a vicious pattern. In town, prices would spiral dizzily, and unemployment would become widespread. The authorities then might requisition bread from another province; but interminable delays in transport, toll charges at practically every turn in the road, and a general psychological incapacity of officialdom to cope with crisis, would delay help until it was too late.

The distinguished French historian Pierre Goubert vividly describes the effects of poor harvests on a clothworker and his family in the town of Beauvais, northwest of Paris. Jean Cocu has a wife and three daughters, the youngest nine years of age. The wife and girls all work at home as spinners. The family earns 108 sols per week, and their staple diet is heavy rye bread. They consume nearly 10 pounds of it per day! With bread at one-half sol per pound, existence is normal. But with the poor harvests of 1693 and 1694, the price of bread rises to 2 and then 3 sols per pound. Piecework for the women declines drastically; Cocu is laid off. He spends his savings; then he borrows. The family must replace bread with items they scavenge: bark, cooked nettles, the entrails of slaughtered animals. Others are in competition with them for survival. Their dignity as artisans shattered, the Cocus are inscribed in the Bureau of the Poor for Beauvais. But the town officials are no more adept than they at obtaining food. The youngest is the first to succumb to malnutrition in March 1694. In May the father and eldest daughter follow. The mother and a single child are left, beggars now. The harvest of 1695 brings relief, and the pair apparently live on for a few more years. But as a productive economic unit, the Cocus are destroyed.[1]

Like Jean and his daughters, tens of thousands of producing consumers were annihilated during the seventeenth century, and their survivors were converted into drones. The human waste was enormous but tolerated. Famines usually were localized calamities. While it took one village a generation to make up its loss, its neighbor might escape unscathed. However, there were sufficient harvest disasters to slow the economic development of nearly every state in Europe.

At least once per decade, famines ignited genuine regional catastrophes by merging with bubonic and pulmonary plague, smallpox, or other diseases. Historical demographers have noted that the combination of famine and epidemic, rather than famine or epidemic alone, produced long-term calamities and more than a single generation of population loss. In such instances marriages were delayed, conceptions and consequential birthrates declined, and death rates increased. Customarily it was towns, overflowing with starving refugees from the countryside, which suffered the worst. From 1649 to 1654 famine and epidemic repeatedly struck the cities of the entire Mediterranean basin. In 1657 they returned and spread to northern Italy. From 1661 to 1671 poor harvests and epidemic battered towns in southern and central Europe; from 1676 to 1685 most of Spain's urban centers could not escape disaster. On the other hand, when epidemic unaccompanied by widespread hunger struck European cities, the wealthy and privileged fled to the safer countryside, accompanied by their baggage and servants. Recalling the plague of 1664 in London, the English writer Daniel Defoe noted that there was no litigation in the city that year; the lawyers were all in the country.

Early in the eighteenth century absolute famine disappeared from most of Europe, and improvements in sanitation and housing construction gradually rescued the west-European city dweller from at least the short-term consequences of plague-provoked epidemic. The rat that carried the contaminated flea found brick walls less congenial than timbered ones, tile roofs less penetrable than thatched ones. In England, the Dutch Netherlands, and France, townspeople dispensed with pigsties in their streets. As the eighteenth century opened, central and eastern Europe still felt the remnants of plague; in 1720 it returned to France's Mediterranean coast.

---

[1] Pierre Goubert, *Cent mille Provinciaux sous Louis XIV* (Paris, 1968).

However, that disaster turned out to be the last major plague epidemic to strike western Europe. Cojoined with famine and other infectious diseases, in its prime the plague had exacted huge tolls. As an example, the catastrophe that struck Spain between 1647 and 1652 took half a million lives.

Germany, Poland, and Spain

During the seventeenth century certain regions of Europe suffered from depopulation in such absolute terms that the consequences were considered national disasters. The three most striking examples were Germany, Poland, and Spain.

In 1648, at the conclusion of the Thirty Years' War, Germany, or the Holy Roman Empire, was the most publicized region to suffer human loss. After three decades of nearly continuous warfare, during which it served as Europe's major battlefield, Germany sank into the peace of exhaustion. In a thick band running from Strasbourg in the southwest to Stralsund in the northeast, 50 to 70 percent of the civilian population either had died or else disappeared along the refugee highways. For civilians the ravages committed by troops in winter quarters were far more severe than battlefield destruction. In the electorate of Brandenburg, counted among the war's winners, half the farms were destroyed. In Württemberg, a zone of passage rather than a theater of operations, 40,000 farms had vanished and the population fell from 450,000 to 100,000. Although rural destruction outweighed urban ruin, proud old medieval cities that had begun to stagnate in the sixteenth century—Magdeburg, Naumburg, and Augsburg, for example—were devastated by the war. Successful sieges of towns might give way to sacks, with the attendant pillage, massacre, and expulsion of inhabitants. In essence, the Thirty Years' War cost Germany 6 to 7 million lives: two-fifths of its rural population and one-fourth of its town dwellers. A population that probably had reached 16 million in 1600 was under 10 million by 1648. Only in 1750 would there again be as many Germans as had existed prior to the Thirty Years' War.

Because Germany suffered depopulation on such a catastrophic scale, most of the three-hundred-odd independent princes who controlled the states of the region thoroughly understood the dictum coined by one of them, the Elector of Brandenburg: "People are the greatest wealth of a country." In their bid to reconstruct their principalities, Frederick William of Brandenburg (1640–1688) and his fellow rulers in Hesse-Kassel, the Palatinate, and Nassau avidly sought immigrants. So did the patricians of the north coastal towns of Hamburg, Bremen, Lübeck, and Danzig, where significant refugee colonies already had settled during the war. New arrivals came from decimated regions of the country, from places where they constituted a persecuted religious minority, and from abroad. Princes courted foreign settlers, especially French Huguenots, Swiss, Dutch, Scandinavians, and Scots, to reclaim what the war had turned into frontier lands. The Hapsburg emperors invited settlement in non-German territories beyond the Carpathian mountains and in Hungary. As a result of immigration and resettlement, during the second half of the seventeenth century Germans comprised a vigorous and geographically mobile population. Although parts of western Germany, such as the Palatinate, would suffer anew from Louis XIV's wars later in the century, after 1648 the German population of central Europe began a slow process of recovery. By 1700 there were 11 to 12 million Germans. This was one-third fewer than at the outbreak of the Thirty Years' War, but it also was over a million more than during the bleakest year, 1648.

Poland was not so fortunate. What Germans had known between 1618 and 1648, Poles were to learn between 1648 and the 1720s. The failure of Polish institutions to create a political order of sufficient resilience to withstand the incursions of rapacious neighbors turned large segments of the country into battlegrounds. Overwhelmingly agrarian, Poland was the chief exporter of grain to northwestern Europe. For more than two generations, Swedes, Russians, Austrians, Saxons, and Prussians would fight over Poland's sources of production and ports of exit. When its aristocracy failed to defend the country, Poland's peasantry paid the price. Areas of tillage were reduced drastically and exports fell. A mid-seventeenth-century population of 10 million was down to 8 million at the end of the Great Northern War (1721). By this time, Poland's surviving peasantry was Europe's most depressed, its political life paralyzed by a landowning class unwilling to grant central government the semblance of national authority, and its fate as an independent state in the hands of rulers in St. Petersburg, Vienna, and Versailles.

Spain also suffered a population collapse in the seventeenth century, and it dragged its south-Italian possessions into its decline. The central region of Castile had been the heart of Spain's sixteenth-century international empire. By the 1590s Castile possessed 6.5 million of the 11 million inhabitants of the Iberian peninsula. A densely settled, arid region, Castile had its population concentrated in towns that fed on the countryside, towns that never developed a sturdy manufacturing or commercial base. Furthermore, rural Castile leaned toward sheep herding rather than tillage, and raw wool was Spain's leading export. In 1609 more than 300,000 Christianized descendants of Moslems were expelled from Spain. These people were small artisans and traders, whose religious loyalties were mistrusted by the Inquisition. Their departure accompanied a general neglect of Spanish agriculture at a moment when population had peaked and military expenditures were outdistancing income from the New World's silver mines. The consequences proved disastrous for future generations. After 1620 Spanish agriculture no longer could feed the Spanish people. The demands of the tax collector and recruiting sergeant drove additional peasants to towns, where high prices for scarce bread proved the rule and where epidemic took its toll. By 1648 Spain had lost Portugal in a successful revolt, and its population fell to under 8 million. Worse was still to come.

During the second half of the seventeenth century, Spain's catalogue of misfortunes seemed endless. The country was beset with a dynastic crisis, its neighbors plotted the dismemberment of its empire, and between 1702 and 1713 war was fought on its soil. A landowning peasantry virtually disappeared. Whatever farms still existed took the form of estates owned by the aristocracy or Catholic Church, and were worked by miserable sharecroppers. Peasant proprietorships covered scarcely 5 percent of the tilled land. Over 150,000 Spaniards belonged to an unproductive clergy. Silver imports from America entered the coffers of Dutch and English bankers and smugglers. Economic depression alternated with equally ruinous inflation. Many of Castile's towns died; the barren, arid plateau which marks the region today took on its familiar contour. There, peasant, shepherd, and artisan gave way to beggar, bandit, and vagabond. By 1715 the most vigorous and mobile elements of Castile's population had drifted to the coastal regions or else secured passage on boats headed for America. Although the periphery bore the seeds of Spain's eighteenth-century recovery, the center had gone through cycles of stagnation and decline. The half century between 1648 and 1700 witnessed a further population decline to 7.5 million. Castile alone lost one-third of its people.

The Remainder of Europe

From 1648 to 1715 the most densely populated region in Europe was the Italian peninsula, and the most densely populated states were France and the Dutch Netherlands. The dominant territorial states were France and the Hapsburg Empire, and the dominant commercial ones were the Dutch Netherlands and England. Except for Italy and parts of France, these places were spared the experience of regular, repeated famines and epidemics; none knew the excesses of perpetually marauding armies. Yet in all of them population growth was slight and in some cases nonexistent. At the close of the period, Italy's population was around 13 million, less than what it had been in 1600. Despite the acquisition of additional territory, France's population hovered between 18 and 19 million, no more than in 1648 and a million fewer than in 1600. The population of the Hapsburgs' German possessions did not rise above 6 million. The Dutch Netherlands and England enjoyed slight population increases: The former went from 1.8 to 1.9 million, and the latter from 5.1 to 5.2 million. Of all the nations of Europe, only the least known and least European, Russia, experienced a sizable population growth, from perhaps 11 to 14 million. It was at this time that the lands leading to the Black Sea, Ukraine, and Lower Volga, the breadbasket of the emerging empire, were settled. But the bulk of Europeans lived in the west, within the radius of an oval drawn from Amsterdam to the Pyrenees, veering westward to include London and southeastern England, eastward to include north-central Germany, the Rhine Valley, and Switzerland, and southward to incorporate Spanish Catalonia and Italy. The region contained eighty to one hundred people per square mile, whereas the remainder of inhabited Europe averaged from ten to forty.

CITIES AND TOWNS

While the overwhelming majority of Europeans lived off the land, it was hunger rather than the search for opportunity that drew most of them to towns. What refugees found in urban communities was not free bread but soaring prices, made all the higher by increased competition for limited stocks. Faced with unemployment as a result of decreasing demand for the products they made, town dwellers despised the new immigrants. Their arrival aggravated problems over fuel, garbage disposal, housing, and water supply. They increased the chance of epidemic. Late seventeenth-century urban society was a human pressure cooker. Periodic crowd-related diseases might reduce the populations, but the megalopolises—Istanbul with its 700,000, Paris and London with their 400,000 each, Naples with its 250,000—made up their losses with new influxes. On the other hand, smaller cities in commercial decline, particularly those that dotted the Mediterranean, failed to recoup their vigor with infusions of rural poor. In fact, during the century the populations of Venice, Rome, Palermo, and Seville declined. By 1700 each had fewer than 150,000 inhabitants. Lyon, Lisbon, Madrid, and Vienna stagnated at 100,000. Valencia, Granada, and Genoa sank to below that. By way of contrast, of Europe's cities during the seventeenth century, none except possibly London could match Amsterdam's demographic and commercial growth. Like other European cities, Amsterdam drew the miserable and infected, but it also attracted the persecuted and ambitious. It prospered as it grew. Its population of 200,000 in 1700 was four times what it had been a century earlier.

Amsterdam, Naples, and Paris

In nearly every way Amsterdam was a unique phenomenon in late seventeenth-century Europe. The city was not subservient to any greater political unit. No king or emperor lorded over Amsterdam. It was the urban heart of the province of Holland, which in turn was the most important of the seven mini-states comprising the United Provinces of the Dutch (or Northern) Netherlands. Holland's leading official was called the grand pensionary, and the province—heavily influenced by Amsterdam—had a major say in selecting the individual who passed for the commander-in-chief of the United Provinces, the stadholder. In its own right the city controlled a worldwide empire of trade and credit. Amsterdam collected its own taxes, administered its own justice, and jealously defended its privileges against foreign powers and the loosely federated government of the United Provinces.

A patrician bourgeoisie of Amsterdam's shipbuilding, trading, and banking interests ruled the city. Responsible for Amsterdam's political independence and economic development, this burgher elite, whose self-confidence has been immortalized in the innumerable portraits its members commissioned, also dictated the cultural tone of the city. Amsterdam's harbor burst with vessels from around the world, and its streets teemed with a polyglot population of refugees from the Southern Netherlands under Spanish control, Protestant and Catholic Germans, Huguenot French, and Sephardic Jews, all of whom found asylum in the tolerant immigration and settlement policies of its government. The city's skilled craftsmen and menial laborers alike eked out wages just sufficient to ensure continuation of a sixty-hour work week deemed appropriate by Amsterdam's ruling patriciate. On their side, the powerful of Amsterdam rarely flaunted their wealth in lavish display. Without retinues of carriages, servants, or retainers, they walked through town amid tradespeople and workers. Lacking spectacular facades, their sturdy and functional houses were built deeply into their sites. Indeed, the physical grandeur of Amsterdam was not represented by private dwellings but rather by its public architecture: the Town Hall, guildhalls, and churches. Of course, it would be an error to say that the economic and governing elites of Amsterdam shunned consumption, for they bought property in the countryside, jewelry for their wives, and annuities for themselves. Nevertheless, the character of the city they built—seventeenth-century Europe's most successful one—bespoke prosperity rather than opulence.

A far different type of city was Naples. Technically, it was capital of the kingdom of Naples, which in turn was part of a Spanish empire in full decline. A Spanish viceroy bargained with committees of local nobles over political power, granting them titles, offices, and tax exemptions in return for guarantees of Spanish sovereignty, and an aristocracy of courtiers, churchmen, and judges contemptuously treated the poverty-wracked majority crammed inside the town walls. This urban proletariat, which sought shelter in tenements, stables, or the streets themselves, had erupted in a massive rebellion in 1647, following a messianic leader, the fisherman Masaniello. For a short time Masaniello controlled Naples as dictator. However, once he was tricked into negotiating with the Spaniards, a mob turned on its leader, murdered him, mutilated his body, and subsequently converted him into a martyr. Masaniello's revolt passed into the countryside where it was put down bloodily, and the city of Naples reverted back to its older subjection. Hunger remained endemic. Skilled artisans verged on starvation. Yet the place remained a magnet for the country poor of southern Italy and Sicily. Peasants, shepherds, sailors, and laborers replenished the dying. By 1715 Naples still was Europe's fourth largest city—after Istanbul, London, and Paris.

Paris lay somewhere between progressive, commercial Amsterdam and chaotic, poverty-wracked Naples. It was capital of Europe's most populous state, yet a city despised by its king. Rather than engage in daily bouts over authority with aristocratic, municipal, and corporate groups in Paris, Louis XIV (1643–1715) preferred to be architect of his own glory. He therefore constructed a spectacular court and administrative center at Versailles, a onetime royal hunting lodge 15 miles to the west. Louis assigned responsibility for controlling Paris to his controller-general of finance, Jean-Baptiste Colbert (1619–1683). That Louis wished to do this is understandable, since in 1648 Parisian magistrates had led a tax revolt against his mother and her courtiers which grew into a horrifying five-year civil war, the Fronde. Fleeing the city as a child, Louis never returned. What he left was a place where contentious groups—merchant guildsmen, craftspeople and artisans, members of religious orders, teachers and professors, royal officials, judges, lawyers, servants, and hangers-on—made their living at the expense of others, guarding special functions and privileges, and pretending that the interdependence which makes urban life bearable never existed.

Colbert attacked what he considered to represent the medieval anarchy of Paris with a series of plans that he hoped would turn the city into Europe's most efficiently run capital—even if its king resolutely refused to reside there. He tore down the old city gates and replaced them with arches in the style of imperial Rome. Other royal monuments and public squares were constructed. Colbert instituted zoning regulations and built tree-lined boulevards for strolling. He founded a professional police force with authority to punish crimes of violence, clean the streets, suppress illicit literature, and stabilize the price of bread. Finding their traditional powers diminished, the old merchant oligarchies protested vigorously. But to no avail. Colbert's agents gained authority for inspecting and controlling Paris's food supply, prisons, and hospitals.

With this shift in responsibility, Paris lost much of its medieval clutter. But it lost some of its vitality as well. The older democratic character of its residential habits disappeared. Sensing the royally sanctioned modernization of their city, its aristocracies forsook the neighborhoods they shared with non-privileged groups in the center and began moving to leafy locales in the western suburbs, where they would construct large, elegant town houses with stables and formal gardens. These became segregated neighborhoods, and by 1715 the aristocratic and administrative transformation of Paris was its most distinctive characteristic. Beyond the teeming streets of its artisan districts, Paris gained a reputation as the place where the political go-getter or noble gentleman on tour had to pass some time. It was there where opportunism and manipulation thrived. Meanwhile, commercial enterprise found Amsterdam and London to be far more congenial places than overregulated Paris, and the French capital's royal patron passed his days in his sumptuous playpen 15 miles to the west.

Urban Transformation

Mortality rates in Europe's preindustrial cities were considerably higher than those in the countryside, and towns had to replenish themselves through immigration or not survive. In 1688 the English statistician Gregory King estimated London's death rate to be 42 per thousand; that of England's villages was 29. Without an annual influx of 1,500 immigrants per year, declining Rome would have disappeared altogether by the end of the eighteenth century. It seems evident that between 1648 and 1715 the inpouring of uprooted rural dwellers changed the character of the large preindustrial cities of Europe. Medieval corporate traditions based on custom and status grudgingly yielded to impersonal contractual relations among individuals, which were guaranteed by governments.

Europe's great cities also had to revolutionize the manner in which they supplied the basic needs of their inhabitants. Instead of relying traditionally on the nearby countryside for food, these cities went afar to corner grain supplies. Paris reached out to Brittany and the Loire River valley, London devoured everything grown up to the Humber River, and the far-seeing elites of Amsterdam controlled the entire grain-producing region along the Baltic seacoast. The need for fuel encouraged Dutch urban capitalists to exploit virgin peat bogs throughout the Northern Netherlands and stimulated the growth of Amsterdam's sugar refining, brickmaking, and brewing industries. London's entrepreneurs developed coal for heating and cooking; once Abraham Darby successfully smelted iron with coke fuel in 1709, coal's use in English industry was assured.

While Amsterdam, London, Paris, and even Naples illustrated the dynamic character of late seventeenth-century urban life, most smaller cities tried to retain something of their medieval corporate traditions in face of the twin pressures of immigration and state domination. In time, of course, every one of these towns developed a distinct personality. Some declined and never recovered. Others transformed into regional ports, trading centers, garrison towns, or administrative centers. The tiny ones depended upon whatever rural industry existed just outside them, guarding their fields and vineyards, their artisans reverting to peasant life at harvest-time. Dependence was mutual, as village wheelwrights, blacksmiths, and other rural laborers provided urban needs at cheap prices.

Of the middle-sized towns, a German one, Frankfurt-am-Main, is representative. In Frankfurt sumptuary codes distinguished the town's social categories. The first category would include the mayor, leading magistrates, guild presidents, physicians, and resident nobility. The second would comprise lesser town councillors, noble immigrants, the wealthiest merchants, and bankers. The third category included lawyers, comfortable tradesmen, and artists. The fourth was made up of smaller traders, messengers, and artisans; the fifth, day laborers and servants. Each category had its own rights and privileges, and it was unseemly for an individual to move from one to another. In towns which were more dependent upon territorial princes than Frankfurt, the ruler's military, church, and court officials found their ranks within the municipal hierarchy. Family connections, the structure of merchant and craft guilds, and historical precedent gave a conservative edge to most of these middle-sized towns. Marginal types such as Jews, actors, tinkers, peddlers, wounded ex-soldiers, and widows were mistrusted and persecuted according to custom. For towns between 10,000 and 50,000 inhabitants therefore, survival in a period of prolonged recession and insecurity meant that elite definitions of respectability and the preservation of status took precedence over thoughts of upward mobility.

THE COUNTRYSIDE

Tradition-Bound Agriculture and the Village

Nearly eight of ten Europeans lived on the land. Except for rare experimental outposts in southeastern England and parts of the Dutch and Spanish Netherlands—where attempts at crop rotation were made and where root crops and clover were introduced to restore soil fertility—the dominant agricultural method was the timeworn field-strip system dependent upon cereal production. On each estate, plots of arable land were divided into three fields (two in southern Europe) that most often alternated annually among wheat, oats, and fallow. Thus, nearly everywhere, between one-third to one-half of the land farmed lay uncultivated so as to recover nutrients and productive qualities. Corn and potato production were still underdeveloped. Dairy products, leaf vegetables, and (except for southern Italy and Spain) fruit were rare. Because cattle raising was largely limited to the eastern and northern edges of Europe—such as Hungary, Lithuania, Denmark, and Scotland—fertilizer was insufficient. The techniques of plowing and harvesting had not changed in over five hundred years. The water-driven mill and wooden plow were basic equipment. Technological limitation helps to explain why in France, continental Europe's most highly developed agricultural state, only half the potentially arable land was actually exploited during the seventeenth century. The remainder was pasture, woods, marsh, or waste. In the Mediterranean, perhaps one-fourth was put to use. East of the Elbe River, it was about 10 percent. Brakes on agricultural productivity held back everything else.

      The agricultural regions of Europe were hinterlands for the continent's towns. Although London, Amsterdam, and Paris began commandeering cereals from relatively distant sources, supplies rarely traveled beyond 50 miles to urban markets. This habitual dependence upon local sources hindered the development of transportation systems for crops and may explain consumer helplessness and governmental panic in times of poor harvests. Moreover, because market-bound produce consisted of highly irregular surpluses, the threat of unrelieved dearth was very real. With an average yield ratio of four parts harvested to one part seeded, a seventeenth-century peasant household, farming 20 acres, fed itself and one to two additional persons. If the yield ratio fell to 3:1, the surplus vanished, and the family's own supply diminished by nearly 20 percent. On the other hand, an increase of the yield ratio to 8:1, an extremely rare phenomenon, might feed the family and ten additional persons.

Average yield ratios are difficult to estimate and even more difficult to evaluate. The highest in Europe were found in England and the Northern Netherlands, perhaps 7:1. More common, however, were the French ratios of 5:1 or the German, Spanish, and Polish ratios of 4:1, yields which barely sustained populations in the best of years and which assured famine in the poor ones. It was their failure to compete in the demand for the abysmal harvests of 1693 and 1694 that doomed members of the Cocu family of Beauvais. Governments knew that increased productivity was essential to eradicate the persistent threat of famine, and during the first half of the seventeenth century had financed drainage projects in the Dutch Netherlands, England, Poland, and France. However, the near universal downturn in Europe's economy after 1650 brought an end to this official experimentation and left landowners to their own devices as far as increasing productivity was concerned.

Lacking a technological revolution, seventeenth-century farmers needed to intensify agriculture so that the harvest might exceed the paltry 5:1 or 4:1 yield ratios. Some possibilities existed. Heavy manuring could have increased production and at the same time reduced the amount of fallow. However, it also would have necessitated converting existing arable land into pasture for livestock, thereby defeating the original purpose. Europeans were aware of other methods of intensifying cultivation, like interspersing nitrogen-fixing peas, beans, and clover with the ever-present cereals, once again reducing the fallow. Or else turnips and clover might have been added to the normal rotation procedure, suppressing the fallow altogether. Moreover, basic agricultural techniques could have been improved upon. Seed might have been planted in rows instead of randomly broadcast; weeding might have been more thorough, plowing more frequent. However, except for England and the northwest corner of the continent, institutional resistance to change held back everything. Landlords leasing plots to peasant villages feared overproduction and price decreases almost as much as they feared famine. Experimentation with noncereal crops might play havoc with their rents, which were almost exclusively paid in wheat or oats.

However, it was the manner in which villages administered production that prevented genuine intensification of agriculture in most of continental Europe. The basic system was called the *common field*. By its terms all arable land was divided into irregular strips, and each peasant cultivator was responsible for various strips which were not contiguous.

The fields were unfenced, and pasture, woods, and wastes were used in common by all the peasants of the village. A village assembly administered planting and harvesting. The entire system demanded cooperation, discouraging individual initiative and intensive labor. Most of all, the need for village consensus stifled change.

On the continent, the village community was the social basis for agricultural activity. The village was recognized in law as a corporate body, woven together by custom, common ownership of equipment and goods, and the parish church. The peasants believed that either they worked together or else starved alone. Generally not even possessing surnames, their individuality was subordinated to their collective obligations, and their social superiors saw them as an undifferentiated mass to be treated at best condescendingly but more frequently with simple contempt. A Prussian pastor in 1684 summarized the patrician's view of the peasantry:

> The peasants are indeed human beings, but somewhat more churlish and uncouth than the others. . . . In his movements [the peasant] would only seldom think of his hat and take it off, . . . but if he does so he turns it round like a potter's wheel, or spits into his hand and polishes it. . . . When they eat they do not use a fork, but they dip their five fingers into the pot. . . . If soldiers steal they do it out of extreme need; but most peasants who help themselves do it out of malice. . . . It is also well-known that those who keep on good terms with the vicar are maltreated by the other peasants, for they give them all kinds of bad names, call them traitors, lickspittles, toadies, talebearers. . . . The peasants have that in common with the stockfish: these are best when beaten well and soft. The dear peasants too are only well-behaved when fully burdened with work; then they remain well under control and timid.[2]

The pastor reveals not only his own prejudices, based on the peasants' lack of social polish, but he also unwittingly shows us something of the peasants' own consciousness of identity. The image of subservience displayed for their betters was one that they despised. In contact with their superiors, they conformed to roles others had written for them. The psychological tension produced must have been very great. Cheating the lord or his bailiff offered some relief—this was the "malice" to which our pastor refers—and genuine revolt, accompanied by looting, murder, and arson, might have provided the ultimate release. This latter possibility existed within the framework of the most stable peasant-landlord relationships. We may well assume that fear of it helped convince the higher orders to

[2] Quoted in F. L. Carsten, "The Empire After the Thirty Years' War," *The New Cambridge Modern History,* vol. V (Cambridge, England, 1961), p. 438.

recommend beating the peasants "well and soft" through hard labor and economic dependence.

Land Tenancy in Western Europe

For those with funds to spare, land was the century's most attractive investment. Wars, social unrest, sluggish demand, and monetary devaluations discouraged large-scale commerce for all but the Dutch and, by the end of the century, the English. Moreover, for the heirs of sixteenth-century families who had grown wealthy through trade or the liberal professions, the ownership of land represented the surest route toward ennoblement and tax exemption. The gift of land was the sovereign's means of rewarding military or administrative service. In the late seventeenth century landowners pushed hard to increase the size of their estates and to raise cereals, not merely for village subsistence but also for sale to urban markets. However, the prevalence of regional famines and underdeveloped transportation methods made it difficult for producers to send their grain to the places that needed it.

English landowners were ahead of their continental contemporaries in the art of estate building. They invested in the reclamation of marshes and swamps and in the exploitation of common lands, woods, and wastes. They also took the lead in experimenting with legumes and root crops so as to cease depending upon the fallow. On the other hand, rather than improve production techniques, magnates in Poland, Hungary, and Russia, who gained control over tens of thousands of acres, extended the use of serf labor. Although a trend clearly existed toward larger estates in the hands of fewer owners, land in seventeenth-century Europe was exploited in a large variety of ways. By 1700, even as wealthy Englishmen evicted renters and enclosed common lands, nearly half the rural population consisted of yeomen who owned or else possessed long-term leases for farmland up to 200 acres or grazing land up to 600 acres. As time would prove, however, this statistic was deceiving. The yeomanry proved to be a declining element in English agriculture.

France provided the model of ownership and tenure for most of western Europe. The estate owner held the right of eminent domain over his property, which was translated into the expectation of rents, dues, and homage from those who occupied it. The owner might lease out an entire estate at long-term rates to a single party, who customarily held a rank in society similar to his own. The lessee could exploit the estate as he saw fit and even sell the lease rights to a third party.

Far more widespread, however, was the leasing system called the *fief roturier*, in which a peasant village assumed collective responsibility over a stipulated portion of the proprietor's estate. In return, the proprietor held certain rights and privileges over the village and its inhabitants. He charged peasants the *cens*, an annual payment recognizing his authority.

Figure 1.1—Illustration by Jacques Lagniet for the Recueil des plus illustres proverbes divisés en trois livres *(Paris, 1657): "The Noble is the Spider and the Peasant is the Fly." While seventeenth-century governments did all they could to stifle criticisms of the established social orders, grievances did find their way into print. This cartoon appeared in a volume of French proverbs. The text in the upper right-hand corner comments on the grasping* seigneur *and pathetic peasant in the following way: "The more one possesses wealth, the more one desires. This poor soul carries everything he has—grain, fruit, money, vegetables. This fat* milord, *seated, ready to take everything, doesn't wish to give him the time of day."*

He held a monopoly over the estate's oven, mill, and wine press, charging villagers a usage fee. He monopolized fishing and hunting rights on the estate, though he might commute them to the village for a price. The same was true for his exclusive right to keep pigeons or rabbits. The landlord controlled and charged fees for the utilization of streams and rivers that flowed through the estate; he could market his own products before the peasants were allowed to market theirs. Above all, the major part of the landlord's investment derived from his keeping a percentage of the village's harvest. Conflicts over dues and privileges were adjudicated in the seigneurial court located on the estate, where the landlord sat as judge.

The individual peasant was responsible for paying his percentage of the village's lease fee and dues to the landlord. He paid an additional percentage to the Church. Whenever the village renegotiated an expired lease with the landlord, the latter would attempt to dig up new dues and charges that, of course, were passed on to the peasant. The peasant hated this endless list of dues with a vengeance. The dues customarily were paid in kind and represented from one-tenth to one-third of his crop yield. He had to pay them in good times and bad, and the landlord insisted that the peasant hand over the seigneurial dues before paying taxes to the king.

On the surface it would seem that the peasant was a helpless renter, saddled with a collection of exploitative obligations that held him in perpetual bondage to the seigneur. In reality, however, the existence and payment of these rents, dues, and taxes were what kept him from slipping down the rungs of peasant society to sharecropper or day laborer status. The fees guaranteed him the right of tenancy, and in the seventeenth and eighteenth centuries the legal concept of tenancy had a vigor and distinctiveness that are no longer apparent today. The tenant held title to his plot, and he could even bequeath or sell it. Once the landlord—a nobleman, churchman, or bourgeois—accepted rents and dues for a piece of his domain, he turned *usufruct* (the legal right to make a profit) over to the tenant. The landlord was entitled to additional dues whenever the tenant sold or willed the property to someone other than his eldest son. But all agreed that the rights of tenancy were as inviolable as the rents and dues that the peasant paid to the seigneur, however large the estate might be, however powerful the landlord, however humble the tenant.

For an estate owner content with a fixed income, the tenancy system provided a means of security that was woven tightly into the structure of west-European rural society. But those who purchased estates as a growth investment during the seventeenth century were not likely to be content with an arrangement that had emerged in conjunction with the economically self-sufficient manorial units of the Middle Ages. Modern-minded landlords wanted to keep the social, economic, and juridical privileges they held over the peasant village, but they also wished to convert the estate into an agricultural factory that supplied grain to distant cities and even foreign states. To accomplish this, they had to regain title to their tenant's plot while at the same time keeping his labor.

In this way seventeenth-century landlords grew reluctant about renewing long-term tenancies, and new estate owners grew reluctant about abiding by tenancy arrangements agreed to by predecessors. They were willing to try their luck in the courts, where magistrates with social views similar to their own might give them a sympathetic hearing. Their aim, and the aim of estate managers whom they often hired in their absence, was to regain the plots of the *fief roturier* and then rent them to former tenants on short-term leases unencumbered by the dues, taxes, and guarantees inherent in the old system. The new rental terms would be simple: 50 to 70 percent of the crop. The estate owner might rent large plots on these terms to the wealthiest peasants of the village, who themselves would hire poverty-stricken day laborers (most likely dispossessed former tenants) to work them. Or estate managers might find their own day laborers to work the repossessed plots. Whatever the method employed, the goal of the modern-minded estate owner was the same—to reduce the medieval forms of land tenancy, based on complex arrangements with inhabitants of the peasant village who were stubborn about reciprocal rights and obligations, and to increase the landlord's direct exploitation of and profits from the arable area. The increased cash income then could be reinvested.

In France, Sweden, the Spanish-held Southern Netherlands, northern Italy, and Germany west of the Elbe River—those parts of Europe with a rich heritage of village tenancy—the *fief roturier* arrangement declined considerably in the second half of the seventeenth century. Village chiefs— those literate enough to handle the contractual details between community and landlord over justice, rents, and dues—rose to newly privileged positions in peasant society. They did so because they took the risk of renting out important blocks of the estate's reserve and hiring their own agricultural laborers.

On the other hand, the mass of villagers found themselves slipping in the opposite direction. They might become small renters, sharecroppers really, dependent upon an estate manager or wealthy peasant for their plot, seed, plow, and beasts, and obliged to turn over more than half of what they harvested. Subject to possible eviction each year, they lost the security the old tenancy arrangements offered. The village bond of responsibility for communal well-being, and for the well-being of widows and orphans, loosened. Village chiefs became economic oppressors. Worst of all, during the periods of recession that dotted the second half of the seventeenth century, onetime tenants might fall clear to the bottom, becoming hired hands or vagabonds, wandering from estate to estate in search of work, dragging along their miserable women and bedraggled offspring. They were at the mercy of any potential employer, but even more so of nature, for they were the most likely victims of famine and epidemic.

Serfdom in Eastern Europe

However depressed in social status, west-European peasants at least negotiated their labor. The new forms of exploitative agriculture assumed the existence of a mobile work force, although in southern Italy, Portugal, and Spain peasant indebtedness to landowners could rivet rural labor to the estate. East of the Elbe River, where the work force was smaller than in the west, estate owners also wanted to fix rural labor permanently to their lands, and they secured legislation from governments that prohibited the movement of agricultural workers. In Denmark, much of northeastern Germany, Bohemia, the Hapsburgs' Austrian lands, Hungary, Poland, the Baltic provinces, and Russia, tenants on estates saw the dues and taxes owed to the seigneur converted largely into labor services on the landlord's own reserve.

Such services might come to four or five days of the total work week. They so overwhelmed all other tenancy responsibilities of the peasantry that historians call the seventeenth and eighteenth centuries in eastern Europe the age of a new serfdom. It was a particularly insidious kind, written into the king's law and protected by the king's troops. In order to succeed, it had to keep peasants tied to the estate. In 1649 a new Russian law code expressly fixed every family chief and his dependents to an estate, and no statute of limitations was placed on the landlord in hunting down fleeing workers. After 1682 the concept of a free peasantry had become so alien to Russian thinking that landlords short of funds were allowed to take peasants from the estate and sell them like cattle to other landlords. In 1650 the Saxon peasant lost the right to leave his estate without the explicit authorization of its proprietor. Three years later, Frederick William of Brandenburg confirmed that every peasant in his electorate was a serf unless a specific title or the landlord's goodwill could prove otherwise. Estate owners in Brandenburg obtained virtual government authorization to evict peasants from their plots and then add the plots to the reserve.

Throughout eastern Europe an inexorable process deprived the peasant family of its liberty, property, and security. The estate owner needed peasant labor, not peasant rents. Importing countries such as Holland and Spain were crying for grain, timber, beer, and wine. So were the new armies and princely courts. The seigneur therefore gobbled up peasant land and added it to his own. He compelled serfs to purchase from him the grain, drinks, and cheese needed for their own sustenance. He served the state as its tax collector. He was delegated control over justice. He ran the village tavern, mill, and store. After 1648 the entire economy of eastern Europe was tilted in favor of the estate owner, and the regime of subjugation and privilege was engraved into the law.

THE FOUNDATIONS AND STRUCTURES
OF SOCIETY

Marriage and Family Life

In town and countryside alike, the shadow of death hovered over most human activities. Only recently have historians laid to rest the myth of the peasant or artisan child marriage which bore fruit in the form of half a dozen sturdy offspring. Had this actually occurred, a crisis of overpopulation, and not demographic stagnation, would have struck Europe during the second half of the seventeenth century. Rural France, which historians have studied in great detail, may serve as an example for western Europe. There, around 85 percent of the peasant population married, females rarely before they were twenty-four, males rarely before they were twenty-seven. Female fertility ceased between forty and forty-five, and interbirth periods averaged no fewer than two years. Statistically, this meant five to seven births per couple. However, death carried off half of those born before they reached twenty. One child in three perished before the age of ten. For mothers the situation was nearly as precarious. In the first two years of marriage, particularly during the first pregnancy or first birth, female mortality was exceedingly high. Moreover, famine, accident, and simply worn-out bodies terminated conceptions, and indeed marriages themselves, before fifteen years had elapsed. In eastern Europe the mortality rates were even more drastic than those in France. However, nearly 95 percent of east-European peasants married, and they did so six to eight years earlier than their French cohorts.

The aristocracy and wealthy bourgeoisie married earlier than the lower classes, and women from these privileged groups were the sheltered childbearing matrons of the age, living from pregnancy to pregnancy, turning each infant over to a wet nurse, and then repeating the process. Throughout Europe the upper classes married in their teens. They averaged a dozen conceptions, eight to ten live births. It is safe to assume that sheer reproductive vitality assured the leadership of the dominant social groups, as long as they could exploit the labor of the suppressed groups for their own maintenance.

For peasant or artisan families, existence was far different. Life was very unstable. Nowhere in Europe did their median life expectancy exceed the age of forty. In France it was thirty-three, in northern Italy twenty-six. Faced with epidemic and contagious disease, villages might experience death in sudden, large doses. Widowhood was common, and at least one in four marriages was a remarriage. Stepparents and half siblings abounded, so that the family was perpetually reconstituting itself. Yet it seems clear that in northwestern Europe and England the modern nuclear family, with the married couple at its core, prevailed. Elsewhere complex varieties thrived:

Multigenerational families lived together, brothers combined households, well-off peasant units included aunts, uncles, and cousins. On the serf estates in eastern Europe, landlords encouraged extended family units to live under one roof. It was a way of consolidating the work force.

Sentimentality and tenderness had little place in the seventeenth-century peasant or artisan family. From infancy on, it was thought that children had to be tamed through sanctions and beatings. Religious teaching tried to moderate domestic brutality. For example, the French *Catechism of Agen* (1677) listed parental duties as providing physical nourishment and religious instruction, correcting "both gently and charitably," and setting a good example. In Protestant countries the authority of the father was reinforced by his role as director of familial religious practice, and parental responsibility included instruction in reading and how to earn a proper living. These moral, religious, and practical prescriptions, however, often were at odds with reality. In tens of thousands of seventeenth-century families it was uncertain that one's childhood would even be spent at home. If economic conditions demanded it, all children except the favorite son might be sent away for training as apprentices or servants, never to return. If they remained in the household, intense sibling rivalries developed over inheritance rights, and a father's economic power over the favored son invited lifelong conflicts within the family. Sharp divisions of labor between husband and wife relegated the woman to responsibility over the children, kitchen, and livestock. Unlike her husband, she had no role in village or guild governance; her social activities were confined to communal labor activities such as washing clothes. While her sons might belong to village clubs, her daughters were trained to follow her path. Unless chaperoned, daughters were to stay at home while their fathers negotiated their future with other elders.

This negotiation underscores the importance of the seventeenth-century family as an economic enterprise. The dowry, an inheritance, and childbearing capabilities were concerns of parents, relatives, and neighbors alike. Of course, the state had an interest too, and in Germany princes and municipal governments withheld permission to marry to propertyless individuals like servants and journeyman workers. Yet the emotional needs of the couple were not totally ignored. By desacralizing marriage, Protestant theologians implicitly admitted the importance of sexual desire. By recognizing divorce (though only for the direst of reasons, such as kidnapping, first-cousin marriage, and female adultery) they suggested, also implicitly, the possibility of domestic incompatibility. While underscoring the sacramental aspect of marriage and thereby refusing to condone divorce, the Catholic Church nevertheless begrudgingly tolerated some marriages without parental consent, provided that the banns were publicly posted and a priest conducted the ceremony. Of course, the ultimate purpose of marriage was procreation. Religious teaching and social practice concurred in considering contraception a mortal sin, abortion akin to infanticide, and a childless couple worthy of pity, suspicion, and ridicule.

Perhaps the most important developments concerning the seventeenth-century family were the increasing privatization of its life and a more active part for the betrothed couple in determining its own future. The evolution of the nuclear family combined with powerful social and religious proscriptions concerning correct sexual conduct to create clear distinctions between the private world of the couple and what members of the village or neighborhood considered the community's business. Protestant and Catholic Churches alike insisted that sexual activity remain exclusively the province of wives and their husbands. Priests and pastors attacked public promiscuity, and their insistence on prenuptial virginity may well have encouraged marriages based on mutual respect.

At the wedding ceremony the betrothed couple assumed a more active role than had been the case earlier. Their mutual vows and exchange of small gifts replaced the giving away of the bride by her father as the central symbolic act; the wedding feast, which had often degenerated into a public brawl, leaving dead and wounded, was tamed. Collective village ceremonies, which might once have expressed disapproval of a marriage through public mockery, were tolerated less frequently. Most significantly, when wife and husband closed the curtain of their bedchamber, they were shutting out village or neighborhood. Their marriage sanctified the legitimacy of their private life, beyond the prying eyes of the community, relatives, or parents.

In the second half of the seventeenth century, therefore, church and state challenged village and neighborhood in exerting tightened legal and moral control over the *public* sphere of marriage and family life. At the same time society was obliged to recognize the legitimacy of the *private,* or intimate sphere. It is possible that both developments benefited the female partner. She became less a piece of property sold by her father to her husband and more a participant in the marriage contract itself. Indeed, surviving archival records reveal brides-to-be renouncing agreements which they claimed were forced on them. In 1667, for example, Savine Dieu, daughter of a garment trimmer in Troyes, France, went to court to break her contract with Joachim Simon, a public letter writer, stating that she had agreed to marry Simon only "out of duty to her father and mother." When her groom-to-be showed little respect for her, Savine responded "with neither inclination nor love"—and she wanted out. Meanwhile, religious and secular authorities reminded husbands that sexual fidelity was a mutual responsibility. Whether such warnings deeply affected traditional male practices is difficult to gauge. Local studies, particularly in England, nevertheless indicate that the percentage of prenuptial conceptions and illegitimate births declined between 1648 and 1715, only to rise dramatically in the second half of the eighteenth century. Both Catholic and Protestant Reformations established models of sexual discipline, and the liberation of attitudes after 1750 was in large part due to the relaxation of religious influences.

The Society of Orders: "Class" and Mobility

In today's world an individual's contribution to the economic life of the state and the material benefits derived from this contribution largely determine one's status in society. Sources and sizes of income generally unite people within a so-called social class and are primary factors in defining lifestyles ind attitudes. During the seventeenth and eighteenth centuries, however, he law did not necessarily group people according to their productive role in the state's economy but rather according to the esteem, honor, or dignity attached to their person—an esteem, honor, or dignity *tangentially* rather than *directly* related to their material well-being.

Society in old-regime Europe was compartmentalized juridically according to a formula of orders and ranks that conformed to the hierarchy God had created in nature. Each rank was conceived of as a distinct entity, with observable standards of dress, decorum, eating habits, and forms of address. Each rank defined the education and the tolerated occupations of its membership. As it was unnatural for a pig to climb a tree and munch acorns, so too was it unnatural for a nobleman to dream of directing a woolens mill. Of course, reality did not always conform to this juridical ideal. Certain historians believe that notwithstanding the carefully worked formulas of legal treatises and habits of deference, a desire to control production and distribution was what guided the activities of all seventeenth-century classes. This need to dominate the field and marketplace lay behind the socioeconomic relationships among landowners, renters, merchants, and artisans, and belied the respectful solidarities suggested by a society of orders. Moreover, making deals and dividing political power with local elites, the absolute monarchies of the Old Regime simply redeployed the so-called apparatus of medieval feudal domination. This viewpoint makes considerable sense, even though seventeenth-century observers themselves viewed socioeconomic relations somewhat differently. For them wealth and power were respected as a *consequence* of rank rather than as a *cause* for it.

Three general categories, each divided into a welter of subcategories, distinguished the members of society. The great categories, known as the Estates, were based on the medieval distinction that had been made among those who prayed, those who fought, and those who worked. The First Estate, the clergy, had the most important duty of temporal existence, the care for human souls. The Second Estate, the aristocracy, bore the responsibility of defending the lives of everyone else. The Third Estate, containing the overwhelming majority, had to feed, clothe, and shelter society.

Within each Estate, distinctions were enormous and represented the overlay of "class" upon juridically defined "order." In Catholic countries, bishops and parish priests stood worlds apart from each other, and even the monastic orders had their own ranks of prestige. Meanwhile, in Protestant countries, the smaller size of the clergy produced a social order that was more homogeneous than in Catholic ones. Concerning the Second

Estate, the typology of aristocracy set court nobles apart from country gentry and, most notably in France, important judges and magistrates formed yet another distinct aristocratic group. Nowhere, however, were ranks so distinctive, subgroups so conscious of their unique corporate characteristics, as in the Third Estate. Middle-and lower-ranked government officials, attorneys, men of letters, merchants, and master craftsmen—all self-proclaimed "honorable men"—distinguished themselves from one another. A physician's wife enjoyed a form of address that was more exalted than a surgeon's. In the innumerable processions that celebrated a holiday or the visit of some dignitary to town, cloth merchants would cede their habitual place in rank to no others. But all the "honorable men" kept themselves apart from shopkeepers, craftspersons, and tenant farmers, not to mention the masses of the *bas peuple* —mechanics, laborers, sharecroppers, and itinerant workers. The law defined corporate personalities for the subgroups, and the members of each subgroup had specific fiscal responsibilities. In the Third Estate, occupation was an obvious determinant of social station, but it was not the exclusive determinant. The geographical region of the country in which one lived, one's religion, property qualifications, and gender all helped to shape one's place.

Although a static, compartmentalized hierarchy built on privilege, esteem, and responsibility was the idealized structure for European society, the aspirations of individuals always threatened to create imbalance in the edifice. The sole possession of money could not transport an individual from an Estate or rank with few privileges and many burdens to one with many privileges and fewer burdens, but the judicious use of money might help. Because rank was associated with a whole code of behavior that included one's dress, language, eating habits, and even posture, it was rare for a single individual west of Muscovy to make a large leap upward—say, from the ranks of the peasantry to a professional or mercantile group. If a merchant acquired some landed property or a government office, however, within two or three generations his descendants might learn the art of "living nobly." Purchasing land and exercising seigneurial rights over a peasant village, they might withdraw from retail commerce and invest discreetly in an overseas commercial venture, the slave trade, or state loans. Or they might sink everything into the rural estate, exploiting it in modern fashion. By now well known in his neighborhood, the family chief might marry off a daughter to a titled clan, petition the king for his own armorial bearing, and doctor a few genealogical charts to show an aristocratic ancestor.

Distinguished service in the king's administration or, especially, his army, could speed up the process. Warfare accelerates social turmoil, resulting in personnel changes in the dominating group. In the Thirty Years' War, German conquerors assumed the land and titles of nearly the entire native Czech nobility; the English Protestant conquerors of Ireland did the same to the Catholic aristocracy there. Old aristocrats constantly complained about the passage of land and titles into the hands of parvenus. By the end of the seventeenth century, the pace of property transfers, very rapid during the social crises from the 1640s through 1670s, had slowed down demonstrably. Nobles, especially newly arrived ones, pressured sovereigns into being more stingy with titles. Furthermore, Europe's emergence from recession by 1730 renewed the pleasures of urban life and the attractiveness of commerce and manufacturing. In France and England especially, but also in western Germany and even Russia, a bourgeois consciousness emerged that no longer needed to ape the aristocratic lifestyle. Until this occurred, however, it was the nobleman's world.

For the largest of society's subgroups, the peasantry, matters were very different. Despite the fact that money alone could not dictate one's social status, the gulf between rich and poor widened considerably during the seventeenth century. West of the Elbe, peasant society was highly complex. The sharecropper had a rude hut and perhaps a scrawny cow and a couple of chickens. The day laborer had even less. On the other hand, the village chief owned a comfortable cottage and rented out hovels to his hired workers. He might control 70 or 80 acres. He possessed half a dozen horses and pigs, twice as many cows, and fifty chickens. He loaned money and rented equipment to his fellow villagers. He purchased their grain and took his chances on the open market. The remaining villagers fit into two or three categories, depending upon the comfort of their houses, number of acres held as tenants, amount of livestock possessed, and non-agricultural jobs pursued.

Generally, sharecroppers and poorer tenants had to supplement their fieldwork by taking in weaving or spinning. Diet helped determine peasant status as well. Most likely the peasant and his family ate less nourishing and less varied food than his grandparents had. Certainly the family ate less meat, and the caloric content of its porridge and bread was below sixteenth-century standards. However, variations were great from country to country and from region to region. English renters ate better than French sharecroppers, and a Polish serf or Sicilian day laborer would have considered the diet of a Dutch truck farmer as positively princely.

The urban counterparts of the peasants—the artisan, shopkeeper, or mechanic—had a more precarious existence than those on the land. During a steady recession the town dweller's rigid wages might be expected to increase in real value. But the period from 1648 to 1715 was a recession punctuated with disastrous crop failures, famines, and plagues. The moment prices rose, demand for items other than food collapsed, and men like Jean Cocu faced disaster. In town during a bad year high bread prices correlated with low pewter prices, which meant that workers were trying to sell their household possessions, and the Jean Cocus of Europe fell into ruin.

It appears that in nearly all the orders a shift away from the middle took place during the second half of the seventeenth century. Within the upper reaches of virtually all ranks, individuals consolidated their positions. A village chief became a little tyrant over his community and on occasion even transformed himself into an estate manager or owner. A comfortable merchant might invest in landed property and redirect the social aspirations and status of future generations of his family. A bishop might accumulate for his diocese and for himself. But tenured peasants, urban artisans, petty gentlemen, and parish priests were sinking. While Jean Cocu starved to death, half a dozen of the elite in his hometown of Beauvais had incomes, mostly in land, that could have fed him and a hundred like him for a normal year.

POLITICAL INSTITUTIONS

Absolutism and Its Limitations

As an institution wielding effective political authority over a large geographical region, the seventeenth-century state lay midway between the feudal monarchies of medieval Europe and the centralized, bureaucratic leviathans that emerged in the Western world just before the French Revolution of 1789. Anomaly and contradiction seemed to govern its structure and administration. The glorified idea of divine right and a Roman tradition of absolute power confronted the reality of a political society where corporate and privileged groups had negotiated contracts and agreements with the state that circumscribed its authority. Chief among these groups were the political Estates, representing the orders of society. But provinces, towns, professional bodies, guilds, and even individuals also had negotiated political and economic power with a sovereign, whose successors were legally obliged to honor the agreement. There were other hindrances to uniformity and centralization. Within a single state, laws, dialects, and weights and measures changed so frequently that travelers might feel they were crossing a new frontier at every hitching post. For that matter, the actual borders between states were ill-defined, vague, and always in dispute. They often were formed when a ruler simply constituted a frontier by building fortresses at strategic points.

In order to collect taxes, raise armies, and dispense justice, generations of governments had divided their states into administrative units. Nearly always, however, these artificial divisions deferred to historical realities and respected another type of regionalization created by custom, a shared past, language, or simply domination by a single great family. In all of the states of the seventeenth and eighteenth centuries, what first strikes the eye are the *historic regions* — unequal in size and diverse in statutory law, each claiming unique judicial rights and fiscal responsibilities. These states-within-states represented perpetual challenges to the centralizing efforts of the sovereign. The empires of both the Spanish and German Hapsburgs contained historic regions that caused rulers particular difficulty in the seventeenth century. Ever in need of funds, the Spanish monarch sold back independence to towns previously absorbed into the kingdom. Even in a relatively centralized kingdom such as France, provincial governments quarreled with one another to a point barely short of war, and the king found himself arbitrating their differences.

Nevertheless, pulling against the guarantees of regional and corporate privilege was a powerful idea—that of a hierarchical political order, at the helm of which stood the sovereign. It was exceptionally rare, even in periods of social unrest and outright civil war, for rebels to dispense with the principle of monarchical or quasi-monarchical authority. Evil advisers might dupe the king, or the sovereign himself might be a wretch. Nevertheless, standing in the wings was a hope, an heir, a successor, legitimized through birth or election, who would set matters straight again. The French philosopher Blaise Pascal (1623–1662) was no friend of absolutism. Nevertheless, he conceded that necessity dictated the existence of a hierarchical political order based on the principle of male hereditary succession:

> Because of the disorderly nature of mankind, the most unreasonable things of this world become the most acceptable. What could be less reasonable than choosing the first son of a king or queen to govern the state? We do not select for a ship's captain the passenger who happens to come from the best family. The principle of hereditary monarchy seems absurd and unjust, but habit makes it reasonable and just. Moreover, just who should be chosen to rule? The most virtuous and most skillful? How do we recognize him? Everyone pretends to be the most virtuous and most skillful. Let us therefore add something beyond dispute. That is the principle of the ruler's eldest son. It is clear-cut. It is incontestable. Reason itself is powerless to do better, for civil war is the greatest of misfortunes.[3]

The overwhelming number of Pascal's contemporaries shared his position. Only England from 1649 to 1660 and the Dutch Netherlands from 1650 to 1672 tried to adopt a form of government that dispensed with a monarch or superaristocrat at the helm; on each occasion the experiment failed. Religion, the Roman legal tradition, and popular legitimation sanctioned the pyramidlike hierarchy. A divine autocrat commanded the universe. He delegated control over humans' secular interests to an agent. Catholic priests and Protestant pastors alike, believing that it was in the interests of the Church to maintain those of the king, never tired of citing scriptural bases for royal authority. The office of kingship was shrouded in mystical religious fervor. The coronation ceremony was a magnificent spectacle built on a miracle. Once rightly anointed, the ruler was supposed to possess the touch that cured the lame and healed the sick. Christ himself had passed on to sovereigns certain of his divine powers. Principles derived from the law of the late Roman Empire held that the maintenance of efficiency and

---

[3] Blaise Pascal, *Pensées,* ed. L. Lafuma (Paris, 1952), p. 158. (Author's translation.)

social peace necessitated placing kings and their delegated officials above the compartmentalized segments of society. In the end, however, even religion and the law provided incomplete bases for maintaining or extending a sovereign's power. He needed the acquiescence of his people. When Louis XIV sent royal agents to the remote province of Auvergne in 1662 to prosecute a group of landlords who were terrorizing their tenants, he was successful because Auvergne's townsmen, clerics, and peasants supported him. Twenty-five years later, when James II tried to use his agents to enforce unpopular royal authority over England, he invited his dethronement.

Estates, Parliaments, and Diets

In the second half of the seventeenth century, the major problems of government were creating a working administration in the interests of the state itself and organizing the resources of the state to exploit opportunities in Europe and overseas. Representative Estates at the national and regional levels were highly suspicious of the methods used by sovereigns and their servants to resolve the problems of government, since this usually meant restricted privileges and increased taxation. Although their function was less to legislate than to petition the sovereign or ratify his decisions, parliaments and Estates in England, the Dutch Netherlands, and Poland resisted the centralizing tendencies of their sovereigns with a good measure of success. Elsewhere, national or regional assemblies maintained their nuisance value, and rulers found it necessary to bargain with them over the distribution of political authority.

Spain never had developed an Estates-General for the entire kingdom, and that of France would not meet again until 1789. Yet regional parliaments in Catalonia, Aragon, Valencia, and Navarre made it impossible for the Spanish Hapsburgs to establish good government, and in 1648 France's provincial Estates and its twelve regional law courts helped provoke the worst civil war in the kingdom's history. The Estates of Hungary made life miserable for the Austrian Hapsburgs, and parliaments in Scotland and Ireland could cause the Stuarts nearly as much difficulty as the English parliament at Westminster.

Nevertheless, by 1715 Estates in most places were on the decline. During his long reign Louis XIV alternately browbeat and negotiated with local elites in his effort to define the locus of political authority in France, while Leopold I of Austria (1658–1705) and Philip V of Spain (1700–1746) used the excuse of war emergency to neutralize the effectiveness of regional Estates in Hungary and Catalonia, respectively. The princes of the Holy Roman Empire constructed their minor absolutisms on the wreckage of both imperial and Estate authority. In Denmark a royalist coup d'etat established the king's unchallenged supremacy; in Russia, Estates paralleling those in the west—that is, built into the constitutional framework of the state—never really developed at any level.

The groups customarily represented by the national Estates were the most highly esteemed elements of the clergy, aristocracy, and urban bourgeoisie. Almost never did the peasants, town craftsmen, or country priests have a voice. The Swedish Estates were exceptional in that the more prosperous tenant farmers had their own House. In England the middling gentry was represented in the House of Commons. However, elsewhere in Europe smaller landlords had to be content with having their spokesmen in regional or provincial assemblies. In Poland and the Dutch Netherlands, the provincial Estates were more important than the national one. A member of the national Polish Diet or Dutch States-General could vote only in accordance with instructions sent from home.

Officers and Commissioners

In order to extend their authority into the economic, political, and spiritual lives of their subjects, governments had to create instruments of coercion. Bureaucracies had to be formed to which the ruler delegated areas of power and responsibility, especially in financial, judicial, and military matters. In the international arena, sovereigns theoretically possessed a plenitude of power. At home their claims as the source of justice, their leadership of the state's Church, and their right to assess contributions from districts, households, and consumers, depended upon the existence of loyal servants possessing the will and means to translate wishes into fact. For most governments, however, the supreme irony was that the sovereign's chief officers wished to restrain his authority rather than extend it.

The court, or royal household, was technically the ceremonial wing of government. The ambulatory monarch, trudging the dusty roads of his kingdom nine months out of twelve, was a thing of the past. By 1648 every sovereign in Europe had a royal residence in a royal capital. Now the landowners came to him. The reasons behind this unending procession are not hard to find: It had grown too costly to maintain a magnificent lifestyle in a provincial chateau; the sovereign wanted a potentially rebellious noble where he could keep an eye on him; and the royal court was the right place to be for the favor seeker. It also was where the sovereign could establish and preside over the most privileged society in the realm, a society governed by unswerving rules of etiquette and precedence and by a steady round of festivities and ceremonies. In Sweden, England, Spain, and Austria, members of the royal household doubled as government officials. By way of contrast, France's Louis XIV tried to distinguish the court from the working bureaucracy. He was successful only in part. Wherever a royal court existed in Europe, it insinuated itself into the structure of the regime. Because courtiers existed within a universe of sinecure, favor, and bitter personal rivalry, they hindered the development of disinterested government.

Rulers' persistent need for cash created a far more pernicious hindrance. In the seventeenth century newly enriched bourgeois subjects craved an elevated social status, but not even the king could sell them prestige willy-nilly. Estate ownership was a path that led to nobility only after several generations. A second path was office ownership. An office was a government post that could be purchased and inherited, like a piece of property. But it also was associated with a public function. In return for specific obligations and periodic financial contributions, the aspiring officeholder obtained a public power from the sovereign. Some officeholders, like the judges of the French sovereign courts, collectors of royal taxes, or managers of state finances, labored long and hard at posts they were proud to own. They even forged a corporate identity, a kind of guild, with holders of similar posts. A type of aristocracy accompanied certain important offices. In France it was called the *noblesse de robe*. For some posts, like a royal chancellorship, presidency over a sovereign court, or headship over the customs collectors, one had to be born noble.

Unfortunately, most individuals invested in offices not to serve the king but to obtain privileges. An officeholder won exemption from most direct taxes and military service. He was subject to a special jurisdiction reserved for members of his group, and he was expected to use his office to earn an income. Tax collectors retained a percentage of their take, judges and their officeholding clerks collected all manner of fees from litigants, and petty officials regularly took bribes in return for a permit or stamp. Therefore, alongside the dignity of function assumed by the great responsible officers of state was the sordid embezzlement of an army of lesser functionaries.

The royal need for funds merged with the hopes of those with some sums to spend, creating an industry that glutted the state with officials while failing to respond to its need for loyal servants. In France or Spain individuals and groups worked as stockjobbers in offices, purchasing dozens of posts from the Crown and auctioning them off at a profit. Two or three individuals might hold the same post, splitting income and fees. While England and Brandenburg escaped the worst calamities of officeholding, critics in Italy, Austria, most of the smaller German principalities, France, Spain, and even the Dutch Netherlands complained about grasping "agents" of the sovereign. Public opinion was expressed in this aphorism: "Each time the king creates an office, God creates a fool to buy it."

The multiplication of offices was antithetical to effective government, and sovereigns knew it. They therefore tried to develop another track of officials more likely to be responsive to the state's interests than the self-serving, corporate-minded officer corps that often worked hand in glove with regional and provincial Estates to thwart royal wishes. This second track of government agents comprised the commissioners. Like officers, they were socially ambitious. Unlike officers, however, their posts were not sold to them, but awarded at the sovereign's discretion. Their tenure never was guaranteed, and disgrace was a daily possibility. But their power and responsibilities were significant. The king tried to make them his closest advisers, and he sent them into the countryside to investigate, cajole, persuade, and browbeat Estates and officers alike. Point by point the duties of commissioners were established in opposition to those of the officers. The commissioners were inspectors and controllers, watchdogs for the sovereign. They supervised local police, exercised control over the domestic militia, investigated the tax rolls, and were constantly looking for new ways to increase royal revenues. They were responsible for developing the economic potential of a region. They proposed land reclamation projects and requested funds for canal and bridge construction.

The number of commissioners was limited, and their influence should not be exaggerated. Although the state tried to educate them for their jobs, their social origins were not very different from most of the officers'. They might emerge from the middling bourgeoisie or the country nobility. Many French *intendants* came from the junior ranks of the law officer corps; others, like Louis XIV's chief commissioners in the province of Languedoc, were sons of parlementary First Presidents. The elector of Brandenburg recruited his from the Estates themselves. Peter the Great of Russia went abroad to find servants for his state. By the early eighteenth century, every country in Europe had its commissioners. In Brandenburg, Denmark, and Russia they overwhelmed the older forms of officialdom. In France and Spain they enjoyed mixed success in their struggles with officers, relying on the strength of their own personalities as much as on the weight of royal authority. In the Hapsburg Empire or Poland, where governments were too poor or too weak and aristocracies were well entrenched, the commissioner corps was very feeble.

One group of commissioners was particularly important—the state servants responsible for raising, feeding, clothing, and equipping the sovereign's army. Noble retinues, town militias, and mercenary bands hired for a limited campaign no longer sufficed for rulers worried about internal revolt and external threats. The second half of the seventeenth century witnessed the rapid evolution of the large standing army. In the sixteenth century King Philip II of Spain had been content to send 40,000 troops to war. Louis XIV needed half a million. Commissioners advised kings on raising the productive capacity of the state in a time of recession, so that the military machine could be supported. They had to tax consumer goods in ways that would allow few or no exemptions. They had to haggle with uniform makers, munitions suppliers, and regimental colonels who hunted down potential troops. They had to make certain that soldiers were adequately trained, drilled, and paid.

Thus, from the middle of the seventeenth century on, governments tried to devise means of creating administrations through which they could wield effective authority. But the modern state did not emerge overnight. The financial poverty of regimes, the shortage of trained and loyal personnel, the inherent difficulties built into a society that tolerated corporate privilege, the idea that a government post was a piece of exploitative property—all of these factors slowed the development of the impersonal, centralized state as we know it. Well into the eighteenth century, court favorites and cliques of royal cousins might topple an able, disinterested minister of state. Even the most skillful royal commissioner had to bribe or grant special favors to local aristocracies in order to extend the king's law. Government agencies still were not systematized according to function. The incessant "special cases" of administrative jurisdiction— entire countries like Ireland or Hungary, provinces like Brittany or Cleves, cities like Barcelona or London, countless villages, as well as socioprofessional groups like clerics, nobles, guilds, landowners, and magistrates—all of these frustrated the extension of the state's control over people's lives. The centralizing sovereigns were the wave of the future in most places. But time and again their efforts were frustrated by dependence upon the habits and institutions of the past.

2

THE AGE OF MERCANTILISM

INDICATORS OF RECESSION

Prices and Money

Except when famine-provoked scarcities made agricultural necessities inordinately expensive, the period from 1648 to 1715 was one of low demand and sluggish prices. This situation contrasted with the sixteenth century, when a powerful inflationary spiral had gripped Europe, prices soared, and wages lagged behind. The influx of bullion from Spanish America, the consequential increase in the supply of money, the heroic attempts of traditional agriculture to feed a rapidly increasing population, and the rising costs of governmental administration and military needs—all had contributed to the sixteenth-century inflation. After 1620, however, the boom was over. The Mediterranean was the first region to sink into recession. Spain's bullion imports fell off, war disrupted commerce, and famine and plague struck hard. By 1648 even distant Poland and Russia felt the shock waves.

The most universal economic indicator of the late seventeenth-century recession was stagnant or falling grain prices. Not all countries were adversely affected, although producing and exporting countries bore the brunt. Between 1650 and 1700, average prices in France fell by 25 percent; in Spain, by 30 percent; in Poland and the Baltic regions, by as much as 40 percent. Peasants dependent upon cereal crops had to revert to secondary jobs like home weaving, tillable land surfaces shrank, and yield ratios fell. On the other hand, importing countries like the Dutch Netherlands benefited from lower prices. Of course, poor harvests temporarily produced dramatic fluctuations. For a short interval, prices would soar out of control, and the results were calamitous. Producers went hungry, and urban wage earners would squander their savings in the mad dash for scarce food. Except for such occurrences, however, agricultural sales remained sluggish. It is no wonder that west-European tenant farmers experienced increasing difficulty in meeting the costs of their fixed rents and dues, and their central- and east-European counterparts sank into serfdom.

Scarce money accompanied the lag in prices and is one factor that explains the recession. Less money reduces purchasing power, contributes to insufficient demand, and leads to a mad hunt for consumers. Peasants find it difficult to keep up their rents and dues, and landlords cut back investment and production. Between 1646 and 1660 the Spanish government recorded bullion imports from America at their traditional receiving station, Seville, as plummeting 90 percent below late sixteenth-century levels. Throughout the sixteenth century the commercially vigorous continent had greedily swallowed imports of precious metals. After 1620 this no longer was the case, exception made for cities in the Dutch Netherlands and, to a lesser extent, London and Hamburg. Moreover, throughout the seventeenth century over a third of Europe's stocks of bullion drained off to Asia and were not replenished. Experiments were made in Spain and Sweden to replace silver coinage with copper; but resultant inflation-deflation spirals in these countries discouraged the practice elsewhere. For a time Sweden had to revert to a natural economy. The government took its taxes in grain, meat, and iron. Soldiers were paid in farm produce. Professors at the University of Lund received their salaries in oats.

Seaborne Commerce and Regional Recessions

For several years historians concluded that the indicators of seaborne commerce confirmed the existence of an unrelieved all-European recession during the second half of the seventeenth century. Now it is clear that such a conclusion should be nuanced. The first set of traditional data concerned the import-export trade of Seville, focal point for Spain's West Indian and Latin American commerce. Between 1601 and 1605 an annual average of nearly 20,000 tons of cargo was registered as leaving Seville for the New World. Between 1651 and 1660 the annual cargo registry was down to 4,559 tons. Between 1681 and 1690 it was 3,898 tons, and between 1701 and 1710 it had plummeted to 1,729 tons. Government figures for American treasure dumped in Seville averaged 11.8 million pesos annually between 1661 and 1665, 6.9 million between 1671 and 1675, 1.9 million between 1681 and 1685, and 0.1 million between 1691 and 1695. Another set of figures holds that between 1600 and 1650, a total of 6,573 ships plied Spain's West Indian trade; in the second half of the century there were 1,835 ships sailing back and forth.

There is, of course, a danger in collating commerce in bullion and luxury products with general economic trends, and during the century north-European smugglers—who left no written records—took over a good share of Spain's commerce. However, a second indicator of seaborne commerce, the toll accounts of the Sound, that narrow strip of water at the entrance to the Baltic Sea, appears to confirm the Spanish evidence. Through the Sound came ships laden mostly with Polish and German cereals, but also with Swedish iron, Russian naval stores, and timber from Scandinavia. First the Danish and then the Swedish government used the Sound's toll charges as important sources of state revenue. Compared to the base year of 1650, there were half as many average annual passages through the Sound between 1655 and 1675, and 40 percent fewer between 1700 and 1720. These two periods were heavily punctuated by warfare, it is true; yet for only eight of the years between 1651 and 1730 did the number of ships passing through the Sound exceed the number for 1650.

This said, historians recently have questioned whether the apparent decline of seaborne traffic to and from Seville and through the Sound are valid indicators of an all-European recession. In the first place, Seville's export registers were based upon merchants' valuations for tax purposes. As taxes increased in the century, so did smuggling and grossly undervalued declarations. Secondly, the weight of transported products is not a very good indicator of their value. In 1600 bottled wines dominated Seville's exports to Spain's American colonies. A century later fine cloths, silks, and fancy lacework from France were important—and pound for pound much more valuable than the earlier cargo. Thirdly, historians have revised their estimates of late seventeenth-century imports of American treasure into Spain through Seville. Official government records announced a precipitous decline, parallel to the fall in Spanish exports. On the other hand, narrative sources, like consular reports and newspaper accounts of ship arrivals, betrayed still considerable remittances—for some years twenty and thirty times larger than official government figures. In addition, ports other than Seville were now siphoning off American silver and gold—Amsterdam in the Dutch Netherlands, Bordeaux in France, and Cádiz in Spain itself.

Concerning the traffic through the Sound, while the average annual number of passages declined in the second half of the century, the actual size of ships increased. Wide-bottom Dutch ships called flutes became the most common carriers. Moreover, the weight and volume of Dutch transport varied little throughout the century; the Dutch share in the carrying trade reached from half to three-fourths of the total. Finally, the rhythm of declining exports from the Baltic to England coincided with an evolving self-sufficiency in that relatively progressive country. In fact, England's prosperity may have contributed to the decline of Baltic commerce. It therefore seems more reasonable to speak not of an all-European recession in the later seventeenth century, but of regional recessions cutting through Spain, much of Italy and France, the Southern Netherlands, parts of Germany, most of Poland, and the other states ringing the Baltic Sea. On the other hand, England and the Dutch Netherlands represented concentrations of prosperity; it was from these places that Europe's eighteenth-century recovery would radiate.

Still, a psychology of hard times gripped most of Europe. Attempts at land reclamation stopped altogether in Italy and slowed down appreciably in France and England. Theoretical works on agricultural improvements were rare. Spanish industry, like Spanish agriculture, was in an advanced state of decay. Toledo silks and Segovia woolens virtually disappeared from the market. The Spanish government tried to revitalize overseas commerce by opening up Cádiz as an entrepôt, but foreigners immediately took over its port trade. Italy, the sixteenth century's most highly industrialized region, became an agricultural backwater. Of her cities, Venice, whose textiles had clothed sultans and kings, showed the most spectacular decline. In the 1680s the output of Venice was one-tenth of what it had been a century before. The city kept up a good front by becoming an aristocratic tourist resort; but Milan, Florence, Genoa, and Naples—to say nothing of Sicily's teeming slums of Palermo and Messina—collapsed with less grace. The entire western Mediterranean was in a state of transition. Its economy had been built on a carrying trade in wheat, wines, olives, woolens, textiles, and glassware. The Barbary Coast, Sicily, and the Near East had supplied the goods; Spain and southern France, the market; and Italy, the carriers. After the 1620s, however, the routes of supply shifted, and the carriers changed as well. Now Dutchmen brought Polish cereals and North Sea herrings to Spain and Italy. What was left of the trans-Mediterranean commerce fell into the hands of the French and the ubiquitous Dutch.

The south-German towns and old Hanseatic League ports on the Baltic-North Sea coast declined too. Of the few German coastal towns that were active, the northeastern grain-export centers of Memel and Gdansk (Danzig) were controlled by middleman shippers from the Dutch Netherlands and England. The south-German towns were in the sinking orbit of Italy. The princes of the Holy Roman Empire, whose political triumph was consolidated by the Peace of Westphalia, supplied limited capital for the establishment of "manufactories" of porcelain at Meissen (1710) or military uniforms at Berlin (1713). On the other hand, the princes exercised an especially nefarious influence over German trade by prohibiting the export of raw materials, neglecting road building, tolerating disunified monetary systems, and setting up customs barriers. They charged tolls for river traffic at every turn.

German princes also protected traditional guild manufacture and tried to suppress unregulated rural industry, especially that of textiles for domestic use. Long-distance overland trade in Germany remained medieval in character, dominated by the periodic fairs at Leipzig, where, for a stipulated few weeks during the year, unmolested buyers and sellers might exchange products varying from textiles to glassware and books. The emergence of Hamburg as an important financial and shipping center was one of the few bright spots on the German commercial scene. However, the shortsighted practices of the princes, the conservatism of the urban guilds, and a shortage of capital, manpower, and national markets conspired to maintain and even accelerate a decline that had already begun on the eve of the Thirty Years' War.

THE COMMERCIAL LEADERSHIP OF THE DUTCH

By 1648 European industrial and commercial leadership had concentrated in new hands. The fastest growing source of copper and iron, as well as timber and tar, was Sweden. England was bidding for supremacy in the manufacture of woolens and worsteds. Its coal and metal industries were growing. In the 1670s England began exporting grain, and it reexported nearly everything else, including tobacco and sugar from America and calicoes and silks from Asia. After 1661 France reorganized its commercial and industrial life. As Louis XIV's controller-general of finances between 1661 and 1683, Colbert laid the ground rules for French development: direct government investment followed by encouragement and regulation of very selective heavy industries such as shipbuilding and of manufactured luxury goods such as quality cloth, mirrors, and tapestries; government pressure to export more manufactured goods than were imported and to import more raw materials than were exported; heroic attempts to force provinces and towns to abolish or reduce internal tolls; and the construction of an overseas empire through trade and colonization.

Republicanism, Fish, and Ships

But for the half century after 1648 the real masters of Europe's economic life were the Dutch. At first glance the circumstances for such control looked highly improbable. Even by seventeenth-century standards, the Dutch political system appeared genuinely medieval, incapable of sustaining commercial leadership. Sovereignty was carved out of a successful rebellion against Spain that had taken eighty years to settle. The chosen form of government was a halfway house between royal and republican, which resulted in a persistent constitutional tension. Moreover, Dutch fears of centralization were as powerful as their horror of royal absolutism. The basis of government was a loose federation of seven provinces, countless free towns, and a buffer territory bordering on the Southern Netherlands still held by Spain. Nowhere in western Europe did regionalism have such a strong bearing upon a state's politics and society. There was no uniform taxation; weights and measures varied among the provinces and towns. Sitting in their various provincial and urban assemblies, a thousand citizens dictated the decisions of their representatives in what passed for a national legislature, the States-General meeting in The Hague.

On the other hand, the Orange family, its legitimacy enshrined in Dutch life because of its leadership in the sixteenth-century revolt against Spain, prevented a more thoroughgoing republicanism. Its leading male member, the prince of Orange, held patronage power over the central offices of state, especially the military ones. He customarily was chosen stadholder (or lieutenant) of Holland, richest and most important of the seven provinces. He headed an aristocratic political party and was very popular with the Calvinist clergy, shopkeepers, peasantry, and urban workers. True, sovereignty officially resided with the States-General, and the individual provinces so jealously guarded the right to elect their own particular stadholders that at no time during the seventeenth century did a single person hold the office in all seven of them. Yet the stadholder of Holland was a prince, and the family he headed possessed a patriotic mystique that was shared with no other party in Dutch public life. The prince of Orange held a court where French was commonly spoken, and foreign ambassadors dealt with him. He was commander-in-chief of the armed forces, and at least four provinces besides Holland customarily elected him their stadholder. It was no secret that the constitutional propensities of the prince of Orange veered toward monarchy rather than republicanism, and the burghers of Amsterdam did all they could to resist his ambitions. In fact, between 1650 and 1672 they managed to prevent the election of a stadholder for Holland altogether.

Despite this tension in Dutch political life, the great burghers of Holland's towns created a trading-banking empire that knew no peer in the century. On the one hand, its basis lay in the growth of commercial fishing and shipbuilding; on the other, in the evolution of a rural society of independent farmers specializing in commercial crops ranging from traditional wheat, barley, and oats to innovative cabbages, beans, and flower bulbs. A merchant marine was constructed that exceeded in total tonnage all rivals combined. A pair of international trading companies and the Bank of Amsterdam capped the empire.

How can we explain this unparalleled energy for gain in an insecure, politically unstable nation of fewer than 2 million? In part it was due to the persistence, courage, and sobriety found among a small people aware that nothing in this world comes easily. The long political revolt against Spain had succeeded because the Dutch were sufficiently prescient to build a natural wall of defense behind the great rivers on their southern frontier and because their superior seamanship and shipbuilding abilities put the enemy on the defensive. Even prior to the rebellion against Spain, the Dutch realized that their future lay in commercial mastery of the sea. The provinces of Holland and Zeeland always had nourished themselves on the fish off their shore. Sometime in the sixteenth century the spawning grounds of Baltic herring shifted southward, creating a surplus catch that could be sold all over Europe. By the middle of the seventeenth century more than a thousand Dutch fishing vessels plied the North Sea and English Channel up to the Thames itself. The Scandia shoals and Norwegian Sea fell within the Dutch orbit.

Their ships were of compact size, up to 30 tons apiece. Each was manned with a crew of ten to fifteen and rigged so ingeniously that the fish could be salted and kept on board until the catch was complete. Vessels were sufficiently supplied with food and water for voyages that might last as many as eight weeks. Once the fishermen, cleaners, and curers finished their specialized tasks on board, the ships returned to port where inspectors would check the quality of the catch and supervise repacking for domestic sale and export. The quality of the catch was uniformly high, and the product commanded premium prices. A full fifth of the Dutch population lived off the herring industry. The catch could average over a quarter million tons per year.

As shipbuilders, the Dutch were so far ahead of their rivals that as late as 1700 one-fourth of the English fleet was made in Holland's yards. In the 1670s the volume of Dutch-owned shipping exceeded that of all the rest of Europe combined. The piers of Amsterdam contained a welter of wind-driven sawmills, winches, and cranes; the skill of Dutch shipwrights, as well as their economy in the use of materials, was admired and envied. The flute was the most celebrated vessel built in Dutch yards. It was a stout, sturdy ship meant to bear heavy and bulky commodities such as the salt, grain, naval stores, and packed fish that were the chief items passing between the eastern Baltic and Mediterranean. Wholly utilitarian, the flute doomed the costly armed merchantman. Everything was sacrificed for the cargo. The hold was enormous, the cabin space minuscule, the crew of minimal size. It weighed from 200 to 500 tons and could be modified for specialty transport, such as timber or whale carrying. Because their merchant marine and shippers commanded the transport and ownership of raw materials from which the flutes were constructed—namely timber, hemp, iron, and pitch from Scandinavia and the Baltic—the Dutch could build a flute 50 percent more cheaply than any other of their competitors. They passed savings in construction and crew costs on to carriers. During most of the seventeenth century, English, French, and even Spanish traders preferred to buy the vessels from the Dutch rather than urge imitations on their own shipbuilders.

In their turn, Dutch carriers could offer merchants the best prices in Europe, and Dutch merchants took advantage of their geographical good fortune to exploit the Netherlands' rivers and adjacent sea-lanes. The provinces of Holland and Zeeland contained the mouths of the Scheldt, Maas, and Rhine rivers. Their coastal towns faced the convergence of the North Sea, English Channel, Baltic and Atlantic routes. At the quays of Amsterdam, Rotterdam, and Schiedam, as well as dozens of smaller ports, Dutch-owned flutes containing Polish and east-German grain, Scandinavian timber, and Baltic naval stores jostled with Dutch-owned trawlers reeking of North Sea herring and Arctic cod. Beside the ships, burghers scurried back and forth arranging sales and exchanges. By 1648 the Dutch controlled northern Europe's grain trade, they dominated the region's commerce in naval stores and iron, and their agents exercised almost complete command over the Baltic export centers of Gdansk and Memel.

Price determined the success of the Dutch shippers. They made large-scale purchases, offered liberal credit terms, provided cheap transport, and relentlessly exploited their sources of supply. They purchased Finnish and Norwegian forests outright. They invested directly in Swedish mines. Not content with simply dominating trade between the Netherlands and the Baltic, they were busy in southerly commerce as well. Three-fourths of the salt sent from Portugal and France to the Baltic was transported on Dutch ships. Half the west-European cloth intended for Scandinavia and eastern Europe was made or finished in the Dutch town of Leiden and its suburbs. The Dutch cornered the production of Tuscan marble. In the course of the seventeenth century they added new products to their commercial repertoire. Sugar, tobacco, and cotton from the West and East Indies were processed in Dutch towns and then sold to foreign merchants. All of this activity stood in marked contrast to the passion for land investment that tied up capital elsewhere on the continent.

Fundamental to Dutch prosperity was the maintenance of open seas and open ports. No people abhorred war at sea more than the Dutch. No people in Europe feared more the development of economic nationalism, as defined by import and export tariffs and the closing of foreign ports to nonnative shipping. Between 1648 and 1721, however, wars tested Dutch ingenuity to its limits—in the Baltic from 1655 to 1660, 1674 to 1679, and 1700 to 1721; in the North Sea and Atlantic from 1652 to 1654, 1665 to 1667, 1672 to 1678, 1689 to 1697, and 1702 to 1713; and sporadically in the Mediterranean. The wars carried to the East and West Indies as well. After the 1670s the Dutch became major investors and participants in the wars against Louis XIV of France. The wars strained their resources while forcing rivals and enemies to develop their own. In 1715 the Dutch still were carrying half of the Baltic's grain and up to 40 percent of the region's timber and naval stores. But the French and English were manufacturing their own flutes now. Moreover, these larger states were beginning to understand a concept that the Dutch had failed to grasp adequately—that fishing, shipping, and investment abroad were not sufficient bases on which to establish a nation's lasting economic strength. The Dutch still controlled the transport of Swedish iron in 1715, but the fact that two-thirds of it eventually wound up in England was most prophetic of all.

Carriers to the World

Dutch merchant-shippers failed to comprehend the significance of the first faint signs of European industrialization. To them a more obvious mark of economic health remained the carrying trade, and Holland's mastery over non-European sources of supply was the sharpest indicator of all. It may seem exceedingly strange to us that Malabar pepper, Yemenese coffee, and Bengali silks—in short, luxury items enjoyed by fewer than 1 percent of Europe's population—should weigh so important. But an age of economic stagnation, when the gulf increases between the whisper-thin layer of the very rich and everyone else, is not one to recognize the long-term advantages of creating a vast market of consumers. Few in the seventeenth century conceived of the market as anything more than war materiel for kings, subsistence foodstuffs for the majority, and luxury items for the wealthy. The boom in the new, inexpensive printed calicoes that the English brought from India in the 1680s caught everyone by surprise. A state's economic strength was supposed to be measured by its share of control over the grain, fish, and luxury trades, and it was difficult to shift one's mentality.

The Dutch never really did. Their handling of overseas commerce, particularly in the East Indies, which they considered their major enterprise, contrasts markedly with their price-cutting techniques in handling the Baltic and North Sea trade. They controlled so completely European imports of pepper from Malabar, Sumatra, and Java, as well as the more exotic Indonesian cloves, nutmeg, cinnamon, and mace, that they might well have experimented with lower prices in order to influence habits of consumption. Indeed, in the eighteenth century, this is what the English and French would do for sugar, tea, and coffee. But the Dutch were very cautious. Even if it meant destroying the stocks already in Amsterdam's warehouses, they kept the price of spices at consistently high levels. A privileged company possessing exclusive rights to overseas commerce from the Cape of Good Hope clear across the Pacific to the Straits of Magellan, ran the Dutch East Indies colony. Directed by seventeen of Amsterdam's greatest merchants and bankers, the Dutch East India Company possessed a spirit of independence that was legion. It could wage war, make treaties, command military units, and supervise conversion of the heathen.

The half century after 1648 was the company's golden age. It was the most important European institution in Asia, and it enjoyed a sphere of interest that radiated out from its headquarters on the island of Java to control the spice trade of the Malay peninsula and Ceylon. Its ships dominated the coastal traffic of India and plied the Persian Gulf. The company enjoyed a major share of Asia's own carrying trade, particularly between India and Japan, and between China and the Philippines. But the spice trade between the East Indies and Europe remained its primary interest, and its guiding philosophy never parted from maintaining enforced scarcities. Nor did the company encourage colonial settlement, and in 1650 the Dutch population in Asia and South Africa was fewer than 10,000.

Such restrictive attitudes proved costly. During the 1690s the Dutch East India Company introduced the Arabian coffee bean into Java. The newly established plantations raised the crop according to the principles established for spice production. Exports of coffee from Java to Europe in 1713 totaled exactly 1 ton. At one point in the eighteenth century, when the company misguidedly feared that the European market would be saturated, it sent orders to uproot the coffee trees in Java and substitute pepper. On the other hand, while the rivals of the Dutch never challenged the company's monopoly over spices, coffee was another matter. The French and English in the Antilles and the Portuguese in Brazil experimented with methods of increasing productivity and influencing European consumption. By the 1730s, west Europeans were becoming accustomed to coffee. However, it was coffee from America, not from the East Indies, that they were drinking. The Dutch had allowed the market to slip out of their hands.

Dutch commerce in the West Indies was built on a less solid foundation than the caution which brought the dignified East India Company such prestige. In the late seventeenth century 2 million Spanish-speaking inhabitants in the New World needed textiles, tools, and manufactured goods that their declining motherland was unable to supply. English and French West Indian planters were creating a vast new sugar, tobacco, and coffee culture; but they desperately needed cheap labor and cheap food for their workers. The Dutch had the ships. It was logical for them to supply the goods. They brought manufactured goods to New Spain and black slaves to the Caribbean. They brought grain, beef, and fish from New England to the West Indies and carried rum, molasses, and sugar back to Europe.

Nearly all of this commerce was accomplished in defiance of trading restrictions that the Spanish, English, and French governments had placed on their own colonists. Much of it occurred during times of war. Rival states considered the Dutch commercial activities to be smuggling, and on occasion they even degenerated into piracy—such as raids on Spanish galleons suspected of containing bullion. For the Dutch, America was a riskier adventure than the East Indies. They depended upon the cooperation of producers and their own ingenuity, bypassing the barriers that governments set in their way. The Dutch West India Company was a colonial power too. Although it conquered Curaçao, St. Eustatius, and other Caribbean islands, it lost New Netherland to the English and Brazil to the Portuguese. Without doubt, its ships indirectly encouraged English, French, and Scottish colonization by providing settlers from Newfoundland to Barbados with European manufactures and by carrying back to the Old World their exportable staples.

Banking and Investment

The fishing industry, shipbuilding, and carrying trade inside and outside Europe helped make Dutch fortunes in the seventeenth century. But this was not all the Dutch accomplished. Amsterdam's insurance house dated from 1598, its stock exchange from 1608, and its exchange bank from 1609. Private Dutchmen loaned funds to chronically impecunious states such as Denmark, Austria, and Spain. One Dutchman, Louis de Geer, ran Sweden's munitions industry. Other Dutch investors held export monopolies in Russian ports and were behind the one truly important land reclamation project of the century, the draining of the Cambridge fens in southern England. When the Bank of England was founded, Dutchmen bought a major interest. While the Dutch state strained its resources beyond repair in forty years of hot and cold war against Louis XIV, individual Dutchmen were investing in French textiles, sugar refining, and shipbuilding; their flutes were carrying powder, matches, and lead to French ports. They were not overly scrupulous about their customers, and the government of tradesmen and bankers understood. One of the happiest investments for Dutchmen remained at home, however, in the exchange bank of Amsterdam. An account in the bank was a mark of true prestige. In the seventeenth century it was Europe's most secure financial institution. Between 1611 and 1701 deposits rose from under a million florins to 16 million. Money placed into the bank could be withdrawn anywhere in the world.

The canvasses of De Hooch and Vermeer may not show it, but there actually were poor people in the Dutch Netherlands in the seventeenth century. Amsterdam had slums that could rival those of Naples and Madrid. Still, the Dutch never starved, and in this fact they were unique among the continent's people. Buying in low season, their merchants stored goods until it became a seller's market. The port warehouses were stocked with munitions, brandy, tobacco, dried herrings, spices, and grain.

As an importing nation, the republic was always prepared for a domestic food crisis, and the Dutch were ever ready to seize the advantage in case of a foreign one. In 1672, on the eve of their costly war with England and France, the Dutch had a twelve-year supply of cereals stored away. Twenty years later, when famine hit Europe, Amsterdam made a fortune in grain sales. By 1715, however, the undisputed commercial leadership of the Dutch was in jeopardy. During the War of the Spanish Succession (1702–1713), Amsterdam's customs receipts declined. They never returned to prewar levels. Conversely, the war created a boom in English shipbuilding. In 1663 the English merchant fleet was 90,000 tons. Fifty years later it had grown more than threefold.

The Dutch Republic exhausted itself financing the allied coalitions against France, and Dutch merchants and bankers increasingly looked beyond the Netherlands for new investment opportunities. They remained loyal enough to Amsterdam's exchange bank, but they were losing faith in their country's commercial future. They grew impatient waiting for famine to make their grain purchases pay off. Leiden's textile industry, mired in the habits of a guild system and scorning technological innovation, looked less attractive than the rapidly developing woolens manufactures of England. The trading habits of the East India Company hardly seemed geared for the modern world. Short on people, lacking natural and agricultural resources, unable to develop new domestic channels for investment, early in the eighteenth century the Dutch Netherlands slipped as an economic power. For other countries, however, emerging from a period of stagnation, Dutchmen with funds were a godsend. Austrian mining, Swedish munitions, French sugar refining, the Bank of England—all owed their eighteenth-century prosperity to the prescience of Dutch investors. This dispersion of resources, costly to the Netherlands, heralded better days for Europe as a whole.

THE BREAKTHROUGH OF THE ENGLISH

The Dutch had consolidated their commercial triumphs within the confines of a traditional seventeenth-century economy. They carried what others needed, provided the essentials of survival for those who could pay, and brought prestige items to the leisured groups. It was left to others to work out the idea of an expanding domestic and export market—one in which modest peasants or craftspeople might desire some sugar to sweeten their coffee or an extra shirt to place on their backs. Around the 1680s English merchants conceived of exploiting this market. Why it occurred in England is an important historical problem. In several ways England was more advanced economically than nearly all the continental states. Its towns and villages had been spared the ravages of war, small industries never had to rebuild from rubble, river transport was easy and customs-free, the land was unforested but contained sufficient ore and abundant coal, and the guild structure was weak. Moreover, both landed and merchant groups shared an interest in commerce, industry, and investment. With its export of woolen cloth, England always had done well enough in Europe's subsistence economy. By 1650 the country had lessened its dependence upon grain imports from the Baltic. Half a century later England was sending its own cereal surplus abroad.

Reexports, Protection, and the Anglo-Dutch Wars

It was neither the export of familiar products nor the expansion of commonplace industries, such as buttons or cutlery, that turned England into the most formidable rival of the Dutch. England's new economic strength derived from obtaining control over the reexport of products coming from the New World and Asia. London became a major entrepôt for sugar, tobacco, cod, cottons, and calicoes. Merchants, carriers, and the government became convinced that not only their countrymen but also the Dutch, French, and Germans—and perhaps one day the Spaniards and Italians—would want new products. Hopeful signs appeared even in an age of recession. From just over a million pounds in the 1630s, between 1699 and 1701 tobacco exports from Maryland and Virginia rose twentyfold. Prior to the 1640s, West Indian sugar was practically unknown in Europe. Between 1699 and 1701 nearly 4 million pounds of it entered English ports. In 1660 calicoes from India were rare and feared by all of Europe's cloth interests. Between 1699 and 1701 over 860,000 pieces reached England. Particularly encouraging was the fact that two-thirds of the tobacco and calicoes and one-third of the sugar that arrived in England between 1650 and 1700 were *reexported* to other parts of Europe. Consolidated statistical estimates verify this evolution. In the 1660s England's total exports averaged £4.1 million per year; total imports averaged £4.4 million. In 1700 the corresponding figures were £6.4 million and £5.8 million. A deficit had been converted into a surplus, and reexports of raw materials, foods, and textiles from the New World and Asia accounted for most of the newly favorable trade balance.

The policies of English governments made certain that English merchants and carriers would be the ones who profited from expanding overseas trade. Between 1651 and 1673 Parliament passed six pieces of protective legislation called the Navigation Acts, all aimed at the Dutch. Essentially, the acts were intended to restrict commerce between English colonies and England to ships bearing the English flag and manned by English crews. This restriction was extended to English trade with Asia, Africa, and the non-English colonies of the New World. To assure English ports of customs receipts and ensure the prosperity of the reexport trade, certain "enumerated articles" produced in the colonies—generally tobacco, sugar, indigo, and dyewoods—were forbidden from going directly to ports other than those in England, Ireland, or an English possession. Imports to England from the continent had to come directly from the producing country or country of normal first shipment, never through another port such as Amsterdam. Specific commodities (timber and naval stores from the Baltic; fruits, wines, spirits, and salt from the Mediterranean) had to be imported on English ships or ships of the exporting country. Foreign merchants sending goods to British North America usually had to pass through an English port first, pay tolls there, and then reload their cargoes on an English ship that would make the Atlantic crossing. Trade along the English coast was to be limited to English vessels.

The restrictive purpose of the Navigation Acts was obvious—to cut into the Dutch carrying trade, especially that part of it destined for England and the English colonies in the New World. The acts succeeded gradually. Between 1660 and 1700 the amount of colonial commerce reexported to Europe through English ports rose fourfold over the previous half century. Tobacco, sugar, and calicoes alone formed two-thirds of this reexport trade. In addition, after 1688 the idea of exclusive and privileged overseas trading companies was modified. Although the English East India Company preserved its monopoly in Asia, merging with its chief rival in 1708, the Royal Africa Company was forced to yield to the principle of unfettered expansion in England's trans-Atlantic commerce. This greatly contributed toward opening up the African slave trade. By 1700 most English foreign trade was available to investors willing to act as individuals or in partnership, as long as they adhered to the government's complex collection of tariffs, navigation laws, and commercial treaties.

Thanks largely to the Navigation Acts, the English government began to view the parts of the empire as interdependent units of production and consumption. Merchants and shippers in the motherland controlled the machinery. Thus, the Devon fishing fleet picked up Newfoundland cod and transported it to Spain and Portugal, returning to England with wine and olive oil. English slavers dumped their human cargo into the West Indies or the southern mainland colonies of North America and picked up raw sugar, tobacco, or cotton for shipment home. In England the colonial products were refined, then either used domestically or sold to the continent. From England the slavers took arms to West Africa in exchange for more blacks. Newfoundland and New England sent fish to feed the cane workers in the West Indies; the islands returned molasses, sugar, and rum to the northern colonies. All the while, England supplied its colonial markets with a stream of textiles, guns, tools, and machinery at prices favorable to producers and suppliers.

The Dutch, against whom the Navigation Acts were mainly directed, tried to circumvent them as best they could. They smuggled textiles and machinery into New England and the West Indies, and their fishermen insisted on pursuing their catch off the English coast. In 1652 war erupted between the Netherlands and Oliver Cromwell's English Protestant republic. Observers were astonished by the struggle between the two European states most alike in religion and political ideology. The Anglo-Dutch War was the first in modern times to be fought almost exclusively for commercial reasons. The English were the aggressors, the Dutch on the defensive. Thirteen years later a second war broke out, when the English fleet attacked Dutch shipping off the coasts of West Africa and North America. On this occasion the Dutch proved that their commercial triumphs had not softened them, and Admiral Michiel de Ruyter conducted one of the boldest maneuvers in the history of modern naval warfare. In 1667 he led his fleet straight up the Thames and Medway, destroyed most of the English navy resting in dry dock, and returned home with a prize warship in tow.

Although the Dutch relinquished New Netherland at the Treaty of Breda (1667), the English still had to recognize Germany and the Spanish Netherlands as within Holland's economic sphere of influence. The Navigation Acts were modified to permit Dutch vessels to carry goods to England from this enlarged trading area. In 1672 a third Anglo-Dutch war erupted, ending in stalemate two years later. For the remainder of the century England and the Dutch Netherlands remained at peace with one another, because the two countries shared a common interest of survival against Louis XIV's France. But the Navigation Acts stood. Throughout the eighteenth century and well into the nineteenth, they represented the cornerstone of British trade and imperial policy.

In the late seventeenth century England's technological development did not yet measure up to the ambitions of its merchants and shippers for serving an expanding market. A hundred years earlier the country had experienced what has been called, with some exaggeration, "the first industrial revolution." Factories were established in the countryside—paper and gunpowder mills, cannon foundries, saltpeter works. By the 1640s England and Wales already produced three times as much coal as the entire continent, but the failure to devise a workable process of smelting prevented the English from becoming preeminent in metallurgy. At length, in 1709 the first genuinely successful smelting of iron with coal took place when Abraham Darby discovered that by precooking his coal he was able to remove most of the impurities that had rendered the ore hopelessly brittle. But even Darby's breakthrough failed to surmount all the obstacles between invention and its full use in manufacturing.

Preindustrial Manufactures and the Consumer-Generated Economy

Between 1648 and 1715 textiles comprised England's chief manufacturing industry. Perhaps it was the greatest industry of any kind in Europe. However, the basis for preparation, spinning, and weaving remained but slightly mechanized. Carding and combing of the fibers were hand processes. Weaving looms were exceedingly simple mills that pounded cloth either with vertically moving pestles or angle-set hammers. Production was decentralized. The merchant-employer bought the raw materials and distributed them to rural laborers, who worked them on ancient family looms during their spare moments away from the fields. Since the jobs were performed on farms and in cottages, the employer was unable to supervise the efforts of the worker, and the quality of the products varied. Without a technological revolution, the industrial factory could not develop. The wholesale change from wood to coal as fuel, the mastery of heavy machinery, and the organization of urban-based centers of complete and supervised manufacture had to await the mid-eighteenth century. Between 1648 and 1715, England was far from becoming an industrial giant.

Nevertheless, an evolution in manufacturing did occur. Quantitatively, it was a general rise punctuated by short-term fluctuations. According to one estimate, in the late 1660s annual woolens exports from England averaged £2.1 million, and between 1699 and 1701 the figure was over £3 million. Heavy and light woolens were sent from the newly developed southwestern port town of Exeter to the Dutch and Spanish Netherlands, Germany, Spain, and Portugal. In addition, England now was producing a greater variety of textiles. Highly finished serge replaced rough kersey. West Indian cotton was introduced into the county of Lancashire. Woven together with linen, it could be used for tapes, ribbons, and garters. Manchester's merchant capitalists thrived in the new manufacture of linen draperies.

Invention and innovation contributed to the expansion of textile production. Using the recently introduced Dutch loom, during the 1690s a single Lancashire weaver could make twelve pieces of ribbon over 400 yards long in two days. In the small towns of Nottingham and Leicester the stocking frame revolutionized hosiery manufacture. Meanwhile England profited enormously from the religious bigotry of France's Louis XIV. The king's premature declaration in 1685 of the disappearance of Calvinism in France brought tens of thousands of skilled Huguenot workers to England, many expert in textiles, book printing, papermaking, and other crafts. In their English asylum they transformed watchmaking, as well as the manufacture of cutlery, fine textiles, and glass, into industries which catered to a larger clientele than had existed prior to their arrival. Instead of simply the great aristocracy, now country gentlemen and even comfortable yeomen, merchants, and professionals hankered for beaver hats, fine woolens and cottons, silks, velvets, and brocades—for themselves, their wives, and their children.

It was during this period that investors and merchants conceived of the market as elastic and expandable. High wages, low food prices, and the disappearance of the fear of famine encouraged English producers to develop the idea of a consumer-generated economy. Of course, the desire to consume was nothing new. In their greedy pursuit of palatial houses, ostentatious furniture, precious jewelry, and exotic furs, the great nobilities of sixteenth-century Europe had few peers in history. However, prior to the late seventeenth century what prevailed was the Dutch conception of consumers serving either as common users of subsistence articles or else as aristocratic purchasers of luxuries. Fashionable economic thought supported this position, considering general widespread spending on material goods to be detrimental to a country's prosperity.

During the 1680s the success of the English East India Company in importing unprecedented amounts of cheap, colorful fabrics from Asia led some economic theorists to rethink their long-held beliefs. In 1691 Dudley North (1641–1691) wrote that "the main spur to Trade, or rather to Industry and Ingenuity, is the exorbitant Appetites of Men, which they will take pains to gratifie, and so be disposed to work, when nothing else will incline them to it." It would be a mistake, of course, to envision "democratic consumerism" as emerging explosively and unchallenged. After all, as much as anything else, such acquisitive egalitarianism might threaten the social hierarchy established and maintained by elites, and the motives of merchants who advocated increased consumption remained suspect. Yet it was abundantly clear that in late seventeenth-century England, trade and preindustrial manufacture were thriving; shippers, merchants, and entrepreneurs were the driving forces behind this prosperity. Employment rose, wages stayed high, markets grew; English yeomen, shopkeepers, their wives and children joined the craze for colorful clothing, coffee, sugar, and tobacco. Had they known what was occurring in this privileged corner of Europe, the misery-wracked Jean Cocus on the continent would have sighed with wonder and envy.

Agricultural "Improvement"

It was during the late seventeenth century that England enjoyed another unique boon: increased agricultural production through more intensive farming and an expanded arable. The consequence was an exportable surplus. These developments necessitated a revolution in thinking fully as important as the one which encouraged an expanding market for manufactures. As was the case on the continent, prices for English cereals were relatively low throughout the century. Whereas the continental European response to low prices was to limit production, in England both the government and landowners opted for another course. It was thought that increased production would make England agriculturally self-sufficient and allow it to escape dependence upon Baltic grain imports. As with textile manufacturing, it was in hope of stimulating consumer demand that agricultural policies evolved. The same wage earner who desired a second woolen shirt would be taught to prefer English wheat bread over imported barley or rye.

Literature speaking of agricultural "improvement" was best represented by John Houghton's *Collection of Letters for the Improvement of Husbandry and Trade,* a newsletter published weekly from 1691 to 1703, which urged the use of clover, lucerne, and turnips as field crops within rotations. The legumes would improve pasturage while the root crops would produce fodder for animals. Nor was invention neglected. Plows were improved, and in 1701 Jethro Tull patented his design for a planting drill that would render obsolete the ancient habit of broadcasting seed indiscriminately. There was experimentation with raising leaf vegetables, hops, and flax. Encouraged by recommendations from the agricultural committee of the Royal Society, England's official agency of scientific inquiry, the potato moved from the garden to the field. The growth of fodder products like turnips resulted in a larger supply of healthy animals, more manure, and better cereal yields. The home market absorbed most of England's increased agricultural output, and the country's exports did not amount to more than 4 percent of its annual production. Yet England no longer had to import grain. Its people learned to expect wheat bread, and they became inveterate beer drinkers. In the 1580s there had been twenty-six common brewers in London; as the eighteenth century opened, there were 180.

The decision by English landlords to opt for intensification, greater yields, and rational stockbreeding placed pressure on the traditional social structures of rural life. Landowners saw a need to increase the size of their holdings through the consolidation of several farms into one. This procedure was called *engrossing.* Landowners also wished to consolidate into compact holdings the scattered strips tilled in time-honored ways by leaseholding village peasants. This was known as *enclosing.* Neither engrossing nor enclosing was new. Since the sixteenth century landowners had tried to secure the advantages that might accrue from assuming common village rights over arable and pasturelands. Following acquisition of the property the landowner would surround his holdings with fences or hedges, plant crops in one area, and raise cattle in another. However, common sense had prevailed against transforming peasant leaseholders into mere renters, agricultural laborers, or vagrants. The social menace produced by the dispossession of large numbers of people was a very real fear. Still, during the second half of the seventeenth century fewer voices were heard against enclosing and engrossing, and it has been estimated that during this period more enclosing took place than at any comparable time before or after.

By 1700 around half of England's arable land was enclosed. Cultivation was extended and estates were enlarged. Landlords replaced traditional tenure arrangements with higher rent charges. To finance improvements they borrowed heavily. In order to better their social status as they invested in modernizing agriculture, wealthy city merchants purchased rural property and became country squires. They, and others like them, showed tenants and renters alike the material benefits of improved farming techniques, higher yields of traditional crops, and experimentation with new ones. Elegant manor houses filled with tapestries, French furniture, marble, and mirrors sprouted throughout the English countryside. Fine gardens, grottoes, and parks embraced the new structures. Improving agriculture became as fashionable as it was profitable.

Banking, Taxation, and Deregulation

The English moved ahead of their commercial rivals in another important way: the creation of a financially solvent state—a government that balanced its books and to which subjects and foreigners loaned funds with confidence. The Dutch had provided the model. They were the first seventeenth-century Europeans to invest safely in government enterprise. During the war against France from 1672 to 1678, the States-General borrowed without difficulty at 4 percent, while the overcommitted Louis XIV could barely find takers willing to finance him at 10 or even 15 percent. Yet when it came to questions of taxation, the Dutch were backward. The provinces possessed the right to bargain with the States-General over their assessment, and this customarily meant the reduction or even removal of quotas. The Netherlands lacked a central agency to supervise the collection of taxes, and the States-General had to depend upon heavy excises on consumer items. These indirect taxes usually were farmed out to individuals who advanced the government a lump sum and then kept most of what they subsequently collected for themselves.

      When it came to taxation the English were only slightly ahead of the Dutch. In fact, until 1692 England's tax revenue probably was the smallest per capita in Europe. It was one-fifth the size of France's. It derived from surcharges on certain consumer goods, customs dues, and direct taxes agreed to by Parliament. Under James II (1685–1688), some reforms were tried. For example, tax farming came to an end, and by 1710 a single royal agency staffed by commissioners, the Royal Treasury, controlled all accounts of collection and expenditure. The costs of the major European wars in which England found itself after 1689 called for a reevaluation of the public's tax-paying responsibilities. To raise revenue, characteristic nuisance taxes were levied, such as duties on windowpanes and houses. The major direct tax, on land rented out, was raised to 20 percent, so that those who best could afford to pay, the great property owners, were the ones who did so. However, taxes still accounted for only half of the state's revenue. The remainder had to come from loans contracted with the public and with chartered companies. Through the Bank of England, founded in 1694, the English developed the most efficient system of state borrowing to date. Individuals would deposit funds into the bank and receive its notes, plus interest ranging from 4.5 to 7.5 percent. The bank proved to be a safe, solid investment. Businessmen in Parliament underwrote it and Dutch capital sustained it. By 1715 England attained a financial equilibrium that avoided overtaxing the poor and undertaxing the rich. Investors showed a confidence in the financial future of the government that paralleled their confidence in the commercial future of the nation.

In several other respects England took on policies that distinguished it from its continental neighbors. Sixteenth-century habits of regulating industry, controlling the supply and movement of labor, and relieving the poor were modified. The last legislative attempt to regulate the cloth industry failed to become law in 1678, and by the 1690s manufacturers and sellers alike preferred to adapt production to market trends rather than adhere to traditional quality specifications dictated for their product. At the same time the government's need for tax revenue in wartime encouraged less fettered production; once peace came in 1713, royal policy protected and stimulated overseas trade through enforcement of the Navigation Acts as opposed to regulatory legislation.

Meanwhile the government let lapse the sixteenth-century laws for the cloth industry which had required fixed terms of apprenticeship, long-term work contracts, and wage ceilings. Now the marketplace was permitted to define wage scales for jobs, many of which were unknown when the older regulations had been promulgated. Concerning the poor, the Elizabethan Settlement Act of 1576, which had commanded parishes and towns to establish workhouses for the unemployed, gave way to the Settlement Acts of 1662 and 1697, which sought to alleviate local indigence by returning the recently arrived poor to the parish of their origin. Workhouses were not eliminated; but the decline of collective social responsibility toward the poor during a period of enclosures and economic restructuring illustrates England's decision to forsake a familiar channel of traditional charity for the still uncharted—but indisputably rougher—waters of individualism and free enterprise.

FRANCE: MERCANTILISM IN THEORY AND PRACTICE

The Anglo-Dutch trade wars of the third quarter of the seventeenth century were the logical consequence of a set of economic theories common in Europe at the time. Fundamental was the notion that the amount of international trade was fixed and that every state must therefore acquire a slice of the world's economic pie at the expense of every other state. Governments were supposed to assure the outward flow of finished products and the inward flow of precious metals and raw materials. They were to protect and encourage manufactures, establish colonies, construct a favorable balance of trade, found privileged commercial companies, and maintain both a strong navy and large merchant marine. Nowhere did these ideas postulate an ever-expanding demand for consumer goods and the interdependence of states in supplying them. Even after English merchants and manufacturers revised their notions about state regulation and popular consumption, they cherished the Navigation Acts and most of the protectionist doctrines on which the Acts had been based. The old theories had a good deal of staying power. It was not until the late eighteenth century that they fell into disrepute, to be replaced gradually by ideas generated by the overarching countertheory of the economic interdependence of nations. Then the economic reformers of the eighteenth century covered the older ideas with a disparaging label: *mercantilism*.

Colbert's Vision

Mercantilist theory and practice should be placed within the context of the age—a time of excessive international warfare, internal political strife, crop failures, severe climatic variations, defective consumption, inefficient distribution, and depressed prices alternating with scarcity-provoked inflation. Governments felt obliged to intervene in the economic life of states in order to find ways of combating the gloomy prospects. Jean-Baptiste Colbert, Louis XIV's controller-general of finance, was the most energetic of the experimenters. He persuaded his king to raise tariffs, regulate manufactures, establish and underwrite commercial companies, and encourage the immigration of foreign craftsmen. He also convinced his king to go to war in order to crush commercial rivals and take over their markets. Louis XIV needed little encouragement to merge his dream of dynastic glory with Colbert's mercantilist vision, and in 1672 king and minister dragged France into war with the Dutch Netherlands. This was intended to be much more than the relatively limited struggles on the high seas that had occupied the English and Dutch in 1652 and 1665. It was planned as a total war, one that would destroy Holland's economic capacity. French intervention thus converted the third Anglo-Dutch war into a crusade aimed at annihilating the Netherlands. The plan was for Louis's army to occupy Rotterdam, Leiden, and Amsterdam. In the end the French failed to accomplish their aim, the Dutch survived, and Colbert had to channel his energies into dredging up war revenues for his marching king.

War was the crudest weapon of the mercantilists. It promised the quickest solution but entailed the gravest risks. Tariff barriers against the manufactured goods of others offered a more subtle approach. Colbert directed French duties primarily at Dutch and English textiles, but he also prohibited Venetian glass and lace from entering the country. Indiscriminately applied tariffs have a boomerang effect, however. The French lists of 1664 and 1667 were so long and the duties so high that the plan amounted to a virtual exclusion of imported manufactures. French merchants who depended upon foreign articles howled in protest. The Dutch reciprocated with their own discriminatory tariff. In 1678 England refused to import

French products. Colbert's bludgeons thus produced a counterattack. To change the metaphor, instead of increasing France's share in the pie, he seemed to be reducing it.

Tariffs are defensive measures, intended to keep capital at home for investment in domestic production. But Colbert believed that the state alone possessed the will to undertake such experimentation. In France, where recession merged with the thirst of moneyed individuals for the prestige of estate or office ownership as opposed to investment in manufacture or trade, the controller-general probably was correct. Therefore the government underwrote an entire series of international trading ventures—the French East and West India Companies (1664), Baltic Company (1669), Levant Company (1670), and Senegal Company (1673). It established luxury workshops that trained artists and artisans in the manufacture of laces, lavish mirrors, and tapestries. It underwrote production of hats, silk and woolen stockings, and draperies. It built cannon and munitions foundries, as well as the great dockyard at Toulon. It paid for navigation improvements for France's major rivers, and financed construction of a canal in the southern province of Languedoc, connecting the Atlantic and Mediterranean for ships up to 200 tons.

Through such projects Colbert hoped to join private to state investment. He could not award titles of nobility to budding capitalists, but he did offer bounties, tax breaks, and control over labor to those who would invest in French shipbuilding, silk production, or sugar refining. Foreigners, especially the ubiquitous Dutch, accepted the offers. The most celebrated of them, Josse van Robais, came to France to build the country's first important textile factory. Everywhere Colbert's method was to award production or sales monopolies, fiscal exemptions, and privileges—as opposed to stimulating competition. The state might honor an entrepreneur with the title of "royal manufacturer" and guarantee him the lion's share of purchases of his product. Bounties and tax exemptions were used to tempt foreign artisans to work in France. Shipwrights, silkworkers, glassblowers, leatherworkers, dyers, and papermakers were recruited from all over Europe. Of course, the privileges they received only served to fragment further a society comprised of bitterly divided groups.

Colbert believed that the state must regulate as well as encourage commerce and industry. The controller-general attacked local toll charges within each of the three major customs districts of the country. He was fairly successful with the inner ring, called the Five Great Farms; but in the outer districts, parlements, Estates, and tax farmers successfully resisted him. He did better, or thought he was doing better, with town industries. First, he revised France's industrial guilds, but not as autonomous organizations. Masters were to make certain that rigorous standards of manufacture were maintained. For cloth manufacture alone there were nearly two hundred rules covering the composition of dyes, thickness and number of threads, and types of tools to be used by artisans. Royal inspectors were dispatched to ensure compliance, and they had to bargain incessantly with manufacturers wishing to modify the rules. An obsessive concern with quality control motivated Colbert's regulations.

Now, when a regime decrees that fabrics made in one place must contain 1,408 threads per cloth, while those made in another must contain 1,216, it stifles individual initiative—particularly among manufacturers in the first location, who may wish to sell cheap cloth. The privileges that Colbert awarded to the book publishers' guild of Paris, which could not hope to supply the needs of the country, had the twin effect of nearly destroying the legitimate publishing industry in the provinces and of turning illicit book production into big business. In the long run, Colbert's regulations over French industry worked against his desire for its orderly, controlled growth. Nevertheless, he did establish a craft discipline and regional specialization unmatched in any other European country. The glass of Saint Gobain, silks of Lyon, tapestries of Beauvais, Chaillot, and the Gobelins factory of Paris, the embroidered cloths of Arras and Carcassonne—all became bywords for quality and beauty among leisured consumers. France became the workshop for Europe's aristocracy. Colbert could conceive of no other kind of market. He set the tone of *luxe* for French products that haunts its industry to this day.

The Heritage of Colbertism

Tradition and, ultimately, royal policies that conflicted with his own, undercut Colbert. Village spinners and weavers hired out by small-time entrepreneurs frustrated his dream of establishing an urban work force under quasi-military discipline. Aware of the strengths of the seigneurial system and the resistance of regional custom, Colbert practically ignored attempts to reform agriculture. After 1672 he paid the supreme price for having pushed his king along the path of martial glory. Increasingly, until his death eleven years later, Colbert had to ignore building up French manufactures and a colonial empire in favor of tracking down money lenders and office purchasers to pay for Louis XIV's military campaigns. The government no longer was able to subsidize the trading companies, and all but the East India Company collapsed. The controller-general even had to ease up on his attack of local toll officials so that the government might be assured of its share in their take. Against his better judgment, Colbert had to tolerate another royal obsession, the persecution of the French Protestant community, mainstay of a host of industries ranging from fine textiles to printing, papermaking, jewelry making, and shipbuilding. The great Huguenot exodus to England, the Dutch Netherlands, the Protestant areas of Germany, and overseas, occurred in 1685–1686, after Colbert's death. Ironically enough, by the end of the century only the restrictive legislation seemed to represent his major legacy.

Some contemporary theorists already saw the shortcomings of Colbertine mercantilism. The great French marshal Sébastien le Prestre de

Vauban (1633–1707) pleaded for a system of priorities that would place the welfare of the laboring poor ahead of a favorable balance of trade. In his *Dixme royale* (1707) and other writings, Vauban advocated state responsibility for full employment even if it meant giving away exports, and he called for a graduated tax based on income, not rank. In the *Détail de la France* (1695), the legal officer Pierre le Pesant de Boisguilbert (1646–1714) pointed out mercantilism's failure to grapple with the issue of maldistribution of wealth. Money, he believed, had become the master of commerce instead of its servant. Boisguilbert wrote that as a first priority the state ought to direct itself toward increasing agricultural productivity. Sturdy peasant proprietors thus would form a natural market for manufacturers. As might be imagined, Colbert's theories found severe critics across the English Channel. In 1691 Dudley North wrote in his *Discourses Upon Trade* that a nation's true economic interest rested on free individual enterprise, not state regulation of production. In the highly controversial *Fable of the Bees* (1714, 1728), Bernard Mandeville (1670–1733) rejected government regulation outright. For Mandeville the excesses of unrestricted individualism must be tolerated because they ultimately would lead to improvement for everyone. "Private vices, public benefits," Mandeville wrote. This stood in contrast with Colbert's doctrine that economic progress originated and evolved only by virtue of the moral energy provided by government control and direction.

Despite the growing chorus of criticisms, Colbertine mercantilism was not a complete failure. The controller-general's grant of free port status to Marseilles in 1669 stimulated the export of French manufactures and the resurgence of French commercial dominance in the eastern Mediterranean. Woolens production in northern France increased significantly between 1680 and 1715. Although most of the chartered overseas trading companies failed, the stimulation of colonial enterprise through government-sponsored exploration and settlement resulted in a thriving community of 15,000 inhabitants in late seventeenth-century Canada, in French control over the Mississippi Valley and Louisiana, successful sugar-growing plantations in the West Indies, and an important presence in southern and southeastern Asia. Colbert refitted French ports, and France's naval fleet was equal to England's until 1713.

Moreover, we should not judge mercantilism entirely by the amount of print and paper expended in the publication of threatening royal decrees. Powerful theoretical pronouncements and fearful commands were the outward masks of French absolutism, often veiling a reality marked by compromise, negotiation, and unacknowledged tolerance. Before embarking on a project, Colbert and his successors habitually consulted with the businesspeople most affected by it. Once a decree was proclaimed, enforcement was another matter. Colbert's fifty inspectors of textile manufacture could not hope to control the multitude of weaving looms scattered in 40,000 French towns and villages. Ignoring the law was commonplace. As an example, although the regime officially prohibited French importation and manufacture of calicoes, these brightly printed cottons proved to be as fashionable in late seventeenth-century Paris as they were in London, where they were imported freely. Then too the regime itself might be complicit in avoiding its own regulations. Early in the eighteenth century the inability of the state-protected and privileged printers of Paris to meet the demand of readers for novels and popular religious books led the government to tolerate counterfeit and semiclandestine editions by provincial publishers— despite the loud complaints of the supposedly favored Parisians. Finally, we must remember that mercantilism never made headway in the largest sector of the economy, agriculture. Production remained local and unsystematized, determined by custom, weather, and the market. Here the French state stood aloof, even more so than the English, where Parliament encouraged enclosure and improvement.

Although Colbertine ideas waned in France during the eighteenth century and England's prosperity centered on unrestricted production and overseas commerce protected by the Navigation Acts, it was Europe's underdeveloped states—Spain, Prussia, and the Hapsburg Empire—which best adapted mercantilist theories to new uses. In these places the energies of the state were put to work in order to subsidize industry and reduce dependence upon imported manufactures. In the ensuing struggles over serfdom and sharecropping, state-organized agriculture was incorporated into neomercantilist thought. Moreover, all eighteenth-century governments, mercantilist or not, placed into the forefront an idea that Colbert would not have been able to contemplate: the interdependence of national economies. This new concept relegated as suspect the Colbertine certainty that a nation's prosperity was fundamentally dependent upon its neighbor's poverty. Neomercantilism was based on hopes of a better material life for the vast majority, something Colbert would have considered unattainable. The controller-general's theories and reforms were the product of a time of pessimism. When all is said and done, they were the alternative to despair.

3

CRISIS AND RESOLUTION: THE WEST

THE MID-CENTURY CRISES

In 1648 the three treaties incorporated into the Peace of Westphalia ended a generation of war in Germany. The armies of Spain, Austria, Sweden, and France withdrew from central Europe, leaving vast areas in ruin. Elsewhere wars either continued or soon flared up—on the Spanish and French frontiers, along the eastern Baltic coast, in Poland, the Ukraine, and on the high seas. But for the overwhelming number of Europe's statesmen, townspeople, and peasants, 1648 was the year of peace among nations.

  Within states themselves, however, matters were far different. While most of Germany sank into the peace of exhaustion, elsewhere civil turmoil either erupted or passed into a new and critical stage. The 1640s and 1650s were decades of rebellion against constituted governments that would know no parallel for another century and a half: revolts of social orders, of regions, of corporate groups; revolts in large measure determined by local conditions, yet somehow feeding on one another, even in an era of parochialism and poor communications. Some historians have interpreted the uprisings as desperate protests of the poor against high taxes in a period of bad harvests. Others have seen the rebellions as motivated by a capitalist-minded bourgeoisie turning against governments committed to a regressive agrarian-based economy and social structure. Still other historians have considered the revolts to have been the response of an exploited, bitter "country" alliance of landowners, townsmen, and peasants against an exploiting group of court nobles, churchmen, and officers. Finally, some scholars have interpreted the last gasps of the Thirty Years' War, the conflict between France and Spain, and the struggles in Poland and the Baltic, as driving desperate corporate groups to rebellion.

  The outbreaks were widespread. No state and few capitals seemed immune. In 1648 riots erupted in Paris and Moscow. In Istanbul the Royal Guard murdered the Turkish sultan, and a few months later the English executed their king. During much of 1649 it appeared that the French monarchy itself was going to be dismantled. The following year armed troops and burghers faced each other in the streets of Amsterdam. On the

European edges of Spain's tottering empire, conflict spread to Naples, Palermo, and Barcelona. In the North, Stockholm and Berlin were scenes of unrest. While major revolt was nothing new to Europe, the almost universal character of the mid-century uprisings was.

THE CROMWELLIAN EXPERIMENT

Civil War and Revolution in England

In 1648 England was in the midst of revolution. Seven years earlier Parliament had destroyed the means by which King Charles I established his personal rule. Royal prerogative courts, royal taxation, and the political power of the Anglican bishops were eliminated. Parliament assumed control over the finances of the country and the military. However, because too many vexing religious and political questions remained unanswered, England did not slip into a comfortable constitutional monarchy. There was little agreement, for example, about what to do with the established and protected Anglican Church. A significant number of politicians, particularly those close to King Charles, wished to do nothing. Others viewed a Church resplendent in its ritual, hierarchical in its order, and privileged in its rewards as more Catholic than Protestant, and vowed to tear it out "root and branch." A second cause of instability was the untrustworthiness of the king. He refused to accept the parliamentary political victory of 1640–1641. Following a botched attempt in 1642 to arrest his leading parliamentary opponents, Charles organized his political and military support and risked civil war. Which side—the king's or Parliament's—was chosen by England's various social groups is a matter of conjecture. Wealthy landlords, poor tenants, artisans, preachers, and businessmen fought on both. Families were divided, as were geographical sections of the country. However, one matter was certain. Charles's counterattack was insufficient. By 1645 Parliament was financing construction of a superior military force, the New Model Army. The army crushed the forces of the king and forced him into exile in Scotland.

But the struggle was not over. In 1647 the Scots returned Charles to England. As Parliament's prisoner, he tried to renegotiate a political settlement. Yet it proved far more difficult than before the civil war. During the two years of the king's absence the country had changed dramatically. Most significantly, an awakening of political consciousness among urban artisans and craftsmen, Protestant sectarian preachers, and small property owners in town and countryside created a situation unique in English history. Even more dangerous was the articulation of radical political and social ideologies within the New Model Army. Simple soldiers seized on the unstable political situation to call for representative government and universal male suffrage. Civilian counterparts, particularly in London, erected pragmatic political programs based on broadened suffrage, a written constitution, and a sovereign House of Commons. Other groups formed: Some advocated the people's occupation of common grazing land; others called for a religious terror unleashed against the "nonelect," approximately 99 percent of the country's population. The Civil War between king and Parliament had given birth to as volatile a social and political atmosphere as England had ever known, something that elites on either side had not foreseen.

The army leadership, behind the country gentleman Oliver Cromwell (1599–1658) and his son-in-law Henry Ireton, was deeply troubled by the rising tide of radicalism among the troops and in the cities. Cromwell and Ireton identified themselves with middling property holders, who had been instrumental in preventing the establishment of a pretentious absolutism by Charles I. An elite nonetheless, this middling gentry believed in parliamentary sovereignty and a franchise extended no further than to men like themselves. In fact, for Cromwell and Ireton only those with a "fixed interest" in the nation—that is, the propertied—possessed sufficient responsibility to govern. More radical programs appeared dangerous to them. A political debate between Ireton and a lesser army officer, Colonel Thomas Rainsborough, in late October 1647, best illustrates the gulf that now separated the different groups which had stood firm against Charles I:

> *Rainsborough*: For really I think that the poorest he that is in England hath a life to live as the greatest he; and therefore truly, sir, I think it's clear, that every man that is to live under a government ought first by his own consent to put himself under that government; and I do think that the poorest man in England is not at all bound in a strict sense to that government that he hath not had a voice to put himself under. . . .

> *Ireton*: . . . I think that no person hath a right to an interest or share in the disposing of the affairs of the kingdom, and in determining or choosing those that shall determine what laws we shall be ruled by here—no person hath a right to this, that hath not a permanent fixed interest in this kingdom.[1]

Ireton's view prevailed. He and Cromwell abolished the soldiers' councils in the army and arrested civilian radical leaders. Shortly thereafter, when the king escaped from his captors and tried staging a countercoup, Parliament had no other choice than to fight. There were scattered uprisings in favor of Charles; but by October 1648 the New Model Army easily crushed his supporters, and Charles again was in the hands of his captors. Even after the pathetic uprising, ostentatiously called the Second Civil War, it remained doubtful whether prevailing political opinion in the country, or

---

[1] Quoted in Barry Coward, *The Stuart Age* (London, 1987), p. 199.

for that matter in Parliament itself, was prepared for what was to come. Convinced of the king's bad faith, Ireton persuaded the army's ruling council to march on London and purge Parliament of those still willing to deal with Charles I. On December 6, troops surrounded the Parliament building. Colonel Thomas Pride, leader of the force, permitted entry only to those members who swore fidelity to the army and whatever policies it would decide. Sixty did so. The remaining 370 MPs either were sent home or else left voluntarily. For the time being at least, the revolutionary generals had erased opposition on both the left and right.

Cromwell, Ireton, the army generals, and "Rump" members of the House of Commons were convinced now of the unredeemed rottenness of the Stuart court, its Anglican Church, and royal institutions of government. They decided to bring the Civil War to its logical consummation. In January 1649 the Rump voted to place Charles I on trial for levying war on Parliament and the kingdom. It appointed a court of high justice to hear the case. The House of Lords refused to participate and was brushed aside as irrelevant. The Rump House of Commons assumed supreme political authority over England. With Cromwell directing the scenario, the outcome of the royal trial never was in doubt. On January 30, 1649, displaying a dignity and resolution that often had betrayed him in less desperate times, Charles I was executed as a treasonous king. With him, the regicides hoped, would perish all the trappings of the English monarchy.

Commonwealth and Protectorate

Thus England became a republic, and its new leadership now had to search for a workable alternative to the old regime. There was a sense of impatience in the country, for the most part expressed in religious terms. A belief that the perfect society was at hand—"a godly reformation"—pervaded popular thought. Deeply Protestant, this ideology emphasized the importance of the inner spirit possessed by every individual and was deeply suspicious of state-imposed Churches and clerical influence. It generally supported limited religious toleration and insisted on the autonomy of religious congregations. It mistrusted the secular past and was highly experimental in its quest for political and social perfection. Among the so-called Civil War religious sects, the downtrodden and women often gained new dignity. Groups like the Quakers aggressively emphasized social equality, and others like the Ranters established a highly permissive sexual morality. Sects like the Levellers attacked law courts and universities as being havens of privilege and corruption, and radical groups like the Diggers built their own little segregated communities, based on universal education and group ownership of property.

The elites in charge of the country were deeply concerned about such outbursts of sectarian experimentation, and persecuted its most dangerous proponents like the Levellers. However, there were other scores to settle as well. The monarchy and House of Lords officially abolished, in

May 1649 England was declared a commonwealth and a council of state took over executive functions. But a residue of Stuart sympathy remained in Ireland and Scotland. Displaying an uncharacteristic intolerance, Cromwell savagely conquered Ireland, where he left a legacy of hatred that lasts to this day. Following the troops, English Protestant immigrants entered the country, dispossessing both native and Anglo-Irish landlords and seizing control of Irish trade. In 1651 Scotland was taken, feudal land tenures abolished, reforms instituted in law and local government, and toleration granted to all Protestant sectarian groups. In England itself large transfers of property took place. Crown lands, Anglican Church lands, and lands of suspected Royalists were seized and sold. Troops received plots in lieu of wages. While some Royalist property owners whose land had been expropriated paid large fines to get it back, others lost their homes forever. The revolution produced a new landholding class of London merchants, lawyers, speculators, and army officers. Shippers and important port merchants now had a government that sympathized with their interests. In 1651 the first Navigation Acts were passed and the Anglo-Dutch War erupted. Within a few months, English sea victories netted seven hundred prizes.

But the outward successes of the Republic were deceptive and only concealed very real difficulties. Chief of these was the impatience of Oliver Cromwell with the agonizing search for a workable political settlement. An obscure country squire, in 1640 Cromwell had entered Parliament and eventually made his career as a gifted political and military strategist in the New Model Army. By 1649 he was its uncontested leader and thereby de facto head of state. He believed in parliamentary government, but was even more convinced of the holy righteousness of military leadership. The army had destroyed the old monarchy and Church. Then it nipped the radical menace. It conquered Ireland and Scotland. For Cromwell it was more than a cold military machine. It was a moral force, "a lawful power," whose duty was to recreate politics and society according to the wishes of God. On the other hand, in its desire to control use of taxation and reduce military commitments, from 1649 to 1658 Parliament became a focal point of opposition to both Cromwell and his army. Exasperated by the Rump's growing antimilitary stance, Cromwell prorogued it in April 1653, and later that year he assumed the new executive office of Lord Protector. He continued to convene parliaments but dismissed them nearly as quickly as they were called. The Instrument of Government, the only written constitution England ever has had, proved ineffective because Parliament challenged the Lord Protector's control over the army. At the local level the rift widened between civilian officials and the military. Unrepentant Royalists became active, and plots were uncovered to bring about a Stuart restoration. Merchants complained about customs taxes, landlords complained about property taxes, and those with administrative experience refused to hold local office.

Finally, Cromwell gave up on civilian rule. To maintain internal security, in 1655 he divided the country into eleven districts, each under the control of a major-general. The military regime was not meant to be permanent, and the major-generals were not supposed to be petty tyrants. They were efficient in extorting tax grants, but their interference in nearly all aspects of civilian life in the provinces and their prudish opposition to taverns, sports, and popular pastimes exacerbated an already tense situation. Many who had supported the idealistic programs of the 1640s puckered at the sour fruit of a grim military dictatorship. As late as 1656, Cromwell might have saved the revolution had he presented the nation with a parliamentary monarchy and himself as king. But his religious and political principles caused him to shudder at royalism in any form, and his chief military supporters vigorously opposed a solution that failed to give the army a central place in government. By 1657 it was evident that the republican experiment was failing. Far from laying the foundation of the New Jerusalem, the 50,000-man army had become an inordinately expensive agency of repression in a country notoriously hostile to centralized control and military politics. Each day the major-generals created additional sympathizers for a Stuart restoration. Not even Cromwell's agreement to withdraw both the major-generals and the Instrument of Government relieved the tension. In exile on the continent, the son of Charles I announced his readiness to return. The crisis broke in the late summer of 1658, when the Lord Protector took ill and died.

Almost immediately the Cromwellian regime fell apart. Troops were unpaid, and the courts were not functioning. Without Cromwell there to patch together differences, the army itself split into factions. Cromwell's son and heir apparent Richard could not weld it back together. Late in 1659, General George Monck, commander-in-chief in Scotland, concluded that the only way to restore order to public life was to reestablish continuity with the monarchical past. Having decided to recall the son of Charles I from exile in Holland, Monck moved his troops southward and entered London unopposed. Monck leaned toward the political solution Cromwell had rejected earlier—a disbanded army and a government that would work out its own balance between king and Parliament. Monck restored the survivors of Pride's Purge to Commons, and those moderate royalists disclaimed their right to vote in the absence of the House of Lords. A new election was held. It returned a heavily royalist Commons. The Lords took their seats in the Upper Chamber. On April 25, 1660, the so-called Convention Parliament met and a week later declared the government of England to be invested in King, Lords, and Commons. A month later, Charles II returned from his travels to take up what he called the twelfth year of his reign. Parliament imposed no new restrictions on the king. He was granted an annual subsidy to pay for the upkeep of his estates, the navy, royal judges, and the diplomatic corps.

Much of the onus for the failure of republicanism must fall on Cromwell. He never was able to extricate himself from the military frame of mind that had produced such a resounding victory over the forces of

Charles I. Although it notably excluded Ireland, his religious tolerance was his most endearing trait. His Puritanism tried to comprehend Protestant points of view from Presbyterian to Quaker, and it was he who brought the Jews back to England after three centuries of exile. But even this tolerance eroded, turning him against those groups that he believed were frustrating God's will—first Roman Catholics and High Church Anglicans, and eventually Presbyterians and Quakers. Cromwell earnestly wished to be a "healer and settler," and during the Republican interlude much was achieved. Many laws were made intelligible, and all in England were declared equal before justice. Medieval monopolies over production and trade collapsed, and the market rather than the guild came to determine the laws of supply and demand. England emerged as a commercial power, with Ireland and Scotland as essential components of a burgeoning empire. Judges learned to depend upon salaries, not litigants' fees, for their income. Finally, though the vicissitudes of Parliament were many and great under Cromwell, the fact that he summoned it time and again, in one form or other, assured its survival as the fundamental repository of the public interest. Cromwell erred in trying to build the Republic on a military foundation, and he never could dispense with the military's arch adversary, Parliament, for very long. In the end it was Parliament, speaking for England, that restored Charles II.

THE STUART RESTORATION

Charles II (1660–1685) and the Cavalier Parliament

Of the two major problems of the Restoration period (1660–1688), the first concerned the religious, political, and civil rights of the so-called Dissenting Protestants—the Presbyterians, Congregationalists, Baptists, Quakers, and others who had dropped out of the Anglican Church's narrowly defined community of true Englishmen in the first half of the century. The reestablished state Church rejected any theological or institutional generosity toward the Dissenters. It offered Protestants unable to conform to the Anglican Church's *Book of Common Prayer* a begrudging, minimal religious toleration while persuading Parliament to prohibit them from worshiping in public and barring them from local political office. Nor could nonconformists serve as schoolteachers or university professors. Nevertheless, the Puritan spirit survived, and around 10 percent of England's late seventeenth-century population remained religiously nonconformist. Meanwhile, complacent and devoid of much spiritual infusion, privileged and corrupt, Restoration Anglicanism lacked the self-righteous zeal of the persecutor. Rather, it stood for a kind of social order under the command of the bishops and landed oligarchs who dominated both houses of Parliament.

The second problem was more specifically political. Would England at last follow most of continental Europe and opt for a strongly authoritarian form of royal government? Most members of the Cavalier Parliament that sat from 1661 to 1678 wanted a Stuart king, for he embodied legitimacy and was a sacred barrier to republicanism. But they also wished to keep the king in tow, out of local government that they themselves ran and out of expensive foreign adventures that threatened to enhance royal prestige. The most effective way to curb royal influence was by controlling its income, so Parliament exercised the power of subsidy over Charles II. It kept Charles' annual income below the £1.2 million considered necessary for him to meet his expenses and limited his additional revenue to a temporary hearth tax and the sales tax on liquor. Parliament withheld all supplementary grants unless a royal accounting was given of how the funds would be spent.

While Charles won larger subsidies than his father, his royal income was insufficient. Between 1660 and 1673 it was half of what Cromwell had controlled between 1649 and 1658. The Convention (1660) and Cavalier (1661–1678) Parliaments made certain that the tax burden fell on the poor through charges placed on consumer goods and individual hearths. Whenever possible, Royalists whose lands had been sold or expropriated in the Civil War instituted legal action to get their property back. Only the wealthiest were successful, however; those who had borrowed in order to pay fines for their land under the Commonwealth and Protectorate discovered that they still were debtors. Thus, on questions of land ownership and debt responsibility, the Restoration Parliaments trod very cautiously. Members were not committed to an ideology of vengeance. While permitting the king to appoint state, Church, and local officials, this loose coalition of courtiers, officeholders, country gentlemen, and merchants wished to steer a course that avoided the shoals of both revived republicanism and Stuart tyranny.

The king was both opportunistic and pragmatic, well versed in the arts of compromise and negotiation, but ever ready to further his cause through more devious means. An intelligent, witty, cynical sensualist who took more naturally to bribes and intrigue than to direct confrontation, Charles II had not enjoyed exile; and he had little desire to risk being sent abroad again. His constitutional powers were significant. In addition to those of appointment, he controlled the militia, could veto legislation, suspend laws, call or dissolve Parliament, and make foreign policy. Initially eschewing confrontation, he preferred to construct a personal following in Parliament and plied its most royalist members with gifts, bribes, and favors. For the first six years of the Restoration, his chief adviser and minister was the earl of Clarendon (1609–1674), a dour conservative holdover from the prerevolutionary years. Victimized by a series of events beyond his power to control—the plague of 1665, the London fire of 1666, De Ruyter's destruction of the English fleet in 1667—Clarendon was suspected of wishing to increase the king's authority beyond proper limits. Impeached by Parliament, Clarendon fled to France, where he wrote both an autobiography justifying his career and a great history of the Civil War.

Clarendon was replaced by five politicians known as the Cabal, which formed a ministerial phalanx around the king. Although members often worked at cross purposes, two of them, Arlington and Clifford, advised Charles to increase his income beyond his financial dependence upon Parliament. They were entrusted by the king to concoct the Secret Treaty of Dover with France's Louis XIV (1670). By terms of the treaty Louis granted Charles an annual subsidy of £225,000, sufficient to increase his income by 20 percent, in return for English support in any future French war with the Northern Netherlands. Furthermore, Charles admitted to being a closet Roman Catholic and agreed to declare his religion openly at the first convenient opportunity. Finally, Louis promised Charles financial and military help in stifling opposition once the moment was deemed appropriate for the English king to announce his Catholicism publicly.

Because it invited confrontation rather than reliance on negotiation and bribery, Charles's customary methods, the Secret Treaty of Dover proved to be a dreadful blunder. Rumors about it leaked out, and fears mounted in Parliament that a re-Catholicized England, the pawn of Louis XIV, was a distinct possibility. In March 1672, without parliamentary consent, Charles declared war on the Dutch. Louis followed suit. Then Charles issued a royal Declaration of Indulgence, which offered religious liberty to English Catholics and dissenting Protestants alike. Penal laws against both groups were suspended, Catholics obtained the privilege to worship freely in their own homes, and Dissenters the right to pray in their own churches. Contemporaries asked what all of this meant. Had the king opted for confrontational "Catholic" policies veering toward absolutism rather than a balanced "Cavalier" program ensuring parliamentary cooperation? Caught between fear and anger, Parliament in 1673 declared null and void Charles's suspension of penal statutes against religious minorities and passed the Test Act, a direct challenge to the king's Declaration of Indulgence. The act stated emphatically that all civil and military posts must be reserved for Anglicans. Charles's younger brother James, a secret Roman Catholic since 1669, promptly resigned as Lord Admiral of the Fleet.

The king knew he had gone too far and beat a strategic retreat. He revoked the Declaration of Indulgence. However, now Parliament was in a confrontational mood. In the sessions of late 1673 and early 1674, MPs attacked the French alliance, the recent marriage of James Stuart to an Italian Catholic princess, and the king's closest ministers. Groups organized in the House of Commons to seek ways of avoiding a Catholic succession to the throne—for, although Charles had fathered at least a dozen bastards, he and his queen had produced no legitimate heir. His brother James was next in line to the throne. Once Dutch propaganda seemed to convince Parliament that the purpose of the Anglo-French alliance was to establish Catholic tyranny in England, Charles withdrew from the Dutch War.

The Cabal broke apart, and Charles selected as chief minister Sir Thomas Osborne, later earl of Danby (1632–1712), an experienced politician convinced that effective royal leadership depended more upon the manipulation of institutions than upon foreign policy adventures or confrontations with the House of Commons. Danby courted whatever sympathizers he could find in Parliament. To hold on to Anglican squires in Commons and bishops in the House of Lords, he enforced the Test Act to the letter. This had the effect of arousing Dissenters. Clubs and coffeehouses in London seethed with political activity. A onetime member of the Cabal, Anthony Ashley-Cooper, first earl of Shaftesbury (1621–1683), sought support for a program that would counter Danby's. In 1678 he called for new elections. Although fewer than half the original members remained, the Cavalier Parliament of 1661 was still officially in session.

While Danby tried to forge a parliamentary following for the king and political opposition took root, a single crucial issue began to assume ominous form. In 1678 Charles was nearly fifty. He had no legitimate offspring, and his brother James, next in line to the throne, was a devout convert to Catholicism. Moreover, James had a young Italian wife. By a first marriage, James had two Protestant daughters, Mary and Anne. Mary was betrothed to the stadholder of Holland, William of Orange. However, in 1678 the possibility of her succession seemed relatively remote. On the other hand, should James sire a son, the boy would have precedence and guarantee England a Catholic sovereign for the next generation. The Parliament and country might accept James, but they would not tolerate the continuation of a Catholic royal line. Charles would not hear of divorcing for reasons of state a barren wife toward whom he had been unfaithful all his life, and there was no sentiment behind legitimizing the king's eldest male bastard, the Protestant duke of Monmouth. So the succession issue began to overshadow all others, and England was seized by a climate of fear for the future. Anti-Catholicism, the country's major popular religious prejudice since the outbreak of the Reformation, turned feverish, even though the actual Catholic population was no more than 2 percent of the total. Still, people asked how Parliament could exclude Catholics from public office and allow James Stuart the highest one of all. On the other hand, if James were denied the throne, would there not be political chaos and perhaps civil war? Already there were signs of preparation for it. Though England was out of Louis XIV's Dutch War, Charles had not disbanded the army. Was it being held in readiness for some kind of coup d'état and the establishment of a pro-Catholic terror?

The Triumph of Charles II

The crisis came to a head in 1679. Taking advantage of the climate of fear, a defrocked priest named Titus Oates, along with a core of associates, claimed knowledge of a great popish plot, in which the king would be murdered. A massacre of Protestants would follow, and Jesuits would turn a re-Catholicized England into a French satellite. Although Oates exonerated James Stuart from direct involvement in the plot, subsequent revelations implicated a close member of his entourage; the mysterious violent death of the Justice of the Peace who had taken Oates's depositions gave rise to national hysteria. Although Oates's accusations had no basis in fact, no one near the king was above suspicion. During the next two years, thirty-five people were tried and executed for their alleged roles in the unproven conspiracy. A new Test Act passed Commons which excluded Catholics from both houses of Parliament; James won exemption by two votes. The crisis mounted with the discovery of Louis XIV's secret subsidy to Charles II, and Danby fell. In a desperate attempt to prevent future revelations, Charles dissolved the Cavalier Parliament and called for new elections.

The election of 1679 returned a majority hostile to the possible succession of James. Shaftesbury organized a political group called the Exclusionists, and their bill to deny James the throne passed Commons in May. Meanwhile, Royalist members claimed that no parliamentary body could tamper with the fundamental laws of succession, accused the Exclusionists of treason, and labeled them *Whigs* after a particularly savage gang of Scottish cattle thieves. The Whigs responded by calling their adversaries *Tories,* after an Irish Catholic guerrilla band. The epithets stuck and gained respectability. Shaftesbury tried to mold a positive program for the Whigs. They were more anti-Catholic and pro-Dissenter than the Tories and inclined to place defined limits on the royal prerogative. They opposed a standing army and liked the idea of frequent parliamentary elections. They also seemed more sensitive than Tories to questions of civil liberties, and they were able to gather petitions and organize popular demonstrations for their cause among people whose limited property qualifications denied them the vote.

Two weeks after the vote on the Exclusion Bill, the Whig-dominated Commons passed the Habeas Corpus Act, whereby a judge could force release of a prisoner if the jailer failed to show cause for imprisonment. Charles accepted the Habeas Corpus Act but would have nothing to do with the Exclusion Bill. To him it was unconstitutional, turning England into an elective monarchy and rendering the king subservient to Parliament. Once more he dissolved Commons. For two additional years the country was deadlocked over the succession issue. Whig-dominated Houses of Commons would offer exclusion bills to Charles, and the king would dissolve the assemblies rather than submit. When one bill made it to the House of Lords in November 1680, the king's influence caused it to be defeated handily. Time proved to be on Charles's side. United in their opposition to James Stuart, the Exclusionists could not agree on who should replace him. Some opted for Charles's daughter Mary, now the wife of Holland's stadholder. Others preferred the duke of Monmouth. Through a pamphlet campaign Tories exploited fears of impending civil strife, and the judiciary stood by the king's insistence of his brother as legitimate heir. Finally, after nearly twenty years of extravagance, Charles learned to live off his own resources and a new subsidy from Louis XIV, thereby ignoring Parliament. After dissolving the body in March 1681, he was in no hurry to call for new elections.

Deprived of their national soapbox, the increasingly desperate Whigs resorted to plots. Implicated behind Monmouth in a foolhardy rebellion scheme, Shaftesbury fled to Holland. Discovery of the so-called Rye House Plot (1683), ostensibly to assassinate both Charles and James on the way back from the Newmarket horse races, resulted in the execution of several leading Whigs, the intimidation of many others, and the disgrace of their cause. By 1685 Exclusionism was thoroughly discredited. The peerage, Anglican clergy, older gentry, and mercantile-financial elites were weary of plot hysteria and desired peace and quiet under strong royal leadership. Charles successfully portrayed himself as the sole harbinger of stability. Collecting his French subsidy, the king kept a small army ready, suppressed the municipal corporate charters for London and fifty other cities, and filled judgeships and other administrative posts with certain allies. Beginning in 1683, hearth and excise taxes were collected directly and efficiently by royal agents. As a consequence, the king's independent income alone was larger than Parliament's subsidy had been twenty years earlier. Dissenting Protestants and Catholics alike were silenced. When Charles died in February 1685, formally affirming his Catholicism, Parliament had not been called in four years. As his brother James succeeded him, the opportunity never looked better for the monarchy to dominate the nation's constitution.

THE GLORIOUS REVOLUTION

James II (1685–1688) and His Fall

An uprising of Scottish clansmen under the earl of Argyll and Monmouth's west country rebellion of disaffected clothworkers and freeholders accompanied the succession of James, but were easily subdued. At first James showed every indication of being moderate and conciliatory. He allowed himself to be crowned according to the Anglican rite and graciously called a new Parliament. The country responded with one that was heavily Tory. Only the most diehard Whigs and Republicans seemed beyond James's reach. The Parliament of 1685 gave James the largest peacetime budget ever enjoyed by an English king. A wave of euphoria and relief swept across England.

Only months after his accession, however, James showed a grimmer face. Argyll and Monmouth were executed. A royal commission rounded up suspected collaborators. Drumhead courts sentenced dozens to death, long imprisonment, or deportation. Increasingly, these "Bloody Assizes" began to look like a convenient way of getting rid of potential opposition, not actual rebels. To contemporaries witnessing the arrival in England of Huguenot victims of Louis XIV's persecutions, James looked less like a middle-aged transitional monarch than a royal revolutionary bent on remaking

England into a Catholic absolutism. He replaced Anglican advisers with Catholics. He demanded that Parliament revoke both the Test and Habeas Corpus acts. He kept the army on a permanent war footing and placed 30,000 troops outside the gates of London. He personally urged conversions to Catholicism and authorized Anglican priests who did so to keep their incomes. He heaped honors on the papal nuncio and kneeled ostentatiously in his presence. In November 1685 he prorogued Parliament. Historical hindsight has been kinder to James than contemporaries were. His major objective was to repeal disabilities and grant full religious and civil rights to English Catholics. Once this was accomplished, he believed that his fellow countrymen would flock to his true religion. However, he grossly miscalculated English anti-Catholicism, and his heavy-handed methods were viewed as steps toward tyranny. By 1687 the national unity that had accompanied James's accession was in shreds. Tories and Whigs, Anglicans and Dissenters, country gentlemen and merchants—all viewed him as a menace.

The leading alternative to James was his elder daughter Mary. Her husband, the stadholder William III, was himself a grandson of Charles I. Meanwhile, James was attacking Anglicanism on all fronts. His Declaration of Indulgence (April 1687) repealed the Test Act and was intended to gain him Dissenter allies by reopening public office to Catholics and non-Conformists alike. A new royal court, the Ecclesiastical Commission, dismissed Anglicans from public posts. In the spring of 1688, the queen became pregnant and seven Anglican bishops, including the archbishop of Canterbury, rejected James's demand that they approve a second Declaration of Indulgence. Their reasoning was that no king of England had the right to overturn an act of Parliament, namely the Test Act. James had the churchmen arrested and tried for seditious libel. A jury acquitted them, the first major legal decision in modern English history to go against the wishes of a reigning monarch. Not even the troublesome news of the birth of James's son could dampen the exultation in London produced by the acquittal of the six bishops and their archbishop. A showdown was inevitable. Wavering Tories hastened to oppose the king. Even some Catholics saw the writing on the wall and withdrew support for James.

On June 30, 1688—the day the seven bishops were acquitted—a bipartisan group of Whigs and Tories representing Parliament, the military, and the Anglican Church opened negotiations with William and Mary. At The Hague, exiled Whigs were convenient intermediaries. The stadholder and James's daughter were asked to cross over to England and rescue Protestantism. Although the "secret committee" of English notables was divided over whether William and Mary should simply compel James to change his ways, establish a regency for the baby prince, or assume the throne themselves, the stadholder was crystal clear in his purpose: to become king of England and bring the country into his life-or-death struggle with Louis XIV. In November 1688 he and Mary sailed for England with 15,000 Dutch troops. As his fleet approached the English coast, an east wind bottled up James's navy in the Thames estuary and kept it from confronting the Dutch flotilla on the open sea. William's force sailed down the Channel, landing on the southern coast at Torbay. The invaders met no opposition. James's army retreated to London and disbanded. His younger daughter Anne went over to the other side. Then the king lost his nerve. Turning authority over to no one, he sent his queen and infant son to France, destroyed the writs summoning Parliament, threw the Great Seal of Justice into the Thames, and joined his family at Louis XIV's court. William and Mary entered London in triumph.

England had no king in residence, but government had to continue. The House of Lords took the initiative to keep the revolution bloodless. The peers called together a convention drawn from the membership of the last Parliament, and negotiations reopened with William and Mary. Ever obstinate and calculating, the stadholder wished above all to get England into the Grand Alliance he was molding against Louis XIV. He therefore would consent to nothing less than joint rule with his wife. The Convention Parliament debated and ultimately accepted William's demand. A legal fiction declared James to have abdicated, thus leaving the throne vacant. Majority Tory opinion held that obedience was due any claimant who guaranteed public order, and with understandable ambivalence awarded title of authority cojointly to William (1689–1702) and Mary (1689–1694). On the other hand, the Whigs emphasized James's breaking the contractual agreement between king and nation and Parliament's right to offer the throne to the most legitimate claimant. They judged the claims of William and Mary equally valid, adding that Parliament possessed the authority to define the scope of royal prerogative powers and to set down a Declaration of Rights governing politics and society.

The Revolutionary Settlement

Such was the basis of the revolutionary settlement. By virtue of the Declaration of Rights (to become a parliamentary Bill of Rights in December 1689), the monarch was enjoined from suspending laws, and the prerogative of royal pardon in particular cases was severely restricted. In all criminal cases the accused had the right to jury trials, and prerogative courts like James II's Ecclesiastical Commission were prohibited. The sovereign had to take a coronation oath upholding Parliament's statutes, and free parliamentary debate was guaranteed. All taxes not sanctioned by Parliament were illegal. No peacetime standing army could exist. William objected to what he considered to be thinly veiled parliamentary conditions placed on his rule, but framers of the Declaration assured him that they simply were restating old laws which had been broken by James. Indeed, nothing except the article on the peacetime standing army was new. Moreover, the monarch retained important powers: the liberty to select his own ministers, formulate his own foreign policy, influence parliamentary elections, and control patronage. The Declaration of Rights confirmed civil rights for English subjects while assuring the mixed and limited nature of the English monarchy. Royal absolutism in the continental manner, fitfully attempted by each of England's four seventeenth-century Stuart kings, was recognized as antithetical to the country's traditions.

Concerning the always inflammable religious question, the Whigs forced through Parliament a Toleration Act amending the spirit, if not the letter, of the discriminatory Test Acts. The new king himself was a Dutch Calvinist, in English terms a Dissenter. He genuinely believed in religious tolerance, and the lessons of the past half century had convinced most Englishmen that enforced religious uniformity could never bring social peace. The solution that appealed to William was "Comprehension"—widening the theological constraints of Anglicanism so as to embrace most Dissenting Protestants within its fold. However, the Anglican lower clergy would not hear of such a compromise. Therefore, the so-called Toleration Act was adopted. Non-Anglicans still were prohibited from holding local civil and political office, but Protestants believing in the Holy Trinity were guaranteed free and open worship. Although Catholics, Unitarians, Quakers, and non-Christians were left outside the provisions of the Toleration Act, restrictions against these groups were not immediately enforced. Roman Catholics were excluded from the throne, and the new coronation oath promised to uphold the "Protestant Reformed Religion." However limited the Toleration Act was, at last it seemed that England's political and social fabric could withstand confessional diversity.

After some wrangling with William, the Whigs won the guarantee of frequent parliamentary elections. They wanted no repetition of the Cavalier Parliament or, what was worse, a king ruling without Parliament at all. In 1694 the Triennial Act called for elections at least every three years (amended to every seven years in 1716). From 1689 to 1713 the needs of war and preparation for war brought Parliament together annually. The increased length, frequency, and regularity of its sittings assured Parliament a central place in the day-to-day functions of government, and pro- and antiwar arguments greatly stimulated the evolution of political parties. Though future ministers might cajole, browbeat, and bribe MPs into sanctioning royal policies, the Glorious Revolution greatly enhanced Parliament's role in government. Parliament had settled the succession question, dampened religious fires, and regulated the royal prerogative. It provided William with the funds to fight his wars and might even impeach his ministers. Surely the king could fill Parliament with his choices, but frequent elections might then undo his packing. After 1689, king and Parliament were undeniably interdependent features of the English constitution.

Mary died in 1694, William in 1702. The couple had no children, so the crown passed on to Anne (1702–1714), Mary's younger sister. Since Anne's numerous offspring had stubbornly resisted survival, the genuine possibility existed that the line descending from James's daughters would end with Anne's death. Therefore, in 1701 Parliament passed the Act of Settlement, fixing the succession in the German House of Hanover, which was directly descended from the first Stuart king, James I. Betraying suspicion of the new continental attachment, the act added that on his own no English sovereign could send troops to war over lands not linked to his crown. Nor could a ruler leave English soil without Parliament's consent.

Although an essentially Whig program dictated the spirit of the revolutionary settlement, Tory support carried it through. Party loyalties and distinctions still were blurred. William III was the king the Whigs had put on the throne, but his activist royal inclinations veered more closely toward a Tory than a Whig position. Still, William could count on the Whigs because they were the fountainhead of his support in the war against Louis XIV. The king was more of a European than an Englishman, with a primary desire to curb French domination over the continent; the long-term effect of English involvement in European politics from 1689 until 1713 was to turn England into a world power.

London's merchants and financiers, as well as the greatest country landlords, loaned the government sums to fight the wars. Customarily, these individuals thought of themselves as Whigs. Others without a direct stake in the wars or in conquering Spain's overseas markets, identified with the Tories. The "political nation" itself was highly circumscribed. About a quarter million males, one of every twelve adults, could vote. Moreover, two-thirds of the electoral districts called boroughs contained fewer than five hundred voters; one-third of them had fewer than a hundred voters. It was not difficult for the Crown or an important peer to control election districts. The limited franchise and unreformed districting placed a high price on votes. By and large, the Tories called for a wider franchise, but both parties represented interests of country proprietors, urban merchants, the armed forces, and civil service, rather than individual constituents.

The revolutionary settlement was respectful of Scotland. William rewarded Scottish loyalty toward his accession by guaranteeing the country's unique laws, its Presbyterian religion, and its independent Parliament. In 1702 the Scots accepted Anne as their queen. However, both English and Scottish-Lowland politicians worried about the loyalty of the wild Highlanders to the Hanoverians. The seventeenth century had been marked by very poor relations—and even open warfare—between the two countries, and in the Highlands there was a strong residue of sympathy for the Stuarts. Fearing Scotland's latent pro-French sentiments as well, English Whigs were convinced of the necessity for union. Surprisingly, in 1707 the Scottish Parliament gave its assent. Its reasons were as much economic as political. The abolition of customs duties meant the free export of Scottish cattle and grain to England and the removal of barriers to trade with the English colonies. In return for yielding its political independence, Scotland gained forty-five seats in the English House of Commons. The country kept its legal institutions and established Presbyterian Church. Membership in

England's privileged trading companies and the benefits of the Navigation Acts were extended to Scottish merchants. The United Kingdom of Great Britain was born.

Ireland was an entirely different matter. The later Stuarts had done nothing to ameliorate the brutality of Cromwell's conquest. Native Catholics wallowed in virtual serfdom. Presbyterians descended from Scottish immigrants in the northern part of Ireland fared somewhat better. English landlords, usually Anglican and often absentee, owned the greatest properties and controlled the Irish Parliament. But the English Parliament considered all Irishmen of whatever religious persuasion with contempt, and in 1690 the Catholic Irish made a fatal error by supporting an abortive effort by James II to reclaim his kingdom. James planned to use Ireland as his strategic base; however, on July 1 William himself defeated James's Franco-Irish contingent at the Battle of the Boyne. English fears of future rebellion provoked a rule of terror and repression. The Catholic population bore the brunt of mistreatment. The so-called Penal Code kept Catholic priests from preaching and Catholic teachers from teaching. Catholic parents were forbidden from sending their children abroad to be educated, and Catholics were enjoined from sitting in the Irish Parliament. Catholics were prohibited from purchasing land, and a child needed only to turn Protestant to dispossess his Catholic father. Professions and most trades were closed to Catholics. To forestall the development of a native Catholic elite, the English determined to keep Ireland's religious majority economically and socially suppressed.

The Protestant Irish had reason for complaint also. After 1690 the Navigation Acts continued to treat Ireland as a foreign country. Its merchants could not sell to England's colonies. The Irish were prohibited from manufacturing woolens; their raw wool was to be exported exclusively to England. Thus Ireland was to live off the sale of raw wool and beef, with its absent landlords pocketing the profits. Even resident Anglicans in Ireland felt like a conquered people, subject to the economic discrimination and political authority of London.

Queen Anne's reign virtually coincided with the War of the Spanish Succession (1702–1713), the struggle William III had inspired against France. An Englishman, the duke of Marlborough, succeeded William as the driving force that brought the anti-French coalition to the threshold of victory. By 1710, however, both Queen Anne and public opinion had grown weary of the war, and the election of 1711 gave the Tories a majority in Commons. Their platform was peace. Anne dismissed Marlborough and packed the House of Lords with Tory peers. In 1712 Parliament and the queen took England out of the war. Two years later, Anne became gravely ill and died at fifty. None of her seventeen children survived her. On her deathbed she regretted that her young Stuart half brother in French exile refused to become an Anglican and return home to claim his crown. But no Whigs and few Tories wanted the Pretender. As foreseen by the Act of Settlement, the elector of Hanover became the next English ruler, assuming the throne as George I. After a century of unprecedented shock and dislocation, the England of 1714 was confident of itself and welcomed the future. Political life was lively, centered around the Whig and Tory parties. However incomplete, the Toleration Act brought a truce to the country's long-standing religious strife. Nobles, gentry, and the propertied middle classes had welded their separate interests into a national program: a political settlement defined by the Glorious Revolution, a social one determined by landed wealth, and an economic one stressing estate building and international trade. An oligarchy ruled the land.

THE DUTCH NETHERLANDS AND THE DEFENSE OF EUROPE

The Dutch Constitution

In 1650 and again in 1672 crises occurred in the Dutch Netherlands. Both sets of events were important politically, but they were not revolutions. The structure of Dutch society was barely affected. Armed battles and large-scale political purges were averted. The crises were consistent with the pattern of Dutch history, a pendulum swinging between the centralizing pretensions of the House of Orange and the oligarchic ambitions of Amsterdam's merchants and shippers. As we have seen (pp. 38–39), the social and political structure of the United Provinces was unique in Europe. An urban patriciate settled largely in the provinces of Holland and Utrecht provided the Dutch with a material standard of life that was the envy of the continent. These oligarchs invested in lifetime annuities and offices, bought shares in the East and West India Companies, built stately town houses, and purchased country properties. Because they overwhelmingly financed the Dutch confederation, the regents of the province of Holland tried to bully or persuade the Estates of other provinces to instruct their representatives in the States-General to vote Holland's way. This usually meant religious tolerance, low taxes, careful foreign alliances, a neutral foreign policy, small army, huge merchant marine, and Dutch mastery over international commerce.

The leader of Holland's delegation to the States-General was a provincial official called the grand pensionary. He customarily prepared resolutions in Holland's name and was entrusted to correspond, in the name of the Dutch Republic itself, with ambassadors abroad. A respected and feared grand pensionary could be extremely imposing in national politics. Offsetting his influence, however, were the two contrary forces of Dutch political life—jealously guarded decentralized structures and the political office of stadholder.

Dutch parochialism was legion. Before making important political decisions members of the States-General had to refer back to the provinces,

Figure 3.1—Painting by Dirck van Delen, "The Great Hall on the Binnenhof During the 'Great Assembly' of 1651." Located in The Hague, the Binnenhof was a medieval castle that housed the Dutch States-General in its central hall. It was an open building, where grave affairs of state were conducted in an atmosphere of commercial sociability. While the delegates debated in the background, booksellers and print vendors sold their items to milling customers whose pets wandered about. Towering above the scene were battle flags captured from the Spaniards in the eighty-year war for Dutch independence, stark reminders that the freedom to conduct business had been hard won. Courtesy of the Rijksmuseum-Stichting, Amsterdam.

and provincial authorities then had to consult town elites. The machinery was cumbersome and secrecy was impossible. Each province awarded a negotiated quota of revenue to the States-General, and tax farmers collected consumer dues. No uniform legal code existed for the United Provinces. For more than a century the country could not even agree on the same date. For example, while Holland and Zeeland had adopted the Gregorian calendar in 1582, the other provinces waited until 1700 before doing so. Politically, what prevented the Dutch constitution from sinking completely into the mire of localism was the stadholderate. In each province this was a medieval office, roughly translated as a "lieutenancy." In the sixteenth-century war of liberation against Spain, the personal heroism and martyrdom of the stadholder of Holland, William the Silent, assured election to the office to future generations of his family. Thereafter the stadholderate would be bestowed on its eldest male member. Four or five other provinces customarily joined Holland in selecting the same individual as *their* stadholder, and the remaining provinces chose a close relative. The States-General customarily granted command of the armed forces to Holland's stadholder, and he controlled most of the major offices put up for sale in the Republic. The House of Orange held large properties in the Netherlands, Germany, and France. It was related to many of Europe's ruling families. The young man who became Stadholder William III in 1672 was the great-grandson of France's Henry IV and grandson of England's Charles I.

Political Turmoil in the Golden Age

The wealth and prestige of the stadholder's family made him very popular among members of the Calvinist clergy, small merchants, petty shopkeepers, artisans, and free peasants—all of whom harbored resentments of one form or other against the urban regents of Holland. The grand policy of the House of Orange was to use the stadholder's prestige to weld the provinces closely together. Although the revolt of the Dutch Netherlands had succeeded by the 1640s, the stadholder, Frederick Henry, wished to continue fighting Spain in order to liberate the Belgian Netherlands to the south. Moreover, following the marriage of his son William to Mary, daughter of Charles I of England, Frederick Henry plotted to rescue that unhappy king from his rambunctious Parliament. All of this bellicosity, however, was contrary to the policies of Holland, particularly Amsterdam's, and the stadholder died frustrated in 1647. The next year the States-General ratified the Treaty of Münster with Spain, thus concluding eighty years of passive and active warfare, and the United Provinces remained neutral during Charles Stuart's agony in England.

   William II (1647–1650) succeeded peacefully to all of his father's offices, including command of the army; but his ambition provoked political turmoil in 1650. William saw himself as a glorious military leader, and his authoritarian personality bore no scruples in wishing to upset the cumbersome constitutional structure of the United Provinces. The immediate cause of dispute with the Estates of Holland had to do with military demobilization. The war with Spain over, the regents of Holland saw no reason for paying their province's customary share in the maintenance of the Netherlands' 55,000-man army. They wished to reduce Holland's contribution unilaterally, without consulting either the States-General or the stadholder. On the other hand, the headstrong William hoped to reopen hostilities with Spain—he already was secretly plotting with France to invade the Southern (Spanish) Netherlands—and he dreamed of sailing to England to avenge his martyred father-in-law, Charles I. William opened talks with Holland over army maintenance; but these quickly broke down, and the young stadholder decided to use force against the recalcitrant province. In July 1650 he arrested six deputies to the Estates of Holland and surrounded Amsterdam with troops brought from the eastern part of the Netherlands, the region most loyal to his cause. Though William released his prisoners, the city government of Amsterdam began arming against him. Civil war seemed near. At this point, however, an act of nature changed everything. William suddenly contracted smallpox and died, leaving a widow childless but eight months pregnant.

A week after his father's death, the future William III (1672–1702) was born. The regents of Holland seized the opportunity of a vacant stadholderate to tip the constitutional balance in their favor, and allies in the other provinces followed suit. The baby prince of Orange was specifically denied the stadholderate and future command of the army. In his place the grand pensionary of Holland, Jan de Witt (1625–1672), assumed control over the republic's destinies. Oliver Cromwell gave De Witt a war he did not want, but the Dutchman masterfully maneuvered through the web of provincial politics and raised a fleet. Through the 1650s the Dutch were able to hold on to the carrying trade of the Baltic and maintain their interests in America and Asia. A second trade war with England broke out in 1665. The Dutch fought well, destroying the English fleet while it lay at anchor in the Thames and Medway. At the Treaty of Breda in 1667 the United Provinces exchanged New Netherland for Surinam in South America, forced relaxation of the Navigation Acts so as to permit Dutch entry into English ports, and had the English recognize the legitimacy of neutral Dutch shipping in wartime.

Domestically, however, De Witt was sitting on a powder keg. Again and again, the inland agricultural provinces chafed at Holland's domination of the confederation. Middling burghers and artisans complained that the regents of Amsterdam were soaking up the republic's wealth. Calvinist preachers denounced De Witt's religious policies, by far the most tolerant in Europe. As the prince of Orange approached manhood, all who were naturally suspicious of the grand pensionary's leadership threw their hopes round William's person. However, remaining hostile to the House of Orange, the Estates of Holland passed the so-called Eternal Edict, thereby abolishing the province's stadholderate altogether. Moreover, the Estates flatly refused to recognize as supreme military commander whoever might be selected as stadholder in any other province. Nevertheless, supporters of William took heart. They closely observed events across the Channel, where the experience of Charles II offered hope that their own leader might not be excluded indefinitely from public life.

As it turned out, it was the crisis of foreign invasion that overturned De Witt's "Regime of True Liberty." In 1670 Charles II concluded the Secret Treaty of Dover with Louis XIV, the intent of which was the destruction of the Dutch Republic. A third trade war erupted with England in March 1672, and shortly thereafter Louis XIV invaded the Netherlands. Unprepared for war, the Republic was traumatized. Rioting erupted. De Witt was blamed for having sacrificed vigilance for profits, and an attempt was made on his life. His enemies seized control of the Estates of Holland

and Zeeland. The States-General recalled how once before the House of Orange had saved the nation, and it asked the frail, shy twenty-one-year-old William to assume his responsibilities to family and country. The Eternal Edict was abrogated and William was invested in the essential offices previously denied him—most importantly the stadholderates of Holland and Zeeland. He was named captain-general of the army and admiral-general of the navy. Orangists took over important provincial posts and sent more Orangists to the States-General. De Witt resigned as grand pensionary of Holland. Falsely accused of plotting William's murder, his brother Cornelius was imprisoned. When Jan went to The Hague to visit him, an ugly mob greeted both brothers. They were blamed for the Netherlands' misfortune, dragged outside Cornelius's prison, hanged upside down, filled with musket shot, and mutilated. On this inglorious note, the Regime of True Liberty fell.

There was no time, however, to meditate on the violence done to the De Witts. French troops had already occupied the three provinces of Overijssel, Gelderland, and Utrecht. A young, inexperienced prince was called on to save the country. That William III managed to do so, while at the same time reestablishing his family's authority over the United Provinces, has made the regime of the De Witts appear shameful by comparison. Dutch patriotic historians call the oligarchic period of 1650 to 1672 a blot on their country's history—materialistic, politically myopic, unwilling to recognize the Anglo-French menace, and thereby inviting disaster. Nevertheless, it was under Holland's peace-obsessed investors and speculators that a very special civilization took root, perplexing and amazing all Europe. For the later seventeenth century, it was as unique as the Dutch Republic itself. Tolerant not only of all Protestant sects but also of Roman Catholics, Jews, and even freethinkers—financing a theater, an international book trade, and the five most innovative universities in Europe, Holland's regents subsidized a generation of unparalleled genius in painting, literature, philosophy, and science. The period known culturally as the Golden Age drew on a spirit of openness. Within it flourished the painters Rembrandt, Vermeer, and Jan Steen, the poet Vondel, the philosopher Spinoza, and the scientists Huygens and Leeuwenhoek. All through the century the Dutch Netherlands were a refuge for the persecuted and endangered: groups from the Pilgrims to the Huguenots, individuals from René Descartes to John Locke. Rich and multihued, Dutch civilization integrated exiles even if it did not assimilate them. As such, it contrasted vividly with the royally stylized classicism taking root in France. It was the genuine legacy of the De Witts.

William III, Stadholder and King

As stadholder, William III either won over key supporters of the De Witts or else placed his followers into town and provincial administrations. Street violence ended. William knew the limits of his authority, however, and he stopped short of trying to convert the Dutch Republic's unwieldy political structure into a streamlined absolutism. The stadholder's overriding preoccupation was military: to mold a European alliance against Louis XIV and persuade the Dutch magnates of banking and trade that it was in their interest to finance the armies of impecunious allies, such as Hapsburg Austria, Spain, and Sweden. William held up the specter of French mercantilism; he offered asylum to Protestant refugees fleeing France. He persuaded his onetime enemies, the oligarchs of Amsterdam, first to pay for the war against France and then in 1688 to finance his expedition to England. The events of 1672 produced no revolution in the Netherlands, but rather only another swing in the pendulum of Dutch history.

William also molded a skillful policy toward England. In 1672 he was fourth in line to the English throne, following Charles's younger brother James and James's two daughters, Mary and Anne. While Charles secretly collected funds from Louis XIV, William reminded Parliament that the Anglo-French alliance might one day backfire on England. In 1674 England withdrew from the third Anglo-Dutch War and three years later the stadholder concocted an important political marriage—gaining the hand of James Stuart's daughter Mary. As James's Catholicism became known, William's betrothal to the Protestant princess assumed greater importance.

Meanwhile Louis XIV's attempt to crush the Netherlands failed. His garrisons were stretched too thinly and the French withdrew from the occupied provinces. The Peace of Nijmegen (1678) recognized the territorial integrity of the United Provinces, and France reduced its tariffs on Dutch goods. Having withstood both English and French attacks on its sovereignty, the Dutch Netherlands achieved the height of prestige. Shortly thereafter William cemented an alliance with England by his own person. In 1685 the duke of York assumed the English throne as James II. Soon James alienated virtually all shades of Protestantism and political opinion in England. Then in June 1688 the birth of his son and the threat of a Catholic succession turned parliamentary leadership toward William and Mary. In November the stadholder responded energetically to the bipartisan invitation to rescue English Protestantism. James fled the country, and Parliament named William co-monarch with his wife.

From 1689 until his death in 1702, William shuttled between London and The Hague. Because of William's absences, Dutch affairs increasingly fell into the hands of the grand pensionary of Holland, Anthony Heinsius (1641–1720). Heinsius was no Jan de Witt. First of all, he was devoted to the stadholder, and as long as William lived, Heinsius prevented the traditional regent-stadholder political rivalry from erupting into civil strife. Secondly, Heinsius was as convinced as William of the moral necessity of the struggle against France. Thanks to his prodding, the Dutch virtually exhausted their material resources in their last war with Louis XIV. However, Heinsius also was enough of a regent to reconstruct Amsterdam's leadership in the confederation.

William died without direct heirs. By previous arrangement a young cousin became stadholder in the peripheral provinces of Groningen and Friesland. Elsewhere, however, plans for a successor to William simply were shelved. The political pendulum tipped again, and for the next forty-five years the republic would live without a stadholder. Holland once more assumed leadership of the Dutch confederation, and carried the brunt of the war effort against Louis XIV. But the Netherlands were rapidly fading as a great power, and the War of the Spanish Succession (1702–1713) proved to be a watershed in the Republic's history. States with more depth in manpower and natural resources outstripped the Netherlands in agricultural and industrial development and were catching up in shipping and shipbuilding. Dutch funds for investment left the country, and the citizenry accepted an existence conforming to the size of the confederation's population and limited by its natural resources and archaic political structure.

FRANCE: THE FRONDE AND THE RISE OF LOUIS XIV

Civil War

In 1648 France's Louis XIV (1643–1715) was a child of ten, and the government was theoretically in the hands of a regency of his closest relatives. In practice, however, the queen mother, Anne of Austria, and her companion, Cardinal Jules Mazarin (1602–1661), ran affairs. Italian born, naturalized in 1639, Mazarin had been Cardinal Richelieu's handpicked successor as first minister of state. Coming to power in 1643, Mazarin continued Richelieu's policy of using a skeletal bureaucracy of intendants and commissioners to challenge the pretensions of nobles and officers holding inheritable posts. However, his style was better suited to bribe, divide, and undercut than to create an institutionalized base of authority. Although Mazarin controlled the princes' Council of State, officeholders, led by magistrates in the Parlement of Paris, stiffened resistance against him. In 1648 revolt erupted.

The indignation of the officeholders was based on self-interest disguised as constitutional principle. In the late stages of the Thirty Years' War, French military expenses were extremely high, and the state was chronically short of revenue for campaigns against the Spaniards. As expedients, Mazarin had created large blocs of posts in the law courts, tax administration, and local governments. He then sold them to the highest bidder. Many offices were duplicated, increasing rivalry and bitterness among their holders and angering clients who had to pay officeholders for services they rendered. Mazarin increased taxes on food and drink. He tried forced loans and hearth taxes. Still, the state could not pay its bills. Finally, early in 1648 he directed the Council of State to impose a new set of taxes on Paris. Then he created yet more offices and increased the renewal fees for older ones. The latter decrees had the effect of lowering the value of offices while at the same time making them more expensive to keep. In addition, office-holders feared a wholesale recall of their posts so that the state could sell them again.

At this point the chief law court of the realm, the Parlement of Paris, stepped in to speak for the officers' interests. The war, an irregular government hungering for revenue, and a countryside suffering from the worst harvest of the century, created an atmosphere of national discontent that the *parlementaires* —themselves the most prestigious officeholders in the kingdom—could exploit advantageously. Already, provincial revolts, en-demic under Richelieu, were spreading toward the capital. The Paris Par-lement refused to register Mazarin's edicts as law. Parlementary leaders then went further, seeking to reverse the absolutist trend in government that had developed in the past half century. They demanded a more active role in making the laws and the right to interrogate councillors of state and minis-ters on policy. They spoke to the wishes of all officeholders by calling for the abolition of the intendants, an end to office duplication, and state recogni-tion of the inviolability of offices legitimately held. Finally, the *parlemen-taires* made a bid at widening their constituency by calling for a lowering of the most important tax in the kingdom, the *taille* (which they and the other officers did not pay), and the freedom of all Frenchmen, irrespective of social rank, from arbitrary arrest. In Paris shopkeepers, artisans, and the unem-ployed prepared barricades. Humble peasants and townsmen—who had built the roads, dug the trenches, and filled the ranks during the cardinal's war with the Hapsburgs—now joined officers and judges of quality in order to change the course of events. All looked to the Paris Parlement as the focal point of opposition to Mazarin and his creatures.

In August 1648 Mazarin bungled an attempt to arrest several lead-ers of the Parlement of Paris, and mobs attacked the royal troops. The great princes at court, traditional malcontents, turned on the cardinal and Anne. Headed by the prince de Conti and the dukes de Longueville and Beaufort, they tried to establish a common front with the parlementary judges and at the same time lead the mobs. Their very lives in danger, Mazarin, the queen mother, and young Louis XIV fled Paris for estates in the country. In October a royal declaration yielded on nearly every point the *parlementaires* had demanded. But Mazarin was simply buying time. He correctly sus-pected that an alliance of princes, magistrates, and the people could not last. Unlike the situation in England, where deep-seated religious, constitu-tional, and political concerns had led to popular support of revolutionaries, in France a handful of judicial officers holding lifetime sinecures had ma-nipulated a dispute over their sources of income into a confrontation over the constitution of the monarchy and the civil liberties of its subjects. As he pretended to give way, Mazarin prepared countermoves. Making peace with the Hapsburg emperor, he moved troops released from German service

toward Paris. The prince de Condé remained loyal and was pl.
head of the army. In January 1649 Condé besieged Paris, and
erupted in earnest.

At this stage the restive princes turned to arms, and th   ..u
parlementary front disintegrated. Some judges joined the princes; others
acceded to Mazarin's promise to bring order out of anarchy. A few damned
both sides while remaining true to the principles of the previous summer.
Aside from a common hatred of Mazarin and a desire to dismember the
state among themselves, the princes lacked a coordinated program. Unquenchable ambition was what drove them on, and their complicated hostilities ravaged the countryside until 1653. Though Mazarin had pulled the
army out of Germany, France remained at war with Spain. Spanish armies,
royal and noble troops, and irregular guerrilla bands cut a swath of destruction. Dismissed troops and peasants driven from ruined estates joined
whatever ragtag group that promised the most booty. The war spared few
regions. In many places food production halted altogether. Crop failure and
famine led to property sales at giveaway prices. For the peasants the civil
war was an unmitigated disaster. Casualties reached 2 million, one-tenth of
the total French population. Twenty-five years later, a spectacular drop in
marriages and births was attributed to the demographic catastrophe accompanying the Fronde.

In the end, Mazarin returned as savior of the state. He skillfully
divided enemies and bribed potential friends. Most *parlementaires* returned
to the royal fold, and by 1652 the country was crying for peace. The
promise of pardon gave the princes an honorable excuse to lay down their
arms, and late in 1652 Paris, the onetime center of resistance, meekly submitted. It took nearly a year to subdue all the provinces; however, with the
fall of the "people's republic" of Bordeaux in August 1653, the Fronde
officially was over.

The Grooming of Louis XIV

The failure of the Fronde prepared the way for Louis XIV's conception of
absolutism. The alternatives offered up by *parlementaires* and princes now
were discredited. Mazarin sought neither revenge nor reprisals. He accepted
a surface reconciliation with the erstwhile rebels and a slow, steady reconstruction of royal power. From 1653 to 1661 the cardinal chose his associates well. Disregarding the princes, he turned to the lesser nobility and even
bourgeoisie for his most trusted servants. He persuaded officeholders and
junior parlementary officials of proven ability to enter the royal service as
commissioners. He bought off local aristocracies with estates and money.
As Louis XIV approached the age of majority, Mazarin developed the cult
of majesty for the young king. In 1654 Louis enjoyed a magnificent investi-
ture ceremony at Reims. The following year he showed what might be
expected when, in full hunting regalia, he burst into a session of the Paris

Parlement and prohibited the magistrates from presenting their legal objections to a new tax edict. In 1659 Mazarin brought the lingering war with Spain to a triumphant end and scored an even more telling diplomatic victory by marrying off Louis to the eldest daughter of the Spanish king, Philip IV. This personal union would make France arbiter of the fortunes of the Spanish empire.

Yet the exhaustion that followed the Fronde only covered up the disorder in French society and government. Taxation was abusive, and offices still were duplicated and sold. The government borrowed money from tax farmers and private combines. It then turned its "benefactors" loose on the peasantry to recoup loans and interest. From the Fronde, Mazarin learned that royal power might exploit the political and social divisions in France. Young Louis XIV would perfect the cardinal's strategy and then insist on his prerogative to mediate the discord. Moreover, as the most populous state in western Europe, a source of vast agricultural and commercial wealth, France offered Louis untapped opportunity. His person might provide the unifying structure lacking elsewhere, and an active, opportunistic monarch might well restore a mood of self-confidence to his people. On March 6, 1661, Mazarin died, willing his superb library to the state that had paid for it. On the following day, the twenty-three-year-old king announced that henceforth he would serve as his own first minister.

LOUIS XIV AND FRANCE: MEDIATIVE ABSOLUTISM

Provincial Elites and Royal Bureaucrats

Louis understood the obstacles confronting him. Above all, he needed to convince corporate and regional elites that royal leadership alone offered the means of serving their needs and meeting their expectations. The king depended upon his agents, the intendants, to assure officers of state that it would be in their self-interest to submit to the royal will. The intendants' essential responsibility was investigative—to watch over the judicial and tax-collecting officers, the courts, militia, and police. With links to the central government assured, the intendants added administrative responsibilities to their investigative ones. In this way they assumed umbrella authority over many aspects of provincial life. They oversaw the payment of town debts, supervised collection of the *taille,* and had the last word in the distribution and collection of new state taxes. They heard complaints of officer malfeasance and seigneurial injustice. They were responsible for public order and maintenance of the militia, as well as for keeping roads and bridges in repair. When troops had to pacify a region, the intendants took charge. If necessary, they supervised martial law. The utilization of the intendants as his *ex officio* agents for justice, finance, and police was the most lasting feature of Louis's administrative reforms.

Although Colbert might dream of a France served exclusively by intendants and their subordinates, his king was more realistic. Louis had no interest in crushing the traditional officers of state. He preferred to coopt the greatest of them with noble titles, military contracts, monopolies over state-generated industrial enterprises, and seats on royal commissions. The king needed state loans granted by officers for his ambitious military and foreign policies, and he desired the association of parlements and Estates in asserting his political will over the country. Therefore he went to great pains to persuade traditional opponents of royal authority that regulated cooperation with the government would bring them greater social and financial benefit than would smoldering hostility, sullen acquiescence, and periodic revolt.

Louis's intendants could never have realized royal objectives without the cooperation of provincial elites. The king's apologists liked to create the impression that a combination of legal argument, military power, and royal magnificence persuaded parlements, Estates, seigneurs, and churchmen that resistance to Louis XIV was hopeless, and therefore the groups which had spent most of the previous hundred years defying royal centralization had no other choice than to embrace late seventeenth-century absolutism. Generally missing from this argument is what local elites gained in return for their support. The *quid pro quo* was considerable, especially in the realms of royally supported economic development and the sharing of public power with the Crown.

Concerning economic development, Colbertine mercantilism revived entire regions just when it was most necessary. In southern France government grants and monopolies encouraged the reemergence of Languedoc's textile manufactures and export of the province's woolens to the eastern Mediterranean. Textile production revived as well in northern France, especially around the cities of Amiens, Rouen, Caen, and Reims. Colbert eliminated import and export duties in the port of Marseilles, and persuaded the king to share construction costs with Languedoc for the Canal des Deux Mers connecting the Mediterranean and the Atlantic, thereby providing easy transport of grain. Although the state-chartered overseas trading companies themselves were short-lived, government investment in forming them stimulated subsequent private funding of large-scale projects in Africa, Asia, and America. In each of these instances—industrial growth, capital improvement, canal building, and overseas investment—the royal government was persuading wealthy individuals to throw in their lot with the regime and thereby profit from its successes.

As far as local government was concerned, Louis XIV informed Estates and parlements that he would not tolerate independent assertions of their authority. Intendants were instructed to exclude uncooperative individuals from these bodies, and the royal signature on a *lettre de cachet* assured the arrest without warrant of a particularly obstinate member. Yet it would be mistaken to consider the *système louisquatorzien* as control through terror. In return for their cooperation, provincial landowners, officers, and guilds were assured royally regulated authority over the king's subjects. Louis XIV sought areas of mutual interest with the parlements, such as persecution of Protestants, and he even provided troops to assist the magistrates. Louis manipulated provincial Estates by allowing them to implement royal laws and collect the *taille,* all under the supervision of the intendants. Officials in the Estates assumed their tasks willingly, for the laws generally benefited them, and income from the *taille* contributed to their stipends. Ecclesiastical elites also profited, as the government awarded funds to bishops and abbots for the reconstruction and embellishment of their residences and churches. Therefore, by offering titles, grants, tax exemptions, and other marks of precedence, the king solidified local hierarchies as long as they remained personally loyal to him and respected his regulatory powers.

Provincial elites stood at one end of Louis XIV's bureaucratic apparatus; centralized departments located in royal palaces at Versailles, Fontainebleau, and Paris stood at the other. No preordained plan guided the construction of the king's officialdom, but four concentric circles seemed to give it definition. First was the Council of State. Presided over by the chancellor of France, the Council prepared and verified laws and heard appeals to the king. In its appellate capacity the Council could nullify decisions of the parlements, review those of intendants, and adjudicate disputes among the great nobility. Its most eminent members included thirty-six prominent officials representing the Church, the old nobility, and the *robe* (or judicial) aristocracy. The Council depended upon the labors of approximately 150 department chiefs and their assistants, plus 400 additional lawyers, secretaries, junior commissioners, and their clerks. The only member of the Council who possessed an irremovable post was the chancellor, and in time his role as administrative coordinator became an empty honor. During the reign of Louis XIV new agencies attached to the Council were established, like the postal service. Others expanded their jurisdiction, as when the Chancery Department assumed control over the licensing and censorship of books.

A second area of royal administration, the day-to-day running of the provinces, was directed by four secretaries of state, each of whom was responsible for a demarcated region of the country. Moreover, the secretaries of state possessed specialized jurisdiction over war, the army, navy, or foreign affairs. They constructed their own bureaucracies in two large wings of the royal palace at Versailles and corresponded regularly with the intendants. The third great administrative agency dealt with government finances. In the 1640s Mazarin had reinforced the authority of royal tax collectors under two *superintendants* of finance. One superintendant, Nicolas Fouquet, presided over collection. The second, Jean-Baptiste Colbert, treasurer of Mazarin's own household and architect of French mercantilism, watched over Fouquet. In 1661 Fouquet's corruption brought him down, and Colbert took over. He suppressed the office of superintendant, and as controller-general of finances assumed direction of a fiscal empire. His specialized subordinates at Versailles oversaw administration of the *taille,* salt tax, the king's estates, fiscal reform, and new revenue-raising methods; intendants and tax collectors in the provinces were in constant contact with Colbert.

A fourth concentric circle was Louis's inner group of ministers of state, the so-called High Council. Meeting regularly with the king at the royal invitation, the ministers generally comprised a few secretaries of state and heads of the great departments. An official of the High Council might direct several government agencies. For example, in addition to finance, Colbert sat on the High Council, ran the naval department, and supervised state manufactures, building construction, cultural institutions, and public works. After Colbert's death in 1683, François-Michel Le Tellier, marquis de Louvois (1639–1691), High Council minister and secretary of state for war, took over the superintendancy of building. The real workhorses of the bureaucracy were mid-level officials, masters of requests of the Council of State, who prepared the royal orders and edicts. The most promising among them became ambassadors, department chiefs, and ministers.

From minister of state to departmental clerk, all members of the bureaucracy served at the royal pleasure, with the knowledge that disgrace and dismissal might come without notice. Actually, the risks were fewer than one might imagine. Louis XIV had a passion for continuity and order in government. During his sole reign of fifty-four years there were only sixteen ministers of state, even with three to five sitting at any one time. Louis's controllers-general of finance, war secretaries, and secretaries of state for foreign affairs averaged nearly eleven years apiece in office. Between 1685 and 1715 the provincial intendants averaged over sixteen years apiece. The king maintained Mazarin's policy of drawing officials from relatively modest social backgrounds, usually the lesser judicial nobility or bourgeoisie.

Two families, the Le Telliers and Colberts, dominated the ranks of Louis's government, eventually creating ministerial dynasties that worked against the king's intention of keeping passive, subservient subordinates. From Mazarin's circle the king inherited as war minister the lawyer Michel Le Tellier (1603–1685). From the age of fourteen Michel's son François-Michel, later made marquis de Louvois, occasionally attended High Council meetings with his father. The two built Louis's army. Surrounded by technicians and strategists drawn from outside the ranks of the *grands,* Le Tellier and Louvois recovered the army from the aristocratic colonel-generals who had purchased regiments and whose loyalty to the Crown never was assured. After 1661 specialized intendants and inspectors clothed, fed, and formulated strategy for an army that in peacetime grew to 200,000 and in wartime reached half a million. The high nobility still led the battlefield charges, but they were subject to the control of the two great war secretaries

and their disciplinarians—Martinet, inventor of cadence; Fourilles, reformer of the cavalry; and Vauban, commissioner-general of fortifications.
The state assumed complete responsibility over military justice, police, finance, dress, and maintenance. Each parish in France had to supply a stipulated share of troops. As the new infantry regiments became the foundation
stone of the French army, the cavalry as preserve of the aristocracy lost
prestige. The artillery, heretofore contracted to civilians, was integrated
into the newly created engineer corps. By 1707, the year of Vauban's death,
over 160 new or rebuilt fortresses surrounded France.

Until his death in 1691, the marquis de Louvois dominated
France's military revolution. He fed Louis's belief in the army as the chief
instrument of royal glory and power, and the war secretary rose to the
central place in the king's government. Finances of state came to be used in
accordance with Louvois's recommendations, and his triumph gradually
was achieved at the expense of controller-general Colbert. Architect of the
Dutch War of 1672, Colbert was no pacifist. However, his major achievement was as developer of royal revenues. Following Mazarin's policies, this
draper's son had the government abandon its dependence upon loans from
corrupt financiers and tax farmers. Taking advantage of public hostility
toward these moneylenders, at the slightest provocation Colbert repudiated
payment to them. The controller-general advised Louis not to renew the
most useless offices of state, to reduce payments to officeholders whenever
possible, and to find loopholes in sales contracts that would restore recently
alienated properties to the state. Abolishing abusive practices and making
certain that most tax revenue actually got to the treasury, during his first
ten years of service Colbert doubled royal income. Mercantilism and restraint combined to bring financial respectability to the French monarchy.

The Dutch war (1672–1678) changed everything, however.
Promising victory daily, Louvois became an appendage to Louis's vanity,
and Colbert was reduced to digging for quick expedients. The controller-
general had to revert to petty, irritating schemes, like taxing household
pewter or raising the excise on salt and tobacco. Serious fiscal revolts
erupted in Bordeaux and Rennes, spreading into the provinces of Guyenne
and Brittany. In 1675 contemporaries spoke of a new Fronde in the western
half of the kingdom. Two armies had to be dispatched to quell the uprisings. As under Mazarin, the state borrowed on anticipated revenues. Royal
subsidies for new industry dried up, Colbert had to scrap his plan for building a merchant fleet, and both the West Indian and Northern commercial
companies collapsed. In 1680 Colbert pleaded for one-tenth of 1 percent of
the state's budget for subsidies to stimulate commerce; he was turned down
and in 1683 died out of favor.

The policy of the Dutch War set the pattern for the remainder of
Louis's long reign. Military needs subordinated all else. The famine and
plague of 1683–1684 introduced an age of trials: declining landed income,
scarce food, greater fiscal burdens placed on the shoulders of a contracting

population. In their search for income, Colbert's successors resorted to the old techniques of currency manipulation and office sales. Tax collectors and garbage collectors, law clerks and funeral criers, judges and wigmakers —all had to buy their posts from the state and pass on their expenses to the populace by way of fees or gratuities. In 1693 a new famine hit, and now not even office purchasers could be found. Intendant after intendant pleaded for the privileged to pay their share of tax burdens.

Attempts at fiscal reform were made. In 1695 the *capitation* was introduced, a head tax exempting only the indigent and the clergy—though the Church was expected to apportion out a lump sum. Abandoned in 1699, the *capitation* then was revived during the War of the Spanish Succession (1702–1713). The *dixième,* the first French tax to be based on voluntary declarations of income, was proposed. Had these two experiments been pursued to their logical conclusion, they might have combined fiscal sanity with social justice. But exemptions based on social rank eventually destroyed the utility of both new taxes, and they simply added to the burden of the *taille* -paying poor. By the time Louis XIV died in 1715, the state was more in the debt of tax farmers and financiers than at any moment since the advent of Colbert. The deficit was an astronomical 2 billion livres.

"Un Roi, une Loi, une Foi"

Louis's ambition to raise up the throne as arbiter of the lives of his subjects was illustrated in two areas of administrative policy: law and religion. From the parlements on down, law courts were made to understand that above all they were arms of royal administration; suspected deviations from this rule meant deprivation of office and exile. For ostensibly supporting the regional tax revolts of 1675, *parlementaires* of Bordeaux and Rennes learned this. On the other hand, as long as the magistrates cooperated with the regime, they were rewarded with co-management of the countryside. Royal troops assisted the Parlement of Toulouse in repressing disorder and brigandage in 1666, and the king protected the magistrates from rival claims of authority by the Estates of Languedoc and municipal council of Toulouse.

Flattering the king with the title "the new Justinian," Colbert wanted codification of the laws to represent the major achievement of the reign. The task was immense. From south to north, contradictory Roman and Germanic legal traditions divided France. Clerical courts ruled for the laity on matters such as marriage contracts. Regions and corporations had their own law. More than eighty different civil codes existed, and procedure varied from place to place. Nevertheless, with a commission of experts, Colbert took on the job of codification. In civil and criminal law he never got beyond establishing uniform codes of procedure. Arbitrary and brutal punishments were left untouched. A code was devised to protect forest lands for eventual use in primary industries such as shipbuilding. A commercial code was drawn up; however, because of religious objections, it refrained from establishing legal rates of interest. A code for the marine appeared in 1680 and one for colonies and slaves in 1685. This last, the *Code noir,* did not reprove slave hunting or slave owning, but at least it insisted on the obligation of masters to provide slaves with food, shelter, and the rudiments of religion.

The royal motto was "un roi, une foi, une loi." If the idea of legal uniformity was dear to Colbert, that of religious uniformity particularly appealed to his king. Claiming political power from God alone, Louis took responsibility for the salvation of his subjects very seriously. He liked to consider himself a kind of super bishop, taking both forms of communion and mediating religious disputes. Louis was convinced of a mission to establish a unity of belief in France, and this led him to quarrel with the pope, with some of his Catholic subjects, and with all of his Calvinist ones.

Early in life Louis offered the Jesuits his confidence in religious matters. In this, as with so much else, he was loyal to the end. In one respect, however, Louis disagreed with his spiritual guides. The Jesuits were uncompromisingly devoted to the pope. They accepted the ultramontane view that all Catholic kings must submit to papal pronouncements on matters of faith and, if necessary, respect the pope's opinions on political questions. On the other hand, Louis's Gallican view stated that where Rome's governance over religious matters clashed with royal policies, national church councils might overrule papal authority. Since the line separating papal from royal responsibilities in ecclesiastical affairs had always been indistinct, church-state relations were essentially a matter of mutual goodwill.

Until the end of the Dutch war, the Jesuits had kept squabbles between Louis and the papacy from degenerating into anything serious. Then Louis claimed the power to collect and retain income for episcopal sees left temporarily vacant because of the death of a bishop. Pope Innocent XI (1676-1689) asked the king to revoke his claim, called the *régale.* In 1681-1682 Louis called an emergency meeting of France's bishops, and the quarrel with Innocent deepened into a full-scale conflict over the entire range of church-state relations. The French bishops affirmed the king's superiority over the pope in all temporal matters and asserted the pope's limited authority in religious ones. They added that decisions of councils of bishops might overturn papal decrees. Undoubtedly many bishops in the great clerical Assembly of 1681-1682 voted more from fear than conviction, and Innocent refused to accept their conclusions. He rejected each of Louis's nominees to vacant sees, and by 1688 thirty-five sees had no bishop. National sentiment rallied round the king; however, Louis was at the point of excommunication, and France was on the road to schism. Fortunately, the king had no desire to effect a Reformation. He was devoted to Catholic theology and to his Jesuits. Moreover, he was worrying about his own soul. He therefore decided to wait for the intractable Innocent to die so he could work out a compromise with a successor. This he accomplished in 1693. He won his point on the *régale* but withdrew official support for his bishops' so-called Gallican Articles of 1682. He promised to cooperate with the papacy and kept his word. The French sees were filled, and the Jesuits breathed more easily.

For most of the reign Louis was obsessed with a group of his Catholic subjects who called themselves Jansenists. Certain theological views and habits distinguished Jansenists from other Catholics. They rejected frequent communion and the efficacy of good works, and their moral asceticism made them hostile to the humanist, worldly wise Jesuits. The Jansenists gave French Catholicism a harshness of tone and appreciation of the tragedy of human existence that appealed to many of the century's most sensitive minds. Certain Jansenists were identified with the opposition to Mazarin during the Fronde, and largely for political reasons Louis developed a special aversion toward them. He translated religious individualism into suspect loyalty to his crown. On several occasions popes had condemned the movement's chief source book, Cornelius Jansen's *Augustinus* (1640), and in 1653 a papal bull formally declared as heretical five propositions supposedly derived from this work.

Because they customarily adopted a Gallican position toward papal authority, the Jansenists might have proven useful allies of the king. However, their leadership was derived from anti-Jesuit intellectuals, parlementary families, and great nobles—groups which Louis identified as unsympathetic to his conception of absolutism. For Louis, Jansenism became a kind of underground church that harbored political and social malcontents, and in the last twenty-five years of his rule the old king tried to wipe out all vestiges of Jansenist thought and belief. His campaign culminated in 1713 when he goaded the pope into promulgating the Bull *Unigenitus,* condemning 101 so-called Jansenist principles of faith.

Louis's attack backfired badly, inviting a revival of political Jansenism in the eighteenth century. On the eve of the king's death in 1715 those excluded from the mainstream of the provincial ruling elites discovered in Jansenism a rallying point against the bureaucratic absolutism that for a half century had constrained and repressed their corporate interests. These individuals included soured parlementary jurists, peeved officeholders, humiliated great nobles, and discontented merchant-shippers. In addition, simple priests in poverty-stricken parishes, harboring an understandable hostility toward the great bishops, abbots, and priors favored by the regime, considered themselves heirs to the Jansenist spiritual tradition. Their resentments were carried to their flocks. In Paris and other cities during the eighteenth century a disrespectful underground Jansenist newspaper circulated widely. It is an oversimplification to trace a straight line between the *Augustinus* and the revolution that exploded a century and a half later. However, in the generation after 1715 Jansenism found renewed strength—indeed, Louis XIV's persecution of it had kept it alive—and it was identified with corporate and popular opposition to the authoritarian political structures perfected by the king.

In 1661 the future of French Calvinism did not appear grim. Although amended by Richelieu, the Edict of Nantes (1598) had held for more than half a century, guaranteeing Protestants religious toleration and civil equality with Catholics. There were nearly a million and a half Huguenots in France. No longer fighters led by potentially rebellious nobles, they were economically self-sufficient professionals, merchants, craftsmen, and peasants. They were concentrated in the western and southern parts of the country, but could be found in smaller numbers nearly everywhere. They were especially important in banking and the law. Loyal during the Fronde, the Huguenot community had integrated itself into the life of the nation as well as could be expected from any seventeenth-century religious minority of 10 percent.

Mazarin treated the Huguenots with benign neglect. Colbert saw them as providing France with the lifeblood of the country's commerce and industry. Early in his personal reign, however, Louis XIV considered the Huguenots to be an affront to his authority. At first he decided to use persuasion, pious example, and bribery to win converts. In the mid-1670s he turned to sporadic harassment. He maintained the Edict of Nantes but interpreted its terms with a rigor that invited persecution, prohibiting everything that was not expressly authorized. Nothing in the charter explicitly stated that the Huguenots might bury their dead by day, so they were compelled to bury them at night. Nothing in the edict expressly opened up crafts and professions to them, so they were excluded from serving as judges, notaries, doctors, booksellers, and printers. Discriminatory tax burdens were placed on them. Endowments for their poor were seized and passed on to Catholics. Huguenot parents were forced to give their children a Catholic education. Their schools and hospitals were shut down, and churches constructed since 1598 were closed as well.

After 1680 the Huguenots were assured a scapegoat role. Catholic assemblies of the clergy and Louvois urged Louis to step up persecutions. Parlements and provincial Estates eagerly cooperated. Huguenot churches were demolished—186 of them from 1681 through 1684. Early in 1685 zealous intendants forced Huguenot families to lodge troops, who were permitted a free hand with their hosts. This latter act stimulated some conversions, which were announced to the king, and a flight of Huguenots from France, which was not. Louis himself was convinced that his policy of persuasion/coercion had worked. By October 1685 he estimated that an insufficient number of Huguenots remained in the country to warrant a charter protecting them. Therefore, the Edict of Nantes was revoked. The rights of Protestants in Alsace were affirmed; but elsewhere in France, orders went out to destroy all remaining Protestant churches and proscribe worship. At the same time that adult laymen were prohibited from emigrating, pastors were given two weeks to leave the country.

Then the dike broke. Perhaps 300,000 Huguenots took flight. Families left by sea and through mountain passes, forests, and fields, heading for places where they could worship in peace. The Dutch Netherlands, England, and Brandenburg took most of the refugees; some did not stop until they reached the shores of North America or South Africa. A disproportionate number of those who left were small merchants and industrialists, sailors, teachers, and craftspersons. They brought the linen industry to England and northern Ireland and helped develop Holland's eighteenth-century publishing industry. Back in France, Louis basked in the light of self-delusion. He struck six medals celebrating the extirpation of heresy, and public reception of the Revocation of the Edict of Nantes was very warm. Poets and painters immortalized the deed.

However, the Revocation of the Edict of Nantes proved to be the most glaring domestic error of Louis's reign. Historians still debate the economic effects of the Huguenot flight on France. Very likely the drop in French agricultural and industrial activity between 1685 and 1715 stemmed more from wartime dislocations and overregulation than from the loss of enterprising subjects. It was in spiritual terms that France suffered its most stunning blow. Europe was weary of religious strife and in the Revocation saw a reversion to the primitive intolerance of the sixteenth century. Pope Innocent himself doubted its wisdom. In England, the Netherlands, and the Protestant states of Germany, the influx of refugees inspired hatred toward Louis and France. In France, Protestantism went underground, and in the mountainous Cévennes region of the south a guerrilla war exploded in 1702, taking two royal armies three years to suppress. In 1715, at the very moment Louis lay on his deathbed, the pastor Antoine Court was presiding over a secret Calvinist synod of ministers in an abandoned rock quarry near the city of Nîmes, the first such meeting since 1685.

The Classical Style

Practically speaking, Louis built his absolutism on the foundations of a loyal bureaucracy, compliant officer corps, and a magnificent court of nobles performing household functions for him. In theory, sometimes the bases were allegorical—the sun surrounded by revolving, dependent satellites; on other occasions they were mythological—the king as Ares, Apollo, or Zeus; most often they were religious. From Louis's childhood the idea had been implanted that the king was the viceroy of God. As chief theoretician of Louis's absolutism, Bishop Jacques-Bénigne Bossuet (1627–1704) specialized in justifying the reign according to divine premise. Louis was priest-king, the anointed of God, successor to Solomon and David. Bossuet wrote of royal power, "It holds the entire kingdom in position just as God holds the whole world."

A passion for setting things in order, the so-called classical ideal, complemented Bossuet's divine-right theorizing. The idea that monarchical power best serves the well-ordered state is as old as the Egyptians, and Colbert subsidized culture to stress the point. Nearly all forms of artistic, literary, and scientific expression depended upon patronage, and the regime made certain that the king's patronage overwhelmed all other varieties. The state founded academies of inscriptions and belles lettres, painting and sculpture, science, architecture, music, and dance. It nationalized the Académie Française, granting its forty members pensions and comfortable quarters at the Louvre palace in Paris. One consequence of this control over culture might be expected: a nauseating monotony of drivel spewed forth from the pen and brush of talentless hacks who knew how to fawn and scrape according to classical rules. Nevertheless, a handful of poets and playwrights also managed to compress a universe of passion, emotion, and human frailty into a framework of disciplined language, strictly defined form, and censored taste.

The classical style was the court style, and the court was Louis's personal work of art. Even before the death of Mazarin, the young king dreamed of settling down in a sumptuous residence of his own. He hated Paris, with its memories of the Fronde, and shortly after his accession decided to convert a modest hunting lodge in a village 15 miles southwest of the capital into a single overwhelming building that would serve both as a seat of government and his home. Versailles would not be just another palace. It was meant to epitomize Louis's domination over nature itself. Imitated by many other princes in Europe, as a colossus of marble and stone it never could be duplicated. The planning got underway in 1668, but it was not until 1682 that the king and court could move in. Louis himself prepared the visitors' guide, and throughout the rest of the reign the work went on. The infant mirror industry, Gobelins tapestry works, and academies of painting and sculpture labored for Versailles without rest. Though Louis himself tired of the palace, Europe's image of him was inseparable from Versailles.

Within the palace walls the king was a demigod. Drawn from the security of their provincial redoubts, the great aristocrats of France were tamed, kept at court, and made financially dependent upon Louis. They became an army of retainers jostling for the privilege to attend the royal awakening each morning or the royal retirement each night, to escort Louis on his strolls, or to be asked to accompany him for a weekend at his more intimate residence at Marly. Ministers, secretaries, and their staffs worked in the government wing of the great palace; the most privileged nobility caroused in the residential wing, enduring an unending round of intrigue, parties, and gambling sessions. The discomforts at Versailles were legion. One froze in the winter and roasted in the summer. In the palace corridors residents mingled with lackeys, peddlers, and prostitutes. Men and women set up camp in antechambers and hallways. A daily coarseness, even criminality, lay behind the superficial pomp and dignity. This was the logical consequence of a situation where several thousand idle individuals milled about, their chief activity to undercut one another and obtain a pension or favor from the king, upon whom all were dependent.

The atmosphere at court evolved with Louis's personality. Prior to the move to Versailles, the court's spirit was licentious and carefree. In the first twenty years of his reign Louis had many loves who effaced his shy, devout Spanish consort. Louis was a patriarch, running the lives of his family, arranging and prohibiting affairs and marriages, and legitimizing his bastards. He turned the latter over to the care of a woman whose moral influence redirected the spirit of both king and court. This was Françoise d'Aubigné (1635–1719), widow of the poet Paul Scarron. In 1673 she was admitted to court and obtained 200,000 livres to purchase an estate. Ingratiating herself with the king, as Madame de Maintenon she became his last mistress. Shortly after the death of Queen María Teresa in 1683, she secretly married Louis.

Under the influence of Madame de Maintenon, the last twenty-five years of Louis's reign exuded an exceptionally rigid, formal religiosity. Personal misfortune—a dozen close family deaths, including those of four heirs to the throne—merged with military disaster to give Versailles its lugubrious tone. Moreover, the court culture no longer set the pattern for the rest of the country, and the criticism of anonymous pens began to rival the empty praise of court hacks. A few challenges penetrated even Louis's gilded cage. In 1693 the abbé François de Fénelon, (1651–1715), later archbishop of Cambrai and member of the Académie Française, wrote a devastating (and anonymous) "Letter to Louis XIV" in which he called France "one great hospital, desolate, and uncared for." Fénelon laid the blame squarely at the royal doorstep.

Fénelon was no isolated malcontent but rather tutor to the king's own grandson, the duke of Burgundy. In 1711, when his pupil was heir to the throne, Fénelon composed the duke's political program, which advocated voluntary taxation voted by provincial Estates, a sum that obviously would render foreign wars impossible to fight; a triennial Estates-General of bishops, nobles, and urban patricians who would participate actively in formulating government policies; and an end to state regulation of commerce and industry. Fénelon wished to reverse the trend of bureaucratic centralization. His economic liberalism looked to the future; his feudal politics, to an idealized past. The untimely death of the duke of Burgundy in 1712 prevented the implementation of Fénelon's program; but along with the antimercantilist fiscal schemes of Boisguilbert and Vauban, it offered institutional alternatives to what Louis and his secretaries had given France over the past half century. Far more worrisome for the government was the resurgence of civil violence. In 1703 and 1707 there were serious provincial revolts.

In the final years of the reign internal discontent and a desperate shortage of revenue forced the government to revise certain of the political and economic principles on which its rule had rested. Old corporate groups like the Parlement of Paris joined the chorus of critics, and even at Versailles the dukes and peers of the realm looked forward to the passing of the old

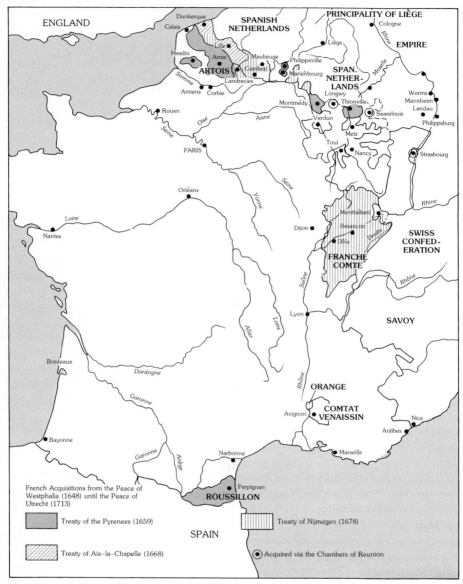

Map 3.1—French Acquisitions, 1648–1713

king. The system created by Louis XIV as the only alternative to Fronde–like chaos was loosening its hold over a society weary of military defeat, religious wrangling, and state bankruptcy. When the king died in apparent remorse on September 1, 1715, it remained an open question whether his successors possessed sufficient initiative and vision to coordinate the activities of the government with the aspirations of its subjects.

THE FOREIGN POLICIES OF LOUIS XIV

Certainly the malaise in France in 1715 was a direct consequence of the human and financial costs of half a century's ambitious foreign policy. To Louis XIV it was a matter of faith that a great king should possess a grand plan for Europe. Louis's plan was a collection of client states tied to France through blood and marriage. This was the logical consequence of a seventeenth-century view that relations among states were legitimate extensions of personal relations among princes. Friendships and animosities determined peace and war. Louis was preoccupied with his international reputation and therefore meddled in the affairs of other states as though they were affairs of his own family—and they often were. Louis, his first wife, and his inveterate enemy, William III of the Netherlands and England, shared a common grandfather, France's Henry IV (1589–1610). The wife of the Hapsburg emperor Leopold I was the stepsister of Louis's queen; the emperor himself was a close relative. To Louis wars were matters of family pride. Because dynastic honor meant so much to him, ruling houses that disagreed with the French interpretation of honor were subjected to abuse and aggression. The last twenty-five years of Louis's reign were dominated by open warfare or alliances that led to warfare. Eventually the mundane idea of a balance of power in international affairs challenged and overwhelmed the French king's grandiose scheme of dependencies and satellites. Although the balance-of-power concept had failed to keep the peace in the ancient Greek world or in Renaissance Italy, after 1715 it seemed the only viable alternative to the dynastic imperialism of a single state; for the next two hundred years its preservation would become the cornerstone of European diplomacy.

Louis XIV, Spain, and the Dutch

The eighteenth-century idea of a balance of power emerged in the following way. In 1648 the Peace of Westphalia had cemented the religious and political fragmentation of central Europe. The Holy Roman Empire no longer functioned as a single political unit. Its German princes were declared sovereign in rights and powers, with standing armies and independent political institutions. The fragmentation of the Empire meant that France was relieved of the pressure of Hapsburg encirclement from bases in Germany, Spain, and the Spanish Netherlands. On the contrary, as "guarantor of the peace of the Empire" and the dominating force over the Rhineland's principalities, France could easily intervene in German affairs if it considered the Westphalia settlement endangered.

      In 1648 Mazarin's emissaries won recognition of French sovereignty over three important bishopric fortresses jutting into the Empire—Metz, Toul, and Verdun—as well as occupation rights over parts of Alsace, thus interrupting Spanish access to the Southern Netherlands from Italy. Desiring additional footholds along the Pyrenees and Belgian frontiers, Mazarin continued the war with Spain. Preoccupied with the Fronde, France had to fight defensively. Once the civil war ended, however, the tide reversed and Mazarin's military alliance with Cromwell in 1657 forced Spain to sue for peace. At the Peace of the Pyrenees (1659), France obtained Roussillon in the south, Artois in the north, and a cluster of Flemish fortresses leading into the Spanish Netherlands. England obtained Dunkirk, which was sold to France in 1662. These provinces and fortified places represented Louis XIV's first substantial territorial acquisitions at Spanish expense. His marriage to María Teresa, eldest child of a weakened Spain's King Philip IV (1621–1665), opened the door to more.

When María Teresa accompanied her debonair groom to France, she gave up all claims to her father's throne. However, Louis wanted to keep the Spanish succession question open, and the inability of the Spanish government to pay for María Teresa's exorbitant dowry provided Louis with an appropriate personal excuse for maintaining pressure. In 1661 Philip's second wife gave him a son and heir; four years later the Spanish king died. The child Carlos II (1665–1700) was a miserable, sickly little monarch, but his tenuous hold on life temporarily dashed Louis's grandiose plans of acquiring Spain and its empire. Undaunted, the French king worked on a more limited scheme. His lawyers cooked up a claim for María Teresa to the Spanish Netherlands and in 1667 Louis sent his troops across the defenseless northern frontier. The French army advanced unopposed. Louis occupied a dozen fortresses and prepared to take the entire country.

Facing this threat, in the Dutch Netherlands a worried Jan de Witt quickly made peace with England and negotiated a defensive alliance with it and Sweden. For the moment Louis halted his aggression. He turned his troops away from the Dutch frontier and opened peace negotiations with Spain. The Treaty of Aix-la-Chapelle (May 1668) ended the so-called War of Devolution, awarding Louis not a contiguous slice of the Spanish Netherlands but rather a dozen unconnected towns and dependencies—chiefly Lille, Cambrai, and Tournai—stepping-stones for any subsequent movement northward. Vauban began fortifying the advanced posts. The war against Spain confirmed the overwhelming superiority of Louis's new 150,000-man army when matched against any one of France's neighbors.

Just prior to the Treaty of Aix-la-Chapelle, Louis's preoccupation with the future of the entire Spanish empire had him propose a partition scheme to his chief potential rival, the Austrian Hapsburg Emperor Leopold I (1658–1705). Like Louis, Leopold was married to a daughter of Philip IV. Though much younger than María Teresa, Leopold's wife (and niece) had not renounced her Spanish claims. In the event of Carlos II's death, the Austrians suspected that they would have to fight France over Spain. With the Turks menacing their southeastern frontier, however, they were in no position to engage in a two-front war. Unsure of what the English and Dutch would do, for his part Louis feared the outbreak of an all-European conflict. Therefore, the French king's secretary of state for foreign affairs, Hugues de Lionne, offered the Austrians a secret deal should the sickly Carlos II die without heirs. France would guarantee Leopold the Spanish throne, Spain's American colonies, plus the duchy of Milan and ports in Italy. For his support Louis would get Spanish Navarre, the Southern Netherlands, Franche-Comté on France's eastern frontier, Naples, Sicily, and the Philippines. The secret treaty was signed in January 1668, and France granted generous peace terms to Spain the following May.

Though a near imbecile and plagued with diseases resulting from generations of Hapsburg inbreeding, Carlos II refused to die. Louis grew impatient. The French king focused his irritation on the Dutch, in his eyes a collection of heretic "cheese and herring merchants" who were foiling his plans for dynastic conquest in the Southern Netherlands. Just as Louis despised Dutch politics and religion, Colbert envied their commerce, which he wished to control. Therefore king and minister agreed on a new adventure, the Dutch War, and Le Tellier mobilized the army. French diplomacy bought off the erstwhile allies of the Dutch, first England with the Secret Treaty of Dover and then Sweden with subsidies and pensions. Louis occupied the duchy of Lorraine and bribed or intimidated the major German princes, including the Austrian Hapsburgs. At length, in the spring of 1672 England and France declared war on the Dutch Netherlands, and Louis himself rode at the head of 100,000 troops.

The Dutch were thoroughly unprepared to defend their country. By the end of June the French army occupied two provinces, and their German allies controlled three others. The Dutch were forced to open the Minden dikes, thus flooding the plain south of the Zuiderzee. The land reclamation work of three generations was ruined, but Amsterdam was saved and the French advance halted. Louis arrogantly spurned the States-General's offer of peace terms and demanded everything between the Rhine and Meuse rivers. His aim was nothing less than the destruction of the Dutch Republic. At this juncture a wave of popular indignation swept through the Northern Netherlands, finishing off the De Witts; William III was invested in the offices previously denied him. In tenacity and diplomatic skill this untested young prince was to prove more than a match for the Sun King. He reorganized Dutch military defenses. Then, skillfully manipulating European fears of French ambitions, he revitalized Dutch diplomacy. Spain and Austria were detached from the French alliance and in 1673 joined William in his struggle against Louis XIV. Many of the French king's German satellites dropped out. In 1674 Parliament forced England's Charles II to conclude peace with the Dutch. As the Austrians attacked from the east and the Spaniards hit from the south, Louis's occupying army in the Dutch Netherlands was dangerously exposed. In order to protect France's borders, he was forced to abandon his territorial gains.

Therefore the short, conclusive war Louis had envisioned dragged on until 1678, costing France a fortune and discouraging Colbert. Because Louis's enemies were even more war weary than France, at the Peace of Nijmegen signed in 1678–1679 the French king secured very favorable terms. He obtained Franche-Comté and exchanged territories on France's northwestern frontier, which defined the border more advantageously for him. Occupied Lorraine remained in his hands. Despite the French gains the Dutch breathed more easily. Their country was saved and France agreed to reduce tariffs directed against their commerce. Above all, the stadholder gained immense prestige throughout Europe. William III had successfully challenged the myth of French invincibility and forged a working coalition against French aggression. For his part, because he had faced up to William's coalition, Louis XIV considered the Peace of Nijmegen a triumph. Perhaps it was. Yet Louis learned that victory by military parade was a thing of the past. To obtain his objectives he would have to resort to diplomatic intimidation or bloody warfare.

Intimidation, the Spanish Succession, and the Peace of Utrecht

During the next nine years Louis tried intimidation. His northern frontier fixed and his splendor confirmed, the French king kept his army, now 200,000 strong, on a war footing and directed his ambitions toward specific objectives in the east. Between France and the Rhine River lay a patchwork of weak principalities, towns, and villages inside the powerless Holy Roman Empire. During the latter stages of the Dutch War this territory had served as a staging ground for allied attacks on France. Therefore during the 1680s French policy was to extend a line of impregnable fortresses along the Rhine's west bank, thereby blocking any potential invasion route. Louis's means of acquiring the necessary territory were crude indeed: annexation of any land possessing the vaguest dynastic or historical link to France or to France's recently acquired possessions. The king established the so-called Chambers of Reunion to decide on the legality of his claims, and somehow the French magistrates selected for the Chambers always ruled in his favor. Then, before the inhabitants of the contested territory could lodge a protest, French troops would move in. The high point of these offensives was the seizure of the free city of Strasbourg, taken in 1681 without even a juridical protest. All of Alsace became French. So did most of Spanish Luxembourg and some of the Saar valley. Brute occupation resolved all ambiguities over rival claims. Louis moved into Italy and threatened the Spanish duchy of Milan.

The Chambers of Reunion extended France's eastern frontier, and Louis reached the height of his power. Although Spain tried to strike back, a short and disastrous campaign in 1683–1684 resulted in a truce whereby both the Spanish and Austrian Hapsburgs were forced to recognize Louis's most recent territorial gains, including Strasbourg. William III found himself diplomatically isolated. In 1685 the Catholic James II became king of England, and Leopold I had his hands full with the Turks. Amsterdam's merchants counseled appeasement of the French. Still, the tide was starting to turn. When Louis XIV revoked the Edict of Nantes in October 1685, Protestant Brandenburg and Sweden signed defensive treaties with the Dutch. Fears of further French aggression in the Rhineland persuaded principalities in southern and southwestern Germany to join the Austrian Hapsburgs, Spain, and Sweden in the defensive League of Augsburg (1686); Leopold's victories over the Turks in 1687 brought other wavering German states into line. French intimidation no longer was bearing fruit. When a disputed election of the new ruler of strategically located Cologne and Liège resulted in the replacement of a French puppet with the Austrian candidate, French troops took Cologne and invaded the Palatinate across the Rhine (September 1688). Louis and Louvois anticipated a campaign of a few months. What they got was the Nine Years' War (1689–1697).

Events rapidly ensured a protracted struggle. Two months after Louis's invasion of the Palatinate, William III sailed his fleet to England and James II abandoned the English throne. Louis expected a new English civil war, but in February 1689 William and Mary peacefully acceded to the throne. In May the Dutch and Leopold signed the so-called Grand Alliance against France. A few months later England, Spain, and Savoy joined. Virtually all the smaller German states became members. The initial aims of the alliance were twofold: to return France to its pre-1659 frontiers and to preserve the English throne for William III. Except for a loose arrangement with the Turks, Louis fought alone. Few realized that western Europe was entering a prolonged period of warfare. With the exception of a single, brief interlude (1697–1702), the struggle of attrition would take twenty-five years. Aims would shift and the stakes would grow higher. In 1702 they included the fate of Spain; seven years later Louis's throne itself was in jeopardy. Two successive allied coalitions (1689–1697, 1702–1713) tested France to the breaking point, and the country wound up fighting for its life. The aging grand monarch endured it all stoically. He felt the shortage of men and money. For the first time he faced military leadership superior to that of his own marshals. The old, quick triumphs gave way to wearisome sieges, scorched-earth tactics, and slow occupations.

In the Nine Years' War, Louis failed to restore James II to the English throne. The fighting mostly occurred along France's frontiers and was largely siege warfare against well-constructed fortresses. There were skirmishes between English and French settlers in North America, as well as in the Caribbean and along the coasts of India. Commanding his forces from Versailles, Louis was very cautious about sending his 300,000-man army into pitched battle. The allies felt likewise, and by 1697 all parties except Leopold I were looking for a way out. A peace conference opened at William III's palace at Ryswick near The Hague, and by terms of the treaty signed there Louis had to concede forward posts in Italy and some German territories which the Chambers of Reunion had granted him. He also recognized William III as king of England. Since this was the first time in Louis's reign that France had ceded land, the peace was not popular at Louis's court. What assured its impermanence, however, was the unsolved Spanish succession issue. By 1697 King Carlos II of Spain was a living corpse. It took a supreme effort for him to move, chew, or mutter. He conserved what energy he possessed for daily meetings with soothsayers and priests. All believed that the Spanish throne would become vacant soon. Then what would happen? Leopold I of Austria already had claimed it for himself and for his second son Charles. Meanwhile Louis XIV eyed it for his grandson, Prince Philip of Anjou.

For three years after the Treaty of Ryswick, diplomats tried to ward off the crisis posed by the ever-imminent death of Carlos II. Various schemes emerged to partition the Spanish empire, and at first Louis behaved cooperatively. The chief opposition to partition came from two camps: that of Leopold I, who considered his son Charles the legal and rightful heir to all of Spain's territories, and that of the Spanish court in Madrid, where there was deep resentment over the distribution by others of Spain's lands and people. Louis XIV resigned himself to the prospect of an Austrian on the Spanish throne, provided that the two parts of the Hapsburg inheritance should never fall to the same individual, and that an adequate share of Spain's possessions should compensate a Bourbon prince. William III leaned toward the French compromise rather than the Austrian position.

Upon the death of Carlos in November 1700, the crisis broke. A month earlier the Spanish king had secretly remade his will, and his court approved it as policy. All of Europe knew that the Spanish position was to keep its empire intact. The shock was Carlos's designation of his successor. It was not Archduke Charles of Hapsburg but rather Philip of Anjou, Louis XIV's younger grandson. Resentful that Spain had become a satellite of Austrian politics, a patriotic faction was the last to win the ear and guide the hand of the moribund Carlos. The designation of Philip stipulated that the prince must renounce his place in the line of succession to the French throne.

When on November 9, 1700, news of Carlos II's will reached Versailles, Louis, his ministers, and family took their time weighing options. The English and Dutch had always supported partition. Would they risk war if France accepted Carlos's testament? Leopold surely would. However, since Carlos II's will had named Archduke Charles as heir to Spain in the event of rejection by Philip of Anjou, Louis really had little leeway. Still, the king spent a week listening to arguments and alternatives. At last, on November 16 he called for silence. He had made his decision. He ordered the doors flung open to the palace reception hall and introduced his grandson to the court and ambassadorial corps as Spain's next king. To quell the fears of the English and Dutch, Louis renounced any intention of meddling in Spanish affairs. Anjou was crowned Philip V. Governments in England and the Netherlands opposed war. The emperor was isolated. It appeared just possible that a feared European conflict over the Spanish succession might be averted.

That it was not must be Louis's responsibility. The calm with which England and the Dutch Netherlands had accepted the will of Carlos II deceived him into believing that once more he might dictate affairs to Europe. He invalidated Philip V's renunciation of his French inheritance. Despite earlier assurances to the contrary, Louis took over the government of the Spanish Netherlands. He had Philip V award France important trading privileges in the Spanish New World, including the monopoly over African slave imports. Overnight, Dutch slave merchants and English traders who had controlled the contraband to South America turned from peace to war. William III in England and Anthony Heinsius in Holland did not need much prodding, for they feared it was the same old Louis. In September 1701 the Maritime Powers renewed the Grand Alliance with Leopold I and proposed a partition of Spain. Philip V might keep the heartland and its overseas colonies; the Spanish and French thrones must be separate; Leopold could have Spanish Italy and the Spanish Netherlands. However, Louis rejected all attempts at negotiation. Instead, he called William a usurper and recognized the son of the late James II as England's rightful king. No act could have better solidified English opinion against France. The accidental death of William in March 1702 made no difference. On May 15, England, the Dutch Netherlands, Austria, Denmark, Brandenburg, and most of the principalities in the Holy Roman Empire declared war on France and Spain.

The War of the Spanish Succession lasted nearly eleven years and so exhausted Europe that no major conflict succeeded it for an entire generation. Battles raged from the Danube to Portugal, in the Caribbean, and on the North American mainland. The victories of the allies at Blenheim-Hochstadt in Bavaria (1704) and Ramillies in the Spanish Netherlands (1706) showed that Louis could find no commanders comparable to the emperor's Prince Eugene and England's duke of Marlborough. Unlike the Nine Years' War, the War of the Spanish Succession was a struggle of movement and infantry firepower. The French were thrown out of the Spanish Netherlands and forced to defend their own fortresses. By 1709 it was clear that the war was being fought not merely over Spain but over the future of western Europe. A catastrophic famine that winter was accompanied by the threat of an allied occupation of France. Louis asked his adversaries for terms, but half a century of dynastic arrogance now produced its backlash. The allies ordered him to recognize the archduke Charles as Spain's king, send a French army to Madrid to depose Philip V, and hand some French towns over to the allies to assure his word. Louis remained too much the dynastic patriarch to turn on his own grandson, and he perceived the award of French territory as the first stage in the dismemberment of his own country. For the first time in his life, he appealed to his subjects. In a circular letter to be read from all pulpits, he explained his course of action. Writing that "justice and French honor" compelled him to continue fighting, he asked for prayers and men.

From 1710 to 1713 matters improved for Louis. The French rallied round their king, and it became the allies' turn to feel war weary. A platform of peace brought the Tories to power in England. Then there were dramatic shifts in Austria. Leopold I had died in 1705; his successor Joseph I, six years later. The archduke Charles became Hapsburg emperor, and neither the Dutch nor English wished to see him add the Spanish crown to his laurels. This would upset the balance-of-power principle as grievously as would a single Bourbon on the thrones of Spain and France. In 1712 England withdrew from the war. Prince Eugene's effort to crush the French in one final battle, at Denain, fell short. The time was ripe for Louis to bargain for more honorable peace terms than those of 1709.

The Treaties of Utrecht and Rastatt (1713–1714) confirmed William III's policy that no single power should be strong enough to exercise hegemony over the continent, and international recognition of the balance of power made peace more durable than had been the case back in 1648. France was weakened but not humiliated. England and Austria were strengthened but not overwhelmingly. Exhausted from having financed the coalition, the Dutch welcomed the lightened responsibilities of a second-class power. To underscore the spirit of balance and compromise, the European parts of the Spanish empire were partitioned among the victors. Philip V kept Spain and its overseas possessions but renounced his claims to any French inheritance. Sicily went to the duke of Savoy, and the Austrian archduke (now Emperor Charles VI) obtained the Spanish Netherlands, Sardinia, Naples, and Milan. Spain ceded Gibraltar and Minorca to England. In 1720 the Hapsburgs and Savoy exchanged Sardinia for Sicily. France gave some advanced posts in the Southern Netherlands to the Austrians and permitted Dutch garrisons to reoccupy the "barrier forts" from which they had been expelled in 1702. In North America, the French abandoned Hudson's Bay, Acadia, and Newfoundland (though retaining some fishing rights) to the English, and in the Caribbean France yielded St. Kitts. Louis XIV kept the vast bulk of what had been recognized as his at the Treaty of Ryswick back in 1697, including most of his acquisitions in Flanders, Alsace, and Franche-Comté. The English gained the best commercial advantages. They replaced France as Spain's most-favored trading partner and gained special privileges in Cádiz, now the major Spanish port for American goods. They won a thirty-year right to send an annual 500-ton slave ship to the Spanish New World.

The Grand Alliance had served its purpose. Its membership differed in religion, domestic social practices, and political ideologies. The partnership had creaked and sputtered. In 1713, when England and the Dutch Netherlands left Charles VI alone to fight Louis, it fell apart. In the end, however, the balance of nations became a deeply entrenched feature of European diplomacy. Trade-offs and partitions became the accepted means of resolving disputes; succession questions were recognized as matters of international concern. Until the 1790s no European power again tried to dominate Europe to the extent the Hapsburgs and Bourbons had done in the century preceding the Utrecht settlement.

DECLINE AND RECOVERY IN SPAIN AND PORTUGAL

The Last Hapsburgs of Spain

Virtually no major European state was spared crisis in the mid-seventeenth century, but some emerged better equipped than others to cope with the challenges of the future. As a political experiment, Cromwellian England proved a failure. However, the Navigation Acts, accompanied by the destruction of guild and corporate interests, opened the gates to economic expansion at home and abroad. In the Northern Netherlands the Regime of True Liberty coincided with a blossoming of Dutch art and thought, and the peace cultivated by the regents of Holland permitted an accumulation of capital resources that financed the great struggle of 1689 to 1713. The chaos of the Fronde cleared the decks for Louis XIV and his intendants and secretaries, leading to the construction of the classic absolutist regime. Compared to these experiences, the recovery of Spain was far more modest.

In 1648 Spain certainly had its share of woes. Both its Dutch and Portuguese possessions were lost. A revolt in Catalonia was seven years old. The Italian dependencies of Sicily and Naples were scenes of uprisings among the urban and rural poor, and a plot had been uncovered to foment rebellion in provincial Aragon. Spain still was at war with France, and as long as this struggle dragged on its retention of the Southern Netherlands was by no means assured. In 1654 Cromwell's England attacked too, blockading much of the Iberian peninsula, seizing Spain's silver transports from America, and eventually allying with France. Without allies, Spain put up a valiant fight; however, its army was unpaid, and after forty years of war the country was exhausted. In May 1659 King Philip IV reluctantly went to the bargaining table and signed the humiliating Peace of the Pyrenees with France.

Spain lost its province of Artois to France, as well as additional patches of territory in the Southern Netherlands and Catalonia. Moreover, Philip IV's daughter María Teresa was betrothed to Louis XIV, thereby ensuring French interference in Spanish dynastic politics. The war with France over, Philip still fought to win back Portugal; but to no avail. When the king died in 1665, he left an empty treasury. During his reign the loss of the Dutch Netherlands and Portugal was confirmed, and other territories were slipping away. On the other hand, the south-Italian revolts were suppressed and most of Catalonia begrudgingly returned to the fold. At least Spain was not going to explode from within. Still, the danger was far from over. Although Philip IV had at least thirty bastards, at the king's death his only legitimate heir was Carlos II, a four-year-old child in terrible mental and physical health. This pitiful consequence of Hapsburg inbreeding was all that stood in the way of a possible dismemberment of the entire Spanish empire. Scheming at partition and succession, between the accession of Carlos II and the Peace of Utrecht in 1713, the great powers of Europe were to remind Spaniards of the humiliating decline of their country. Yet it also was during this period of economic difficulty and international impotence that Spain faintly began to sense recovery.

Like France, in theory Spain was an absolutist state. The system depended upon a bureaucratic mechanism radiating from the king in Madrid. However, Spain differed from France in a fundamental way. Its constituent parts were autonomous. Although sovereign in the various regions of Spain, the king had to govern according to the separate laws and traditions of each major section of the country. In practice, again like France, effective government depended upon the political interplay between royal commissioners and regional aristocracies, Catholic Church leaders, urban oligarchs, and tax farmers. However, except for the central region of Castile, local officials in Spain had much greater governing authority than was the case in France. The northern province of Navarre still called itself a "kingdom," with its own laws, coinage, and administration. The same was true of the northeastern province of Aragon. The Basque provinces enjoyed the status of independent republics, and the Spanish king there was viewed as nothing more than a feudal lord. Before being officially recognized as king a new sovereign was supposed to visit personally the three constituent parts of eastern Spain—Catalonia, Valencia, and Aragon —and swear fidelity to their Estates while upholding their privileges. By way of contrast, in the central core of Spain, the provinces of Old and New Castile, a strong king was an imposing force. Castile possessed the largest population, heaviest tax burden, and administrative responsibility over a world empire. Still, even in Castile the monarchy had to respect aristocratic interests, because it was only through the cooperation of local elites that effective government was possible.

Nevertheless, the king was the hub of government, and Spanish history did not lack for energetic, politically active kings. Unfortunately, Carlos II was condemned by Philip IV's incestuous marriage with his fourteen-year-old niece to a life of physical misery and mental incompetence. Called "the Bewitched" by his subjects, at four Carlos was unable to walk, at nine he remained illiterate, at fourteen he dribbled constantly, and at twenty-five he could not stand upright. He probably was sexually impotent. He neither traveled nor attended government meetings, and royal documents customarily bore facsimiles of his signature. In face of such royal inaction the burden of directing the country and empire fell to rival factions at court, and a privileged minority of great nobles and churchmen occupied the top rungs of administration. There was little distinction between the king's household and the apex of his government. Possessing inherited titles, rents, and pensions, the grandees closed off advancement by others. Barely a chance existed for a Le Tellier or Colbert to rise through sheer competence from obscure origins to high position. The middle and lesser levels of the Spanish bureaucracy were occupied by the *letrados,* individuals with some canonical or legal training who owned their offices and, as notaries, lawyers, and judges, created their own small spheres of influence. The *letrado* class reinforced bureaucratic parasitism.

The central government was composed of councils with both regional competence (councils for Castile, Aragon, Italy, the Southern Netherlands, lost Portugal, and the Indies) and functional responsibility (councils for war, finance, and the Inquisition). Councillors jealously guarded their posts as property and considered colleagues to be rivals. Although a Council of State dealt with international issues, there was no cohesive body of officials akin to the French High Council that could break through the rivalries of jurisdiction and responsibility inherent in semiautonomous government units and make rapid decisions. A minister, three secretaries, and the royal confessor served as a central mail bureau, shuffling dossiers and orders back and forth from council to council, transmitting the advice of councils to the king, expediting letters and edicts. Council advice was often ignored in favor of the programs of individual grandees at court, chief of whom was the *valido,* or royal favorite. For most of Carlos II's reign, *validos* and their factions ruled the country.

What sort of country was it? Recently, the prevailing view of late seventeenth-century Spain as a land sunk in clerical-aristocratic lethargy, economic nonproductivity, and disastrous monetary inflation, has given way to a more nuanced interpretation. Throughout the reign of Carlos II, Castile was indisputably in decline. There the tax demands of the big landowners, Church, and state had crushed the free peasant proprietor; the law further accelerated rural Castile's depopulation by giving preference to livestock raising. Where farming remained, yield ratios for cereals were a pitiful 4:1, tools were primitive, and mule-drawn machinery exhausted the topsoil. Between 1650 and 1700 not a single new work on agricultural improvement was published. Towns failed to take up the slack. Nearly every sector of urban industry remained depressed, with textiles, metallurgy, and shipbuilding showing the worst record. In Seville and Cádiz, Castilian ports which held the monopolies over transatlantic commerce, smuggling, fraud, and tax evasion were perfected. In these towns foreigners replaced Spaniards as the merchant aristocracy.

By way of contrast, northeastern Spain, particularly the province of Catalonia, showed signs of life during the second half of Carlos II's reign. Following the French example, royal commissions for trade offered tax exemptions and monopolies to individuals and groups who invested in manufacturing there. Artisans and merchants from the Southern Netherlands and France were granted royal contracts for glass-and crystal-making, paper manufacture, and textile production in Catalonia. During the 1680s the northeastern region escaped the deflation which plagued Castile. Agricultural prices remained stable and new land was opened to cultivation. Seaborne commerce in textiles, spices, and fish brought activity to the seaport of Barcelona, whose traffic in the 1690s doubled from what it had been at the beginning of the century. Catalonia's energetic shippers sought commercial openings with America.

Neighboring Valencia had a different problem, the need to recover from the loss of a quarter of its population during the expulsion of the Moriscos (Christianized Moslems) back in 1609. New immigrants arrived but found themselves bound to a seigneurial agricultural system to which they paid as much as half of their harvest in taxes, rents, dues, and tithes. Failing to obtain redress in the courts, in 1693 the Valencian peasantry staged a rebellion against its landlords—the most serious one in Spain during Carlos II's reign. The army eventually suppressed it and the government awarded an amnesty. In the long run little changed. However, like Catalonia's more peaceful challenge to fatalistic decline, the Valencian revolt sought better times, relief from the gloom that had plagued Castile and its dependencies for nearly a century.

However, Castile was the heartland. Even in decline it had two-thirds of Spain's population. However, the Hapsburgs' failed mission to reshape Europe during the first half of the seventeenth century left Castile weakened and bitter, and the American colonies no longer felt obliged to mine wealth unceasingly in order to support a decadent, stagnating society across the Atlantic. After 1660 Castile wished to withdraw unto itself, but the Crown's futile efforts to regain Portugal bled the region militarily and fiscally; Castilians no longer could sustain the chronically bankrupt Spanish Crown with taxes of American imports. In fact, profits from them were funneled to foreigners. To obtain loans from English and Dutch creditors, the government promised them anticipated returns taken from the American treasure fleet. Two-thirds of American silver imports were pledged in this way. Militarily, matters were not any better. The futile Portuguese campaigns of 1660 to 1664 exhausted Castile, and the region could not provide the government with adequate revenue for Spain's territorial losses to France in 1667 and 1678. Over the next ten years Castile suffered natural calamities in the extreme: flood, drought, earthquake, epidemic, and pestilence. A quarter million people died prematurely. For those who survived, a brutal cycle of deflation and inflation crippled the economy.

During the 1690s the Spanish monarchy reached the nadir of its fortunes, and the country's entire tax revenue was mortgaged in the form of annuities paid out to lenders. While Dutch and Italian bankers underwrote costs of running the empire, court grandees and (after 1689) Carlos's German queen manipulated Spanish politics. Meanwhile, the Spanish Church—

a massive organization of at least 150,000 clergy, plus retainers—offered the populace the consolation of a hundred feast days per year and ritual burnings of converted Jews served up as scapegoats for national misfortune. Yet even in this dark period there were some glimmers of hope. Weather improved and epidemics abated. If Spaniards continued to be hungry, at least widespread starvation was averted. The government tried economic reform, devaluing the currency, ordering the circulation of gold and silver, and stabilizing prices. It also reduced annuity payments to the most speculative lenders.

Revival and Philip V (1700–1746)

Paradoxically enough, it was the deepening crisis over the succession of Carlos II that presaged national revival. Patriotic Spaniards finally became aware that they were losing control of their country's destiny. It was clear that the ailing Carlos never would father an heir. Both Louis XIV and Leopold I had compelling claims to a vacant Spanish throne. Yet most of Europe shuddered at the thought of such a monumental accretion to either the kingdom of France or the Hapsburg Empire. As a compromise, in 1698 Louis and the Dutch agreed to a scheme whereby the young Joseph Ferdinand, electoral prince of Bavaria, would be declared heir to Spain and its non-European empire, with the remainder being divided between Leopold I's younger son Charles and the French dauphin. The Spanish Council of State rejected the partition out of hand and secretly named the Bavarian prince alone as successor to Carlos II. However, early in 1699 Joseph Ferdinand died and Louis, William III, and the Dutch worked out a second partition, dividing Spain and its empire between Leopold I's second son, the archduke Charles, and the French dauphin. Because he did not like Charles's share, Leopold would have nothing to do with the treaty, and the Spanish government rejected it as well. However, time was running out for Carlos II. Despite the labors of exorcists, the bewitched king slipped toward death. The pope encouraged him to keep Spain intact. On October 3, 1700, the Council of State drew up a new, secret will. It named Philip of Anjou, younger grandson of Louis XIV, as sole heir to the Spanish throne. Less than a month later Carlos was laid to rest.

Though bitterly contested by the Austrian Hapsburgs, the crown of Spain remained on the head of Philip V throughout the war of 1702–1713. In the end, however, Spain's first Bourbon king was unable to prevent the division of the European sections of his empire. The Treaties of Utrecht and Rastatt awarded Gibraltar and Minorca to Great Britain. The Southern Netherlands, Sardinia, Naples, and Milan went as consolation to the Austrian Hapsburgs. The newly established kingdom of Savoy obtained Sicily. Philip V's court was not at all pleased with the Utrecht settlement, and in the first half of the eighteenth century Spain was the most dissatisfied member of the European family. At home, however, early eighteenth-century Spanish governmental institutions gave way just enough to allow the monarchy to convert the notoriously autonomous councils of government into interdependent ministerial departments on the French model. For the most part, the administrative changes were largely on paper, for the grandees and *letrados* still dominated the personnel. But the new structures were put to good use later in the century.

More important was Philip's handling of the problem of provincial autonomy. Northeastern Spain's economic revival, first noticeable around 1690, halted temporarily during the War of the Spanish Succession. Dismayed and hoping for greater freedom, the nobility and municipal oligarchs of Valencia, Aragon, and Catalonia threw in their lot with the Hapsburg archduke Charles, and Philip V considered them in revolt. Valencia and Aragon were subdued in 1707, but Catalonia held out past the Utrecht settlement. In 1714 Barcelona fell to Philip's troops. With the defeat of Catalonia, the institutions of all three northeastern provinces were modified. A captain-general from Madrid assumed wide executive powers, and the region was divided into administrative districts that cut across traditional provincial frontiers. As breeding ground for Catalan patriotism, the University of Barcelona was suppressed and the Estates and autonomous councils of Catalonia dissolved. Administrative use of the Catalan language was prohibited. By 1716 the regional independence of the northeast was foredoomed. The difficulty was that the most economically backward region, Castile, now was imposing French administrative practices on the vital periphery. The Catalans called Madrid their leech. Spain was not yet a nation, but an awkward beginning had been made.

Portugal

On the other hand, a successful revolt against Spain in 1640 and the reconquest of Brazil from the Dutch in 1654 assured Portugal's future and compensated for colonial losses in India, the East Indies, eastern Africa, and along the Persian Gulf. Between 1650 and 1715, Portugal's population hovered at 2 million. Although attempts were made to create glass and textile industries through state grants and foreign experts, Portugal's prosperity derived overwhelmingly from its enormous American colony. Brazil's sugar, produced with the labor of half a million African slaves, brought prosperity to the aristocratic and clerical elites of late seventeenth-century Portugal. Then, in 1692, gold was found in Brazil, stimulating a great rush there and creating unprecedented opulence in the motherland. England, whose ties with Portugal were sealed with commercial privileges and a royal marriage (Charles II and Catherine of Bragança), swept the small overripe kingdom into its economic orbit. In 1703 the Methuen treaty awarded the Portuguese a near duty-free English market for their sweet wines. In turn Portugal accepted British woolens and gave English merchants rights of participation in the Brazilian trade. Great Britain assumed responsibility for defending Portugal, and a landholding alliance among king, nobles, and churchmen ruled the country. The Catholic Church owned two-thirds of the rural property and supported half the population. Compared to Castile, taxes were low. In 1715 Portugal was a stagnant, feeble, and complacent country, stuffed with piety and the wealth of Brazil.

4

CRISIS AND RESOLUTION: THE CENTER AND EAST

THE COMPROMISE OF POWER IN CENTRAL EUROPE

During the second half of the seventeenth century west-European governments worked out arrangements with traditional political and social elites, whereby aristocracies were promised degrees of local control over the countryside in return for recognition of their governments' overarching legal, fiscal, and military authority. Louis XIV best perfected these arrangements with Estates, parlements, landed aristocracies, and great churchmen; governments in Spain, the Dutch Netherlands, and England exercised variations on the theme. Intended to avert the civil strife that had plagued Europe during the 1640s and 1650s, the arrangements generally were successful. Governments solidified their political control, and regional aristocracies enjoyed wealth and prestige through the exploitation of both rural labor and overseas investment.

Between 1648 and 1715 similar compromises of power occurred in central, northern, and eastern Europe. As a consequence, peasantries customarily lost more control over their own lives than they did in the West. During the first half of the seventeenth century landowning nobles in the less commercially developed parts of Europe, sitting in government councils and in provincial or national assemblies, had been the chief obstacles to the emergence of absolutist regimes. These aristocrats cast a wary eye on extensions of political power by elector, king, or emperor. However, they also firmly desired to maintain and extend their control over a servile, legally subjugated labor force needed to plant and harvest grain for an international market. In return for increased fiscal, administrative, and military command over the machinery of state, after 1648 rulers in central and eastern Europe guaranteed their aristocracies vast seigneurial powers over peasant labor. Leashed tightly or loosely by their sovereign as the case might be, landlords ran local affairs. Rural workers fell into neoserfdom, without civil rights, often used and sold like beasts.

Denmark-Norway

Denmark offers the classic example of this compromise of power. In 1648 the Danish-Norwegian monarchy was Europe's oldest and most dominated by an aristocracy. About 150 families owned half the land in Denmark and controlled all local administration, including civil and criminal justice. A Diet of three Estates, dominated by the nobility, chose the king. Only the underpopulated Norwegian part of the kingdom was free of such domination. There a peasant society created its own structures in which rich farmers, not titled aristocrats, controlled poor ones.

In 1648, Frederick III (1648–1670) became king of Denmark-Norway, a weakened state of fewer than a million people whose participation in the Thirty Years' War (1626) and brief struggle with Sweden (1643–1644) had resulted in embarrassing defeats. Between 1655 and 1660, two more lost wars against the Swedes cost Denmark a province in Norway, fertile wheat-growing lands across the Sound, and control over the tolls which merchant ships paid for transport through the narrow waterway into the Baltic Sea. The nobility had fought very poorly in all of Denmark's seventeenth-century wars, yet it also refused to yield on its important tax exemptions. When the national Diet met in Copenhagen in September 1660, the treasury was empty, the nobility continued to insist on its privileges, and the lower Estates were in an ugly mood. Clergy and burghers urged King Frederick to impose a consumer tax on everyone, and royal advisers asked him to declare the monarchy hereditary. When the noble Estate balked, Frederick took a huge gamble. To prevent the aristocratic landowners from going home for assistance, he slammed shut the gates of Copenhagen. Then the king summoned the loyal burgher militia of the capital and declared the Danish crown both hereditary and absolute. Finally he disbanded the Diet.

In the next five years King Frederick successfully consolidated his daring coup d'état. Following a glorious coronation, an absolutist constitution was drawn up. Even for the seventeenth century its award of unlimited legislative, judicial, and administrative authority to the king was remarkable. By its terms, if a sovereign felt obliged to place voluntary restrictions on his own power, his heir had no need to abide by them. The Diet disappeared, the aristocratic Royal Council was reduced to a service household, and a skeletal salaried bureaucracy was established to run the state's fiscal, judicial, and administrative agencies. The king reserved the right to name town officials, and a new royal tax was placed on all towns and all lands.

Aware that they had been outfaced, the landlords swallowed the pill rather than risk revolt. Yet by no means had they lost everything, for Frederick III had no social revolution in mind. In order to win support of elites he sold state-owned lands to old nobles, newly made ones, and absentee townsmen alike. Landowners negotiated tax exemptions for themselves (though not for their peasants), and no effort was made to tamper with their seigneurial rights over the peasantry. In the state land survey of 1682, 97 percent of the rural properties belonged either to the king, nobility, or absentee townsmen. Old nobles merged with ambitious parvenus to form the royal bureaucracy, and their tenants had to pay taxes both to king and seigneur. Encouraging investment on the mercantilist model, the Crown formed privileged East and West India Companies, a slave-trading company, and monopolies for fishing and for commerce with Russia. Frederick III's absolutist formula for Denmark thus awarded dependent elites sufficient local authority, prestige, and profits so that the aristocracy accepted the compromise, and the system continued unchallenged for the next three generations.

The Holy Roman Empire

The political and social example of Denmark was repeated, though less brutally, in many of the principalities of the Holy Roman Empire that tried to rebuild from the wreckage of the Thirty Years' War. The Empire itself persisted as the great fiction of European politics. Although an imperial constitution, Diet, and law courts existed, the Peace of Westphalia had destroyed the Empire as a working confederation of independent central European states. The emperor and his princes distrusted one another, as did the princes and elites of the free towns. Inside Germany, Catholic and Protestant princes, or ecclesiastical and secular ones, were mutually suspicious. It was nearly impossible for the emperor to raise taxes, get laws passed, or raise an army. No imperial foreign policy existed. Genuine sovereignty in Germany resided in the governments of the three hundred-plus states and cities that filled the Empire, and the political trend within these states was toward constructing individual princely absolutisms. The princes preferred to keep the Empire weakened. So did Louis XIV, who consistently interfered in affairs there, buying off princely clients and turning them against the emperor.

In those regions of the Empire which had lost from half to two-thirds of their prewar population, the manpower shortage was critical. Princes needed taxpayers, noble estate owners needed labor, and it was in the interest of both ruler and landlord to keep tax-paying peasants from fleeing to the anonymity of towns. In some parts of Germany, like Westphalia, the prince was benevolent, encouraging the restoration of deserted peasant holdings to peasant proprietors. In most other places, however, ruler and landlord conspired to fix the peasantry to the soil. For example, the Labor Ordinances of the electorate of Saxony (1651, 1661) forced peasants and their children to work noblemen's lands before they could touch their own small plots; the elector of Brandenburg approved when the Estates of his territories of Mecklenburg and Pomerania prohibited peasants from changing their residence without express landlord consent. In return for concessions that ensured their absolutism, princes throughout the Holy Roman Empire guaranteed aristocratic landlords the labor of a servile peasantry, thereby sealing the fate of thousands who might otherwise have taken advantage of society's general impoverishment to bargain for their liberty.

Brandenburg and Its Great Elector

Frederick William, elector of Brandenburg and duke of Prussia (1640–1688), wished to establish strong political authority over the mosaic of rural regions and corporate towns that recognized him as sovereign. Apart from the person of Frederick William, no unifying principle tied his lands together. They were scattered from Cleves on the Rhine River to East Prussia on the Niemen, and were separated from one another by many states and principalities over which Frederick William had no authority whatsoever. In the heartland, the electorate of Brandenburg, territorial Estates and town councils initially withheld from Frederick William the right to grant and spend tax money, make clerical appointments, and recruit for local bureaucracies and defense. Frederick William's authority was stronger in Prussia, where his family, the Hohenzollerns, owned vast properties with direct control over peasants. However, the Thirty Years' War cost dearly, depopulating Brandenburg by as much as 50 percent, and Frederick William sought control over the tax-collecting apparatus of all his territories along with an army devoted to his person.

As a tool and agency of government, a loyal military could be very useful to the elector, for it alone might coerce the Estates into making political and fiscal concessions. In 1650 the elector wished to go to war, but the Estates of Brandenburg refused him subsidies. Wrangling continued until 1653, when a compromise was reached. In return for six years of guaranteed funds, Frederick William recognized blanket tax exemptions for all estate owners in Brandenburg. Only townsmen and peasants were to foot the bill. Furthermore, the elector agreed to acknowledge formally the principle of *Gutsherrschaft*—the landlords' economic jurisdiction over their peasants, which carried with it civil and criminal control—and he recognized serf status for all peasants unable to produce contractual evidence to the contrary. Whenever a Junker, a noble landowner in Brandenburg, dispossessed a peasant, the elector agreed to look the other way. Landlords might demand unlimited services from their peasants, and were permitted, duty-free, to export grain and wool while importing wine, salt, and cloth.

In this way the aristocratic landlords of Brandenburg were assured of being the dominant economic and social element in the country. It may first appear that they got the better part of their bargain with the elector. However, Frederick William won a free hand in building his army, used it wisely against the Swedes in 1658, and maintained most of it in peace as a lever for further subsidies. After 1660 he informed the Estates of Brandenburg and East Prussia that his request for subsidies no longer was negotiable. He hired loyal Junkers as his commissioners and had them ride out into country districts, an armed company behind, to make certain his decrees were obeyed. Eventually, Frederick William transformed the Estates of Brandenburg into regional assemblies beholden to him. East Prussia submitted less willingly, and he had to use military force there to tame the Estates. Although Frederick William had difficulty cowing his more distant domains in western Germany, he set the pattern of social order for his eighteenth-century successors. Each element within society had a distinctive function. The peasantry bore the overwhelming fiscal and labor burden. All townsmen were to pay purchase taxes on the articles they used. Landed aristocrats and a few ennobled commoners worked for the state as fiscal and judicial agents. They led the troops and controlled the peasantry. In each territory a kind of intendant, called the *Statthalter,* served the elector and was assisted by a local elite of councillors.

Up from 2,000 in 1656 to 45,000 in 1678, the army welded together the elector's domains. The War Commissariat, a governmental agency that supervised lodging, supply, and food for the troops, as well as collection and expenditure of taxes, became the regime's most important administrative agency. Early in the eighteenth century, the *Amtskammer,* the treasury accounting for income and expense, merged with the War Commissariat in Berlin, thereby guaranteeing the indissolubility of the military, fiscal, and financial offices of the state. Half of Brandenburg-Prussia's revenue was funneled back into the army. A special tax on every cow, pig, or sheep slaughtered had to be paid to maintain the troops. Moreover, Frederick William imposed a severe regime of military discipline on his beloved army.

The elector wished to professionalize his army, and in time the officer corps became a kind of aristocratic guild with young nobles serving as apprenticed cadets prior to securing their own units. A military-style discipline and devotion to the Hohenzollerns were supposed to set the tone for the civil service. This service was not so incorruptible as nationalist Prussian historians would like us to believe; for even in Brandenburg, public office was a convenient way to build private fortunes. However, Frederick William's budding bureaucracy was the envy of most neighboring states and enabled the elector to be the most efficient absolute ruler of his generation. Commissioners were expected to be dutiful governors, revenue collectors, and judicial and customs officials. With grants of land they controlled the countryside in the elector's name. By and large, Frederick William was popular enough to command their loyalty, if not their affection.

The elector worked hard to rebuild Brandenburg from the damage of the Thirty Years' War. He was sincerely interested in economic improvements and tempted rural immigrants with special tax exemptions. He built the Oder-Elbe canal to divert downriver traffic away from the Swedish port of Stettin and encouraged both tobacco raising and truck gardening. By prohibiting imports of woolens and dressing his army in home-produced dark blue uniforms, he ensured the growth of a blossoming textile industry. State-protected glass, iron, and copper industries emerged. The elector's religious policies marked him as the most tolerant ruler of his age. Principle and social pragmatism guided him. Lutherans and Calvinists comprised the religious majority in his domains, but pockets of Catholics, Mennonites, and Protestant sectarians unwelcome elsewhere found refuge with the elector. He opened Brandenburg to French Huguenots, Austrian Lutherans, Polish Unitarians, and even Jews. A devout Calvinist who had spent his formative years in Holland, Frederick William conceived of a new university with a faculty drawn exclusively from victims of religious or political oppression. He endowed Catholic as well as Protestant churches and schools.

The fundamental political achievement of the Great Elector was to mold the patchwork of regions he had inherited into a collection of provinces overseen by his personal army and bureaucracy. State service would weld together different regional aristocracies in common purpose. In his foreign policy the elector wished to be an influence in the Holy Roman Empire second only to the Hapsburgs, and he wanted to make Brandenburg a Baltic power. However, he commanded an underpopulated and underdeveloped state dependent upon foreign subsidies. Therefore momentary expediency rather than long-range planning dictated his alliances, and Brandenburg remained a bit player in late seventeenth-century power politics. Its role in the alliance against Louis XIV netted it nothing, and its occupation of the Swedish Baltic port of Stettin (1677) only lasted two years. Frederick William's major achievements in foreign affairs were the acquisition of Eastern Pomerania and European recognition of his sovereignty in East Prussia, where he no longer had to play vassal to the king of Poland. However much the Great Elector considered his work incomplete, by the time of his death in 1688 the Estates of his territories were humiliated and the aristocracy had been coopted into creating an absolutist regime on solid military and bureaucratic foundations.

Frederick I, King in Prussia (1688–1713)

The Great Elector's son Frederick III (after 1701, Frederick I in Prussia) reigned between a constructive, diligent father and a brutally strong son. Under him, Brandenburg was added to the list of small German states dazzled by the splendor of a royal title and royal trappings. For recognition of the coveted title of king in his East Prussian domains, Frederick accepted Emperor Leopold I's invitation to join the Grand Alliance against Louis XIV. In 1701, at enormous cost, Frederick dragged his court from Berlin in Brandenburg to the East Prussian capital of Königsberg for a lavish coronation. Returning to Brandenburg, he embellished Berlin with gardens, buildings, and statuary and invited the eminent scientist-philosopher Gottfried Wilhelm Leibniz (1646–1716) to become charter president of the state's new Academy of Sciences. With its unique programs in comparative religion and jurisprudence, secular history, and experimental science, the University of Halle was founded under Frederick's patronage.

In his efforts to create a Prussian Versailles, Frederick was largely frill. In one respect, however, his vanity bore fruit. He was the first Hohenzollern to view his collected domains as an indissoluble entity. Not even the Great Elector, who had tried to divide his lands among the children of his two marriages, possessed this vision. Frederick's first political act, to throw out his father's will, proved to be his most important one. His own son's first act was to get rid of his father's court. By 1713 the state of Brandenburg-Prussia was well established in Europe. It had been true to the alliance against Louis XIV. Fighting from Naples to Ramillies, its military units performed courageously under Marlborough and Prince Eugene. Succeeding his vain and spendthrift father, Frederick William I decided to restore the country to its proper financial moorings.

From Hapsburg Domains to Danubian Monarchy

Although the Holy Roman Empire was impotent, because of its association with the Austrian Hapsburgs it retained a role in European politics. Except for a brief interlude in the eighteenth century, the senior male Hapsburg was regularly elected its emperor. If it could strengthen his own hand as mediator and conciliator in Germany, the Holy Roman Emperor stimulated discord among the princes, particularly the powerful ones. But a more promising method of improving his constitutional position in Germany was to increase his control over the dynastic lands of his own family—kingdoms, duchies, and principalities scattered throughout central and southeastern Europe, and lying both inside and outside the Holy Roman Empire. When confronted with unrest or revolt within their dynastic territories, the Hapsburgs instituted variations on that compromise of power we have previously noted. They purchased loyalty to their dynasty by yielding degrees of autonomy to regional elites. However, because this loyalty failed to translate into support for a unitary political ideal, it remained incomplete and inadequate. Regional Estates, diets, and seigneurial aristocracies were invited to share fiscal, judicial, and administrative power with absentee nobles at court in Vienna who simultaneously ran territorial departments. Meanwhile the emperor and his advisers could only hope to dominate each region singly, while pleading with local aristocracies to pay their share for the maintenance of the whole. With an empire containing widely different ethnic groups and nationalities separated by language and religion, the Hapsburg emperors governed through special constitutional agreements and by manipulating opportunity as best they could.

The heartland of the eighteenth-century Hapsburg domains radiated south, north, and east from the Danube River valley to comprise dozens of regions with different ethnic, linguistic, and religious traditions. Between 1657 and 1711 the Austrian Hapsburg emperors Leopold I and Joseph I accumulated more territory in Europe than any other reigning dynasty, and at the Peace of Utrecht and Rastatt (1713–1714) the addition of most of Spain's Italian territories and the Southern Netherlands further complicated this multinational empire. Although the seventeenth-century Hapsburgs learned that military repression was a far less successful means of averting regional revolt than the cooption of elites, unlike Frederick William of Brandenburg or even Louis XIV of France, they were unable to persuade aristocracies that service to the ruler's person might evolve into service to the Hapsburgs' empire as a whole. Absentee landlords from Bohemia, Moravia, Hungary, Austria, and elsewhere, who were drawn to the Hapsburg court in Vienna to run the bureaus overseeing the regions of the empire, successfully constructed departments independent of one another but closely bound to tax-collecting and judicial authorities at home. The aristocracies of the empire generally were proud of Hapsburg territorial accumulation. However, they had no desire to consolidate or integrate their bureaucratic departments in the name of an imperial common good. In fact, their jurisdictional rivalries actively worked against such an aim.

Far from Vienna, in lands whose social structure rested on rural bases, magnates and gentries remained effective barriers between the government and its subjects. In Austria proper, as well as in Silesia and the Alpine valleys, local nobles and clergy collected rents, tithes, and taxes from tenants. In Bohemia, Moravia, the Balkans, and Hungary, noble landowners held the power of life and death over their serfs. There peasants had to devote three to five days of free labor to lords who administered the state's revenue, exercised imperial and private justice, and monopolized mills, taverns, stores, and seed supplies. In these places the nobility paid no taxes, and made certain that the peasant's contribution never left the region. Meanwhile, puny subsidies from Estates and diets of the empire could not meet the costs of the conquering Hapsburg armies, so the emperor begged from the English and Dutch or borrowed at exorbitant interest rates from his own aristocracy. The Hapsburg Empire was no more than the sum of its parts, and two reconquests—the first of Bohemia and the second of Hungary—provide instructive examples of how the failure of institutional reform dulled the dazzle of outward military success.

Bohemia, Hungary, and the Balkans

In 1648 Bohemia was the largest entity among the Hapsburg possessions. Its unsuccessful attempt to wrench free a generation earlier had turned it into a conquered province, shorn of the political privileges it formerly had enjoyed. The Bohemian crown became hereditary in the house of Hapsburg, Catholicism was declared the only legal Christian religion, the sovereign in Vienna replaced the Bohemian Estates as the source of legislation and appointment, and for legal and administrative purposes the German language was imposed on the primarily Slavic country. Mercenary chiefs, who had served the emperor during the Thirty Years' War, took over the properties of those Czech magnates who had rebelled against him. They were accompanied by German peasants who resettled abandoned manors.

Despite the reduced influence of the older agencies of Czech nationalism, such as the Diets of Bohemia and Moravia, it would be a mistake to say that German immigration permitted the Hapsburgs to absorb these regions into the Austrian empire. Far into the eighteenth century Czech aristocrats still managed to dominate the Bohemian chancellery in Vienna and its regional offices in Prague. They still ran the Bohemian Diet and collected the state's taxes. After 1648 the Hapsburgs sold additional crown lands to Bohemian nobles, who ostentatiously reconverted to a peculiarly Czech form of Catholicism that had thrived prior to the Reformation. Towns declined, as did the lesser gentry; the peasantry remained enserfed; the manor was the basic unit of government. By 1715 a coalition of great Czech nobles, absentee in Vienna or enjoying their vast properties at home, had regained control of the country in the name of the Hapsburgs.

The Hapsburg reconquest of Hungary took a somewhat different form, although the results were familiar. Following the death of Emperor Ferdinand III in 1657, it took Leopold I a year to accumulate all his titles, including the electoral one of Holy Roman Emperor. But the Hapsburg domains had been relatively free of crisis since the end of the Thirty Years' War, and Leopold concentrated on establishing a front line of defense against the Turks who occupied half of his kingdom of Hungary. The great Hungarian magnates and lesser gentry urged Leopold to mount a full-scale offensive to free the country from the Turks. However, his more modest aim was a truce legitimizing the current frontier. An inconclusive battle with the Turks at St. Gotthard, while heralded as a great victory by the Hapsburgs, at least provided the truce sought by Leopold. In 1664 the Treaty of Vasvár acknowledged Ottoman control over their occupied half of Hungary, and the Turks agreed not to encroach further on Hapsburg territory. Hungarian nobles, the Magyars, were infuriated by what they considered to be Leopold's betrayal of their interests.

Relishing "liberties" dating back to the thirteenth century, including the right to resist their Hapsburg sovereign when they considered themselves betrayed, in 1665 malcontent elements of the Hungarian nobility staged an ill-conceived revolt against Leopold. The emperor suppressed it easily, tried its perpetrators in an Austrian court, and executed four of them. The unsuccessful rebellion gave Leopold the opportunity to occupy the non-Turkish part of Hungary with German troops and attempt to teach a lesson to his recalcitrant subjects, who controlled and collected taxes, ran their own armed forces, directed local affairs, and mercilessly exploited their peasants. A military governor took over, and suspected sympathizers in the abortive revolt found their lands confiscated. The Hapsburgs demolished Hungarian institutions and until 1678 ruled through terror.

However, holding Hungary permanently this way was impossible. Between 1678 and 1683 guerrilla warfare erupted, and Leopold opted for a negotiated settlement. He had little choice. The Turks were preparing a new offensive against the Danube basin. In July 1683 they had to be repulsed from Vienna itself. Four years later, the Hapsburgs reached an agreement with the Magyars. Property confiscations would cease, and the Austrians promised to liberate the entire country from the Turks. They guaranteed Magyar landlords the state's backing in the economic and social subjugation of the peasantry. Serfdom was acknowledged officially. In return, the Hungarians had to recognize that their crown was hereditary in the Hapsburg house, and they gave up their long-coveted right to resistance. The Hungarian Diet was restored but made to understand that Hapsburg requests for subsidies were to be taken seriously. German troops would remain in Hungary, and in 1699 the Hapsburgs liberated the southern part of the country from the Turks. It was incorporated into the new constitutional statute.

For certain Magyars, steeped in the folklore of Hungary's medieval independence under aristocratic rule, any compromise with the Hapsburgs was tantamount to defeat. In 1703, led by the magnate Ferenc II Rákóczi (1676–1735), they staged a new rebellion. It began as a patriotic uprising, uniting all social groups and religious faiths against "Germanization." However, Leopold and his successor Joseph I divided and conquered, and the Peace of Szatmár (1711) confirmed the agreement of 1687. This time the Hapsburgs were magnanimous, cajoling and flattering the greatest magnates by offering them administrative posts in the Hungarian chancellery in Vienna. The magnates' preponderant role in the Hungarian Diet was confirmed, while Hapsburg law protected both their seigneurial powers and native offices. The cost to the magnates was cheap—guarantees that they would not resort to arms in future disputes with the Hapsburgs. Meanwhile, in the remote corners of rural Hungary, the gentry grumbled that the natural leadership of the country had sold out to its historic oppressors. From their vantage point there was some truth in the assertion. For the Hapsburgs and the great Hungarian nobility, however, Szatmár proved to be a successful reconciliation. For the next two generations Hungary would be quiet.

Without the revival of Austria's international posture, Emperors Leopold I and Joseph I could not have pacified Hungary. They profited from their leadership role in the Grand Alliance against Louis XIV, but even more remarkable was their liberation of the northern Balkans from the Turks. In 1683 the Turks broke the truce they had signed with Leopold back in 1664, and renewed their drive northward. By July their force of 200,000 soldiers, artisans, merchants, and camp followers reached the gates of Vienna. Leaving the capital in the hands of the town garrison, Leopold called on the Christian princes of Europe to relieve the defenders. The city was about to fall in September, when an army led by Duke Charles of Lorraine and King John Sobieski of Poland swept down from the Kahlenberg heights and routed the Ottomans. The Hapsburgs rallied, offered their compromise to the Hungarians, helped the pope organize a holy league against the Turks, and forced the Peace of Karlowitz (1699) on their foes. Hapsburg control over Transylvania and nearly all of Hungary was assured, and subsequent victories over the Turks in 1717–1718 added the most fertile regions of Serbia, the rest of Hungary, and parts of Wallachia and Moldavia to the spoils gained at Karlowitz. Within a generation the Hapsburgs had replaced the Turks as the predominant Balkan power, and their thoughts of carrying a crusade to Istanbul itself seemed realistic.

ECLIPSIS POLONAIE

A Kingdom of Nobles

During the second half of the seventeenth century the course of Polish history was fraught with crises. Although Polish kings would have welcomed a compromise of power resembling the Hapsburg solution, nothing of the sort ever emerged. The country was effectively an aristocratic republic with an elected king, possessing a constitutional structure as complicated as that of the Dutch Netherlands. Unlike the United Provinces, however, Poland's socioeconomic structures were not commercial but agrarian. A rural aristocracy dominated the country's regions, enserfed its peasantry, and paralyzed central government. Noble estate owners viewed their use of power as a supreme virtue and saw no necessity for compromise, regardless of the king's desires. Without the consent of his aristocracy, the king of Poland had no army, no income, and no bureaucracy.

After Russia, the Commonwealth of Poland-Lithuania was Europe's largest country. In 1648 its population was 10 million, but fewer than half were ethnic Poles. In the north, east, and southeast, respectively, lived large groups of Lithuanians, White Russians, and Ukrainians—self-contained minorities understandably hostile to the emergence of whatever Polish national consciousness a strong ruler might inspire. Throughout Poland ethnic Germans lived in hundreds of their own enclaves. Religious diversity added to ethnic diversity. A half million Jews held tightly to their distinct religion and culture in villages and small towns that dotted the eastern part of the country. The most enterprising of them oversaw the estates of absentee magnates. Poles and Lithuanians usually were Catholic, White Russians were Orthodox or Uniate, and Germans were customarily Lutheran.

Great magnates so dominated their regions that the government of Poland was nearly as decentralized as that of the Holy Roman Empire. Furthermore, all the aristocratic magnates possessed their retinues and private armies. The gentry of their region were their men, not the king's. The great nobles controlled local diets and could form legally recognized confederations to resist the king or one another. The magnates endowed churches, constructed fortresses, and founded towns. Along with the hierarchy of the Catholic Church in Poland, they comprised the upper house of the national Diet. The king was obliged to select his high officials from among them. They supplied him with subsidies and an army, both infinitesimal in size. Representatives of the lesser nobility, the gentry, sat in the lower house of the national Diet. Both houses elected the king and wrung from him a pledge to do nothing that would upset the constitutional status quo. In 1652 the national Diet adopted the *liberum veto,* thus ensuring a power vacuum at the center. Hereafter, not only was unanimity of both houses necessary to pass any major piece of legislation, but a single adverse vote was sufficient to nullify all previous legislation passed at the session and dissolve the Diet. Thus government was effectively paralyzed. Between 1655 and 1717, forty-eight of the fifty national Diets convoked produced no legislation. Foreign powers bribed Diet members and manipulated confederations. No other European state was subjected to more outside interference in its affairs than Poland.

The inability of the Polish king to raise an army forced him to depend upon large bands of seminomadic warriors to defend the southern frontier against the Turks. The Cossacks—horsemen, lumberjacks, herdsmen, hunters, and petty traders—lived, or rather roamed, along the Dnieper, Don, and Volga rivers in Poland and Russia. All who wearied of the constraints of sedentary existence, including runaway serfs, freebooters, and criminals, joined the Cossacks. Technically, they owned no land and paid no dues or taxes. By 1648, however, the westernmost ones showed signs of settling down, and so-called registered Cossacks found winter shelter in Polish towns. As they took up farming on frontier lands, they came into conflict with the great Polish magnates of the Ukraine. The latter, large-scale grain producers for the west-European market, wished to exploit these virgin lands themselves and press agricultural Cossacks into serfdom.

From Decline to Catastrophe

In 1648 clashes between Cossacks and Polish magnates erupted into social warfare. The Cossack leader Bogdan Chmielnicki (1595–1657) invited Ukrainian peasants to join the revolt, which became an enormous rural uprising. Moslem Tatars from the Crimea allied with the rebels. Chmielnicki's motley army turned on magnates, their rent collectors, the Catholic clergy, and Jews. The Cossack leader hoped to carve an independent Ukrainian republic from the southeastern part of Poland, but he also knew it was only a matter of time before his ragged support would melt away. Therefore, in 1654 he revised his earlier plans and promised Tsar Alexei of Muscovy tax collection rights in the parts of the Ukraine controlled by the Cossacks and the lion's share of lands taken from the Polish magnates. In return the tsar was to protect the Cossacks and recognize their liberties.

For the Poles this meant war with Alexei, and during the next fifteen years Polish history was a litany of misfortunes. Cossacks and

Russians plundered the Dnieper River valley. A second front opened in Lithuania; Janusz Radziwill, the leading magnate there, dreamed of detaching Lithuania from the commonwealth with Poland and becoming its king. In 1655 Sweden entered the war to seize Poland's territory on the Baltic and beat the Russians to Warsaw. Looting and burning Catholic churches as they traveled, the Swedes occupied Warsaw and Cracow. The Polish king, John II Casimir (1648–1668), had to flee the country. Although Brandenburg joined the invaders, neither the Austrian Hapsburgs nor the Dutch desired to see Poland devoured, and they pursued ways of maintaining the integrity of the commonwealth. Polish resistance finally coalesced, and in 1660 Sweden and Brandenburg ceased fighting. The Cossack-peasant alliance disintegrated, though the war with Muscovy dragged on until 1668. When the Treaty of Andrusovo finally ended the conflict, Poland was saved from dismemberment. The price, however, was an enormous loss of life, especially among Jews massacred by the Cossacks. Poland provisionally ceded half the Ukraine to Muscovy.

Twenty years of war guaranteed Poland's place as prize pawn on the European chessboard. Socially, the regime of rural servitude hardened. The country had lost valuable territory and nearly 30 percent of its population. Driven from their ruined villages, tens of thousands of peasants and hundreds of gentry were floating through the countryside in search of food. The winners were the great landlords who occupied deserted properties and offered a hovel to poor creatures with no choice than to sell away a lifetime in service dues. Polish patriotism had expressed itself not in social or constitutional reform but rather in widespread persecution of Protestants, Germans, and Jews. Regional diets remained in force, preventing any semblance of central authority. Meanwhile an attempt by John II Casimir to abolish the *liberum veto* and select his own successor resulted in a magnate uprising and the king's abdication in 1668. Exiled from his country, four years later he died in a French monastery.

The international reputation of King John III Sobieski (1674–1696) as a Christian warrior has created his image as the most popular king in Poland's history. However, he did little to halt his country's decline in European politics. Sobieski stemmed from the immensely wealthy magnate aristocracy of the southeastern Polish borderlands, and he was obsessed with fighting Tatars and Turks. Once elected king, he put his own private army at the service of the commonwealth and urged his fellow magnates to do the same. Aristocrat to the core, Sobieski never wished to strengthen central political institutions, including the monarchy, and his anti-Moslem concerns blinded him to the far greater threats to Poland of Sweden and Muscovy. Therefore, when Leopold I called on help from Christendom in 1683 to prevent Vienna from being seized by the Turks, Sobieski marched 30,000 Polish troops across the Carpathian mountains, took command of the relief force outside the Hapsburg capital, and on September 12 saved the city.

However, Sobieski never took advantage of the luster accruing from his triumph to strengthen the Polish state. In 1686 he allowed Muscovy's occupation of half the Ukraine to become permanent, and he paid little heed to Hapsburg victories in Hungary. Use of the *liberum veto* regularly broke up national Diets, provincial nobles raised troops and taxes on their own, the great magnates employed the royal army for private purposes, and the king ultimately retreated into private life on his elegant estate outside Warsaw. Meanwhile Poland's rapacious neighbors—Brandenburg, Sweden, Austria, and Muscovy—signed treaties with one another guaranteeing the commonwealth's status quo. This meant preserving the privileges of the magnates, keeping the monarchy impotent, and assuring Poland's financial poverty.

Following the death of John III Sobieski in 1696, the Diet was unable to agree on a successor. Two magnatial cliques brought Poland to the brink of a new civil war. As candidate of one of the groups, the elector of Saxony rushed to the capital and was crowned. Assuming the throne as Augustus II (1697–1733), he offered his new subjects a tempting economic union of Saxon industry and Polish agriculture. Moreover, Polish ports gave Saxony an outlet to the sea. Dazzled with his new crown and blind to Poland's traditional weaknesses, Augustus extended his expansionist vision northward.

At the time of Augustus's accession Peter I and Karl XII took command of Russia and Sweden respectively. Twenty-four years old, overshadowed since childhood by his aunt and mother, Peter was anxious to prove himself. On the other hand, Karl was an untried adolescent of fifteen. Sweden's territories were scattered from the eastern reaches of Finland to a few miles from the Dutch frontier, and the underpopulated Scandinavian state seemed unprepared to defend them. Augustus therefore tempted both Peter and the king of Denmark with shares of Karl XII's inheritance, all the while grossly underestimating Karl's extraordinary capabilities and overestimating Russia's strengths. War came to the North, and in 1700 the Swedes annihilated the Russian army at the Battle of Narva. Karl smashed his way into Poland, deposed Augustus, occupied most of the country, and set up his own puppet king, Stanislaus Leszczynski.

As in the 1650s, remorse, followed by an indignant wave of patriotism, settled over the Polish aristocracy. Peter recovered, and the magnates pleaded with him to rid Poland of the Swedes. The country became a battlefield again. In 1709 Karl XII's army met disaster in Russia, Leszczynski in turn was deposed, and Augustus II restored. However, the tsar had no interest in becoming a disinterested liberator. He saw Poland as a conquest and King Augustus as his puppet. To pay for his continued struggles against the Swedes and Turks, he forced war contributions on Poland. Peter encouraged magnatial rivalries and refused to remove Russian troops from Polish soil. Augustus II was forced to abandon ideas about abolishing the liberum veto and reforming the monarchy. He became another in the long line of Poland's frustrated kings, channeling his energies from futile politics to the production of three hundred illegitimate children. While its king trundled from bedroom to bedroom, Poland's fate was sealed. Little more than a generation after Augustus's death in 1733, the commonwealth's neighbors, now too civilized to fight over Poland, began dividing the country peaceably among themselves.

SWEDEN'S AGE OF POWER

In Poland no true compromise of power emerged. Instead an aristocracy shackled both king and peasants, and foreign powers manipulated politics for their own ends. In Sweden, however, a clever king, Karl XI (1660–1697), outmaneuvered his magnates without sacrificing the country's peasants. Karl manipulated the political and social forces of his realm so skillfully that not even military disaster in the following reign could undo his work. Although the royal personality would be effaced during much of the eighteenth century, the king's bureaucracy still ran the country and society rested on the freest peasantry in Europe.

Royal Decline and Recovery

In 1648 Sweden was the dominant power in northern Europe. The eastern two-thirds of the Scandinavian peninsula was the heartland, a vast, thinly peopled country of a million inhabitants. On the eastern and southern shores of the Baltic lay the rest of the Swedish empire: Finland, Ingria, and Estonia bordering Russia; Livonia bordering Poland-Lithuania; and western Pomerania, Bremen-Verden, and Wismar in Germany. Sweden controlled the important German port of Stettin, and it held two Norwegian provinces. The bases for these scattered territories were fragile, for Sweden was poor, agrarian, and underpopulated. Its forests and iron mines depended upon Dutch capital, and as long as its ports and seas remained open to their commerce, the Dutch and English tolerated Sweden's makeshift empire.

Sweden's rural society more resembled that of western Europe than that of neighboring Brandenburg, Denmark, or Poland. Its peasants were not serfs. Significant numbers held full ownership of land; others leased property from the aristocracy or the Crown. Royal peasants even sent representatives to the national Diet, meeting in Stockholm. Most noble estates were modest in size, and the greatest Swedish aristocrats did not control regions and clients. Nor were they great officeholders, as in France. Rather, they were devoted to the sovereign and served the Crown in both the army and Royal Council. Of course, they sat in the national Diet, but so too did free peasants, the Lutheran clergy, and a small group of burghers.

Between 1650 and 1680, however, the delicate balance of traditional Swedish society was nearly upset. During the Thirty Years' War, Queen Kristina (1644–1654) desperately needed cash, and she therefore sold crown lands to nobles at cut-rate prices. She also rewarded faithful military officers with large tracts in Finland. Free peasants leasing alienated state properties now found themselves beholden to new landlords, veteran officers of the recent war, men who had seen serfdom in Germany and western Poland and were eager to apply it to Sweden. These new estate owners began charging their tenants with dues and services heretofore unknown in Sweden. Kristina did little to avert this social reaction. If anything, the idea of a splendid magnatial nobility appealed to her inclination of transforming backwoods Sweden into a dazzling baroque kingdom whose aristocratic residences, theaters, and libraries would be the envy of the North.

When the Swedish Diet gathered in Stockholm in 1650, the Estates of peasants, clergy, and burghers pleaded with the queen to take back the lands she had awarded to the nobility. Because Kristina was contemplating abdication and wished to name her cousin Karl Gustav as successor, the queen promised to heed the aggrieved commoners. Once Karl Gustav was officially recognized as her heir, however, she did nothing about the land grants. Alienation of state properties continued unabated. After his accession in 1654, Karl X Gustav (1654–1660) tried to slow down the process, but war with Poland and then Denmark further strained the country's resources. Although the Danish war went well for Sweden, which conquered Denmark's provinces east of the Sound and controlled most traffic through it, the premature death of Karl X Gustav in 1660 left a political power vacuum—a four-year-old child as successor. The newly enshrined magnatial aristocrats prepared to take charge of the state. Some even dreamed of converting Sweden into a monarchical republic on the Polish model.

In a social sense they nearly did so. Between 1660 and 1680, the peasants sank more deeply than ever into debt and resignation. They were subject to the landlord's civil and criminal jurisdiction and could be evicted without notice. As the magnates grew richer, the state grew poorer. In 1674, however, the aristocratized Royal Council committed a fatal blunder. It involved Sweden in a new war with Denmark and Brandenburg that the country could not afford. When peace arrived five years later, Sweden managed to keep its empire intact, but the state was on the verge of bankruptcy.

No longer a child, Karl XI had proven himself on the battlefield and was determined to take command of his country. In 1680 he called together the Diet, ostensibly to find a way to pay the outstanding war bills. The lower Estates surprised even the king by their boldness, suggesting a wholesale reacquisition of alienated state lands and establishment of an absolute monarchy. Even the gentry who served in the army and civil service and whose wages were in arrears, joined the cry. The great magnates had had their day. A royal survey disclosed that over 72 percent of the land now was owned by the nobility. For the remainder of his reign the king repossessed great estates that the Crown had lost within the past half century, and he promised the peasants that he would not abandon them to serfdom as long as they paid state taxes, rents, and dues. They willingly exchanged masters. The nobility was told to be satisfied with traditional careers in the army and royal administration, and Sweden entered a period of rigid austerity.

Despite the vigor of his *Reduktion,* Karl XI was no royal revolutionary. He did not abolish serfdom in Livonia and Estonia. Within his empire he actually created six hundred new nobles and redistributed expropriated estates among them. However, these properties were kept relatively small in size, and in return for them, owners were to work for the king and administer royal farms. Peasants too bought lands, and by 1700 free farmers, the aristocracy, and Crown each owned one-third of Sweden's cultivated land. The king avoided borrowing from foreigners but encouraged their investments. During Karl XI's reign Sweden's iron exports doubled. The army was rebuilt, with each province providing regiments of infantry recruits. Every draftee was granted a cottage and a small piece of land as payment and remained in the reserve force until he was fifty-five. Adding these recruits to the professional army gave Sweden in 1697 a well-trained force of at least 90,000 men. Karl XI's economic reforms were accomplished without bloodshed. The aristocracy was tamed and the peasantry was rescued from impoverishment and exploitation. Four years before Karl XI's death a grateful Diet declared him "by God, nature, and the Crown's high hereditary right . . . an absolute sovereign king, whose commands are binding on all, and who is responsible to no one on earth for his actions."

The Nordic Meteor

When Karl XI died at forty-two in 1697, he left an heir of fifteen and a state seemingly prepared to defend itself. Shortly thereafter Frederick IV of Denmark, Augustus II of Poland, and Peter I of Russia were eager to test its will. These rulers counted on a Swedish aristocratic revival that would overturn Karl XI's reforms, weaken the state, and invite foreign intervention. But they underestimated the new king. Descended from a line of warriors, reared in the Lutheran piety of a court that rejected learning and the arts, Karl XII (1697–1718) quickly showed talent as a gifted and impetuous military commander. The aristocracy of his empire supported him, and the Swedish peasant army fought with courage and skill. A brilliant battlefield strategist, at the age of seventeen Karl forced Denmark out of the coalition with Russia and Poland. Several months later, in November 1700 at Narva in Estonia, he surprised a Russian army five times the size of the Swedish force of 8,000. Aided by a snowstorm that blew into the faces of the Russians, he scored such a decisive victory that Peter abandoned the battlefield, his army in ruins. Within half an hour, 15,000 Russians were dead and 20,000 taken prisoner. Europe was stunned. William III and Louis XIV both courted the teenaged warrior, but Karl had little interest in the Spanish succession question. He still had a score to settle with Augustus II. The Swedes poured into Poland, deposed Augustus, and forced a rump Diet to elect Stanislaus Leszczynski as king. Karl left Stanislaus a Swedish occupation force. Then he turned his attention to the Hapsburgs, scolding Emperor Joseph I for mistreating his Protestant subjects. For all his military daring, Charles bore a religious strain in his politics that was reminiscent of another age. His hatred of Augustus II was inflamed by the fact that the Saxon was a renegade Lutheran turned Catholic for the Polish throne. Joseph promised that he would treat non-Catholics in a more kindly way. Once more Karl moved eastward.

Peter's recovery after Narva forced Karl to confront the Russians. The tsar had learned that without a complete overhaul, his army never could stand up to a disciplined, well-trained force. From scratch, Peter built a volunteer infantry, then a commissariat, and finally an artillery. He systematized the peasant levy and established a school of tactics for young officers. In 1703 he scored a couple of small successes against the Swedes in Ingria and defied Karl by projecting the construction of Russia's new seat of government on soil claimed by Sweden. In September 1707 Karl moved across Poland at the head of 43,000 troops. His goal was Moscow. However, in the face of disease, bad weather, and Polish guerrilla resistance, the Swedish advance bogged down. It took ten months to reach the Dnieper River, still in Poland. In July 1708, as his supplies dwindled, Karl received an offer of help from the Cossacks, who accused Peter of interference in their affairs. The Swedish king decided to cut a wide detour through the Ukraine, where he might find food and link up his forces with both the Cossacks and a second Swedish army moving down from the Baltic.

At this juncture, however, the Swedes suffered from misfortune and miscalculation. As they retreated, the Russians burned the countryside. Repeated sniper attacks wiped out nearly half the force sent to relieve Karl, and the Cossacks did not help. The terrible winter of 1708–1709 struck the Ukraine early. After eight years in the field, Karl's surviving troops longed to go home. Still the king would not deflect from his goal. Although the Swedes already had lost over half their army and the king himself was badly wounded, Karl challenged Peter to fight. As the Swedes besieged the town of Poltava, the Russians finally attacked. Outnumbered two to one, their king incapacitated, hungry, tired, and without supplies, the Swedish army came close to pulling off yet another miracle. Carried from place to place on a litter, Karl defied death itself. However, the Russians wore down their old tormenters, and with a thousand survivors the Swedish king fled into Turkish territory.

Poltava heralded the end of the Swedish empire and the beginning of the Russian one. Russia, Denmark, and Brandenburg seized Sweden's Baltic lands. Peter cleared Poland of Swedish troops, deposed Stanislaus Leszczynski, and reestablished Augustus II. In September 1714, after a series of fantastic adventures among the Turks, Karl decided to return home. With two companions it took him two weeks to cover 1,350 miles incognito. Undaunted as ever, he was filled with plans and projects. Stralsund, his last German port, fell to the Prussians; but he believed that a new victory would revive his countrymen. The Danes had always been his easiest victims, so the king pulled together his last army and marched across the frontier into Danish-occupied Norway. In December 1718, while besieging the fortress of Fredriksten, a stray bullet finally caught up with the Terror of the North. Upon Karl's death, his generals called off the campaign and the army went home. Two years of negotiations confirmed most of Sweden's wartime losses: Hanover took Bremen-Verden; Prussia took Stettin and half of Swedish Pomerania. Peter saw his hold confirmed on Ingria, southeastern Finland, Estonia, and Livonia. Like Denmark, Sweden was finished as a great power.

Karl XII left a disputed succession. The Diet elected the king's sister Ulrika Eleanora (1718–1741) as queen but hedged her powers and threw out the absolutist blank check presented to Karl XI back in 1693. However, Sweden did not revert to the chaos of Poland. For more than fifteen of his twenty-one years as king, Karl XII had been out of the country, and a loyal bureaucracy had run the government. From 1718 to 1772, the four-Estate Diet and civil service shared political responsibility, and the monarchy was eclipsed. Sweden's eighteenth-century foreign policies were tailored down to its size and strengths. Ultimately the social-administrative reforms of Karl XI proved to be a far more enduring legacy than the military adventures of his warrior son.

FROM MUSCOVY TO THE RUSSIAN EMPIRE

The Original Character of Muscovy

In 1648 Moscow was worlds apart from Paris, London, or even Warsaw. Nevertheless, it shared severe social tensions with these other capitals. Lacking Diets, Estates, or a legal tradition, Muscovy was unlike any other European country. In the sixteenth century its tsars had developed the concept of a pure service state in which clearly defined social groups owed to their imperial majesty a set of obligations peculiar to their station. Theoretically the tsar owned the state, and all subjects were required to serve him by giving of themselves or of their property. Aristocrats were to lead the tsar's armies and administer his government. Peasants were to render labor services to noble landowners and pay taxes to the tsar. Townsmen provided the ruler with a percentage of the revenue they derived from commerce. The tsar possessed the power to identify the privileged elements of Muscovite society. To the nobility and Church he donated property and peasants. He bound the peasantry to lord and land, and then left administration of serfdom to private law. The tsar could grant monopolies, estates, and titles to foreigners who established foundries and iron works or who directed the export-import trade. Towns had no municipal liberties. The state channeled and directed internal commerce. In 1654 an imperial decree accomplished what Colbert could never do in France. It abolished all internal tolls.

Theoretically a despotism, the state nevertheless possessed internal checks to restrain it from becoming a model of ruthlessness. The tsar's government was poorly organized and, except at the very top, devoid of hierarchical structures. Departments were created to respond to the needs of the moment and then retained. In the 1680s eighteen separate bureaus competed for the management of army affairs. Coordinating departmental duties was foreign to Russian tradition, and sheer distance permitted the provinces to maintain their own rhythms of existence. This autonomy was especially significant with respect to extracting money and services from subjects. The tsar refused to create a western-style office-owning corps of aristocrats to whom he might alienate degrees of political authority in return for financial support. Instead he appointed governor-intendants to oversee taxation and justice, and these officials ordered landowners to have their peasants pay taxes and serve in the army. Once more, however, Russia's distances weighed against the smooth functioning of such a coercive enterprise. Summoned to Moscow by the governor-intendant, recalcitrant landowners would be lectured on the necessity for their dependence, and then ordered home to force their peasants to pay lapsed taxes to the state. For a decently respectful period the gentry would obey, but inevitably old habits of neglect reemerged.

The Orthodox Church also served as a counterweight to the idea of cold imperial despotism. The model of church-state relations was Byzantine. The tsar controlled and protected the Church, but in Muscovy very little distinction existed between secular and religious matters. Any religious dispute, even one concerning ritual or dogma, had the potential for becoming an affair of state. Because Russian Orthodoxy lacked systematic theological or scholarly foundations and essentially was a folk religion, the danger was very great that schism could erupt into civil strife. Therefore both tsar and Church officials tacitly agreed to avoid tampering with icon worship, ritual custom, or liturgy. During the sixteenth century the Church had grown very wealthy. Tax-exempt monasteries and priories were granted vast estates complete with serfs. Moreover, the Orthodox patriarch was a political figure of the first order. He dominated the religious life of the tsar's family, outranked all other imperial dignitaries, and participated in the promulgation of government decrees. Before the reign of Peter the Great the symbiotic relationship between the religious and the political meant that civil authorities might order and stage religious processions, while, on the other hand, no major political decision could be made without the involvement of Church officials.

Tsar Alexei (1645–1676)

In June 1648 riots broke out in Moscow over the imposition of extraordinary taxes on households heretofore exempt from paying them. The government could cope with petty tradesmen and artisans; however, once the palace guard joined the discontented Muscovites, matters became critical.

Crowds burned the houses of unpopular officials and lynched two of them. For four days Moscow was in flames, until the personal intervention of Tsar Alexei ended the destruction. Although the Moscow riots failed to spread to the countryside, they convinced the tsar and his advisers of the need to invite groups to the capital and present the government with lists of grievances. The makeup of the assembly turned out to be overwhelmingly aristocratic and rural, and in January 1649 the tsar responded to its concerns with a law code that became imperial Russia's *de facto* constitution, surviving until 1833. The Code of 1649 froze society, confirming the subservience of all elements to the state. Only the service nobility and Church could own land and peasants. Burghers were tied to their place of residence, with foreigners and country people prohibited from competing in town commerce. The Church no longer could acquire tax-exempt properties, and a new government department was established to oversee Church administration. Serfdom was enshrined as an immutable institution, with the peasant and his entire family tied to a landlord's estate. Should the serf run away, the landlord's claim to possess him would never lapse.

The Code of 1649 did not stifle unrest in Muscovy's empire. On the contrary, its repressive terms probably encouraged uprisings a year later in the independent-minded cities of Pskov and Novgorod. When Bogdan Chmielnicki's war against Poland threatened to spill into Russia, a nervous Alexei formed an alliance with the Cossacks. Moreover, during the 1650s the intertwining relations between the political and the religious in Muscovite society aggravated another set of tensions. The origins lay in the rise in influence of the tsar's good friend, the monk Nikon (1605–1681). Nikon was a religious reformer absolutely convinced that the only way Russian Orthodoxy might achieve intellectual parity with Protestantism or Catholicism was by liberating itself from dependence upon folk ritual and magic and bringing it closer to its Greek roots. As an energetic and well-respected abbot, in 1646 Nikon gained access to the tsar. He shortly became Alexei's confessor, then metropolitan of Novgorod, and in 1652 patriarch of Moscow.

Nikon prepared to purify Church and society in ways reminiscent of his contemporaries in Cromwellian England. Vodka consumption was reduced, musical instruments destroyed, and a campaign launched to reshape ritual. A new service book was drawn up, deemphasizing or eliminating what Nikon considered to be superstitious forms of worship. Imposed on the country clergy, the reforms provoked widespread hostility among those who viewed the reduction of the number of hallelujahs and genuflections in the Orthodox service as tampering with God's law. Tens of thousands refused to part with what they called the "Old Belief." They politicized their religious protest by abandoning their villages and escaping to the Cossacks in the south or to the wilderness in the east. Nikonites were accused of having been seduced by the devilish triad of Catholicism, science, and geometry. Increasing in number and vigor, Old Believers became the caretakers of an indigenous anti-Western tradition that considered itself more authentically Russian than the tsarist regime itself. They also became the great frontier pioneers of Russia, first colonizing Siberia and the southeast, crossing mountains and seas, ever moving on when the arm of the state came too close.

Although Nikon's political ambitions led to his disgrace, in the late 1660s social, political, and religious unrest erupted in widespread violence. In this instance the origins lay far from the capital, 600 miles southeast of Moscow, in the valley of the Don and Volga rivers, where escaped serfs and Old Believers came in contact with Cossacks paid by the tsar to protect Muscovy from the Tatars. The Don-Volga Cossacks had been free horsemen, shunning agriculture for animal raising and plunder; but the arrival of tens of thousands of newcomers encouraged the rapid development of unaccustomed dependencies and house-owning traits among them, that threatened to destroy the egalitarianism of their rough frontier society. All that was needed to ignite the explosive situation was a charismatic leader promising to end oppression and restore true Cossack freedom. In 1667 a repentant house-owning Cossack named Stenka Razin offered that leadership, and within a year his large band of horsemen and former peasants seized control of the western and southern shores of the Caspian Sea well into Persian territory. Razin then turned his horde abruptly toward Moscow, with the apparent intention of overthrowing the tsar and his government. Ex-soldiers, Dnieper Cossacks, country priests, overburdened townsmen, and enserfed peasants joined Stenka Razin's crusade. He sought help from the disgraced Nikon, who refused the invitation. To many others, however, Razin was a saint, a deliverer, promising to end serfdom and religious schism, and replace despotism with assemblies of the people.

At its height Stenka Razin's uprising involved several hundred thousand and was the most spectacular popular rebellion in seventeenth-century Europe. As the human wave pushed toward the northwest, estates went up in flame and towns fell. In 1670, however, Razin lost control of his following. Tensions erupted between Cossacks and newcomers. Razin was betrayed, captured, carted off to Moscow, tortured, and publicly executed. His splintered forces still terrorized the countryside but no longer posed a threat to the regime. Soon they disintegrated altogether.

The service nobility was amply rewarded for remaining loyal to Alexei. The Code of 1649 stood, and the landlord was ensured total property rights over those who worked his estate. By 1680 Russian society seemed to rest securely enough on the foundations of a complex political compromise among elites, consistent with trends in central and eastern Europe. In actuality, however, the structure was extremely fragile. Taxes were irregularly collected, Old Belief remained a religious threat, and primitive Cossack democracy a political one. Even Alexei's greatest military triumph, the conquest of the Ukraine, was fraught with danger, for it introduced into Muscovy Polish notions of aristocratic independence that were contrary to the ideology of the service state, and the consequent growth of Western cultural influences at the tsar's court widened the gap between elite values and popular traditions. In Muscovy the forging of instruments of coercion, which might convert absolutist claims into reality across millions of square miles of desert, forest, and ice, was as yet incomplete.

The Rise of Peter the Great

Alexei died in 1676. From his first marriage a girl, Sophia, and two boys, Feodor and Ivan, had survived. From his second marriage to Natalya Naryshkin, a son, Peter, was born in 1672. Feodor succeeded his father, but the young tsar died in 1682. Ivan was mentally incompetent. Since the Russian state possessed no law of succession, such a situation customarily degenerated into palace intrigue with its attendant political murders. Peter's mother Natalya and her family proposed the ten-year-old boy as the new tsar. The patriarch of Moscow gave his blessing, and a mob of Naryshkin followers, hurriedly labeled the "Assembly of the People," acclaimed Peter. However, Sophia did not relish being thrust aside so easily. Controlling the palace guard, she and her lover, Prince Vasili Golytsin (1643–1714), murdered all the Naryshkins they could find. Miraculously, Peter and his mother were spared. To avert the inevitable backlash, Sophia proposed an imaginative compromise. Peter and his dim-witted stepbrother Ivan would be recognized as co-tsars and Sophia would serve as regent. This was appropriate enough for state occasions, but Sophia's real aim was to keep Peter out of the picture as much as possible.

Between 1682 and 1689 Peter and his mother were forced to live on a village estate a few miles outside Moscow. Left to his own devices, the boy roamed the countryside and caroused in the "Foreign Suburb," located midway between his residence and the capital. For two centuries several dozen west-European merchants, technicians, and army officers had resided there, insulated from Russians whom they despised and who feared them. Learning to share their prejudices toward his countrymen, Peter struck up friendships with several soldiers of fortune. From them he learned the rudiments of military tactics and developed a passionate interest in naval matters. Peter learned a little German and Dutch, but his education was hardly regular. His mother could not control him, and Sophia kept him at a distance.

An artisan and bully, Peter drilled his companions, terrorized peasant girls, and built sailboats. Paradoxically enough, the regime of Sophia and Golytsin prepared Russia for Peter in several ways. Golytsin envisioned an aggressive foreign policy. He wanted to draw the Muscovite state closer to Europe and develop contacts with the Orient. He wished to introduce Western technology to backward Muscovy and considered the greatest aristocrats (the boyars), the Orthodox Church, and palace guard as the chief obstacles to progress. Time, however, was not with Golytsin. In 1689 his enemies staged a countercoup and deposed Sophia. The regent was placed in a convent and her Western-looking adviser was exiled to Siberia.

Natalya Naryshkin offered the face of respectability to the corrupt gang of nobles who had seized the government, and young Peter moved closer to the throne. In 1694 his mother died, followed two years later by Peter's half brother Ivan. A vigorous young man of twenty-four, Peter was sole ruler at last. His pent-up energies exploded in every direction.

A New European Power

Peter was the first European ruler to commit mind and heart almost exclusively to the technological improvement of his state. His motives were clear-cut. The modernization of Russia was the surest way to tighten his hold on the country and impress the country on the world. That Russian society and civilization might resist his vision was irrelevant. He would perfect the implements of power at his disposal and bend the nation to his purpose. He never swerved from his faith in providing example from above. Near the close of his life he wrote, "Our people are like children who would never set about their ABC's unless their master compelled them."

Force of arms offered a shortcut to national goals, one of which was to turn Muscovy into a sea power. The country did not even possess an ice-free port. Swedish-controlled Finland, Ingria, Estonia, and Livonia closed off the Baltic. Tatar Crimea, a tributary state of the Turks, controlled the entrance to the Black Sea. The Ottomans blocked passage to the Mediterranean. To the tsar the Crimean bases seemed the most vulnerable points. In 1696 Peter captured the seaport of Azov and began to build a fleet. He planned harbors for the Don River and a canal link between the Don and Volga. However, since the eastern Mediterranean was in the hostile hands of the Ottoman Turks, this opening still appeared to be a dead end. Then, in 1697, a more promising opportunity beckoned. Karl XI of Sweden recently had died, and Augustus II of Poland suggested to Peter the division of Sweden's Baltic empire. Agreeing to the scheme, the tsar abruptly shifted focus. The Baltic, not the Black Sea, would be his window on the West.

For Peter, the Great Northern War began disastrously in 1700, with Karl XII's victory over the Russians at Narva. Peter eventually wore down the undermanned Swedes, but not until 1721. Even after the Russian victory at Poltava in 1709, it took twelve additional years to dispossess Sweden of its Baltic territories. Peter nevertheless lived long enough to see the Peace of Nystad (1721) affirm his major foreign policy goal.

From Viborg to Riga, Russia replaced Sweden on the Baltic littoral, and Poland was turned into a diplomatic pawn. Flushed with his victory at Poltava, Peter had hoped to outflank the Hapsburgs in liberating the Balkans from the Turks. In 1711 the tsar moved his army into Moldavia. He expected the Christian populations to rise up against the infidel and welcome the Russians as their saviors. However, this scenario failed to materialize. Peter overextended his forces, and the Turks surrounded his entire army on the Pruth River. The tsar had to surrender or face annihilation. He returned Azov to the Turks, thereby closing the Balkans and Black Sea to Russian expansion for another half century. However, on a third front, along the Caspian Sea, Peter was more successful, taking strips on the southern and western shores from the Persians.

Peter understood that conquest might make Europe fear Russia but never welcome it. The tsar longed to divest the West of its suspicions of Russian power and scorn for Russia's institutions. By borrowing experts and techniques from Europe, he believed he could strengthen the state and at the same time integrate it into the community of nations he so envied. Peter was convinced that he might accomplish his aims through personal example and thus embarked on two "Great Emissaries" to the West, the first in 1697 and the second in 1716. During the first voyage he traveled as a private person, working with his hands at the dockyard of the Dutch East India Company, spending fifteen weeks in an English shipbuilding town, and observing Parliament. On the return journey home, via the Netherlands, Leipzig, Prague, and Vienna, he contracted expert seamen, gunners, shipwrights, mathematicians, surgeons, and engineers, who followed him shortly, carrying their books and instruments.

In Vienna, Peter learned that the officers of the palace guard were meddling in dynastic politics again. Goaded by boyars worried about the tsar's apparent impiety, devotion to foreigners, and mistreatment of his wife, four regiments revolted. Peter rushed back to Moscow, only to find that the uprising already had been suppressed. Suspecting a conspiracy to place Sophia on the throne, Peter decided to settle the matter of palace revolts once and for all. Fourteen torture chambers were erected outside Moscow. Dismissing the entire Moscow guard, considered by Peter to be poor soldiers and worse plotters, the tsar wiped out its leadership. Charges were filed, court martials were held, and hundreds were whipped, garroted, beheaded, hanged, or buried alive. Peter had an execution block set up directly outside Sophia's convent window. At this moment the first contingent of Western experts arrived.

Peter and the Making of Russia

Any summary of Peter's internal reforms runs the risk of suggesting that they were conceived in a reasonably systematic fashion. Nothing could be further from the truth. One order might contradict another, and none ever considered the psychological unpreparedness of the Russian people for change. Although it was characteristic of Peter to emphasize the outer, superficial, and symbolic aspects of modernization, such as trimming robes or clipping beards, other changes were far more shattering and created the matrix into which modern Russia was molded. Peter consulted neither intermediate political bodies nor entrenched social groups. With the stroke of his pen the tsar dismissed overlapping boyar councils and erased provincial governments. In 1700 he divided the country into eight regional districts with a governor and staff for each. After the defeat of the Swedes at Poltava these eight districts were further divided into smaller units, and local landlords administered them by means of a rigidly hierarchical order of state service. Responsible only to the tsar, they were to collect taxes, grain, and soldiers. Those older officials accustomed to pocketing the lion's share of revenue grumbled, but they did not resist.

Peter also streamlined the central administration. He appointed a cabinet (called the senate) of nine trusted men to handle day-to-day affairs and execute the tsar's orders. Peter had no patience with the interminable deliberations of the old boyar councils. The senate better suited the needs of crisis government, and the councils thus were doomed. Provincial officials sent reports to senate members, who dispatched agents and spies to the provinces. Even the senators were subjected to scrutiny by Peter's fiscal agents and by the procurator-general, the second most important political figure in the empire. The tsar also established departments called colleges, each with specific functional authority over foreign affairs, the army, navy, mining installations, and manufactures. Each college established systems of procedure, including majority rule, and made long-term recommendations. Administrative business was to take place only in government offices, and in 1720 the General Regulations of bureaucratic procedure were formally adopted. Thus Peter offered Russia for the first time the framework of a coordinated governmental apparatus, even though the country lacked trained personnel to fill it. Peter imported technicians and army officers, but creation of a disinterested civil service was another matter. The tsar's cronies rubbed shoulders with haughty boyars ill-fitted for their new roles. Personal allegiances and family connections among the service nobility continued to plague government. Social tensions and mutual jealousies abounded. Neither corruption nor human inefficiency could be erased overnight.

Old Muscovite society had not only distinguished among peasant, townsman, and noble but also contained recognized categories of peasants. These were slaves, serfs, freeholders, and colonists. Each group accordingly paid specified types of household taxes to the government. The Code of 1649 had gone far toward creating a uniform serf-peasantry, and Peter completed the job by substituting for the old impositions a single poll tax on 5 million male family heads. With the peasant village now in bondage to landlord and state, Peter went after the privileged members of Russian society. By prohibiting the division of private estates, the tsar channeled the younger sons of landlords into the army, navy, and civil administration.

Peter inherited the concept of a service state and imposed it on a reluctant society. By institutionalizing a system of ranks that corresponded to the military's, Peter formalized the status of Russia's elites. Of the fourteen grades denoting civil rank, the highest eight conferred nobility. Aristocrats were urged to compete for the top grades, and everyone understood that devoted state service was the only avenue to recognized social distinction. In

Social

this way the tsar controlled the social hierarchy, and at the same time energetic individuals irrespective of bloodline could rise through the ranks.
Both military and state service were lifelong, beginning at age fifteen; personnel could be sent anywhere in the empire. Discipline and honor thus replaced
rebelliousness and indolence as cultural norms for the Russian aristocracy,
the reward for which was control over the country's serfs.

Taxes

Peter made sure that taxes were collected. Between 1710 and 1724
state revenues tripled, and despite war the budget was balanced. Nor did the
industrial primitiveness of Russia daunt the dynamic tsar. He had inherited
a substantial mining enterprise in the Urals, but the sheer size of the country and its lack of a communications network assured the existence of
hundreds of self-supporting economic units dependent upon handicraft
production. However, peasant villagers could neither clothe Peter's army
nor make sails for his navy. Therefore the tsar ordered the construction of
specialized factories, encouraged foreign investment, and had state-owned
serfs trained to specialize as iron workers, cannon founders, and textile
laborers. Vagrants, poor women, and orphans were put to work. The best-
developed industry, iron production, spread from Perm in the Urals to the
region around Lake Onega and St. Petersburg. A former peasant, Nikita
Demidov, was the industrial genius behind the growth of Russia's heavy
metals. By the mid-eighteenth century the country produced as much pig
iron as the rest of continental Europe combined.

Peter was almost wholly responsible for the birth of his country as
a commercial power. Prior to his reign, Archangel, the only important
port, was controlled by Dutch and English tradesmen, who handed the
Muscovite government a pittance in customs revenue. The acquisition of
Sweden's east-Baltic empire altered the picture completely. Suddenly the
great entrepôts for Polish grains—the towns of Riga, Reval, and Viborg—
were in Russian hands. Peter envisioned the Baltic regions as the nerve
center of his country. Out of the ice and mud taken from the Swedes would
arise its living monuments, the capital of St. Petersburg and naval base of
Kronstadt. No insulated Versailles, St. Petersburg was to be Russia's hub of
world commerce, a royal residence, and an administrative capital. Peter
offered monopolies to businessmen willing to establish themselves in St.
Petersburg. He began building a network of canals linking the Caspian Sea
to his new city. During his own lifetime Peter saw St. Petersburg emerge
from nothing into a busy port. In 1713 a single ship laid anchor there, but
in 1725 the number rose to five per week. Of course, no Amsterdam or
London could be created overnight. Yet St. Petersburg's merchant community was comprised mostly of Russians who developed connections with
Turkey, Persia, central Asia, and China; who gained control of the iron,
pitch, and tar production of the hinterland; who persuaded Peter to finance
the Bering expeditions that would charter the straits between Siberia and
Alaska; and who even planned an East India Company. Russians were

learning the techniques of Western commerce, and this brought Peter immense satisfaction.

In other respects, however, the breakthrough was less promising. The ships that left St. Petersburg, Riga, and Reval laden with iron, naval stores, wheat, and silks, were seldom Russian. Russians still were too unskilled to undertake banking and insurance. Nevertheless, none of Peter's contemporaries understood bootstrap economics as well as he did, and St. Petersburg offered the enterprising individual an unparalleled opportunity at entrepreneurial pioneering. The state provided incentive, monopolies, and privileges. Within a generation St. Petersburg became Russia's most cultivated and beautiful city.

Of the Russian institutions that opposed Peter's projects, at the forefront was the Russian Orthodox Church. It was the most privileged institution in Russian society, with an income barely touched by taxation and lands tilled by hundreds of thousands of serfs. Its hold on the people was unrivaled by any secular ideology the tsar could hope to conjure. Peter himself was a believer. His letters were filled with biblical allusions, and he was genuinely interested in missionary activity among the non-Christian peoples of his empire. However, he feared and hated the institutionalized Orthodox Church. To him the patriarchate of Moscow, seat of Church government, was obscurantist, corrupt, and an obstacle to his vision of a new Russia. The patriarch Adrian despised foreigners, repudiated any change in Russian life, opposed the "Great Emissary," and scolded the tsar for his promiscuous private life.

When Adrian died in 1700, Peter decided to bring the Church into his net of activity. He delayed nominating a new patriarch and instead picked a layman as temporary administrator. Citing as his reason the financial crisis following the defeat at Narva, he commanded Church revenues to be diverted to the government's use. No other European sovereign could have succeeded at this, but Peter maintained the so-called emergency until 1721. Then he dissolved the patriarchate altogether and replaced it with a holy synod, a committee of eight priests of unquestioned loyalty with a layman presiding. This was nothing more than a faceless body subservient to the regime. The synod took command of the essentials of Church organization and government and controlled income, appointments, and building construction. It oversaw the education of priests and ordered the clergy to stress morals and patriotism instead of ritual and prayer. Peter allowed the number of monks and nuns to dwindle through natural attrition and appointed army veterans to monastic vacancies. By passively accepting Peter's humiliating blows, official Orthodoxy showed the tsar that he had nothing more to fear from it. Meanwhile traditional folk religion persisted. Old Believers fled the regime of the "crowned Satan" for the relative freedom of the Arctic and Siberia. Those who returned paid discriminatory taxes and helped widen the gulf between those who honored the values of Old Muscovy and the Westernizing courtiers, bureaucrats, and industrialists who comprised the core of the tsar's service elite.

Additional resistance and personal misfortune marred Peter's last years. Between 1719 and 1726 an estimated quarter million serfs fled eastward. They participated in rebellions in the provinces of Smolensk, Muscovy, and Nizhny Novgorod. Despite the failure of their own uprisings between 1707 and 1710, the Cossacks were always restless. Finally, there was the problem of the great Muscovite aristocracy, the only element of the old privileged society that Peter had neither destroyed nor mastered. Their government councils dissolved, the boyars grumbled over their place in the Table of Ranks beside foreigners and the self-made men of the new bureaucracy. The Muscovites resisted passively, resigned to riding out the Petrine storm. Time, they believed, was on their side. Moreover, they had a potential leader. Alexei, Peter's son by his first marriage, passionately hated his father. When Peter chose a former Lithuanian camp follower as his second wife, Alexei decided that, given the chance, he would undo all his father's work. This meant abandonment of St. Petersburg and the Baltic and restoration of the government to boyar councils.

Although the aristocracy chose to await Peter's death, Alexei was less patient. Intimidated by Peter's rages and threats of disinheritance, in 1716 the tsarevitch fled the country. First he sought refuge in Vienna, at the court of his brother-in-law, Emperor Charles VI. Peter sent emissaries after him, and they finally chased him down in Naples. Alexei returned to Russia, where father and son staged a tearful reconciliation. However, haunted by prospects of Alexei's accession, Peter succumbed to a morosity that nearly broke him. Finally, he had Alexei arrested and ordered the application of torture so as to learn the tsarevitch's genuine motives. The questioners proved too conscientious, and in 1718 Alexei died under the strain. It was political murder, and Peter's responsibility was total. Peter died eight years later without naming his heir, and once again a succession crisis loomed. The senate quickly set up the tsar's widow Catherine as empress, but she died in 1727. For the next fourteen years, faction and clique fought bitterly over the Petrine inheritance; the country never was in greater danger than during this time.

Most of the revolution held, however. The Muscovite boyars misjudged the intentions of the bulk of the country nobility. That the gentry had been bludgeoned into service by the tsar there is no doubt. That its members considered many aspects of this service oppressive, particularly the years in the army and the drudgery of tax collecting, is beyond question. That they feared the regime at St. Petersburg also cannot be denied. However, the Table of Ranks made certain that the highest offices of state would be open to the most able and most ambitious. No longer would they serve as the exclusive preserve of well-connected boyars. In the orderly service state Peter desired, an obscure squire might realistically contemplate becoming a general, senator, or department head. During the eighteenth century the meteoric careers of provincial landlords and rise of an occasional serf sufficiently illustrated the paradox inherent in Russian society—frozen by law, yet mobile through circumstance. Peter the Great's obsession to catch up with the West became an essential element in Russia's complex heritage. Traditional complacency and isolation yielded to a spirit of competitiveness in which individual ambition, channeled through service to the state, might produce vast rewards. Peter fulfilled a compromise of power Russian style, one which worked to the mutual advantage of the regime and landholding gentry. On the other hand, its victims were the ancient boyar families, Orthodox churchmen, a tsarevitch, and several million peasants.

5

EUROPE AND THE WORLD

During the second half of the seventeenth century relations between the European states and their advanced posts in America, Africa, and Asia assumed wider dimensions. Mother countries demanded agricultural products and raw materials from their colonies either for sale at home or reexport abroad. These goods were to be transported on the motherland's ships, manned by her crews, and financed by her investors. Colonists were supposed to purchase manufactured and industrial products from the motherland. Around the 1670s calicoes and cottons from Asia and coffee and sugar from America began finding a European market. This enriched commerce necessitated efficient exploitation of native labor in the Orient and slave labor across the Atlantic. European rivalries, particularly between France and its enemies, extended to the colonial world. Now European armies fought pitched battles overseas, and warfare tightened the bonds between motherlands and their colonies. Finally, the age witnessed an extension of Catholic Europe's religious mission to the world, particularly in the direction of Asia. The effort dramatically brought home lessons about the perils of evangelization and affected Europeans themselves in ways that missionary priests could never have foreseen.

ATLANTIC IMPERIALISM

North America

From the beginning the penetration by Europeans of mainland North America extended the rivalries and conflicts of the Old World. By 1648, Spain seemed firmly in control of Mexico, had a foothold in Florida, and Spanish Franciscans were conducting an unchallenged mission to the native populations of the present-day southwestern United States. Elsewhere in North America, however, particularly in the vast territory extending from the mouth of the St. Lawrence River to the backcountry of Virginia, adventurers and settlers from half a dozen European states transferred their political, economic, and religious struggles and initiated new ones with native American inhabitants. France had a difficult time defending its interests in Canada, especially Acadia, from English incursions. The Dutch encountered similar problems in their underpopulated agricultural estates in the Hudson River

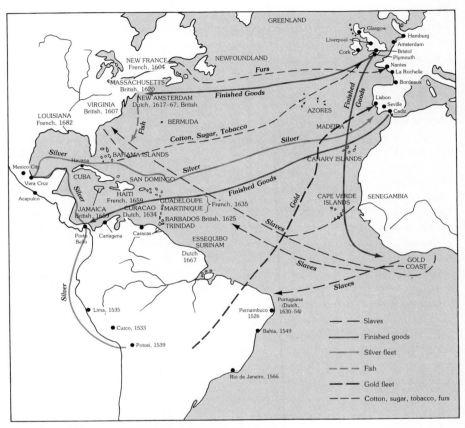

Map 5.1—The New World in the Seventeenth Century

valley and thriving little port of New Amsterdam; to the south, along the Delaware River, the Dutch, Swedes, and English were lively rivals.

Alone among the Europeans it was English-speaking peoples who made the firmest commitment to conquest and settlement. A royal colony since 1624 and controlled by aristocrats, Virginia by 1650 had a white population of 20,000. Despite a high mortality rate, thanks to immigration the colony was growing rapidly. Tobacco planters and young migrants working as indentured servants formed its Anglican, hierarchical, and over-whelmingly rural population. Although enslavement of black Africans was yet to become a major factor in the lives of Virginians, domination of non-Europeans took the form of violent relations with native Americans. Indian battles and massacres punctuated Virginia's early history, and in the

1670s the penetration of new immigrants toward the west presaged additional disturbances. Moreover, in 1676, led by Nathaniel Bacon, Virginia frontiersmen, tenants, and indentured servants staged an armed revolt against the Tidewater aristocracy. The civil strife petered out quickly following Bacon's death from malaria; but Virginia's political leadership hereafter recognized the interests of an expanding white population—now 40,000—by encouraging western settlement at Indian expense and by extending the practice of enslavement of blacks transported from the West Indies and Africa itself.

Adjoining Virginia was Maryland, granted by Charles I to his favorite, Cecilius Calvert in 1632. Largely Catholic, Maryland also was dependent upon the vagaries of tobacco production. By way of contrast were the dissenting Protestant settlements of New England, originally founded as a temporary Puritan experiment, prior to the immigrants' hope of the mother country's eventual conversion to Calvinist godliness. English stockholders in the Massachusetts Bay Company turned governing rights to the colony over to its settlers, who were ruled by a General Court elected by all males belonging to approved Puritan congregations. Freemen elected their governor. The Puritans completed their break with the Anglican Communion, and their faith assumed a covenant with God resembling that of the Old Testament Jews. Despite attempts of the Puritan leadership to maintain religious orthodoxy, breakaway movements proliferated. In 1636 Roger Williams left to found Rhode Island, and in 1648 all Puritan congregations obtained the right to independence and equality. During the 1650s numbers of Puritans returned to England to assist Cromwell; but the failure of the Cromwellian regime and the subsequent Stuart Restoration produced a new wave of immigration, sanctioning the permanence of the Puritans' American adventure. In 1660 Connecticut won a royal charter and defined its boundaries. Consciously breaking with European habits of landlord oppression, aristocratic hierarchies, and impoverished tenancies, New Englanders were building a society based on extreme Calvinist religious values, unrestricted land ownership, and self-governing towns. This activity did not necessarily suggest equality of wealth or status, but their "City upon a Hill" was intended to fulfill a utopian ideal.

By way of contrast, the later Stuarts envisioned the English mainland colonies of North America very differently from the settlers. For Restoration governments—as indeed it had been even for Cromwell's—the colonies *in toto* represented the centerpiece of an evolving imperial network that was subordinate to England and subject to its laws. This modern conception of colonialism was at odds with the rejection by those settlers of any relationship to the motherland rendering them either economically or politically inferior. The English colonies had been founded as discrete units, protected by individual charters that determined their governance, and colonists resented whatever might threaten their religious traditions or economic concerns. Tensions existed among the different colonies themselves, between poor settlers and wealthy ones, and between European immigrants and native Americans. Meanwhile Charles II's practice of granting huge tracts of royal land to favorites—entire provinces in the case of New York seized from the Dutch in 1664, as well as Pennsylvania and New Jersey—contributed to eroding the king's authority in North America. Yet English enforcement of the Navigation Acts, particularly with respect to customs collection, was bound to prove explosive and even led to violence in North Carolina and Maryland. The most economically diversified colony, Massachusetts Bay, wished to develop its own manufacturing in defiance of the Navigation Acts and of the subordination of colonial interests to imperial ones.

The Lords of Trade in London comprised the chief policymaking board for America. In 1684, on the insistence of James, duke of York (and governor of the New York colony), the Lords tried to establish a Dominion of New England that would revise, and ultimately dispense with, the individual charters held by Massachusetts Bay, New Hampshire, Connecticut, and Rhode Island. When James became king of England a year later, he intended to investigate all the North American colonial governments with an eye toward dissolving the twelve provincial assemblies and awarding their authority to tax, legislate, and select judges to royally appointed governors and councils. James also promised the colonies religious toleration, which Protestant settlers feared was a convenient screen for Catholic missionary activity and implantation.

Certain that a union under absolute royal leadership was necessary, James II annulled the charters of Massachusetts Bay, New Hampshire, Connecticut, and Rhode Island. In 1687 James's own proprietary colonies of New York and New Jersey were attached to the enlarged Dominion of New England. Sir Edmund Andros, a devoted courtier, was named its governor. Massachusetts Bay became a sullen, embittered place. Its farmers, frontier dwellers, fishermen, and urban craftspersons joined Puritan leaders recently dismissed from the old colonial assembly to resist the Dominion. When Boston learned of James's supposed abdication early in 1689, the city exploded with joy. New Englanders proclaimed their solidarity with the Glorious Revolution, and Governor Andros was arrested and shipped back to England. William and Mary restored charters to Connecticut and Rhode Island. Massachusetts Bay conceded property rights rather than religion as the chief basis for suffrage, and accepted a new charter sanctioning both a Crown-appointed governor and representative assembly. Having displaced native American tribes from the eastern seaboard, by 1689 nearly a quarter million English-speaking settlers dwelt in semiautonomous, overwhelmingly Protestant colonial societies, united only in their determination to defend their distinctive ways of life.

North of New England, Acadia and New France formed a completely different world. Louis XIV had little interest in his unexplored Canadian possessions which in 1660 were occupied only by 2,000 non-Indians, mostly missionaries and trappers. However, Colbert saw a place for them within his mercantilist system. New France could supply fish and leather for West Indian sugar plantations, and the colonies could serve as dumping grounds for French manufactures. However, New France first would have to be settled. Despite Louis's avowed reluctance to encourage emigration, adventurous noblemen and military officers were attracted by the prospect of extending the seigneurial system to the New World; by 1680, Canada's French population had grown to 10,000. Although England's acquisition of New York in 1667 barred French advance southward along the St. Lawrence River, the expansionist vision of the royal intendant, Jean Talon (1665–1672), and then the military governor of New France, Louis de Buade de Frontenac (1672–1682), led to exploration and claims to tracts bordering the Great Lakes and the Mississippi. While the French alternated skillfully between coercion and negotiation in their dealings with native Americans, the English became hemmed in between the Atlantic and the Alleghenies. In 1682 the French explorer Robert Cavelier de la Salle reached the mouth of the Mississippi and claimed the lands on both banks in the name of his unappreciative king. In contrast to New England's compact network of farms, towns, and fishing villages, New France remained a long thin string of isolated fur trapping stations and villages running over 300 miles across the wilderness, from Trois Rivières and Montreal through Quebec to Hudson's Bay. The enormous Louisiana territory contained only a few fortified places. Wherever the French settled the land, a seigneurial class tried to oversee a peasant society and dominate relations with native Americans; the peasants in turn longed for the woods while the Indians resisted through diplomacy or force.

The War of the League of Augsburg (1689–1697) brought the English and French colonists into open conflict. New Englanders hoped to conquer Canada, and the French dreamed of a descent on Boston and New York; but neither side possessed sufficient troops and arms. At the Treaty of Ryswick the old boundaries remained intact, and the French still blocked the westward expansion of the English coastal colonies. Meanwhile, as the interdependence between colony and motherland continued to grow, William III and the Whigs looked on colonial political autonomy as skeptically as James II and the Lords of Trade had. Pressures once more mounted to abrogate the colonial charters. Before any policy decisions could be made, however, a new war in Europe extended to America. In 1711 an Anglo-American army left Boston to conquer New France but was shipwrecked in the St. Lawrence estuary. Campaigns took the form of murderous frontier raids and reprisals. Both sides made alliances with native Americans and exploited tribal rivalries. At the Peace of Utrecht in 1713, Louis XIV gave up Acadia and Newfoundland. Deeply French and Catholic, most of Acadia's 5,000 inhabitants now had to submit to English Protestant rule. However, the rest of Canada still was French, and French claims to the Mississippi Valley remained in full force.

By 1713 the white population of New France reached 19,000, but the demographic preponderance of the English colonies was overwhelming. Their population now had reached 400,000. They had always been uncompromisingly particularistic about their habits and institutions. New Englanders reveled in their universal literacy, dissenting Protestantism, vigorous town life, and local self-government. Unlike the slaveholding planter gentry of Virginia and the Carolinas, they had no desire to submit to England's economic needs or emulate the motherland's aristocratic style of politics. New York and New Jersey were too royalist for them, Maryland too Catholic, and Pennsylvania too Quaker. At the same time, throughout all of English North America tensions again were rising between the wealthy coastal settlers who controlled colonial assemblies and the unrepresented pioneers pushing toward the wilderness. For the moment the new Hanoverian dynasty in England promised to let matters rest. Nevertheless, the terrain was prepared for additional aggression against Indians, for political and commercial disagreements between the colonists and the homeland, for social and economic disagreements among the colonists themselves, and for renewed conflicts between French and English settlers.

Latin America

By 1648 European civilization in Florida, Mexico, and South America was nearly 150 years old. The lands in the New World claimed by Spain contained between 3 and 4 million people, nearly half the population of the motherland itself. Eighty percent of Spanish America's inhabitants were indigenous; the remainder were whites, Afro-Americans, and people of mixed racial stock. The Spanish colonies represented the most important transplantation of European culture anywhere in the world, and this repeopling already had produced the most devastating demographic holocaust in modern history. On the eve of colonization, Mexico and Peru had Indian populations of at least 35 million people. During the sixteenth century European epidemic diseases against which they had no immunity, deteriorating food supplies, unsuccessful rebellions against Spanish rule, and forced population movements had reduced the number of Indians by more than 90 percent. In the face of this unparalleled human catastrophe very little recovery was made during the succeeding four generations, and survivors were reduced to the status of tribute payers and labor suppliers for white ranchers and mine owners.

Although the original conquistadores had seen themselves as semifeudal overlords weakly bound to their king in Madrid, it was Spain's seventeenth-century misfortunes that loosened the motherland's grip on the New World. Interlopers successfully challenged Spain's trading monopoly, and the Spanish colonial administration governed by the Council of the Indies in Seville no longer was able to regulate Latin America's plantations, silver mines, and towns. Colonists perfected the arts of smuggling and tax evasion. Meanwhile seventeenth-century Mexico and Peru were themselves in deep economic crisis. Labor shortages were felt in agriculture, mining, and manufacturing. Food and silver production declined. Its own population stagnating, Spain was unable to supply the cheap labor demanded by America, and colonists resorted to importing West African slaves. Because the Spaniards had failed to develop African supply stations, the government leased out short-term monopolies to the highest bidder in human lives. At various times slave-merchant companies from Portugal, England, Genoa, and Holland held the supply contract, called the *asiento,* but smugglers from everywhere responded to Spanish America's desperate need for labor.

An American–born colonial aristocracy often infused with Indian blood, the Creoles filled the vacuum left by Spain. Though the viceroys of Mexico and Peru generally were drawn from Europe, town councils and municipal magistracies were packed with Creole officeholders. Supported by a wealthy and influential clergy, during the second half of the seventeenth century the Creoles established the pattern of life in colonial society. In Mexico its economic base originally had been the *encomienda,* a form of tribute and labor obligations paid by Indians working on cattle ranches and farms. However, as the labor shortage increased during the seventeenth century, the enormous landed estate, the hacienda, came to define the terms of working conditions. Tilled by wage-earning, debt-bonded, or enslaved laborers, Mexico's haciendas were put together by Creoles or were awarded to grandees who never left Spain. Important as it was in Mexico, in Peru silver mining was the motor force of the economy. High in the Andes, 16,000 feet above sea level, the silver metropolis of Potosí was the largest seventeenth-century city in the New World. In 1650 its population was 160,000, composed overwhelmingly of Indians who labored six days per week in the mines under appalling conditions. Although Potosí was a testament to European greed and corruption, during the seventeenth century its productive capacity was clearly in decline—4.7 million pesos in 1600, 2.9 million in 1650, and 1.3 million in 1700—and technology proved insufficient to halt its collapse. Remittances to Spain sank and transatlantic trade fell. Meanwhile, commerce flourished between the different parts of Spanish America and helped to stimulate the economic independence of the colonies.

Theoretically at least, Spanish America was built on racial foundations. For example, persons of mixed blood were supposed to be excluded from the universities and professions, and degrees of racial purity helped define social status. Often possessing some Indian ancestry, however, Creoles quite understandably had ambivalent feelings about race. Unlike their counterparts in British North America, Spanish colonial males had few qualms about sexual union with Indian women and had fathered generations of children of mixed blood. Moreover, Creole mythology established the Indian of the preconquest period as a dignified and aristocratic personage. With the arrival of African slaves a further element of racial and cultural blending was introduced. Therefore by the beginning of the eighteenth century Spanish

Americans had a clear sense of their distinctiveness with respect to the mother-land. They believed that their culture, architecture, learning, and piety easily equaled Spain's.

Even officeholding helped forge an American identity. Creoles liked to envision Mexico and Peru as semiautonomous realms with their own bureaucracies and governments, tied only by bonds of loyalty to the sovereign in Madrid. All government posts, except the top one of viceroy, were sold, and officeholders were businessmen out to maximize economic profit and political power from them. The traffic in offices was notorious. Court favorites obtained offices from the king and sold them to speculators, who in turn found Creole purchasers. The holders of offices associated with legal or political duties thus procured pieces of the king's authority. They would charge customers for services provided, and in this way large sums of money went into favor-creating enterprises that aggravated the exploitative character of life in the colonial world.

For forty of the years between 1648 and 1713, Spain was at war. Privateering off the Latin American coasts became more organized and periodically interrupted commerce. At the Peace of Utrecht the allies left Spanish America intact, with the English and Dutch preferring to cut through the paper monopoly of Spanish trade rather than assume the responsibilities of governing lands whose natural resources appeared to them to be exhausted. After 1700 Philip V sought to reform colonial institutions, and he did manage to slow down the sale of offices. He also planned to introduce French-style intendants to attack corruption, and he made genuine efforts at appointing qualified adminstrators to the highest colonial posts. Renewed measures were taken to protect the American coasts against smuggling. However, Creole society resisted any concerted attempt at re-strengthening the bonds between motherland and colony, and eighteenth-century Spain lacked the sustained vigor to force the issue.

Portugal also had a major interest in colonial America. In 1630 the Dutch had managed to seize control of Portuguese Brazil, but in 1654 Portuguese colonists there completed a successful nine-year revolt and restored the sprawling, barely explored colony to the motherland. The indigenous population always had been much smaller than that of Mexico or Peru, and European settlers maintained a coastal civilization built on a sugar-tobacco economy fed by regular infusions of slave labor from Portugal's African stations of Angola and Mozambique. By the mid-seventeenth century Brazil had become Europe's major supplier of sugar. Though more sparsely settled, Brazilian coastal society resembled that of Spanish America. Both were dominated by a landed aristocracy that was suspicious of the motherland and contemptuous of the lower orders. In the 1680s, however, Brazil experienced a boom that knew no parallel anywhere else in the colonial world and transformed it into a huge pioneer country. Not content with settling the coastal regions, Portuguese adventurers pushed deeply toward the west and south, where they cleared land for cattle raising and leather production.

However, gold was what wrote the longest chapter in Brazil's colonial history. As far back as the sixteenth century, handfuls of tough, lawless men searched the São Paulo plateau for precious metals. A few made strikes, but the majority either perished in the wilderness or returned to the sugar and tobacco plantations, where they became foremen and slave drivers. In the 1680s, however, hinterland strikes increased in frequency, immigrants and coastal inhabitants caught the fever, and they moved westward toward the Minas Gerais and Matto Grosso. Up to 30,000 gold seekers, dragging twice as many black slaves behind them, pushed on to the foothills of the Andes. Portugal took its percentage from the strikes and tried to tighten its control over the colony. Between the 1690s and 1715, it received as much gold from Brazil as Spain had received from all of its possessions in the previous 140 years. Gold was Portugal's milch cow. It created the Portuguese wine industry and helped pay for the armies that wore down Louis XIV. In Brazil's interior it forged a frontier world more individualistic and unruly than the stagnant, settled coast, and served as the magnet for subsequent waves of immigration.

The Caribbean

The deterioration of the Spanish navy opened the Caribbean to adventurers from all over Europe, and rival governments moved in for the spoils. With the near-total eradication of the indigenous populations on the Leeward islands of St. Christophe (St. Kitts), Martinique, and Guadeloupe, the French constructed a flourishing economy based on slavery and sugar. To prospective settlers the isles were far more attractive than Canada, and by 1650, 15,000 Frenchmen and 12,000 African slaves lived and worked there. In 1664 Colbert decided to regulate the immigration, economy, and political status of the French Antilles, and he sent a viceroy to establish order in the islands. A governor general and intendant established residences on Martinique, and the French West India Company was formed to monopolize trade.

When investment in the company proved inferior to expectations, in 1674 the islands were opened to all French vessels. Martinique and Guadeloupe were large and fertile. Sugar could be grown cheaply. Moreover, their location northeast of Caracas made them ideal way stations for smuggling goods into Spanish America. As the French Antilles became the focal point for privateering in the Caribbean, merchants and shippers from all of Europe urged their governments to exploit the region at Spain's expense. Between 1655 and 1670, England seized Jamaica, eastern Honduras, and the Bahamas. The Dutch held Caracas, the Danes settled the Virgin Islands, and the French captured Haiti. The European powers even devised ingenious means of dividing islands. For a time the French shared St. Christophe with the English and St. Martin with the Dutch.

As was the case nearly everywhere else, in the West Indies England proved to be France's chief rival. The Peace of Utrecht confirmed the English presence and guaranteed the *asiento* slave-supply monopoly to English merchants for thirty years. On the English islands themselves colonial legislatures controlled by white sugar-growing elites dominated politics, while the demands of the slave-laboring economy created a vibrant Afro-Caribbean culture. The white planters tried to imitate the aristocratic lifestyles of the English gentry, but lacked the commercial energy and literary culture of their compatriots back home—or, for that matter, of those on mainland North America. At least half were illiterate, and the thoroughly exploitative nature of a sugar-growing economy accentuated class distinctions between the great plantation owners and lesser ones, all of whom nevertheless owed their decadent existence to the labor of Africans brought against their will.

The Caribbean was the late seventeenth-century nerve center of the so-called Triangular Trade. Controlling West African port stations, the Dutch collected slaves for the West Indies. The slaves worked the plantations, which sent raw sugar and molasses to Europe's Atlantic ports. There the cargo was refined or converted into rum. The emptied ships then headed to West Africa for more slaves. Newfoundland cod fed the Afro-Americans, and cheap European cloth dressed them. The French isles had the best-developed commerce in sugar and slaves, though Dutch shippers derived the greatest profits from it. New England merchants defied the Navigation Acts by heading straight to Martinique for sugar and molasses. They willingly supplied the French planters there with fish, wheat, meat, tools, and timber.

Skillful at cutting production costs, the French planters passed on savings to whoever wanted their sugar. English merchants from Jamaica and Bermuda purchased raw sugar from the French and sold it illegally in London for less than the price asked by their own planters. Caught between high production costs and the loss of all their markets, English planters on Jamaica and Bermuda pleaded with Parliament to enforce commercial prohibitions between New England and the French Antilles. In the years following the Peace of Utrecht, they were instrumental in fomenting international tensions wholly out of proportion with their government's interests. Conflicts were provoked between Britain and Spain over their smuggling, then between Britain and France over their rivalries with French planters, and finally between Britain and the North American colonists over the latter's insistence on trading for the best price irrespective of the nationality of the partner.

AFRICA

To seventeenth-century Europeans there were three Africas. North of the Sahara lay the Africa of Islam. Its eastern fringe was Egypt, a province of the Ottoman Empire but in reality divided among semi-independent prefects whose civil wars kept the country in perpetual chaos and out of touch with the Mediterranean world. West of Egypt lay Tripoli, Tunis, and Algiers, technically Ottoman regions as well but in reality autonomous provinces under native governors called beys. Despising and fearing the coastal inhabitants, Europeans called this entire region Barbary. Under Barbary's flags, Turks, Arabs and renegade European Christians turned piracy into a major industry. So successful were they that they created the opulent city of Algiers, whose population in 1700 reached nearly 150,000. West of Algiers lay the sultanate of Morocco. Between 1672 and 1727, the sultan Moulai Ishmael created an empire that drove southeast to the Sudan. He developed Moroccan society, creating his capital, Meknes, into an African Versailles ringed with fortresses. Sudanese blacks formed the bulk of his 150,000-man army. Moulai Ishmael conceded two trading stations to the Spaniards and one apiece to the English and Portuguese. Periodically, he would skirmish with the Europeans in their enclaves; but above all he desired civilized relations with their governments. For European arms and munitions he exchanged African cloths, indigo, ivory, and dates. He suppressed piracy and fought Barbary's freebooters. He prided himself on running the only indigenous African state with regular diplomatic contacts with Europe.

South of the Sudan lay black Africa. For centuries nomadic Arab slave hunters had eaten deeply into the vitality of the central part of the continent. However, the gravest menace of all proved to be the European slavers. The Portuguese dream of a Catholicized black civilization stretching from the Cape Verde Islands to Angola sadly yielded to the incentive of profits in human flesh, and the Portuguese won the dubious distinction of being the first Europeans to transform black Africa into a reservoir for America's servile labor. To be fair, the influence of Europeans was not entirely negative. They did introduce Africans to crops transplanted from America, and two of them—maize and manioc—became invaluable supplements to the African diet. However, it was slavery, the traffic in human beings, that came to dominate Europe's economic relations with west-central Africa, and would continue to do so until the mid-nineteenth century. After 1600 the Dutch took over the slave trade along the Guinea coast, and after 1715 the French and English became the great European traffickers there. Promising rewards in rum and guns, the traders incited native chiefs against one another and bought prisoners of war. Europeans rarely penetrated beyond the coastal stations. In eastern Africa, Arab merchants displaced the Portuguese as the leading slave traders.

It is impossible to calculate the toll Africa had to pay for a forced emigration that could reach 100,000 per year and that in the eighteenth century averaged 75,000 people annually. Very likely its long–term social and economic impact was more pronounced in the regions where the Africans landed than in those they left behind. In all, perhaps 15 million Africans arrived in America against their will, and at least as many died somewhere en route. Those rounded up were often young men from defeated armies and young women with the best chances of procreating. The region that suffered the most severe loss was the coastal plain between the western border of modern Ghana and the eastern border of Nigeria.

Population loss because of the slave trade was not the sole cause of Africa's underdevelopment. In addition, two and a half centuries of warfare among rival rulers seeking European guns, liquor, tobacco, and shoddy consumer goods, and willing to exchange human beings for these articles, brutalized human relationships in west-central Africa. Traditional political practices in settling disputes gave way to European-style military solutions with their attendant atrocities. Formed to resist the Europeans, tribal confederations failed to hold together and were sucked into the ambitious rivalries of the whites. Moreover, rulers of the Ashanti, Oyo, Benin, and Dahomeyan kingdoms along the Gulf of Guinea regulated the interior trade and profited from slave sales, at least until they were themselves swept away by nineteenth-century forms of European imperialism based on partition. Once the slave trade came to an end, Europeans were able to redirect their investment practices in west-central Africa; however, having concentrated on a single export commodity for four centuries, Africans discovered that they had nothing more to offer.

On the entire continent the southern tip alone served as a base for European settlement in the seventeenth and eighteenth centuries. Since the days of da Gama, the Portuguese had stopped periodically along the Cape of Good Hope on their way to southern Asia. By 1600 Dutch, French, English, and Scandinavian ships were doing the same. In 1649 a Dutch crew forced to winter at Table Bay asked the East India Company in Amsterdam to occupy the region, and three years later the company sent eighty employees led by Jan van Riebeeck to build a fort and supply station for traveling vessels. Once released from their company contracts, some of Van Riebeeck's men obtained land and the title of "free burghers." In order to clear fields the Dutch landed slaves from Dahomey and Angola, and land was enclosed for cultivation. By 1680 more than 600 Dutch and German settlers had arrived.

Differing from the earliest immigrants who had built stately homes in Cape Town and became involved in trade and government, the second wave of Europeans was land hungry. Moreover, they were searching for a spiritual climate more receptive to their fundamentalist Calvinism than the tolerant Arminian Netherlands. In 1688 a boatload of Huguenot refugees from France joined them. Pushing into the interior, the pioneers broke with their European origins to a greater degree than did the English, French, and Iberians in seventeenth-century America. Sustained by religion, one group became settled farmers on properties averaging fewer than 200 acres. Another group comprised the "Trek Boers," or migrant farmers, who longed for the frontier. These people considered themselves a race apart, a new chosen people. Their initial tolerance of the black Africans gave way to powerful sentiments of racial superiority. They took slaves, encroached on pasturelands of the Africans, and forced tribal chiefs to submit to European overlordship and law. European diseases, particularly smallpox, further weakened African society. The whites took up cattle grazing on properties in excess of 6,000 acres. By 1715 they had pushed northward and eastward through the mountain passes, overwhelming Bushmen and Khoikhoi (Hottentots) to find good ranching country beyond the reach of the East India Company that administered the coastal station. By now the European population of South Africa had reached 3,000. At the close of the eighteenth century it would increase fivefold.

ASIA INSIDE EUROPE: THE OTTOMAN TURKS

An Unstable Political Culture

During the seventeenth century the Ottoman Turks were the only Asians to dominate significant numbers of Europeans. From its cosmopolitan capital of Istanbul, abutting on the Bosporus at its entrance into the Sea of Marmara, the empire stretched eastward toward vaguely defined boundaries along the Persian Gulf and south of the Caspian Sea, exerting hegemony over the entire Middle East and Anatolia, laying claim to Egypt, and calling the North African Barbary States vassals. The Turks considered the eastern Mediterranean, Black Sea, Red Sea, and west Caspian as their waters. The heartland of the empire was in the Balkans, where Ottoman rule extended over Christian Greeks, South Slavs, Croats, Slovenes, and Magyars. The height of Ottoman power had been the sixteenth century. Yet early in the 1680s one final lunge extended its northwest frontier a bare 80 miles from Vienna, and in 1683 the Turks besieged the Hapsburg capital itself. The peoples subject to the Ottomans numbered from 25 to 30 million, belonging to assorted cultures and nations that grudgingly submitted to a tribute-collecting army of occupation, grasping governors, and provincial chiefs. The Turks could offer their subjects neither a moral nor legal justification for empire. The only reason for conquest was the extension of Islam, and even here the Turks no longer forced the issue.

Lacking a priesthood, the Ottoman Empire could not be called a theocracy in the western sense. Nevertheless, Islam permeated all Turkish institutions. The fundamental reference for settling legal and administrative questions was the Koran, and the sultan's decrees were based on his reading of Islam's holy book. Because they were also descended from Abraham, Christians and Jews were tolerated, though they had fewer rights and responsibilities than Moslems. They might participate in government, largely because the older Turkish aristocracy now revealed less aptitude for administration than it had during the sixteenth-century Golden Age. Expelled Spanish Jews and Moriscos proved a boon to the Ottomans, providing them with artisans, merchants, administrators, physicians, and sailors.

The appeal of the warrior state to European talent is a thread running through Turkish history.

The empire was built on regional self-sufficiency and the tribute of subject peoples. During Europe's sixteenth-century expansion, wheat, wool, copper, and precious metals from Turkish-controlled lands were exported to the West, creating scarcities and lost tax revenues that grievously affected the Ottomans several generations later. In addition, because the empire thrived on conquest, peace glutted Istanbul with bored troops and provided opportunities for intrigue, political murder, and revolt. Provincial military officers, *sipahis,* tried to control hundreds of clients and their men. The Balkans replenished the army every generation. During five-year intervals up to 15,000 able-bodied Christian boys were taken from their parents and reared in special camps as Moslems. They were granted legal and social privileges and taught an esprit de corps. They formed the sultan's elite guard, the Janissaries, 200,000 strong. In the seventeenth century, however, far from being the bedrock of the sultan's power, the Janissaries were the most dangerous element in the state. If the sultan was unable to pay their wages regularly, which became common, their discipline grew lax, and they became a restless force for sale to the highest bidder.

Combined with the liberty of each sultan to interpret the Koran according to his own political ends, the lack of binding constitutional principles and legal understandings between ruler and subject made the Ottoman state seem like a hopeless tyranny to Europeans. Moreover, in the seventeenth century political factionalism became particularly virulent. Since there was no rule of succession, relatives of the reigning sultan built their constituencies at court and in the harem and outbid one another for Janissary support. Government degenerated into a welter of intrigue and instability, which had serious consequences for the empire. In the Balkans, Transylvania, and Moldavia, Christian subjects edged toward autonomy under native chiefs; on the eastern frontier the Persians gained control over most of Iraq. In the 1630s an energetic sultan, Murat IV, temporarily regained command of the state through a program of terror. After 150 years of warfare he forced the Persians to make peace. The Ottomans recovered Iraq and the route to the Persian Gulf. On Murat's death in 1640, however, anarchy renewed itself. In 1648 unpaid Janissaries deposed and murdered his successor, Sultan Ibrahim.

Revival, Defeat, and Transformation

A six-year-old child, Mehmet IV (1648–1687), was placed on the throne and for his safety was locked in his late father's harem. For the next eight years the empire reached the nadir of its fortunes. Thirteen grand *vezirs,* roughly equivalent to prime ministers and titular army commanders, rose and fell. Bread riots were endemic in Istanbul, revolts broke out in Anatolia and the Balkans, a war with Venice went very badly, *sipahis* became petty tyrants in the provinces, and sectarian dervishes stirred up religious passions and social unrest. Finally, early in 1656 a seventy-nine-year-old former *sipahi* and tax official, Mehmet Köprülü (1583–1661), now living in retirement in Albania, was appointed grand *vezir*. Technically the sultan's slave, Köprülü took advantage of the political crisis to demand total administrative power. The adolescent sultan Mehmet IV agreed to stand by him. Sick of the murderous instability of recent years, Janissary officers did also. Köprülü pitilessly purged government councils and eliminated all potential opposition. He restored Transylvania to Ottoman suzerainty, chased the Venetians from the Dardanelles, and put down a revolt in Anatolia—shipping back to Istanbul the severed heads of 12,000 suspected rebels. Köprülü's methods were completely ruthless, but they saved the state. In 1661 the old man died, and his twenty-six-year-old son succeeded him as grand *vezir*.

Fazil Ahmed Köprülü (1635–1676) was an urbane, cultivated statesman and gifted military commander. He would serve as grand *vezir* for fifteen years, restoring order in the army and temporarily reestablishing imperial control under his guidance. He attained his aims through political skill rather than terror and shored up Ottoman control at the expense of his European enemies. He fought the Hapsburgs in the Balkans, solidifying Turkish power in Hungary and Transylvania; he took Podolya from Poland and established suzerainty over the Ukraine; and he skirmished with the Russians. Buoyed by success, Fazil Ahmed set his sights on the habitual and elusive goal of the Ottomans, Vienna itself. Its conquest, he judged, would shatter the Hapsburgs and ensure Turkish control of the Balkans and Hungary for generations to come.

While preparing his campaign, however, Fazil Ahmed died. In 1676 his brother-in-law Kara Mustafa replaced him as grand *vezir*. Kara Mustafa preserved the idea of a renewed offensive toward Vienna, and the great Magyar rebellion against the Hapsburgs provided him with the opportunity. Conspiring with Hungarian chiefs who preferred loose Ottoman suzerainty to tight Hapsburg control and encouraged by Louis XIV's assurances that the Austrians could not fight a two-front war, Kara Mustafa gathered together a magnificent cavalcade of 200,000 and in July 1683 reached the outer walls of Vienna. Instead of storming the city, the grand *vezir* adopted the strategy of a deliberate siege. The Hapsburgs gained a respite, and Emperor Leopold pleaded with the princes of Christendom to save his capital from the infidel. A relief force of Bavarians, Saxons, and Poles reached the Danube early in September. On September 12 the Christian army swept into Kara Mustafa's camp and scattered the besiegers, softened by two months of inactivity. Abandoning tents of silk, treasures of gold, and thousands of slaves, the Turks fled in panic. In November at Gran the Christian allies smashed through the Ottoman defenses, and the twin defeats became the worst military catastrophes in Turkish history. For the disgrace Kara Mustafa was strangled.

This time, however, no change in leadership was able to renew the empire. Louis XIV made peace on the western front, freeing up Hapsburg forces for Balkan service. Moving to the offensive, the Austrians captured Buda in 1686 and smashed the Ottomans at Mohàcs, where Hungary had lost its independence a century and a half earlier. Istanbul was in panic, and Mehmet IV was deposed. Although the Ottomans staged one of their amazing military counteroffensives, reestablishing their defense line on the Danube, recovery proved short-lived. In 1696 Peter the Great took the port of Azov, and a year later the Hapsburg commander Eugene of Savoy destroyed the Turkish army at Zenta. For the first time in their history the Turks sued for peace (Karlowitz, 1699). The terms were disastrous. The Ottomans acknowledged the loss to the Hapsburgs of Transylvania, nearly all of Hungary, and parts of Slovenia and Croatia. The Venetians took Dalmatia, the Morea, and the Aegina. Poland retook Podolya; the Ukraine was lost. In 1702 the Ottomans signed away Azov to the Russians. No longer were the Turks a menace to Europe. They were on the defensive, and their empire was clearly disintegrating. Although the Ottomans' surprising victory against Peter the Great on the Pruth River (1711) temporarily halted Russia's foray through the eastern Balkans, the Austrian advance was inexorable. In 1718 the Hapsburgs took control of all of Hungary and a substantial part of Serbia, including the Ottomans' west-Balkan capital of Belgrade (Treaty of Passarowitz).

Battlefield defeat not only shrank the Ottoman Empire, but it also changed its character. Janissaries came to prefer shopkeeping and petty trades to war, and the military vitality of the state was sapped. In the European provinces still under Ottoman control wealthy Greek Christians and *sipahis* rivaled one another for tribute-collecting rights over sullen populations. A new generation of Ottoman *vezirs* broke with centuries of diplomatic isolation and for the first time sent ambassadors to Europe. In place of leading armies through the Balkans the sultan and his court retired to Istanbul and Adrianople, where they indulged in extravagant dances, concerts, and Chinese shadow plays or else took their martial glory vicariously by cheering on favorite participants in mock sea battles fought in the Dardanelles.

Above all, humbled by military defeat, the empire opened up to the West. French-inspired palaces arose around Istanbul, filled with statuary, parks, and fountains. A mania for tulip cultivation and an appreciation of nature captivated the upper classes. Coffeehouses and cafés became social centers for the people. European furniture, clothing, decorative arts, and printing presses were imported, and for their part European writers, artists, and composers developed a curiosity about the nonmilitary aspects of Ottoman life. For the Hapsburg and Russian regimes, however, policies of liberating the Balkans submerged all interest in Turkish culture. Emperor and tsar urged Greeks and South Slavs to throw off three centuries of infidel rule. Meanwhile the Turks' defensive posture hardened and its

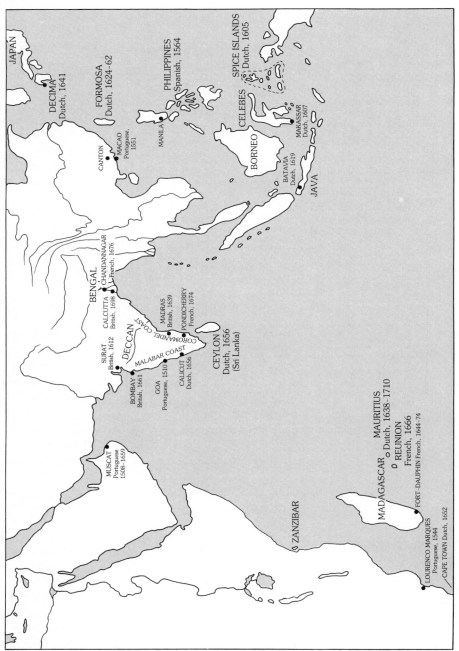

JAPAN

DECIMA
Dutch, 1641

FORMOSA
Dutch, 1624–62

PHILIPPINES
Spanish, 1564

SPICE ISLANDS
Dutch, 1605

CELEBES

CANTON

MACAO
Portuguese,
1551

MANILA

MAKASSAR
Dutch, 1607

BORNEO

BATAVIA
Dutch, 1619

JAVA

BENGAL

CHANDANNAGAR
French, 1676

CALCUTTA
British, 1698

MADRAS
British, 1639

PONDICHERRY
French, 1674

DECCAN

COROMANDEL COAST

SURAT
British, 1612

CEYLON
Dutch, 1656
(Sri Lanka)

BOMBAY
British, 1661

MALABAR COAST

GOA
Portuguese, 1510

CALICUT
Dutch, 1656

MUSCAT
Portuguese
1508–1659

MAURITIUS
Dutch, 1638–1710

REUNION
French, 1666

MADAGASCAR

FORT-DAUPHIN French, 1644–74

ZANZIBAR

LOURENCO MARQUES
Portuguese, 1544

CAPE TOWN Dutch, 1652

Map 5.2—European Colonies and Trade Centers in Asia

central government weakened. By the time of the French Revolution, Europe's ancient terror was a generation away from becoming its sick man.

EUROPE AND THE ORIENT

Dark fortresses in the Canadian wilderness, sprawling sugar plantations in the Haitian countryside, tidy farms in the Transvaal, and massive silver mines on the heights of Potosí—these characterized the triumph of European arms over nature and non-Europeans. The pace of conquest varied, yet it was an inexorable process that would assume full force in the eighteenth and nineteenth centuries. The indigenous peoples of America and black Africa were the earliest and most important victims of the tide; on the other hand, even though Europeans gained commercial preeminence in Asia, civilizations there discouraged colonization and resisted evangelization.

India and Indonesia

Initially, it appeared that India would offer an opening. During the second half of the seventeenth century the Mughal Empire reached its greatest point of expansion, but at the same time it weakened itself irreparably beneath the pressures of religious and ethnic strife. Following a bloody succession crisis resulting in the imprisonment of his father and deaths of three brothers and a son, Shah Alamgir (born Aurangzeb) (1658–1707) seized the throne as Great Mughal. Alamgir was a fanatical Sunni Moslem, whose persecution of non-Moslem vassals resulted in revolts among the Sikh, Rajput, and Maratha peoples of India; for the last twenty-five years of Alamgir's reign civil war wracked his empire. Had he known the scale of Alamgir's campaigns, his contemporary Louis XIV would have been dumbfounded. They easily cost 100,000 lives per year. Alamgir's tent cities surrounding his battlefields measured 30 miles in circumference, and were serviced by half a million camp followers. Fifty thousand camels and 30,000 elephants were used in battle. Worst of all, the war costs in grain, silver, and accompanying plagues were astronomical. When Alamgir died near ninety, remorseful and penitent, he left an exhausted empire. Moreover, the Marathas were not beaten and they controlled central India's Deccan plateau. In the northwest Sikhs and Rajputs renewed the fight against Moslem domination.

Alamgir's costly struggles in the name of religious fanaticism invited exploitation of the divisions in his empire. By 1700 there was no shortage of Europeans prepared to attempt just that. More than two hundred years earlier the Portuguese captain Vasco da Gama had sailed his two surviving vessels into Calicut harbor, and during the sixteenth century Portugal obtained commercial concessions and the right to establish trading stations along the coast of the subcontinent. Spices brought enormous wealth to Portugal's kings. With the incorporation of Portugal into Philip II's Spanish empire in 1580, Spain's enemies began encroaching on its Asian trade. The Dutch and English were the most active assailants, their East India companies fighting the Spaniards, Jesuit missionaries, and each other. The English built "factories" at Surat, the Mughal's principal port, then at Bombay, and finally at the village of Madras. Meanwhile the Dutch sent south-Indian slaves and cotton cloth to their Spice Island plantations. By the 1670s all that remained of da Gama's heritage were the outposts of Goa and Diu on the Indian Ocean, with their distinct Indian-Catholic-Portuguese culture.

Taking advantage of the west-European craze for brightly colored light textiles, the English successfully exported Indian calicoes to Europe. Actually their operation on the subcontinent existed by default, as an answer to Dutch development of spice plantations on the Moluccan archipelago and in Indonesia. Following several years of inconclusive skirmishes with Shah Alamgir, in 1690 the English East India Company was awarded a privilege to found a new base upriver from the Bay of Bengal. This was Calcutta. Ten years later its English population numbered 1,200. European settlement was urban and wholly dependent upon trade. Merchants lived communally, the warehouse serving as focal point of their existence. They married Indian women, particularly Goans, wore Indian clothes, and enjoyed Indian food. Absorbing the material aspects of Indian culture, they took more than they gave, exporting textiles and introducing the pajama to Europe. Occasionally European artillerymen, architects, and physicians arrived to serve the Indian aristocracy. The French followed the English, their East India Company forming an arm of Colbert's overseas colonial policy. Each firm had a resident governor general, and each was expansionist. The French established trading stations at Pondicherry, just below Madras, and at Chandannagar in the Bengal.

The weakening of the Mughal empire drew the French and English into the web of Indian politics. As south India broke free and the Marathas caused trouble in the Deccan, emerging Persia threatened Mughal control of the north. In their seaport settlements Europeans sided with Indian factions and constructed forts to protect their trade lanes. In defense of Bombay, the English fought pitched battles against the Marathas. They coined money, raised Indian troops, and made treaties. Between 1689 and 1713 Europe's wars reached India, forcing the rival commercial companies to pursue native allies aggressively, and peace in Europe did not necessarily extend to India. Either as employees or as soldiers of their respective companies, adventurers arrived, their individual greed feeding traditional national rivalries. The French were the most aggressive. While the Persians sacked the Mughal capital of Delhi in 1740, Benoît Dumas, governor of the French East India Company, was forging alliances with the Great Mughal's vassals, creating battalions of Hindu troops, enjoying the title of nabob, and extending French influence from Bengal to the gates of Bombay. The colonial

Figure 5.1—Illustration by Wenceslaus Hollar in J. Nieuhoff, An Embassy Sent by the East India Company of the United Provinces to the Grand Tartar Cham [Khan], or Emperor of China Delivered at Pekin by Peter de Goyer and Jacob de Keyzer in 1655. *(1673). Temporarily holding a trading post on the island of Taiwan, Dutch East India merchants desired commercial ties with the Manchu conquerors of China. This title page engraving portrays the young Manchu emperor Shunzhi as a fearsome world conqueror, heir to Ghengiz Khan. Under the subsequent reign of Kangxi, for Europeans the warrior image of the emperor gave way to a philosophical one. The Great Khan was transformed into the Oriental sage.*

population of Pondicherry grew to 50,000. French seizure of the islands of Mauritius and Bourbon in the Indian Ocean provided way stations to the subcontinent's ports. To the English this no longer appeared to be commercial competition but rather a French bid to succeed Mughal rule, and they determined to resist it.

Nothing comparable to the Mughal empire faced the first Dutch merchants in Indonesia early in the seventeenth century. The small Moslem sultanates that had thrived on the localized spice trade wanted no more than commercial dealings with the Dutch. With the establishment of their East India Company in 1621, the Dutch began purchasing plantations. They exchanged Indonesian silks, spices, and pepper for Persian coffee, Indian cottons, and Chinese porcelains. Then they sent all these products to Europe. By the 1680s most of Indonesia's sultans were Dutch vassals, retaining internal sovereignty and enjoying the Europeans' "protection" in return for yielding a monopoly over stipulated exports. The Hollanders made no secret of their aim of pure economic exploitation. After a generation of contact and even intermarriage with the natives, the company's planters and merchants sealed themselves off from Indonesian society. Lacking the manpower to exercise total control over sources of production, the Dutch concentrated on carrying and selling goods. Until the mid-eighteenth century, their East India Company dominated Asia's carrying trade from Sri Lanka to Japan, and it controlled shipments to Europe of Indonesian pepper, nutmeg, and cinnamon. As in the Baltic and Atlantic, the Dutch role in the Far East was to ship products, particularly the products of others.

China

While the late seventeenth-century Europeans in India faced a declining empire, those who penetrated China found one on the ascendancy. In 1644 the Ming dynasty had succumbed to a recently formed confederation of invading northern tribes, the Manchus. The Ming emperor and most of his court committed suicide; in 1662, the year following Louis XIV's accession to absolute rule in France, an eight-year-old Manchu prince, Kangxi (1662–1722), became emperor of China. His impact on eastern Asia proved at least as great as the Sun King's on western Europe. During his sixty-year reign, Kangxi eradicated the vestiges of Ming resistance, wiped out a serious rebellion in south China, conquered Taiwan, and successfully wooed Chinese intellectuals through his respect for Confucian principles. Like Louis XIV, he subsidized classical forms of literature and learning. Pacifying the tribes of central Asia, he set the stage for the greatest territorial advance in China's history, which by the mid-eighteenth century reached the borders of India and turned southeast Asia from Burma to Vietnam into tribute-bearing states.

Under Kangxi, Manchu China entered its golden age. The state was reconstituted along military lines. Ming aristocrats lost their privileges,

Manchu army officers doubled as government officials, and Manchu soldiers took over the best lands. The conquering minority attempted to maintain its own racial and cultural distinctiveness. Its members were exempt from taxation. They kept their own language, dress, marital customs, and religious practices; they were prohibited from marrying Chinese women. On the other hand, for the Chinese the Manchu conquest was a rude shock. Thousands of bureaucrats chose suicide; others participated in fruitless guerrilla warfare. The Chinese peasantry probably welcomed the new regime. Out of the social turmoil of the 1640s emerged free tenancies and even independent peasant ownership. The Manchus preserved certain traditional Chinese institutions if they might be useful to the state—the civil service examination system or orthodox Confucianism, for example. Kangxi himself remained true to his warrior origins and spent several months each year at the head of his troops. His proudest accomplishment remained the taming of Mongolia. He was sincerely interested in both Buddhism and Christianity and took European Jesuits as advisers. It was this tolerant, cultivated side of the emperor that captured the imagination of eighteenth-century Europe, which envisioned him as the archetypal Oriental sage, a philosopher-king.

Manchu China was open to Europeans, but it also had the power to resist them. The Portuguese were permitted a trading outpost in the port city of Macao, but the Dutch had to abandon Taiwan during the Manchu conquest of the island. Russia was the only European state with which China had regular diplomatic contact. Inconclusive border skirmishes gave way to the Treaty of Nerchinsk in 1689, which maintained the caravan route from Moscow to Peking and defines China's northern frontier to this day. After 1702 the English, French, and Dutch began carrying Chinese tea to Europe. Though the Dutch had been transporting porcelain, lacquer ware, silks, and plants to Europe for several generations, a seemingly insurmountable problem inhibited the establishment of genuinely great commercial ventures with China. Except for gold and silver, the Manchus wanted few things that Europe could offer. Until the English East India Company was able to dump Indian cottons and opium into China, the great tea trade remained in its infancy, emerging only at the end of the eighteenth century.

Japan and the Philippines

Just as China slowly opened, Japan rudely closed. The emperor resided in the royal city of Kyoto, and his mayor of the palace, the shogun, oversaw the Council of State, ministers, and provincial governors. Until the middle of the sixteenth century, great landowners aided by their military retainers, the samurai, ran Japan. Civil war was endemic. The Japanese aristocracy had just finished another cycle in 1603, when Tokugawa Ieyasu became shogun. He forced the surviving landlords to assume government posts and spend every second year at the administrative capital, Yedo (Tokyo). All the landholders in Japan, including the powerful Buddhist orders, saw the reins of state service tightened around them. As the Tokugawas froze the social life of the state, defining specific roles for samurai, nobles, merchants, and peasants, they moved to save Japan from foreign contamination. In 1638 Japanese were prohibited from leaving the country, except by specific dispensation. European merchants and missionaries were expelled. Only a few Dutch, clustered together on a tiny island in Nagasaki harbor, where they could have no contact with the population, were allowed to remain. Japanese Christianity, which had 300,000 converts at the beginning of the seventeenth century, was suppressed. Martyrdoms reached 40,000, perhaps the most ruthless persecution ever committed against a Christian community. Meanwhile, only a few Dutch ships exchanged Japanese copper for Indian textiles and Indonesian spices. Until Commodore Perry boldly sailed into Nagasaki harbor in 1853, the West showed little interest in a nation that feared and scorned it.

In the Philippines, where sixteenth-century Spaniards had discovered a less sophisticated culture than what they found in India or China, around 1,200 Europeans settled in. By the 1620s, two generations after their arrival, the Spaniards had Catholicized 2 million Filipinos. They superimposed a centralized administration on the islands but handed local power over the populace to Europeans or Filipino elites who were assigned huge estates according to the *encomienda* system. The estate owner collected tribute and taxes, paid wages at his discretion, and controlled local justice. The Spaniards wished to exploit the Philippines as a commercial link between the Orient and Latin America. Each year a single galleon legally crossed the Pacific for Mexico laden with Ceylon tea, Indonesian spices, Chinese silks, and Siamese teak. Merchants in Manila served as middlemen, distributing Asian textiles for American use. The Dutch tried to involve themselves in this transport as well, but Chinese insistence on American silver in exchange for their textiles was a limiting factor. The Spanish government opposed the drain of precious metal toward Asia, but colonists in Manila and America wanted it extended, and an extraordinary contraband trade, valued at 10 million pesos annually, submerged the transport of the single legal galleon. Therefore, until the American veins were exhausted, the colonials prevailed over the homeland's interests. The only Asian country where Europe's religion gained more than a tenuous foothold, the Philippines experienced an exploitation of the land that resembled the Latin American plantation, and the colony served as a commercial link between the world's oldest civilization and its youngest.

THE MISSIONS

In the New World

During the sixteenth century Portuguese missionaries had evangelized successfully in America and Asia. On the other hand, in black Africa the zeal to win souls soon was overwhelmed by the lust to chain bodies, and the slave trader superseded the efforts of priests. In the New World, the earliest Portuguese and Jesuit missionaries tried to defend Indian converts from exploitation by plantation owners, ranchers, and mining bosses. However, the great influx of Africans into Latin America made evangelization both more important and more difficult. To slave masters, lessons on the equality of souls before God smacked of subversion, and the missions worked out a compromise with social realities. Declared incapable of sustaining themselves physically, Africans were said to need masters who would treat them with firm paternal benevolence, while nourishing and clothing them adequately. They were to be baptized and taught the elementary rudiments of Christian faith.

Uncomfortable with their accommodation of black slavery, missionaries in the New World worked hard to prevent the indigenous populations from falling into the same dismal social category as the unfortunate Africans. Beginning in the 1520s, Franciscans and Dominicans established parishes for Indians in Mexico and Peru. In 1610 Jesuits constructed a refuge for them—self–contained and self–supporting communities—in Paraguay, where European colonists could not enter without permission of the governing Fathers. Most white immigrants considered the missionaries as meddlers, needlessly complicating social and economic relations that of necessity were based on separatism and inequality. The Catholic episcopal hierarchy in the New World often shared the position of the settlers. Nevertheless, the Jesuit missions in Latin America kept the spark of conscience flickering in a society dependent upon servile labor.

North of Mexico, Europeans generally displayed less humanitarianism toward native Americans than did the Jesuits of Paraguay. Considering Indian religions as the source of savagery, initially Catholic friars and Protestant pastors alike linked conversion with their so-called civilizing mission. For their part, with diametrically opposed views of the world, nature, and immortality, Indians treated Christian ritual and theology with incomprehension or contempt. As an example, the Pueblos of the southwest conceived of their land as a communally controlled environment whose nature spirits commanded duties and provided rewards of prosperity and harmony. Then Spanish priests informed the Pueblos that the same land had been created by a remote deity and belonged to a far-off human king who demanded tribute. Pueblo religious leaders challenged the Spaniards, and proceeded to ridicule baptism, Catholic processions, and the mortification of the flesh. They blamed drought on neglect of traditional Pueblo ceremonies. The Spaniards responded with force. In 1675 their royal governor suppressed Pueblo traditions and executed medicine men. The Indians retaliated by burning churches, and those who had been baptized plunged into rivers to wash away the Christian taint. Around 1700 Spanish Franciscans occasionally adopted a less brutal formula than their predecessors, mixing religious instruction with lessons in European agriculture. In Florida and Georgia, though most notably not in California, they employed utilitarian measures as opposed to pure physical and psychological coercion.

Encountering the belief systems of the Algonquian and Iroquois nations of eastern Canada, French Jesuits in New France operated differently from the Spaniards of the Southwest. Intelligent and well educated, the French Fathers appreciated the sophistication of Indian religion and looked for points of correspondence between it and Catholic doctrines. Meanwhile, in the rough frontier society of woodsmen, fur trappers, and traders—where theological subleties had little place—Indian belief systems penetrated deeply. Even the inhabitants of the more Europeanized towns and villages of Quebec might learn to tolerate native American religion without understanding it. In Calvinist New England, however, such acceptance was considered ungodly weakness. Certain that they were building a New Jerusalem and possessing a Bible-centered preaching tradition, the Puritans might sympathize with native American habits of divine respect and gratitude; however, the objects of Indian devotion—dozens of spiritual forces called *manitous,* located in the sky, wind, corn, and people— appeared to the English as idolatrous. To them Indian medicine men who cured the sick and interpreted dreams were charlatans. Worse, people who painted their faces in joy or mourning, who celebrated festivals by dancing and throwing their possessions into the fire, who treated the land not as a source of goods but as a sacred space, and who changed dwelling according to whim or the season, were not easily understood by sober, acquisitive, sedentary English Protestants.

Therefore, the Puritans denounced American Indian religion as readily as they had repudiated the rites and habits of European Catholicism or Anglicanism. The Puritans possessed no storehouse of images, feast days, and music which the friars had used to tease the emotions of potential Catholics. All the English possessed was the Word, and at that, they were reluctant about translating it into Indian languages. In fact, English Puritans and Anglicans alike seemed less interested than Jesuits and Franciscans in converting the Indians at all. When they did make the effort, they insisted that the Indians abandon their culture. In place of the rich symbolic and communal life they had left behind, Indians were to settle in English-style towns, dress like Europeans, and learn how to pray.

Ultimately religious incomprehension combined with European land hunger to produce armed conflict. In 1675 the Wampanoag chief Metacom forged an alliance with other tribes and attacked farms and villages throughout New England. The devastating two-year struggle, called King Philip's War, cost 5 percent of the adult white population of Massachusetts and Rhode Island; the Indians lost 30 percent of their people. At best tension, at worst warfare, now dictated relations between Protestant Europeans and the native peoples of eastern North America. As shattered tribes retreated westward—pursued by white settlers and fur traders alike —European disease, social custom, economic habits, and alcohol took their toll of Indian cultural autonomy, and the dream of Christian conversion, however misguided, was relegated to the far background.

The Jesuits in Asia

In Asia, where the missions often encountered highly developed religious codes, the initial successes of the Portuguese and Jesuits were gratifying. By 1600 there were 300,000 Christian converts in Japan, an equal number in India, and a million and a half in the Philippines. China appeared ready for evangelization. Asians often had social or political reasons of their own for converting. For example, in India, Christianity was attractive to low-caste women who wished to marry Portuguese. In Japan the Westerners' religion won over landowners and samurai who wished to illustrate their independence of the shogun or Buddhist monks.

During the seventeenth century the Jesuits were responsible for Catholicism's Oriental mission, and Protestantism made virtually no impact. The Jesuits considered the missionary techniques of their predecessors to be superficial. They insisted that converts learn the roots of basic doctrine; but as in Canada they also adapted doctrine to accommodate native habits, customs, and traditions. Rome praised the attempt to make new Catholics comprehend as well as believe, and initially the papacy showed itself remarkably tolerant of Jesuit respect for Asian cultures. By 1700, however, philosophies of evangelization that called for the converts' total submission to orthodox doctrine challenged Jesuit methods. Stemming from Saints Paul and Augustine, these Dominican ideas represented a purer approach to winning souls than that employed by the Jesuit Fathers. But they also cost the Church Asia.

In India the basic difficulties concerned the caste system and native beliefs in pantheism. During the first half of the seventeenth century, an Italian Jesuit, Father Roberto di Nobili (1577–1656), insisted that Christianity's future in India depended upon its penetration of Hinduism. Therefore, Nobili tolerated the caste structure and began preaching to members of the highest one, the Brahmins. An aristocrat from Rome, Nobili adopted the dress and habits of a holy man living in prayer and penitence. He resided in a rude hut, lived on vegetables and water, and passed his days in contemplation. He learned Indian dialects and read Indian poetry. Brahmins visited Nobili and admitted him to their caste. He translated the Psalms into Tamil. Claiming that he had brought a fifth Veda that complemented the four books of Hindu teaching, Nobili baptized Brahmins. When he discovered a Hindu rite that even he could not accommodate to his syncretic Christianity, he called it a political or social custom. Conscious of his rank in Indian society, Nobili kept his distance from native inferiors. He proferred them Communion on the end of a long stick or left the wafer at their door.

Nobili's techniques illustrated all the dilemmas Christianity would have to face in the mature civilizations of the Orient. His mission on the Malabar coast won 100,000 converts, but other priests denounced him as a secret Hindu. Asked for an opinion several times, the papacy approved

Nobili's methods but in 1645 and 1649 noted the incompatibility between Christianity and the caste system. Nevertheless, Nobili's disciples followed in his footsteps, and by 1700 nearly a million Indians had accepted Catholicism. In Rome, however, a mood was developing against the Jesuit missions. Based on Dominican jealousies and opposed to the practice of religious syncretism, it stressed the need for pure and total conversions. Reporting on the missions in India and China, in 1704 a papal legate, Charles Maillard de Tournon, recommended condemnation of the Jesuits' so-called Malabar rites, calling them contrary to Catholic orthodoxy. With a million souls at stake, Rome fell short of invalidating the conversions already made. In 1745, however, Pope Benedict XIV formally declared the hostility of the Catholic Church to caste distinctions and Hindu customs. New conversions ceased, and old converts returned to the ancestral faiths.

The hostility of the Japanese Tokugawa ruling house to both Buddhism and Christianity was political. Christianized landlords and Buddhist monks had opposed the growth of the centralized state, and the shoguns persecuted their enemies ruthlessly. Officially proscribed and amply supplied with martyrs, Japanese Christianity went underground. By way of contrast, seventeenth-century China opened the gates to evangelization. In their commercial enclave at Macao, the Portuguese had made a few thousand converts. Ingeniously accommodating Catholicism with Chinese customs and beliefs, however, it was the Jesuits who made the greatest progress. Their skill in medicine, mathematics, and astronomy gave them access to the imperial court, where they became privileged subjects.

As early as 1600 a pair of Italian Jesuits had introduced the Ming aristocracy to a Christianity that gave highest priority to principles of divine justice and divine reason. Their immediate successors imitated these displays of outward respect for Chinese civilization, donned the costume of the scholar aristocracy, kneeled during audiences with officials, spoke humbly of themselves, and addressed their hosts with accepted forms of exaggerated praise. The Jesuits tolerated ancestor worship as a practice intended to teach respect for one's heritage, particularly useful in maintaining the social order; they even tried to accommodate nature worship with Christian principles. High Ming officials converted to Christianity. Following their conquest and a brief period of official hostility, the Manchus welcomed the Westerners. Father Adam Schall (1591–1666), superior of the mission to China, was named mandarin of the first class and was appointed chief of the imperial department of astronomy, an important post in a country where astrology was a passion.

Ingratiating themselves at the court of Emperor Kangxi, the Jesuits also went out into the country. They built churches and by 1670 had won 300,000 converts. They served the emperor as military engineers, artillery experts, and diplomats. They helped negotiate the Treaty of Nerchinsk with the Russians. In 1692 a French Jesuit used quinine to cure Kangxi of a severe illness, and in gratitude the emperor officially proclaimed the liberty of public Christian worship throughout China. The Jesuits had reason to hope that they were forging an Oriental Constantine.

Not only did the Jesuits bring Christianity to China, but they also brought China to Europe. In doing so, they impelled an intellectual mutation that had been taking root since the Thirty Years' War. To the troubled European society of the late seventeenth century, the Jesuit image of a near utopian civilization governed by moral sages uncorrupted by intolerance, passion, or material desire, offered a refreshing contrast. Kangxi was viewed as a philosopher-king whose sense of justice and virtue made Leopold I or Louis XIV seem like moral pygmies. Europe swallowed fact and fancy about China. For the first time, a significant body of Western intellectuals cast doubts on the ethical superiority of their own civilization. Paradoxically enough, this was occurring at the moment when the very same thinkers were producing rational explanations about the physical universe that Eastern sages could not hope to match.

European Self-Doubt and the Loss of China

Convinced of their technological and methodological superiority over all other peoples, Europeans were starting to question the value of all the new knowledge if one did not know how to live. For many the most disturbing immediate problem posed by the discovery of China was its impact on the historical veracity of the Bible. According to the calculations of the Jesuit scholar Martini, the Celestial Empire had been founded 660 years before the accepted date of the biblical deluge. However, Chinese annals contained no reference to the Flood. Could it therefore have been merely a local episode, important only to the Jews and their immediate neighbors? Some scholars estimated that East Asian civilizations were flourishing even before the accepted date of Adam's Fall. Was it possible then that Adam was the ancestor of the Jews alone, and not of humanity at large? China past and present either was calling to question the universal character of Christianity, or else it was placing doubt on the accuracy of biblical chronology.

The seeds of self-questioning that the Jesuit image of China had planted in Europe coincided with a growing mood in Rome for investigating Jesuit missionary practices in Asia. Dominicans and Franciscans who themselves had practiced mass conversions in the Philippines now insisted that Jesuit-tolerated Chinese nature and ancestor worship were polytheistic. The Jesuits responded that in their hearts the Chinese worshiped the true God. They insisted that gentle prodding rather than wholesale condemnation of Chinese customs would result in the conversion of millions. The Jesuits pointed to encouraging signs: For example, during the funeral procession for one of their number in 1688, imperial guards marched behind banners of the Virgin and child Jesus. Four years later the emperor gave his blessing to free Christian worship. By 1701, 244 Chinese churches were serving the country and more than one hundred European missionaries were traveling through the land.

In Europe, however, the tide had turned against the Jesuit missions. In 1700 theologians at the Sorbonne in Paris condemned ancestor worship and other "Chinese rites." Four years later the papal legate de Tournon, fresh from his investigation of Jesuit practices in India, arrived in Beijing. De Tournon's arrogance so irritated Kangxi that the emperor expelled him from the country. In 1707 Pope Clement XI declared the Chinese rites idolatrous and ordered the Jesuits to repudiate them. Kangxi was infuriated that Europeans who could not even read Chinese characters were condemning practices that he himself considered to be civil, not religious, customs. The emperor expelled missionaries who abided by Rome's decisions. By now, however, the Chinese themselves were questioning the compatibility of Catholic orthodoxy with their traditions. They recalled that even some Jesuits had once depicted them as unimportant minor descendants of Old Testament Hebrews. Moreover, the dualism of Christian theology was unintelligible to them; the exclusiveness of the Western religion was repugnant; its glorification of poverty presented a danger to society. Even China's earlier receptivity to European technology and the fruits of inductive reasoning waned, and the country turned its back on Western-style modernization.

Paradoxically, while Europe's religious leadership lost touch with China, Europe's leisured classes became infatuated with the East. Outward trappings of Chinese civilization became the rage. Porcelains, lacquerware, furniture, and the architecture of the pagoda and pavilion captivated Europe's aristocratic tastes. Oriental flora and fauna were imported and came to adorn arboretums and zoos in London and Paris. Great atlases of China, India, and the Pacific were printed. Learned societies published papers on East Asian customs, and novelists gave birth to the Oriental tale. Except for the clergy, the West's reception to the East remained warm. Above all, it was China that was considered wise, with much to teach. The philosopher Leibniz planned on importing Chinese scholars for the instruction of Europe's statesmen and thinkers. He dreamed of a new international language of the learned based on Chinese ideograms. In the end Rome's feud with the Jesuits provided eighteenth-century sinophilism with its genuine cutting edge. Admitting the value of the East became a way of identifying what was wrong with the West. By virtue of their image of the Orient, early Enlightenment thinkers, pro-Chinese and hostile toward Rome, created what they wished their Europe would become.

6

THE AGE OF REASON

TRADITIONAL RELIGION AND CHALLENGES TO ITS AUTHORITY

Late Seventeenth-Century Christianity

For the overwhelming majority, religion remained the most important cultural force in European life. The decisions of governments often were based on religious motives, and scientists and philosophers had to consider the religious climate of their societies before daring to publicize their discoveries. The year 1648 witnessed the settlement of a religious war, and in 1715 religious crises were smoldering in places as far removed as France and Russia. The European penetration of the Orient depended upon missionary activity and foundered on the shoals of religious controversy. In 1654 Queen Kristina of Sweden abdicated for religious reasons; in 1688 King James II of England was deposed for them. Most rulers believed that God had chosen them to govern. The Hapsburgs considered divine intervention to have been responsible for their successes over the Turks, and even the idea of a crusade still flickered. Women and men remained willing to endure persecution and death for their beliefs. Everywhere devout sectarians challenged the conscience and stimulated the anger of the majority: Puritans and Catholics in England, Huguenots in France, Pietists in Germany, Lutherans in the Hapsburg lands, Old Believers in Russia.

Catholicism retained a remarkable vitality. In Spain, Portugal, and Austria, magnificent baroque abbeys and churches soared in testimony to the triumph of the Counter-Reformation. In these countries a comfortable and wealthy Church owned up to half the land and collected the tithes of an overburdened peasantry. On the other hand, France revealed Catholicism's contentious side. There king challenged pope, saintly men and women challenged king, and the religious controversies of the day filtered down into the parishes. Among Europe's Catholic peasantry, religion was all-consuming and laden with folk custom. Believers sacrificed animals to the Virgin, prayed to the new moon, and worshiped the sources of streams. They made curative pilgrimages to sites of miracles. Yet popular religion had its learned side as well. Book peddlers carried to villages sacks filled with saints' lives, collections of psalms, catechisms, and stories linked to Christ's nativity, death, and resurrection. A literate villager or priest read the little books aloud, and listeners would venerate the crude woodblock illustrations of biblical events and martyred Christians accompanying the text. The faithful believed in the necessity of witch-hunts and resisted the Church's attempt to stamp them out. Satan was everywhere, and his creatures had to be eradicated. Thus social nonconformists, the mentally unbalanced, vagabonds, widows, heretics, Gypsies, and Jews were scapegoats on whom people thrust responsibility for their own private sins.

After 1650 the Church made a supreme effort to spiritualize peasant Catholicism by attacking its magical content. A better educated clergy was sent to rural parishes, emphasizing scriptural teaching, the sacraments, and the catechism. The Church attacked semipagan folk festivals and declared war on the veneration of accumulated bric-a-brac that had transformed churches into sacred warehouses. As royal confessors and school teachers, Jesuits reinvigorated Catholicism. They were receptive to the new science and led the Catholic reconquest of Bohemia, Poland, and Hungary. They had ambitions for Russia and, as we have seen, led the Christian penetration of the Orient.

In Protestant Europe the prince was chief administrator of a country's Church, even though he might not share the confession of the majority of his subjects. For the people, however, deviation from the majority usually spelled civil disabilities, special taxes, and occasional expulsion. Habitual subservience of Protestant Churches to the prince might conceivably lead to religious indifference or Catholic advance, particularly in the Lutheran regions of Germany. By reading decrees from the pulpit, helping recruit for the army, preparing tax lists, and registering births, marriages, and deaths, the German Protestant clergy doubled as political functionaries. Each Sunday without fail, pastors preached the virtues of integrity, submission, and obedience.

It was within this environment of orthodox sterility that Pietism emerged as the continent's most important example of Protestant revival. Pietism was a grass roots movement of individual believers desirous of restoring zeal, passion, and social concern to both Lutheranism and Calvinism. Most Pietists invigorated the traditional confessions, but others splintered off into new sects. Firebrand preachers and tireless hymn writers inspired the flock. Fellowship centers admitted all social elements to their halls, from nobles to vagrants. Thousands learned to read their Bibles in the movement's primary schools. Pietism extended into Scandinavia and Holland. It inspired Methodism in England and the Great Awakening in America. In Germany, Pietism rescued Protestantism from the stranglehold of the state, offered the laity a deep religious experience, and even provided a semblance of cultural unity to a Germany fragmented into hundreds of rival political pieces.

Despite Nikon's reforms and the passion of Peter the Great, Eastern Orthodoxy knew nothing comparable to the renewed spiritual vigor of either the Jesuits or Pietists. What stood for revival in the Balkans and Russia were popular movements which resisted liturgical or administrative Church reforms. In lands under Turkish occupation Slavic Christians resented that their Church, suffering its Babylonian Captivity, was headed by a Greek puppet of the sultan residing in Istanbul. This patriarch and his officials collected the sultan's tribute, recruited for his armies, and sought ostensibly to purify Slavic folk rite and liturgy by introducing Byzantine forms of worship. Because of this, the Balkan peoples welcomed Tsar Peter as their liberator from the infidel and his Greek servants. However, deep in the Russian heartland, many who saw Peter firsthand regarded him very differently—indeed they considered him an anti-Christ, who kept Nikon's liturgical changes, poked fun at services, cut beards, expropriated monasteries, and dominated Russia's Church administration. Far from St. Petersburg and its Western-inspired sophistication, the reaction set in. Priests simply ignored the reformed rites, stuck to traditional forms of prayer, and insisted on the magical properties of their service. Thus Holy Mother Russia engaged in a conspiracy of unresponsiveness that would pay dividends in subsequent generations. In Russia as well as the Balkans, cultural nationalism had religious roots.

The Challenge of Philosophy

Despite signs of spiritual revival in the late seventeenth century, secular values gradually were replacing religious ones as major influences on European life. By 1715 it had become unfashionable to go to war in the name of rival Christian creeds, and within states themselves a few princes noted the political and social impracticality of inconveniencing religious minorities. In their quest for new settlers the German rulers of Brandenburg and Saxony deemed religious affiliation to be a private, not public, matter, a position which the Dutch had long accepted. Christian benevolence persuaded England's Oliver Cromwell and Sweden's Karl XII to respect the religious convictions of most other Protestants. Whatever discomfort English Catholics suffered was due more to their suspect politics than to their religious practices. Nevertheless, because credal affiliation could easily be confused with political loyalty, bigoted rulers like Louis XIV or Leopold I failed to see how non-Catholics could ever be loyal subjects, and even Cromwell had ingrained doubts about non-Protestants.

Despite this, however, the notion was in the air that religious association might be irrelevant to citizenship. Nurturing such a position was an accompanying movement that subjected religious practice to rigorous critical analysis, ridiculing unproven credulity and weakening traditional belief. Out of the carnage of the Thirty Years' War and Puritan revolution emerged the first generation of European intellectuals to repudiate witch-hunts, scorn oracles, and deny the supernatural message of comets. Contempt for superstition evolved into doubts over more hallowed forms of dogma, especially beliefs which appeared to contradict the course of natural phenomena. Late seventeenth-century Europe's most honored scientist, Sir Isaac Newton (1642–1727), considered himself a devout Christian, and his incessant labors on biblical chronology revealed him to be a highly pedantic one. Still, Newton's theories of the physical universe rendered it impossible for him to accept the dogma of the Holy Trinity, and his honesty was respected. In light of Newton's successful career, intolerance was placed on the defensive.

The well-publicized attitude of the French philosopher René Descartes (1596–1650) offered an important theoretical justification for religious tolerance. In his *Discourse on Method* (1637) Descartes gave rational supports for the existence of God. Insisting, however, that his overriding concern was with matters of knowledge and not belief, he avoided submitting questions of dogma to rational scrutiny. According to Descartes, such questions were the business of the individual believer alone. However, Descartes's desire to examine everything else was unacceptable to the Catholic Church, which sensed the potential danger of summoning its privileges, customs, and institutions before the bar of reason, and the *Discourse on Method* was placed on the Church's *Index* of prohibited books. The condemnation proved futile. Dutch, French, and Swiss presses poured out editions and translations. By the end of the century Cartesianism was a respected philosophical school, and in Catholic France it even became dominant. Moreover, it served the cause of toleration. The argument went: If one allowed religious dogma to be exempt from rational analysis, a humanly contrived institution, the state, had no business determining which religion was correct and which was false.

In England a rival philosophical school, empiricism, offered an even more perplexing hypothesis. Rejecting Descartes's position on innate ideas, empiricism held that experience alone determines the sum of our knowledge. Therefore, should not religious truth, like knowledge, derive from voluntary and universal consent? Should not religion submit to tests of reason, experience, and faith? According to empiricists, the immense variety of religions ought to cast a long shadow of doubt on the absolute validity of any single creed, the will of princes and opinions of theologians notwithstanding.

The father of modern empiricism, the Englishman John Locke (1632–1704), remained an Anglican because Anglicanism best responded to his own experience. Locke, however, saw no motive for refusing to respect the contrary beliefs of others. Furthermore, Locke conjured up the idea of a widespread "Invisible Church," a voluntary association of individuals united in their desire to worship God. Locke's position was compatible with that of Leibniz, who spent a lifetime seeking common religious ground for Protestants and Catholics. Moreover, Jesuits in the Orient, who tried to accommodate Catholicism to principles shared by reasonable, civilized pagans, emphasized the syncretic, or embracing aspects, of their religious beliefs.

Most important of all, a quest for *natural* religion captivated intellectuals of the period. Scientists and philosophers sought out religious precepts that governed the human consciousness as universally as the laws of motion were shown to govern the physical world. The traditional Christian story of fallen humanity, subjected to evil earthly forces and needing a redeemer outside nature to attain salvation, gave way to a notion of the individual as God's pampered child, placed on the earth expressly to unlock divine secrets within nature. "The heavens declare the glory of God" became the watchword of the spokespersons of natural religion. Because God must embody supreme reason, a Christian cosmology suffused with corruption no longer made sense. Rather, the majesty of God manifested itself in natural laws. Physical scientists became the theologians of the future, authoring bombastically titled texts such as *Physico-Theology, or a Demonstration of the Being and Attributes of God from His Works of Creation.* Others might use mathematical formulas to justify particular confessional viewpoints. However ludicrous the approaches appear to us today, religion was being emancipated from terror, fear, and prejudice. Moreover, an especially critical eye now was cast on the teachings of both Protestant and Catholic Christianity.

For good reason, guardians of the Christian tradition were worried. The bitter Jesuit-Jansenist controversy, revocation of the Edict of Nantes, and Rome's mishandling of the Chinese rites controversy invited attacks on traditional dogmatism. One of the most effective critics was the journalist-pamphleteer-scholar Pierre Bayle (1647–1706). A Huguenot from southern France, Bayle knew intolerance firsthand. While Bayle fled the persecution of Louis XIV and found refuge in Rotterdam, a less fortunate brother lost his life to the *dragonnades.* The stadholder William III liked Bayle's sardonic denunciations of the French king and his offensive against Catholic dogma. However, Bayle's submission of biblical history to the severe tests of reason and scholarship proved too radical even for enlightened Holland, and his vitriolic pen cost him a university professorship.

Still, Bayle remained active. He argued that atheists might possess moral codes as elevated as those of the devout. He wondered whether God could be either all-knowing or all-benevolent, when He had done nothing to prevent Adam's Fall. In his *Historical and Critical Dictionary* (1695–1697), Bayle spared no sanctimonious tradition, no inconsistent or intolerant doctrine, no barbarity committed in the name of divine revelation. Bayle doubted every unproven hypothesis and submitted all to reason's test. To his hypercritical and skeptical mind, proof by universal consent simply meant that everyone could be wrong. Treading paths even Descartes called off limits, this independent thinker insisted he was a Christian. His Christianity, however, could never be the repository of unquestioned tradition and fundamentalist belief.

Nor could it be for his Catholic contemporary, the French Oratorian priest Richard Simon (1638–1712). Expert philologist and ancient historian, Simon is one of the founders of modern biblical scholarship. His histories of the Old and New Testaments (1695, 1697) largely rejected literalism in favor of allegorical and symbolic interpretations. Catholic orthodoxy tried unsuccessfully to silence him. Like Bayle, Simon protested his good faith. He was certain that by excluding myth from Christianity he was performing a service for belief.

However, biblical scholarship could not long remain in the hands of critics who nevertheless wished Christianity well. Louis XIV's personal confessor, Bishop Jacques-Bénigne Bossuet (1627–1704), thundered, "A great battle is being mounted against the Church, under the banner of Cartesian philosophy." For Bossuet, applying to religion the reasoned proofs of scientific inquiry would lead either to skepticism or to sophistry. The Churches might bid good riddance to Saint George's dragon, the portable head of Denys the Aeropagite, and the half-pagan mythologies of folk religion; but could Genesis, biblical chronology, or the Incarnation itself survive the probes that now were entering the body of Christian lore? Was it really necessary for science and mathematics to pinpoint the celestial position of paradise? Orthodox hierarchies agreed with most Pietists, Jansenists, and Old Believers that reasoned criticism was the devil's curse. For the first time since the fourth century, Christianity was placed on the defensive. This time the threat was from within.

THE GOD OF THE PHILOSOPHERS

Hobbes and Spinoza

For philosophers compelled to explain the reciprocal relationships between humanity and God in terms conforming to reason, it no longer was a question of God the savior. What mattered to them was God as author of nature's laws. Such thinkers wished to enter where Descartes had feared to tread. They would construct entire theologies in accord with the universe of measured facts. The dangers were obvious. For example, once the English philosopher Thomas Hobbes (1588–1679) concluded that only matter conformed to objective reality, he lost God altogether. However, in the seventeenth century atheism based on a materialist worldview won few converts. Much more appealing was the search for a rationally explicable God. Such a quest might be pursued according to Descartes's instructions for abstract reasoning, or else it might derive from the formulas of empiricists, born of experience and pragmatic need. Whatever the approach, the minds and eyes of most European intellectuals between 1648 and 1715 were focused on the author of nature. Whether or not this deity satisfied emotional or existential needs was parenthetical.

The system of Baruch Spinoza (1632–1677) was among the most important of the new creeds. Born in Amsterdam to a family of Portuguese

Jews who had fled persecution, Spinoza imbibed both his ancestral religion and the new science. The conflict of his learning became readily apparent, and at twenty-four Spinoza was expelled from the synagogue for expressing ideas antithetical to Judaism. He spent the remainder of his days at his trade of lens grinding and at working out a metaphysics, ethical system, and political theory. The audience of this humble renegade Jew was impressive. He knew the de Witts personally and corresponded with princes, Leibniz, and the secretary of England's Royal Society. Fearing that an official academic position might compromise his liberty of thought, he declined a professorship at the University of Heidelberg. His career exemplifies the evolution of the philosophers' Europe, a republic of letters where customary political, religious, and social barriers had fallen.

Spinoza made his reputation with an impressive critique of Descartes's thought. The sharply dualist nature of mind and body did not convince him at all; nor could he dispense with God as an active agent operative in the physical world. Nevertheless, as a rationalist Spinoza had little use for unproven scriptural claims, miracles, a personal savior, and established Churches. He envisioned God as primary reality, not necessarily creating the universe and then standing aside but identical with the universe, immanent in both matter and thought. People were part of God, indistinct from Him, modes of divinity, as it were. Spinoza was a pantheist, with a spiritual home neither in Judaism nor Christianity, and he was anathema to the Cartesians. Above all, Spinoza was a moralist and builder of a powerful ethical system. If God was all, the individual, indistinct from God, would reject the folly of personal desire and not be tormented either by guilt or sin. That individual would opt for spiritual communion with other creatures, recognize the unproven subjectivity of sectarian theologies, and depend completely upon the God of divine reason. The lifetime of the perceptive individual would be spent in contemplation, study, and the perfection of personal morals.

Leibniz

Because the concept of God the creator was so deeply ingrained in the Western religious tradition, Spinoza's pantheism was usually misconstrued as atheism. Fellow philosophers asked how morality could be built on anything except divine commandments. How much safer it would be to use Cartesian principles as proof not only of God's existence but also God's workings. This is what a French priest, Nicolas Malebranche (1638–1715), attempted to do. Malebranche concluded that divine intervention was what made the body obey the mind's will. Certainly nature functioned according to God's laws, but human action necessitated the occurrence of countless little miracles. To some rationalists this constant intervention smacked too much of mysticism, while the Catholic Church condemned Malebranche for his loyalty to Descartes. Nevertheless, European intellectuals hungering to make Cartesian rationalism compatible with Christian belief chose Male-branche as their high priest. His fame was such that Chinese philosophers asked the Jesuits about him. Above all, he frustrated the spread of Spinoza's theories.

Meanwhile other alternative explanations of the philosophers' God were catching hold. The most important of these was promoted by Leibniz. Scholar, courtier, and diplomat, advocate of religious union, founder of symbolic logic, and co-discoverer with Isaac Newton of infinites-imal calculus, Leibniz stood on the peak of Europe's intellectual life in the late seventeenth century. His correspondence was large and influential. He founded learned academies and contributed more to the free exchange of ideas than anyone else of his time. Because he could not abide Spinoza's pantheism and Malebranche's elaborations of Descartes seemed contrived to him, he developed his own overarching conceptions about the workings of the universe and God's role in them.

Entranced by the concept of infinitesimals and the discovery of both microscopic cells and spermatazoa, Leibniz theorized a universe filled with imperceptible, self-contained metaphysical organisms called monads. Operating independently, these were the necessary agents of divine cre-ation. Yet it also was absolutely essential for monads to relate to one an-other. How, for example, could mind perceive tree? Leibniz held that it was God who synchronized the movement of monads. For every perception within a monad at a given time, there arose a corresponding perception within another monad. Taken as a whole, the activity of monads fulfilled the divine plan of preestablished harmony. God acted freely to foreordain this most systematically logical of worlds, and God is benevolent.

Vulgarized for popular consumption, Leibniz's notions brought him enormous popularity during his own lifetime and after his death. They were the source of one of the most self-satisfied attitudes of mind in West-ern intellectual history. Faith in preestablished harmony guaranteed a suffi-cient reason for why anything should be as it is, since God knew and planned for the best. Leibniz's enthusiastic disciples attributed to him the resolution of the problem of evil. For them, confidence in the ability of divine intelligence to manipulate monad after monad according to a provi-dential pattern was a tempting means of explaining away the most seem-ingly incomprehensible horror, without reference to bothersome points on the origins of evil and human corruption. Leibniz's most celebrated work, *Essays of Theodicy* (1710), and subsequent commentaries on it, went through dozens of editions.

Pascal

Their criticisms of established religion notwithstanding, the rational philosophers often looked like old-fashioned sectarians hurling their per-sonal interpretations of truth at one another. To complicate matters further, some, like Leibniz, paid lip service to traditional Christian formulas while actually disbelieving them. More than most, John Locke was disturbed by the difficulties of reconciling reason with revelation. He accepted the validity of certain extrarational ideas on the basis of what he called their clarity, but he was uncomfortable doing so. On the other hand, the Frenchman Blaise Pascal stands out as a chastened rationalist who, having served science and tested some philosophic theologies, ultimately found them wanting. Pascal returned to Christianity simply because, in his view, it best explained the human condition. Born in 1623 and living only 39 years, Pascal haunted subsequent generations long after Malebranche's occasionalism and Leibniz's monadology had lost their disciples.

As a brilliant young mathematician, Pascal had spent much time reading the critics of orthodox Christian doctrine. In 1646 Jansenism attracted him, and his *Provincial Letters* (1657) provided a highly effective polemic against Jesuit theories on grace and salvation. Following a brush with death, Pascal underwent a mystical experience during which he was overwhelmed by a sense of human weakness. He offered himself to the Christian God of mercy and spent the remainder of a life wracked with pain and illness composing epigrams that reduced arguments to a few trenchant words or sentences of revelatory insight. After his death several hundred of these were found. First published in 1670, Pascal's *Thoughts* have become one of the masterpieces of French literature. Systematizing them is impossible, but they prove that Pascal never truly abandoned the reasoning process in favor of pure mysticism. Like Descartes he subjected all knowledge to question and doubt. Applied to nature and nature's God, however, reason taught Pascal nothing. Instead of gaining a sense of security from the celestial harmonies uncovered by philosophers, Pascal found himself "engulfed in the immensity of spaces whereof I know nothing, and which know nothing of me. I am terrified. . . . The eternal silence of those infinite spaces frightens me."

Examining the human condition, Pascal discovered that however much individuals claimed reason as justifying their behavior, their true motives customarily were passion and self-interest. Observing that all he knew affirmed a pessimistic view of human nature, Pascal pleaded with philosopher, skeptic, and unbeliever to take a leap of faith in the Christian God of mercy and forgiveness. If this God exists, he wrote, all is won. If God does not exist, nothing is lost. But to a generation of intellectuals who failed to share Pascal's fears, his wager made little sense. He wanted to address himself to the intellectuals of his day, to point out the folly of their rational cosmologies, and to win them back to an existential position that he considered consistent with humanity's genuine state. But he was both too late and too early. Euphoric over the use they could make of mathematics and empirical science, Pascal's contemporaries were caught up in the excitement of discovery rather than the bewilderment of doubt. The secularization of European culture was quickly becoming a fact.

THE SCIENTIFIC CULTURE

The Geometric Spirit

That Pascal's plea went unanswered was partly due to a new approach toward scientific inquiry that had emerged in the first half of the seventeenth century. A procedure emphasizing systematic analysis and experiment turned previously accepted conclusions about the workings of nature into apparent guesses built on casual observation. The idea of the universe as a living, breathing organism, comprehended according to its qualities or principles of behavior, where miracles and spontaneous generation were accepted, was repudiated in favor of a conception of the universe as a celestial machine, understood only through measurement, calculation, and quantitative prediction of its working parts. A new method of inquiry, commencing with axioms, definitions, postulates, and hypotheses, and concluding with experiments and proofs, was enshrined as the only legitimate means of discovering certainty about how the observable world functioned. Mathematics would compel nature to unlock its secrets.

By 1650 devotees of the new method, labeled "the geometric spirit," comprised the most important intellectual community in Europe. Members visited and corresponded, exchanged theories in books and letters, and acquired a fraternal esprit de corps that transcended national boundaries, traditional religions, and political ideologies. They prided themselves on creating a new culture, a republic of letters. At the same time, however, the gulf between themselves and the overwhelming majority of Europeans had become immense and, by their own decision, unbridgeable. For the first time since the fall of the Roman Empire an intellectual elite was pursuing approaches to God, man, and the universe that the rest of Europe could barely comprehend, much less share. Nor did the new elite mask its contempt for the older culture.

The protectors of the older culture were the universities and Churches. With a few notable exceptions, European universities in the mid-seventeenth century remained medieval institutions. Nonexperimental science had a revered place in the mathematics quadrivium, and Aristotle's natural philosophy still dominated the arts. Scientific education took the form of lectures and commentaries on the ancients, such as Euclid, Ptolemy, and Galen. At the Sorbonne in Paris, Descartes was condemned, and William Harvey's theories on blood circulation rejected out of hand. The contempt of university-educated physicians for surgeons empirically trained in modest surgical colleges hindered the development of modern medical practice.

Professors in the older universities, who might be receptive to certain new theories, did not dream of pursuing them in their research. They only asked for the right to offer mathematical and empirical methods as possible alternatives to Aristotle and the ancients. The new science made slow inroads in the traditional repositories of learning. Yet there were a few advances. The admission of Isaac Newton and Edmund Halley to the faculties of Cambridge and Oxford Universities respectively, linked these hallowed institutions to research conducted in London by the Royal Society. Guided by a progressive physician, Hermann Boerhaave (1668–1738), Leiden University in Holland incorporated physiology, chemistry, botany, and physics into its medical program. Nevertheless, Leiden was exceptional. Most older universities were bound by their corporate character and traditions, and their faculties were filled with pompous beadles entrenched in privilege and thriving on academic ritual.

It was in Germany that the modern state-sponsored university emerged. At Halle in Brandenburg (1694) and later Göttingen in Hanover (1737), faculty were civil servants, the brainpower of the emerging state bureaucracies. Professors were to do original research and use it as the basis for instruction. To the political authorities they submitted regular reports of their work and their students' attendance at lectures. Although the professor as state servant was to have tragic consequences for modern Germany, during the eighteenth century the faculties of Halle and Göttingen rose to European preeminence. Princes paid for their libraries and scientific equipment. Professors ranged freely over a panorama of scientific and humanistic learning. There the cooperative research seminar was born, prototype for the community of scholars unencumbered by the past.

Nevertheless, it was outside the universities that the new culture became genuinely fashionable. Wishing to bask in the sunlight of their beneficiaries' discoveries, princely patrons subsidized private research. Under government protection learned academies emerged. The model was the Accademia del Cimento of Florence (1657–1667), supported by the ruling Medici family, where professional scientists met for the exclusive purpose of conducting cooperative experiments and publishing their research. The most spectacular new organization of this type, the Paris Academy of Sciences, was underwritten by Louis XIV himself. For about eight years a group of Parisian savants had been meeting irregularly. Then, in 1666 Colbert offered them a place on the king's payroll, comfortable living and working quarters, and the promise of an astronomical observatory. Members of the Paris academy comprised a privileged elite, but their lives were regimented. They had to live in Paris, meet twice weekly, and adhere to government-defined work schedules. The academicians understood the price of royal patronage, but only rarely did Louis's bellicosity and intolerance cost him a scholar. From the beginning the Paris academy stressed the useful aspects of research, and its concern for technology and public demonstration of experiments opened scientific inquiry to a wider audience than had been the case earlier. Because of the academy, the new culture appeared less mysterious, less subversive, and more respectable.

The Royal Society in London was quite different from the Paris academy. Private individuals, not the state, subsidized it. Chartered in 1662 and publishing its *Philosophical Transactions* from 1665, the Royal Society remained both underfinanced and free from political influence. Presided over by Isaac Newton from 1703 to 1727, it was particularly revered in the world of early modern science. Of primary importance were its experiments in mechanics and optics, but the Royal Society also promoted useful medical practices, such as smallpox inoculation. Elsewhere in Europe, where absolutist princes hankered after investments in prestige, the French institution rather than the English one served as the prototype. In underdeveloped states an academy could become an important agency of government. Peter the Great's, established in 1725, supervised education, book publishing, and technological innovations. In more advanced states provincial academies blossomed. They specialized in science but also contributed to local history and folklore. By 1760, France alone had forty such institutions.

The most important generation in the history of science had been that of 1620 to 1650. During this period Galileo, Kepler, Harvey, and Descartes rejected the formulations of Aristotle, Ptolemy, and Galen that had defined scientific inquiry for nearly fifteen hundred years. Doubt, experiment, observation, and reason now overwhelmed the prestige of the past, and demands for precision caused scientists to concentrate on the concrete and measurable. Laggard as it was, technology after 1650 showed concern for exactitude too. Scales, barometers, compound microscopes, and telescopes were perfected. In 1656 the Dutch physicist Christiaan Huygens (1629-1695) demonstrated how the isochronism of the pendulum could be incorporated into a mechanical clock, thus creating a measuring device that all could use. Exactitude extended into the human sciences. In 1690 Sir William Petty (1623-1687) published his *Political Arithmetick,* the first serious estimate of the population of England based on the country's occupational groups. The prestige of the measuring scientist had never been higher. The French academician Bernard de Fontenelle (1657-1757) wrote, "A work on morals, on politics, and on criticism, perhaps even on eloquence, will be better . . . if it is written by a geometer."

Newton

The central scientific event of the entire century was the discovery of a mathematically and empirically verifiable law of motion that confirmed a mechanistic interpretation of the universe. *The Mathematical Principles of Natural Philosophy* (1687) of Sir Isaac Newton became the point of reference for all the exact sciences. Newton synthesized the advances in celestial mechanics that had been developing ever since the problem of a mathematically defined force of attraction in the universe had been touched on two centuries earlier. He proved that bodies in the heavens and on earth were subject to the same laws of motion.

Newton's great synthesis emerged in two bursts of creativity, each lasting approximately a year and a half. The first occurred in 1665-1666, when Newton was in his early twenties. He already had rejected the

Aristotelian theories on planetary movement. Moreover, the unverified Cartesian hypothesis of a universe filled with celestial fluid, sustaining the sun and planets, seemed to him absurd. Cartesians, Newton thought, made the error of trying to perceive the universe in its entirety rather than observing its particular phenomena. In Newton's view, only a meticulous analysis of the particular could lead to a valid explanation of the whole. Reflecting on his conclusions drawn in 1665–1666, Newton later wrote, "[I] compared the force requisite to keep the Moon in her Orb with the force of gravity at the surface of the earth, and found them to answer pretty nearly." But "pretty nearly" was not mathematical proof of a theory of universal gravitation. Newton could go no further in his calculations, and for the next twenty years he worked mainly on calculus, optics, and alchemy.

Many others remained profoundly disturbed when mathematical and empirical investigation failed to support Descartes's hypothesis of planetary movement. Newton's contemporaries Robert Hooke (1635–1703) and Edmund Halley (1656–1742) wrestled with alternatives illustrating the mutual attraction of heavenly bodies, but verifiable proofs eluded them. In 1684 Halley went to Newton with his dilemma. To his surprise, he learned that Newton had worked with the problem of motion twenty years earlier but then quit on it. Halley urged Newton to take up his work again. Because the old notes were lost, Newton began afresh. This time the route proved smooth and he published his findings. In fewer than three years *The Mathematical Principles of Natural Philosophy* became known to the community of science. Aware of the distance of the earth to the moon, computing the lunar orbit, and checking his computations against observed facts, Newton discovered that, according to his theorem of inverse squares, a single law of motion existed and held as true for the transits of planets as for a falling body. Thus Descartes's general appreciation of nature was confirmed, even as the details of his hypothetical vision of planetary motion were rejected.

Newton's discovery electrified European intellectuals. If he was correct, the idea of celestial uniqueness had to be discarded. What was true of bodies seen through the telescope applied as well to bodies seen through the microscope. England honored Newton with a seat in Parliament, knighthood, directorship of the royal mint, and presidency of the Royal Society. He became the first natural philosopher to be so treated by his country within his lifetime. English, Dutch, and many German scientists accepted the theories of the *Mathematical Principles*. For political reasons, however, the Paris academy refused to abandon Descartes, and the French universities stayed with Aristotle.

Although Newton had confirmed that the mathematically deduced and empirically observed were the twin measures of reality, he shunned a purely materialist conception of the universe. He offered an olive branch to the defenders of the older culture by postulating the existence of a divine mystery behind the marvelous mechanism of the physical world. God was not simply a watchmaker who created His masterpiece and then stepped aside. God was living and real, though to be sure closer to the scientist-philosopher than to the theologian. In his *Optics* (1704), Newton wrote, "The main business of natural philosophy is to argue from phenomena without feigning hypotheses, and to deduce causes from effects, till we come to the very First Cause, which certainly is not mechanical." Newton's legacy was to have uncovered, through the application of mathematics, systematic observation, and experiment, a reasoned harmony behind the surface disorder of the physical universe. Treated as a seer by his allies and as an occult magician by his enemies, he admittedly did not work in a scientific void. Throughout the second half of the seventeenth century a wide range of cumulative advances in mathematics, chemistry, geology, medicine, and biology accompanied work in celestial physics, all of which helped confirm the mechanistic interpretation of the universe.

The Limits to Discovery

Challenging Descartes, scientists known as the *corpuscularean theorists* had already created an intellectual mood that would be receptive to Newton's theories. To Cartesians the hypothesis of a universe of densely packed, constantly moving coarse and fine particles, all immersed in a celestial fluid, denied the existence of a vacuum. Such skepticism was in keeping with Aristotelian thought. However, between 1644 and 1654, working in controlled laboratory environments, experimenters such as Pascal and the Italian Evangelista Torricelli (1608–1647) disproved the Cartesians. Torricelli's method was to fill a tube with mercury, place his finger over the open end, and invert the tube so that its mouth was submerged in a dish of mercury. Removing his finger from the tube, Torricelli found that the mercury level had fallen and he had created a vacuum. Pascal confirmed this experiment by measuring mercury levels atop a French mountain, the Puy de Dôme, and discovering that air pressure there was less than it was at sea level. Cartesians claimed that "subtle matter" had caused the change, but increasingly their reasoning, unverified through experimentation, sounded nonscientific. The capstone for the corpusculareans was achieved when the Englishman Robert Boyle (1627–1691) proved that the volume of gases varied inversely according to the amount of air pressure on it. Like Newton, Boyle rejected unverifiable Aristotelian-Cartesian conceptions.

Just as the Cartesians had been wrong in denying the possibility of a vacuum, so did the universities err in reducing matter to the four elements of fire, air, earth, and water. This ancient way of analyzing matter lay at the heart of the qualitative explanations. Fire was dry and hot, earth dry and cold; air was moist and hot, water moist and cold. Matter reacted in predictable ways not because of physical laws but because, like human beings, it longed for certain states. A stone fell because it yearned for earth; smoke rose because it yearned for air. In *The Sceptical Chymist* (1661), Boyle ridiculed the qualitative explanations of the workings of matter, and he tried to remove chemistry from the domain of the magical and sinister. Boyle's achievement, however, remained incomplete. He never was able to systematize according to their physical properties what he called "primitive and simple . . . unmingled bodies," and he never quite forsook the kitchen for the laboratory. Alchemy tempted him, as it did Newton, causing him to work at cross-purposes. Still, Boyle never tired of emphasizing the possibilities of science, and he was convinced that the new learning awarded a greater glory to God. He set aside a sum to pay preachers to lecture on the compatibility of science and Christianity. His enthusiasm misapplied, it was said that few doubted the existence of God until the Boyle lecturers set out to prove it.

What we today call the biological sciences were in their infancy. They too became indebted to a mechanistic outlook and experimental methodology. When he outlined his theory of blood circulation in 1628, William Harvey had liberated physiology from its ancient Galenic standard; during the second half of the century the microscope became inextricably linked to physiology. Thoroughly entranced by the microscopic, a Dutch draper, Anton van Leeuwenhoek (1632–1723), had used lenses to test the quality of cloth. He began assembling his own, perfected a 300-power instrument, and delighted in entertaining his acquaintances with the wriggling universe beneath the glass. In his lifetime he made at least 240 microscopes and insisted that he had observed the perfect form of a sheep in an embryo one-eighth the size of a pea. Though an amateur, Van Leeuwenhoek nevertheless gave the first complete descriptions of both spermatazoa and protozoa. He even began classifying bacteria into species, and he corresponded regularly with the Royal Society, which published his articles and elected him to membership. Upon his death the society obtained his treasured instruments.

Despite their innovators, physiology and biology lacked universally accepted and verifiable principles of classification. Physics at least had its geometrized superstructure built on a comprehensive body of precise, ascertained facts. On the other hand, life scientists groped amid conflicting systems, names, and descriptions. They were looking for a *natural* system of classification that would uncover the genuine, unifying relationships of living things. In botany matters were particularly critical. The passion for collecting Europe's flora and fauna and the discovery of exotic plants made it imperative to establish principles of classification. An intuitive genius, the Englishman John Ray (1627–1705) classified nearly 20,000 identifiable plants according to their community of origin. Ray was the first to use the term *species* in this way, and his French contemporary Joseph Pitton de Tournefort (1656–1708), a professor at Paris's Royal Plant Gardens, developed the term *genus* for a definable group of related species. Finally, in the next generation, the Swede Karl Linné (1707–1778) brought the work of Ray and Tournefort to a triumphal conclusion. Linné's most lasting innovation was in nomenclature, the binomial system of categorizing. The first word was generic, shared with other species (*Rosa*); the second represented the species itself (*carolina*).

A belief in the fixity of species presented the study of vertebrates with an obstacle that Newton's triumph seemed to make all the greater. It was not until after 1750 that the concept of evolution challenged the idea of unchanging order in nature. Before this occurred, biologists believed that they had to work within a system analogous to the regularized, harmonious universe of physical matter uncovered by the Newtonians. Since this universe was based on the principle of static reality, with change abhorrent to its workings, the celestial physicists saw little need to challenge the view that the earth was 5,700 years old, and that all plant and animal life in existence around A.D. 1700 had been present at the dawn of creation. Geologists, however, were making discoveries that upset such complacency. They found in various layers what they thought to be skeletal remains of creatures no longer in existence. These discoveries challenged biblical chronologies and turned the Flood of the Book of Genesis into merely the latest of a series of ancient marine catastrophes. Scientists started asking, How many extinct creatures once roamed the earth and swam in its waters? In 1710, addressing the Paris academy, Fontenelle underscored the role of fossils in natural history: "Here are new species of medals whose dates are more important and more certain than all the Greek and Roman medals combined." The Newtonians had provided momentous alternatives to time-honored theories; but in the wake of their discoveries, others were asking highly troubling questions.

By 1715 the idea of a universe that works had replaced the idea of a universe that feels. In his theoretical writings Descartes had insisted on the substitution of fact for imagination, and Newton took him at his word. As a consequence, deduction, observation, and experiment emerged triumphant. To be sure, the future branches of modern science still were at different stages of development. Physics and mechanics were the standard for all the rest. The sciences of classification were groping for methodologies, and geology was in a perplexed state. Despite the air pump, microscope, and other instruments of measurement, technology remained too undeveloped to affect the lives of the majority of Europeans. In the 1690s attempts were made to find new sources of power by applying steam to the piston and cylinder, but it was not until 1712 that the imaginative English blacksmith Thomas Newcomen (1663–1729) harnessed steam power sufficiently to make an engine of limited use. Around the same time the passion for improvement reached into agriculture, the area which touched most closely on the well-being of society.

As previously noted, at the turn of the eighteenth century English landowners, borrowing Dutch ideas on intensive cultivation, began abandoning the fallow for systematic methods of crop rotation. The New Husbandry operated on a cycle of clover, wheat, turnips, and barley. No one yet understood just why clover and turnips invigorated the soil, but observation and experiment proved that they did. In the 1720s, when the English gentleman farmer Jethro Tull (1674–1741) showed that pulverizing the soil produced effects similar to manuring it and invented the horse hoe to effect his ideas, a long-delayed marriage between science and agriculture seemed to be approaching reality. Though technology still lagged behind theory, methodology and newly acquired optimism for the future linked Newton to Newcomen and Tull.

EMPIRICISM AND THE HUMAN SCIENCES

The subjection of the physical universe to mathematical and empirical analysis inspired seventeenth-century thinkers to apply reasoned judgment to ethics, political theory, psychology, and jurisprudence. Spinoza, Malebranche, and Leibniz were confident that they would solve metaphysical problems as comprehensively as the celestial mechanicians were solving physical ones. What was needed were careful definitions, tightly reasoned analyses, geometrical demonstrations, and meticulous observation of God's work through nature. That scientific and philosophical problems might call for differences in approach was barely conceivable to thinkers flushed with the power of the new methodology. Although some tried to use mathematical formulas to prove the existence of good and evil in people's hearts, it became clear that empirical study was more useful than abstract analysis in probing the realities of human existence and one's place in the social and political environment. Observation and experiment enjoyed places of honor, especially as checkpoints, in the findings of the great theorists of matter; the less developed sciences of biology, chemistry, botany, and geology were almost entirely dependent upon empirical techniques. By 1715 psychological, social, and political theories as well were awarding precedence to the world of observable fact.

The Senses and Human Understanding

Three Englishmen—Francis Bacon (1561–1626), Thomas Hobbes (1588–1679), and John Locke (1632–1704)—spanned nearly five generations of empiricist thought. Bacon set down the guidelines. He assumed that the sum total of phenomena was finite; observation and the collection of facts formed the basis of inductive proof; experiments must be deliberate and rationally conceived; and the ultimate end to knowledge was humanity's mastery of nature. Bacon's secretary, Hobbes, disregarded the immaterial side of Cartesian dualism, believed that reality consisted exclusively of matter in motion, was persuaded that universal laws had nothing to do with reality, and placed all on the side of the senses. Unlike Bacon, Hobbes was interested in the reactions of people battered about by a universe of fleeting matter. Responding entirely to the needs of the senses, the Hobbesian individual was constantly in competition with other humans. Knowledge was uncertain. Religion and morality were intended either to counteract the most ruthless aspects of competition or else subject some individuals to the rule of others. Profoundly pessimistic about humankind, Hobbes nevertheless insisted that his conclusions were based on painstaking observation of his fellows and a careful reading of history. His own life affirmed his faith in uncertainty. A defender of Charles I, he fled to France in 1640. However, Cromwell invited him back, and his masterpiece, the *Leviathan,* was published in London in 1651. Although Charles II protected Hobbes, his materialism earned him the reputation of a dangerous character, and his enemies called the great plague and fire of London divine retribution for his presence. Timid by nature, yet repudiating nothing he had ever written, Hobbes died in 1679 at ninety-one, certain that experience justified his pessimism.

For nearly half a century the life of John Locke overlapped that of Hobbes. The two thinkers lived through the Civil War, Interregnum, and Restoration. Like Hobbes, Locke experienced political exile, and the two shared a belief that the primary way to learn about humanity and the world was empirically. But here all resemblance stopped. Hobbes was convinced of the instability and unpredictability of life, of the individual's unquenchable egoism, and of the inevitability of social conflict. On the other hand, Locke left room for hope. His *Essay Concerning Human Understanding* (1690) was meant to refute Descartes's principle of innate ideas and to show that trustworthy knowledge derived exclusively from human experience. Locke agreed with Hobbes that simple ideas were products of our senses. He added, however, that individuals reflect on simple ideas and refine them. Locke was vague as to how the mind sorts out and arranges the products of experience, and what he called the principle of innate rationality appears to be human conscience. This rationality transforms our sense-derived ideas into complex ones, and the complex ideas become the guides for our conduct, morality, law, religion, politics, and aesthetics.

Locke developed a related theory of overpowering consequence. He theorized as follows: Since we are so dependent upon our senses for ideas, our environment molds us. Conversely, our complex ideas, the product of our "reflective experience," may transform and ameliorate our environment. A generation reared on Cartesian faith in reason, dazzled by the discoveries of the celestial mechanicians, and increasingly skeptical about traditional theologies and original sin, took to Locke's sanguine empiricism with an enthusiasm that the pessimistic Hobbes could not have expected. Locke's *Essay* represented a revolutionary event in the history of ideas. Upon its hypotheses and conclusions arose the fundamental liberal belief in moral and material progress. Though Locke stated that the concept of God was the clearest complex idea one could hold, his psychology was uncompromisingly secular. Humanity alone controlled its destiny.

Just as Descartes, Spinoza, Pascal, Bossuet, and Leibniz were keenly interested in political theory, so too did Hobbes and Locke apply their secular empiricism to politics. No one lived in a political vacuum. All knew how rebellion, revolution, and regicide had plagued the first half of the seventeenth century. Although international warfare rather than internal revolts dominated the second half, thinkers remained obsessed with the fundamental political questions of the legitimacy of sovereignty, purpose of government, and proper role of the subject.

Political Thought: Bossuet and Hobbes

Theorists of divine-right absolutism such as Bishop Bossuet, court preacher at Versailles, had what they believed to be unchallengable answers to these questions. For them governments were obviously ordained by God, and subjects were obliged to obey these governments. Nothing could be clearer than the words of St. Paul, whom Bossuet quoted in his *Politics Drawn from the Very Words of Holy Scripture* (1709): "Let every soul be subject to the higher powers. For there is no power but of God and the powers that be are ordained by God. Whosoever therefore resisteth the power resisteth the ordinance of God." Hereditary monarchy was the most appropriate "higher power." It offered a parallel to the divine order and was chosen by God for ancient Israel. Far from resting his argument exclusively on biblical fundamentalism, however, Bossuet also showed that individuals instinctively craved paternal government, that absolutism was the best insurance against division in the state, and that hereditary rule was the "most natural and self-regenerating kind." Distinguishing between absolute and arbitrary government, Bossuet reminded princes that they must respect the fundamental laws of the state and the property of their subjects. Nevertheless, against an unjust ruler the subject might make nothing more than respectful remonstrances. Antithetical to scripture and violating public order, civil disobedience was intolerable. The ultimate weapons of a suffering populace were prayers for the tyrant's conversion.

Like Bossuet, Hobbes was a convinced believer in absolute government, though his method of justification did not endear him to divine-right theorists. Hobbes's thought had little room for the Christian God, and his world was suffused with swirling matter and individuals who followed their instincts and responded to their senses. The political theory of Hobbes's powerful work, the *Leviathan,* derived from the book's cosmology. Hobbes began by placing the individual within a hypothetical environment that preceded the establishment of political society. In the Middle Ages such an environment had been linked to a natural state, the Garden of Eden, where humans behaved according to natural laws ordained by God.

Early in the seventeenth century the Dutch political thinker Hugo Grotius (1583–1645), while not dispensing with the device of a state of nature, secularized the principle of natural laws by postulating them on the workings of human reason. Even if God did not exist, Grotius hypothesized, the laws of nature stood, being indistinguishable from moral principles. Like Grotius, Hobbes described a state of nature which was not dependent upon God. Here, however, all resemblances between the two theorists ceased. Devoid of either moral or divine laws, Hobbes's state of nature was a microscopic version of his universe. Within it individuals obeyed their private instincts and were restrained only by fears of reprisal and of their own violent death. Scoffing at the idea of a social instinct that, according to Grotius, drew people into cooperative activities even before the formation of organized society, Hobbes envisioned the state of nature as a state of "war of every man against every man." There, "the notions of right and wrong, justice and injustice, have no place." Mere existence was conflict, "and the life of man, solitary, poor, nasty, brutish, and short."

Inside Hobbes's state of nature the freedom of one individual threatened the survival of everyone else. Then, for a moment—according to Hobbes the single most important instant in human history—people applied their powers of reason to their need for self-preservation. Among one another they agreed to surrender their liberty and "confer all their power and strength upon one man, or upon one assembly of men." This act of self-preservation created a "mortal god," the great Leviathan, the omnipotent state. Its sovereignty was absolute and its power unlimited. It defined justice, morality, and religion; it made no reciprocal concessions to subjects. Its purpose was wholly to maintain order and avert dissension. Mass rebellion against it was social suicide, for such activity would result in a return to the murderous state of nature. Only when the sovereign failed to provide necessary security did a rationale exist for subjects to transfer authority. Unpleasant as the *Leviathan* was, as a piece of political philosophy it represented a landmark. Out went the religious, moral, feudal, and constitutional underpinnings of the state. In came a total, self-sustaining view of political authority.

Hobbes broke with the past in another way. For him, political society originated as a voluntary association of individuals, equal in their freedom and misery. Neither religious commandment nor moral vision lay behind the social act. The state and its laws were artificial creations, and Hobbes saw no need for subjects to urge rulers to govern according to principles higher than utilitarian ones. For him, natural laws never really existed. Subsequent thinkers, however, revived them and made them indisputably secular, embodying humanity's inherent and pristine rationality. Because natural laws were positive, even benevolent, it was the duty of government to preserve their character. Faith in the reality of natural laws was consistent with faith in the reality of the mechanical workings of the universe. It also was consistent with faith in natural religion that philosophers and deists extolled. Almost in reaction to Hobbes's gloomy prospects, the idea of a voluntarily contracted society merged with a revival of natural law theory to create a set of political ideas which placed unprecedented confidence in the capacities of human beings to work out their own destinies.

The Natural Law Theorists: From Pufendorf to Locke

The theorists themselves did not comprise a homogeneous group. One school argued that strong government provided the most effective instrument for expressing natural law and defending natural rights. The most celebrated spokesman for this position was a Saxon professor and jurist, Samuel von Pufendorf (1632–1694), who served two of the most effective rulers of his day, the Great Elector of Brandenburg and Karl XI of Sweden. For Pufendorf, as for Hobbes, people established political society as a vehicle for restraining themselves. Yet the purpose of government was protective, not repressive. For this reason subjects made a second contract, this time with their newly appointed government. The subject affirmed loyalty to his ruler; the ruler agreed to respect the natural rights of the subject. Pufendorf's view appealed to the princes of the Holy Roman Empire, who believed they were protecting their subjects from social anarchy while defending them from the pretensions of the emperor. In the mid-eighteenth century, the so-called enlightened despots of central Europe also drew their rationale for absolutism from Pufendorf.

A second body of natural law theorists did not share Pufendorf's elevated view of the powerful state. On the contrary, these critics considered it politically naive to entrust governments with defining and then defending natural rights. They considered absolutist regimes to be less interested in protecting subjects than in maintaining authority. Constructed on principles of rigid hierarchy, these governments existed in order that the few might dominate the many. By way of contrast, however, the people— and the people alone—must define the meaning of natural rights and laws. This doctrine originated in England during the 1640s, a time when revolution was giving birth to Europe's boldest political climate. Its primary advocates, the Levellers, held that because the laws of nature were established on the collective reasoning power of mankind, it made no sense to delegate to a political regime the right to reinterpret the laws. The people must remain sovereign.

If reason rules the state of nature and political society represents such a threat to natural rights, why bother to form governments in the first place? In his *Commonwealth of Oceana* (1656), James Harrington (1611–1677), an old crony of Charles I who refused to choose sides in the Civil War, responded with the view that all regimes—monarchies, aristocracies, or republics—are beholden to the propertied and exist to defend the interests of landowners. For Harrington this was how it should be. In the next generation, more clearly than Harrington had done, John Locke incorporated the protection of property rights into a political theory supporting natural rights. Locke's amalgam appealed to the victors in the Glorious Revolution of 1688–1689 and became the commonplace for the English ruling classes of the eighteenth century. Because he hated absolutism and said so, Locke also became a model for continental liberals. His legacy was to show that both security and freedom were compatible features of civil society.

Locke's *First Treatise on Government* and a good deal of the *Second Treatise* were written between 1679 and 1683 in order to refute Sir John Filmer's advocacy of divine-right monarchy. Unfortunately, the last four years of Charles II's reign were bad ones for opponents of absolutism. A physician with a research post at Oxford University, Locke was associated with Shaftesbury and the Whigs. Fearing imprisonment during the Tory reaction of 1683, he fled to Holland. Political exile nurtured his distaste for unregulated governments, and the fall of James II brought him home in 1688. Thereupon he polished up and published his two treatises. For the remainder of his life Locke lived quietly near London, in contact with scholars, scientists, and politicians, enjoying fame as the founder of empiricist psychology and the leading theoretician of the Glorious Revolution.

Locke's *Second Treatise* (1690), his more important one, opens in the state of nature, where "everyone has the Executive Power." Freedom there is not the anarchic and obliterating kind outlined by Hobbes, but rather a natural freedom defined by natural law. In Locke's state of nature it is human reason which interprets natural law. Any individual who constricts the freedom of another is committing a transgression. However, distinct disadvantages exist in the state of nature. The laws of nature are not written, nor is there an impartial judge who can try and punish transgressors. An aggrieved party has no other choice than to fight it out with his attacker in much the same way states do in the "community of nations," where no supranational court of justice exists. Locke insists, however, that in the state of nature, reason guides individuals and conflict is the exception. As evidence, people remove raw materials from nature, apply their labor to these materials, and convert them into useful products. This activity gives the individual title to property. "As much land as a man tills, plants, improves, cultivates, and can use the product of, so much is his property. . . . God gave the world to men in common. . . . He gave it to the use of the industrious and rational, and Labor was to be [mankind's] title to it." To guarantee themselves a juridical device that will protect their natural and material possessions, individuals create civil society.

A contract among individuals forming civil society marks the first step out of the state of nature. The second step occurs when society institutionalizes protection by authorizing government. The purpose of government is the establishment of a legislature and magistrates "with authority to determine all the controversies and redress the injuries" individuals might suffer at each other's hand—in other words, to guarantee natural rights and rightful property. While Pufendorf glossed over the fact that the state itself might present the greatest danger to rights and property, Locke saw it clearly. The relationship between the citizenry and legislature was not indissoluble. Government was a trust: "The Legislative acts against the Trust reposed in them, when they endeavor to invade the Property of the Subject, and make themselves, or any part of the community, Masters or Arbitrary disposers of the Lives, Liberties or Fortunes of the People." But who should determine whether government has overstepped its bounds? "To this I reply," wrote Locke, "the People shall be judge." Breaking with Hobbes and Pufendorf, Locke approved of throwing out the rascals, either through elections or other means. Rid of repressive government, the people do not fall back into a state of nature. The first contract stands. Civil society must simply establish another government, more worthy of its trust than the preceding one.

Therefore, within society and under government, Locke's individual retains as far as possible the rights held in the state of nature. Eighteenth-century Whig aristocrats assumed that Locke's "people" were the "political nation," that is, those who possessed valuable amounts of landed property. These were the individuals with most to gain from a benevolent government and most to lose from a repressive regime. The propertied made certain that the "Legislative" in England represented their interests and voted according to their wishes. They also used Locke to justify both social and economic inequality. However, Locke's heritage extended far beyond the elegant country houses of the English gentry. Frederick the Great might discover his spiritual ancestry in Pufendorf. On the other hand, American and French revolutionaries found theirs in the timid Oxford don whose major concern remained citizens' rights and not subjects' duties.

BAROQUE, CLASSICISM, AND REALISM

Italian Baroque and Its National Variants

The years 1648 to 1715 were filled with contradiction and paradox. Economic decline, depopulation, war, famine, and disease formed a backdrop for a series of intellectual triumphs unparalleled since the Golden Age of Athens. Art and architecture concretely illustrated the self-confidence of elites and their intoxication with power. The governing form of artistic expression was called baroque. It derived from the Italian Renaissance, took hold around 1620, became an international style at mid-century, and influenced painting, sculpture, and architecture until the 1750s. It was soaring, dynamic, and passionately intense. It stressed curves and shadow, avoiding clear lines and sharp contrasts. Seeking to capture the fleeting moment, or else the act of revelation or climax, baroque enjoyed its greatest prestige in religious sculpture and building.

Baroque's most celebrated practitioner was Giovanni Lorenzo Bernini (1598–1680), for half a century the papacy's official artist. Bernini sought to capture the heart of the viewer by dazzling the senses. The tombs that Bernini sculpted for Popes Urban VIII and Alexander VII dramatically revealed subjects surprised by death, underscoring the inexorable fact of mortality. By way of contrast, his "Saint Theresa in Ecstasy," her heart pierced by the shaft of divine love, subtly intertwined the facts of spiritual and erotic rapture. In all of Bernini's pieces, it is sensuality that dominates. As an architect, Bernini—as well as his contemporary and rival Francesco Borromini (1599–1667)—designed churches that twisted, curved, and soared toward the Roman sky. Bernini's masterpiece was the staggering square that faces Saint Peter's basilica in the Vatican, bordered by freestanding open colonnades, four deep, that embrace the beholder. Never before or since has an ellipse of columns been used with such daring and effectiveness.

Baroque's influence spread from Muscovy to South America. The Jesuits adopted it as the official style for their churches, and the reconstruction of central Europe after the Thirty Years' War was largely the work of baroque-inspired architects. The Hapsburgs used baroque as a visual means of linking together into a common civilization the diverse people of their empire. In the most southern Catholic regions, particularly Spain and Latin America, baroque churches assumed fantastic proportions. They were riotous and bombastic, flinging passion and eccentricity into the face of the beholder. They went far beyond Bernini's intentions and illustrated the degenerate form into which the style could fall. On the other hand, baroque was more restrained in the Protestant North. The Great Fire of London in 1666 necessitated the reconstruction of the English capital. Christopher Wren (1632–1723), mathematician, charter member of the Royal Society, and engineer as well as architect, proposed a whole new baroque city. However, Parliament commissioned him with the more modest task of rebuilding or restoring some fifty churches ruined by the fire. Chief of these was old Saint Paul's Cathedral. Wren envisioned a new edifice, Protestantism's response to Saint Peter's. It took nearly forty years to complete the job. Wren worked empirically, modifying and changing details as the building went up. What emerged was not a clumsy hodgepodge but a masterful blending of earlier classical, Gothic, and Renaissance styles that gave a unique tone to English baroque.

French baroque assumed such distinctive national characteristics that it has been given its unique label: classicism. Obsessed by the achievements of the ancients, Louis XIV personally preferred rectilinear shapes, order, and harmony to the less disciplined, sensuous, soaring forms of Italian baroque. Yet the emergence of French classicism preceded Louis, as the early seventeenth-century architect François Mansart and painter Nicolas Poussin deviated from baroque forms. Under Louis, a rigorously defined court style established itself, and royal institutions were built to enforce a dictatorship of taste.

Colbert was assigned to harness art, and he accomplished the task in his customary regulatory manner. In 1663 he awarded a constitution to the

Academy of Painting and Sculpture, already fifteen years old. To be assured commissions in Louis XIV's France, an artist had to be in good standing with the academy and obey its aesthetic standards. Other academies regulated dance, music, and architecture. The painter Charles Lebrun operated the state-financed Gobelins tapestry works, controlling a multitude of sculptors, painters, weavers, and cabinetmakers. The French Academy of Rome was founded to train young French artists in the heart of ancient classical— and modern baroque—civilization. A symbolic confrontation between Italian baroque and the French style occurred in 1665 when the 67-year-old Bernini was commissioned to rebuild the Louvre palace in Paris. Arriving in the French capital, the passionate and independent-minded Italian was flabbergasted to discover French artists and critics laboring within the confines of Colbert's bureaucratically defined canons of taste. Unruffled, Bernini presented his flamboyant sketches to Colbert and Louis, who ultimately rejected them for the more classical and less expensive designs of a French artist. Bernini cast the mold for his famous bust of the king and indignantly left for home.

French classical architecture challenged baroque by emphasizing reason, regularity, and conformity. To reflect seventeenth-century standards of palatial grandeur, it nevertheless had to borrow from baroque sources. One building, the royal palace at Versailles, showed how baroque and classical might coexist in the most spectacular way imaginable. From the moment of its conception Versailles was to be monumental as form and symbol, the costs of its construction unaffected by falling revenues and economic recession. Louis XIV detested Paris and longed to live in the grand manner on a country estate. His father had built a hunting lodge 15 miles southwest of the capital. Early in the 1660s the lodge was modified into a place for official receptions. Then in 1669, Louis decided to construct his new residence on the site. What he envisioned was the playground for his court and the central offices of his bureaucracy.

The architect Louis Le Vau preserved Louis XIII's hunting lodge but dwarfed it inside an enormous U-shaped edifice. The most active period of construction took place between 1669 and 1684. Between 1679 and 1689 the formal gardens were laid out. Great open courtyards were carved from marble and stone in order to stage theatrical performances and to celebrate births, marriages, and military victories. The three-storied building and its enormous facade flanked by a pair of wings exuded baroque magnificence while classicism reigned inside. Lebrun and his decorators filled the walls with vivid allegorical paintings favorably comparing Louis XIV to the gods and heroes of antiquity. Noble, placid statuary brooded over the scene. A great canal was dug through the palace grounds, and the completed gardens were models of symmetry and order. The town of Versailles was built, wholly dependent upon the needs of the palace. The ensemble represented total mastery over nature, revealing cold, ruthless, mechanical power. Filled with pilgrims, Saint Peter's square vibrated with life. On the other hand, the great courtyard at Versailles was a stage setting and the palace itself a monument to artificiality and ritual. Though housing a government, Versailles seemed divorced from the real world. As architecture it was Europe's most oppressive masterpiece.

Baroque painting was symbolic, allusive, and decorative. Its intention was to seize the fleeting moment. The sixteenth-century picaresque studies by Michelangelo de Caravaggio and the overflowing church walls and ceilings by Corregio were its sources. After 1648 church interiors in the Mediterranean, the Hapsburg Empire, and South America drowned the beholder beneath heavy cloud formations, gesticulating figures, and flowing draperies. A pompous aristocratic society adored these decorative renderings of spirituality. Once more the French offered a classical variant, indeed an alternative, to the Italian style. Lebrun and the Academy of Painting pursued the notion that the ancients had perfected beauty through a balance of realism and ideal form, and adapted this aesthetic concept to late seventeenth-century tastes. Chief among the French classical painters was Nicolas Poussin (1594–1665), who spent forty years in Rome for inspiration. Paris merchants, parlementary judges, and court aristocrats bought Poussin's pastoral scenes and dignified mythological subjects bathed in cool, light colors. Claude Lorrain (1600–1682), another Frenchman living in Rome, seconded Poussin with pastoral subjects that greatly influenced west-European landscape gardening. Poussin and Lorrain equated reason with nature and nature with virtue. While late baroque offered overripe magnificence as an alternative to war and uncertainty, classicism yielded escapist arcadias.

Besides classicism, another variant of baroque painting took root in the Dutch Netherlands—in the native landscapes of Jacob van Ruysdael (1628–1682), domestic scenes of Jan Vermeer (1632–1675), and late portraits of Rembrandt (1606–1669). The Dutch artists were the first to work exclusively for an open market, not for a specific patron. No academy bound them to regulations governing subject matter or technique. They drew from the world, all the while experimenting with color, light, shadow, and technique. What resulted was an explosion of artistic creativity unparalleled in the century.

Vermeer and Rembrandt were the greatest painters. Born in 1632 in Delft and dying there forty-three years later, Vermeer painted no more than sixty canvasses in his lifetime. His subject matter was limited to domestic scenes in two small rooms in his modest provincial house. The furniture and people hardly ever change. Women working in the kitchen, making lace, or playing a musical instrument possess a disturbing air of silent mystery, and in their day Vermeer's paintings did not sell very well. However, no painter has ever understood better than Vermeer the interaction of light and space or the subtleties inherent in the most ordinary scenes of life. Vermeer's masterpiece was a landscape, the "View of Delft," an artistic victory for expression and understanding as complete as Newton's.

On the other hand, Rembrandt began his career as a baroque artist. Born to a Leiden miller's family in 1606, he studied art in Amsterdam and settled there in his mid-twenties. In 1632 he skyrocketed to fame with his group portrait "The Anatomy Lesson of Dr. Tulp," commissioned by the physicians represented in the painting. Then personal misfortune struck him hard in the form of financial difficulties and the premature deaths of his beloved wife and several children. Wealthy burghers grew less interested than before in his overly introspective portraits of them. His "Night Watch" perhaps is the greatest of all baroque paintings; yet his ultimate fame was not through depiction of the grandiose and elegant but rather through analysis of the tragedy and turmoil of the inner self. Rembrandt's last portraits and religious scenes brought out his true genius, a psychological perception softened by comprehension and tenderness, uncompromisingly poignant evaluations of human fallibility and grandeur.

Literary Baroque and Its Classical Alternative

In the late seventeenth century the subjects of painting were illustrated according to baroque, classical, or realistic techniques. Literature showed similar trends. By 1648 baroque writers had created a common style that transcended differences in language, religious tradition, or social and political circumstance. The religious allegory was an excellent subject for baroque expression. In *Paradise Lost* (1667), for example, John Milton (1608–1674) depicted the rebellion of the angels and fall of humanity in a grandiose poem, a Protestant response to *The Divine Comedy*. Across the English Channel, the Dutch epic poet Joost van den Vondel (1587–1679) first celebrated the political triumph of the United Provinces and, subsequently, in his work *Lucifer* (1654), stressed religious themes very similar to Milton's. By way of contrast, in *The Pilgrim's Progress* (1678), the self-educated tinker-preacher John Bunyan (1628–1688) brought the allegorical fantasy of the baroque to the lowest rung of literate English society. Bunyan's artistic re-creations of abstract Christian principles derived straight from the medieval morality play; yet the passion, conflict, and digressive story line are indisputably baroque. In addition to *The Pilgrim's Progress*, vulgarized courtly romances fascinated village audiences throughout England, the Netherlands, and France. Both reader and listeners would virtually memorize the dog-eared volumes, and oral tradition passed the stories on to the next generation.

Built mostly on the 2,500 plays of Felix Lope de Vega (1562–1635), Tirso de Molina (1584–1648), and Pedro Calderón de la Barca (1600–1681), by 1648 Spain's literary Golden Age had peaked. The sacred dramas of these three, which were allegorical representations of the Eucharist, Bible stories, and saints' lives, remained as popular as their secular plays emphasizing patriotism, chivalry, and virtue. The Spanish dramatists were more than moralists. A deeply religious spirit and sense of guilt over the vanity of the world etched their way into Spanish baroque theater, perhaps the playwrights' reaction to the collapse of their country after its sixteenth-century flash of splendor. Spanish baroque influenced French theater in the work of Pierre Corneille (1606–1684), whose characters were beset with excruciating choices between emotion and duty. However, in Corneille's plays the Spaniards' skepticism about life is missing. Moreover, the Frenchman leaned heavily on classical subjects, since they were the only ones that the academic arbiters of national taste considered sufficiently dignified to be represented by tragedy. Convention also required Corneille to write in Alexandrine verse. He rejected stage violence, limited stage action to twenty-four hours or less, and constructed plots on logic and argument as opposed to atmosphere and visual mood. Corneille's inspiration was baroque, but his universe was classical.

The seventeenth-century literary tradition of central and eastern Europe emphasized baroque seasoned with folk realism. Germany's most important writer was Hans Jakob Christoffel von Grimmelshausen (1625–1676), whose adventure novel *Simplicius Simplicissimus* (1669) owed much to the immensely popular extravagant romances of France and Spain. The setting of *Simplicissimus* is Germany of the Thirty Years' War, and its basic theme is survival in the jungle of the world. The protagonist is the obverse of the dignified Corneillian hero. His fantastic, vulgar, and shocking adventures are told in a style that is both naturalistic and bitterly ironic. In its extravagance *Simplicissimus* was baroque; however, its exposé of war and concern for the common man's instinct to survive give it a very realistic turn.

While Corneille was a baroque writer constrained by a classical mold, his younger French contemporary Jean Racine (1639–1699) revealed how elevated a literature might emerge from pure academism. Racine's most prolific periods coincided with the construction of the chateau of Versailles. However, the playwright's work gave a depth and substantiality to the classical style that formal gardens, placid statuary, and arcadian harmonies could not hope to match. Racine wished to analyze emotions rather than illustrate them, and the individual confronted by a hopeless destiny fascinated him. Racine's major works dealt with tragic heroines— *Bérénice, Phèdre, Esther,* and *Athalie.* The French Academy limited the vocabulary he could legitimately employ, and like Corneille, he was restricted to the unities of time and space defined by Aristotle. He had to write in Alexandrine verse, and all his plots were derived from classical or biblical themes. The results were remarkable. The reasoned tone, intellectualized emotions, and obsession with dramatic unities reduce action to pure dialogue. Scarcely a playwright has written better poetry than Racine about the individual's hopeless struggle against fate. True to Jansenist theology all his life, Racine applied severe discipline and singular direction to his masterpieces of character analysis. He developed the classical literary style to its fullest bloom. Its very restrictiveness afforded him the opportunity to concentrate, analyze, and dissect.

In France, classicism produced theoreticians for whom clear thinking and expert craftsmanship were the hallmarks of literary art. These attributes were particularly necessary to forms like the funeral oration, court sermon, maxim, and even personal letter, all of which were converted into art forms during Louis XIV's reign. Dramatist, poet, and theoretician, John Dryden (1631–1700) was England's greatest exponent of classicism. Few were more skillful than Dryden in applying verse to heroic drama. Most other English classicists wrote formally correct works to combat what they believed to be Shakespeare's baroque excesses, but they lacked the incisiveness, depth, and subtlety of a Racine.

The greatest comic author of the century, Molière (1622–1673), wrote his plays while remaining true to the French Academy's classic rules. Born Jean-Baptiste Poquelin to a family of Paris merchant upholsterers, Molière rejected his father's business in 1643 and established a traveling theatrical company. Following a lengthy period of tours throughout France, in 1658 he had the opportunity to perform for Louis XIV. First employed by the king's brother, Molière subsequently won a place on the royal payroll. One of the few original spirits in Europe's most convention-bound court, Molière had his troupe play whatever he wrote. His comedies were satirical, picking apart miserliness, hypochondria, status seeking, religious hypocrisy, and the foolishness ingrained in the learned professions, particularly law and medicine. Although he gained enemies among professionals and churchmen, Molière knew the limits of his freedom and he never touched politics. His comedies usually take place within the confines of the bourgeois family, so that king and court could enjoy the humor without embarrassment. As a professional actor, Molière knew firsthand what it meant to suffer outside the mainstream of society, and his plays penetrate deeply into the ironies of human existence. Mocking excess, he exposed society to analysis and criticism. His most attractive character was the practical, quick-witted servant girl whose refreshing authenticity contrasts with the pedantry and floundering of her social masters.

Although baroque and classical remained the dominant forms of seventeenth-century European literature, a restless desire to break out of traditions and habits gave rise to experimental approaches that defy classification. At the century's close the popularization of science itself had become literature. In his *Conversations on the Plurality of Worlds* (1686), Bernard de Fontenelle tried to make the Copernican-Cartesian universe intelligible to nonscientists. The *Conversations* took the form of five dialogues in a moonlit garden between a beautiful marquise and her tutor. Never before had instruction been made so entertaining. Fontenelle also wrote about the possibility of life on other planets. His *History of Oracles*

(1686) attacked superstition, and his *Origin of Fables* (1724) criticized the supernatural sources of religion. During a lifetime that lasted an entire century, Fontenelle pleaded for the unrestrained right to explore new cultural vistas. He spoke up for experience and common sense; he was skeptical about the past and optimistic about the future. He did more than anyone else of his time to increase public awareness of the unfolding scientific civilization. Fontenelle merged a trenchant critique of existing institutions with a profound hope for discovering reasonable, authentic, and happier alternatives. Along with Bayle, Locke, and Leibniz, Fontenelle laid the groundwork for the eighteenth-century Enlightenment.

P A R T

AN AGE OF HOPE AND REVOLUTION (1715–1789)

7

THE PEOPLE, THE LAND, AND THE STATE

POPULATIONS: RURAL AND URBAN

The Indices of Growth

By 1720, and especially after 1750, Europe's "long century" of very slow population growth was over. The 100 million Europeans alive at the beginning of the eighteenth century left between 190 and 200 million descendants at the end. Another 30 million people of European origin were settled on five other continents. Only China, whose eighteenth-century population tripled to over 300 million, exceeded the European rate of increase. Although statistics for the period are estimates and trends varied widely, most eighteenth-century couples in Europe continued the reproductive habits of their ancestors. Peasant women still married in their middle or late twenties and averaged three to five births. However, no longer did one-fourth of their infants perish in their first year. No longer were half of them dead by age twenty. During the eighteenth century the first-year mortality rate dropped below 15 percent, and the chances were seven in ten that a peasant infant would survive adolescence. Thus, of the half-billion Europeans born, 40 to 50 million were spared who would not have reached adulthood a century earlier. Those who reached twenty-five could count on living ten years longer than their parents had. Half of them would reach sixty. For the first time in European history, people began rejecting the presence of death. Death became a private family matter, not a public ceremony. It was shunted aside, hidden from view, thrust out of consciousness.

More elemental physiological reasons than medical progress lay behind increased life expectancy. Preventive medicine, such as widespread inoculation against smallpox, still lay in the future. Although efforts were made even in the countryside to replace semimagical folk formulas with professionally prescribed remedies, curative medicine remained the privilege of the rich. Hospitals were places where one awaited the end. The most elementary rules of personal hygiene, such as regular bathing with soap, were largely ignored. Although the ravages of plague largely passed after the 1720s, crowd diseases such as influenza, smallpox, typhus, and dysentery still struck hard. However, because they were better nourished, Europeans born after 1720 resisted disease more successfully than their seventeenth-century predecessors.

Earlier we noted how from 1648 to 1715, limited agricultural productivity restrained population growth. For most of this period Europe's farming frontier receded from what it had been in the sixteenth century. Except for England and the Dutch Netherlands, regional dearth could easily grow into widespread famine, with weakened survivors easy prey for disease and epidemics. After 1700, however, opportunities increased for extending cultivation and settling new areas of Europe. The Russian Ukraine, Hapsburg Hungary, Swedish Finland, and East Prussia were such regions, and in the course of the eighteenth century Europe's cultivable space nearly doubled. In western Europe intensified methods of crop raising increased productivity. From Ireland to Russia new crops were introduced, such as the potato, corn, and rice, diminishing consumer dependence upon other cereals. Improved roads and waterways, reduced or eliminated customs tolls, and more effective state intervention in times of regional dearth, facilitated agricultural transports and saved countless thousands. While it is overly simple to see in the eighteenth century a steady, progressive increase in food supply, the fact remains that people were better fed than their parents and grandparents had been. They survived, married, and reproduced.

Expansion and Control

The growth of central and eastern Europe is most striking. In 1700 the population of Hungary, recently liberated from the Turks, was a million and a half. Germans and Slavs poured in. By 1800 Hungary held over 6 million. Frontier areas such as Finland and eastern Germany saw populations triple. The newly opened southeastern plains of Russia witnessed demographic increases of 10 percent per year. Rulers thought they saw a link between extended or improved agriculture, expanding populations, and a strengthened state. The Hapsburg emperor Joseph II (1780–1790) ennobled a propagandist for clover cultivation. Frederick II of Prussia (1740–1786) and Catherine II of Russia (1762–1796) encouraged immigration, paying for the costs of displacement and promising new subjects religious freedom, fiscal exemptions, and even serf labor.

In western Europe, population increases were less dramatic than in the eastern frontier regions, but the social consequences proved more telling. England and Wales had under 5.5 million in 1700. Despite emigration to the New World, a century later they held 9 million. During the same period the population of France rose from 19 million to 28 million. Neither country possessed virgin lands to accept additional people. In fact, after 1760, England's rural population declined markedly. While "improving" English landlords increased agricultural productivity with fewer hands, the dispossessed rural poor could secure passage to America or migrate either to London or the industrial boomtowns. On the other hand, French peasants found emigration less possible or attractive than their English counterparts, and there were fewer industrializing places to absorb them. Tenaciously, French men and women tried to stay on the land, but the competition for scarce plots drove up rents past what most could afford. By the 1780s a French rural population of unprecedented size and in exceedingly difficult straits lay at the root of a profound social crisis. Never before had France experienced such a large population at the point of indigence—perhaps 10 million people. In 1789 the coincidental merging of a political and constitutional crisis with a social and economic one produced a national explosion. Though revolution failed to occur in either the Italian states or Spain, growing populations of rural poor nevertheless presaged mounting social tension. During the eighteenth century Italy's population rose from 13 to 17 million, Spain's from 7.5 to 10.5 million.

Relatively few observers pinpointed the inherent dangers of dramatic population growth until the English economist and social critic Thomas Malthus (1766–1834) published his *Essay on Population* in 1798. Malthus was among the first to make a mathematical correlation between food supply and demographic expansion. He believed that from generation to generation the production of food might be described in arithmetical progression (1, 2, 4, 8, 16); at the same time, births occurred in geometrical progression (1, 2, 4, 16, 256). The major checks on growth would be the familiar ones: war, famine, and epidemic. Nineteenth-century so-called progressive theoreticians built their own implications on to Malthus's findings. They believed that the best way to avoid a future universal calamity was by keeping the poor at subsistence levels. Let nature take its course and seize the weak.

Between 1715 and 1789, however, a few west-European regions seemed to have taken voluntary steps to avoid the Malthusian peril. The Dutch Netherlands were commercially rich and urban; Denmark was agriculturally rich and rural. During the eighteenth century the Dutch population increased only from 1.9 million to 2.1 million; the Danish population rose only from 750,000 to under 900,000. Prosperous Lombardy and Tuscany witnessed population increases that were proportionally smaller than the so-called backward areas of Sicily and Naples. Within larger states certain well-to-do provinces grew less rapidly than others. The reasons were neither high mortality nor fears of catastrophe. These regions had no agricultural frontier and were not industrializing rapidly. While opportunities were limited, residents lived well enough. They appear to have instituted family planning in order to keep things that way.

Urban Developments

Poor country people often try their luck in town, whether or not the town can absorb them. West of the Elbe River, urban growth again became important. London and Paris became metropolises. The English capital grew from 400,000 in 1700 to nearly a million a century later. Paris contained 400,000 in 1700 and 700,000 in 1789. London was a royal capital, great international port, and hub of world finance. Paris was Europe's cultural center, an aristocratic residence, a lawyer's town. Both cities had great floating populations. Filth and overcrowding were endemic. Though deaths probably exceeded births in both cities, immigration from the countryside more than made up for losses. In the 1770s two of every three inhabitants of London or Paris had been born elsewhere.

Nor were these the only metropolises of Europe. Istanbul rivaled London in size, and by 1800 Naples contained over 400,000 souls. With insufficient commerce and little culture and industry, both of these cities were baskets for the poor. By 1800 fifteen additional cities had populations exceeding 100,000. In 1700 there had been only seven. Berlin, Vienna, Warsaw, St. Petersburg, and to a lesser extent Moscow, owed their growth to government. They were administrative centers or royal courts. On the other hand, after London and Paris, the most vigorous west-European cities over 100,000 were either ocean or river ports: Barcelona in Spain, Marseilles and Lyon in France, Amsterdam in the Dutch Netherlands, and Dublin in Ireland. However, not even these cities were representative of eighteenth-century Europe. Most urban populations lived in towns under 100,000. During the seventeenth century such places in western Germany, France, Spain, Italy, the Southern Netherlands, and the London basin had lagged in development. After 1740 many revived, largely as markets for grain and cattle, as centers for administering both government and country estates, and as residences for entrepreneurs, craftspeople, and shopkeepers.

Around 1770 a new type of city emerged in northwestern England, the Austrian Netherlands, and northern France: the industrial town, a place far different from the administrative-commercial agglomerations that Europe had known since the Middle Ages. These new towns were to become living embodiments of the most important displacement of population Europe had experienced since the fall of the Roman Empire. The industrial city was not entirely the consequence of the Industrial Revolution. As late as 1800, most of the industrial population of Great Britain still clustered around textile mills or iron and coal mines in the countryside, whose source of power depended upon fast streams. Nevertheless, the rise of Manchester, from 20,000 to just under 100,000 in the course of a century, coincided with its emergence as a great textile producer. Between 1760 and 1800, Birmingham, Britain's major source of light metals, doubled in population. So did the shipbuilding city of Liverpool. As fossil fuels and mechanically powered machinery were introduced, factories were born and suburbs grew around them. These cities were genuine boomtowns, traps for the new industrial poor, lacking housing, sanitation, or breathing space. Well into the nineteenth century, deaths there outstripped births; but the countryside still fed them its surplus. Although the saying "Alcohol is the quickest way out of Manchester" stems from the 1850s, it was already a fact in the 1770s.

A DECLINING PEASANTRY

East-European Serfdom

Despite population shifts toward towns, eighteenth-century Europe remained overwhelmingly rural. Even in the highly urbanized Dutch Netherlands, half the people lived in the countryside. In England, seven in ten did; in France, four of five. Eastern Europe was practically townless. In 1726, 97 percent of Russia's people were on the land; seventy years later, 95 percent. On the continent land tenure systems consolidated in the seventeenth century were perpetuated in the eighteenth. East of the Elbe River a largely unfree peasantry labored for noble landlords who enjoyed legal, economic, and judicial powers over their workers. Except in Prussia, the landlords might be immensely wealthy and powerful. Three noble families controlled all the land in the Polish Ukraine. One of them, the Potockis, had 3 million acres and 130,000 serfs. The Hungarian Esterházy clan ran 7 million acres, and the properties of the Lithuanian Charles Radziwill absorbed six hundred villages. In Russia, 15 percent of the estate owners held 80 percent of the serfs. Law and custom kept the great properties intact, and heirs usually were prohibited from dividing estates for sale.

Protected by the law, landlord aristocracies institutionalized serfdom. In Poland peasant males spent four days per week on the estate owner's domain. In Russia the serf was constrained to work his own tiny garden plot by night. In Bohemia, if a peasant was half an hour late for work on the domain, the landlord's bailiff charged him with an additional seven hours of free labor. Social relationships fed on a psychology of mutual distrust and fear. Masters suspected bailiffs, and bailiffs held villages collectively responsible for the misdeeds of individual peasants. Village chiefs, serfs themselves, were caught between the contempt of the bailiff and mistrust of their fellows. The favorite folk hero in eastern Europe was the bandit, who, beyond the realm of the law, was beyond the realm of subjugation. Runaway peasants joined the bands of those who attacked merchants and manor houses. East of the Elbe, poor harvests and the threat of famine easily ignited collective passions. Between 1762 and 1772 alone, the Russian army confronted forty different regional uprisings.

Yet such revolts had little effect on the static quality of east-European rural life. Raising cereals for distant markets, the estate owner preferred to control production rather than parcel out plots for money rents. The serf's pitiful patch remained the legal fiction recognized by government and landlord in return for the labor services expected of him. Without even this speck of land, tens of thousands of serfs worked merely for a hovel and bread. The estate owner customarily denied peasants the right to acquire their own tools. Collecting taxes for the government, serving as magistrate and police chief, he remained an impenetrable wall between regimes and the most numerous body of their subjects. Serf agriculture was as wasteful as it was degrading. Eighteenth-century domains might expand in space, but their per-acre yields remained as limited as they had been in the Middle Ages. The open-field system left one-third of the strips fallow every year. The active strips alternated between spring-sown barley and oats and autumn-sown wheat and rye. The permanent pasture provided insufficient fodder, and mechanized improvements were virtually unknown. An innovation like manuring the soil was considered an act against nature or crime against God.

Hapsburg Reforms

Midway into the eighteenth century, some central- and east-European governments attempted to improve agricultural productivity. The Hapsburgs brought clover from their Belgian possessions and planted it in their German ones. Frederick II of Prussia virtually had to shove the potato down the throats of his peasants; however, by 1770 its cultivation assured the conquest of absolute famine. Genuine social and economic reform was a far thornier issue than the introduction of fertilizing agents and new foods. However, governments had considerable self-interest in modifying or eliminating serfdom. Peasants able to sell crops on the open market would have cash for state taxes. Free from threats of eviction or sale, with additional time to till their own plots, peasants might become more efficient, trustworthy, and intelligent cultivators. All of this worked toward a prosperous state, but it also worked against social custom and the privileged status of rural aristocracies.

It was the Austrian Hapsburgs who took the lead in chipping away at the foundations of serfdom. They began in Hungary, where vast immigrations of Germans and Rumanians had created an unprecedented ethnic diversity. This new settlement invited Vienna to reassess landlord-peasant relations. The traditional arrangement had been the classic east-European formula: enserfed cultivators tilling tiny plots leased by the peasant village. For their land, peasants gave the estate owner free labor services, certain stipulated dues, and a share of the crop. They also contributed state taxes, which the landlord was exempt from paying, and a tithe to the Church. Landlord justice controlled peasant life, sales of individuals were possible, and the scale of dues and services varied according to what the individual landowner believed he could get.

Following an investigation of rural conditions that genuinely shocked her, in 1769 Empress Maria Theresa (1740–1780) issued an edict guaranteeing Hungarian peasants the right to leave their holdings upon expiration of the contract with their landlord. Although the empress had no wish to abolish peasant labor on the landlord's domain, such work was limited to two days per week and four in emergency situations. Imperial officials, not the landlords or their bailiffs, were to enforce the edict. Not yet free tenants, Hungarian peasants at least were released from the bonds of landlord arbitrariness. Between 1771 and 1775, the Hapsburgs extended the Hungarian decrees to their German territories. In all cases the spirit of the legislation was not to abolish peasant dues and services but to regulate and reduce them.

By way of contrast, Maria Theresa's son and successor, Joseph II, desired genuine emancipation. In 1781 the emperor abolished personal labor services in Bohemia. Four years later Hungary's peasants were liberated as well. The final step came in 1789, with the conversion of all personal services and multifarious peasant dues into money payments. In place of these obligations, peasants were to give the landlord a rent approximating 17 percent of their annual income. The state was guaranteed an additional 12 percent. The sums were the equivalent of two working days per week— according to peasants, much too high a compensation, and according to their landlords much too low. In Hungary both social groups rose in armed revolt. Joseph died prematurely in 1790, and his successor was forced to repeal the antiserfdom decrees. It would take another half century before the Hapsburg peasantry gained its absolute freedom. This notwithstanding, the Josephian laws represented the most important step taken in eighteenth-century Europe to liberate a servile work force through means short of political revolution.

The role of the state as arbiter of landlord-peasant relations became an accepted fact in several other eighteenth-century European states. The reformist example of the Hapsburgs influenced governments in Denmark, Savoy, and the German state of Baden to abolish serfdom. Although Frederick II of Prussia and Catherine II of Russia limited their activity to the realm of good intentions, public opinion in their countries gradually considered serfdom to be a problem rather than an institution. In Poland, where forced rural labor was more deeply entrenched than anywhere else in Europe and where the central government was thoroughly incapable of defending the most elementary rights of the peasantry, a reformer wrote, "We have imposed upon our serfs the intolerable burden of an enslavement that has no counterpart elsewhere in Christendom."

West-European Tenancy: The French Example

Therefore humanitarian motives joined pragmatic ones in questioning and modifying timeworn practice. West of the Elbe River, peasant-landlord relations were more complex than in eastern Europe. In parts of Germany, Italy, and France, serfdom still existed; but no more than 10 percent of western Europe's peasantry was subjected to its restrictions. Tenancy arrangements varied from country to country and from region to region. In southern Italy, Sicily, Spain, and Portugal, sharecroppers and landless migrants were the rule. Though technically free to move, they nevertheless were so poor and dependent upon estate owners that their misery could not be distinguished from that of the most downtrodden Polish serf. West-European governments rarely intervened in peasant-landlord relations. Tenants tried to defend their holdings in law courts. However, what satisfaction could they obtain from judges who themselves were landlords? Moreover, rural populations were expanding. Larger peasant families meant split inheritances, and split inheritances meant smaller, less productive plots. By the tens of thousands, peasant tenants had to sell out. Wealth was concentrated in fewer hands, and the number of landless rose. The latter comprised a particularly embittered group, relatively young in age, increasingly poverty-stricken, conscious of deteriorating social-economic conditions, and, as consumers, hard hit by mounting prices.

France offers the classic case of the declining eighteenth-century tenant farmer. In 1789 more than 22 of 28 million people lived on the land. French peasants were highly sensitive to their place in society. Though details of their obligations varied from place to place, they knew that they bore the overwhelming share of their country's taxes. They alone paid the *taille,* the state's tax on possessions and agricultural production. While other social groups had won exemption, for peasants the "revolutionary" contributions demanded by Louis XIV had become additions to the *taille.* Along with others, peasants paid consumer taxes for salt, shoe leather, playing cards, drinks, tobacco, and iron implements. They were aware that the state did not take these taxes directly but rather farmed them out to wealthy individuals who kept the major share of them in return for a fixed contribution to the government. Peasants paid a tithe to the bishop of their diocese, knowing that only a tiny fraction of their contribution would ever return to their parish to pay the priest and provide relief for the destitute. Most of the tithe supported the bishop himself, his episcopal administration, and wealthy abbeys. If peasants were sharecroppers, they paid half or more of their crop in rents to the estate owner, plus sums for seed, tools, and the use of animal power. If they were long-lease tenants, they paid not only rents but also a welter of dues for use of the estate owner's mill, oven, and wine press. Peasants also performed a stipulated amount of road maintenance on the estate. It is true that these latter dues and services, the product of an age when the estate was a self-contained, self-sufficient community, were not a very great economic burden. Yet it was all the more galling to see greedy landlords charge legal experts to hunt down neglected dues in musty charters and then demand back payment for ten, twenty, or even fifty years. In good times and bad, peasants bore a threefold burden to state, Church, and landlord. They might see their entire income seized by grasping hands.

After 1740, French tenancies declined in both number and size, and tenant farmers who sold out were reduced to sharecropping or migratory labor. In the name of improvement, some landlords tried to take over pastures administered in common by the peasant village. Consumer pressures caused the price of agricultural products to rise, and the large-scale exploiter derived the biggest profits. Until 1775, he lived in a golden age. Rents were up, prices were good, and enclosures were increasing. Between 1776 and 1789, however, a series of poor harvests in most parts of the country ended the period of agricultural prosperity, and estate owners tried to make up for underproduction with an even more vigorous assault on long-term tenancies. They increased rents and dues at a time when the small cultivator had less to sell. As scarcity-provoked high prices forced consumers to spend a disproportionate share of their incomes on bread, they could not afford clothes. The textile entrepreneur sent out less material to be spun and woven in peasant cottages, and another source of rural income was cut. Nevertheless, peasant obligations to state, Church, and landlord remained as high as ever.

The bitterness of cultivators was directed at those who demanded payments from them. They believed that a conspiracy of government officers, tax farmers, intendants, high churchmen, and landlords was intent on securing their destruction. They tried to fight back. The social climate of the 1780s illustrates not only an unprecedented rise in peasant-landlord lawsuits but also an increase in rural violence, brigandage, and simple peasant "usurpations" of pieces of the domain, seigneurial hunting grounds, and contested pastures. Late in 1788 the government admitted the rapidly deteriorating climate in the countryside and called on each parish in France to list and collect specific grievances. But the time for discussion was past. With thousands of onetime tenants taking to the road monthly, those still on the land reacted in spontaneous and violent desperation. During the summer of 1789, a widespread peasant revolt destroyed the remnants of the feudal regime.

Agricultural Revolution in England

In eighteenth-century England the communal patterns of rural life changed more dramatically than was the case in France, and the period has been called an age of agricultural revolution. By 1700 numerous English estate owners farmed directly with hired labor, but most leased plots to tenants residing in country villages. Like their west-European counterparts, the most privileged members of village society in England claimed immunity from arbitrary eviction and willed plots to heirs and widows. On taking over a new plot, they customarily were exempt from the irritating dues and services that continental landlords milked from their tenants. English freeholders did not have to pay any annual rent, and they had the right to vote in county elections. Beneath this cream of English peasant society were less privileged tenants, sharecroppers, and landless villagers.

Despite distinctions in material wealth and social rank, all English peasants derived a sense of communal security from the village. The village was responsible for assuring that no member suffered from excessive need. Although enclosures continued apace during the late seventeenth century, in the Midlands and southern England open strips of land often surrounded the village. While tenants considered themselves individual owners of stipulated strips, village governments controlled the sale of crops and distribution of livestock. Moreover, the village represented the peasant in disputes with the estate owner or his steward. Landlords grumbled over the wastefulness of open fields and the anachronism of village controls. England's population was growing; the continent was crying for grain and bread. After 1700 "improvers" showed how turnip cultivation could better yields when rotated properly with barley, clover, and wheat. The mechanical drill made possible more regular sowing and breaking up of the soil. For these innovations to work, however, it was necessary for the scattered strips to be consolidated into single plots, and the owner himself had to have the final say in cropping and stocking. Most important of all, among politicians and landowners alike a psychological mood had to triumph that emphasized intensive exploitation and profits as opposed to the maintenance of collective village security.

As we have seen, already in the 1660s this mood was growing. Prior to 1700 half of England's arable land was enclosed. During the eighteenth century the process was completed. Six million additional acres of common pasturelands and forests were enclosed and developed. After 1760 individual acts of Parliament largely replaced lengthy parish negotiations as a quick means of decreeing enclosures. During the first half of the century, only 115 Parliamentary enclosure acts were passed. In the 1760s, there were 424; in the 1770s, 642; from 1800 to 1810, 906. In the redistribution of enclosed fields and common lands, tenants technically were entitled to their plots; however, the disposition of land involved expensive litigation, and construction of fences and roads involved costs that most village governments could ill afford. Small farmers therefore sold out to landlords or to the most enterprising of their own kind. In the dawning world of capitalistic agriculture the self-employed cottager became an anachronism, and the enclosure movement destroyed the traditional village community. Landless farmhands now, most of its inhabitants became renters or rural wage earners hired to work new areas brought under cultivation. The less fortunate were thrown on the parish, several of which might combine to establish workhouses, and countryside industrialists took advantage of the recently liberated labor.

Those able to profit from enclosures were the big winners. Free to experiment, "improving landlords" often increased productivity in ways unimaginable a generation earlier. Thomas William Coke of Holkham made marginal lands so profitable that in forty years he was able to increase rents nearly ten times over. He gave his renters long leases and insisted that they follow his prescribed model of cultivation. In Leicestershire, Robert Bakewell crossbred stock for superior traits and kept them alive through the winter on grass and root crops. His methods spread, and within a short time England was raising animals for food whose size flabbergasted Europe. At the Smithfield market, oxen that had averaged 370 pounds in 1710 were averaging 800 pounds in 1795. Calves went from 50 to 150 pounds, sheep from 38 to 80 pounds. The agricultural revolution had created a paradoxical situation in England. The destruction of the village dislocated society. Thousands were dumped into parish workhouses; tens of thousands drifted to the misery of towns. Yet practically no one was starving. Absolute famine was considered an unacceptable scandal, the sign of a barbaric past age. People were eating white bread, not rye. Cottagers and laborers alike knew the taste of roast beef and beer.

A TRIUMPHANT ARISTOCRACY

Complexity and Paradox

The core of Europe's peasantry, serfs and small tenants might well have regarded the eighteenth century as a new iron age. They were the losers in a time of relative prosperity. For the aristocracy, however, the three generations between 1715 and 1789 represented a moment when landed wealth created a sense of incomparable refinement and luxury.

In most of eastern Europe the greatest landlords comprised the aristocracy. Members enjoyed an inherited superior social position which they attempted to translate into political power. Through their nominees they controlled regional political assemblies. Where a national parliament or diet existed, they sat in it themselves. The sovereign awarded them the best posts in the army, civil administration, and Church. They owned the countryside and had controlling interest in rural industry. Fifteen magnatial families comprised the aristocracy of Poland. Around them, seeking favors, gifts, and appointments, swarmed their clients—a country gentry 700,000 strong. Many of these petty nobles were threadbare; half were without land. Parting from its rebellious traditions, the eighteenth-century Hungarian aristocracy constructed fantastic residences in and around Vienna and began priding itself on its service to the Hapsburgs. Meanwhile, the Magyar gentry stayed home, took over the reins of district government, and criticized the assimilation of its natural leadership.

In eighteenth-century Russia a similar court aristocrat/country noble breach widened. Provincial landlords technically served the tsar by collecting his taxes, administering his justice, and running his regiments. However, they considered the ruling elite at St. Petersburg as distant, decadent, and foreign. With its French manners, German music, and self-conscious cosmopolitanism, it indeed was. Of the European rulers east of the Elbe, only the king of Prussia successfully merged great aristocrats and country nobles into performing dutiful civil and military service to the state. There regional assemblies either were eradicated or else shorn of their independence. Their personnel were transformed into functioning units of the bureaucracy. Old Junker families and petty nobles alike learned to share a mentality based on loyalty to the king and duty to the state.

In western Europe distinctions between powerful aristocrats and mere nobles were more subtle and complex than in eastern Europe. Landed estates in the West rarely reached proportions that set apart magnates from everyone else. Few aristocrats could count on their wealth and influence to draw swarms of noble clients to their side. Furthermore, unlike the East, the West was filled with towns and cities whose patricians, while not technically noble, possessed an inherited political power marking them as aristocrats. Great Britain had a titled nobility of only 200, but its ruling aristocracy of 75,000 controlled local politics and sent representatives to govern the country through Parliament. In the West, neither excessive propertied wealth nor a title guaranteed aristocratic status. Unlike the east Elbian regions, a wealthy bourgeois in France or west Germany might purchase a landed estate, call himself marquis, and add "de" or "von" to his surname. In time king or prince might even confirm him in his nobility.

Nevertheless, only an important army commission, government post, seat in a provincial Estate, or judgeship in a law court brought aristocracy to the new landlord. After 1740 the aristocratically controlled society of western Europe grew more self-consciously exclusive than ever. Those seated at its peak noted an ever-increasing number of young, literate, nonprivileged individuals beginning to question the foundations on which the structure itself was composed. Rulers called on aristocracies to increase their financial responsibilities to the state; some princes challenged them in their political privileges. The predictable reaction of aristocrats was to underscore the exclusiveness of their station, frustrate reform, and, where possible, unleash a counteroffensive of their own.

Aristocratic Reaction or Defense of Privilege?

One means by which aristocrats fought back was their effort to make length of noble pedigree the ultimate requirement for public office. For example, after 1760, the parlements of France were demanding four generations of nobility for new members. After 1781 the same restrictions were to apply for admission to military academies. Half the best administrative posts and most of the top military officerships were reserved for families possessing noble status for at least two hundred years. Under Louis XVI (1774–1792), neither a prerevolutionary bishop nor intendant emerged from the bourgeoisie. French aristocrats (and several present-day historians) defended such restrictive policies by noting that it was a way of assuring professionalism in government or military service. By demanding a history of several generations of such service from aspirants, elites guaranteed that family merit rather than money would determine one's qualifications. In this way, it was argued, parvenu nobles as well as tradesmen's sons were to be excluded, a policy considered necessary in a country where one-fifth of the noble families had attained their status only within the past two generations.

Elsewhere in western Europe, parallels with France could be found. After 1720, Sweden's monarchy weakened and the country reverted back to the rule of the great families. The constitution was aristocratized, and only the existence of a strong civil service prevented slippage into a political climate resembling Poland's. In England an aristocratized House of Commons spoke for the country gentry. The latter and their most prosperous tenants comprised the majority of an electorate of 250,000, and in 1776 it was estimated that 5,723 voters, nearly all gentry, chose half the members of Commons. Technically, English merchants could purchase country estates and adopt the ways and habits of the aristocracy. Conversely, the country gentry might invest in trade. For generations this interchange of city/country, middle-class/aristocratic wealth had contributed to the fluidity of English society. After the 1740s, however, the gentry began obstructing the lines between the moneyed and landed interests. Merchants and industrialists found it more difficult than before to acquire country estates. Rural gentlemen grew reluctant to send their sons to town and learn about business. Instead, they went straight into Parliament, where they distinguished their interests from those of the older, numerically fewer men of commerce. In the English counties the aristocratized society was just as noticeable. After 1750, engaging in commerce or manufacturing disqualified an aspirant for the post of justice of the peace.

In England, the aristocracy was the government. This also was true in Poland and the continental urban republics, such as Geneva, Venice, or Berne. On the other hand, assimilating aristocracies into absolute monarchies was fraught with tensions. For example, on March 3, 1766, King Louis XV of France, a ruler who disliked political confrontation, addressed the Parlement of Paris in the following way:

> Sovereign power resides in my person alone. . . . I alone possess the independent and indivisible power to legislate. By my sole authority the officers of my courts proceed, not to form the law, but to register, publish, and execute it. . . . All public order emanates from me; and the rights and interests of the nation, that some dare to separate from the monarch, are necessarily united with my own, and reside wholly in my hands.[1]

---

[1] Quoted in J. Flammermont and M. Tourneaux, *Remontrances du Parlement de Paris au XVIIIᵉ siècle* (Paris, 1895), Vol. II, pp. 557–558. (Author's translation.)

This berating of France's most prestigious corporate aristocratic body ushered in a lingering constitutional crisis that would contribute to the dissolution of the ancien régime a quarter century later. The king's speech was a pronouncement of unadulterated absolutism, of a kind that his great-grandfather, Louis XIV, liked to represent. As we have seen, in practice Louis XIV was subtle, combining persuasion, bribery, and force to convince parlementary aristocrats, the so-called *robe,* that they should accept royal dominance. He had converted once rebellious great aristocrats, the *sword,* into dependent courtiers at Versailles. Finally, Louis XIV's country nobility was placated with provincial and military officerships and seigneurial control over the peasantry. Even prior to the Sun King's death, however, once silenced aristocrats begin stirring against the absolutist ideal. After 1715 robe and sword aristocrats mingled socially, intermarried, and in the 1750s together resurrected some of the political ideology of the Fronde. In eighteenth-century dress, its message was a sovereignty shared by the king on one hand and parlements, provincial Estates, high clergy, and important officers on the other.

The Parlement of Paris took the lead in demanding the right not only to verify legislation but also to participate in its formation. However, the parlementaires had no intention of extending either legislative privilege beyond their own corporate body or of converting their antiabsolutist ideology into a movement advocating profound political and social reform. They blocked reform as vigorously as they blocked attempts by nonaristocrats or recently ennobled ones for membership in their body. Responding to a royal attempt in 1776 to improve the tax structure, abolish the guilds, and do away with compulsory peasant labor in building roads, the speaker for the Parlement of Paris read, "Any system which, in the guise of humanitarianism or improvement, causes a well-ordered monarchy to establish an equality of duties among men, thereby destroying necessary distinctions, will lead to anarchy. . . . The lower orders of the nation, unable to render the state distinguished service, acquit themselves through their tribute, industry, and corporal labor.[2]

Thus after 1750 constitutional tensions simmered in several parts of Europe, pitting kings and their ministers against lay and clerical aristocracies. Although the major source of conflict was constitutional, the need of rulers for money played a large role as well. Between 1715 and 1740, most sovereigns refrained from costly wars. For the next half century, however, international rivalries erupted into terrific military struggles. The Anglo-French competition for empire revived, an aggressive Prussia upset the equilibrium in central Europe, and Hapsburg and Russian aggression extended into the Balkans and Poland. Great armies and fleets had to be

---

[2] Solonelle remontrance du Parlement de Paris, 4 March 1776. Quoted in *Documents d'histoire vivante de l'antiquité à nos jours* (Paris, 1968), Vol. IV, p. 27. (Author's translation.)

built and maintained. Governments demanded that aristocrats yield needed revenue, and the privileged groups resisted with equal firmness. In England, for example, the gentry-controlled Parliament refused to reassess the value of land for tax purposes, even though no adjustments had been made since 1692. Consequently, the government sought other means of revenue, like tax stamps on articles of general consumption. This infuriated non-aristocratic Englishmen and helped drive colonists in North America into rebellion.

In France the Crown wished to correct obvious inequities in the *taille,* the tax paid by peasants. It also wished to establish a property tax without exemptions. The Parlement of Paris, provincial parlements, and officer corporations united in resisting any major fiscal reform, and in 1787 an Assembly of Notables summoned by Louis XVI declared that only an Estates-General possessed the authority to resolve the government's financial predicament. The king eventually yielded, and the convocation of the Estates-General inaugurated the French Revolution.

In the Hapsburg lands virtually the entire nobility was exempt from direct taxation in 1740. From peasants and townsmen, regional aristocracies collected what they thought the government needed to support a court, maintain defense, and pay officials. In general this was rarely sufficient. By 1790, however, the Crown had made significant gains. It managed to collect its own revenues rather than accept the pittances sent by aristocratic agents in the countryside, and under Joseph II state income rose by 70 percent. Noble land was duly registered as taxable and at the same rate as inheritable peasant properties. It is not surprising that uprisings in Hapsburg Hungary and Belgium in 1789–1790 were led by disgruntled aristocrats and country gentry. Elsewhere in Europe governments intent on economic reform faced inevitable aristocratic opposition, but even aristocratized Churches felt the sovereign's demands. The king of Naples began taxing his clergy; Joseph II of Austria and Catherine II of Russia seized monastic lands that they termed useless and then sold or redistributed them to the laity.

Formation of a Service Elite

Aristocrats resisted rulers, but also served them. Participation in government was the ultimate mark of social leadership, and most members of a diet, parlement, or Estate would protest loudly if one likened their protection of privilege to acts of political obstructionism, much less disloyalty. Venal officers, whose fiscal, judicial, or administrative posts provided income in fees and bribes, insisted that they were devoted servants of their sovereigns. More worthy of the name, however, were those officials whose posts were not owned as inheritable property but rather were revocable and conditional on the administrative effectiveness of their occupiers. This alternative bureaucracy of royal commissioners and secretaries had blossomed in France and Prussia in the late seventeenth century and became the lifeblood of royal administration in the eighteenth. Rulers in the Hapsburg Empire, myriad states of Germany, north Italian principalities, Spain, and Russia established their commissioner corps.

As the king's superior agent in each of thirty-four administrative districts within the country, the French intendant was the prototype commissioner—overseeing military recruitment, apportionment of the *taille,* collection of direct taxes by officers, and the regulation of trade, industry, and agriculture. Under Louis XV (1715–1774), the post of intendant grew exceptionally prestigious, and the brightest young members of the *robe* aristocracy aspired to serve. Often blood relatives of parlementary elites, French intendants displayed initiative and independence in their work, and the king often selected his chief ministers from among them. Thus the great constitutional and political struggles of eighteenth-century France involved aristocratic personalities serving different sides. As ministers, commissioners, and courtiers, one group banked its future on the side of royal authority. As parlementaires and officers, the other group sought to moderate absolutism through oligarchic means. Ideology divided families, and individuals themselves changed sides. This notwithstanding, the function of high administrative, judicial, and military service had become the monopoly of the aristocracy to an extent unmatched in modern French history.

The eighteenth-century French bureaucracy failed to welcome earnest, ambitious nonaristocrats to responsible posts. The same was true of its Prussian counterpart. Many Prussian noble families were quite poor, and the country possessed no magnatial landowning class around which clients could hover. Once the Great Elector and his two successors had tamed the country's regional diets and assemblies, aristocratic service in the central government and the military virtually became the only paths to recognition. The administration of districts, towns, and royal lands, as well as the responsibility for tax collection, the fostering of industry, and internal colonization, necessitated the labors of at least five hundred senior and several thousand junior officials. The governmental bureaucracy in Berlin, the tax collecting agency, and the military needed expert personnel. Landowning nobles were to monopolize the most important posts, and noncommissioned army officers dominated the lesser ones. Their assigments could be revoked, and little scope for individual initiative was permitted.

Furthermore, regulations from Berlin were explicit; commissioners were poorly paid and trained to spy on one another. Nevertheless, Junkers called into the civil service of Frederick the Great took pride in knowing that their bureaucracy was the least corrupt and most efficient in Europe. The king repaid them by acknowledging their mastery over peasants on their manors and by fitting society around their needs and code. Frederick enjoyed the security of reigning over a docile, well-integrated working aristocracy. On the entire continent only the esprit de corps of the Prussian military rivaled that of the Prussian bureaucracy, and in fact service in the army generally overwhelmed all other aristocratic duties. In 1739 no commoners served among the 34 Prussian generals, 1 among the 57 colonels, and 8 among the 108 majors. Half a century later, there were but 6 commoners among the 732 senior officers in the Prussian army.

Peter the Great also had wished to convert the Russian nobility into a state-serving aristocracy. He destroyed the old boyar councils, reorganized administrative and military structures, and created the Table of Ranks of obligatory imperial service. No ancient charters of privilege protected Russia's aristocrats. They were creatures of the tsar and his needs, and one's place in the Table of Ranks rather than hereditary title conferred status. Russian nobles in turn demanded the establishment of an educational system which would teach their children the skills for rising in the Table of Ranks.

During the forty years after Peter's death, a period largely marked by palace coups and political instability, aristocrats worked at evading the compulsory aspects of state service. During the reign of Elizabeth (1741–1762), they won a twenty-year time limit; in 1762, Tsar Peter III granted them the privilege of withdrawing from service at any time they wished. A quarter century later, Tsarina Catherine II wished to break down the barriers separating the Europeanized St. Petersburg aristocracy and the country gentry by conceding additional privileges to the entire Russian noblesse, erasing its dependence upon the sovereign and converting it into a caste apart. The Table of Ranks stood, but hereafter the Russian aristocracy became a legitimate corporate body. The envy of west-European counterparts, Russian nobles might now run their provincial and district assemblies, control the military, and fill the inner councils of the tsarina's government. Only they could acquire or own lands with serfs and build rural factories. They were exempt from taxes and corporal punishment. If accused of a crime, they were tried by their peers alone. The cultural consequence of establishing a noble Estate in Russia was the introduction of European ways to the countryside in the form of books, music, theater, and polite conversation.

Spain had the largest per capita nobility in western Europe. The northern part of the country was filled with hidalgos, pauperized nobles who might eke out a living as blacksmiths or stonemasons, hardly an aristocracy. By way of contrast were the *títulos,* who owned the best land and held social power by dominating the seigneurial system. They administered justice, controlled offices, collected taxes, and imposed dues and services on an impoverished peasantry. Some, like the duke of Medinaceli or count of Altamira, controlled tens of thousands of peasants and were absentee landlords, enjoying court life in Madrid. Most others lived on their estates as petty sovereigns. During the second half of the eighteenth century, parts of Spain, most notably Valencia, knew a feudal reaction similar to the one in France. Landlords tried to reclaim or reinforce privileges over their peasants and stimulated both lawsuits and hunger riots. The Crown's reaction was weak, resisted by courtiers who of course were seigneurs themselves. Army officer-ships also were hereditary, although an aristocracy of merit was taking hold in the civil service. There talented hidalgos rose to become intendants and ministers. By no means did they wish to open important government posts to commoners; however, they—and their sympathetic late eighteenth-century king, Carlos III (1759–1788)—considered dutiful state service rather than bloodline as justification for upward social mobility.

On their hereditary German lands the eighteenth-century Haps-burgs tried to create the nucleus of a civil service, its members either chosen from the older nobility or else raised to noble status. These district officials took over public welfare responsibilities resembling those of the French intendants. Urged by the Hapsburgs to submit to the will of Vienna, the Hungarian gentry resisted them as interlopers or traitors and looked with envy on aristocratic justices of the peace of the distant English countryside who took no orders from any reform-minded central government. No mon-arch dared threaten the justices with armed intervention. As unpaid coun-try gentlemen serving for life, their idea of administration was to fulfill duties as described by common or statute law. They knew that the law, made and interpreted by Parliament, was the work of those who shared their interests and rank.

Therefore, while eighteenth-century aristocracies consolidated their position as the dominant force in society, their role in government was ambivalent. In England and Poland they *were* the government. In Prussia they served willingly. Under Catherine II they helped convert the Russian Empire into an aristocratized state. In France, Spain, and the Hapsburg Empire they proclaimed devotion to monarchical principle while alternately serving and challenging absolutism. Not necessarily the wealthiest individ-uals in European society, aristocrats were indisputably the most privileged. In most Catholic countries, they also dominated the high clergy. Their social and economic strengths were engraved in the land they owned or controlled and in the day-to-day power this afforded them over the lives of those who worked the soil.

A RESILIENT BOURGEOISIE

The Traditional Third Estate

While eighteenth-century aristocracies consolidated their social leadership, Europe's north-Atlantic states found individuals establishing lucrative careers in trade, the professions, and industry. In constructing their governmental bureaucracies the rulers of France, Prussia, Austria, and the smaller German states needed trained and educated lower echelon officials, secretaries, and clerks which traditional aristocratic or noble sources were unable to supply. The emergence of the eighteenth-century middle class corresponded to the growth of economies and bureaucracies. Of course, the social, economic, and political importance of the bourgeoisie was nothing new. Medieval Flanders and the north-Italian communes had prospered on middle-class commerce and preindustrial manufacturing. Merchants and guildsmen had built the civilization of the south-German cities. The roots of France's parlementary aristocracy were bourgeois, as was a considerable segment of England's landed gentry. In 1726 Daniel Defoe reminded English aristocrats all too willing to forget their origins that "the tradesman's children, or at least their grandchildren, come to be as good gentlemen, statesmen, Parliament men, privy councillors, judges, bishops, and noblemen, as those of highest birth and the most ancient families."

Certainly the topmost layer of the eighteenth-century bourgeoisie possessed a material lifestyle which, family pedigree and noble quarterings aside, was similar to that of wealthy aristocrats. The regents of the Dutch Republic and the pompous burghers who filled the council seats of the urban republics in the Holy Roman Empire, Switzerland, and north Italy, were unquestionably non-noble aristocrats. In France bourgeois individuals might purchase certain stipulated offices, especially municipal ones, and thus acquire limited prestige through government service. They also might buy rural estates and become seigneurs, beleaguering unfortunate tenants with rent hikes or long-forgotten dues responsibilities. A group of bankers and financiers distinguishable as "bourgeois living nobly" constituted the dominant economic element in French society. Its members had reaped fortunes by supplying Louis XIV with loans and provisioning his troops. In return, they were permitted to keep the lion's share of the state's "indirect" taxes, customs receipts, and sales taxes that everyone paid on salt, tobacco, wine, liquor, leather, iron, paper, and cloth. With their private administrations of receivers, controllers, clerks, and troops, these financiers, the Farmers General, formed a state within a state. Eighteenth-century Frenchmen of all social groups detested them, but their wealth brought them large landed properties. Nobles took their daughters as wives, and Louis XV took their daughters as mistresses.

Municipal regents and Farmers General comprised a non-noble upper crust that was aristocratic, privileged, and well entrenched. Just beneath it, among the shipbuilders, arms makers, international traders, and important textile manufacturers of the north-Atlantic states, the temptation of an aristocratic lifestyle and hope of entering the charmed circle itself remained powerful. However, in a world governed by aristocratic values, where an industrialist or merchant was held in contempt by those above him, to attain aristocracy meant rejecting bourgeois occupations. In France, whenever reformers tried to establish a noblesse of great international traders, they were repulsed by aristocrats. Numerous businessmen accepted this fact of life and therefore invested their hard-earned capital in aristocratically acceptable enterprises, such as country property or office. Others, however, challenged the contempt of social superiors with a scorn of their own, based on a self-conscious morality set apart from the idleness and superficiality of their so-called aristocratic betters. An emphasis on orderliness, thrift, piety, and industriousness was intended to create a sense of individual self-worth and at the same time indicate the moral distance separating proper bourgeois from those above. Moreover, during the second half of the eighteenth century, tension between social orders was aggravated by increasing numbers of both aristocratic and nonaristocratic males surviving adolescence and receiving good educations. They expected jobs commensurate with their training and abilities, but first-rate opportunities in government, the military, and Church failed to keep pace with the numbers seeking them. Attractive posts became virtual preserves of the aristocracy, thus contributing to the status anxiety and moral self-righteousness of the ambitious bourgeoisie.

However, the overwhelming majority of Europe's bourgeoisie did not live opulent, comfortable lives as shipbuilders, speculators in sugar, or traffickers in slaves. They did not commission their solemn portraits for posterity, nor did they build stately town houses. Their lives and interests were parochial, and their dealings rarely extended beyond their town or street. It is very difficult to depict the average burgher, whose place on the social ladder of the Third Estate had as many rungs above as below. From country to country, particular conditions defined the middle-class member. In England one might be a small merchant manufacturer of cotton cloth, distributing and collecting goods from fifty cottage weavers scattered outside his town. In Spain the prototypical bourgeois was much poorer, living out a dull, rhythmical existence mapped out by guild, Church, and king. In Germany small merchants and master craftsmen alike mingled traits of sobriety with grudging deference to superiors and haughty authoritarianism toward inferiors. For example, a Leipzig bookseller worked regularly from seven in the morning until eight at night, shunned card games, and never set foot in a tavern. On Sundays he went to church, read a newspaper, and strolled around his town. In the summer he would treat his family to a few trips into the countryside, where they would drink a bottle of wine. Once per year he would take his apprentices for a 2-mile drive in his carriage. Moving eastward toward the serf societies of Poland and Russia, burghers became rarer in number and were even considered alien. Polish petty commerce was in the hands of Germans and Jews; in Hungary, Germans and Greeks were the tradespeople.

The "New" Bourgeoisie

The eighteenth century witnessed an evolution of two categories of bourgeois, distinguishable in wealth and lifestyles from the topmost ranks of middle-class society and differing as well from the merchants and master craftsmen who had formed the nucleus of Europe's urban life since the Middle Ages. The first category, intimately linked to the growth of governmental bureaucracies in central Europe, contained lawyers, clerks, treasury agents, and other trained officials who served as subordinate members of the departments and boards established by the Prussian Hohenzollerns, Austrian Hapsburgs, and German territorial princes. Aristocratic commissioners, weaned away from diets and Estates in order to serve sovereigns more directly, needed expert advisers and administrators. Princes trained them in new schools and universities. The three-hundred-odd independent German states, each with a specific jurisdiction, necessitated civil services that contained far more officials in proportion to the general population than at any other time in the region's history.

Governments expected honorable service from their middle and lower rank civil servants, who were given tax exemptions and special privileges. Like their Junker superiors, Prussian state workers were trained to follow orders and perform their tasks meticulously. Yet members of the civil service were not necessarily dull automatons. Throughout Germany in the eighteenth century, bureaucrats founded reading rooms and reading societies. They patronized the theater and opera. Their culture was more political and more cosmopolitan than that of the older mercantile/master-craftsman bourgeoisie. By learning French and copying French fashions in furniture, dress, and eating habits, they aped their aristocratic superiors. Yet after 1750, this newly educated, "official" bourgeoisie responded positively to the German literary revival and proved receptive to proposals extending religious, civil, and political liberties to others.

The second category of evolving bourgeois emerged from industry. A major goal of government in eighteenth-century England was to increase private profit and ensure economic development. Indeed, an argument for the enclosure acts was that the legislation established conditions for accumulating excess capital for investment outside agriculture. Traditionally, the chief area of investment had been overseas trade. By 1700 European demand for Indian cotton goods had persuaded investors to subsidize cotton cultivation elsewhere. Money was channeled into West Indian plantations and the American South; Africa provided the slave labor for planting and picking. Most important, the raw goods then would be shipped to England for processing and manufacturing. Peasant and, later, factory labor created Britain's new textile industry. In the late eighteenth century the cheap cotton clothes manufactured in the regions of Liverpool and Manchester were intended to cover the backs of the English and, even more importantly, were to be shipped to Europe and America. Between 1750 and 1770 the export of British-made cottons grew tenfold. Inventions greatly accelerated the pace of spinning and weaving: among the first were the flying shuttle (1733), waterframe, and spinning jenny (1769–1770); and a decade later, the spinning mule and power loom.

Even before the 1780s, the decade of England's celebrated takeoff into industrial revolution, adventurous entrepreneurs in textiles could become rich very quickly. Not much capital was needed to start. Market demand brought profits, and there was no shortage of labor. Manufacturers sent out the goods to be spun to peasant cottages. Once mechanized weaving permitted the realization of maximum profits by concentrating equipment and workers in one place, the modern factory was born. Industrial capitalists assumed responsibility for housing workers, paving roads, and providing a modicum of law and order, thus creating the factory town. The rising bourgeois industrialist spread from England to northern France and Belgium. In addition to textile plants, collieries and ironworks developed. Here, too, England took the lead, and invention stimulated production. Newcomen's steam pump permitted deeper reaches into the mines without flooding them; the Darbies learned to smelt iron with coke instead of forest-denuding wood for charcoal. In the second half of the eighteenth century, England bounded into first place in iron production; after 1781, Watt's rotary steam engine assured the industrialist the power by which he was to supply the world.

The Paradoxes of Bourgeois Culture

A bourgeois culture accompanied the evolution of bourgeois social groups and transcended national frontiers, occupations, and at times even the barriers between Estates. A Prussian civil servant or Manchester cotton manufacturer might share aspects of this culture with a French notary, book publisher, "philosophic" abbé, "liberal" nobleman, or even "enlightened" yeoman. Lacking a precise ideology, the culture must be defined as an evolving consciousness. It fed on several seventeenth-century sources, chiefly the skeptical tradition of Descartes and Bayle, the empirical psychology and political liberalism of Locke, and faith in the great scientific discoveries. Nourishing it further were the works of eighteenth-century writers who tempered trenchant criticisms of humanity's present lot with poignant hopes concerning its future possibilities. It is foolhardy to envision armies of bureaucrats, businessmen, and professionals joyously leaping into their Spinoza, Newton, or Locke every time their occupational cares afforded them a moment's respite. Nonetheless, during the eighteenth century a mental attitude was shared by many middle-class people who rejected a culture directed by the conservative forces of Church and guild and who were growing impatient with the preeminence of aristocratic values and aristocratic social-political leadership. The new mentality possessed many inner contradictions, but in general it called for freer trade and manufacture, religious tolerance, the thawing of barriers to upward social mobility, and the opening of political life to more widespread participation.

In France this critical spirit grew most forceful and bitter, reaching upward into segments of the nobility and downward into segments of the peasantry. As early as the 1740s, the aristocratic marquis d'Argenson termed as worthless those grand seigneurs who based social status and political power on their "dignities, wealth, titles, offices, and functions. . . . If you

Figure 7.1—"Group Portrait," François-Hubert DROUAIS, Courtesy of the National Gallery of Art, Washington; Samuel H. Kress Collection. During the second half of the eighteenth century the middle classes of western Europe developed self-conscious cultural norms that emphasized domestic sentimentality within the confines of the nuclear family. Artists like the Frenchman Drouais catered to such tastes. In this painting the female figure dominates. Her role, however, is clearly defined: wife and mother.

listen to these individuals, . . . you will hear that they are the foundation of the state. . . . I understand that a good race of hunting dogs should be preserved; but when they degenerate, we drown them." The peasant father of the writer Nicolas Restif de la Bretonne added, "My son, we are non-noble and proud of it. The non-noble is the man par excellence. It is he who pays the taxes, works, sows, harvests, trades, builds, and manufactures. The right to be useless is a poor right indeed!"

However disenchanted they might have been with a world governed by aristocratic privilege and rank, few eighteenth-century bourgeois dreamed of leveling society altogether. Their envy of land, the traditionally aristocratic source of wealth, was strong, and the aristocracy's reluctance to allow their social and political advance was what turned them against that order. Moreover, a smugly bourgeois sense of corporate virtue made members of the middle class suspicious of the humble peasant or artisan, who were distinguished scornfully as the "people." Voltaire, one of the most important formulators of the bourgeois consciousness, wrote, "The people will remain ignorant and weak-minded, always needing to be led by a small number of enlightened men." It nevertheless remains true that between 1750 and 1789 bourgeois discontents were directed more toward aristocratic leadership than toward the lower social orders. In North America the discontents merged with political grievances into a colonial revolt. In England, Ireland, the Dutch Netherlands, and the city of Geneva, the discontents hardened into movements against the political status quo. In France they were the necessary catalyst for a great revolution, one which became international in scope during the waning years of the century.

THE WORKING CLASSES

Traditional Labor in Decline

The great social dramas of the eighteenth century concerned the crisis of the peasantry, offensive of the aristocracy, and disaffection of the bourgeoisie. Seemingly overshadowed by these movements, Europe's artisans and laborers found their lives changing rapidly. From Yorkshire to the Urals the worker in traditional rural industry was customarily a peasant who supplemented his income or kept himself alive in the slack season by producing objects destined for sale. In a corner of his cottage was a primitive loom or spinning wheel. Wives and daughters sewed. Villages involved in textile production witnessed significant immigration during the eighteenth century; those wholly dependent upon agriculture stagnated or lost populations. Women and men who descended into coal mines or iron pits were customarily peasants or rural serfs, as were those who labored in glassworks, forges, and paper mills that dotted the countryside. Skilled artisans, such as the cutlers near Sheffield in England, Solingen in Germany, and

Nogent in France, the linen weavers of Silesia, and even the watchmakers of Geneva, were part-time workers from the fields.

In those towns of western and central Europe where guild control was strong, a clear-cut hierarchy of labor existed. Fiscal and judicial privileges protected certain trades. Contract and statute dictated the terms of apprenticeships, and mutual-assistance organizations served journeymen. The craft guild represented labor's aristocracy and was most highly developed in the oligarchy-controlled towns of southern Germany, northern Italy, Switzerland, and the Netherlands. On the other hand, the French guilds formed the channel through which royal government exercised its surveillance over industry.

Clannish rather than competitive, with masters fixing both prices and production, with style and quality rigidly adhered to, guilds stood for the economic order of the past. During the eighteenth century, relations between master and worker degenerated. At the same time barriers between them grew. Masterships became hereditary, and except for a fortuitous marriage, journeymen found it nearly impossible to rise through the ranks. Consequently, worker class consciousness increased, and the protective associations of journeymen often assumed a militant character superimposed on their traditionally benevolent one. In France, master craftsmen asked the government to suppress these primitive trade unions, and in the Holy Roman Empire an edict of 1731 deprived them of their legality. In the Empire journeymen were wanderers, carrying their skills from town to town and across territorial frontiers. However, governments became suspicious of these rootless, contentious young individuals, and they soon were forced to report to police when arriving in or departing from a town.

By 1715 guild-dominated industry in England had deteriorated, and it was declining in Germany. In most places east of the Elbe, it never had existed. After 1750 the French government turned against the guilds and in 1776 dissolved most of them. All regimes saw guilds as weights chained to the neck of industrial development, their production methods and corporate structures incapable of meeting the consumer needs of growing populations. Moreover, they shielded masters from the state's judge or tax collector. By offering subsidies to individual manufacturers or industrialists, governments bypassed the guilds. In this respect the Prussian state was Europe's model, organizing manufactures in Berlin and coal mines in Silesia. Capitalists were encouraged to hire wage labor. In eastern Europe the state gave them serfs.

Emergence of the Factory

During the eighteenth century the factory gradually replaced both rural-based cottage industry and the guild workshop. The effects can be seen in urban development. The growth of innumerable eighteenth-century towns was identical with the influx of working-class populations. In northern

France the laboring population of Sedan comprised 800 in 1683. A century later it was 14,000. In present-day Belgium the textile and metallurgy complex round Verviers and Liège employed 100,000 people. Cotton finishing brought similar numbers to Barcelona and Manchester. As their numbers grew, people gravitated toward industrial centers. On the eve of the revolution of 1789, 2 million French workers were devoting more than half their laboring time to industry, and nearly half the adult population of England was producing goods that others sold.

The nomadism of unskilled and semiskilled laborers began to overwhelm the craftsperson or journeyman tours of previous ages. In England the movement was from south to north, toward the new manufacturing centers of Manchester, Birmingham, and Leeds. In France it was toward Lille, Lyon, and the Ile de France. In Spain and Russia the pull was eastward, in the first instance toward Barcelona and its textile production and in the second toward the Ural mountains and their iron mines. In Germany it was in several directions, toward the Rhine valley, Saxony, and Silesia. Not even the borders between states stopped these human migrations. Saxons, Styrians, Piedmontese, and Carinthians went wherever there were mines. Swiss cotton workers flocked to France, Belgium, Saxony, and Silesia.

The immigrant to town or mine had to develop different work habits from those employed for generations in the countryside. A small-time entrepreneur employing a few peasants in a backyard shed was bound to be close to his workers. The work week was long but flexible. Employer and employee might well leave for half a day to see an itinerant circus or attend a cockfight. Later they would make up for lost time with three or four feverish eighteen-hour workdays. The factory's claims to efficiency changed all that. The impersonal engagement between worker and foreman meant 7 A.M. to 8 P.M., Monday through Saturday, with an hour of unpaid time for meals. In the factory and mine, women and children endured equality of toil, though at a fraction of the man's salary. Pay might be based on the worker's productivity, it might be a weekly or monthly wage, or else it might take the form of an indemnity against housing, food, and tools which the owner supplied, thus reducing the worker to a state of perpetual indebtedness. Fines for alleged worker negligence, absenteeism, or defective products cut further into wages.

Salaries varied from region to region and from industry to industry. By 1780, French engravers, watchmakers, and cutlers were earning six to eight times more than spinners and weavers in country districts. At the same time, English day workers in textiles earned five to six shillings per week, skilled weavers in Leeds earned eight to ten, and Newcastle coal miners, fifteen. During the eighteenth century salaries rose, though at a rate half that of prices and one-fourth that of agricultural rents. Between 1740 and 1790, the purchasing power of Spanish workers dropped by nearly a third. In the industrializing regions of France, the loss was rarely less than 25 percent. The indices of precarious existence, while not so murderous as in the seventeenth century, nevertheless had not disappeared. A poor harvest meant skyrocketing bread prices, and this meant low demand for textiles and industrial goods. Widespread layoffs followed, and hunger returned as a haunting fact of life. In 1789 workers in Paris were spending up to 90 percent of their salaries for bread. In normal times, the average was 50 to 60 percent.

Hunger was not the sole oppressor of the new factory hand. Throughout Europe, aristocratic governments and bourgeois industrialists agreed that no distinction existed between laboring classes and dangerous classes. Legislation was intended to ensure docility. French workers could not quit their factory jobs without the consent of their employers. When they changed residence, they had to present certificates of good conduct to the police. They could neither assemble nor strike. They had to be off the streets by 10 P.M. England, the German and Italian principalities, and Spain had similar laws. Nevertheless, illegal worker organization took place. Englishmen in textiles, hatmaking, paper manufacturing, and small metallurgy took the lead, although what they formed were in themselves corporate elites, intended for the most specialized and best-paid workers and excluding the laboring masses. In most of Europe, workers were weak and unorganized. Their class consciousness was mounting, but it was less than employers and governments thought. Journeyman associations still fought street battles with each other. The semiskilled in factories scorned newcomers from the countryside. A dexterous cutler had nothing but contempt for a humble domestic spinner. Worker unrest before 1789 took the form of bread riots and vague mob action. Only rarely did it demand amelioration of actual labor conditions. It took the French Revolution and its aftermath to instill in the working poor a conviction that organization and collective action were the path toward social and economic justice and, eventually, to political power.

8

THE ENLIGHTENMENT

THE TRIUMPH OF PRINT CULTURE

The Evolution of Literacy

History records the first printed book in Europe, Gutenberg's *Bible,* as appearing in 1456. During the next century and a half the availability of paper, use of inks, and development of the hand press and movable type permitted the publication of 100 million books and at least as many printed laws, decrees, news sheets, broadsides, pamphlets, and tracts. In Europe's cities the publishing industry was born, replacing manuscript reproduction that had been the monopoly of rural abbeys and monasteries since the early Middle Ages. The Protestant Reformation used print culture to spread its message, and it is impossible to conceive of the scientific revolution without the easy communication among scholars permitted by the dissemination of books, journals, articles, and printed correspondence. Although enterprising publishers distributed the psalms, prayer books, catechisms, fairy tales, and popular romances to a larger clientele than ever before—to readers whose grandparents would have considered the written word as a kind of magic—literacy in Europe prior to 1700 remained restricted to fewer than 15 percent of the total adult population. Governments and churches alike tried to limit access to reading skills and to keep literacy as the monopoly of political, social, and cultural elites. Moreover, regimes limited publication rights to works advocating conventional and established ideas; they attempted to control the book trade through preventive censorship and printing monopolies awarded to "safe" publishers. Governments also punished with jail terms or galley service all authors and printers of books published without prior approval.

However, during the eighteenth century national debates throughout Europe challenged the idea of maintaining large illiterate populations, while public demand greatly weakened the practice of official censorship. Critics showed that those few places which had experimented with mass literacy or schooling campaigns—the Dutch Netherlands, Sweden, Denmark-Norway, Scotland, and some German principalities—were not producing rebels but rather productive, self-reliant, and loyal subjects. In fact, the *least* politically reliable populations—in Russia, the Hapsburg Empire, and the lands bordering the Mediterranean Sea—seemed to be those with highest incidences of illiteracy. Governments understood that the written word might be used to promote correct thinking and that linguistic uniformity was related to political stability. Therefore, wherever it was practicable and within means, regimes established elementary schools to teach reading skills in the national language, thereby eradicating local tongues that set apart subjects from one another and from the tax collector or recruiting sergeant.

Efforts at increasing literacy bore mixed results. Generally, they were more successful in urban areas than in rural ones, and more men than women learned to read and write. For example, in Amsterdam by 1780 around 85 percent of the potential bridegrooms and 64 percent of the potential brides were able to sign the city's marriage register. In mid-century France one male in three was literate, compared to one female in eight. Social status was indicative too. In the French city of Lyon, by 1750 only 20 percent of the women categorized as bourgeoise were considered illiterate. However, half the wives of artisans were, and of the town's poorest women, only one in five could sign her name. Certain rural regions did make the most dramatic gains. For example, in 1750 one Prussian peasant in ten could sign; fifteen years later it was one in four; by the end of the eighteenth century, nearly one in two. Greater progress was made in teaching people to read than to write, and village social circles like the French *veillée* or German *Spinnstube* (spinning group) developed the activity of reading aloud during idle periods in the winter months. By and large, at the outbreak of the French Revolution northwestern Europe was on the verge of becoming a literate society. Half the males and one-third of the females could sign their names. The percentages were even higher for those who could read, at least in a rudimentary way. In Sweden, lowland Scotland, and parts of England, Germany, the Dutch Netherlands, and northeastern France, up to 80 percent of the population could decipher markings on a page. On the other hand, in Russia, Poland, most of the Hapsburg Empire, Spain, and southern Italy, literacy rates ranged from virtually nil to 10 percent. Without question by 1789 the most dramatic feature of the literacy map of Europe was the sharp contrast from place to place.

The World of Books

By 1750 Europe's publishing industry was adapting to the growing market for books in several ways. Interlopers broke down corporate monopolies, and traditional means of distribution such as exchanges at the annual book fairs of Leipzig and Frankfurt yielded to larger scale and longer distance sales practices. Authors escaped censorship policies by having their books printed abroad and then reexported to their home country, whose publishers— smelling a certain bestseller—subsequently produced illicit pirated editions. Books used as entertainment and as guides to worldly success now stood side by side with books considered necessary for one's spiritual guidance. One consequence of this development was the growth in popularity of scientific and historical texts, as well as a new literary form, the novel. No longer concentrating on a humanist intelligentsia of churchmen, academics, government officials, and students, publishers began treating readership as several distinct markets: relatively unlettered readers of popular romances, folk tales, and catechisms; somewhat more sophisticated readers of almanacs, how-to books, simple abridgments of classics (known as chapbooks), Bibles, and psalters; relatively well-educated readers of novels, histories, and vulgarized science; and finally, professionals, readers of specialized works. Books successfully rivaled experience as legitimate means of acquiring both skills and knowledge.

From country to country the book trade evolved differently; yet there also were patterns common to most. In a bureaucratized monarchy like France the state tried to coopt authors and publishers alike through a complex network of privilege. Officers of the publishers' guild of Paris formed an arm of the royal administration, visiting the city's printers once every three months to make sure that each shop possessed the requisite number of presses and type fonts. Paris guildsmen also exercised police powers over printers and booksellers in the countryside, and their near monopoly over publishing all new books and exercising continuation rights for printing older ones, made them dictators of the trade. On their side, however, provincial publishers responded by reprinting works of popular devotion and by making both counterfeit and illicit editions. Moreover, across the frontiers—in Switzerland, the Low Countries, and Rhineland principalities—French exiles, often Huguenot Protestants, established their own semiclandestine publishing industries and sent books, pamphlets, engravings, and tracts back into France. These included so-called "philosophic" works, a shorthand description for disrespectful and often pornographic attacks on church and state. The French police used ingenious devices to track down these uncensored books; however, in face of an insatiable public demand for scandal, their efforts were doomed to failure.

Well into the seventeenth century London's Stationers' Company and Parliament's Licensing Act had established government-supported habits of monopoly and censorship for England that paralleled those in France. During the reigns of William and Mary, however, the controls broke down, and the central events of eighteenth-century English book history concern the evolution of press freedom and copyright. The Copyright Act of 1710 theoretically allowed authors proprietary claim to their work. However, in return for getting printed, authors customarily ceded this claim to a publisher, who, appealing to Common Law, would do all in his power to hang on to it in perpetuity. Competing publishers issued challenges, and finally in 1774 the House of Lords proclaimed a 28-year copyright limitation, after which any published work might enter the public domain. Moreover, authors successfully interpreted copyright as a guarantee of their intellectual property. Seeking the highest price, they bargained with publishers over transferring their copyright; or else they might keep it, print their books on their own account, and sell them on a subscription basis. With the emergence of a lively periodical press and widespread interest in the novel, English publishing flourished in Europe's freest intellectual climate.

  The Holy Roman Empire was a book pirate's dream. There was no central censorship authority, only local ones, and competition among the Empire's princes encouraged both literary productivity and counterfeit editions. Unlike their English counterparts, however, German authors failed to bargain for the best price and generally had to be satisfied with a publisher's honorarium, descended from the patronage system. On the other hand, while King Carlos III of Spain granted a publishing monopoly over liturgical books, reprints, and translations to the Royal Company of Printers and Booksellers, he also awarded Spanish authors de facto copyright, namely exclusive license to print their original works. With Europe's smallest per capita literate population and a publishing industry created and controlled by the state, Russia nevertheless knew the evolution of a merchant-writer elite struggling for independence of its imperial sponsor—and eventually becoming its adversary. In several ways the Scandinavian states made the most progress applying literacy to cultural and political development. Early in the eighteenth century the governments of Sweden and Denmark-Norway encouraged mass literacy, believing that existing orthodox political and religious beliefs might be reinforced through print. For a time this policy was successful. However, by the 1770s both state and church were losing control over censorship, newspapers as well as books began circulating freely, lending libraries were built, and populations were reading more critically than ever before.

The Birth of the Modern Press

Critical and useful reading was an essential component of cultural life during the second half of the eighteenth century as print culture assumed the responsibility for reflecting on social practices and public affairs. Customarily it was the newspaper and journal of opinion, prototypes of the modern press, that took on these issues. Although journals and newspapers appeared nearly everywhere in Europe, they thrived especially in the Holy Roman Empire and in England.

  For a Germany divided into countless petty states and lacking a central capital city, newspapers and journals formed networks of communication—the primary means of disseminating information, literary news, and political opinion. Public officials and professionals alike wrote for these periodicals, subscribed to them, discussed their contents, and broadened their political horizons. Political issues like the emergence of Prussia and revitalization of Hapsburg Austria directly affected subjects of the Holy Roman Empire; the first partition of Poland (1772), American War of

Independence, and growing financial crisis in France greatly interested readers. Moreover, newspapers and journals offered legitimate means of discussing administrative, fiscal, and economic reform within the states and cities of the Empire itself, provided that editors posed questions in a manner that would not threaten the powers-that-be.

By 1785, 151 newspapers were publishing in Germany and had a weekly circulation of 300,000. In addition, during the course of the century 4,000 additional journals of opinion appeared—more than 1,200 new ones in the 1780s alone. The most widely read periodicals were the so-called moral weeklies, journals of manners with useful advice on issues ranging from household management to proper social behavior. A second type was the all-purpose magazine, containing information on inventions, literature, and both scientific and medical discoveries. Finally, during the 1770s the German political press came into its own. Average press runs of the journals of opinion were 2,000 to 3,000 per issue; however, at least ten readers would devour any single copy, especially by virtue of their participation in the 400 reading clubs scattered throughout the Empire. Inside the clubs subjects of particular interest mentioned by the journals became topics for structured discussion and debate. Journalists obtained access to government documents. They published statistics and contributed to bringing politics out of the secret chambers of princes and into public view. For example, E. Brandes, editor of the highly popular *Berliner Monatsschrift,* criticized the backwardness of the imperial constitution, serfdom, the death penalty, and the guilds. During the 1780s nearly every political journal in Germany was debating the issue of divine-right authority and discussing natural law alternatives. This notwithstanding, in most cases German journalists were uninterested in revolutionizing politics. Nor, however, were they willing to accept absolutism blindly. They cooperated with the political authorities of the Empire. Many were themselves state officials. They had to submit to censorship controls. Addressing the public directly, they nevertheless considered themselves to be the standard-bearers of reform.

Journalists in England were much less respectful of authority than their German counterparts, and their language of political reporting was unrestrained. Critics viewed the eighteenth-century English newspaper as "the subtle poison that creeps imperceptibly through every vein; the Seed of Jealousy, Revolt, and Civil Discord; and at least the Parent of Treason, if not the Offspring of it."[1] On the other hand, English supporters of freedom of the press called it "the Palladium of all other English liberties." By 1760 at least fifty periodicals were publishing in London alone, a provincial press

[1] [Charles Lloyd], *A Defence of the Majority* (London, 1764). Quoted in Eckhart Hellmuth, "'The Palladium of All Other English Liberties': Reflections on the Liberty of the Press in England During the 1760s and 1770s," in E. Hellmuth, ed., *The Transformation of Political Culture: England and Germany in the Late-Eighteenth Century* (Oxford, 1990), pp. 472–473.

was growing, and newspaper subscriptions reached 200,000. A grave conflict over government restrictions of the press occurred in 1763, when John Wilkes (1727–1797), an MP representing the London suburb of Middlesex, used his newspaper, the *North Briton,* to accuse King George III of wishing to reestablish a Stuart-type despotism. The government's reaction to Wilkes was remarkably inept and turned him into a martyr for press freedom. In order to close down the *North Briton,* a "general warrant," naming no one personally, was issued. Wilkes was arrested, and his house was ransacked by searchers. He fought back in the courts. When the government maintained that the *North Briton* had jeopardized national security, Wilkes responded that general warrants jeopardized individual liberty. The case dragged on until 1769, but Wilkes ultimately was vindicated. General warrants were declared illegal, Wilkes won damages, and the English press gained a Europe-wide reputation for expanding political discourse and molding public opinion through lively commentary and moral censure of public figures—the king not excepted.

As governments observed nervously, journals and newspapers were established throughout most of eighteenth-century Europe. Those published in France were officially licensed and rigorously censored; but, as with books, French-language newspapers and periodicals published abroad escaped scrutiny and circulated inside the kingdom. The most important one, the *Gazette de Leyde,* generating from the Dutch academic town of Leiden since 1677, became Europe's newspaper of record. It provided readers with a detailed chronicle of events and was sought after by individuals as different as Thomas Jefferson and Louis XVI. By the time of the French Revolution, Lisbon, Madrid, Paris, Copenhagen, and St. Petersburg had their dailies or semiweeklies—some livelier and freer than others, yet all offering news and interpretations to increasingly inquisitive and politically aware populations.

THE RELIGIOUS CULTURE

The Christian Churches

Between 1715 and 1789, religion remained the dominant cultural force in the lives of most Europeans. The majority of books printed were devotional works, evangelization was active, and Churches tried to purge folk religion of what theologians considered to be pagan elements. Governments served the faith by enforcing respect for the sabbath and vigorously punishing transgressors. In Germany and Scandinavia, Pietists kept alive the flame of Protestant revivalism. In England, Methodist preachers carried the religion of the heart to thousands of villagers, the lost souls of the coal pits, and the slum dwellers of the teeming new industrial towns. In Italy and France, Catholic Jansenism revived. Monastic and priestly scholarship thrived. At their abbey at Saint-Germain-des-Prés in Paris, the Benedictines of Saint-Maur produced meticulous critical editions of the Church Fathers and medieval history. The history of the Roman emperors by the French Jansenist Le Nain de Tillemont (1637–1698) inspired Edward Gibbon to write his *Decline and Fall of the Roman Empire* (1776–1788), and the Italian priest Ludovico Muratori (1672–1750) obtained an unsurpassed collection of the antiquities of medieval Italy.

Nevertheless, the period was not a religious age. Established Churches lacked independent leadership. Eighteenth-century popes were especially weak and ineffective and were chosen mainly because they were aristocrats. Bishops in France, Spain, Portugal, and the Hapsburg Empire found it efficacious to bend to the wishes of their rulers when the sovereigns' orders contradicted those of the pope. In Protestant England, Prussia, Sweden, and Denmark, the Church was an agency of government. Such subservience sapped organized religion of much spiritual vigor.

As a comfortable, drifting institution, the Church of England offered the most notorious example of a religious institution that somehow had lost its sense of mission. Most English bishops were politicians, using their places in the House of Lords to advance to lucrative sees. The king reserved the best sees for favored aristocrats, but no village curacy escaped the patronage and favor seeking that marked political life. Anglican clerics had relatively little to do and did not even need to reside in the parish that they ostensibly served. Often neglecting the timeworn Christian dilemmas concerning sin and redemption, eighteenth-century Anglican leaders made a religious virtue of political or economic success. In this they were not alone. Even the Protestant Dissenters fell under the spell of worldly wisdom. Denied full civil rights by law and excluded from the universities, they attended their own academies, and many turned their vital energies away from religion to business, scholarship, and science.

The failure of Anglican leadership and secularization of Dissenter ideals successfully ended the religious conflict that had plagued English life for more than two centuries; but it also left a spiritual vacuum in eighteenth-century English Protestantism, made all the more critical by the social dislocations of the agricultural revolution and beginnings of industrialization. With its stress on worldly virtues, the Established Church barely addressed the needs of poverty-stricken immigrants moving to mine and town. Successful Dissenting Protestants forsook fire-and-brimstone evangelism for the cooler principles of Deism, or else drifted back into the Anglican fold and its promise of social and political privilege. For many the celebrated couplet of Alexander Pope summed up the essence of their religious convictions:

> For modes of faith let graceless zealots fight
> He can't be wrong whose life is in the right.

On the other hand, England did contain a few sensitive spirits who founded charity schools for the poor or devoted themselves to missionary work. And others, frustrated by the lukewarm conformism of Anglican religious life, rediscovered sin and portrayed it in a manner comprehensible to the poor.

One such individual was John Wesley (1703–1791). Sons of an Anglican priest and his iron-willed wife, John and his brother Charles attended Oxford University in the 1720s. Their acts of self-mortification and penance made them oddities among their fellow students, but at Oxford they also found a handful of like-minded souls. One was George Whitefield (1714–1770), who tried to convince them of the emotional power of open-air evangelizing among the poor. Unconvinced, the Wesley brothers left England to do missionary work in the North American wilds of Georgia. However, they discovered that devotion to the formal rites of Anglicanism was out of place in a rough frontier society, and they returned to England with a sense of failure. In May 1738, however, John underwent a mystical experience based on total submission to Christ. Shortly thereafter, Whitefield's address to the Kingsfield coal miners near Bristol created a national sensation, and John joined his old friend in open-air preaching.

Wesley's life now was transformed. His zeal drew followers, but the distinctive organizational lines on which he constructed his movement provoked the hostility of the Anglican bishops. As a consequence, Methodism evolved into a Protestant sect with its own habits and hierarchy. Wesley ordained a clergy. Between the day of his mystical experience and that of his death 53 years later, John Wesley traveled nearly 250,000 miles and delivered over 40,000 sermons. He went to the darkest slum and remotest village, preaching a basic message of sin, salvation, and rebirth, and urging on his listeners a morality founded on thrift, abstinence, and work. Methodism's political and social messages were profoundly reactionary. Under his leadership, the movement was hostile to education and accepting of child labor. It was theologically fundamentalist and intolerant of non-Protestants. Because it channeled the material misery of the poor and weak into other-worldly hope rather than this-worldly change, Methodism unwittingly served the forces of economic expansion and political status quo.

For eighteenth-century Protestantism the great event was the rise of the Wesleyites and their German counterparts, the Pietists. For eighteenth-century Catholicism it was the fall of the Jesuits. Both events derived from the weakness of venerable religious institutions—in the one case national Protestant Churches, in the other the papacy. Here, however, any parallel ceased. Individual Protestants might abandon older sects in favor of smaller groups of like-minded souls. However, dispossessed Jesuits had nowhere to go—unless it was to Protestant countries, where they might continue their teaching mission as long as they abandoned their religious one.

After 1715, rulers in Catholic Europe waged a relentless campaign against papal influence in national affairs. They expropriated monasteries and convents, nominated bishops and abbots, and their theorists on church-state relations called the pope an Italian politician, the Roman Curia his fifth column, and the Jesuits his shock troops. By the 1740s, the Jesuit question had become the most serious matter of all. Jesuits' hold on secondary school education was firm. They knew too much about the molding of young minds and had enemies everywhere. Memories of the Chinese and Malabar rite controversies remained fresh, and even the pope's esteem for them had fallen. Following some official harassment, in 1759 the king of Portugal expelled them from his country and colonial possessions. Five years later, after an official examination of the Jesuits' constitution found the Order to be subservient to a foreign power, Louis XV expelled it from France. In 1767, the rulers of Naples and Spain followed suit. Finally, in 1773, submitting to the bullying of princes, Dominicans, and Franciscans alike, Pope Clement XIV suppressed the Jesuits entirely. Religiously indifferent non-Catholic sovereigns like Frederick II and Catherine II invited notable ex-Jesuits to Prussia and Russia, where they became pioneers in the establishment of state-supported public school systems.

Churches on the Defensive

Established eighteenth-century Churches had to endure more than evangelical challenges or princely incursions into their spiritual authority and organizational structure. During the century, skepticism about the claims of orthodox doctrine became a central feature of European intellectual life. While the overwhelming majority remained attached to the beliefs of their parents, for numbers of comfortable and literate individuals indifference or even hostility to Christian tenets was increasing. In Protestant countries, natural religion infiltrated official orthodoxies. The decline of de facto censorship in several Protestant states led to publication of deistic writings. Influenced by Newtonian physics and astronomy, these works established God as a providential watchmaker who had set the universe running for the best and invited individuals to revere divine providence by adhering to a very brief and reasonable set of rules for human conduct. Old credal distinctions were to be abandoned; people were to be socially useful and charitable toward one another. For many European intellectuals, the Alexander Pope couplet cited earlier became a guide to life.

Deism penetrated Catholic and Protestant Europe without distinction. In France, the young baron de Montesquieu wrote in his *Persian Letters* (1721) that the most certain way of pleasing God was "to observe the rules of society and the duties of humanity." Voltaire added that the meaning of religion is "to be a good husband, good father, good neighbor, good subject, and good gardener." Abbé Noël-Antoine Pluche's best-selling *Spectacle of Nature* (1732–1742) held that divine providence's only request of humanity was contentment with one's lot. Such dismissal of dogma in favor of a complacent, optimistic ethic touched the beliefs of the rising body of civil servants in Prussia, northern Italy, and the Hapsburg Empire. In France, however, early eighteenth-century Deism evolved into an aggressive anti-Catholicism, largely because the official French Church resisted deistic calls for instituting religious tolerance, considering it a threat to the social order. Faced with accusations of heresy and worse, French Deists exposed clerical institutions and practices before the bar of reason. Materialists and atheists joined, and the Church was thrown on the defensive.

Timeworn Christian attitudes and practices were forced to confront philosophic alternatives supposedly derived from common sense and social utility. Critics called original sin morally reprehensible and the Trinity an affront to principles of logic. Biblical explanations of natural phenomena were accused of retarding scientific progress, and those poor souls who practiced the contemplative life and took seriously the vows of poverty, chastity, and obedience were accused of denying their genuine humanity. Eighteenth-century *philosophes* confronted Christian teachings by stressing the legitimacy of guiltless happiness, physical pleasure, and worldly culture. The French *Encyclopédie* (1751–1772), an immense collaborative effort of more than two hundred experts, observed, "Who can deny that the arts, industry, the taste for fashion—all those things which are beneficial to commerce—are not a genuine boon for nations? On the other hand, Christianity, which condemns luxury, at the same time weakens and destroys those things that depend upon it. Through its renunciation of vanity, it introduces laziness, poverty, the abandonment of everything—and in short destroys the arts."

Sporadic attacks by rulers on clerical wealth and religious societies, critiques by the encyclopedists of ecclesiastical institutions and Christian values, the penetration of deistic ideas in literate society, and the emergence of a respectable materialism—all these factors grievously weakened the underpinnings of traditional religious life. The advances of Methodism and Pietism notwithstanding, society was turning sharply toward the secular, especially in the fashionable circles of western and central Europe. The same critical turn of mind that questioned divine-right rule and blind acceptance of slavery and serfdom now was challenging both religious dogma and practice.

THE SCIENTIFIC CULTURE

The Practical Mission of Science

During the eighteenth century the progress of science best realized the concern of Europeans for a rational, socially useful approach toward life. The scientist had achieved cultural parity with the theologian and, after Newton, even became a new kind of folk hero. Because inquiry had not yet diverged into esoteric specialties, curious amateurs still could understand what scientists were doing. In Europe and the Americas scientific academies arose, explaining technique and discovery through public lectures, demonstrations, and courses. Admission to the academies required no special expertise, participants from all social classes met on an equal footing, and in a few instances women were welcome. Journals and magazines circulated, publishing the latest findings and the correspondence of scientists. Since agreed–upon fundamentals did not yet guide most subdivisions of science, serious amateurs and charlatans alike could captivate public interest. Paris was Europe's center for spectacular pseudo-scientific displays. There abbé Jean-Antoine Nollet (1700–1770) passed electrical charges through companies of royal troops and volunteers while onlookers gasped in delight. In the hands of Nollet electricity became a fashionable toy, and dinner parties became occasions for charging up. However, public obsession with science could easily lead to misrepresentation—magic for moderns though considered far more certain in results than medieval incantations. Charlatans used elaborate contraptions to commune with the dead or with other worlds. They pretended to cure ancient diseases through magnetism or electricity and formed secret societies that incurred the suspicion of respectable academies and government authorities alike. Notwithstanding official disapproval, a gullible public paid handsomely for their services.

Writings on pure science now formed a branch of literature. Following on the work of Fontenelle and abbé Pluche, the English radical theologian and political theorist Joseph Priestley (1733–1804) set the tone for popular scientific explanation with his *History and Present State of Electricity* (1767). With unparalleled verve an entire generation of remarkable French scientists insisted on using the vernacular rather than scholarly Latin in announcing and propagating their findings. So self-assured were they that in confirming Newton's theory of gravitation, the astronomer Pierre-Simon Laplace (1749–1827) proposed science as humanity's next religion. For Laplace the successful mission of science was to have "dissipated the fears of celestial phenomena and to have destroyed the errors born of being ignorant of our genuine rapports with nature, errors and fears which will revive promptly if the flame of science is ever extinguished."

Much of eighteenth-century science was directed toward the concrete and empirically derived. The passion for measurement and calculation markedly affected the least defined subdiscipline, chemistry. As late as 1750, earth, air, fire, and water still were considered elements. The phlogiston theory, initially expounded in 1697, held that all combustible bodies expelled an inflammable substance on burning. For a metal to be reduced to elemental earth, its phlogiston first had to be released. The theory dominated much of eighteenth-century chemistry, and the successful isolation of gases such as chlorine and manganese occurred virtually as fortuitous accidents. Priestley managed to isolate oxygen in 1774; however, he remained chained to the phlogiston theory. He called oxygen "new air."

Successfully isolating nine gases, Priestley's discoveries lacked plan. They occurred as accidents or surprises.

On the other hand, the Frenchman Antoine Lavoisier (1743–1794), indisputably the century's greatest chemist, removed the last vestiges of magic from his chosen branch of science. He isolated oxygen from both air and water, underscored the active role of the gas in calcination and respiration, and destroyed the phlogiston theory. Lavoisier proved that matter is indestructible and gave to chemistry its nomenclature (the list of elements) and its means of expression (the binomial equation). The forty memoirs that Lavoisier wrote for the Paris Academy of Science tightly coordinated his work into a systematized whole. His *Elementary Treatise on Chemistry* (1789) remains the eighteenth century's landmark of scientific publishing. A Farmer General and director of the state's saltpeter works, Lavoisier was a part-time experimenter. He wished to convey his view of the larger perspectives of science to laypeople. His basic tool was the scale, and he was guided from start to finish by the hypothesis that matter might change form but neither augment nor diminish.

Genius applied to painstaking observation and experiment permitted Lavoisier to grant scientific respectability to chemistry. Similarly, the patient laboratory work of the Dutchman Petrus van Musschenbroek, Frenchman Charles Coulomb, and Italian Luigi Galvani converted electricity from its role as a fashionable toy and paved the way for Alessandro Volta's discovery in 1800 of the inductive charge and invention of the electric battery. Meanwhile, processes of heat fascinated both the public and experimenters, even though precise and universally accepted measures of temperature eluded scientists. A professor of chemistry and anatomy at Glasgow University and discoverer of carbon dioxide, Joseph Black (1728–1799) was puzzled by the length of time it took ice to melt or boiling water to evaporate into steam. Black observed that a "capacity for heat" caused mercury to heat and cool much more rapidly than water. He was particularly astonished to find that capacity for heat had nothing to do with the weight or density of the substance involved, and he discovered how to measure the specific heat of a substance by comparing it to the heat of water. Black's work turned the study of heat into a careful, exact science. Specific heats were worked out for liquids, solids, and gases. Instruments were devised for measuring thermal expansion. In a rare case of theoretical and technological interdependence, James Watt used Black's researches in his invention of the separate condenser for the steam engine.

Challenges to Religion and Newton

"Collect experimental evidence and shun the spirit of system-building." Despite this advice by the French naturalist Georges-Louis Leclerc, count de Buffon (1707–1788), those who collected objects and determined the age of fossils, rocks, and the earth itself insisted on challenging sacrosanct systems. None was more vulnerable than the chronology of the Bible, and Buffon was loath about taking his own advice. While writing his massive natural histories of animals and birds, in 1778 Buffon composed his *Epochs of Nature,* covering the origins and fate of the earth and life upon it. According to Buffon's calculations, more than 60,000 years earlier a comet had crashed into the sun, spewing forth a chunk of molten matter which formed our planet. Seven historical stages followed, each cooler than its predecessor. The process was continuous and unalterable, and Buffon volunteered the gloomy conclusion that in 88,000 years the earth would grow too cold to sustain life. Divine intervention had no role in Buffon's story, and he earned the condemnation of the Sorbonne's theologians. Though government censors prohibited the *Epochs* from appearing in France, clandestine editions entered the country and translations flooded Europe.

Eighteenth-century Europeans were introduced to a concept of geological evolution that challenged not only Genesis but also the concept of a static Newtonian world machine. Buffon's exciting hypothesis of the earth's development stimulated thinking on species development. As early as the 1750s the French mathematician Pierre-Louis de Maupertuis (1698–1759) proposed that climate and opportunities for nourishment helped determine the variations of animal life. Poorly constructed types degenerated or perished; the fortunate survived. Maupertuis suggested a common ancestor for both the horse and donkey, and Buffon held that the same might be true for humans and monkeys. However, neither theorist advanced much further. Already the earth had been reduced to a speck located in a cosmically remote solar system, its birth and history attributed to impersonal natural causes. However consonant with the spirit of empiricism, eighteenth-century scientists were reluctant about applying similar causes to human development.

Medical Practices

As a pragmatic branch of scientific inquiry constructed on a foundation of observation and experiment, eighteenth-century therapeutic medicine increasingly was served empirically. Although medical students at the Sorbonne in Paris still had to spend two years listening to the syllogistic debates of professors before touching a cadaver, anatomy, chemistry, and botany nevertheless were introduced into the curriculum. So were visits to the sick in the city's charity hospitals. Europe's first university-sponsored medical clinic was established in Vienna in 1754, and Paris followed suit in 1770. The French specialized in studying childbirth. Thanks to government-sponsored midwife tours of the French countryside, where mothers-to-be and local practitioners learned safe techniques, the lives of thousands were spared. Medical journals were founded as outlets for publishing research, and a representative dedicated physician like the Swiss Simon-André Tissot (1728–1797) preached the virtues of smallpox inoculation, published a widely distributed manual for treating the rural poor, and inveighed against what he perceived to be the debilitating consequences of masturbation. Throughout western Europe surgeons began to obtain reluctant recognition from the medical profession of their contributions to the healing arts.

Despite the evolution of diagnostics and the symptomatic observation of heart disease, diabetes, typhoid fever, and some forms of tuberculosis, no innovative theoretical vision as yet guided therapeutic medicine. Many physicians still believed that the illness itself was purgative, ridding the body of unwanted elements, and that high fever was an unmistakable sign of release. They were reluctant to attack symptoms too quickly or to suppress fever through artificial means. The most common therapy either allowed nature to take its course or else assisted natural purgation through bleedings, diets, and thermal cures. Although a few priestly confessors might still advise the gravely ill to swallow neck crucifixes, such bizarre remedies were sinking into the realm of abandoned superstition. Pearls and viper's skin lost their miraculous powers.

In this period modern preventive medicine was born. Physicians advised governments on quarantining inhabitants to ward off the ravages of epidemic, and governments began removing responsibility for public health from religious bodies. Travelers were required to carry certificates of health, and doctors wrote treatises on hygiene disseminated by schoolmasters and priests. The century witnessed the world's first massive campaign of disease prevention, namely the struggle against smallpox, and individuals sensible to the curative powers of medicine started expecting better treatment. By the 1770s it was considered a public scandal for four sick persons to occupy the same bed in Paris's largest charity hospital, the Hôtel Dieu. A generation earlier, such crowding would have been accepted practice. English private philanthropy constructed clinics in London and other urban centers. In Hapsburg Austria, Emperor Joseph II ordered the construction of state hospitals in larger towns and decreed compulsory hygiene lessons for the poor. Even the imprisoned and insane won medical treatment as a basic human right.

Science and Technology

The eighteenth century also witnessed adolescent flirtation between theoretical science and applied technology. Traditional technology customarily had been oriented toward warfare. For example, during the struggles of Louis XIV the rapid-fire rifle had dethroned the slow-shooting musket, and the invention of the cartridge permitted a soldier to fire three rounds per minute. Two generations later, however, demand for sources of power indicated to a few visionaries the need to link technology with the laboratory. It was not easy to do so. The relationships between empirical scientists and inventors often had been strained. The maker of machines was considered either a tinker or grubby profit seeker, supposedly lacking patience for painstaking research into the underlying processes of nature. This conflict helps explain why the eighteenth-century chemical industry was so far in advance of chemical theory. Chlorine was used as a bleaching agent before laboratory scientists understood just why it was effective.

On their part, European artisans mistrusted scientists. Artisans worked in closed communities which jealously guarded industrial secrets. The monopolistic production techniques of these communities offered little incentive for change, for cooperation with theoretical scientists, or for assisting consumers in the easy and inexpensive acquisition of goods. Nevertheless, critics were determined to link artisanal technology more closely with science and make its fruits better known to a wider audience. No one was more eager to accomplish this than a French cutler's son, Denis Diderot (1713–1784), co-editor of the century's most important book, the folio-sized twenty-eight volume *Encyclopédie,* subtitled *A Reasoned Dictionary of Sciences, Arts, and Crafts.* Diderot adored technology and invention. He devoted large sections of the *Encyclopédie*'s eleven volumes of plates to illustrating industrial and mechanical processes. He also had the amateur's passion for pure science and invited the best theorists in Europe to contribute to his book. The result of Diderot's labor was not necessarily the trusting marriage he had foreseen, but rather a difficult and unnatural union, with artisans remaining suspicious and frightened. Diderot's collaborator, the mathematician Jean Le Rond d'Alembert (1717–1783), nevertheless remained hopeful, writing, "it most likely is among artisans that we can find genuine proofs of the wisdom of the human mind." Even as publication of the *Encyclopédie* got underway, the fashionable Paris Academy of Science undertook its own *Descriptions of Arts and Trades.* By 1788, the academy's venture had reached eighty-eight folio volumes. However much its practitioners resented it, artisanal culture was becoming absorbed into the all-encompassing world of science.

However, it was Europe's economic advance, and not its scientific progress, which explains the eighteenth-century technological breakthrough. Foreseeing the use of a great reservoir of raw cotton in America if only mechanization could assist hand labor, English investors actively encouraged invention. From John Kay's perfected flying shuttle of 1733 through Samuel Crompton's spinning mule forty years later, technology revolutionized England's textile industry. Spinners learned to produce yarns nearly as fine as handcrafted Indian cottons. The thread makers were in advance of the weavers. In 1800, however, the pastor Edmund Cartwright put together a mechanical weaving machine to which he eventually applied steam power. The development of his machine was rendered possible by perfecting malleable iron for its construction.

The quest for power sources preoccupied inventors throughout the century, and science eventually came to technology's aid. James Watt (1736–1819) worked as an instrument maker at the University of Glasgow. One day in 1763, while repairing a model of Newcomen's steam engine, the young Watt was appalled by the heat wasted as a result of the need to cool the hot cylinder with a jet of cold water discharged inside it. After consulting with the university professor Joseph Black, Watt was able to condense the steam outside the cylinder. Then he fitted a jacket round the cylinder and employed steam instead of atmospheric pressure to force the piston downward. Armed with a patent, Watt began building steam engines for Matthew Boulton, a Birmingham industrialist. In 1782 he patented a double-acting engine which obtained twice the power. In 1788 the rotary steam engine was standardized, and by 1800 the Watt-Boulton partnership had created more than five hundred machines.

Even before Watt's remarkable discoveries, visionaries dreamed of steam-powered transportation. In 1763 the French military engineer Cugnot built a three-wheeled cannon bearer to support a modified version of Newcomen's engine. The contraption moved at less than 3 miles per hour, and it was necessary to stop it every fifteen minutes to feed its furnace. Steam-powered land transport made little headway, but by 1780 several experimental ships were plying French rivers. Nor was steam power the sole means of propulsion that caught imaginations. On August 27, 1783, before a delirious Paris crowd of a quarter million, the French physician Jacques Charles launched a hydrogen-filled balloon into the atmosphere. It reached 3,000 feet, then tore apart, and dropped to earth 15 miles from the capital, astonishing peasants who thought the moon was falling. Three weeks later, before King Louis XVI and his court at Versailles, the paper manufacturer Etienne Montgolfier launched and landed a balloon containing some caged animals. On November 21 of the same year, the young physician Jean-François Pilâtre de Rozier and his friend the marquis d'Arlandes entered a balloon basket in Paris, spent half an hour in the air, and landed 6 miles from their starting point. Two years later, as he tried to fly over the English Channel, Pilâtre de Rozier was victimized by a torn balloon and became aviation's first martyr. By this time, however, other humans already had flown across the English Channel, and shortly thereafter the military once more put technology to use. In 1794 the armies of revolutionary France were using air transport for reconnaissance missions.

The overwhelming number of mechanical and industrial inventions either were English or French. Capital investment was missing elsewhere, and the agrarian states of central and eastern Europe participated minimally in world commerce. Bohemian and Silesian textiles, Solingen cutlery, Russian draperies, and the manufacture of lace, clocks, mirrors, and glassware depended largely upon a dispersed labor force and the traditional manufacturing methods of rural-based industry. Prussian soldiers spun cotton in their barracks, prisoners at Spandau prison in Berlin worked with wool, and orphans in the asylum at Potsdam made lace. Except for England, where faith in consumption flourished, entrepreneurs lacked confidence in an international market and continued to depend upon traditional village handicraft to work their raw materials. In England, however, entrepreneur inventors learned how to consult scientists and persuaded wealthy individuals to be bold with their investments. Not everyone grew rich overnight. Occasionally disaster struck, as the oversupplied cotton industry revealed in 1792. Nevertheless, in the long run gambles paid off handsomely. Early in the nineteenth century England's industrial power helped defeat Napoleon. Subsequently it was to create an empire of unprecedented proportions.

THE SPIRIT OF THE PHILOSOPHES

Cultural Cosmopolitanism

For a literate west-European public, reason had become autonomous, and neither theology nor metaphysics was needed any longer to sustain it. Experiment and observation, the techniques of eighteenth-century science, now were established firmly as the essential means for acquiring knowledge. Ideally, whatever hypotheses failed to submit to their test were suspended or rejected as unworkable. It is, of course, nonsense to suppose that the philosophes had rid themselves totally of phlogiston theories of the mind. Even with untrammeled reason as their guide, their prejudices ran deep. They failed to understand the emotional needs that attracted civilized people to Jansenism, Methodism, or Pietism, and with the sweep of a facile generalization they would condemn an entire epoch such as the Middle Ages. Although the philosophes never established a formal school of thought, for the first time since Rome's fall, secular and secular-minded intellectuals demanded responsibility for Europe's cultural guardianship. They defined the boundaries of knowledge and the means for attaining truth. Committed to liberty of thought and expression, they expressed their opinions in epic poetry, satire, the essay, novel, and even the dictionary.

For what did the philosophes stand? In 1715, at the dawn of the Enlightenment, the marquise Anne-Thérèse de Lambert (1647–1733), a Paris bluestocking who afforded advanced thinkers the protection of her home, stated that the philosophes intended "to clothe reason in all its dignity and restore it in its rights by shaking off the bonds of tradition and authority." West European in character, the Enlightenment fed on English sources, particularly the empiricism of Locke and scientific certainties of Newton, and it took deepest root in France. Nevertheless, there also was an American Enlightenment and a Scottish one. Sympathetic German, Swedish, and Italian intellectuals were in regular communication with French colleagues. Progressive nobles in Poland and Russia lined their shelves with volumes of Enlightenment thought. Following the example of their king, Frederick II, Prussian bureaucrats became familiar with the new ideas, and the warnings of their empress Maria Theresa notwithstanding, Austrian civil servants did as well.

The state had a significant part in fostering Enlightenment thought. Frederick and Tsarina Catherine II of Russia (1763–1796) offered subsidies to philosophes and made them welcome at court. In France a hierarchy of state-supported academies encouraged the study of history, literature, and science. Aristocrats participated in these organizations, and several of the Enlightenment's most important thinkers were nobles. Readings and debates were held in the comfort of aristocratic salons. Yet we cannot say that the movement had the unquestioned blessing of the powers-that-be, any more than we can label it as aristocratic or bourgeois in scope. Its chief audience crossed class lines and was composed of skeptical, literate, reform-minded women and men possessing faith in science and technology and in the power of human reason to better the world.

Of course, these individuals had to be able to afford the luxury of books and possess the sufficient leisure time to read them. They were court nobles and civil servants, tax officials and army officers, worldly abbés and progressive pastors, salon hostesses and booksellers' widows. They belonged to scientific and cultural clubs throughout urban Europe and to Masonic lodges which grew rapidly after the 1730s. They not only purchased books but also subscribed to newspapers and journals. In England, *The Spectator,* founded in 1711 by Joseph Addison and Richard Steele to popularize science, literature, and ideas, attained a circulation of nearly 30,000. Its French counterpart, the *Mercure,* was sold in fifty-five towns by 1774. Elsewhere in Europe, circulation figures for cultural journalism dropped as one headed eastward, forming an accurate gauge of both the spread and depth of Enlightenment thought and controversy.

Not merely representing the supreme intellectual effort of ancien-régime society, the Enlightenment also underscored the inner contradictions of that society. The philosophes chipped away at both ecclesiastical and aristocratic privilege, the two most important institutional pillars of the eighteenth-century world. The intent of most critics was not revolutionary. Rather, the philosophes advocated social and political reform, so that science and reason might develop untrammeled, and individuals like themselves might achieve proper recognition for their usefulness. They were elitist, but what they most seemed to advocate was a meritocracy and at least qualified equality of opportunity. They mistrusted the uneducated: "It is not a question of pleasing the people, but of doing what is good for them," wrote the marquis Marie-Jean de Condorcet (1743–1794), one of the most humane of the thinkers. Most philosophes supported strong government, even absolute government, if regimes would attack privilege and social abuse as vigorously as they would protect civil liberties. Most philosophes despised war as a crime against reason and humanity, though they courted favors and protection from warring sovereigns. While sharing their readership's contempt and pity for the "lower orders," the philosophes nevertheless indignantly denied that they were replacing one set of prejudices with another. They proclaimed that they were addressing humanity at large.

Montesquieu

Charles-Louis de Secondat, baron de Montesquieu, was born near Bordeaux in southwestern France in 1689. His family belonged to the *robe* aristocracy, and he was educated by Oratorian priests, the rivals of the Jesuits. Then he studied law. At twenty-five, he replaced his late father as a councillor in the Parlement of Bordeaux, and three years later obtained a late uncle's parlementary office as president. In 1716 he joined the newly established Academy of Bordeaux and became one of its most active members, reading papers on physiology, physics, and biology. While tempted by the delightful obscurity of a comfortable judicial life on his beloved native soil, Montesquieu also yearned for a literary career, the salons of Paris, and foreign travel. In 1721 he published anonymously in Holland the *Persian Letters,* an irreverent political and social satire that took to task French political and cultural institutions. Four years later he resigned from Bordeaux's Parlement and embarked on a lengthy tour of Europe, particularly enjoying his stay in England.

At thirty-five, Montesquieu was elected to the French Academy. However, once word got around that he had written the *Persian Letters,* Louis XV refused to sign the warrant of admission. Received eventually, Montesquieu passed the remainder of his life alternating among his travels, elegant town house in Paris, and the family's country château at La Brède. In 1748 his masterpiece, *The Spirit of the Laws,* appeared. He composed the article "Taste" for the *Encyclopédie* and in 1755 died in Paris—in Christian sanctity, said one witness; as a true philosophe, retorted Voltaire.

In the *Persian Letters,* Montesquieu exploited an Oriental tale to describe the "enlightened" reactions of a group of Persians confronted by the brutalities, inconsistencies, and irrationalities of life in eighteenth-century Europe. The device was entertaining and allowed Montesquieu to escape personal responsibility for the ideas expressed by his characters. Montesquieu's Persians envisioned the pope as "an old idol who is doused with incense out of habit . . . but who no longer is feared." As for the king of France, he "is a great magician. He exercises an empire over the minds of his subjects. He has them think whatever he wishes. If he possesses only a million écus in his treasury and needs two million, he simply persuades them that one écu is worth two and they believe him." The *Persian Letters* stood out as a bold statement against despotism, papal claims to temporal authority, the arbitrariness that passed for justice in France, and the worst features of financial speculation.

Behind the *Persian Letters* lay a belief that identifiable and defined causes, not blind chance, form our institutions and beliefs. In his *Considerations on the Causes of the Grandeur and Decline of the Romans* (1734), Montesquieu applied his ideas to a single historical circumstance. Finally in *The Spirit of the Laws* (1748) he wrote that the institutions of a people are the exterior manifestations of specific circumstance and habit, such as climate, quality and size of land, population, occupations, religion, wealth, and social customs. By noting that in some countries there may be "natural" reasons for slavery or polygamy, Montesquieu denied any intention of justifying these institutions. Rather, he was merely seeking out the reasons for them. A man of the Enlightenment, Montesquieu nevertheless was a moralist, with a clear sense of what *ought* to be. In *The Spirit of the Laws* he devoted considerable space to evaluating the nature of political constitutions and the effect they ought to have on the laws of a people.

In judging any society, political liberty stands out as Montesquieu's ultimate moral criterion. Eschewing determinism, he wrote that liberty can survive only through a conscious effort at balancing the ambitions of contending political forces. If one force goes unchecked, despotism threatens. Montesquieu thought he saw such a balance being practiced in the government of eighteenth-century England, where he observed function and power divided among Parliament, king, and judiciary. In Montesquieu's view each body made certain that none of the others overstepped bounds of authority. Idealizing the unwritten English constitution, Montesquieu accepted the political compromise, horse trading, and corruption that played such a significant part in daily government. He considered these political habits as the consequence of Britain's constitutional balance. When he called on the so-called intermediary powers in France—namely the high clergy, great nobility, and parlements—to check the despotic tendencies of absolute monarchy, Montesquieu's aristocratic prejudices probably got the better of him. Except as it applied to small republics, he opposed democracy nearly as vigorously as he hated despotism. Nor did he say much about forswearing social privilege. Nevertheless, the disciplines of modern sociology and political science are in Montesquieu's debt. With the precision of a physical scientist, he ingeniously manipulated empirical data, and he perceptively analyzed the sociological factors which lay behind laws and institutions. His most lasting contribution was the priority he awarded to civil liberties. In this respect, Montesquieu not only was a worthy descendant of Locke but also an inspiration to those who followed him.

Voltaire

No eighteenth-century figure tried more forcefully than Voltaire (1694–1778) to implement Montesquieu's principles on civil liberties. Born François-Marie Arouet to a comfortable Paris lawyer and a woman descended from the petty nobility, Voltaire became the Enlightenment's best pamphleteer and most tireless warrior against institutionalized injustice. While in his teens he gained the reputation of a quick-witted, acid-tongued man about town. For allegedly insulting the regent of France, he spent most of 1716 in the Bastille. Once released, he became well known as a writer of classical tragedies, but his penchant for wrangling with influential politicians earned him two years (1726–1728) of enforced exile in England. The

English impressed him, as they would impress Montesquieu several years later. Back in France, Voltaire published an adulatory essay on English customs, the *Philosophical Letters* (1734). However, his acknowledged writings, anonymous pieces, and spoken comments continued to anger important officials of church and state. The *Philosophical Letters* were condemned by the Parlement of Paris, and a copy was ceremonially shredded and burned in the courtyard of Paris's Palace of Justice. At the age of forty, Voltaire again feared for his safety and withdrew from Paris to the country estate of his companion Émilie du Châtelet, near France's eastern frontier. For several years the pair entertained an array of guests and studied Newtonian science, history, and philosophy.

Envying the limelight, in 1739 Voltaire abandoned country life and for nearly a quarter century served as unofficial roving ambassador for the republic of letters. Sovereigns and aristocrats fought for his favors, and his international reputation reached its height. The writer enjoyed the protection of out-of-sorts royalty like the duke du Maine, illegitimate son of Louis XIV, the duchess, and Stanislaus Leszczynski, former king of Poland. Genuine rulers courted him too. For three years Frederick the Great served as his host in Berlin, though the pair parted company on very poor terms.

Voltaire fantasized himself becoming an enlightened seigneur. He purchased several properties and in 1760, aged sixty-five, settled down on his estate at Ferney in southeastern France, close to the Swiss border. There he supervised a permanent community of around sixty, which grew its own crops and had its own handicrafts, library, and theater. Visitors, supplicants, and guests poured in; pamphlets and letters poured out. Ferney became Europe's clearinghouse for causes. Voltaire concentrated on rehabilitating the reputations of victims of intolerance, such as Jean Calas, a Protestant merchant executed for having allegedly murdered a son who contemplated conversion to Catholicism, and General Lally, scapegoat for the loss of India to the British. In warring for the individual, Voltaire hoped to reform the system. His efforts did help to reduce secret trials and vindictive judicial punishment. Just prior to the revolution of 1789, Protestant civil liberties were restored in France. Persuaded to visit Paris in 1778, Voltaire was acclaimed with banquets, receptions, concerts, and plays he had written decades earlier. The trip was his last. Utterly exhausted and crowned with an aureole of glory, he bade farewell to a life he had so cherished. His remains were placed in the Pantheon, resting place for France's great.

The intellectual development of Voltaire is attested to by his fifty volumes of published writings and a hundred more of correspondence. His religious views became more radical as he grew older. Through the 1730s he consoled himself with faith in "Newton's God"; but even during his years of scientific experiment with Madame du Châtelet, he suspected that the universe was something less than a playground built for humanity's enjoyment. Too many innocents suffered without apparent cause; there was too much confirmation of the reality of evil. Between the premature death of Madame du Châtelet (1749) and a catastrophic earthquake in Lisbon which took 20,000 lives (1755), Voltaire suffered from bouts of profound pessimism. He found some solace in scholarship and wrote his great histories, *The Century of Louis XIV* (1751) and the *Essay on the Habits and Customs of Nations* (1756). Incapable of escapism or passivity, however, the old man recovered. His brief novel *Candide* (1759) counseled the active, useful life as solace in the face of incomprehensible misfortune, and for nearly two more decades he directed his most spirited attacks against the cruelties of religious fanaticism. Clinging to the straw of a skeptic's vague, ill-defined God, he assumed fanaticism to be far more dangerous than atheism. At seventy-four he wrote, "I only preach the adoration of God, goodwill, and indulgence. Armed with these sentiments I challenge the Devil, who doesn't exist, and the real devils, who exist only too well." Defense of individual liberties remained his chief cause. Yet he was no democrat. He believed in the mission of intellectuals to influence the powerful. For Voltaire, enlightened and absolute princes were necessary to check the passions of priests and the people alike.

Diderot

For all of Voltaire's destructive wit and irony, he was not the boldest thinker of the French Enlightenment. In this respect Denis Diderot (1713–1784) outstripped him. Diderot came from a provincial artisan family. As a child he was precocious, and in 1722 his parents sent him to a Jesuit school for training as a priest. Diderot continued his studies in Paris, secured a master's degree at the Sorbonne, and promptly lost his religious faith. Next he tried a legal career. Finding it unstimulating, during the mid-1730s he favored a bohemian existence in the capital. Earning his living as a translator and anonymous author of soft-core pornography, between 1746 and 1749 Diderot also composed some essays that spoke lightly of Christianity and suggested that practical morality had little to do with divine law. For his writings, Diderot found himself in trouble. One work was publicly burned, and its author was thrown into Vincennes prison. Once released, Diderot continued to write "dangerous" books anonymously; but other facets of his immensely creative personality also surfaced. He composed art criticism and wrote plays that replaced the aristocratic formalism of the French classical tradition with a sentimental style underscoring bourgeois virtues. He made friends with bankers and Farmers General and welcomed a pension provided by Russia's Catherine II. Most significant of all, for more than twenty-five years Diderot took charge of the *Encyclopédie,* overseeing publication of the enormous work with the dedication of a parent saddled with a brilliant and thoroughly wayward child.

    As we have seen, the *Encyclopédie* was an exhaustive compilation of current scientific and technological data. In the hands of Diderot and his

Figure 8.1—Illustration of "Agriculture, Working the Field" by the engravers Defehrt and Prevost from the Recueil de Planches, sur les Sciences, les Arts Libéraux, et les Arts Méchaniques, avec leur Explication, *in* Encyclopédie, ou Dictionnaire Raisonné des Sciences, des Arts et des Métiers, *Vol. XVIII (Paris, 1762). As chief editor of the* Encyclopédie, *the eighteenth century's most ambitious publishing project, Denis Diderot merged actual work processes with his utopian vision. Considering French agricultural practices to be socially reprehensible and economically retrograde, he offered an alternative which was both modern and romantic. In this engraving the field labor is well organized and cooperative. The medieval chateau lies in ruins. Fields are enclosed by hedgerows, and the tools, such as Jethro Tull's light plow and the abbé Soumille's mechanical seeder, are recent inventions. Courtesy of Dover Books,* A Diderot Pictorial Encyclopedia of Trades and Industry, *edited by Charles C. Gillispie (New York, 1959), vol. 1.*

co-editor for several years, the mathematician d'Alembert, it tried to be considerably more—namely an attempt to place all human creativity in the service of what the pair and their collaborators perceived to be untrammeled reason. Most *Encyclopédie* articles reflect on facts. In the subscribers' prospectus Diderot wrote that the editors assumed no prior knowledge on the part of readers, that any single article might expand on another, and that, except for the specialist, the book could take the place of one's entire library. Cropping up periodically are criticisms of Christianity, divine-right monarchy, metaphysics, and other "un-reasonable" institutions or attitudes of mind. Diderot did not impose ideological or theoretical limitations on his contributors, but the immense *Encyclopédie* clearly illustrated that a common attitude of mind had swept over a broad section of Europe's intellectuals. Virtually all the contributors, French and non-French alike, were moralists and teachers, who believed in the virtues of literacy and proper education. The majority shared a faith in the workings of science and technology. For them, reason was no cold abstraction. They exalted in the pleasures and passions of life. Above all, they addressed themselves to an idea of humanity undivided by national, religious, or racial prejudices, and drawn together by proofs of natural equality, natural rights, and natural law.

For Diderot, the *Encyclopédie* was not only a monument to truth but also a hornet's nest of trouble. Clerics, politicians, and jealous rivals made for enemies everywhere. Twice the project was stopped by government order. In 1759 the French Royal Council finally revoked the publication permit altogether, accusing the *Encyclopédie* of having caused "irreparable damage to morality and religion." The Catholic Church denounced the work and threatened to excommunicate all who possessed or even read it. Anxious contributors, as well as d'Alembert, defected. Nevertheless, Diderot labored on, collecting materials, writing dozens of articles himself, setting up pages, and semisecretly preparing the illustrative plates. The first edition of text was surreptitiously printed in 1765, and the plates were finished seven years later. The publishing event of the century took twenty-five years to complete, and all 4,225 original subscribers or their successors obtained their sets. Between 1776 and 1782, reprints, imitations, and pirated editions found their way into libraries across Europe—from Dublin to Moscow and beyond. Thomas Jefferson paid for his with 15,000 pounds of tobacco. A set was ordered for the Cape colony in southern Africa. In all, more than 25,000 *Encyclopédies* were published before 1789. For those unable to afford sets, the periodical press lifted excerpts and printed them.

While editing the *Encyclopédie,* Diderot composed personal works that were radical and materialistic. Rather than risk scandal by publishing them, he left most in manuscript form where they remain testamentary evidence of his evolving thought. Whether advocating a "natural" morality in sexual relationships, suggesting biological evolution based on natural selection, or wrestling between amoral cynicism and sentimental conformity as life's guides, Diderot argued with disarming sincerity. Meanwhile, built as it was on facts, his *Encyclopédie* remained a monument to combative reason, passionately espoused. So representative of the Enlightenment was Diderot, that his colleagues addressed him alone as Le Philosophe.

Secular Humanitarianism and Philosophical History

By the 1760s many literate Europeans believed that enlightened public interest might provide an adequate basis for private morals. Complementing this idea was the conviction that legislation and proper education could reform the worst social evils. A repentant French tax farmer, Claude-Adrien Helvétius (1715–1776), not only urged the extension of educational benefits to wide segments of the population but also advocated reformation of the curriculum. For Helvétius, the traditional catechisms of priest and schoolmaster were to be scrapped. What the child needed was less religion and more reading and arithmetic. Helvétius added that lessons in morals should be based exclusively on the public interest. Such ideas bore fruit as eighteenth-century governments initiated national, secular educational programs suited to the needs of the state. In Portugal a widely traveled pressure group of French-inspired intellectuals lobbied for the elimination of Catholic-dominated education, and in the Dutch Netherlands schemes for a universal elementary school system were put into practice. Danish initiatives for school reform were intended to transform a newly liberated peasantry into a self-reliant social class. The government of Savoy began licensing teachers and supervising student examinations. Following the dissolution of the Jesuit order in 1773, Poland organized a national educational commission that supervised teacher training, reformed pedagogical methods, and hired textbook authors.

Contrasted with the record of previous centuries, eighteenth-century state-inspired elementary school reforms were impressive. Nevertheless, European culture was above all elitist, and the energies of governments were directed more toward assuming control over the secondary school and college educations of potential civil servants, legal experts, and liberal professionals than in teaching peasants to read and write. The Jesuits had dominated secondary school instruction in most Catholic countries until 1759, after which European rulers began exiling the 20,000 Fathers and taking over control of their schools. Replacing the Jesuits was a tall order, for they had directed nearly 700 establishments in Europe and Latin America. The results were mixed. While the French state failed to organize a smooth transition, the Austrian Hapsburgs established teacher-training colleges, founded new university chairs, reformulated secondary school curriculum in favor of modern subjects, and reduced religious education to moral lessons emphasizing submission to proper authorities. The atheist Prussian king Frederick II welcomed former Jesuits to his Protestant country as long as they excluded Catholic instruction from their teaching mission. Elsewhere in Germany, as well as in England

and Scotland, nonconformist Protestant sects established private academies for students whose religious beliefs denied them admission to traditional schools and universities. The academies taught Dissenter beliefs, of course; but more importantly they also emphasized modern science, modern languages, and history. In England, Nonconformists made wealthy in trade and industry generously supported the academies.

The promise of state-directed education reform led Enlightenment theorists to hope that political authorities would experiment with other reforms as well. The preoccupation of the French government with the peasant question was due largely to the influence of a body of economic thinkers called physiocrats. The spiritual father of physiocracy was Louis XV's court physician, François Quesnay. In 1774 another prominent physiocrat, Anne-Robert Turgot (1727–1781), rose from his post as intendant of Limoges to become state controller-general of finance. French reformers linked the problems of stagnant agriculture to the government's chronic need for money. They also proposed capitalist land development as practiced in Britain and advocated the free internal movement and export of grain. They insisted on the elimination or at least reduction of seigneurial privileges and the imposition of a single tax based on landed rents. The physiocrats hated tax farmers and the guilds. To them, mercantilism, which still defined the course of French economic life, was outmoded and detrimental to progress. Turgot's twenty-month stint as controller-general, from 1774 to 1776, gave physiocrats the chance to begin working on what they called the "natural order" of economic development. In the end, however, the force of corporate, guild, and seigneurial privilege brought down Turgot and defeated French physiocracy.

Economic reform in central Europe proved more successful than in France. In the Hapsburg Empire, where university professors of economics doubled as ministers of state, the task was to increase agricultural production that was meager and based on serf labor. The reformers in the Hapsburg lands were more pragmatic and less ideological than the French physiocrats. They were more insistent on state involvement and administrative efficiency than on free trade and laissez-faire production methods. Moreover, they had support from the top. Their emperor Joseph II (1780–1790) encouraged his experts because he wished to destroy the social barriers to economic growth, and the abolition of serfdom in 1789 was the culmination of Hapsburg economic reform.

Unlike the reformers in the Hapsburg Empire, the Scotsman Adam Smith (1723–1790), was neither a neomercantilist nor a politician. He was professor of moral philosophy at the University of Glasgow, and his epic *Wealth of Nations* (1776) became a primer for the emerging industrial civilization. Like the French physiocrats, Smith illustrated how a highly regulated economy might frustrate agricultural development. Unlike most physiocrats, however, Smith was friendly toward commerce, and for his followers laissez-faire became a byword. A humanitarian, Smith predicted the exploitation of industrial workers and saw the need of government to protect them. Moreover, for Smith, the state was essential not only to prevent monopolists from getting a stranglehold over a nation's economy but even more fundamentally to put laissez-faire on an operating basis. State controls over the sale of land had to be abrogated, restrictions on grain exports removed, and duties on imports abandoned. Smith urged governments to médiate benevolently, encouraging industrial growth and free trade and, where necessary, eradicating special interests. Regimes never again should concern themselves with minute mercantilist regulations. As for humanity's material future, Smith was an unrepentant optimist.

Secular humanitarianism permeated the century's most celebrated analysis of criminal law and procedure, *On Crimes and Punishments*, published in 1764 by a twenty-six-year-old Italian from Milan, Cesare Beccaria (1738-1794). Within Europe, judicial torture still was being used to extract confessions, punishments rarely conformed to crimes, and trials commonly were secret judgments based on circumstantial evidence and unreliable witnesses. Influenced by Montesquieu, Voltaire, and Helvétius, Beccaria wrote that punishment ought to serve not as an act of vengeance but rather as a deterrent. It therefore must be suitable, prompt, and certain. Penal codes, Beccaria contended, must be defined clearly, so that would-be criminals were aware of the risks involved. Beccaria had no use whatsoever for judicial torture. Fearing prosecution for his work, he published it anonymously. The French translation, however, skyrocketed the obscure young Italian to renown, and he was feted by philosophes and enlightened rulers alike. Although Beccaria never again wrote anything comparable to *On Crimes and Punishments,* the Austrian Hapsburgs recognized his contribution by awarding him a professorial appointment and high government post in Lombardy. His legacy lay in the development of state criminal codes, establishment of courtroom procedural reform, and abolition of judicial torture.

Penal reform and code building wedded Enlightenment humanitarianism to the desire of goverments for intensifying command over state institutions and citizens' lives. Religious tolerance fulfilled a similar purpose. Eighteenth-century sovereigns began seeing religious bigotry not as guaranteeing cultural unity but as an impediment in the quest for useful, obedient subjects. A generation after Louis XIV called the Revocation of the Edict of Nantes the triumph of his reign, French government officials were complaining about the loss of 300,000 enterprising and industrious subjects. By the 1750s writers everywhere were attacking forced conversions and civil disabilities based on religious preference. Although English Catholics—and especially Irish ones—still suffered for their religion, dissenting Protestants in the British Isles were attaining material and professional success. An underpopulated state, Prussia encouraged the immigration of religious minorities, and several German princelings imitated Frederick II's indifference to the private religious practices of his subjects. As British Catholics began to regain their civil rights, French Protestants won their revenge over Louis XIV. Despite episcopal protests, in 1787 their religion obtained recognition by the Crown.

Cradle of the Counter-Reformation, the Hapsburg Empire offered the century's most spectacular example of religious tolerance. The empire itself was religiously pluralist, with its Catholic majority and pockets of Orthodox, Protestants, Moslems, and Jews. Shortly after succeeding to his mother's titles and lands and despite the warnings of his advisers, Joseph II issued a series of sweeping toleration edicts. Offered to all religious groups, whether Christian or not, were freedom of public worship, the right to hold land, the enjoyment of schooling, and entry into the professions, public office, and the military. The emperor's intentions were purely utilitarian— to facilitate the formation of loyal subjects.

At the same time, Joseph ensured the subservience of Catholicism to the state. The clergy was prohibited from writing to the pope without government permission; bishops had to swear an oath of allegiance to the regime; pious lay brotherhoods and contemplative monastic orders were suppressed; state seminaries were established to educate priests; religious processions and church services were regulated, sermons censored, and civil marriage validated. Joseph was no Voltairean; his Catholicism was sincere, and he warned Protestant pastors lest their diluted zeal degenerate into "rational paganism." In his own time, Joseph was accused of using religion to further the aims of the omnipotent state, and his Belgian subjects greeted his reforms with armed revolt. However shocking Joseph's regulations must have seemed to many of his contemporaries, in historical perspective his edicts of toleration remain the ancien régime's most visionary testaments to Enlightenment zeal. It was government's way of fulfilling the promise of the philosophes.

Viewing reason as a weapon rather than a process, eighteenth-century reformers hoped not only to correct and modify institution but also to rewrite history in the service of their perceived truth. Of course, scholars had long used the past to justify the present. From St. Augustine to Bossuet, historians had served Christian revelation. Following Pierre Bayle's footsteps, the "philosophical historians" of the eighteenth century laid claim to objectivity and roundly denounced fable masquerading as fact. They held that human records alone formed the basis of historical material, and they widened the scope of these records to include sociological, economic, geographical, and literary sources. If their wide appreciation of sources permitted them to study non-European civilizations more objectively than predecessors had ever done, their preconceived skepticism of Christianity forced them to downgrade the epochs of the Old Testament and Middle Ages. They also believed that history must tell a lively story and rejected fact grubbing for its own sake. They loved pagan antiquity and initiated the serious study of the recent past. Voltaire was their pioneer. In his *Century of Louis XIV* (1751) and *Essay on the Habits and Customs of Nations* (1756), Voltaire emphasized the contribution of the arts, sciences, and secular institutions. Postulating the universality of human nature, he neverthe-less categorized heroes and villains according to his own secular system of values. Concerning the avowed intentions of his subjects, he was ever skeptical.

Voltaire's British successors, David Hume (1711–1776) and Ed-ward Gibbon (1737–1794), were more flexible than he was in their attribu-tions of both historical motive and cause. In his *History of England* (1754–1762), Hume even doubted whether the historian ever could deci-pher either spiritual or secular plans in the development of humanity. On the other hand, in his *Decline and Fall of the Roman Empire* (1776–1788), Gibbon did not shrink from generalization and, in fact, leveled a sharp indictment at Christianity for contributing to the collapse of classical civi-lization. The greatest of the eighteenth-century historians, Gibbon was more subtle and even more skeptical than Voltaire. He wished to instruct and explain but doubted whether his historical lessons would reform any-one. For Gibbon, although Rome's decline and fall was a story of epic proportions, neither Christianity nor the Germans alone had caused it. The matter was more complex. From Montesquieu, Gibbon learned that climate, geographical factors, the size of the empire, exhaustion of economic re-sources, and human folly also had done their share.

THE LATE ENLIGHTENMENT AND ROMANTIC REACTION

Initial Doubts

As a state of mind applying empirical techniques to life's questions, the Enlightenment was not all-conquering. The success of Methodism and Pi-etism clearly exemplified the liveliness of religious sentiment throughout the century. Books of mysticism and prayer, such as *A Serious Call* in England or *The Conducting Angel in Christian Devotion* in France, were bestsellers for decades. In artistic expression the cultural strengths of reli-gion were obvious. Painting and sculpture were less dependent upon bibli-cal themes than previously, but music was another story. The chorales of Bach, oratorios of Handel, and masses of Mozart merely represent the peaks. Virtually every composer of the century tried to attain the sublime by appealing to the religious sensibilities of listeners.

Reaction to the Enlightenment was not confined to religious re-sponses. Voltaire himself doubted whether in the long run humanity would be beholden to reason, but he kept right on fighting injustice. Hume skepti-cally found so-called pure reasoning to be no less based on custom and habit than was religion. In the mid-1760s the Paris salon of a self-declared Ger-man noble, Paul Thiry, baron d'Holbach (1723–1789), discussed the power of pure matter, aimlessly directed, in controlling the universe and dictating our destinies. In his unpublished writings Diderot privately echoed similar sentiments. Their fatalism notwithstanding, Holbach and Diderot emphasized that the individual must enjoy total moral and political liberty. Each attacked the restrictive institutions of his day, and though falling short of a call for political revolution, Holbach's *System of Nature* (1770) is replete with "what ought to be's." The perception of a new kind of society characterized late Enlightenment thought, and utopian fantasies such as Louis-Sébastien Mercier's *The Year 2440* (1773) were in vogue. Some writers, like the Frenchman Gabriel Bonnot de Mably (1709–1785) or Englishman Richard Price (1723–1791), found inspiration for change in the successful American Revolution. As early as the 1750s, Mably had written, "Choose between revolution and slavery; there is no middle course."

Others, like Jeremy Bentham (1748–1832), rejected the Enlightenment's cherished natural law in favor of an ethic based on untrammeled individualism; the marquis Donatien-Alphonse de Sade (1740–1814) interpreted moral liberty in terms of unbridled personal sexual fulfillment. Still, prior to Jean-Jacques Rousseau's formal challenge to the moral legitimacy of reason, neither skepticism, materialism, nor sadism offered an adequate synthetic alternative to the Enlightenment's passionate attack on traditional value systems and its attempt to reconstruct the universe on the suppositions of the intellect. A few anticipated Rousseau's ideas, questioning whether the faculties of mind provided adequate tools for the exploration of human experience. For example, the heroine in Pierre Marivaux's novel, *The Life of Marianne* (1731–1741), declared, "As far as I am concerned, only feeling can give us reliable information about ourselves, and we must not put too much trust in what our minds twist to their convenience." The French moralist the marquis de Vauvenargues (1715–1747) added, "Reason betrays us more often than nature does." Diderot defended the passions as inspiring a desire for happiness, and Edmund Burke (1729–1797) added that no reasoned balance sheet of pros and cons could ever hope to provide a more sincere guide to human conduct than feelings. Though Rousseau himself never completely rejected reason as a means of tempering the wishes of the heart, for him neither empirical observations of society nor utilitarian approaches to conduct could resolve the truly basic dilemmas of human existence. For Rousseau such dilemmas were moral ones, and only a spontaneous inner voice, uncoerced by either church or state, might resolve them. Therefore natural feelings were infallible guides to moral action.

Rousseau

During the 1760s and 1770s, Jean-Jacques Rousseau (1712–1778) dominated the cult of sensibility. The movement was rooted in France, deeply affected England, and inspired Germany's cultural awakening. It influenced court fashions at Versailles, became the basis for the literature and art of romanticism, and was the source of the century's most complete philosophical synthesis, that of Immanuel Kant (1724–1804).

In 1749 Rousseau first set down his personal challenge to Enlightenment assumptions. His irregular, adventurous life had brought him from an abandoned childhood in Geneva to the bohemian quarters of Paris, where he associated with Diderot and other representatives of the high Enlightenment. Along the way he had composed operas, poetry, and plays, taught music to the children of the wealthy, served as secretary to the French ambassador at Venice, and developed a liking for the amenities of civilization. On a morning in October 1749, he walked from Paris to suburban Vincennes to visit Diderot, who had been imprisoned for "dangerous writings." The journey was long and the day was hot, so Rousseau brought along a magazine to read. In it he noticed an essay contest inviting contributors to respond to the question, "Has the restoration of the arts and sciences contributed to the improvement of mankind's morals?" As Rousseau wrote twenty years later in his autobiography, his mind "was dazzled by a thousand lights," his head swam, and he sank down beneath a tree to regain his composure. "If I had ever been able to write a quarter of what I saw and felt under that tree, how clearly would I have explained all the contradictions of the social system! With what power would I have exposed all the abuses of our institutions, how simply would I have shown that man is good by nature, and that only institutions have made men evil!"

Rousseau composed his essay, won first prize, and broke with polite society. He dressed plainly and soberly, rejecting friends, sinecures, and gifts. To support his mistress and himself, he copied music. Taking up a solitary, wandering life, between 1755 and 1762 he published the four works that made him a household word among literate Europeans and marked him as a singular watershed in the history of modern thought: the *Discourse on the Origin and Foundations of Inequality* (1755), *Julie, or the Nouvelle Héloïse* (1761), *Émile* (1762), and the *Social Contract* (1762). The first three had an immediate effect on his generation; the fourth became a bible for revolutionaries thirty years later. In all four books Rousseau's thematic message was clearly stated: The humanity found in nature is unspoiled, virtuous, and noble. The individual there is not stained by original sin, but sins consciously in creating civil society; for he or she constructs something that is artificial, built on pretense, and prospering through lies. Obviously, humanity cannot simply return to the woods. It is within one's power, however, to remodel the world in a manner conforming to humanity's original psychological state, where feeling and conscience rather than intellect and reason guided all actions. Rousseau removed moral direction from the hands of priest and king. Unlike his encyclopedist contemporaries, however, he refused to delegate it to the care of an intelligentsia. Each individual must be at liberty to construct a moral vision, conforming to what was best within one's self.

In the *Discourse on the Origin and Foundations of Inequality,* Rousseau held that once humanity renounced a casual, wandering, propertyless existence, social interdependence produced social problems unknown in the state of nature. Above all, these problems had to do with property. Rival claims to what is "mine" stifled the sentiment of natural compassion and made individuals "avaricious, ambitious, and evil." Conflict ensued between the first occupier and the strong; blood was shed. Thus for Rousseau, Hobbes's anarchic state of nature is in fact the first stage of human society. It is impermanent, however, because the wealthiest subsequently are able to persuade the poor that it is in the interest of all to recognize the legality of property and establish government to protect it. This sounds like the reasonable Lockean contract, but Rousseau claims to know better. In his ringing style he wrote that the law now "changed a clever usurpation into an irrevocable right, and for the profit of a few ambitious men henceforth subjected the whole human race to work, servitude, and misery."[2]

This no longer was injustice coolly analyzed by Montesquieu or subjected to the satirical wit of Voltaire. This was fire. Although its vision of humanity's current state was pessimistic, the *Discourse on the Origin and Foundations of Inequality* left some hope for redemption in the future. Its form lay in the moral and political rededication of the individual to his or her community. Later, in the *Social Contract,* Rousseau would illustrate what he meant by this rededication. Meanwhile, from 1758 to 1760, he wrote two works leading directly to his great political testament. The first, *Julie, or the Nouvelle Héloïse,* was an epistolary love story that affirmed morality as an innate rather than a calculated principle. It also rediscovered the countryside and underscored the links between the individual's physical and spiritual environment.

Tens of thousands drank in the potion of the *Nouvelle Héloïse* with its elevation of virtue, emotion, and nature. In France alone between 1761 and 1789, it went through seventy editions. Rousseau's second work in this period was *Émile,* essentially a treatise on education. Rousseau agreed with the philosophes that formal schooling ought to be more than fact grubbing and the catechism. For him as for them, education must bring about the moral elevation of the individual and hence the renovation of society. However, in his description of the teacher's function, Rousseau broke with his contemporaries. Rather than a master conditioning the child's social and intellectual environment, Émile's tutor was to permit his charge to grow autonomously, uncorrupted by the forces of conventional society. Free the child, Rousseau urged; let it explore nature and express its imagination. To be sure, Rousseau was referring to *male* children. Little girls were to be

---

[2] *Discourse on the Origin and Foundations of Inequality Among Mankind,* ed. Roger D. Masters (New York, 1964), p. 160.

trained to please men and serve their vanity by remaining docile and learning domestic tasks.

Feminine subjugation notwithstanding, for progressive middle-
and upper-class families, *Émile* stood for a new freedom. Many tried to
adopt its principles. A section in *Émile* which appeared to avow a Spinoza-
like pantheism brought Rousseau grief at the hands of religious authorities,
and he found little sympathy among his old philosophe acquaintances. Personally and ideologically he had broken with them. They had placed reason
on a pedestal; he seemed to be giving all to sentiment. They held that
human nature did not change; he considered it historically mutable. They
spoke for the virtues of urban civilization, social intercourse, technological
improvements, and a world controlled by scientists and philosophers. He
advocated a return to nature, solitude, introspection, and the simple life.
Misunderstanding and personal clashes widened the gulf. Most important,
it was becoming evident that two diametrically opposed views of the world
confronted each other. For Rousseau, however much they denounced the
injustices of the ancien régime, Voltaireans still profited from the system.
They visited and lectured royalty, invested in land and industry, and hoped
for the triumph of a meritocracy heavily influenced by themselves. For his
part, by 1762, Jean-Jacques considered the system unreformable. The sole
option lay in complete moral revolution.

The *Social Contract* represents Rousseau's vision of the new order.
Of all his works it had received the least notice prior to 1789; but in the
revolutionary 1790s, Rousseau's name became indissolubly associated with
his political theory. As the crowning achievement of the school of natural
law, the *Social Contract* forged an original conception of society and politics. Moreover, in it Rousseau amended the pessimism of the *Discourse on the
Origin and Foundations of Inequality*. In the *Social Contract* he wrote, "The
transition from the state of nature to the civil state produces a quite remarkable transformation within man—i.e., it substitutes justice for instinct *as the controlling factor* in his behavior, and confers upon his actions
a moral significance that they have hitherto lacked."[3] As instinct becomes a
social force, the individual's spirit is emancipated and one's conscience is
absorbed into the general will of the community. Because Rousseau saw in
the social-political world of the eighteenth century a congeries of petty,
warring pressure groups, the general will cannot be merely the sum of the
desires of society's members. On the contrary, in Rousseau's new order,
privilege had to be eliminated completely, economic differences reduced,
luxury abandoned, and every member guaranteed equality before the law.

Rousseau coined the apparent paradox that individuals who yield
to the community really give themselves to no one. He hoped that a com-
munitarian spirit would guide the actions of all of society's members, and

---

[3] *The Social Contract,* ed. Willmoore Kendall (Chicago, 1954), pp. 25–26.

he believed that it certainly would do so for the majority. The genuine social contract took the form of a pledge to pursue the general will. The general will is sovereign; governments are not. Once regimes start claiming sovereignty, they become usurpers and tend toward illegal despotism. At this point the people should toss out the rascals and replace them. For Rousseau, governments have no sacrosanct character. They are simply a necessary evil.

The *Social Contract* concerned the reconciliation of authority and liberty. For Rousseau, the general will did not enslave society. On the contrary, individual freedom perishes when one person is subjected to another. In the eighteenth-century world, this was everywhere present; in Rousseau's utopia, this was impossible. There a common law to which people voluntarily consent binds them to a common social life. Rousseau is not gentle to those who refuse to respect the legislation deriving from the general will. Those who find it impossible to accept the deistic assertions and beliefs implicit in the civic religion of the state are to be banished. Those who accept and later reject the civic religion are to be put to death. Moreover, the tactical device of an all-wise lawgiver who divines and then implements the principles of the general will is as troubling as is Rousseau's quest for moral absolutes and perfection in politics.

What led Rousseau to sanctify the general will was his unquestioned faith in the moral sense of the individual. True freedom is legal obedience which the individual voluntarily imposes upon one's self. Because apostates to the civic religion have transgressed the law, Rousseau treats them harshly. Their subversive activity places the entire community in mortal danger, and they must be disposed of. However much twentieth-century regimes have twisted this argument to justify genocide, we cannot blame Rousseau for subsequent totalitarian perversions of his thought. On the contrary, he was the first modern political thinker to underscore the absolute legal and moral equality of all citizens—*male* citizens, to be sure. His most impassioned indignation was reserved for those who would degrade others for reasons of birth, religion, or race.

Preromanticism

Rousseau spent his last years, from 1770 to 1778, in Paris and in a small house on a friend's estate in the countryside. He wrote his *Confessions,* an autobiography seeking to justify his life and vilify false friends, and he had few visitors. By this time, however, the two *Discourses, Émile,* and the *Nouvelle Héloïse* had turned him into a living legend. His influence extended into rivulets running throughout Europe. His works were translated in England, where preromantic sentimentality already had created a sensation in the novels of Samuel Richardson (1689–1761) and where the melancholic sides of emotion found expression in the poetry of Edward Young (1683–1765) and Thomas Gray (1716–1771). In England, too, Methodism's particular spirituality accommodated Rousseau's claims to the heart and reverence for nature. As English writers discovered a vigor and honesty in the deeds of primitive peoples and medieval ancestors, a Highland Scotsman, James Macpherson (1736–1796), took advantage of the cult for the "wild and coarse" by supposedly rediscovering the bardic songs of pre-Roman Britain. Most proved to be forgeries, Macpherson's own creation, but no matter. The "Ossianic Poems" (1765) became the rage, an amalgam of emotion, sensibility, and quest for the mysterious that rejected neoclassical formulas.

Rousseau's vision also was welcomed in Germany. In 1768 the journalist-jurist Justus Möser (1720–1794) published a history of his native principality of Osnabrück in which he illustrated the influence of folk traditions on the customs and government of the community. Although the Osnabrückers did not necessarily represent the historic reality of the social contract in action, Möser's idealization of a vigorous, egalitarian past stood in stark contrast to the existing imitation French courts of aristocratic Germany or the numbing, socially frozen towns. Möser himself remained personally respectable, but certain of his youthful contemporaries who achieved maturity in the 1770s literally went wild with emotion. These were the participants in the *Sturm und Drang* movement—literally "Storm and Stress" rebels—who rejected the powdered wigs of conventional society, wore their hair long, and cried out their suffering in terms more pantheist than Christian. Frustrated by a stratified society and its aristocratically dominated politics, Germans like the young Johann Wolfgang von Goethe (1749–1832) and Johann Christoph Friedrich von Schiller (1759–1805) turned to pure literature, especially the novel and theater. Their tragic heroes deeply feel spontaneous inner needs, but a cold, mannered world frustrates and eventually kills them. To the preromantics, the genuine problems of life were moral, not lending themselves to empirical observation. Alone, an inner voice showed the way to correct judgment; neither state, church, nor philosopher could impose its will on the conscience of the individual.

At the close of the century the East Prussian philosopher Immanuel Kant (1724–1804) grappled with many of the issues unleashed by Rousseau, defined the frontiers of empirical knowledge, and achieved a metaphysical synthesis for human thought and action. Kant established separate realms for pure reason and practical reason, or ethics. Knowledge of the external world had to do with phenomena alone, and the body's organs of perception conveyed no direct knowledge of the essence of a perceived object. Thus the external world is reduced to what is measurable, and the human observer conducts measurements by imposing subjective dimensions of space and time. Although objective reality may lie outside the scope of human intellect, the mind possesses a vast power of intuitive awareness, and duty is a consequence of this awareness. A "categorical imperative" derived from within ourselves spurs us to moral action. For Kant as for Rousseau, only conscience can sanction moral law. The individual is a morally autonomous creature with self-imposed obligations. Functioning within the confines of these restraints is the essence of true freedom.

With its emphasis on the unchanging quality of human nature and the influence of environment, Enlightenment thought was highly cosmopolitan. Voltaire, Helvétius, and the encyclopedists prided themselves on serving no specific nation. Their avowed intention was to liberate all of humanity. In reality, of course, they embodied an emerging consciousness that wished to submit tradition-based value systems to the test of reason and social utility. Furthermore, with Paris as its capital and the salon as its workshop, the Enlightenment had a distinctly French tone. "I have passed half my life wishing to see Paris," wrote Prince Henry of Prussia, brother of Frederick the Great, "and I pass the other half wishing to return." By mid-century, however, European opinion was becoming less flattering. To many it seemed that what Louis XIV had failed to accomplish by force of arms, namely the French conquest of Europe, Voltaireans and encyclopedists were doing with the pen.

In Germany the preromantic reaction to the Enlightenment turned against France. *Sturm und Drang* Germans exaggerated the contrasts between reason and sensibility as though they alone had discovered passion, and they emphasized a new kind of moral liberty—namely the liberty of genius to rise above the natural rights the philosophes ascribed to everyone. Even German extollers of reason and realism, like the dramatist Gotthold Ephraim Lessing (1729–1781), denounced French intellectual hegemony. Lessing pitted the raw genius of his native language against rule-laden French classicism, and German poets and scholars alike glorified the distant medieval past when the national culture seemed both whole and untainted.

Though the most vociferous preromantics were Germans expressing hostility to the French Enlightenment, identifying the new movement as simply an aberrant example of cultural nationalism does it an injustice. The power of preromanticism lay in its ability to restore the nonrational aspects of human nature to intellectual respectability. Nevertheless, with the German philosopher Johann Gottfried Herder (1744–1803), one of the original subscribers to *Sturm und Drang*, preromanticism rejected the cosmopolitan and empirical claims of the Enlightenment in favor of an organic and evolutionary interpretation of cultural development. While appreciating the influence of environment, Herder refused to believe that savages could be civilized through the mere application of will. Human nature, he believed, is not so universal, and the individual is the product of an historic community from which one never can be completely divorced.

For Herder, cultural forces, particularly language, are what determine the individual's relationship to community and to the world. Language is not merely a vehicle for expression, but rather the very repository of a nation's culture, joining together those who share it and keeping out those who do not. In each language, Herder believed, there exists a kind of mystique that conditions the thought and action of a people. He wrote,

"Each nation speaks in the manner it thinks and thinks in the manner it speaks." The *Volk* share a common language, transmitting fable, folklore, and historic memory to future generations. The case for Germany particularly saddened Herder because during the eighteenth century political barriers and social cleavages divided the authentic *Volk*. On the other hand, Herder considered a multinational, multilingual state such as the Hapsburg Empire to be a monstrosity. Herder himself was no racist, nor did he believe in the superiority of one *Volk* over another. In stressing human diversity and placing emphasis on the uniqueness of national traditions and characteristics, however, Herder broke with Enlightenment cosmopolitanism. His exclusion of the Frenchified aristocracy and wandering rabble from the authentic German *Volk* surely supplied future racists with a good supply of poison. Yet Herder possessed enough of Enlightenment goodwill to state that each nation contributed to human brotherhood if only through its distinct gift of culture.

THE ART OF LIVING AND THE LIFE OF ART

Fashion and Function

For land-owning aristocrats and well-off urban bourgeois, the eighteenth century brought improvement in the quality of life, and the philosophes were nearly unanimous in their defense of comfort. In the domestic sphere, a quest for graciousness gave birth to the dining room and to the art of French cooking. Because city life placed a premium on space, rooms were toned down in size, heated properly, and given specific functions. The spectacular marble staircases and open galleries of the baroque age yielded to tasteful and intimate salons intended for the art of polite conversation. Blended woods replaced stone interiors, mirrors and bookcases became standard items of furniture, and cushioned Louis XV chairs supplanted the stylized, comfortless seventeenth-century models. Exotic items such as Chinese cabinetry, Persian carpeting, and Turkish sofas penetrated town houses and country estates alike.

Fashion no longer was the monopoly of royal courts and capitals. It extended to the provincial towns of western and central Europe. On the continent, urban elegance emerged as the new standard; in England the pleasures of country life offered an unparalleled example of rural graciousness. Though the poor knew only necessity, not style, for the upper tiers of the west-European peasantry, comfort definitely had become a consideration in housing. In French, Belgian, and German villages the solid stone and brick cottages of the eighteenth century still stand. They possessed large windows, and at least half the rooms could be heated. Each room had a specific function and contained sturdy, homemade utilitarian furniture and household wares, genuine beds and chairs, tables and tools differentiated for use either in eating or working. It would be too easy to exaggerate. For the majority of Europeans, eighteenth-century housing was substandard. Yet, of the peasant houses standing in 1800, 60 to 70 percent had been built within the previous half century. They were larger and better made than those they had replaced. They became genuine centers of family life, fulfilling an elemental need for shelter and just comfortable enough to serve as places for conversation and work, where the generations might gather and, in the complete sense of the term, live.

Just as functionalism found its way into the humble peasant cottage, it also contributed to the evolution of the eighteenth-century town. The tasks of postwar reconstruction, the creation of princely residences and administrative-judicial centers, and the growth of town populations gave rise to government-sponsored urban planning. A capital created out of swampland, St. Petersburg was Europe's most spectacular example. Peter the Great had dreamed of a Baltic Amsterdam, a place independent of Russia's half-Oriental architectural past. Under Bartolomeo Rastrelli (1700–1771), chief architect for Tsarina Elizabeth, baroque and neoclassicism found receptive homes in St. Petersburg. The tsarina demanded spacious palaces for summer and winter. Rastrelli built the one at Tsarskoye Selo outside the city and the other in the heart of the capital. The Smolny Convent, aristocratic residences, and dozens of other buildings turned the Russian capital into the Enlightenment's architectural gem—by 1800 a living, vibrant city of 200,000.

Imitating Versailles, the princely court cities of Germany witnessed an orgy of construction, while older capitals such as Paris, Nancy, Copenhagen, and Brussels were refurbished with government buildings and roomy squares crowned by equestrian statues of the reigning sovereign. For professional and bureaucratic elites, elegant residential quarters arose. Late eighteenth-century Vienna would have been unrecognizable to a resident of the little polygon that had been besieged by the Turks a century earlier. Lisbon's Commercial Square, reconstructed after the earthquake and fire of 1755 and surrounded by solid ministerial palaces, had nothing in common with the medieval town buried beneath the ashes. Across the Atlantic, Rio de Janeiro was modeled after Lisbon, and the new American capital at Washington would be based on the planning of a French-born designer, Pierre-Charles L'Enfant, himself inspired by the regularities of classicism.

From Baroque to Gothic Revival

Baroque survived in the early eighteenth-century residential and church architecture of Austria, Bohemia, and south Germany, where the style literally exploded in testimony to the revived fortunes of the Hapsburg Empire. The summer palace of Prince Eugene of Savoy, the Belvedere of Vienna, consisted of magnificent pavilions ending in sharp-ridged corner towers crowned with cupolas. Surrounded by stately formal gardens and an artificial lake, the place was a fairyland for triumphal entries, feasts, and receptions. As for religious architecture, the Karlskirche of Vienna, or even more graphically the fortresslike monastery at Melk, seated on a ridge high above the Danube, evoked Hapsburg religious militancy—"Arise, arise ye Christians!"—the battle cry of 1683. Inside Melk, however, was a paradise of music-making cherubs, an orgy of angelic decorativeness. Profuse statuary and gilded busts added to the sensual impact.

Though the Hapsburgs proved that baroque could prosper in the eighteenth century, it was not the Enlightenment's style. English aristocrats felt more comfortable emulating the dignified domestic habits of ancient Roman senators than playing deified baroque heroes, and their architects pored over volumes written by sixteenth-century Italian predecessors who had studied classical ruins firsthand. One of these Italians, Andrea Palladio (1508–1580), became the authoritative word for the architecture both of English country houses and Virginia plantation manors. Facades would resemble Renaissance-inspired antique temple fronts, and a grandiose sense of order became the primary canon of good taste. A new kind of garden, which tried to reflect the beauties of nature rather than represent the architect's mastery over her, surrounded these noble residences.

In this way, solid Palladian grandeur became the English artistic response to baroque ostentation. However, it was not the only one. In France, southern Europe, parts of Germany, and Latin America, baroque itself was refined, lightened, and transformed into an exquisite style known as rococo. Parisian tapestry weavers, cabinetmakers, and bronze workers molded the shapes of shells, scrolls, and leafy branches into dazzling and ornate compositions. Of course, rococo could easily degenerate into spiritless tinsel and flash, and as early as 1750, many continental architects considered it too frivolous a style to inspire building construction. In reaction, they preferred pure line, and their quest led to an interest in undiluted ancient Greek and Roman art, the older the better. Purity was defined as simplicity and sincerity, freed from unreasoned aberration or academic rules. During the 1750s and 1760s, the ruins of Pompeii and Herculaneum were uncovered. Interest extended to the Doric ruins in southern Italy and Sicily, and the German archeologist Johann J. Winckelmann (1717–1768) formulated an aesthetic code based on the ancient Greek masterpieces, which found wide acceptance throughout the remainder of the century.

Until the 1750s, the tastes of aristocratic patrons and purchasers largely dictated the evolution of painting styles. They particularly liked rococo. Owners of manors and town houses wished to decorate their walls with pastoral fairylands where ladies were forever beautiful, lovers always graceful, and life itself a minuet performed by sensuous shepherds and shepherdesses. Aristocratic demand for frivolity eclipsed the sober requests of the great old patron, the Church. Clever technicians profited from the rococo fad, but very few painters were sufficiently talented to turn the make-believe into timeless art. One exception was Antoine Watteau

(1684–1721), who worked mostly for noble patrons in Paris. Watteau's universe was a pastel-colored earthly paradise of idle young dreamers, but it also possessed sufficient melancholia and mystery to make the place appear interesting. With Watteau's successor, François Boucher (1703–1770), mid-century France's most fashionable painter, sex moved into the gardens and parks. Boucher was a boudoir artist, and the jaded Louis XV admired his nudes of teenaged royal mistresses idealized as Aphrodites. The greatest of the rococo painters was J.-H. Fragonard (1732–1806). Fragonard lived in the twilight period of the style, imparting to its innate delicacy vibrancy and even robustness. When it no longer was popular, he adapted his talents to portraiture and landscapes.

Rococo painting outlasted rococo architecture, but by the 1770s Enlightenment intellectuals and social critics concluded that its fanciful-ness could never adequately express their practical concerns. In England the dignified portraiture of Sir Joshua Reynolds (1723–1792) and his school made rococo superfluous; in Italy, under the brushes of the Venetians Canaletto, Francesco Guardi, and Giovanni Tiepolo, baroque monumental-ity never conceded to rococo grace. Increasingly popular as an architectural style, in the second half of the century neoclassicism also found expression in painting. The Frenchman Jacques-Louis David (1748–1825) espoused stoic virtues so convincingly that after 1790 the revolutionary regime adopted neoclassicism as a weapon of visual propaganda. Yet even prior to the French Revolution, David's sober political statements were challenging competing styles. Court painter under Louis XVI, David predicted things to come. Nothing contrasted more vividly with rococo frivolity than David's manifesto, the "Oath of the Horatii" (1785), where the stern, sober lesson of patriotism submerges all other human sentiments, even filial love.

Rather than epitomize Enlightenment, David presaged revolution. Between rococo make-believe and neoclassical heroics stood the middle ground of realism. Quiet scenes of contemporary life or the imparting of moral lessons appealed to philosophes advocating commonsense virtues. The greatest English realist of the century, William Hogarth (1697–1764), was an unashamed moralist best known for his serial engravings that taught the rewards of virtue and consequences of sin. The most important French realist, Jean-Baptiste-Siméon Chardin (1699–1779), was subtler than Hog-arth. An artisan's son who preferred painting to a craftsman's trade, Chardin rejected Watteau's dream world and the historical subjects favored by the French Royal Academy of Painting. First he concentrated on the realism of still life and subsequently scenes of ordinary people engaged in ordinary tasks. Mastering texture, light, and color to evoke emotions through understatement, Chardin can be compared favorably to Vermeer. His "Saying Grace" transposes a humble dinner rite into pure poetry; the "Return from Market" turns a tired young housewife into a timeless em-bodiment of domestic virtue. Chardin's portraits of little boys building card houses or spinning tops represent acts of intense mental concentration.

They conform to the Enlightenment's adulation of intelligence and to its concern for the concrete.

Neoclassicism in architecture and realism in painting evolved as the visual aesthetic standards of the Enlightenment, consistent with the clarity of a Voltairean tale or article from the *Encyclopédie*. But we must not oversimplify. Side by side with Montesquieu, Gibbon, and Lessing there existed an extraordinary popular longing for literary sadism that antedated the unhappy marquis by a full half century. In the visual arts, pornographers had no shortage of aristocratic and bourgeois patrons. An underground book trade with illustrations portraying the abysmal cruelty or sexual depravity of courtiers flourished everywhere in Europe. Still, for most of the eighteenth century, socially sanctioned art followed generally accepted principles. The artist must study nature and classical antiquity. "Style" was a quality handed down through the generations. Rule books like Palladio's were acceptable guides for beauty. In all countries, annual art exhibitions encouraged conformity to academic tastes, whether rococo, neoclassical, or realist. Until the 1790s relatively few artists disputed the accepted bases. Those who did spoke to later generations, not to contemporaries.

Among the challenges to the canon, a few merit specific mention. Around 1770 an English gentleman, Horace Walpole (1717–1797), built a country manor with gothic spires and medieval turrets. His fellow aristocrats, schooled in classicism and convinced that gothic was synonymous with poor taste, considered Walpole an eccentric. Yet a generation later, the gothic revival was in full swing. During the 1780s a younger contemporary of Walpole's, William Blake (1757–1827), began confronting conventional Enlightenment aesthetics with mystical writings and accompanying engravings of nightmare and fantasy. Blake self-consciously set himself against the principles of Great Britain's Royal Academy of Painting. Beside Blake were several landscape painters who rejected arcadian and pastoral scenes in favor of depictions of nature in all its power and violence. Some ceased relying on traditional rules of craftsmanship and insisted that their imagination and inner eye sufficed. A few theoreticians even questioned the old regulations. For example, as early as 1757, Edmund Burke wrote that the sublime, as distinguished from the pretty, might use terror and awe to impart visual pleasure. During the 1770s and 1780s a new spirit, later identified as romantic, was seeping into the realm of aesthetics. At the outbreak of the French Revolution, the artistic assumptions of the past three hundred years were being challenged from all sides.

The Enlightenment's Musical Voice

Curiously enough, just as general agreement on what constituted beauty in the visual arts began to break down, music internationalized. Borrowing from folk and classical traditions and injecting great doses of original genius into their works, three generations of German composers overcame the theoretical struggles that had pitted national schools against one another and established the standard for European musical composition. Technological development was important too. Orchestras were enlarged; the organ, harpsichord, and clavichord were perfected. The oratorio and fugue forms matured. Above all, the century witnessed the triumph of opera. Born in baroque Italy during the early 1600s, opera originally had been conceived as court entertainment to celebrate marriages, baptisms, and military triumphs. By the 1670s, however, public opera houses were built in the larger Italian towns, and Italian troupes carried this secular liturgy to northern capitals. Wherever performances were open to all elements of society, opera houses were arenas where audiences mingled loudly, played cards, drank wine, and made love. The bustle ceased only at the moment when grand arias were sung. Tied down by convention, the Italian-inspired opera was made for singers. Dramatic action and psychological characterization were secondary, and within performances production managers loved to stage diversionary extravaganzas, such as ballets, fireworks, or aquatic spectacles.

What eighteenth-century composers accomplished was to transform opera into genuine musical drama, so that it became the theater of the Enlightenment. In England, John Gay (1685–1732) derived his inspiration from popular traditions and invented the ballad opera satirizing London lowlife. In Italy and France, the simple, melodious, realistic *opera buffa* succeeded baroque's ornate and rigidly structured *opera seria*. When the director of the Hapsburg court opera Christoph Willibald Gluck (1714–1787) proclaimed that the aim of his new piece, *Orfeo ed Euridice* (1762), was to strive for aesthetic truth rather than simply compose set arias, he started a revolution. Gluck blended choral singing and instrumental music into his operas, creating greater unity to both text and music. Most fortunate of all, Gluck was succeeded by the century's most complete musical genius, Mozart.

No previous century was more an age of music. Johann Sebastian Bach (1685–1750) transposed the musical culture of the German people and Lutheran church service into magnificent universal statements; George Frideric Handel (1685–1759) perfected vocal music, particularly the oratorio, and placed his adopted England on the musical map; Franz Josef Haydn (1732–1809) did more than any other of his contemporaries in converting the string quartet and symphony into the forms we know today.

But the most representative musical spokesman for the Enlightenment was Wolfgang Amadeus Mozart. He was born at the height of the movement, in 1756, and he died at its twilight, in 1791. As virtuoso and composer, Mozart was history's archetypal prodigy, his early life a ceaseless round of voyages and concerts. At Christmas 1763, he played before the French court at Versailles. The following Easter, he astounded the English royal family. Before he was eight, he had performed on the harpsichord, violin, and organ before the elector of Bavaria and Empress Maria Theresa.

Between the ages of six and twenty-one, he had written half his repertoire. Mozart's reception by aristocratic Europe ought to have awarded him a life of ease and patronage, of a kind enjoyed by far less gifted artists. Indeed, in 1771, after hearing Mozart's organ performance at the funeral of his predecessor, the new archbishop of Salzburg offered the seventeen-year-old composer-performer the post of concertmaster. Though his patron proved to be a tyrant, Mozart behaved as the dependent artist in an aristocratic world.

However, in 1781, he quit his post, bade farewell to Salzburg, and left for Vienna, where he hoped to live exclusively off his talent. It proved to be a fatal mistake. He matured so rapidly that his work was at least a decade ahead of its time. Audiences accepted it but as often were puzzled by it. Rejecting the aid of would-be benefactors, insisting that genius must be free to survive, and exhausted by his perpetual struggle against poverty, Mozart died prematurely in 1791. He was thirty-five.

The most versatile composer of his century, Mozart also was its most accomplished dramatist. From *The Abduction from the Seraglio* (1782), through *The Marriage of Figaro* (1786), *Don Giovanni* (1787), and *The Magic Flute* (1791), his uncanny ability at penetrating and contrasting character through the most beautiful melodies ever written mark him as a singular phenomenon in the history of creativity. He was no political revolutionary, but the social message in his operas was unquestionably dissatisfaction with the status quo. Moreover, his greatness does not rest exclusively with the operas. We must add his chorales, so melodious that sober clerics were reluctant to admit them into churches, his forty-one symphonies, the concerti for keyboard, strings, and wind instruments, and the string quartets and quintets. Every line that Mozart wrote betrayed a confidence in human transcendence and moral perfectibility, a faith that links him not only to the philosophes but also to Rousseau and Kant. Unlike the Romantics who came after him, Mozart did not employ music to confess the personal longings and torments of the artist. (Two of his most jubilant works, the Jupiter Symphony and Requiem Mass, were written in the shadow of a miserable death.) Rather, Mozart used music to reconcile the spiritual dilemmas of life and death, mystery and reason, laughter and tears. His vision was the Enlightenment's vision, suffused with grace, vigor, passion, and, above all else, with a confidence in humanity's ability to transcend the darkness of its soul. More profoundly than any other of his contemporaries, Mozart expressed the aspirations and affirmations of the age. He was the Enlightenment's last spokesman and its most soaring voice.

9

THE ANCIEN RÉGIME TRIUMPHANT (1715–1763)

GREAT BRITAIN: THE AGE OF WALPOLE AND THE RISE OF PITT

The Eighteenth-Century Constitution

British commercial and aristocratic elites gathered in the harvest of the Glorious Revolution, establishing economic expansion and maintenance of a political status quo as national goals. However, to view eighteenth-century Britain solely in terms of capitalist growth and political management would ignore two important aspects of the country's national life which had emerged during the previous three reigns: the guarantee of civil rights for English subjects and the emergence of a powerful military state fueled by taxes.

In the first instance, by 1714 all Englishwomen and men, not merely privileged groups, were free from arbitrary arrest and imprisonment. Provided that their words did not breach the peace, they were permitted to speak or write what they pleased. An independent judiciary and local self-government were the two benchmarks of public life. While civil freedoms did not exist for Irish Catholics under British rule and while the death penalty for more than two hundred offenses was the chief means of keeping property safe, the government nevertheless was loath to raise the necessary police force to track down potential offenders. Nor did the king possess a network of prying officials that resembled continental intendants. Whatever smacked of direct royal control was suspect.

Still, Britain was a much stronger state in 1714 than had been the case half a century earlier. More than twenty years of warfare against Louis XIV produced an unprecedented militarization of public life, and this would continue on an even vaster scale during the eighteenth century. The British navy would come to dominate the Atlantic and Indian oceans, as well as the Caribbean and Mediterranean seas. British armies would fight on three continents. The Navigation Acts would define the extent of economic warfare in Europe, America, Asia, and even Africa. All of this was made possible through increased taxation, the growth of a national debt, and the emergence of a bureaucracy which organized and maintained the country's fiscal and military commitments. Powerful though it might have been, however, the British state never became absolute over the lives of its subjects. Just as landowners, industrialists, merchants, and financiers accommodated themselves to the economic benefits of an expanding empire, their scrutiny of political issues, insistence on parliamentary consent, and demands for tax accountability would not countenance unconstitutional assertions of state power.

An independent judiciary and lively system of aristocratic self-government comprised one side of public life in eighteenth-century Britain. A world of patronage, management, and graft comprised the other. The king himself had to pay a royal fish-bearer for bringing him a carp caught in the royal pond. A bishop who changed sees was expected to donate sums of money to a regiment of courtiers. Contractors who supplied uniforms and weapons to the military had to pay off government clerks and ministers. The mentality of payment for services rendered was etched deeply into public life. Nor was Parliament immune. In order to obtain desired revenue and laws, the king's ministers needed parliamentary allies. To get themselves elected, MPs needed a pliable electorate. It was at the highest levels of government that the system of patronage and management became a fine art.

The source of revenue and legislation was an unreformed Parliament. Each of England's forty ancient counties sent two representatives to the House of Commons, and the twelve Welsh counties sent one apiece. Fifty additional MPs sat for cities, and the universities sent two more. The remaining 203 sat for boroughs, towns, and villages of widely varying size and population. Except for the exclusion of females, no nationwide standard defined suffrage in the boroughs. In some, voter residence was obligatory; in others, nonresidents outvoted residents. Some borough electorates were in the pocket of a great family. Others were up for sale regularly. Southern and southwestern England were overrepresented; in the newly settled regions in the Midlands and Yorkshire the opposite held true. A borough might contain several thousand voters or, as was the case, a single one. Since political power was essential for attaining social influence, and since control over legislation and state finance determined the nation's future, the English aristocracy worked hard and long to control borough representation in the House of Commons.

Local squires and nobles flattered, browbeat, and bribed voters. For their part, voters were less interested in national issues than in payments granted by candidates for support. Until the 1730s the rivalries for borough seats were keen. Afterward, money told its tale. The wealthiest patrons secured their strongholds and selected friends and relatives for Commons. It was not difficult to win and hold a borough with a small electorate. In 1715, sixty seats were contested in boroughs with fewer than four hundred voters. In 1761, only fifteen were. The system invited collusion between the king's ministers and many members of the House of Commons. At the borough level, a squire or magnate desired jobs and favors for his clients that only the court, chief dispenser of patronage, could supply. In return, the court and ministry needed the laws and funds that the borough MPs could deliver. The parliamentary votes of representatives from the controlled boroughs thus became the fulcrum on which rested the stability of eighteenth-century English political life. Meanwhile, the most important magnates found their way into court and the royal ministry. There they could reassert control over their MPs through the award of offices, sinecures, and pensions. As secretary of the Board of Trade for nearly a quarter century, Thomas Pelham-Holles, duke of Newcastle (1693–1768), dispensed favors with an uncanny eye for detail. He cemented the alliance between the government and borough patrons. Though individual ministers and country magnates might have disagreements, the court-country alliance worked so well that during the eighteenth century no general election ever went against a sitting ministry.

Of course, independent voices remained outside the control of patrons and prevented the House of Commons from becoming a complete agency of the executive or simple avenue to preferment. For example, the ninety-two representatives from the counties of England and Wales, the knights of the shire, took special pride in the exercise of independent political judgment, and county elections were customarily more honest than borough elections. The knights distrusted magnates and political operators, inveighed against borough mongering, and opposed both standing armies and continental entanglements. Because their own friends, relatives, and constituents expected jobs and rewards, these so-called Independents tolerated much of the system and stayed in the Whig and Tory parties. Nevertheless, during most of the eighteenth century they were critics and watchdogs of executive power, thereby assuming a role that in earlier times had been the responsibility of the entire House of Commons.

Executive power was far from negligible. Most of the 220 members of the House of Lords were pliable, and both Commons and Lords were technically the king's high courts. The courts of law interpreted the king's justice, and the court of exchequer collected the king's revenue. Selecting his own advisers and delegating authority to those he trusted, the king alone made political decisions. In point of fact, of course, England was no continental absolutism. The king's advisers had to cooperate with Parliament in order to work within a framework of what was politically possible. If a series of parliamentary defeats over individual bills informed a royal ministry that it no longer commanded a majority in Commons, either the ministry had to steer a new course or else several of its members had to resign. On the other hand, very few MPs made careers of overturning ministries, and even fewer were so bold as to prescribe advisers for the king. Regular, continuous opposition to the ministry still smelled like treason.

When people spoke of the Government, they customarily meant the king and his ministers. Because the old councils of nobles had become too large to function effectively in matters of diplomacy and national security, early in the eighteenth century King George II (1727–1760) and his trusted confidant, the Whig politician Robert Walpole (1676–1745), began leaning heavily upon a small group of eight to ten men. This inner cabinet gained control over much royal patronage and formulated important domestic and foreign policy positions. Its members met informally, often at dinner, and had access to secret papers. In time, cabinet ministers developed the principle of consensus and collective responsibility. If a single member disagreed with his colleagues over an important matter, he had to resign. Once agreement was reached, the cabinet member possessing most influence with the king requested the sovereign's assent, though it was not always easy to obtain. Once royal approval was won, cabinet, courtiers, and allies in the House of Lords started guiding the proposal through Commons, where the regime of patronage and management was put to the test. As long as Walpole commanded the confidence of both king and Commons, he successfully manipulated cabinet government. Policy lines he considered essential became those for Britain. He wished to conciliate the landed gentry, keep taxes at acceptable levels, foster trade and commerce, and avoid costly wars. Speaking for the oligarchs, neither Walpole nor his immediate successors intended to establish a ministerial despotism, but rather contented themselves with manipulating the king's influence in Parliament and the country. They knew that they were answerable to the nation's elected officials.

The Hanoverian Succession and Robert Walpole

When Queen Anne died in 1714, the fifty-four-year-old elector of Hanover became George I of England (1714–1727). Most Whigs accepted this and considered a Protestant succession an act of faith. Newly rich and newly powerful, the Whigs had a healthy respect for Britain's commercial expansion. They wanted a limited monarchy and saw a need to protect the civil liberties obtained in the seventeenth century. On the other hand, the Tories mistrusted the new Hanoverian dynasty. They were attracted to James II's young son in continental exile and drank toasts to "the king across the waters." However, the Stuart Pretender's refusal to abandon Catholicism disqualified him from the throne. The 1715 election brought a large Whig majority into Commons, and an uprising led by a pair of misguided Tory leaders in the name of the Pretender failed miserably. With Toryism thus discredited, in control of Parliament and emerging as defenders of the Glorious Revolution, the Whigs considered the future to lie in their hands.

By 1719, however, storm clouds appeared. As chief guardian of the Utrecht settlement, Britain incurred expensive military commitments, and the Whig leadership was searching for a way to reduce the national debt. A group of merchant investors, consolidated as the South Sea Company, proposed a fantastic scheme. The group offered to pay the debt if government securities would be transferred into South Sea Company shares. Transfixed by the vision of turning a huge debt into an outlet for credit, Parliament approved the idea. When shares in the company were placed on the open market, a speculative frenzy swept across England. By June 1720, shares in the South Sea Company were selling at ten times their face value. Other fly-by-night companies formed to take advantage of the mania. Then the bubble burst. The South Sea Company intended to invest in Latin America, but shareholders began to doubt whether the plan ever would bear fruit. They started selling, first to make a profit, then frantically to salvage what they could. The value of company shares plummeted. Ruined investors called for the heads of culprits. It became apparent that members of the royal household had initiated the selling wave. The Whig leader, the earl of Sunderland, the chancellor of the exchequer, and two royal mistresses were implicated. King George had to reconstruct his ministry. He asked Robert Walpole, a Whig politician unstained by the scandal, to form a government and salvage a situation dangerous enough to threaten the Hanoverian succession itself.

Walpole removed the court from the stench of scandal and returned the country to stable financial moorings. Instead of depending upon unlimited credit, Walpole reduced the national debt through a reserve fund fed with regular infusions of tax revenue. This restored investor confidence. He used patronage and persuasion to construct networks of support in both houses of Parliament. Out to make England safe for country gentlemen like himself, Walpole also helped its tradesmen and manufacturers by abolishing most export duties and instituting tariffs on imports that competed with home production. Walpole's pet scheme, developed in the 1720s and proposed in 1731, was to abolish the land tax, an idea warmly supported by most of his fellow gentry. He hoped to replace it with sales taxes on consumer articles. The idea itself was not new, for France and Prussia depended heavily upon excise revenue. In England itself beer, ale, spirits, and paper had long been taxed. Walpole began by reintroducing the excise on salt and extending it to tobacco and wine. His fellow gentry dreamed of the day when it would attain a privileged fiscal position heretofore enjoyed by continental aristocracies.

Supported by the king and most of Parliament, Walpole underestimated the fury of nonaristocratic resistance. Opposition was most vocal in the press, liberated since 1688. In coffeehouses, voters and the unenfranchised alike gathered to protest the possible ramifications of the excise. To many, such taxes signified a new tyranny, with paid thugs probing private warehouses and shops ostensibly in search of contraband. London's merchants led the opposition. Some spoke of armed resistance. Walpole knew he had crossed the line and withdrew his proposal. For the remainder of his tenure in office he refrained from introducing legislation that threatened to extend government. Preferring to manipulate institutions rather than over-turn them, he lived by his motto: "Let sleeping dogs lie."

Walpole's belief that England could live without a land tax was based on his vision of his country's place in the world. An advocate of conquest through trade and a supporter of the Navigation Acts, Walpole also wished to avoid renewing the military conflicts which had made Britain a major power. Therefore his foreign policy sought to preserve the Peace of Utrecht, and he desired French cooperation toward this goal. For a dozen years after 1713, Austrian-Spanish enmity threatened to plunge Europe into new wars. The Hapsburgs were not reconciled to their failure to secure the Spanish throne, and the Spaniards resented the partition of a once great empire. Concerted efforts by Britain and France kept the peace, but in 1725 Spain settled with the Hapsburgs and turned its wrath on England. In defiance of Spanish navigation laws, the English were smug-gling slaves and goods into Latin America. The Spaniards tried to stop this contraband by attacking British merchant vessels. They also demanded the return of Gibraltar. Hostilities between Britain and Spain erupted in Febru-ary 1727, but the French managed to arrange a cease-fire. In 1731 Spain agreed to settle reparations for damages done to British shipping, while Walpole acted as honest broker over conflicting Austrian-Spanish claims in Italy. As France permitted its fleet to deteriorate, a reassertive England was becoming the main arbiter of peace in Europe.

As long as England and France pursued common goals, Walpole considered matters manageable. He supported naval construction but hoped to avoid committing British troops to a continental adventure. Since George I and II remained electors of their ancestral German principality of Hanover, the possibility of English intervention in Europe was ever present. In 1733 an international dispute over the Polish succession brought Austria, Russia, and Prussia into a conflict with France. The Spanish Bourbons supported their French relatives. Though Walpole kept England aloof, at the conclusion of the Polish succession war in 1735 the friendship of Spain and France held firm. Meanwhile the sources of Anglo-French friction grew more apparent, particularly in Canada and the West Indies. The Bourbon monarchies recog-nized a common need to contain England's growing power in Asia and Amer-ica, and Walpole had to face the prospect of major new wars.

Mid-Century Conflict and William Pitt

The Spaniards reasserted their pressure, attacking and boarding British mer-chant ships suspected of engaging in illegal Latin American trade. Mean-while in England a new generation of Whig politicians surfaced, critical of Walpole's cautious diplomacy and fed up with his stranglehold over domes-tic affairs. Calling themselves Patriots, the aggressive young Whig back-benchers believed that war with France and Spain was inevitable, and Britain could best protect its commercial interests through strikes on the high seas and seizures of its enemies' colonial outposts. William Pitt (1708–1778), whose family had reaped a fortune in India, was the most impassioned parliamentary spokesman for the Patriot cause. Never warm to Walpole, London's merchants and English West Indian planters adopted Pitt as their own. Playwrights and journalists alike mercilessly lampooned the ministry as corrupt and cowardly. In 1738 a British naval captain named Robert Jenkins testified before a House of Commons committee that several years earlier a Spanish boarding party had taken control of his merchant ship, tortured his crew, and lopped off his own right ear. Throughout the 1730s similar incidents had occurred, with Walpole insisting that they were the price of the dangerous game of smuggling, not a cause for war. The Patriots seized the affair of Jenkins's ear as symptomatic of freedom of the seas and the struggle for empire. Cries of "Protect the flag!" overwhelmed Walpole's pleas for moderation. His old safe parliamentary majorities evaporated. Country gentlemen and even old cronies deserted. King George commanded him to have the Spaniards stop searching English ships on the high seas, or else he would support the war party. Put to the test, the great political strategist was unable to keep the peace. In 1739 open warfare flared up between England and Spain.

What was to be a quick and glorious naval-colonial war merged with a bitter struggle on the European continent, and England became embroiled in a series of very costly conflicts. French armies threatened Hanover, and George II had to beg for the electorate's neutrality. Forgetting Walpole's efforts at royal-parliamentary cooperation, the Patriots bristled at the Whig leader's halfhearted prosecution of the sea war. In February 1742 he and his government resigned. England's continental entanglements grew as complex as they had been during the years of William III. Nearly 16,000 troops were sent to defend the Dutch Netherlands from the French; Parliament awarded the Austrian Hapsburgs a subsidy of £500,000; and Hanover's army was in British pay. In 1745 the French defeated a British army at Fontenoy in the Austrian Netherlands, and a rebellion in the name of the Stuart Pretender erupted in Scotland. However, public dissatisfaction did not reach the point of repudiating the Hanoverian dynastic settlement, and the "revolt of the '45" disappeared into the annals of lost hopes and romance. In the end the individual who profited most from the nation's troubles was not Bonnie Prince Charlie, but rather William Pitt.

Pitt complained that the government's miscalculation had been to fight continental and sea wars that lacked clear national purpose. In Pitt's imperial vision, Britain's natural enemies were France and Spain, and the country's unwavering goal ought to be colonial-maritime supremacy. For him British involvement in Europe needed not to provide soldiers in defense of Hanover, but rather should have subsidized useful allies. Reluctantly, George II took Pitt into his government, and between 1746 and 1755 Pitt converted his vision into a national crusade. London's commercial interests and the country's landed gentry alike became convinced that Britain's imperial destiny and commercial power were indissoluble. Most important, they were willing to pay for it. Pitt allowed other politicians to bring off an empty-handed peace in 1748. In 1755 he even left the government; but he knew he would return. That very year fighting broke out between English and French colonists in North America, and shortly thereafter Frederick II of Prussia again plunged Europe into a continental war. On this occasion Britain had a clear idea of its national priorities, and the moment was ripe for Pitt to make good his claim: "I know that I can save the country and that I alone can!" George II asked him to form a government, and Britain accepted Pitt's promise that an age of grandeur lay at hand.

FRANCE: FROM THE REGENCY TO THE SEVEN YEARS' WAR

The Regency

Because Louis XIV had brought the country to the brink of military and financial disaster, the old king's last years were met with scorn. Louis's death in 1715, after a personal reign of fifty-four years, seemed the opportunity for a fresh start. Smallpox had removed all of Louis's adult heirs from the scene, and the new king was a five-year-old child. Those who had been shunted aside in favor of Louis's bureaucratic absolutism drew hope that their voices would be heard once again. They included courtiers resentful at having been reduced to gilded housekeeping at Versailles, *parlementaires* itching to have their rights of protest restored, and important clerics dreaming of the day the French Church would cease to be servile to the government. Other groups, such as regional Estates, financiers, writers, artists, and intellectuals, were aware that an era had passed, and lacking the imposing presence of the Sun King, the facade of conformity and absolutism might well collapse.

Louis had designated his nephew, Philip, duke d'Orléans (1674–1723), to serve as regent during the minority of Louis XV. A council of princes, headed by two illegitimate sons of the old king, was to join Orléans in making executive decisions. However, Orléans refused to take orders from the grave. To solidify his own future and outface the royal bastards, his major rivals for the throne in case of Louis XV's death, Orléans invited the Parlement of Paris and leading courtiers at Versailles to share in his government. Out went Louis's two sons, along with most of his veteran ministers of state.

In came the *Polysynodie,* a system of autonomous advisory councils for the regent, manned by courtiers and including a few parlementary magistrates and former royal secretaries. Unfortunately, Orléans was unable to make the *Polysynodie* function. Cliques formed, personalities clashed, and the courtiers proved incapable of sustained work. The only councils which managed efficiently were those few run by former secretaries. In 1718 four councils were dissolved. Five years later, the *Polysynodie* was abandoned and the old ministerial system restored.

The major problem of government was financial. In 1715 the national debt stood at 3.5 billion livres, and the anticipated tax revenues for the next two years had already been spent. The government could neither meet its interest on loans nor pay officeholders their stipends. Worthless paper money circulated. If holders ever were to demand payment in specie, the government would have had to declare national bankruptcy. The *Polysynodie*'s Council of Finances therefore embarked on a policy of retrenchment, monetary devaluations, and attacks on speculators and Farmers General. Loans were recalled at a fraction of their face value. By 1717 the French debt had fallen by a third, but it still was an astronomical 2 billion livres. The traditional expedients exhausted, the regent sought advice from individuals who considered themselves experts in state finance, particularly the use of credit. In this way he discovered John Law (1671–1729).

Law was a Scottish goldsmith's son who had settled in Paris late in Louis XIV's reign. His suspicious successes as a card shark led to his expulsion from the capital, but in 1715 he returned to Paris and gained access to the regent. He proposed an economic program that was both bold and archaic, combining appeals to individual greed with a systematized monetary and banking system for the country. Unlike the Netherlands and England, France possessed no national bank. Wealth was fragmented and controlled by corporate groups. Law surmised correctly that while the state was poor, the country was rich. The key to reform therefore lay in the stimulation of credit possibilities. A central bank was necessary to control gold reserves and invigorate investment in colonial commerce. Then the public debt itself could be converted into shares in a state-underwritten trading company, and the company in turn might become the sole creditor of the state. Law's schemes carried into fiscal policy too. He desired a single land tax, which would eliminate the need for tax farming, painful excises, and the exemptions enjoyed by individuals, social groups, and geographic regions.

The regent permitted Law to establish a bank. By 1717 it was emitting bills of exchange which the state accepted as payment for taxes. Next, Law established the Company of the Occident with a monopoly over the commerce of Louisiana. Rival financiers protested, but the regime conspired to have the Company of the Occident absorb all other international trading companies in France. Law's organization dominated the state's colonial commerce. In 1719 the regent removed from the Farmers General the right to collect the state's indirect taxes, passing it on to Law. Converting to Catholicism, the Scotsman was named controller-general of finance and minister of state. Thus, within four years the state's responsibility for France's economic life had fallen into the hands of a single individual.

The success of the experiment now depended upon the will of investors. At first matters looked promising, as sellers of landed estates threw their resources into Law's bank and company. Caught up in the spirit of optimism, Law planned canals, roads, and new projects for commerce and industry. However, in late spring 1720, just as English investors were becoming wary of their own South Sea Bubble, the bottom fell out. Investors demanded quick development of the Company of the Occident. Exploiting a virgin colony like Louisiana, however, could not be accomplished overnight. Settlers had to be found, lands peopled, and ports built. Law counseled patience, but nervous shareholders began selling out. Throughout the summer of 1720, investors rioted in the capital. Desperately, Law tried to save his system by pouring everything he owned into the bank and company. The regent abandoned him, and the state stopped honoring his bank notes. Shares in the company became worthless. Stripped of authority, Law fled the country.

John Law's system had reduced the state debt by one-fourth, but at the same time ruined hundreds of investors. Bitter memories remained in France. Throughout the eighteenth century, potential investors mistrusted state credit institutions and shuddered at thoughts of a national bank. They returned to the tradition of placing their funds in land, buildings, and offices, or else they dabbled in shipbuilding and overseas ventures. While wars and economic expansion contributed to inflationary spirals and mounting government deficits, the state's income failed to rise proportionately. Nonetheless, there were a few positive signs. The government enacted Law's plans for road construction and canal building. By 1789, France had Europe's best network of internal communications. Restored, the older commercial companies breathed new life. While many were left with worthless shares in the Company of the Occident, those who had bought and sold early enough found themselves rich, and the top layers of society received doses of new wealth and new blood.

Cardinal Fleury and the Emergence of Louis XV

Though the failure of the *Polysynodie* and John Law's system did not destroy the regency, its adventurous spirit rapidly dissipated. Worn out by physical excess, Philip of Orléans died in 1723, leaving France poorly governed and half bankrupt. Louis XV still was a minor, and the country desperately needed a no-nonsense regime that would live according to its means and acknowledge the state's financial obligations. In 1726, Cardinal Hercule de Fleury (1653–1743), the king's former tutor and at seventy-two the most powerful voice in the Royal Council, assumed control over the government. Like Walpole, Fleury wished to avoid adventure abroad and maintain social peace at home. Selecting political associates with views as conservative as his own, Fleury restored collection of the indirect taxes to the Farmers General, and the currency was stabilized according to the gold standard. No revolutionary schemes were tried for increasing government income—just tight controls over private loans, royal lotteries, and the clergy's "gift." In the tradition of France's great minister-churchmen, Fleury was ruthless toward his enemies. He had Jansenist priests silenced, exiled unfriendly members of the Paris Parlement, and closed the Club d'Entresol, meeting place of "advanced" political thinkers who were overly critical of the regime.

Unlike Walpole, Fleury had no parliament to cajole and no electorate to pacify. As long as he enjoyed the young king's confidence he was secure. He had luck too: agreement with England to keep local conflicts from erupting into generalized warfare, a series of good harvests until 1738, and prospering coal and textile industries directed by the state. Budgets were balanced, Paris glittered, provincial towns like Rennes, Lyon, Bordeaux, and Dijon witnessed construction booms. Trading in West African slaves and West Indian sugar, France extended its colonial power. Its Atlantic ports thrived. Under skillful governors, important advances were made in India.

By 1740, however, Fleury was eighty-seven. Louis XV was thirty. The recent death of the Hapsburg emperor Charles VI provoked an international crisis, worsened by the deepening naval war between England and Spain. Several years earlier, France had played a halfhearted role in the War of the Polish Succession, and now young bellicose courtiers around Louis XV urged the king to be rid of his aged preceptor lest the country suffer a new diplomatic or military defeat. Like his great-grandfather, Louis XV had strong personal loyalties, and Fleury survived in office until his death in 1743. By this time genuine power had fallen to hawks at the French court, led by the count de Belle-Isle. Belle-Isle dragged the country into an anti-Austrian coalition with Prussia, Spain, Sardinia–Savoy, and Bavaria. French troops were committed to fighting in Germany, while in America and Asia, French and British forces confronted one another. Therefore, following more than twenty years of relative success, the post-Utrecht settlement, built on Anglo-French cooperation, cracked. Appeals to national honor overwhelmed the work of both Fleury and his friend Robert Walpole.

When Fleury died in 1743, Louis XV (1715–1774) at last wished to direct the government in fact as well as in name. Lacking his great-grandfather's ability to neutralize factions and dominate advisers, Louis quickly fell victim to ambitious counselors. He submitted to courtiers, ministers, and royal mistresses alike and followed conflicting lines of policy at the same time. Consequently, the king was mistrusted and his government became weak. French diplomacy reacted confusedly to initiatives taken by other states. The corporate elements in French society, particularly the clergy and parlements, reasserted themselves. Declining military leadership, new financial difficulties, revived regionalism, and a near civil war inside the French Church produced many unforeseen problems. Because of weakness at the top, nearly all of them remained unresolved. Lazy and vain, thoroughly spoiled since infancy, Louis XV sought shelter from political responsibility in childish pleasures and sexual adventures.

Inherently timid, on occasion he might conjure up a majestic attitude. But Louis truly disliked being king and would have been happier as an intriguing, cynical courtier. Unfortunately, neither Louis nor France possessed the option.

During the War of the Austrian Succession (1740–1748), France's ally Frederick II of Prussia, who started the conflict by seizing the Hapsburg province of Silesia, held on to his acquisition and converted his small scattered kingdom into a contending power. Although French armies held their own in the European theater, at the peace conference of Aix-la-Chapelle, French diplomats gained nothing. In 1748 some of Louis XV's advisers recommended reviving the English alliance. Across the Channel, however, Pitt and the Patriots constantly stirred up anti-French public opinion, for they knew there was an empire to win.

France at Mid-Century

At the conclusion of the Austrian Succession war, France's main problems were internal. Because the indifferent king would appoint no prime minister, strong-minded department chiefs tried to fill the vacuum. The war had produced a new fiscal deficit, and Jean-Baptiste Machault d'Arnouville (1701–1794), controller-general of finances between 1745 and 1754, attacked the problem in a spirit of reform. As Machault correctly saw it, the difficulty lay in distribution of the tax burden. Residents of certain towns, all aristocrats, all clerics, and many officeholders were exempt from paying the main source of state revenue, the *taille*. The *taille* was inefficiently collected, and the burden for paying it fell on the countryside peasants, particularly those living in the regions of France known as the *pays d'élection*. Farmers General were adept at raking in indirect taxes on salt, customs receipts, and articles of consumption. But as private collectors, the tax farmers, not the state, derived major profit from receipts.

Machault understood that only a major tax reform, converting heretofore exempt groups into contributors and loosening the stranglehold of the tax farmers, could cope with the fiscal problem. He also wanted the Church and regions where provincial Estates still met to increase payments to the state. In May 1749 the controller-general of finances therefore proposed to the king the *vingtième,* a 5 percent tax on revenues acquired from real estate and office ownership. The controller-general insisted that no region and no social group should be exempt from payment. Once Louis XV approved the plan, a storm of protest erupted among privileged groups. The Parlement of Paris declared its unqualified opposition; the Estates of Artois, Brittany, and Languedoc rejected the new tax out of hand, and so did the leadership in the French clergy. The royal court was divided. The influential royal mistress, Madame de Pompadour, supported Machault, as did most of the philosophes. On the other hand, Louis XV's family, led by his daughters, stood behind the clergy and Estates.

The king wavered and then sank under pressures. In December 1751 he declared ecclesiastical properties exempt from the *vingtième,* and eventually the provincial Estates escaped too. Thus the teeth were removed from Machault's scheme. Temporary *vingtièmes* were subsequently levied in wartime—once in 1756 and again in 1760. However, these were momentary expedients and amounted to tinkering. For the remainder of the ancien régime no all-out confrontation of time-honored privileges would be made in the name of fiscal justice, and the Crown's timidity ensured the government's poverty.

The failure of the *vingtième* exemplified the regime's lack of nerve. So did a crisis over the Parlement of Paris. As magistrates of the leading law court in the realm, eighteenth-century *parlementaires* conceived of restoring the principle, popular in the Fronde, that they should participate in legislative and executive decision making. Provincial parlements customarily supported this position, although they were wary of making the Parisians overly powerful. During the 1750s, a constitutional issue in religious disguise set parlements against the royal government. In 1713, Louis XIV had persuaded the pope to issue the Bull Unigenitus, condemning Jansenism as a heresy; however, the declaration failed to clear France of individuals attracted to Jansenist theology. Moreover, large numbers of the lower clergy—hostile to the wealth, moral laxity, and religious indifference of their superiors—found Jansenism attractive and called for wider participation in church affairs. They added that the Bull Unigenitus compromised the independence of the Church of France and strengthened the hand of untrustworthy Jesuits.

Eighteenth-century Jansenism split the French Church. Anti-Jansenist bishops hounded suspected Jansenist priests and ordered the clergy to refuse last rites to communicants harboring Jansenist ideas. Meanwhile, the religious conflict politicized when the Parlement of Paris took the side of the Jansenists and, in April 1753, merged support for the heretics with a claim as repository and defender of the kingdom's fundamental laws. By means of a "Grand Remonstrance," the jurists declared that in pursuit of its constitutional duty, the Parlement of Paris might legitimately countenance resistance to the Crown. Angrily, Louis XV exiled the parlementary leadership from Paris. In retaliation, judges throughout France went on strike. The nation's courts were paralyzed, and the mood of the country suggested a new Fronde in the making. As popular opinion supported the Parlement of Paris and Jansenism, the government backed down. Exiled *parlementaires* returned to Paris, and the Crown agreed to stop the Jansenist witch hunt. Dismayed, Louis XV wrote that the *parlementaires* would not be satisfied until they "led me by the nose. . . . They will wind up wrecking the state." He had a point. Composed of selfish, proud, and venal aristocrats, France's parlements had little interest in deep-seated reform. Nevertheless, their rhetoric had become quite radical, invoking the word *nation* to represent an interest higher than any jurisdiction or institution. Unwittingly perhaps, the parlements sowed the seeds of resistance to royal authority and desacralized the absolutist pretensions of the Crown.

By the mid-1750s the elements of a potentially explosive situation were present in France. The country was divided religiously, the government's fiscal problems were unresolved, the regime itself had exposed the social injustice of the tax system, and the parlements were questioning the absolute nature of the monarchy. An indecisive king headed a weak, drifting government, and in "enlightened" circles a contrary public opinion was forming. Soon military defeat would add to France's woes.

THE HAPSBURG EMPIRE AND PRUSSIAN KINGDOM

Charles VI and the Pragmatic Sanction

By 1713 the House of Hapsburg was reestablished as a great power. It had scored victories over Louis XIV on its western front and defeated the Turks decisively in the Balkans. With 24 million subjects, the empire of Charles VI (1711–1740) comprised four basic segments: the hereditary Hapsburg German lands of the center; Bohemia with its dependencies of Moravia and Silesia; Hungary with its outlying regions of Slovenia, Croatia, and Transylvania; and the exterior dependencies ranging from Belgium in the northwest to Milan, Naples, and Sardinia in Italy. The Belgian and Italian lands represented compensation for the loss of the Spanish inheritance. The Treaties of Karlowitz (1699) and Passarowitz (1718) stabilized the southeastern frontier at the expense of the Turks.

Economically, the far-flung empire was underdeveloped, although it possessed vast potential for commerce and industry. In the style of high baroque the imperial capital of Vienna was emerging from the backwater to present an imposing facade of strength and power, and the court of Charles VI was a focal point for a cosmopolitan aristocratic culture that outdistanced even Versailles in many respects. Revenues collected from distant estates were used to build lavish residences inside or near Vienna, which housed German, Slavic, Hungarian, and Italian magnates called to serve in the individual imperial chancelleries. This drawing of talent and wealth to the Hapsburgs' capital suggested that the time was ripe for the emperor to take the next step and merge the semiautonomous governmental departments. However, by personality and inclination Charles VI was no organizer. He obstinately refused to establish a bureaucracy.

The tastes of the emperor were aristocratic, and he took for granted the feudal, ethnic, and constitutional divisions of his lands and people. For Charles, central government meant the existence of separate departments for the various regions, each agency responsible for maintaining the district concerned and independent of any other. Though departments might work at cross-purposes, Charles made no effort to create institutions common to all the regions. Nor did he invigorate the few that already existed. He left the Estates and diets intact. Worse, he neglected the army laboriously built over the past half century, permitting it to sink to a force of 80,000 ill-trained, ill-equipped troops. Charles's quest for new revenues was unaggressive, and a disproportionate amount of state income went into maintaining his court. As a result of the emperor's passivity, France and England emerged as the dominant diplomatic players in early eighteenth-century Europe, and the Hapsburgs were confined to the sidelines. This was most evident in the 1730s. A halfhearted attempt by Charles to establish a state-financed trading company working out of Belgian ports came to nothing, the dynastic aggressiveness of the queen of Spain, Elizabeth Farnese, ended Hapsburg preponderance in southern Italy, and even the recent great triumphs over the Turks seemed in jeopardy. During a Hapsburg-Ottoman war from 1735 to 1739, the Austrian army was trapped in Belgrade. To win its release, Charles had to relinquish what he had gained at the Treaty of Passarowitz twenty years earlier.

The paradox of Charles VI's reign was that the weakened condition of his empire was directly attributable to his obsession with maintaining its integrity. He sought agreements from his family, from the imperial Estates, and from the powers of Europe that would guarantee the Hapsburg succession to his direct heirs. The roots of the emperor's obsession went back to 1703, when his father, Leopold I, had designated a line of succession in case neither Charles nor his elder brother Joseph sired male children. Leopold designated the daughters of Joseph as having imperial priority over whatever daughters Charles might sire. Ruling from 1706 until his death in 1711, Joseph had two daughters and no sons. Appropriate to the line of succession, Charles replaced his brother as emperor. At the time he was childless but determined to have a say in his own succession. This meant, of course, disregarding his late father's will. In the Austrian and Bohemian lands of the empire it was taken for granted that a reigning monarch could name his successor, previous wills notwithstanding. On the other hand, the Hungarian Diet claimed the right to select its sovereign should the male Hapsburg line die out. To guarantee his own line and avert a possible civil war over the succession, in April 1713 Charles replaced the Leopoldine declaration with his famous Pragmatic Sanction. The lands of the Hapsburg Empire were declared indivisible. Should Charles sire only daughters, the eldest one would succeed as legitimately as a male to all possessions. Only failure to produce an heir would be sufficient reason for the Hapsburg heritage to pass on to others.

In 1717 a son recently born to Charles died in infancy. Shortly thereafter two daughters were born, and there were no further offspring. The emperor passed the remainder of his life seeking assurance of his daughters' heritage. No female had ever headed the house of Hapsburg. To many, its possibility now was a sign of divine displeasure and an invitation to political disaster. Therefore, Charles went after written guarantees. Since the Pragmatic Sanction was, in the first place, a family compact, the emperor had to secure the assent of Joseph I's two daughters and their husbands. One husband was king of Bavaria and the second was king of Saxony. Both would benefit from their wives' claims, and both coveted the title of Holy Roman Emperor. Nevertheless, Charles won family agreement not to challenge his selection of heir. Next, Charles got the regional Estates to accept the Pragmatic Sanction as a law of his empire. Before accepting, the Hungarians extracted concessions. Charles agreed to convoke their Diet regularly, to rule Hungary according to that kingdom's own laws, and to permit the Hungarian Diet to apportion its own war contributions. By 1725 the Pragmatic Sanction had become part of the Hapsburg imperial constitution.

In persuading the European powers to recognize the document, the price greatly outweighed the result. For the assent of Saxony and Russia, Charles had to enter two costly and fruitless wars, the first over the Polish succession (1733–1738) and the second against the Turks (1735–1739). To obtain the agreement of England and the Dutch, Charles sacrificed the overseas commercial company he had projected in Belgium. For France to sign, Charles had to persuade his son-in-law to surrender the duchy of Lorraine and accept, as compensation, the Italian province of Tuscany. Nevertheless, on the eve of his sudden death in October 1740, Charles VI considered his diplomacy a success. His eldest daughter, Maria Theresa, a young woman of twenty-three, succeeded to all her father's lands and titles.

Maria Theresa (1740–1780) and the Defense of the Empire

The peaceful accession of the princess proved illusory. The collapse of the Hapsburg army in the recent Turkish war graphically illustrated Charles VI's neglect of military responsibilities in exchange for what Prince Eugene of Savoy called worthless scraps of paper. Moreover, the state's treasury was empty, the government was demoralized, and Austria's European rivals were eager to find reasons for repudiating the Pragmatic Sanction. In France, Belle-Isle's war party was pressuring Louis XV to lead an anti-Hapsburg coalition; the king of Bavaria, Maria Theresa's cousin, was collecting votes to support his claims to head the Holy Roman Empire; the Spanish Bourbons prepared to clear the Hapsburgs entirely out of Italy; and the king of Prussia demanded the cession of Austrian Silesia.

Before all the pressures the young empress displayed remarkable firmness. However, a few short weeks after her accession the blows rained down. In December 1740, Frederick II of Prussia, himself on the throne but a few months, invaded Austrian Silesia and quickly occupied its capital, Breslau. The king of Saxony repudiated his wife's assent to the Pragmatic Sanction. Both France and Bavaria signed an offensive alliance against Austria. Soon Spain and Saxony joined. With the French war party directing the show, the allies agreed to partition among themselves all the Hapsburg possessions, except Austria proper and Hungary. Late in July 1741 the French and Bavarians marched off to war. The Bohemian cities of Prague and Linz fell to the invaders. The Bavarian king, Charles-Albert, cowed the Bohemian Estates into deposing Maria Theresa and declaring him sovereign. In February 1742 the majority of Germany's electoral princes chose Charles-Albert as Holy Roman Emperor. Spanish troops attacked Hapsburg possessions in northern Italy. Belgium was threatened. Observers believed that if she could salvage as much as Spain had saved in 1713, Maria Theresa would be fortunate.

The major ally of the empress was England, both distant and untrustworthy. Fearful of losing Hanover, George II now threw his support to Charles-Albert as Holy Roman Emperor. Meanwhile, Maria Theresa tried desperately to raise an army. Summoning the Hungarian Diet, she made a dramatic personal appeal to the Magyars. Raising her infant son Joseph high above her head, she cried that her throne and the child's rightful heritage lay in Hungarian hands. The dignity, honesty, and beauty of the empress proved irresistible. The Magyars vowed to defend her with their life and blood. Far fewer than the 100,000 Hungarian troops promised Maria Theresa ever arrived, but those who came fought well. Moreover, the gesture of solidarity on the part of the Hungarian Diet raised the prestige of the empress in her beleaguered domains and on the international scene. The Austrian crown Estates sent troops. Public opinion in England rallied to her favor and English subsidies paid for her campaigns. The War of the Austrian Succession went through several stages before the conclusion of peace in 1748. Reluctantly, Maria Theresa had to concede Silesia to the Prussians, though this was all she lost. Her lands were cleared of invaders, and her empire was saved. After the death of Charles-Albert of Bavaria in 1745, her own husband Francis was elected Holy Roman Emperor.

The near collapse of the Hapsburg Empire was a lesson not lost on Maria Theresa, and the postwar period was the crucial watershed of her long reign. She needed to break with the complacency of her father's time, reduce regional separatism, and translate mere affection for the dynasty into unified state policies. Therefore, she began building a national army and centralized bureaucracy, both of which were essential if she were to regain Silesia. A national military academy was founded, regular camps and maneuvers established, and officer training systematized. In place of the voluntary contributions sent to Vienna by Estates of the empire, which paid for but a fraction of the 100,000 troops needed to defend the borders, the government proposed a military maintenance tax on all property owners. Although the regional Estates were permitted to make the property assessments on their own, the central government was to be guaranteed ten years of stipulated income. Property owners growled. Those in Hungary purchased exemptions. However, other regions of the empire submitted; funds were assured the army, a force of 175,000 was built, and a beginning made in welding together the empress's disparate heritage.

The need for trustworthy allies was as essential as military preparedness. Back in 1740, Britain had been the Hapsburgs' sole friend against a hostile Europe. However, Maria Theresa's advisers correctly surmised that, Hanover notwithstanding, in the long run the island kingdom would be concerned primarily with trade and colonies, not with Austrian interests in central Europe. At the Treaty of Aix-la-Chapelle in 1748, the British advised Maria Theresa to accept the loss of Silesia. Hapsburg diplomats noted that Austria was useful to Britain only as a means of keeping France bogged down in a continental war. Therefore, after 1748, Austria sought to replace the pact with Britain with a new bloc of alliances. For her part, Maria Theresa remained committed to the restoration of Silesia and destruction of Prussia.

The Diplomatic Revolution

A brilliant, egotistical, and eccentric statesman, Count Wenzel von Kaunitz-Rietberg (1711–1794), was entrusted with the empress's hopes. A product of the Enlightenment, Kaunitz envisioned diplomacy as an exact science controlled by adept manipulators such as himself. After 1748 his scheme was to coordinate Russian policy with Austria's, wean away France from its alliance with Prussia, and use the power of the three continental states to destroy Frederick II. Because France had been a traditional enemy of the Hapsburgs for three hundred years, this strategy represented not merely a shift in diplomacy but a revolution in thinking. Nevertheless, it appealed to Maria Theresa. As ambassador to Versailles since 1750, Kaunitz labored at winning trust at the French court, but made little headway. In 1753 he returned to Vienna to head the Hapsburg foreign office. During the next two years Kaunitz's diplomatic efforts remained frozen. Worsening British-French relations suggested that Europe's next war would not be in Europe but rather overseas.

Still, the old continent contained plenty of flashpoints of worry and mistrust. For several years an important ingredient in France's diplomacy had been to bar Russia's westward expansion. Meanwhile, Britain's chief concern had been over possible Prussian aggression with respect to Hanover. Eager to counterbalance France and win protection for Hanover, in 1755 Britain offered to subsidize much of the Russian army. For his part, the Prussian king himself was consumed with fears. Aware of Maria Theresa's unrelenting plans for revenge and the hatred of the Russian tsarina Elizabeth toward him, Frederick II envisioned Austrian and Russian armies overrunning Prussia and then swallowing it completely. Therefore, he looked for friends.

Frederick went to great lengths to convince the British that he had no hostile intentions regarding Hanover and even offered to defend the electorate against possible French attack. The British listened. Austria displayed no intention of defending its Belgian territories from possible French occupation, and for London's business interests the Low Countries might well become a French dagger aimed at English hearts. Therefore, to protect Hanover, forewarn France, and keep Germany neutral, Britain proposed to Prussia the Convention of Westminster (January 1756), a vague promise of mutual goodwill. In America and India an undeclared Anglo-French war was erupting. Frederick promised to do what he could to keep the conflict from inflaming Germany.

Moderate though it was, the Anglo-Prussian convention upset Europe's delicate equilibrium and played into the hands of Kaunitz. The Hapsburg foreign minister redoubled efforts at courting France, dangling vague promises of Belgium and the Polish throne before Louis XV and Louis's family. As soon as news of the Convention of Westminster reached Versailles, the French king showed uncharacteristic rage. By signing an accord with England, Frederick II was displaying contempt for his old ally, France, and at the same time seemed to be ordering Louis XV to stay out of Germany. His pride assailed, Louis denounced the Prussian king. Kaunitz considered the moment appropriate to balance the Convention of Westminster with an Austrian-French defensive alliance. France accepted it unhesitatingly. Ratified in May 1756, the First Treaty of Versailles guaranteed mutual assistance of 24,000 troops or a money equivalent should one of the signatory parties—France or Austria—be attacked by a third power. Specifically excluding the Anglo-French war already raging, on the surface the treaty was innocuous. It did not necessarily commit French intervention in Germany, much less assistance in the destruction of Prussia. In the succeeding months France declined Hapsburg invitations to take military action. Still, the First Treaty of Versailles marked a turning point in the history of European diplomacy.

In this manner the celebrated "diplomatic revolution" of the eighteenth century took effect. Two traditional enemies, France and Austria, now were allies. Hapsburg policy was the centerpiece: the recovery of Silesia and end to Prussia. France's goals were less clear. Allied to the Austrians, the French now could make no claims to Belgium; a costly diversion in Germany would serve no national purpose; and France already had its hands full in a murderous colonial war with the English. All that Kaunitz now needed were for the Russian piece to fall into place and for Frederick to act accordingly. He did not have to wait long. Furious, the Russian court considered itself betrayed by British duplicity and withdrew its offer to protect Hanover. Even without British subsidies, it intended to fight the Prussians.

Then there was Frederick. The Prussian king possessed an uncanny ability for personalizing enmities with his fellow sovereigns so that, irrespective of geopolitical objectives, their raw emotions would drag their states into conflict. Maria Theresa and Elizabeth of Russia loathed Frederick. Now Louis XV did too. Russia and Austria affirmed their solidarity and threatened mobilization the following spring. The horrified Prussian king envisioned the dismemberment of his country. He had lost his only continental ally, France. In its place was Britain, tied by the loosest of alliances. Since striking first had worked back in 1740, Frederick gambled again. He saw Saxony as the most likely jumping-off point for an allied invasion. It also was a convenient route into Hapsburg Bohemia. Hoping to knock out Austria before any coalition against him jelled, in August 1756 Frederick ordered the Prussian army into Saxony. His son married to a Saxon princess, Louis XV stood firmly with Maria Theresa. Refusing to be intimidated, the Hapsburg empress rejected all of Frederick's demands for an armistice. She told her generals to fight. The empress, Tsarina Elizabeth, and Louis XV converted the First Treaty of Versailles into an offensive alliance, and the most prolonged and destructive conflict eighteenth-century Europe had yet experienced, the Seven Years' War, was underway.

Frederick William I (1713–1740) and the Emergence of Prussia

How could Prussia, considered no more than the underpopulated and scattered domains of the Hohenzollern family, unleash two of the eighteenth century's most titanic wars? In 1713 Frederick William I had become king of East Prussia, but the proliferation of titles he held elsewhere in his domains suggested that regional political bodies might yet establish limits on his governing authority. This was more apparent than real. Frederick William was less subservient to provincial Estates than were his neighboring sovereigns in Poland, Saxony, or the Hapsburg Empire. His grandfather, the Great Elector, had stifled the political independence of his dominions, leaving successors free to levy consumer taxes and war subsidies. Moreover, the Great Elector had superimposed a loyal bureaucracy on the old officialdom, and a devoted army supported his authority. Military strength, bureaucratic efficiency, and tight control over economic resources turned the Hohenzollern domains into an administratively sound absolutism. Aristocrats and ambitious commoners alike banked their futures on serving the sovereign; the clergy, merchants, and peasants had no other choice.

Frederick William I deserves personal credit for fulfilling the work of his grandfather. A field commander in the War of the Spanish Succession, he was a "Sergeant King," accustomed to giving orders and being obeyed. He expressed himself coarsely and opted for simple manners and plain tastes. A Pietist Lutheran influenced by Calvin's teachings, he hoped to serve his God by performing human duties as faithfully as possible. He expected as much from his subjects. Frederick William reveled in his role of harsh taskmaster. The king might be seen in the streets of Berlin, swooping down on loiterers, beggars, and prostitutes alike, striking them with his cane and urging them to take up honorable tasks. "Salvation is God's business," Frederick William exclaimed, "but all else is mine."

The king was aware that sophisticated contemporaries sniggered at his boorish personality. Mistrusting those around him, he preferred to work at daily business alone in his study. In his youth Frederick William had seen Prussia tied to a pair of great European conflicts. It belonged to the coalition against Louis XIV, and had joined Russia against Charles XII. Prussian troops fought well, but their continued use nearly always depended upon foreign subsidies. Convinced that the state's own resources must be capable of supporting its defense, Frederick William constructed his regime on twin pillars of military strength and economic self-sufficiency.

Building the army was a labor of love. Frederick William was one of Europe's first rulers to wear a uniform regularly, and he was most at ease carousing with career officers over beer and tobacco. The army of 40,000 that he had inherited in 1713 contained too many foreign mercenaries for his liking. Private contractors raised and paid troops, and local district responsibility for levying soldiers had fallen into disuse. Frederick William went to work on military reform. Prussian nobles were prohibited from serving in foreign armies, a cadet school was opened in Berlin, and the relationship between the Junker landowners and officer corps became a seamless web in the social fabric of the state. In 1733 the military recruitment system was reorganized. Most of the domains were divided into districts of approximately 5,000 households. Every district was responsible for replenishing regiments stationed within or near it. Once sufficiently trained, peasant or artisan recruits were released to perform their civilian tasks. They were, in effect, soldiers on leave. In the fields or at their workbench they wore a uniform ribbon, a constant reminder of their essential duties. During the fall and spring they returned to their military units for six weeks of drill.

By no means was this a system of universal military service. Burghers, university graduates, and workers in high-priority industries had exemptions. Even a few geographical regions escaped the cantonal recruitment system. The lowest ranks of society filled the regiments, and the highest ranks led them. As a group, the Prussian aristocracy was relatively poor. For younger sons unable to survive on the land, service in the armies of foreign princes had long provided an occupational outlet. When Frederick William I closed off this channel, established his cadet school, and constructed a military state, it became obvious to Junkers that service in the king's army had become enshrined both as a social obligation and mark of rank. The Prussian officer corps developed its distinctive characteristics as the country's elite corporation, rooted in social privilege and fulfilling the political aims of the monarchy. Prussia's industrial development also was aligned to the country's military growth. Powder factories and ironworks arose to supply the army, and the textile industry clothed it. Five-sevenths of the government's revenues were channeled back into the military machine. By 1740, over 80,000 well-trained troops were afoot. A state that ranked thirteenth in Europe's population contained the continent's fourth-largest standing army. This military force no longer depended upon foreign subsidies. It was self-sustaining.

Displaying scorn for those he called "ink splashers," Frederick William nonetheless understood that only a well-oiled government machine tended by an efficient bureaucracy could harness the resources needed to maintain his beloved army. The king was interested in financial and administrative reform, sought to increase agricultural and industrial production, and stimulated both immigration and internal colonization. The Hohenzollerns were Prussia's greatest landowners by far, working one-third of the peasantry. As soon as he became king, Frederick William declared all royal property to be inalienable and indivisible. Instead of leasing these lands to Junkers on a long-term basis, as had been the case previously, Frederick William opted for short-term contracts at high rents, or else he hired bailiffs to exploit the crown estates directly. As a consequence of the changes in land tenure practices, income increased. So did tax revenues. The burden of the country tax, the so-called contribution, fell exclusively on the peasantry. It averaged nearly 40 percent of the peasant's net yield of his small personal plot. A second tax, the excise, fell on townspeople. It was imposed on their food, drink, and goods. In 1713 only three of Frederick William's provinces were subjected to the excise. He subsequently extended it to all the regions. During the king's reign, government revenues doubled, and they were sufficient to pay for the army.

Reduced expenses accompanied the increased income. By abolishing his father's lavish court, Frederick William set a personal example, and he insisted that town commissioners collect the excise with a minimum of graft and expense. Believing that centralized and controlled administrative practices could best pull revenues into government, the king established a single all-encompassing board of control for the kingdom, the General Directory. Meanwhile, different town and country administrations were fused with regional departments, one for each of the kingdom's seventeen provinces. Everywhere civil servants were subjected to group discipline and collective responsibility. Individual initiative was discouraged; the common purpose was to raise revenue for military needs. Not even a senior official of the General Directory could act without the consent of his three colleagues on the board—and, of course, the king. Under such a system, without an arch bureaucrat on the throne, the government was doomed. Fortunately for Prussia, no eighteenth-century monarchs took their absolutism more seriously than the Hohenzollerns. They nurtured a state for which military discipline, subordination, and centralization became bywords. The feudal agrarian regions east of the Elbe River yielded easily. Like his predecessors and successors, Frederick William had some difficulty coercing the urban populations in Prussian enclaves along the Rhine River valley, but he succeeded.

A feared and demanding father to his subjects, Frederick William was a timid diplomat who suspected that cunning foreigners wished to use his beloved army for their own ends. Ever respectful of hierarchy, as elector of Brandenburg he maintained a correct relationship with Charles VI, who, as Holy Roman Emperor, was his suzerain. When Frederick William signed the Pragmatic Sanction without conditions, the Hapsburgs miscalculated his deference as a sign of weakness and treated him with disdain. Other powers, however, were aware of the shifting balance of forces in central Europe. Ever seeking protection for Hanover, Britain sought a double marriage with Prussia—first uniting the prince of Wales, heir to the English throne, with Frederick William's daughter, and next wedding the Prussian crown prince to George II's daughter. (As Frederick William and George were brothers-in-law, the marriages would cement an already existing bond.) However, Frederick William feared the elegant amorality of English court life, and in 1730 suspended the project. For the eighteen-year-old crown prince Frederick, the king's decision was a crushing blow. From childhood Frederick had suffered from the brutality and ridicule of his boorish father, and now a brief moment of liberty was denied him. The prince tried to flee the kingdom, and thus provoked the major family crisis of his father's reign.

The personality conflict between Frederick William I and his son is one of the great dynastic dramas of modern European history. Nineteenth-century Prussian historians turned it into a moral fable for schoolchildren: the struggle between the duty-bound, tough, realistic father and the hyper-sensitive, intelligent, artistic prince, followed by the prince's desperate flight. But the flight fails. The boy is caught, chastised, and punished. He is treated as a common army deserter and forced to witness the execution of a coconspirator, his best friend. Then, by stages, Frederick learns that his destiny to become Prussia's king must take precedence over his inclination to play music, write poetry, and read philosophy. His inner rebellion subsides, he takes his father's choice of a plain German princess as his wife, he learns about administration, and he becomes a soldier. Convinced that Frederick's change of heart is genuine, the king is reconciled with the crown prince. Knowing that the state is in safe hands, Frederick William can die in peace. Obedience and duty triumph.

The affair was more than a parable for children. Frequently, individuals and groups opposing the policies of a reigning sovereign might rally round an unhappy heir, forming a lair of malcontents bent on treason. Only a generation earlier, Peter the Great and the aged Louis XIV had suspected this. In England, Leicester House, where the prince of Wales lived, was a hotbed of opposition to Walpole. Frederick William feared that dangerous cliques might use the crown prince to destroy his own accomplishments. As the king's apprehension mounted, he became more abusive. The attempted flight was the climax. Whether the crown prince's repentance was as genuine as nationalist Prussian historians depict it is irrelevant. He never became a carbon copy of his father and may well have continued hating him. But he did learn how to rule.

Settling down on a country estate in 1737, Frederick delved deeply into the classics and writings of the Enlightenment. He corresponded with Voltaire and even wrote a piece of political philosophy refuting Machiavelli. The hope of his father, Frederick, probably the most intelligent crown prince in modern European history, became the darling of the philosophes. They asked whether, once on the throne of Prussia, he might combine reason, humanity, and absolutism in enlightened fashion. What intellectuals missed, unfortunately, was Frederick's profound cynicism, which provided a cutting edge to his belief in duty. Even as he wrote of his ideals in the *Anti-Machiavel*, even as he poured out heart and hopes to Voltaire, Frederick was developing a deeply held principle of the state as a moral end in itself. Considering himself Prussia's first servant, Frederick believed that the king must not only encourage trade and industry, maintain the social fabric, and protect the country from rapacious neighbors; he also must be prepared to add to the state's resources by any means deemed appropriate.

Frederick II Comes of Age

Frederick knew that his father would leave him a large army and a full treasury. While the philosophes naively cheered him as one of their own, the crown prince spent long hours analyzing the weaknesses and strengths of the other European powers. He saw the Anglo-French entente unraveling; and he observed the tensions between England and Spain, feebleness of Poland, and insecurity of Hapsburg Austria. He sensed that a generation of relative stability in Europe was ending, and that boldness would pay dividends. On May 31, 1740, Frederick William I died. Several months later, Emperor Charles VI was dead as well. Converting a long dormant territorial claim into a pretext for aggression, King Frederick seized the Hapsburg province of Silesia. Though few European sovereigns took Charles VI's Pragmatic Sanction seriously, the suddenness of the Prussian descent was stunning. A secondary upstart power had attacked Europe's most prestigious empire. Charles VI left Austria weaker than it had been in a century, Silesia possessed mineral and industrial wealth exceeding all of Prussia's, and the strategic location of the region permitted future expansion to the south and east. An opportunity for aggrandizement beckoned. In December 1740 the Prussian army marched. Six months later, the shock had worn off, and nearly everyone else was joining in for the spoils.

Frederick wanted a quick victory in a limited war. With Silesia in tow, he offered Maria Theresa money, a Prussian alliance, and his vote for her husband in the upcoming election for Holy Roman Emperor. But he would not yield a foot of conquered territory. The young empress scornfully rejected Frederick's entreaties, stating that to do so would betray the labor of her father's life, his Pragmatic Sanction. So she decided to fight. However, French and Bavarian plans to partition the Hapsburg Empire sent events out of control, and the empress was in no position to confront

Map 9.1—Expansion of Russia in Europe, 1689–1796

France, Bavaria, Saxony, and Spain—in addition to Prussia. In 1742 she was forced to make peace with Frederick, thereby acknowledging the loss of Silesia. As ally of the French and Bavarians, Frederick later was forced back into the fray, and in 1745 Maria Theresa had to reconfirm Silesia's loss. Though Prussian diplomats did not even attend the peace conference at Aix-la-Chapelle in 1748, representatives of the other European powers recognized as an accomplished fact the seizure that had initiated the War of the Austrian Succession.

After 1748 Maria Theresa was obsessed with recovering Silesia and destroying Prussia. She prepared for the next war by building an army and a system of alliances. Frederick II was aware of her fury, but even more he feared a hostile alliance in which France and Russia would be serving Austrian ends. Between 1748 and 1755 he tried to persuade the great powers that he now was Germany's peacekeeper. But his past record left Europe unconvinced. All through the War of the Austrian Succession, Frederick had been a very poor ally. To Louis XV, Prussia's Convention of Westminster (1756) with England, however defensive it looked, was yet another betrayal. It drove France into Austria's arms. Like Maria Theresa, Tsarina Elizabeth of Russia despised Frederick, welcomed the eradication of the Prussian state, and broke with Britain because of the Convention of Westminster. Austria's Kaunitz tore Prussia's diplomacy into shreds, and late in August 1756 Frederick had no other choice than to resort to arms. Unlike the invasion of Silesia sixteen years earlier, his decision was born of desperation, not jaunty self-confidence. The new war he unleashed was nothing less than Prussia's struggle for survival.

THE EVOLUTION OF RUSSIA AND THE SEVEN YEARS' WAR

Russia Enters Europe

A major factor in the collapse of the post-Utrecht settlement for Europe was the emergence of Russia. Peter the Great's journey in 1697 had been largely symbolic, but the construction of his new capital and his triumphs in the Great Northern War meant that Russia was aiming due west. During Peter's reign Russia sent diplomats to all corners of Europe, and the empire's commerce expanded with Hapsburg Austria, England, the Dutch Netherlands, and France. Although the days were over when European sovereigns were so little aware of Russia that they would write to tsars long dead, the empire still was a partially known quantity and thereby feared. Some of the difficulty had to do with the country's bizarre political history after Peter's death. Between 1725 and 1762 seven tsars or tsarinas succeeded to the throne, often through murder and violence. Russia lacked an accepted system of dynastic succession. The fledgling bureaucracy built by Peter succumbed easily to clique and faction. While guards regiments and palace favorites made and unmade rulers, no regular administrative staff existed to keep government on an even keel. The French ambassador to St. Petersburg sneeringly remarked, "The master here is the one with bayonets, a cellar filled with vodka, and gold."

During the fifteen years after Peter's death in 1725, the tsar's reforms seemed to have become a dead letter. Favorites replaced the senate, the aristocracy made important strides in escaping required state service, and for a time, between 1727 and 1730, resurgent boyars even moved the capital back to Moscow. During the reign of Anna Ivanovna (1730–1740), Peter's niece from the Baltic duchy of Courland, German adventurers poured into government and exploited Russia as a colonial conquest. Anna's death produced a year of immense political chaos, terminating in 1741 when a guards regiment established Peter's daughter, Elizabeth, as tsarina.

Elizabeth (1741–1762) threw out the Germans and promised to be faithful to her father's heritage. She restored the aristocratic senate as the principal governmental institution, possessing autonomy in routine affairs but deferring to the tsarina's sovereign power when it came to making ultimate decisions. As part of a cultural revival, the educator Ivan Shuvalov and humanist-scientist Michael Lomonosov founded the University of Moscow. Russian aristocrats were persuaded to start ironworks, distilleries, tanneries, and textile mills. A government bank opened to loan funds to investors. A model of sensual excess and extravagance, Elizabeth broke with her father's policies in one important way. In order to retain the loyalty of the Russian aristocracy, she acceded to its desires, chief of which was limiting the duration of compulsory state service. During Elizabeth's reign it was reduced to twenty years. As nobles were granted additional time to manage their estates, serfdom, the social base of Russia, became more hardened and ruthless than ever. In the recently settled fertile regions of the Ukraine, work service obligations were raised to six days per week. Where they could, landlords extracted cash dues from peasants. The recalcitrant were tried in makeshift courtrooms on estates and could be deported or imprisoned at the master's will.

Because of Russia's internal instability, European governments shied away from it. However, the declining status of Poland, Sweden, and the Ottoman Empire also underscored Russia's growing importance. Between 1725 and Elizabeth's accession, one of Peter's German imports, Heinrich Ostermann (1686–1747), directed the country's foreign policy. Ostermann's aims were to preserve Russia's conquests along the Baltic, maintain its influence in Poland, and keep up pressures against the Turks. Since these ambitions coordinated with Austrian intentions, the two powers remained cordial. However, Russia's relations with France were very poor. Traditional enemies of the Hapsburgs, the French were friendly toward Sweden and the Ottomans.

In 1733 the death of Poland's king, Augustus II, provoked an international crisis. The Crown was elective and the election open to bribery. France desired the restoration of Karl XII's former puppet, Stanislaus Leszczynski, now father-in-law of Louis XV. Meanwhile, the Russians and Austrians supported the son of Augustus II. In a mood of national resurgence, the Polish Diet elected Stanislaus, thus provoking the Russians to move an army toward Warsaw. Faced with a hopeless war, the Poles reversed themselves and named the Russian candidate as king. Nevertheless, Austrian and French forces already had clashed in Germany, and Russian regiments were sent to assist Charles VI. Never before had Russians fought so deeply in Europe, and the entire continent grew restive.

Before a massive all-European struggle ensued, however, Stanislaus withdrew his candidacy; Augustus III was crowned, and the crisis subsided. Russia's participation in the War of the Polish Succession was the country's first step in becoming enmeshed in pan-European diplomacy, and as a consequence Ostermann obtained a commercial treaty with England. In 1735 he assisted the Austrians against the Turks, but so dismayed were the Russians with the poor Hapsburg performance that in 1740 they made no move to save Maria Theresa's empire from partition. After Ostermann's fall during the succession crisis of 1740–1741, Elizabeth behaved scrupulously. She promised the Hapsburgs aid in any subsequent conflict, explicitly excluding the present one. For all but one year of European warfare between 1740 and 1748, Russia studiously avoided direct involvement, and even sat out the negotiations at Aix-la-Chapelle.

Nevertheless, Europeans respected the Russian army, and after 1748 the wooing of Russia became a diplomatic preoccupation. While Kaunitz tried to maintain Austro-Russian friendship, in 1755 the English agreed to subsidize Elizabeth's army in return for Russian protection of Hanover. Much to the chagrin of Frederick II, this placed a Russian force on Prussia's frontier and Russia's Baltic fleet was kept on constant alert.

Already at war with France in India and America, the British questioned whether their Russian alliance would hold Frederick in check in central Europe. Moreover, British diplomats underestimated Frederick's morbid fears of a coordinated Austro-Russian attack on Prussia, during which Britain might unwittingly foot the tsarina's bill. The Prussian king had to dissociate Britain from its old alliance with Austria and its new one with Russia. He believed he could not count on French help. Therefore, he proclaimed to Britain his unaggressive intentions in Germany and, to underscore his point, signed the Convention of Westminster (January 1756) with the British.

Frederick considered the convention a clever maneuver. Prussia and Britain would protect central Europe from any would-be aggressor. Meanwhile George II thought he was obtaining double protection for Hanover. However, Tsarina Elizabeth considered the British agreement with a king she despised as base treachery. Much to Frederick's pleasure, she repudiated her pact with Britain, thereby losing her army's paymaster. At the moment of

Frederick's seeming diplomatic triumph, disaster struck. Four months after the Convention of Westminster, France and Austria signed their treaty of friendship, and Russia moved into the Franco-Austrian camp. Sensing a triple-pronged attack on Prussia, in August 1756 Frederick launched his preventive war against Austria. France stuck by its new ally, Austria. In February 1757 Russia joined Austria in order "to reduce the king of Prussia within proper limits," and in March Sweden became party to the coalition. Finally, in May, the Second Treaty of Versailles officially converted Austria's defensive pact with France into an offensive alliance.

Faced with the German war it had wished to avoid, Britain reluctantly subsidized the Prussian army. Meanwhile, the mutual fears, distrust, and ambitions of the European powers thrust Russia into continental affairs. Despite long-standing apprehensions about the intrusion of this half-Oriental, politically unstable despotism, whose existence was built on the subjugation of millions, the die was cast. Russian armies now would fight across European battlefields, and Russian participation would be crucial to any diplomatic resolution. Just as Russia's presence helped precipitate the Seven Years' War, its premature withdrawal in 1762 ultimately became the key to ending the conflict.

The Seven Years' War

Essentially, the Seven Years' War was Prussia's struggle for survival. Scattered in patches from the Niemen to Rhine rivers, the Prussian state was geographically artificial and insecure. It either had to expand or disintegrate. The coalition against Prussia had naked territorial ambitions. The Austrians wanted Silesia, Russia coveted East Prussia, France desired Prussia's Rhineland regions, and Sweden was after Pomerania. The Second Treaty of Versailles, committing 100,000 French troops to Germany, openly invited partition of Prussian territories. Frederick's attack on Saxony brought most of the German principalities into the war on the coalition's side, and England's George II considered Prussia's position as hopeless. To save his electorate of Hanover, George wanted to open immediate negotiations with Austria and France. However, his chief minister, William Pitt, committed his government to saving Prussia and counseled courage and patience.

With its unexpected twists of fortune, the Seven Years' War reads like melodrama. Initially, the allies fielded 450,000 troops to Frederick's 143,000, and in the first year of the war, the Prussians suffered near disastrous setbacks. They failed to help Hanover when an English-Hanoverian army was defeated by the French; the Russians occupied East Prussia; the Swedes debarked in Pomerania; and for a time, in October 1757, the Austrians occupied Berlin. In Prussia's darkest hour, however, Frederick's redoubtable army reorganized and under the direct command of the king scored a pair of victories that have become classics in the annals of land warfare. The first, on November 5, 1757, was at Rossbach, in Saxony, against a coalition of French and imperial forces; the second, a month later, was at Leuthen, in Silesia, against the Austrians. On each occasion, the discipline and courage of the outnumbered Prussians responded magnificently to the tactical skill of their royal commander.

Frederick's victories averted the immediate destruction of Prussia and turned the struggle into a war of attrition. Despite its numerical superiority, the allied coalition quickly revealed cracks. Austrian military leadership was mediocre, the Russians never moved without receiving express orders from distant St. Petersburg, and the French generals were hindered both by divisive diplomacy at Versailles and a public opinion supportive of Frederick's cause. Faced with a titanic colonial war with the British, as early as 1758 the French government began looking for a way out. France reduced its financial commitment to Maria Theresa, and Russia and Austria became the major participants on the allied side. As long as Frederick could raise troops, England subsidized the Prussians to the tune of £670,000 per year and kept an Army of Observation in western Germany. But Prussia was running out of soldiers. A costly defeat against the Russians at Kunersdorf in August 1759 erased the effects of previous victories, and by 1760 Frederick had fewer than 100,000 troops left. With his recruiters driving unwilling Saxon and Silesian peasants into battle, the Prussian king wrote despairingly, "To tell the truth, I believe all is lost. I shall not survive the ruin of my country." While Frederick contemplated suicide, only Austrian and Russian disagreements over where to strike next delayed the end. The Austrians insisted on liberating Silesia, but the Russians delayed in Saxony. Frederick held on, declaring that "fortune alone can deliver me from my present state."

Indeed, fortune smiled through the battle smoke. Early in January 1762 Tsarina Elizabeth died. Her successor, Peter III, a fanatical admirer of the Prussian king, ordered his generals to cease hostilities. By May, Russia was out of the war. Sweden withdrew as well, and France had no more will to fight. Lacking the resources to crush Prussia alone, late in 1762 Maria Theresa reluctantly opened talks with the Prussians. In February 1763, at Hubertusburg, Maria Theresa had to confirm the territorial integrity of the Prussian state, including Silesia. Prussia was saved, but at a terrible price. One-tenth of its population perished in the war, and Frederick wondered whether the final chapter in his country's history had been written. Soon Prussia's relations with England turned sour, France would not even accept a Prussian diplomatic mission, and both Saxony and Austria remained inveterate enemies. Desperately in need of an ally, Frederick turned to his old nemesis, Russia. He dangled a tempting prize, the impotent kingdom of Poland. For the next generation, the history of central and eastern Europe centered on schemes which would result in the partition of that unhappy country.

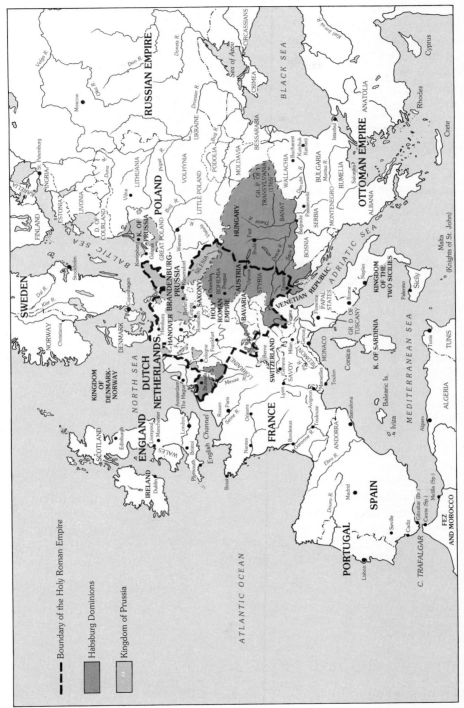

Map 9.2—*Europe in 1763*

Boundary of the Holy Roman Empire

Habsburg Dominions

Kingdom of Prussia

RUSSIAN EMPIRE

SWEDEN

POLAND

OTTOMAN EMPIRE

FINLAND

NORWAY

KINGDOM OF DENMARK-NORWAY

DENMARK

BALTIC SEA

ESTONIA

LIVONIA

D. OF COURLAND

LITHUANIA

VOLHYNIA

UKRAINE

LITTLE POLAND

GREAT POLAND

K. OF PRUSSIA

PODOLIA

BESSARABIA

MOLDAVIA

WALLACHIA

CIRCASSIANS

BLACK SEA

CRIMEA

Sea of Azov

ANATOLIA

CYPRUS

RHODES

CRETE

BULGARIA

RUMELIA

SERBIA

MONTENEGRO

ALBANIA

BOSNIA

BANAT

GR. P. OF TRANSYLVANIA (1765)

HUNGARY

ADRIATIC SEA

VENETIAN REPUBLIC

PAPAL STATES

KINGDOM OF THE TWO SICILIES

NAPLES

SICILY

PALERMO

MALTA (Knights of St. John)

BRANDENBURG-PRUSSIA

HANOVER

DUTCH NETHERLANDS

ENGLAND

SCOTLAND

IRELAND

WALES

NORTH SEA

SAXONY

SILESIA

BOHEMIA

HOLY ROMAN EMPIRE

AUSTRIA

BAVARIA

ILLYRIA

STYRIA

SWITZERLAND

LORRAINE

SAVOY

PIEDMONT

K. OF SARDINIA

CORSICA

MONACO

FRANCE

SPAIN

PORTUGAL

GR. D. OF TUSCANY

FLORENCE

ROME

FEZ AND MOROCCO

ALGERIA

TUNIS

MEDITERRANEAN SEA

ATLANTIC OCEAN

English Channel

Balearic Is.

ANDORRA

GIBRALTAR (Br.)

CEUTA (Sp.)

MELILLA (Sp.)

C. TRAFALGAR

Istanbul

Salonika

Belgrade

Bucharest

Passarowitz

Moscow

St. Petersburg

Stockholm

Christiania

Copenhagen

Hamburg

Königsberg

Gdansk

Warsaw

Berlin

Dresden

Prague

Vienna

Pest

Buda

Cologne

Frankfurt

Breslau

Geneva

Berne

Milan

Venice

Genoa

Turin

Naples

Lyons

Avignon

Marseilles

Toulon

Paris

Rouen

Orléans

Nantes

Bordeaux

Toulouse

Brest

Plymouth

Bristol

London

Manchester

Liverpool

Edinburgh

Dublin

Amsterdam

The Hague

Brussels

Madrid

Seville

Cadiz

Lisbon

Barcelona

Tunis

Algiers

Volga R.

Oka R.

Don R.

Donets R.

Dnieper R.

Dniester R.

Bug R.

Pripet R.

Dvina R.

Vilna

Niemen R.

Vistula R.

Oder R.

Elbe R.

Weser R.

Rhine R.

Danube R.

Drave R.

Save R.

Theiss R.

Tisza R.

Seine R.

Loire R.

Garonne R.

Rhone R.

Meuse R.

Ebro R.

Douro R.

Po R.

Maritsa R.

Prut R.

Sereth R.

Kuban R.

Kerch

Kizil Irmak R.

Dal R.

Klar R.

303

THE ANGLO-FRENCH STRUGGLE FOR EMPIRE

The Sources of Rivalry

A week before the Treaty of Hubertusburg brought peace to Europe, the Peace of Paris settled the colonial and maritime aspects of the Seven Years' War. What climaxed at Paris in February 1763 was a half-century competition for empire between England and France. Since 1755 the rivalry had degenerated into a death struggle. There were three major geographic regions of conflict: North America, the Caribbean, and India. In North America, British acquisition of Nova Scotia and Newfoundland in 1713 was to have offered protection to New Englanders who felt threatened by French domination of Canada. However, the deep thrusts of French explorers into the Mississippi Valley and the threat of potential French settlement there rekindled fears of hostile encirclement among English colonists along the Atlantic seaboard.

Meanwhile, in the Caribbean after 1713 the French successfully developed sugar plantations tilled by West African slave labor. France controlled the large islands of Guadeloupe and Martinique, half of Santo Domingo, and a host of smaller possessions. Caribbean sugar represented one-third of French international commerce, and in Europe nearly 3 million French investors, traders, shipbuilders, and workers in ports and refineries owed their livelihoods to exploitation of the tropical islands. At the same time, English West Indian planters considered French initative to be dangerous and called on Parliament to stifle it. They demanded enforcement of the Navigation Acts and suppression of illicit commerce between New Englanders and the French islands.

India was the third major area of Anglo-French rivalry. As in North America and the Caribbean, recent French advances presaged trouble. At first the British East India Company was content to develop seaborne and inland trade around "counters" at Madras, Bombay, and Calcutta. On the other hand, taking advantage of the power vacuum following the death of Shah Alamgir in 1707, the French counterpart of the English company made a series of military arrangements with Indian princes and extended its influence across the entire middle belt of the peninsula. Commanded by French officers, Indian auxiliaries fought for warring nabobs and rajahs. Director of the French East India Company from 1735 until 1741, Benoît Dumas bartered military assistance in return for commercial privileges. Honored as a vassal by the Great Mughal himself, Dumas was named nabob of the Carnatic. He controlled a string of treaty ports, and Indian princes considered him an equal.

Although France was Europe's most aggressive colonial power, Spain remained its largest. The Spanish empire extended from the Philippines to Africa. Not only did it incorporate most of South and Central America, Mexico, and Florida, but it also penetrated deeply into the unexplored reaches of Texas, California, and Arizona. Cuba and Puerto Rico were the largest of Spain's Caribbean possessions. Among the remaining European powers, only the Dutch and Portuguese still held significant overseas territories. By finally adding coffee cultivation to spice production, the Dutch East India Company tried to revive a slumping Indonesian economy. Holland retained footholds in Sri Lanka, southern Africa, Curaçao, and Guiana. Portugal's future largely depended upon Brazilian gold; yet scraps of past glory also existed at Goa in western India, Macao on the South China Sea, and the African possessions of Mozambique and Angola.

Eighteenth-century English politicians contrasted the political, economic, social, and cultural disunity of their North American colonies with what appeared to be a well-integrated, militarily sound French administration in Canada. The French built the New World's most powerful fortress, Louisbourg, on Cape Breton Island in the St. Lawrence estuary, and their posts of Fort Niagara and Fort Pontchartrain on the Great Lakes guaranteed them command over the Ohio and Mississippi valleys. Of course, British strengths were evident too. There was no question of reducing the navy, which during the War of the Spanish Succession had more than doubled in size. The Bank of England advanced enormous sums to the government, invigorating investment in overseas commerce. Between 1713 and 1740, London emerged as Europe's principal port of exchange for wheat, West Indian sugar, Indonesian spices, Indian textiles, and Virginia tobacco. Most significant of all, during the first half of the eighteenth century the population of British North America alone was rising by more than 30,000 per year. The settlers consumed 10 percent of the mother country's exports and formed a defensive bulwark against France and Spain.

Despite the fiasco over the South Sea Company in 1720, the English continued to experiment with credit and the company maintained its monopoly over African slave sales to Spanish colonials in the Caribbean and South America. English merchants were permitted the annual dropping of general cargo to Spanish Americans and smuggled additional goods to Creoles. The Madrid government hated the trade concessions as reminders of the humiliations suffered in the Spanish Succession war and complained about the smuggling. The British government showed little inclination to investigate Spanish complaints, its position being that if Spain was unable to supply its own colonists, Madrid should not insist on near-exclusive trade rights. So the Spaniards took matters into their own hands.

Their coastal cutters stopped and searched merchant vessels, abusing British crews. Such a boarding party had provoked the incident over Captain Jenkins's ear. All through the 1730s British smuggler-planters in the Caribbean, South Sea Company traders, London merchants, and the Patriots of the House of Commons cried for retaliation against Spanish searches. Greed and appeals to national honor cost Walpole control of Parliament, and in 1739 Britain slipped into open war with Spain. The anticipated easy conquests never materialized, and Frederick II's unexpected invasion of Silesia late in 1740 embroiled Britain in both a continental and colonial struggle. British attacks on Spanish ports in the Caribbean proved futile. In India the British trading counter of Madras fell to the French; in North America an expedition of New England militiamen captured Louisbourg. Just as it appeared that Britain might prevail in North America, the peace congress opened at Aix-la-Chapelle. To the disgust of New Englanders, the British government restored Louisbourg to the French in return for Madras. In the treaty neither French claims to the American hinterland nor the Spanish right to search at sea were mentioned.

The Great Colonial War (1755–1763) and Its Aftermath

For Britain and France the period between 1748 and 1755 was no more than an interlude between colonial wars. In India it was not even that. While the Mughal empire disintegrated, the rival European commercial companies armed their preferred clients and even fought alongside them. By 1751 the French East India Company controlled virtually the entire eastern coast of the subcontinent, from the Bengal station of Chandannagar to the Carnatic. Madras was isolated, and French influence penetrated deeply into the interior. Nevertheless, the British also were learning the techniques of alliance building and puppet forming. A former clerk in the East India Company office at Madras, Robert Clive (1725–1774), won a commission in a company regiment. He proved so successful fighting the French and their clients that in 1754 the director of the French company, Joseph-François Dupleix, was recalled in disgrace. Dupleix's successor tried to work out a sphere-of-influence treaty with the British; however, by the time the document was ready in December 1755, war between the French and English had erupted in America. The issue of European supremacy in India was left to force of arms.

The British colonists in North America felt betrayed in 1748 when Louisbourg was restored to France. With the St. Lawrence and Mississippi valleys still in French hands and the French laying claims to land along the Ohio River, the gates of settlement were closed to British colonials. The French built a military post at Fort Duquesne, just down the Ohio River from Lake Erie. Virginians and Marylanders considered it a dagger pointed at their hearts. Individual English colonies challenged French claims to the Ohio valley. In 1754 Virginia sent a force led by the young George Washington against Fort Duquesne itself, but it was beaten back. Jealous that Virginians' success might be achieved at their expense, other English colonists were not brokenhearted by Washington's defeat. Benjamin Franklin of Pennsylvania tried to overcome mutual jealousies by proposing a pooled force of colonial militias, but his idea ran against the shoals of particularism. The paralysis of the colonial assemblies abdicated genuine decision making to London. It was at this juncture that the British government made its momentous decision for America.

When the duke of Newcastle said, "Let Americans fight Americans," he expressed the traditional viewpoint. Colonists were supposed to defend themselves from local attack, and British military responsibilities were limited to keeping sea-lanes open. Loosely tied to these tactics was a general British policy which tried to link America to a global economic policy defined by the Navigation Acts. Late in the 1740s, however, William Pitt had challenged Newcastle's defensive approach, calling it cowardly, shortsighted, and contrary to Britain's imperial destiny. Pitt considered such destiny and Britain's commercial interests to be inextricable. Both would profit immensely from a showdown colonial war with France. Shifting focus from Britain's traditional sphere of interest in the Caribbean, Pitt saw control over Canada as the key to the empire's future. The conquest of this unexplored wilderness would place North America's fish and fur trade in British hands; the French West Indies would lose their source of cheap lumber and their sugar prices would mount accordingly; France would be bereft of a potential Canadian market for its manufactures and a source of material for building its ships. Finally, British North Americans at last might feel secure.

Although Pitt himself was out of office in 1754, his Patriot supporters demanded that troops be sent across the Atlantic. When the news arrived of Washington's defeat at Fort Duquesne, even Newcastle came around to the position that British North America was endangered. The mainland colonies were envisioned as the heart of Britain's entire colonial system, and their needs no longer could be shunted aside. Pitt took up his theme again: Two million British subjects considered themselves directly threatened. They deserved the Crown's protection.

Early in 1755 General Edward Braddock led a small British expedition across the Atlantic; its assignment was to drive the French out of the Ohio valley. Logistical problems and command disputes led to a humiliating defeat in which Braddock was killed. The French seized Fort Oswego on Lake Ontario, and New England felt engulfed by a French shadow. As war erupted in Europe in 1756, however, these fears proved to be exaggerated. Tied down to a costly campaign in Germany, the French were unable to summon resources and will for a protracted colonial war. Clive's victory at the battle of Plassey (June 1757) sealed the fate of Bengal and, eventually, of colonial India. France virtually abandoned the subcontinent and the great gains made there since 1713. Nor did it commit a royal army to North America. Returning to the ministry in 1757, Pitt urged a Canadian showdown. King, Parliament, and public opinion were behind him, and 35,000 troops were dispatched to America, the largest single trans-Atlantic military expedition that had ever been made. In 1758, Louisbourg and Fort Duquesne fell to the English. The latter was renamed Fort Pitt, and the Ohio valley was opened to English settlement. An abortive attempt to invade England in 1759 resulted in the destruction of the French Atlantic fleet, thus denying France's American possessions reinforcements and naval support.

The French military commander in Canada, Marquis Louis de Montcalm, tried to concentrate his outnumbered forces along the St. Lawrence River, and in late spring 1759 the British made their major assault. A flotilla of 50 warships and 8,500 troops left Louisbourg and sailed up the St. Lawrence estuary toward Quebec, capital of French Canada. For two months, the town was besieged. Because its citadel was located at the tip of a rocky peninsula whose cliffs jutted 200 feet into the St. Lawrence, the place was virtually impregnable. On September 12–13, however, the English commander, thirty-two-year-old James Wolfe, selected by Pitt over far more experienced officers, led a daring climb up over the cliffs west of Quebec and attacked Montcalm's surprised forces just beyond the city walls. The Battle of the Plains of Abraham cost the lives of both Montcalm and Wolfe, but decided the fate of Canada. Quebec fell to the British; Montreal surrendered a year later. New Englanders might breathe more easily, and the path to the West was secured. By 1762, Britain's overwhelming sea power led to the fall of Martinique, Havana, and Manila. When the peace conference at Paris opened in 1763, the British held all the trumps.

Pitt had wished to crush the French and dictate terms, but in 1761 he was out of office again. A negotiated settlement surrendered to Britain Canada, all territory east of the Mississippi River, Cape Breton Island, and France's smaller Caribbean possessions. In Africa, France ceded the Atlantic slave station of Senegal. The British East India Company gained control over the Deccan and Carnatic. France's ally Spain yielded Florida to Britain, and the French compensated the Spaniards with the grant of Louisiana. Britain restored the sugar isles of Martinique and Guadeloupe to France and allowed French-Canadian fishermen catch privileges in the Gulf of St. Lawrence. Five unfortified trading stations in India remained in French hands, and Spain was given back both Cuba and the Philippines.

The Peace of Paris was one of the great political settlements of the eighteenth century. Britain acquired an American empire stretching from the Atlantic seaboard to the Mississippi and from Hudson's Bay to the Florida keys. The British East India Company was Europe's most powerful colonial force in Asia. Although Pitt's dream of empire had become reality, vast new problems were arising. Following the war, England's military expenses became extraordinary. A sense of national humiliation fed French pride, dictating plans for revenge. Moreover, with the French barricade to expansion gone, British North Americans gained a confidence and self-determination that were expressed in a chorus of criticism against the motherland's increasingly clear imperial mission. Only thirteen years separated the Peace of Paris from the Declaration of Independence, but these were years of escalating bitterness and mutual recrimination. Pitt himself romanticized over the Americans and their bearing of British civilization into the wilderness. He had fought the French so that the Americans might feel secure. He wished the colonists well in their determination to make money; but he had no intention of going further. Just after the signing of the Peace of Paris, a contributor to the *London Chronicle* summed up the attitude of official Britain: "The colonies were acquired with no other view than to be a convenience to us, and therefore it can never be imagined that we are to consult their interest preferably to our own."

Such commentary meant that America was to receive Britain's unemployables and supply the motherland with primary articles like tar, sugar, and tobacco. Americans were to purchase Britain's manufactures, especially its woolens. Parliament might impose indirect taxes on the colonials. The ships that traversed the Atlantic were to be British built, manned, and owned. Future parliamentary legislation was intended to protect Britain's interests. To the British government, the fruits of 1763 confirmed the integration of North America into a worldwide colonial system. Most Americans resisted this, abstracting into terms of freedom and tyranny what the British considered to be questions of profit and empire. Furthermore, as Professor Palmer has noted, in all the colonies, but especially in New England, there was "no particular sympathy for the forces that had triumphed in English life since 1660, notably the aristocratic and Anglican governing class, nor did what they know of the realities of parliamentary politics inspire them with much confidence."[1] Just as the British Parliament insisted on America's place in the empire, Americans were coming to realize that they did not wish to be governed by the British Parliament at all. Passions rose. A problem quickly degenerated into a quarrel, and the quarrel yielded a revolution.

---

[1] R. R. Palmer, *The Age of the Democratic Revolution*. Vol. I, *The Challenge* (Princeton, 1959), p. 159.

10

THE DECLINE AND FALL
OF THE ANCIEN RÉGIME

ENLIGHTENED DESPOTISM

The Meaning of Enlightened Despotism

Disillusioned with what they considered to be the excesses of the French Revolution, several nineteenth-century historians devoted scholarly careers to studying the political institutions of eighteenth-century Europe. These historians posed the following questions: Did the monarchies of the ancien régime possess sufficient vigor and will to respond to the needs of peasants burdened by personal servitude and desiring legitimate property rights? Could kings fulfill the ambitions of middle-class subjects eager to expand individual commercial and industrial capacity while acquiring measured doses of political responsibility? Could royal ministers convince aristocracies resentful of losing power and privilege that compromises were necessary to assure survival of existing political and social structures? These historians concluded that, given a chance, late eighteenth-century monarchies might have reformed themselves and society without recourse to revolutionary bloodshed. They noted that most regimes of the time possessed a moral purpose and public conscience that distinguished them from their self-indulgent predecessors. The scholars coined a term for most of these monarchies. They called them *enlightened despotisms.*

Without a doubt, European rulers between the 1760s and the outbreak of the French Revolution included several remarkably intelligent women and men, assisted by vigorous ministers, advisers, and consultants. Reared in the Enlightenment's community of culture, rejecting pompous courts for intimate salons spiced with intellectuals, and taking a lively interest in literature, music, and the arts, the enlightened despots broke with a traditional aristocratic lifestyle that held intelligence in contempt. They applied empirical skills to statecraft, and several equated the use of reason with programs for humanitarian reform. Believing that it is easier to persuade a prince than convince a nation, philosophes struck up personal and epistolary acquaintanceships with sovereigns and urged rulers to consider the state as a public trust. By so doing, sovereigns were asked to implement

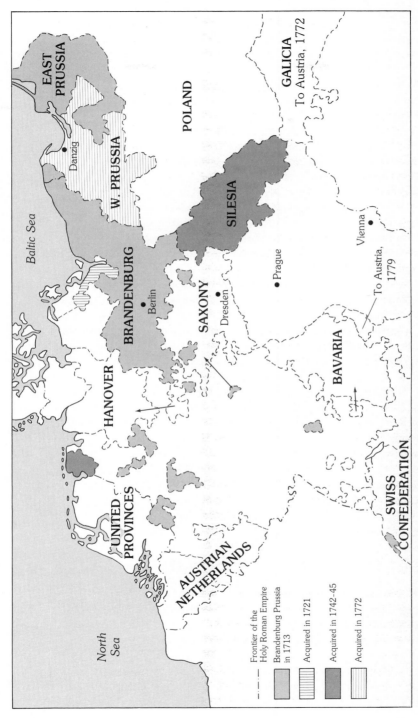

North Sea

Baltic Sea

EAST PRUSSIA

POLAND

GALICIA
To Austria, 1772

Danzig

W. PRUSSIA

SILESIA

Vienna

Prague

BRANDENBURG

Berlin

SAXONY

Dresden

To Austria, 1779

HANOVER

BAVARIA

UNITED PROVINCES

SWISS CONFEDERATION

AUSTRIAN NETHERLANDS

- — · — Frontier of the Holy Roman Empire
  Brandenburg Prussia in 1713
  Acquired in 1721
  Acquired in 1742-45
  Acquired in 1772

Map 10.1 — Expansion of Brandenburg-Prussia in the Eighteenth Century

religious tolerance, expand educational systems, improve and humanize legal procedure, centralize the administration, raise the peasantry to dignity, and better the economic situation of the country. Such programs, of course, were not particularly original, and it is tempting to disregard the entente between rulers and philosophes as a meaningless exchange of flatteries. Still, the Enlightenment gave rulers a vocabulary. They proclaimed themselves "citizens," "virtuous," and "sensitive" to human needs and public welfare. Moreover, even when they were at war with one another, enlightened despots exchanged ideas and techniques of government. The Hapsburgs imitated Prussian administrative models, Catherine II of Russia adopted Austrian educational reforms, and nearly everyone took bits and pieces from British agricultural, commercial, and judicial practice.

At the same time that sovereigns desacralized their own persons, encouraged individual economic initiative, and supported the equality of subjects before the law, they molded an institution that potentially was far more repressive to human liberties than any other previous agency had been under the corporate-ridden, privilege-bound ancien régime: the modern bureaucratic state. Under the enlightened despots the state was to assume social, political, and religious responsibilities formerly held by priest, village, town, landlord, province, guild, or Estate. The state would assure the health, wealth, wisdom, and security of its citizens. State intentions would be expressed lawfully, to be sure. Experts and specialists, not an arbitrary tyrant, would draw up the regulations. The end would be the public good. As far as was socially safe, privilege would be attacked.

The spirit behind enlightened despotism was paternalistic. To reforming sovereigns, the old corporations had never known what was good for society at large. The individual needed direction and control. Therefore, enlightened despots placed more urgency in maintaining sound administration than in protecting civil liberties. As one of Joseph II's experts, the cameralist writer Johann von Justi, put it: "A properly constituted state must be exactly analogous to a machine, in which all the wheels and gears are precisely adjusted to one another; and the ruler must be the foreman, the mainspring, or the soul—if one may use the expression—which sets everything else in motion."

Frederick II and Prussia (1740–1786)

Enlightened despotism arose in the underdeveloped, agrarian regions of Europe, where landlord aristocracies had long been the fiscal, judicial, and legal intermediaries between the people and the state. Because of this, political reality limited royal spheres of action. Although Frederick II believed that all private property in Prussia was held in trust to the state, he made no attempt to expropriate Junker lands or eliminate Junker privilege. On the contrary, Junkers headed Frederick's bureaus and departments, collected his country taxes, and led his armies. Frederick believed that in the reconstruction of Prussia after 1763, the aristocracy had to be integrated within absolutist political structures. As reward for their diligence and loyalty, the Junkers ruled the peasantry and were trained in modern universities and military academies. For Prussia enlightened despotism definitely meant the well-ordered state, and the king was its first servant. Just beneath him was the aristocracy.

The peasantry also served. Like his great-grandfather, the Great Elector, Frederick welcomed rural immigration. After 1763 the state awarded loans and gifts, tens of thousands of homesteads were staked, the potato and sugar beet cultivated, and both moors and swamps reclaimed. Frederick promised new settlers that they would not slip into serfdom. When Prussia acquired the Polish province of West Prussia in 1772, a new wave of immigrants poured in. By the time of the king's death in 1786, every fifth Prussian belonged to a family of colonists.

Still, this invitation to pioneering failed to reform profoundly the social bases of rural life. The old link between the landholding aristocracy and military was overwhelming. On the land and in the army, serf remained beholden to Junker. Except in East Prussia and Silesia, the land tax fell exclusively on peasants. They gave three to four days of their work week to landowners and built Prussia's roads. On private estates Junkers were the law, and Frederick merely assured the peasants that their tiny plots would not be added to the landlord's domain. On crown lands Frederick guaranteed serfs hereditary tenure rights, and their obligations at least were put in writing. Instinctively, Frederick might have wished to ease the peasant's lot. Reason told him, however, that this would compromise the rights of the aristocracy, and in the king's view Prussia owed its survival to Junker landlords and Junker officers.

Burghers served as lower rank bureaucratic personnel and as taxpayers. Although Frederick discouraged burgher acquisitions of land and after 1763 dismissed faithful officers from the army on the grounds of being non-noble, the king did appreciate skilled artisans and craftsmen. He kept them out of the military; but even in giving birth to Prussian industry, Frederick revealed his aristocratic bias. Silesia, which had cost him so much, possessed a rich tradition of textile manufacturing. The province was the heartland of Prussia's wealth, and Frederick promised subsidies and manpower to Junkers if they would develop linen and woolens production there. But while granting capital, credit, and buildings, the state was careful to limit and control productivity. Textile mills, sawmills, distilleries, and brick factories were established on rural estates, but little individual initiative was encouraged in urban centers. Frederick was obsessed with certain luxury manufactures like silks and porcelain. His inspiration was Colbertine France, not Hanoverian England. Heroic efforts at canal building, making the Oder River navigable, exploiting Upper Silesia's mineral deposits, and opening a state bank, bore fruit. While a tariff wall surrounded Prussia, a newly built merchant fleet carried estate-produced grain to the West.

Frederick tried to use bureaucratic forms to perfect the authoritarian structures of his dynastic inheritance. The king dispatched orders through the General Directory, but in his haste to get things done he superimposed new functional departments of commerce (1741), war supplies (1746), excises and tolls (1766), mines (1768), and forests (1770) on the regional competencies of the General Directory. To a greater degree even than his father, Frederick worked alone. During the annual mid-June review of ministers, the king met with his department chiefs. Budgets were approved and affairs discussed. As the ministers returned to their Berlin offices, Frederick withdrew to his own palace study at Potsdam. Until the following June, all government transactions were communicated in writing.

Members of the General Directory and department chiefs sent the king reports and requests; on his part Frederick issued streams of royal commands. Order and regularity defined procedure, and delays were not tolerated. Since Frederick was an impatient man and a very quick thinker, the system functioned efficiently. At Potsdam, Frederick's life was the model of controlled discipline. He lived there alone, with neither court nor etiquette, never observing a religious holiday. Meanwhile out in the provinces, the "ink splashers" were inured to the system. When, on August 17, 1786, no commands emerged from Frederick's palace chambers and couriers arrived in the provinces with empty bags, all officials surmised the reason. The king was dead.

Ruler for nearly a half century, Frederick imprinted his style on Prussia. He fulfilled his father's program of instilling in his people the values of duty, self-sacrifice, and obedience. The bureaucracy and army remained the twin pillars of the state. Even after the Seven Years' War, military expenses accounted for 70 percent of the national budget, and soldiers with their dependents accounted for one-fourth of Berlin's peacetime population. All his life the king held military values in highest esteem. As he grew older, Frederick lost touch with French philosophes and cared little about his enlightened reputation. Cynicism engulfed the aged ruler, and he mistrusted everyone. He feared that the army was going soft and worried whether Prussian institutions would long survive him. Later events justified his concern. Without Frederick's taskmaster spirit, the Prussian state of the next generation collapsed beneath French revolutionary and Napoleonic armies. Curiously enough, what survived were the legal code and educational system, the two elements that parenthetically gave a humane tone to Prussian life.

Frederick intended his reforms to strengthen the autocratic state, and it was a happy coincidence if any particular measure might benefit his subjects. He believed in a social contract with his subjects, but it was to be interpreted in an authoritarian manner. The people delegate to the sovereign absolute rights of maintaining the laws, governing them, and defending them from aggressors. The prince is first servant of the state. In practice this meant organizing society in a legal and systematic way, and Frederick was determined to rule a well-ordered and policed state. From his father he inherited an able minister of justice, Samuel von Cocceji (1679–1755), who had long recognized that law in the Hohenzollern domains was a hodge-podge of local habit and custom, with cases piling up for years and proce-dure tied down by conformism, ceremony, and graft. From 1746 to 1755, Frederick and von Cocceji created an interlocking court system at local, provincial, and central levels. Judges became salaried officials and fee tak-ing was prohibited. University education for judges became compulsory, and incompetents were dismissed. Thus the judiciary ceased being a corpo-rate guild.

Even though he scolded and dismissed judges, Frederick insisted that the law be independent of the sovereign. Therefore, he generally did not intervene personally in court cases. The fact that Prussia had no unified body of jurisprudence embarrassed the king, and he had a group of experts work on defining both criminal and civil laws. In this way, Frederick be-lieved that absolutism might be justified constitutionally. For example, for the past century Prussian rulers had been collecting taxes without popular consent, and Frederick desired to see this practice confirmed by the laws. The laws also must define social rank and obligation. The aristocracy was to be enshrined as Prussia's privileged Estate, its landholdings juridically pro-tected and its members controlling the kingdom's chief civil and military posts. Burghers and peasants were to retain subordinate status.

To some liberal thinkers such deference to absolutism and hier-archy might have seemed betrayal of Enlightenment principles; but the Prussian law code, finally promulgated in 1794, at least humanized crimi-nal procedures and recognized the individual's freedom of religious choice. Torture was abolished, penalties were intended to discourage future crimes rather than punish past ones, and the code reasserted Frederick's earlier indifference to any subject's religious preference. In terms of enlightened thinking, this last feature cannot be underestimated. Religious tolerance lay at the heart of Enlightenment thought, and Prussia was Europe's most tolerant state.

Frederick also had a lively personal interest in educational reform, believing that proper education was imperative in training subjects for their calling. Disabled and retired soldiers were appointed as village school-masters, teachers' colleges were founded, and the state introduced a uni-form inspection system for elementary schools. Frederick welcomed Jesuit refugees as teachers if they agreed not to proselytize for Catholicism. Prus-sia's universities received generous state grants for bright students, as well as funds for construction, books, laboratories, and professors' salaries. Nevertheless, political censorship limited areas of genuine free inquiry, and the essential purpose of education in Prussia, as with so much else, was to provide human talent for the proper operation of a static, paternalistically driven country. Innovation always remained suspect; duty was enshrined as the supreme national virtue.

Catherine II of Russia (1762–1796)

The philosophes gave Frederick a better press than he deserved, but Catherine II of Russia was their darling. The empress knew how to cater to intellectuals and invited several to her court at St. Petersburg. Born Princess Sophie in the tiny German principality of Anhalt-Zerbst, at sixteen she married Peter the Great's grandson, namesake, and heir to the throne. Arriving at the Russian court in 1744, Sophie shed her name and Lutheran religion. The world she discovered in St. Petersburg was rife with brutality and intrigue. Since Peter's death in 1725, favorites and guards regiments had made or toppled five rulers. One of the victims, Ivan VI, was rotting in prison; three of the others were dead. Peter the Great's daughter Elizabeth had been tsarina for three years.

Like his wife, Crown Prince Peter was not a native Russian. As duke of Holstein he had been raised in a German Protestant environment and considered his adopted land and its institutions to be barbaric. For more than a decade the court of Catherine and Peter was an island of unconventional thinking as well as a den of political faction. Sharing a dislike for Russia's traditional friendship toward Austria, the couple preferred an alliance with Prussia. Catherine admired Frederick II, and Peter worshiped him. However, Elizabeth loathed the Prussian king and the young court made little headway in efforts to influence Russia's political or cultural development.

Sympathy for Frederick and impatience with the slow pace of Russian westernization were insufficient to create affection between Peter and Catherine. Moreover, the crown prince showed signs of madness. After 1755 he became openly abusive toward his wife, preferring to pass his days playing with toy soldiers and his nights in sexual encounters with masked servants and chambermaids. For her part, Catherine found solace in the arms of court lovers. Unlike Peter, she perfected her Russian, ostentatiously performed the Orthodox rites, and played on Elizabeth's heartstrings. In January 1762 the tsarina died, and the throne passed to Peter. On becoming tsar, Peter immediately withdrew from the Seven Years' War. Needing allies at court, he exempted the Russian nobility from state service. This was the culmination of recent trends. In 1736, Tsarina Anna had reduced the serving period to twenty years, and Elizabeth had contemplated rewarding war veterans with blanket exemptions. However, because he laid claim to Church income, brought Holsteiners to court, and publicly humiliated Catherine, Peter discovered that his generosity was insufficient to win the Russian nobility. Late in June 1762 a guards regiment controlled by Gregory Orlov, Catherine's present lover, led her to the Cathedral of Our Lady of Kazan, where she was proclaimed sole ruler. The church and senate confirmed the usurpation. A week later Peter died under mysterious circumstances, and in 1764 the imprisoned former tsar, Ivan VI, was murdered.

Initially indebted to the guards regiment who had placed her on the throne, Catherine II wished to build a firmer base of support. For three years she bided her time, then in 1767 perceived an opportunity. What stood for a legal code in Russia was the document of 1649. Since that time a chaotic mass of contradictory legislation had accumulated. Catherine saw the need for consolidating it, but with a novel twist. She herself would write the preamble to the new law code and then request both experts and representatives drawn from various segments of Russian society to draft, discuss, and ratify the document.

The tsarina set to work on her preamble, called the "Instruction," the likes of which Russians had never before seen. Half the paragraphs were lifted directly from Montesquieu's *Spirit of the Laws* and Beccaria's *On Crimes and Punishments*. The "Instruction" blended reason, humanitarianism, and pragmatism. Because of Russia's size, Catherine wrote that the needs of impartial justice dictated absolute government. Nevertheless, subjects were to be equal before the law, torture and inhumane punishments eliminated, and religious minorities tolerated. Catherine admitted that serfdom contradicted the spirit of liberty. Yet serfdom was so closely tied to the fortunes of state and society that the public good discouraged wholesale enfranchisement. The tsarina wrote that the objective of absolute government was not to "deprive individuals of their natural freedom, but to direct their efforts toward the highest degree of human happiness. . . . It is not possible that this will please flatterers who repeat daily to the sovereigns of the world that peoples are created for the sovereigns' sakes. On the contrary, we believe that we exist for our peoples, and are proud to say so."

The majority of the delegates who served on Catherine's Legislative Commission were elected by their peers. Of the 560 members, more than one-third were townsmen and 80 were peasants from crown lands. The landowning aristocracy was represented by 160 delegates and the government by 28 "experts." No privately owned serfs came, and only one churchman. The commission sat for a year and a half but accomplished very little. A law code based on principles of the west-European Enlightenment proved to be beyond its reach, and delegates droned on about personal or group concerns. In the minority, landowners learned that theirs was not the only interest group in Russia. Even without participation of serf and priest, the commission revealed a complex society steeped in tradition and inertia. It taught Catherine a great deal about her adopted country, and by having the deputies solemnly recognize her enthroned presence, she legitimized the coup d'etat of June 1762.

Once she dismissed the Legislative Commission, Catherine decided that her authority, absolute in theory, needed to be confirmed by the privileged members of Russian society. Increasingly, she used the country nobles as the base of her power and in 1785 rewarded them with legal exemption from all compulsory service, direct taxation, corporal punishment, and the billeting of troops on their estates. Country nobles could dispose freely of their lands, build factories on their estates, sell their products without government interference, and own property in towns. As in western Europe, nobility was declared hereditary and confirmed as a corporate body. In each province, nobles were the state's key administrative personnel. Perhaps, as some have claimed, Catherine was merely replacing Peter the Great's iron fetters with silken cords. Nevertheless, by codifying aristocratic privilege in the Charter of 1785, Catherine assured herself of loyal administrators and officers. Hereafter, country nobles identified their fortunes with the empire's.

Catherine accompanied the codification of noble status with an administrative restructuring of Russia into fifty provinces, each subdivided into districts. The extension of state control was provoked by Pugachev's rebellion, which inflamed Russia's eastern provinces in 1773. The rebellion was even more serious and widespread than Stenka Razin's had been in the seventeenth century. It began among the Cossacks of the Urals when Catherine revised the autonomous status of the free horsemen. The Cossack leadership submitted, but the rank and file refused. Instead, they began fighting government troops. Emilian Pugachev (1726–1775), an army deserter, organized the Cossacks by proclaiming that he was Peter III, not at all dead but back to regain his throne. He then urged serfs to destroy their landlords, promised non-Russian tribes an end to harassment, and told Old Believers that he would tolerate their faith. By 1774 Pugachev had managed to appeal to every discontented element in Russian society, and he was welding together a revolutionary program. He maintained an imperial court, and said he would abolish serfdom, end both taxation and military conscription, and liquidate the gentry aristocracy.

First Pugachev's motley forces moved northwest, toward the Volga, and Moscow primed for an attack. Estates were seized, manors burned, and owners lynched. The regular army had to be recalled from the front to face the huge band. Pugachev then retreated southward, toward his home country in the Don valley. As desertions grew, he was betrayed and handed over to Catherine's generals. Transported to Moscow in an iron cage, Pugachev was displayed publicly, then hanged, quartered, and burned. His rebellion was the last major organized rural uprising under the old Russian monarchy. Nevertheless, until the emancipation of the serfs in 1861, dozens of lesser revolts plagued governments, and for a century to come the "peasant problem" would be the overriding social issue in Russia.

Catherine herself deepened the dilemma. The Legislative Commission of 1767 had raised false hopes. Although its convocation endeared Catherine to west-European intellectuals, during her reign lords might imprison serfs at will, and serfs lost even the right to appeal mistreatment to the public authorities. The tsarina extended serfdom into the newly cultivated Ukraine, and she awarded favorites and lovers great tracts of state-owned land along with peasants. Nearly a million people were thrust into privately owned serfdom, where they could be torn from the land and sold as slaves. After Pugachev's revolt, Catherine suppressed whatever humanitarian instincts she might once have had and became a hardened reactionary. She persecuted the most celebrated spokesman for the Enlightenment in Russia, Nikolai Novikov (1744–1818), and she sent to Siberia the author Alexander Radishchev (1749–1802), whose volume *A Journey from St. Petersburg to Moscow* (1790) reflected on the injustices of serfdom and rapacity of local officials. She blamed the French Revolution on Freemasonry, her onetime philosophe friends, and the weakness of Louis XVI's government. She ordered Russian students abroad to return home, banned French newspapers and magazines, and increased the secret police. All her life Catherine enjoyed the bric-a-brac of Enlightenment culture—the Sèvres china, English gardens, and imported French clothes; however, the last years of her reign were etched in repression and fear.

Hapsburg Enlightenment (1740–1792)

Shrewd, opportunistic, and intelligent, Catherine was a consummate actress. By way of contrast, the Hapsburg empress, Maria Theresa, Catherine's contemporary until 1780, was authenticity incarnate. Reading no philosophes and abhorring most of them, Maria Theresa believed quite simply that the state had a moral obligation to protect its peasantry, and to accomplish this goal it must tighten the reins of governmental authority over the multinational landholding aristocracies of her empire. It is essential to recall how widespread this empire was. The central European regions consisted of three blocks of territory: the Austrian family lands, the Bohemian ones, and the kingdom of Hungary; then there were the peripheral possessions, the largest of which included Belgium, the Tyrol, Croatia, Slovenia, Lombardy, and Transylvania. Finally, there were the collateral territories, of which Tuscany was most important. The Hapsburg Empire contained a bewildering collection of ethnic and national groups, all differing from each other in language, religion, and social custom. How could government introduce innovation and order? Maria Theresa's professional advisers used appeals to natural law, economic doctrine, or imperial sovereignty as justifications for reform. For the pious empress, Christian responsibility was sufficient reason for humane action.

Maria Theresa's regime chipped away at the foundation of serfdom. Bohemia and Hungary contained serf-based economies, where an impoverished peasantry weighed down by labor services tilled huge noble-owned estates and were chained to the land by virtue of legal obligations. In Austria the peasants usually owned their own land, but still paid labor services. If the state could not abolish peasant dues and services owed to aristocrats outright, at least it could regulate and reduce them. Following a dreadful famine and serf revolt in Bohemia, in 1775 labor services were restricted there to three days. In selective instances, the services were abolished in favor of cash payments. Fiscal reforms complemented social ones.

For the first time in its history, the government at Vienna gave an accounting of its resources and expenditures. After 1763 attempts were made to coordinate the empire's provinces within an economic network, the goal being a free trade area. Hungary was to be its heart, the source of agricultural production and market for manufactures. In Church matters, the influence of the Jesuits was reduced and eventually abolished. Forms of ostentatious piety were discouraged in favor of an internalized Catholicism advocated by Jansenist theology and by the reduction of papal influence suggested by the bishop of Trier, J. C. N. von Hontheim. Underdeveloped monastic estates were expropriated. With the establishment of a state ministry of education, Jesuit professors were expelled from colleges and universities. The classical curriculum was replaced by courses in political science, applied mathematics, and modern languages.

Hated though Prussia was, Frederick II's upstart kingdom provided Maria Theresa's ministers with the inspiration for several types of reform. Its Protestant Pietist schools offered the model for curricular changes in elementary education. The state assumed the Church's role in censoring books, and the literary monuments of the century were translated into German. Maria Theresa's high officials, appropriately called "the Great Ones," were far more secular-minded than the empress herself and took charge of the expulsion of the Jesuits. Seized Jesuit properties formed the source of the state's education fund. Following the loss of Silesia, military modernization became absolutely essential, and here too Prussia provided the model. In the hereditary Hapsburg lands conscription was introduced, as were demarcated recruiting districts.

Maria Theresa died in 1780, never doubting the moral vision of her secular and religious policies. The eldest of her sixteen children, Joseph, succeeded her. Not quite forty, Joseph was experienced in the responsibilities of government. On his father's death in 1765, he had been elected Holy Roman Emperor. His mother named him co-regent over her Hapsburg lands, and he commanded the Hapsburg army. A restless, unhappy prince, Joseph had urged his mother to attempt more extensive reforms than she dared. Maria Theresa had acted from pragmatism and necessity; Joseph saw the world in much more doctrinaire fashion. He hated the Magyar gentry, whose tax exemptions and control over the Hungarian countryside were extensive. He berated Maria Theresa, insisting that peasants throughout the empire still possessed insecurity of tenure. For more than a decade his impatience produced hostile scenes at court. At last in 1780, Joseph had his chance. With due respect, he buried his mother and set to work.

Joseph II (1780–1790) was the most impassioned and least understood of the so-called enlightened despots. Because Joseph lacked Catherine's charm and Frederick's intelligence, the philosophes never were comfortable with him. Because he lacked his mother's pious warmth, his subjects feared him. Joseph's younger brother, Grand Duke Leopold of Tuscany, himself a progressive reformer, created the unflattering historical image of Joseph: an arrogant, bad-tempered sovereign who "tolerates no contradiction and is imbued with arbitrary, brutal principles." More accurately perhaps, the Belgian aristocrat and man of letters, Prince Charles-Joseph de Ligne, wrote that Joseph II "desired the greatest authority so that others would be deprived of the right to do harm."

Working incessantly, bitterly unhappy in his personal life, Joseph believed that the state bore an obligation to impress moral example uniformly on its subjects. His concern for human dignity was sincere, expressed symbolically when he commanded abolition of the practice of kneeling before one's social superiors, or else expressed ringingly through his great decrees declaring religious tolerance and an end to serfdom (see pp. 209, 257). Too frequently, however, the compulsion to make his authority stick turned Joseph into a spiteful man. His insistence on German as the administrative language for the heterogeneous empire irritated Italians and Croats, the transfer of the Hungarian crown from Budapest to Vienna angered Magyars, and the conversion of the unused imperial palace at Prague into an armory insulted Bohemians. The emperor lacked the gentle touch, and this proved his undoing.

Joseph's nine-year reign concluded with revolt in Belgium and unrest in Hungary. The Belgian uprising was led by a clergy resentful of Joseph's interference with Catholic liturgy and religious practice, such as de-Latinizing the Mass, banning pilgrimages, and suppressing the monastic orders given to the contemplative life. The Josephian state assumed the Church's responsibility for relief of the poor and hospital care. It declared marriage a civil contract. Imperial decrees ordered Church hierarchies to take orders from the state, not the pope, and priests were told to sermonize on good citizenship rather than salvation of souls. The government started paying priests' salaries, assumed control over seminaries, and removed Catholic teaching from several universities. Far from Vienna and preaching to an intensely pious population, the Belgian clergy resisted the Josephian decrees. Privileged corporate groups in Belgium—provincial Estates, guilds, and burgher fraternities—supported the bishops. In 1789 an insurrection expelled the Austrians.

In Hungary the causes for unrest were political rather than religious. In the absence of a national Diet which had ceased to meet in 1765, effective government in Hungary fell to local assemblies of country gentry. Joseph correctly accused these assemblies of representing only vested interests, of repressing the peasantry, and of having no concern for the general well-being of the empire. In 1785 the emperor started overhauling Hungarian institutions. He divided the country into ten new administrative districts, with attention paid neither to geography nor to historical tradition. German-speaking commissioners were sent into Hungary and bypassed the assemblies in preparing a proportional land-tax project intended to sweep away the aristocracy's fiscal privilege and domination of the peasantry. At this point, the Magyar gentry considered its nation in danger, began arming, and asked Prussia for help. By 1788 matters were extremely grave. Bogged down in a new Turkish war, Joseph could scarcely cope with an insurrection. He might have appealed directly to the Hungarian peasantry, but he feared igniting popular will. His goal was revolution from above. He therefore made a strategic retreat. Critically ill, he agreed to summon the national Diet. In January 1790, he suspended most of his administrative reforms; by the end of the month, he was dead.

Clerical and aristocratic reaction defeated Joseph in Belgium and Hungary, but even in his German domains a shortage of crusading bureaucrats rendered it impossible to enforce the imperial decrees. The Hapsburg universities produced several brilliant, dedicated officials imbued with Josephian ideals; but these men were needed in Vienna's central bureaus. In the countryside local landed aristocrats recruited from dormant regional Estates would not enforce orders abolishing serfdom, denying their own tax privileges, and inviting the settlement of religious and ethnic minorities. Lesser officials were as poorly paid as their Prussian counterparts while lacking Prussian devotion to state, sovereign, or public welfare. Just before his death, Joseph lamented, "There is an absolute lack of men to conceive and will. Almost no one is animated by zeal for the good of the fatherland; there is no one to carry out my ideas."

Leopold II (1790-1792), Joseph's younger brother, reaped the bitter harvest. Grand duke of Tuscany since 1765, Leopold had himself earned a reputation as a progressive sovereign. On becoming ruler of the entire Hapsburg Empire in 1790, however, Leopold had to lay to rest many of his ideas. Joseph's revolution from above had failed. In France, a National Assembly formed from dissatisfied elements in the traditional Estates-General was extorting a constitutional regime from Louis XVI. Leopold decided to bargain with the diets and Estates in the customary Hapsburg manner. He insisted on retaining censorship and education as state activities, most of the toleration decrees stood, and new owners kept the greater share of the expropriated monasteries.

However, the laws abolishing aristocratic privilege and peasant servitude, the heart of Joseph's program, were repealed. The Hapsburg peasantry had to wait until 1848 for the end to seigneurial dues and services, and the domination of provincial government and society by the aristocracy survived as long as the empire itself. Still, in 1792 the Hapsburg peasantry enjoyed far greater security of tenure than had been the case half a century earlier, and imperial law, rather than landlords' whim, protected even the most downtrodden. On the other hand, Leopold's relative success in Tuscany suggests that small states lacking the cumulative inertia and resistance of powerful aristocracies might respond more willingly to autocratic reform than large empires. With modest aims, extending from introduction of crop rotation methods to the granting of religious tolerance, several princes in the Holy Roman Empire succeeded as enlightened despots. Only rarely did these rulers tamper with the social order, and none sought to modify the aristocratic-absolutist political balance by experimenting with citizen participation in government. In Scandinavia, however, eighteenth-century governments were more ambitious. Their encroachments on noble privilege unwittingly laid the social foundation for the bourgeois regimes of the nineteenth century.

Enlightened Despotism in the North (1770–1792)

By 1770 Danish absolutism took the form of a cozy alliance between a royal administration of great landlords and an aristocracy of lesser property holders enjoying social and fiscal privileges. The Danish peasantry was enserfed. Then, a young Prussian physician, Johann Struensee (1737–1772), who had recently saved the king's life and become the queen's lover, skyrocketed to power. Despising aristocratic royal councillors, Struensee had them dismissed. For eighteen months he became virtual dictator, mingling tight-fisted political authority with an enlightened social program. Elegant, refined, and iron-willed, Struensee reduced the peasants' service obligations to their landlords and abolished commercial monopolies. In 1772, however, his enemies caught up with him. Convicted of high treason and illicit relations with the queen, who herself was exiled, Struensee was executed. For a decade the old order was restored. In 1784, however, another royal adviser, Count Andreas Bernstorff (1735–1797), progressive and more patient than Struensee, took up the reform program. Within ten years grain and cattle were circulating freely throughout the kingdom, mercantile privileges and serfdom were abolished, and an effort was made to institute a proportional tax on incomes. Absolutism and reform worked hand in glove until 1848, when the revolutionary movement of that year instituted constitutional government for the kingdom.

For half a century after the death of Karl XII, a loose affiliation of influential landowners, military officers, and government administrators controlled Sweden. The two kings of the period, foreign-born nonentities, were elected by the four-chambered Diet, and the political life of the nation, like that of England, revolved around elections to the Diet. Coffeehouse rallies, party programs, political campaigning, and purchased votes became the norm. Foreign governments bribed Diet members, who called such awards healthy for the nation's economy. After 1763, however, the upper aristocracy, customarily identified with the Hat political party, tried to establish permanent control over great military offices, seaborne commerce, and the king's Council of State. The lesser nobility and clergy, identified with the Cap party, resisted. The election of 1765 brought the Caps into power. They adopted a progressive agenda, virtually abolishing censorship, liberalizing trade, and reducing military expenses. However, the Caps found it difficult to consolidate their political victory, and encountered the resistance of the great aristocrats. Political and social conflict, complicated by Russian, Prussian, and Danish intervention in Swedish affairs, threatened to destroy the constitutional balance of the state. There was talk of a possible partition. Then, in the midst of the crisis, the Swedish king, Adolf Fredrik, died in 1771 and was succeeded by his son, Crown Prince Gustav.

Gustav III (1771–1792) was intelligent and eager to end party wrangling. Inspired by the philosophes and his uncle Frederick the Great, he tried a royal power play. Hats and Caps could agree on nothing, and the Diet was paralyzed. In August 1772 the young king mounted his horse and, followed by a contingent of royal troops, rode into the streets of Stockholm exhorting the citizenry to help him deliver the country from calamity. The melodramatic appeal worked. On royal order the Diet threw out the aristocratic constitution of 1720, and Gustav was given absolute powers. For the next fifteen years he modified Swedish institutions, awarding a range of civil liberties to the populace, reducing the Council of State to an advisory capacity, and winning powers over both taxation and legislation. Rather than destroy the old aristocracy, Gustav followed the seventeenth-century practice of Louis XIV. He converted it into an embellishment of his court.

As long as the king enjoyed the backing of Sweden's burghers, freehold peasantry, and lesser aristocracy, his revolution was safe. Gustav also had an ambitious foreign policy, built on memories of Swedish greatness and far too costly for current resources. Going to war against Russia with neither Diet support nor an adequate military budget, he faced an army mutiny and was fortunate to come away with an empty-handed peace in 1790. However, the ill-advised war did bring Gustav one major dividend. Invoking emergency necessity, in 1789 the king effected a new coup d'état at the expense of the Swedish aristocracy. Clearing the Diet of the noble Estate, Gustav offered religious tolerance and civil equality to all subjects, permitted nearly anyone in the country to acquire landed property, and further centralized royal power.

Aghast at its disestablishment, a band of erstwhile great nobles plotted desperate measures against the royal revolutionary. In March 1792 one of their number assassinated Gustav. Disturbing as this was for the king, for Swedish history the plot was of minor consequence. Gustav's successor was able to retain the constitution of 1789. Invigorated by their improved status, burgher, clerical, and peasant Estates resisted an aristocratic reaction. No longer a dominant power in Swedish national life, the nobility retreated into sullen acquiescence. The French revolutionary wars and Napoleonic adventure hastened the social dominance of the bourgeoisie in the nineteenth century.

Enlightened Despotism in the South

A Mediterranean version of enlightened despotism existed in Italy, Spain, and Portugal, where the Catholic Church and landed nobility possessed large rural properties and enjoyed widespread tax exemptions. Although peasants were not legally enserfed, most were landless sharecroppers or indebted tenants. Flights from rural poverty customarily placed them in the teeming slums of the Mediterranean's cities, where they endured brief and miserable lives. King Charles IV of Naples-Sicily (1735–1759) had been a reform-minded prince, attacking ecclesiastical privilege and forcing the clergy to pay taxes on their properties. In 1759 Charles was called to succeed his half brother as king of Spain, leaving an energetic first minister, Bernardo Tanucci (1698–1783), to oversee reform in Naples. Tanucci waged a courageous political and economic struggle against the Church, landlord oligarchs, and a privileged judiciary; but the failure of his king, Ferdinand I (1759–1825), to support Tanucci with sufficient vigor ensured the economic domination of the great estate owners, and he fell in 1776. Tanucci's immediate successors kept up the good fight, proposing a general primary educational system, opening the state's courtrooms to the peasantry, and abolishing the Inquisition in Sicily. Despite the fact that Naples produced more theoretical reformers than any other eighteenth-century Italian state, entrenched privilege and the threat to monarchy posed by the French Revolution closed the door to genuine social reform.

In most of the remaining states of Italy, bureaucratic administrators rather than idealistic intellectuals bore the major responsibility of reform. In Milan the Verri brothers served the Austrian administration well; in Savoy-Piedmont, a small underpopulated state with a highly sustained program of change, the long reigns of two kings—Victor Amadeus II (1675–1730) and Charles Emanuel III (1730–1773)—were geared less toward Enlightenment and more toward increasing both royal revenues and military power. By way of contrast was Tuscany, where Grand Duke Leopold (1765–1790), younger brother of Joseph II, read the philosophes deeply and attempted to create a just political equilibrium between government and its subjects. This led Leopold to free the grain trade, end tax farming, abolish the guilds, and empower state bureaus to collect a single land tax, pet project of the French physiocrats. Leopold had as much interest in civil liberties as he did in economic reform. The Tuscan criminal code of 1786 abolished both judicial torture and the death penalty, and Leopold was the inspiration behind a constitution by which the grand duke's power to wage war, make foreign alliances, raise troops, oversee state expenditure, and forge laws would be shared with deputies elected by the most prosperous citizens. Varied sources influenced Leopold, including English common law, Swiss cantonal democracy, and the constitution of Pennsylvania. That his own document lay stillborn was due to the opposition of Joseph II, who desired Tuscany to be integrated within the larger Hapsburg political system, one that was paternalistic rather than participatory.

Serving as king of Naples-Sicily, Charles IV had understood the difficulties in bearing reform to an ignorant, economically retrograde region where the Church was too wealthy, the aristocracy too entrenched, and the people overworked and poverty-stricken. Becoming Carlos III of Spain (1759–1788), he faced a familiar domestic situation. On the other hand, compared with the shambles of 1713, Spain's international reputation had improved. Under the new Bourbon dynasty, the country revived as a Mediterranean power. The loss of Belgium and territories in Italy reduced state expenses, and Catalonia experienced a resurgence of textile manufacturing and tighter coordination with Madrid's policies. In Catalonia strong-willed royal ministers and a commissioner bureaucracy imposed themselves upon officeholders, local aristocracies, and cumbersome government councils.

With twenty years of royal experience behind him, Carlos III knew that he could not turn Spain upside down. However, he did choose ministers skillfully, whether intellectuals like Pedro Campomanes or Gaspar Jovellanos, politicians like José Moñino, or grandees like the count of Aranda, and he was able to identify the weakest sides of opposition to attack. Government councils, noted for privilege and administrative delay, were reduced to routine chores. The Jesuits were suppressed and the state took over the Inquisition. Carlos and his ministers knew, however, that Spain's problems involved more than a cumbersome administration or overly ripe Church. At the core the difficulties were economic and social. Land was scarce and expensive. Much of it was owned by the aristocracy and remained unexploited. Rents rose higher than prices. Short-term leases victimized tenured peasants, and the landless ones were even worse off. A dramatic population increase was creating a massive proletariat. How were these people to live? How were they to be fed?

Following severe riots in 1765–1766 caused by food shortages and skyrocketing prices, Carlos developed an agrarian program which sought to extend cultivation. Unused rural lands owned by towns were ordered enclosed and sold. The Crown supervised reclamation projects in Castile, and proprietors whose estates were undeveloped because they lay in the path of the sheep runs of the *Mesta,* the powerful pastoral corporation, were granted enclosure rights. None of this greatly changed the social pattern of Spanish agriculture, for the beneficiaries were improving landlords, not small tenants. Moreover, the regime was reluctant to foment aristocratic unrest by tampering with seigneurial dues and existing property rights. Nevertheless, more land was put to use, and reduced state taxes on business transactions liberated commerce. Ports other than Seville and Cádiz were permitted to trade with Spanish America. In the colonies the introduction of royal intendants reduced corruption. After a century of humiliation at the hand of foreign competitors, Spain once more was supplying its people with home-produced goods—cottons from Catalonia, silks from Valencia, and ironware from the Basque provinces. Industrial wages lagged behind prices, and manufacturers dictated labor terms. Before his death in 1788, Carlos III could look back at thirty years of controlled achievement. Dependent upon ministerial elites, progressive landowners, and officeholding *hidalgos,* the king's reform program was certainly paternalistic. It mistrusted the people and had no intention of adjusting its sources of sovereignty. By way of contrast, a year following Carlos's death, neighboring

France would declare as illegitimate any reform program *not* based on popular will. The repercussions in Spain would be the end of enlightened royal experimentation.

Between 1755 and 1777 Portugal witnessed a frenzy of antiaristocratic, anticlerical terror masked as enlightened despotism. Certainly the terrain was ready for a ruthless and energetic reformer to take charge. The country basked in the unearned wealth of Brazil, but the gold arriving in Lisbon was squandered in palace-building projects for the king and his aristocracy, or else siphoned off to Britain. With their own laws and privileges, foreign merchant communities virtually ran the commercial economies of Portugal and Brazil. Numbering 200,000 of a total population of 3 million, the Portuguese clergy owned two-thirds of the land and controlled the country's universities. Nearly half the adult population toiled on Church-owned estates. The papacy was influential, the Jesuits powerful, and the Inquisition effective. Theoretically at least, Portugal was an absolute monarchy whose national Diet had not met since 1697. However, King José I (1750–1777) preferred hunting and the opera to statecraft. Enlightened despotism in eighteenth-century Portugal therefore became inseparable from the activity of a single individual, Sebastião de Carvalho e Melo, marquis of Pombal (1699–1782), onetime ambassador to London and Vienna and supervisor of the reclamation work in Lisbon following the city's devastating earthquake and tidal wave of 1755.

Under Pombal's guidance, the rebuilding of Lisbon converted the ruined town into a jewel of enlightened urban planning. Lawyers, architects, engineers, and surveyors inventoried property rights, cleared out devastated neighborhoods, created grid streets, and implanted the city's new heart: Commercial Square on Lisbon's waterfront. Becoming uncontested dictator of Portugal's national life, Pombal also urged populating Brazil through native-colonist intermarriage and African slave imports. He abolished the Brazilian missions of the Jesuits and set up privileged merchant companies intent on dislodging British and Dutch traders from the huge Latin American colony. National monopolies were to control the sale and export of Portuguese sweet wine, the consumption of which had become the obsession of eighteenth-century English gentlemen. When the tavern owners of the northern city of Oporto rioted to protest state-ordered reduced numbers of them, Pombal reacted brutally—hanging and quartering the chief suspects, imprisoning others, and exiling the rest to Africa and India.

Energetic activity and brutal repression of opposition became the hallmark of the Pombalian regime. A botched attempt on the king's life in 1758 resulted in the brutal elimination of two of the country's leading aristocratic families. Then there were the Jesuits. Portugal became the first Catholic state in Europe to seize their property and expel the order. When the pope protested, Pombal broke off relations with Rome. Church and aristocracy fell into line. Further state monopolies were awarded to those who would start woolens, linen, paper, and glass manufacture. The educational system was secularized. Although he burned the works of Locke, Voltaire, and Rousseau, Pombal possessed sufficient Enlightenment zeal to abolish the legal distinction between the "Old" and the "New" Christians, the latter descended from Moslems and Jews, and he freed children of slaves in Portugal.

Such whiffs of humanitarianism notwithstanding, Pombal bequeathed a legacy of fear. Shortly after the death of his king and protector in 1777, he fell from power. A general amnesty caused hundreds of his victims to pour out of obscure prisons, and the old ex-minister was tried for corruption and abuse of power. Ostentatiously declaring that he had taken all his orders from José I (which no one believed), Pombal published his defense. It was translated into nearly all European languages and served as enlightened despotism's ultimate apology. Himself obtaining a royal pardon, the eighty-two-year-old Pombal died in 1782. Although badly shaken during a quarter century of ruthless battering, Portugal's alliance of pure-blooded aristocrats, clerical grandees, and foreign merchants tried to revive. However, the traditional elites no longer had a monopoly over the country's economic and cultural life. Pombal's neomercantilist state companies perished with the minister's fall, but their ennobled administrators and favored merchants remained dominant forces. They continued to control gold imports and the wine trade, and they derived huge profits from their soap and tobacco monopolies. They were as much the beneficiaries of Pombal's "despotism" as they were of his "enlightenment."

The Balance Sheet

Unlike their nineteenth-century predecessors, historians today can describe the varieties of enlightened despotism without any particular ideological agenda. However, there is little consensus concerning the significance of so many different royal programs. Some scholars believe that enlightened despotism actually weakened absolutism because it acknowledged natural law as the basis of monarchy and stressed the sovereign's duties rather than his privileges. The Scandinavian experience seems to confirm this position. On the other hand, few rulers and ministers disposed more freely of the lives and wealth of their subjects than Catherine II, Joseph II, Frederick II, or Pombal. In relinquishing the privileges of divine-right rule, eighteenth-century political leaders also relinquished divine right's constraints: adherence to immanent moral law, fear for one's soul, and respect for the long-standing rights of corporate groups. When all is said and done, the primary interest of rulers lay in the enhancement of state power. The rights of the individual were parenthetical. The question of whether these darlings of eighteenth-century progressives were also the ancestors of modern day totalitarians is worth pondering.

Enlightened despotism certainly institutionalized reform from above and, in most instances, bolstered monarchical authority. Appealing as

Map 10.2—The Partitions of Poland

they did to social contract theory and expressing concern for general welfare, rulers won new revenues and exploited the state's power over society. But how far could they go? All sovereigns ultimately had to weigh institutional and social tradition against the price of public welfare. Where tradition was strong and protected by constitutional guarantees, as in the Hapsburg Empire, an aggressive form of enlightened despotism like Joseph II's produced violent opposition and ended in tragedy. Frederick the Great was more fortunate than Joseph. Frederick's predecessors already had incorporated local aristocracies into state service, and the king consolidated the process. Although conciliation of aristocracies compromised with privilege, few enlightened despots could afford to ignore this technique. They cajoled the wealthiest elements of the state into administrative service, land improvement, and industrial enterprise. The enlightened despots ruled underdeveloped countries. They desperately needed money and expertise. They found resources wherever they could.

Of course, they were not convinced social revolutionaries. By 1791, faced with a revolutionary menace that threatened to topple absolutisms and aristocracies alike, rulers again were conceding privileges to traditional elites in return for political support. Leopold II let lapse Joseph II's decree abolishing serfdom, Catherine II's Charter for the Nobility sanctified the corporate personality of the Russian aristocracy, and the Prussian Code of 1791 guaranteed aristocratic leadership over society and the state. The radicalization of the French Revolution assured the death knell of enlightened despotism. Monarchs and aristocrats alike recognized a common need for survival. Before outlining the popular challenge to the old order, however, we must observe the actions of enlightened despots in diplomacy and war. Here they greatly resembled unenlightened predecessors.

THE PARTITIONS OF POLAND AND THE EUROPEAN EQUILIBRIUM

Frederick II's Grand Idea

War convinced the enlightened despots of the need to exploit the economic resources of their states, and at the same time the rulers looked beyond their borders for cheap opportunities to add to their resources. While Frederick the Great vowed never to repeat the near disastrous experience provoked by his seizure of Silesia, he also recognized that common interest might tempt fellow sovereigns to cooperate with him in aggressive diplomacy. In Prussia, Russia, and the Hapsburg Empire, eastern Europe contained highly ambitious states. At the same time, in Poland, Sweden, and the Ottoman Empire it contained highly vulnerable ones. After 1763 Fredrick needed allies badly. Therefore he merged Prussia's interests with those of his strong neighbors at the expense of his weaker ones.

The kingdom of Poland represented the major objective in Frederick's thinking, and to Russia and Austria he proposed formal partition of that unhappy land. Now, dividing the possessions of a defeated power was nothing new. In 1713–1714 the victors expropriated Spain's European colonies, and eight years later it was Sweden's turn to lose nearly all of its empire. In 1741 half a dozen European states were prepared to devour Maria Theresa's inheritance. Twenty years later, Russia, Austria, and Saxony intended to make Prussia the victim. It was accepted that overseas colonies were the rightful spoils of war, as France discovered at the Treaty of Paris in 1763. However, Frederick's scheme for partitioning Poland was different from what had occurred previously. In the first place, it was unrelated to war; in the second, predatory neighbors hankered after parts of a sovereign European state in order to prevent the seizure of the whole by any one of them. Diplomats congratulated themselves that no major power would emerge dissatisfied, the balance of power would be maintained, and a source of future conflict avoided.

Another reason for Frederick's bold maneuver had to do with the temporary dissociation of the west-European powers, particularly France, from continental entanglements. France's inability both to fight a colonial war with Britain and remain a useful ally of the Hapsburgs had been a major disappointment between 1755 and 1763, and for the next quarter century the essential theme of French diplomacy would be maritime and colonial hostility toward England. This meant that France's traditional European clients—Poland, Sweden, and the Ottoman Empire—could not count on its diplomatic or military support. Facing this, Frederick felt less pressure than ever about reshaping east-central Europe without recourse to war, a virtual necessity in any case, because of Prussia's terrific human loss in the previous European conflict.

As early as 1752 Frederick had coveted the Polish province of West Prussia, standing between his own provinces of Pomerania and East Prussia. It offered him badly needed territorial unity and possible control of the lower Vistula, the heartland of Poland's grain-exporting economy. Preoccupations in the Seven Years' War prevented Frederick from attaining his objective. Following the conclusion of the conflict and the death in 1763 of Poland's king, Augustus III, events fueled Frederick's ambitions. Poland's weakness was notorious. The country's magnates controlled its elected king, and a *liberum veto* in the Diet permitted any member to exercise a personal veto over legislation. Through bribes and browbeating, foreign powers intervened in Poland's political life. Frederick and Catherine II were influential in the election of a Polish magnate (and ex-lover of the tsarina), Stanislaus Poniatowski, as the country's next king. Poniatowski, however, proved less pliable than his patrons imagined he would be. Suspicious of the intentions of both Russia and Prussia, Poniatowski implored Polish patriots to arm themselves against aggression by rapacious neighbors. He tried to introduce financial and military reforms. Catherine warned Stanislaus that he was playing with fire, and to emphasize her point she stationed 30,000 Russian troops inside Poland's borders.

Frederick became wary. Russia's traditional policy had been to keep Poland weak and dependent. However, the Russian foreign minister, Nikolai Panin, wished to fit a strengthened, though servile, Poland in a northern alliance system directed against France, Austria, and above all, the Turks. Panin hoped to draw Prussia, Denmark, Sweden, and Britain into his scheme. For his own security, Frederick made a treaty of friendship with Russia in 1764. Denmark joined a year later. However, Britain had no desire to bankroll the Russian army again, and Frederick merely wanted Russia's protection of Prussia, not a grand alliance that might engulf him in unforeseen conflict. Therefore, in order to thwart the integration of Poland within a Russian satellite system, he attempted to persuade Catherine of the wisdom of partition.

Although the tsarina coveted eastern Poland, Frederick at first enjoyed little success. Then, in 1767, a reversion of religious tension in Poland provoked an uprising. Nearly 250,000 Protestants lived in northwestern Poland, and over 600,000 Russian Orthodox resided in the east. Both minorities felt themselves persecuted by the Catholic majority, as did the Jews scattered in ghettos throughout the country. Unlike the Jews, however, the non-Catholic Christians had powerful protectors. Prussia was to look after the interests of Protestants, Russia those of the Orthodox. This always had been another convenient pretext for interference in Poland's affairs. When Frederick and Catherine pressured the Polish government into extending freedom of worship and admission to public offices to Christian dissenters, Catholic magnates, gentry, and priests protested. Proclaiming national revival, deliverance from foreigners, and deposition of puppet kings, in February 1768 a resistance movement formed at the fortress town of Bar in southeastern Poland. Other patriotic groups declared solidarity with the Bar patriots and merged into a General Confederacy. Non-Catholic minorities feared a massacre. Since the General Confederacy was led by Poland's greatest magnates, politics added to the religious tension. Orthodox peasants in the Ukraine rose up against their Catholic masters. Russian military commanders egged on the rebelling serfs, who crossed the border into Turkey and burned manor houses. Russian troops also violated Turkish sovereignty, and the Ottoman government impetuously declared war on Catherine.

The Russo-Turkish war took time to begin. Once started, however, Catherine's forces scored sensational victories. In 1770–1771 her army took the Danubian principalities of Moldavia and Wallachia and penetrated the Crimea. The Russian fleet sailed into the Baltic, down the English Channel, along the Atlantic coastline, eastward through the Mediterranean, and destroyed the Turkish navy off Asia Minor. Istanbul was threatened. Alarmed by these unforseen Russian triumphs in southeastern Europe, the Hapsburgs began conversations with their bitter enemy, the Prussian king, and Frederick himself dispatched his brother Henry to St. Petersburg to argue for a Polish partition. Initially, Henry got nowhere; but Catherine soon understood that the unilateral aggrandizement of Russia at Turkish expense was much more likely to provoke a European war than a mutually considered diplomatic solution of the Polish problem. Early in 1771, rejecting the advice of Panin, Catherine suggested that Russia and Prussia help themselves.

The breakthrough thus made, a Russo-Prussian partition convention was signed. However much the Hapsburgs disliked further accumulation of Prussian territory in this way, Austria joined the discussions. Considering the partition of Poland a crime, Maria Theresa told Kaunitz, "I am ashamed to show my face." But she went along. Before the armed might of the three great powers, the Confederacy of Bar collapsed. In August 1772 the partition was sealed. Surrounded by Russian guns, the Polish Diet ratified the act. Frederick obtained West Prussia, Russia took Poland's northeastern provinces, and Austria gained a large triangle in the southern part of the country. Poland lost 50,000 square miles and 4 million people, a third of the country.

Russia's Advance and Poland's Disappearance

One major reason that Prussia and Austria pressed for the partition of Poland was to divert Russia's attention from the Balkans. However, this failed to occur. Catherine's territorial demands on the Turks were so great that peace negotiations between Russia and the Ottomans broke down in 1773, and it was only Catherine's preoccupation with Pugachev's rebellion at home that slowed further Russian advances in the Balkans. In June 1774 the Ottoman Empire sued for peace, and the Treaty of Kutchuk-Kainardji confirmed most of Catherine's war aims. The Crimea, a vassal state of the Turks since the fifteenth century, became independent, presaging eventual Russian annexation. Russia obtained the northern coastline of the Sea of Azov, some Black Sea coastline, and the ports of Azov and Taganrog. Russian ships won free navigation of the Black Sea and unrestricted entry into the Mediterranean. The Ukraine now was completely open to exploitation, and the tsarina obtained the right to "protect" Orthodox Christians in Istanbul itself, a pretext for further intervention in Ottoman affairs.

For Catherine this was but the beginning. Her faithful adviser Panin fell into eclipse and was succeeded by a court lover with grandiose schemes, Grigori Potemkin (1739–1791). Under Potemkin's influence, Catherine planned to dislodge the Turks from Europe altogether, take Istanbul, and reestablish a dependent Byzantine Empire for her grandson Constantine. In 1781 Catherine proposed to Joseph II a secret alliance, the end of which would be partition of the Turks' Balkan principalities. To pacify the French, Catherine hinted at an offer of Egypt. She had something for Spain and England too, should these states resist her proposed rearrangement of the eastern Mediterranean, grandly labeled the "Greek Project."

Fanciful though the Greek Project might have been, Joseph took it seriously. In 1783 Russia occupied the Crimea and started exploiting it despite the sultan's objections. Catherine now possessed sufficient naval bases for a seaborne attack on Istanbul, and she hastily was constructing a Black Sea fleet. In spring 1787 Catherine was Joseph II's host on a magnificent imperial tour down the Dnieper River and into the Crimea. The Turks panicked and in September 1787 again declared war on Russia. Fearful that Catherine would unilaterally seize the Balkan prizes, Joseph honored his secret alliance with her. Initially, Austrian military performance was disastrous, and Sweden offered a costly diversion by declaring war on Catherine and threatening St. Petersburg itself.

By 1789, however, the Russians were pushing back the sultan's armies. Ill, preoccupied with rebellion in Belgium and unrest in Hungary, Joseph could offer Catherine very little help, and his successor, Leopold II, withdrew from the war in July 1790. Faced with some British pressure to come to terms, the tsarina decided to delay any triumphant ride into Istanbul. Hostilities subsided in August 1791, and in January 1792 Russia made peace with the Ottomans. Catherine contented herself with Turkish recognition of Russia's annexation of the Crimea and the Black Sea coastline between the Bug and Dniester rivers. For the moment the Greek Project was put aside. Nevertheless, its genesis had given birth to the "Near Eastern problem," which would preoccupy European diplomats for most of the nineteenth century.

Thus, for the third time since 1740, Frederick II's desire to secure Prussia's future had set off a string of developments that escaped his control. As Russia attempted to dislodge the Turks from Europe, the Polish chapter was far from finished. The partition of 1772 created a movement of national revival in Poland that was remarkably different either from the desperate scapegoat hunting of the seventeenth century or the religiously intolerant Bar Confederacy of 1768. Every politically conscious Pole knew that constitutional weakness and magnatial jealousies had turned the country into its neighbors' prey. History revealed how for two centuries the great powers had exploited Poland's internal divisions, culminating in the disaster of 1772. Although Catherine's ambassador was de facto ruler of Poland after the partition, the tsarina herself was preoccupied with other matters. Within Poland the national Diet proceeded to restrict the authority of the provincial diets and attempted to strengthen central institutions. The king regained his right to mint money, and both hearth and import-export taxes were reintroduced. Following a series of economic reforms, by 1790 Poland's national revenue was twice what it had been two years earlier. Certain social reforms were attempted. The gentry was permitted to engage in commerce, and landlords lost the privilege of executing their serfs at will. The *liberum veto,* right of confederation, elective monarchy, and fifty regional assemblies were denounced as banes to good government.

Certainly, powerful magnates had a vested interest in the old liberties, and many preferred the traditional anarchy to reform. A few, however, became convinced nationalists and concluded that hereditary monarchical government and a strong army were the country's only hope against continued humiliations and foreign intervention. They had reason to fear the worst. Russian troops still were stationed in the country, and Prussia wanted more than its share in the partition of 1772. Catherine began observing Polish developments closely, and she disliked what she saw. Particularly ominous was the fact that a growing number of Polish reformers in the Diet had been visiting western Europe, had read the works of the Enlightenment, and were openly enthusiastic about revolution in France. On May 3, 1791, the Polish Diet unfurled its crowning achievement, a new constitution. The government was confirmed as a limited monarchy, hereditary in the House of Saxony. The king's job was to execute the Diet's laws. The traditional Estates of society were confirmed, but the landless portion of the gentry lost its political privileges. The *liberum veto,* confederacies, and confederation parliaments were abolished. Deputies to the new national legislature were no longer bound by the wishes of the provincial diets sending them there.

The constitutional reforms were modest enough. They left Poland in the hands of its traditional elites, and serfdom was untouched. However, the document infuriated Catherine. By 1792 the French Revolution was entering its radical phase, and the tsarina was certain that its democratic spirit had infected Poland. As soon as she signed the Treaty of Jassy with the Turks, the tsarina responded to the appeals of some unregenerate magnates and once more intervened forcibly in Polish affairs. The constitution of May 3 was abrogated, and in March 1793 a second partition was effected by Russia and Prussia. The Russians got the lion's share of territory and people. Poland was left a rump. Civil rebellion against the Russian occupiers was crushed in 1794, and the eastern powers agreed on a final partition. Squabbling over who should take what delayed the final solution, but by 1797 Poland had disappeared from the map of Europe.

The Bavarian Annexation Affairs: 1777–1785

However reluctantly, Hapsburg Austria had been a partner in the first partition of Poland largely because Prussia was a key participant. Maria Theresa never reconciled herself to the loss of Silesia and considered Prussia to be an outlaw state. Kaunitz, however, was more realistic than his empress and by the mid-1770s knew that Silesia would never belong to the Hapsburgs again. He therefore was on the lookout for an equivalent territorial compensation so that Austria might regain lost prestige in Germany. An opportunity seemed to beckon in 1777 with the death without heirs of the elector of Bavaria. The prosperous electorate lay just west of Austria and was a strategic link between Hapsburg territories in Germany and Italy. Kaunitz doubted Austria's chances of obtaining Bavaria, but Joseph II was optimistic and aggressive. The designated successor as elector, Charles Theodore of the Palatinate, had little stomach for challenging the Hapsburgs, especially after he accepted Austrian offers of financial maintenance for his swarm of illegitimate children. He ceded one-third of Bavaria to Austria and agreed to yield the rest in the future. As Austrian troops began occupying Bavaria, it appeared that the Hapsburgs had scored a diplomatic triumph. However, France reacted coolly to the annexation, and Prussia mobilized its army in protest. In July 1778 Frederick invaded Hapsburg territory.

No one, however, wanted war, least of all Maria Theresa who had considered the entire Bavarian annexation scheme as harebrained from the start. France and Russia proposed mediation, and their solution was forced on Joseph. The Hapsburgs obtained a small sliver of Bavarian territory, so that the emperor might avert total humiliation. Still desiring the electorate, however, in 1784 Joseph proposed the Austrian Netherlands to Charles Theodore in a straight exchange. From Joseph's point of view, it was a sound deal, ridding him of a distant, rambunctious set of towns and provinces that were exceptionally hostile to his reform program. Once Frederick again showed disfavor, no other European power supported Joseph, and his project fell through. On his·deathbed in 1786, the Prussian king was determined to leave to posterity a check on Joseph's ambitions. Along with Saxony, Hanover, and several other German states, Prussia signed a mutual defense pact, and a secret clause specifically mentioned protection of Bavaria's integrity. Thus Frederick the Great's life ended on a note of supreme irony. The figure most responsible for the destruction of central Europe's political equilibrium now produced a high-minded defense of the territorial rights of the small defenseless states within the Holy Roman Empire.

The Anglo-Bourbon Rivalry: 1763–1790

Between 1763 and the French Revolution, the forefront of European diplomatic and military activity was the eastern half of the continent. Western powers refrained from coming to the aid of either the Poles or Turks. Britain was preoccupied with deteriorating conditions in America, and difficulties there invited its old adversaries, France and Spain, to try to settle scores. Because the colonial triumph of Britain had been so complete during the Seven Years' War, both Bourbon powers were in a vengeful mood, and an alliance made in 1761, known as the Third Family Compact, tied the two countries to a common anti-British policy which lasted more than twenty years.

The militarization of eighteenth-century Britain resulted in creation of the world's most potent naval force. After 1763 the French foreign and naval minister, Duke Étienne-François de Choiseul (1719–1785), sought to reduce English maritime supremacy by virtue of a furious catch-up program. In 1770 Choiseul considered France ready again for war; however, in a bitter policy debate, Louis XV disagreed and dismissed him. French financial weakness and common concerns with Britain over the deteriorating situation in eastern Europe produced a brief period of better relations between the two powers; however, their points of rivalry and historic enmity prevented any genuine cooperation. Britain's troubles in North America produced colonial rebellion in 1775, opening up windows of opportunity which no French foreign policymaker could ignore.

From the beginning, American revolutionaries sought help from France. Charles Gravier, count de Vergennes (1717–1787), foreign minister for the new French king, Louis XVI (1774–1792), was sympathetic. Vergennes considered the loss of British North America as essential for restoration of the world's colonial balance and as a prelude to reestablishing French power (and British interest) in Europe. The first partition of Poland and Russian gains in the Russo-Turkish War (1768–1774) greatly disturbed Vergennes, who in the long run desired Anglo-French cooperation to counterbalance the aggression of Russia, Prussia, and Austria. Initially he persuaded Louis XVI to provide the Americans with money and weapons. During the summer of 1777 American privateers were using French ports. In February 1778 France signed military and commercial treaties with the colonists. Five months later France was at war with Britain, and in April 1779 Spain joined its Bourbon partner.

Without a single continental ally, Great Britain now had to fight a world war against France and Spain. This diminished somewhat the centrality of the American theater. Except for a ludicrous attempt at invading England in 1779, French military strategy was initially cautious and concentrated in the West Indies. By 1781, however, France was thoroughly committed to the cause of the Americans, and the French fleet prevented the arrival of British reinforcements at Yorktown (October 1781), the decisive battle in the War of American Independence. Meanwhile, Europe's smaller neutral states had difficulty protecting their shipping lanes, and of all people, Catherine II emerged to champion their cause. The tsarina's so-called League of Armed Neutrality (1780), including Russia, Denmark, Sweden, Portugal, and the Dutch Netherlands, proved to be more a reflection of anti-British principles than a true naval alliance. However, it did lead directly to the Fourth Anglo-Dutch War (1780–1784), which proved to be a disaster for the Netherlands' shipping.

By 1782 the major belligerents wanted peace. Britain had lost the thirteen colonies, and France was financially exhausted. A fresh British government sought reconciliation with the Americans and Anglo-French cooperation in Europe. Therefore, the loss of the colonies excepted, the Treaty of Versailles (September 1783) made only minor territorial adjustments. The French obtained the West Indian island of Tobago, Senegal in West Africa, and some fishing rights off the Newfoundland coast. Spain obtained Minorca and Florida, but not Gibraltar, its chief desire. The European signatories guaranteed the frontiers of the new American republic. For Great Britain the loss of the thirteen colonies surely was a defeat; however, since both France and Spain had practically bankrupted themselves during the war, worse was avoided.

In December 1783, at the age of twenty-four, William Pitt the Younger (1759–1806) became Britain's prime minister. He desired a peaceful foreign policy and an energetic commercial program. A favorable trade agreement with France in 1786 (the Eden Treaty) lowered many tariffs between the two countries and provided a vast market for British manufactures. This was followed by treaties with the Dutch Netherlands and Prussia. Even a conflict with Spain in 1790 over trading rights along the northwestern coast of North America worked to Pitt's advantage. Spain refused to accept revolutionary France's assistance, and resolution of the so-called Nootka Sound affair gave Britain access to the long coastline between Alaska and California. By now, however, French domestic events were working toward a realignment of European politics. Pitt still desired peace, but by 1793 Britain would be forced into war—allied with its traditional enemy, Spain—against Spain's longtime partner, France. However, this no longer was France of the Bourbons, but a renegade republic which had just executed its king, and in so doing became the pariah of Europe.

THE CHALLENGE TO THE OLD ORDER: IRELAND, BRITAIN, AND AMERICA

The New Political Language

The first partition of Poland, the Greek Project, the Bavarian affairs, and Anglo-Bourbon colonial rivalry fit into the traditional pattern of international politics under the ancien régime. Motivations were dynastic, territorial, and economic. Except for Catherine's propaganda campaign about liberating Balkan Christians from Islam's yoke or fellow Orthodox from Polish persecution, ideological factors were of little importance.

However, the second partition of Poland in 1793 was a different matter. Catherine brutally destroyed the Constitution of May 3 because she believed that the Polish reform movement was part of an international conspiracy set on destroying the political and social equilibrium Europe had known for the past five hundred years. The tsarina thought she saw a sinister new plant rising from the traditional societies of Europe. Its roots were widespread and difficult to locate, but the shoots were growing fast. They threatened to choke the older foliage that had flourished through the cultivation of royal-aristocratic politics characteristic of the European garden.

Indeed, by the late 1760s increasing numbers of Europeans no longer were considering concepts of the Enlightenment as mere theoretical abstractions. In the aftermath of the Seven Years' War, the most titanic struggle ever fought according to the ancien régime's rules of correct political behavior, an alternative language entered the sphere of public discourse. It did not address dynastic rights and aristocratic privilege but rather spoke to civil liberties, social justice, and popular sovereignty. If Catherine thought that she beheld dangerous ideas in the petitions presented to her Legislative Commission of 1767, she probably was mistaken. However, there was considerable evidence elsewhere that the political winds were changing.

Novels and political tracts alike were glorifying the autonomous personality unfettered by the shackles of traditional religion, politics, or social practice. In academies, reading clubs, salons, cafés, and Masonic lodges, individuals deprived of active political participation were debating the legitimacy of privilege, bases for sovereignty, and sources of property.

Occasionally debate exploded into action, as in the Polish national revival of the 1780s. Although the American Revolution put Europe's traditional elites on notice that an age of momentous change was at hand, the old continent felt rumblings before 1776. Eight years earlier the better born burghers of Geneva, heretofore excluded from aristocratic town councils, demanded a political voice in them and obtained it. During the next decade it was the turn of artisans and shopkeepers to lobby for greater participation in government. Meanwhile, in the United Provinces of the Netherlands, professionals, merchants, and intellectuals alike established a Patriot political party in opposition to the stadholder and aristocratized town councils that ran the country. Inspired by the Americans and supportive of their cause, the Dutch Patriots grew more numerous in the 1780s, armed themselves, and relieved William V of the stadholderate of Holland. Utrecht got a popularly elected municipal council, and the regent aristocracy of the Netherlands grew very nervous. So did Prussia's new king, Frederick William II, brother-in-law of the deposed stadholder. In 1787 Frederick William marched 20,000 troops into the United Provinces, restored William V, and Patriots fled abroad.

Rebellion in Ireland

Between 1770 and 1778, Ireland was a volatile country. On the one hand, the Catholic majority, 70 percent of the population, had no political rights and few civil ones; on the other, Anglican landlords, one-tenth of the people, owned five-sixths of the land. A third religious group, Presbyterian Protestants descended from Scottish immigrants, numbered 20 percent of the population and were customarily farmers in Ulster holding short-term leases, or else artisans and small traders. The Presbyterians believed that the Irish Parliament, meeting in Dublin, was concerned exclusively with the interests of the great landlords, and they were correct. The Parliament was a rotten institution controlled by a hundred of the largest property owners. However, the landlords themselves complained that decision-making responsibility resided not with the Irish Parliament at all but with the English House of Commons, whose trade laws were intended to protect British merchants and injure Irish interests. Therefore in Ireland several tiers of dissatisfaction overlapped each other. The Anglican aristocracy desired autonomy for the Irish Parliament and freedom for trade; the Presbyterian minority desired to make the Irish Parliament more representative; and the Catholic majority suffered from atrocious political and social subjection.

In 1778, a new crisis struck the country when North Americans, in revolt against Britain, ceased importing Irish linens and food products. Meanwhile, the British released troops stationed in Ireland for service in America, and the Irish prepared for impending French attacks. Native militiamen, largely Presbyterians, were recruited to defend the country. By 1782 there were 80,000 of these armed "Volunteers." Under pressure of events in America, the British government offered some legislative independence to the Irish Parliament. This satisfied Anglo-Irish oligarchs, but leaders among the Volunteers demanded more, namely complete reform of the Parliament in Dublin. The Presbyterians held a Grand National Convention to drive home the message to the aristocracy. Armed weavers, artisans, and small traders demanded political representation. The convention threw some scraps to the Catholic majority, chiefly the right to buy land, but showed little genuine interest in ending the practice of Catholic subjugation. However, the Irish Parliament itself refused to become more representative because, as one insensitive landlord put it, its unwritten constitution was "the admiration and envy of all nations and ages."

Getting nowhere, once the American war was over the Presbyterian Volunteers refused to disband. They urged reform of the Parliament at Dublin. Meanwhile, among the Catholic majority, political consciousness took shape and the British government did what it could to manipulate Irish religious divisions. Presbyterians and Catholics could not agree on the extent of Catholic emancipation, particularly the thorny issue of Catholic participation in any reformed Irish Parliament. By 1789, however, the French Revolution and its principles of universal political rights had captivated Irish Presbyterian leadership in Ulster. Two years later Catholics and Protestants cooperated in founding the Society of United Irishmen, its central principles based on France's Declaration of the Rights of Man and the Citizen. For the moment unable to use religion to divide the Irish, Britain conceded voting rights to Ireland's Catholics. By 1793 the United Irishmen were demanding a democratic republic free from sectarian wrangling.

England: "Wilkes and Liberty"

Before the rebellion in America, several efforts were made to amend England's political institutions. One was the king's. A vigorous, authoritarian young man, George III assumed the throne in 1760. While he had been crown prince, courtiers unable to penetrate the curtain of Whig authority had gathered round him and were now royal advisers. Like George himself, this group wished to free the Crown from what it believed to be the control of the Whig magnates and by so doing purify English political institutions. After forty years of placemaking, out went Newcastle. Out went many others. Not even Pitt the Elder survived the royal housecleaning.

The Whig idea of government had long held that control of patronage, social prominence, and party solidarity entitled political groupings the right to royal favor. On the other hand, George III wished to use royal favor to award patronage and social prominence to parliamentary loyalists. Therefore, like Charles II before him, the king tried to construct his own party in Parliament, where dedicated servants would do the royal bidding. Time, however, was not on George's side. The unpopularity of the Peace of Paris in 1763 forced from office his prime minister, the third earl

of Bute; and a rapidly escalating crisis in North America aggravated ministerial instability. George found himself enmeshed in aristocratic politics,
and the prestige of the Crown was victimized. Disgusted with an unedify-
ing political struggle between George and the Whigs, newspapers and
speakers demanded widened participation in politics. An unprepared king
and Parliament were suddenly called on to answer a critical question: Could
England truly be a free country while it maintained a restrictive franchise,
tolerated rotten boroughs, and accepted the politics of patronage?

While George proposed one way of changing status quo politics,
John Wilkes (1727–1797) offered another. A flamboyant, energetic adven-
turer who was elected to the House of Commons in 1757, Wilkes sat for
Middlesex, a London suburb with a relatively wide franchise. He was an
imperialist, eager to crush France in the Seven Years' War and was bitterly
disappointed when George III dropped Pitt in the midst of the struggle
(October 1761). While in Commons, Wilkes founded the *North Briton,* a
importunate and immensely popular newspaper. The *North Briton* was
wildly patriotic, distrustful of George III, and the government's reaction to
Wilkes over the affair of Number 45 in April 1763 (see p. 235) proved to be
remarkably inept. The journalist-MP became a martyr.

As he fought his case, Wilkes widened the scope of the issues. He
lectured and pamphleteered against the king, the king's friends in Parliament, and the unreformed constitution. For his troubles Wilkes lost his
parliamentary privilege, was wounded in a duel, survived an assassination
attempt, fled to France, and was expelled from the House of Commons.
Although Middlesex returned him to his seat in 1768, Wilkes's colleagues
refused to admit him. The procedure occurred a second, then a third time,
and finally Commons declared Wilkes's losing opponent from Middlesex
the borough's legal representative. Wilkes himself was arrested for sedition
and jailed for twenty-one months. He became a focus for discontent all over
England and beyond. Workers protesting bread prices rioted in his name.
Those demanding parliamentary reform and even Americans across the sea
called themselves Wilkesites. In 1769 some of his English backers established an organization called Supporters of the Bill of Rights, the first such
group to demand parliamentary reform. Petitions urged Wilkes's reinstate-
ment and he was vindicated. In the end, Wilkes became a national hero, lord
mayor of London, a sitting MP, and co-author of the first, and unsuccessful, bill advocating parliamentary reform. His newspapers began reporting
debates in the two Houses.

Prior to the 1790s, no figure in eighteenth-century Europe had
done more than Wilkes to organize public opinion beyond its traditionally
accepted political bases to become a factor in national life. The various
Wilkes affairs had given the lie to the benevolent reputation of the British
constitution. Parliament's stands against Wilkes showed it to be unrepre-
sentative of constituencies, dependent upon its royal patron, corrupt, prej-
udiced, and deathly frightened. If Parliament had erred in succumbing to

the government's vendetta against Wilkes, in the quarrel with the Americans its blunders were compounded. The great imperial crisis between 1764 and 1782 unveiled additional symptoms of Britain's constitutional malaise.

The Crisis in North America

In 1763 Bute's successor as prime minister, George Grenville, inherited a huge war debt. Furthermore, Grenville believed that English country gentlemen were paying too much of it (around 15 percent of their income went to taxes), and North Americans were paying too little. For their part, the colonists were very eager to settle territory newly conquered from France. To Grenville this meant expensive armed conflicts against Indians, which he did not want. Therefore, the minister declared a moratorium on westward expansion in North America. He then moved to suppress smuggling in American ports, enforced the Navigation Acts, and in 1765 proposed a stamp duty on newspapers and legal documents for the colonies. Parliament passed the Stamp Act. English residents had been paying such taxes for three-quarters of a century; however, the North Americans exploded in fury. To them the Stamp Act was tyrannical, and they responded accordingly.

However much the colonies differed from each other in religion, culture, and social custom; however much westward-looking pioneers scorned their coastal creditors or Virginia planters misunderstood Connecticut free farmers, Grenville's actions and Parliament's support encouraged solidarities in the New World and marked its distinctiveness from the Old. In no way was this more apparent than in political institutions. For Ireland a parliamentary act early in the eighteenth century at least had made clear Dublin's subservience to Westminster. For the American colonies, no such act existed. On one hand, colonists considered their right to representation in their colonial assemblies as a consequence of their rights as Englishmen. On the other, Westminster called on colonists to acknowledge subjection to a British Parliament in which they were not directly represented. Therefore, very early in the game, the economic problem of parliamentary taxation of the colonists veiled a deeper political issue: namely, Parliament's *right* to tax them. Americans believed that raising revenue was their prerogative alone. As John Adams said in 1765, "A Parliament in Great Britain can have no more right to tax colonies than a Parliament in Paris."

In the colonial clamor against the Stamp Act, American merchants boycotted British goods; shopkeepers and workers intimidated stamp distributors; and rioters in Massachusetts destroyed the home of the royal lieutenant governor. Nine colonial legislatures collectively denied Parliament's right to tax Americans. Feeling the pinch of the American boycott, England's shippers called for repeal of the Stamp Act. Caught in an impasse, Grenville's ministry resigned in 1765. Its successor, led by the marquess of Rockingham, advised expediency, and the king asked Commons to repeal the act. Accomplished in March 1766, the repeal avoided an open break;

however, the question of political authority remained unresolved. In fact, Parliament explicitly underscored its right "to make laws and statutes of sufficient force and validity to bind the colonies and people of America, subjects of the crown of Great Britain, in all cases whatsoever." In Britain, those who backed Wilkes and detested the unreformed nature of Parliament sympathized with the colonists. By emphasizing the legality of duties that regulated trade and admitting the illegality of duties that raised revenue, Pitt and his followers sought a compromise.

As Britain's postwar debt grew, Parliament in 1767 voted a series of regulatory import tariffs for the Americans, the so-called Townshend duties. Addressing themselves to political theory and insisting on the general illegality of taxation without representation, the colonists saw no distinction between Townshend's duties and Grenville's stamp tax. Between 1768 and 1770, relations between the government and colonists deteriorated again. Boycotts against British goods produced more incidents. Political groups formed in America and talked of separation from Britain. In March 1770, British troops in Boston fired on a crowd harassing them, and five colonists were killed. They became martyrs. Once more, the British tried conciliation. Another new ministry, that of Frederick, Lord North (1732–1792), withdrew the Townshend duties on all articles except tea.

Nevertheless, no atmosphere of mutual trust existed. Colonists accused the British of removing the Townshend duties in order to destroy American manufacturing with a flood of cheap articles. Nearly everywhere in America, politically radical "committees of correspondence" thrived. By 1773 Massachusetts alone had eighty of them. Incidents multiplied. A British revenue ship burned mysteriously in a colonial harbor; the British government dismissed the popular Benjamin Franklin as colonial postmaster. When the East India Company reduced its price of tea so drastically that American smugglers and middlemen alike were threatened with extinction, colonists in New York, Philadelphia, and Charleston refused to unload the product. In Boston they boarded the loaded ships in the harbor and threw £15,000 worth of tea over the side.

Conservative American merchants and political radicals forged a common cause, and in Britain the government was exasperated. Early in 1774 the king wrote, "The die is now cast. The colonies must now submit or triumph." Orders from Britain closed the port of Boston. The colonial charter for Massachusetts was suspended, and the commander of royal troops in America was appointed governor of the colony. Parliament extended French Canadian civil law and toleration of Catholics into the region between the Ohio River and Great Lakes. Americans in New York, Connecticut, Massachusetts, and Virginia interpreted this as a conscious attempt to discourage westward expansion.

In May 1774 the Virginia House of Burgesses called on representatives from all the colonial legislatures to attend a Continental Congress. Pennsylvania offered Philadelphia as the site. All but Georgia sent delegates.

Moderates at the Congress asked for recommendations that would restore harmony to Anglo-American relations without sacrificing the "just rights and liberties" of the colonies. Delegates from Massachusetts and radicals from elsewhere pointed out that as a consequence of the recent "Intolerable Acts," Massachusetts had neither rights nor liberties left. The Continental Congress condemned the Intolerable Acts and rejected the principle of parliamentary supremacy over the colonies. In England, Pitt (now Lord Chatham) and Whigs like Edmund Burke urged repeal of the Intolerable Acts. Lord North refused. The Continental Congress disbanded, and the colonial legislatures sanctioned its work. A new boycott of British goods occurred.

Large-scale violence broke out in America the following April when the Massachusetts governor, General Thomas Gage, lost 250 men (one-tenth of the entire royal detachment in the colony) during a fruitless quest for arms supposedly stored by the colonists at Concord. Lord North and Parliament now spoke openly of rebellion in America. In May 1775 a second Continental Congress meeting in Philadelphia disclaimed any intention of seceding from Britain and pleaded with George III to intervene with Parliament on the Americans' behalf. However, these sober conservatives also organized a Continental Army drawn from colonial militias and asked the Virginia planter George Washington (1732–1799) to lead it. By autumn of 1775 uprisings drove out all the royal governors. As the British withdrew their detachments from the colonies and tried to blockade the American coastal ports, most colonists clung to the hope that George III still might persuade Parliament to recognize the legitimacy of their cause. However, by January 1776 they understood that confidence in the king was an idle dream, and the tremendous public reception of the pamphlet *Common Sense* by the former exciseman Thomas Paine confirmed the new mood. Paine called George a morally despicable fool, "the royal brute of Great Britain," and the British House of Commons an "aristocratized tyranny." Bitterly attacking all monarchy in general, Paine demanded immediate separation from England.

On June 28, 1776, Thomas Jefferson of Virginia, John Adams of Massachusetts, and Benjamin Franklin of Pennsylvania submitted a draft declaration of independence to the Continental Congress. A week later, the declaration, with amendments, passed. The political theory of the document paraphrased Locke's philosophy of natural rights. The government of Great Britain had violated its compact with the governed, and the Americans had no recourse except to break their ties. The declaration enumerated a list of specific grievances. In essence, of course, the colonists were de facto independent before July 4, 1776. Powerful as Britain's militarized state had seemed to the world, the machinery of the old Whig government was intended to manage English society rather than rein in an empire. For George III and Parliament to choose now to rule America from London was a belated attempt to reconquer what already had been lost.

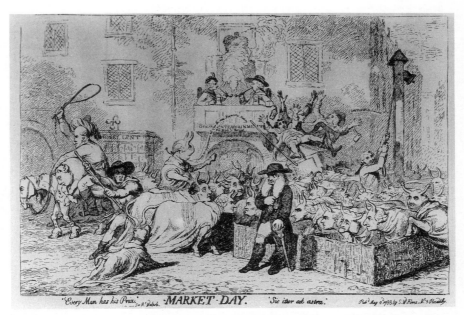

Figure 10.1—Cartoon by James Gillray, "Market Day: May 2, 1788." Last in a line of great eighteenth-century English satirists, Gillray pilloried church, state, and society for more than thirty years. In this cartoon, Gillray attacks the venality of the House of Lords, whose members appear for sale in the Smithfield cattle auction. The dour keeper in the foreground, holding his moneybag, is Lord Chancellor Thurlow, and King George III himself appears on the left, slung across a nag ridden by Warren Hastings, conqueror of India, who was about to be tried in the House of Lords for alleged corruption. William Pitt the Younger relaxes with his pipe and a beer on the balcony in the center, while Edmund Burke—Hastings's major accuser—is toppling into the pen. Courtesy of Dover Books, The Satirical Etchings of James Gillray, *edited by Draper Hill (New York, 1976).*

For six years, from 1775 until October 1781, reconquest eluded the British. Although Washington experienced troubles in raising an army and maintaining patriotic ardor among the Americans, Britain's difficulties proved insurmountable. The country was diplomatically isolated, its logistics and supply a nightmare. France, Spain, and the Dutch Netherlands recognized American independence and declared war on Britain. The scare of a French invasion of England silenced colonial sympathizers in Parliament and business. Nevertheless, while Anglican churchmen and country squires fearful of democratic contamination urged pressing the fight, the armies sent over the Atlantic lacked sufficient naval support to carry the day.

After 1780 Lord North himself doubted Britain's capacity to win the war. When General Charles Cornwallis and his force of 7,000 troops got themselves entrapped at Yorktown on the Virginia coast in October 1781,

North lost heart completely. His ministry fell the following March, and George III instructed his new government to seek terms with the Americans. By virtue of the Treaty of Versailles, Britain recognized the new nation. The distant Mississippi was set as its western boundary, the Great Lakes its northern one, Florida its southern. For the United States and Great Britain the difficult task at hand was to construct a new political relationship based on the search for common, yet independent, interests.

The First Reform Movement and Pitt the Younger

The Irish troubles, Wilkes, and the successful American Revolution made it clear that the halcyon days of the Whig oligarchy were past. Nor had George III been able to supplant oligarchic rule with royal leadership. But how was Britain to be governed? The question now was more serious than ever. Speaking for a new generation of Whig politicians, Edmund Burke offered a dignified and aristocratic program he called "Economical Reform": Reduce the influence and power of the throne, ensure honesty in Parliament, and allow its natural leaders to rule. Burke left room for the vision of a great British empire and for humanitarian treatment of Irish Catholics, but he could accept neither electoral reform nor the end to rotten boroughs. To do so, he claimed, would betray the prescriptive wisdom of the past. Burke mistrusted reason in politics, and he considered natural rights as illusions. His position was summed up in small gestures that would purify existing institutions, such as reduction of the number of sinecures in the royal household and prohibition of government contractors from sitting in Parliament.

On the other hand, the so-called dissenting academies already had produced genuine radicals. Because of their non-Anglican Protestantism, graduates of the academies were excluded from the universities and the civil service. Deeply influenced by Enlightenment thought, they believed in the inexorable advance of reason and equated virtue with one's value to society. Philip Doddridge, Joseph Priestley, and Richard Price, the leading Radical Dissenters, spoke for economically successful and politically unenfranchised tradespeople, merchants, craftspersons, and freeholders. They were pro-Wilkes and pro-American; they wished to abolish pocket and rotten boroughs, end patronage and management, establish annual responsible Parliaments, and give every male adult the vote. During Lord North's ministry (1770–1781) radicalism took root, and after 1778 it became dangerous. Unsuccessful in reforming institutions, radicals began thinking of replacing them. Some proposed an alternative to the unreformed Parliament, a grand national association of landowners, chosen by popularly elected county associations.

The association movement, revolutionary because self-appointed leaders were addressing themselves as the people's will, climaxed during the darkest period of the American war. It attracted discontented MPs and magnates, as well as the disenfranchised and opportunistic. From 1779 to mid-1780, dozens of meetings were held and many ideas posed. Although the influential Yorkshire leadership backed away from "associations" and instead proposed increasing the number of sturdy independent county MPs in the House of Commons, old-fashioned borough politicians sensed that a world was ending. Suddenly, in June 1780, an outbreak of savage violence in London, the Gordon Riots, frightened many moderates away from re-form. Ironically, the riots had nothing to do with the reform movement. They were directed against recent parliamentary efforts to assimilate Eng-lish Catholics into civil society. Catholic neighborhoods were burned down, jails broken into, and 2,000 prisoners set loose. Until the army restored order, John Wilkes himself led the militia to harness the mobs.

The rioting cruelly hurt the associationists' cause. As rioters, the people were viewed as incapable of political responsibility, and Burke's tinkering was accepted. Unable to find a stable ministry, in December 1783 George III reluctantly asked William Pitt's son to form a government. The younger Pitt's youth, vigor, and idealism seemed to signify a new begin-ning, and the reformers thought they had found a second life. Previously, Pitt had backed parliamentary redistricting, elimination of the most rotten boroughs, a program of free trade, and an end to the slave trade. He under-stood that industrialization and empire demanded a redistribution of politi-cal and social power in Britain.

However, Pitt was no revolutionary. His programs were not in-tended to democratize England but rather to release the country from aris-tocratic Whig control and give mercantile-industrial interests a larger voice in its future. Failing to get Parliament to eliminate either the rotten bor-oughs or slave trade, Pitt did persuade George III to pack the House of Lords with wealthy merchants. His India Act (1784) left patronage for the colony in the hands of the East India Company's directors, while granting overall administrative responsibility to the government. Pitt balanced gov-ernment debts at last, simplified customs duties, and reduced consumer import charges. Negotiating the tariff-reducing Eden treaty with France in 1786, he buried the last vestiges of British mercantilism. Enjoying the confidence of the king and keeping his distance from the Whig magnates, Pitt thus made England as safe for commerce and industry as it once had been for the landed gentry.

For the moment, a wave of material prosperity drowned out the radicals' cries for political reform, but the world beyond England also was changing. Between 1789 and 1792, momentous events in France destroyed the ancien régime there, and English radicalism revived in support of the French Revolution. Pitt determined that political unrest must not undo his work. He therefore asked the landed gentry and great merchants to cooper-ate in safeguarding England's institutions and keep the country out of foreign entanglements. As late as February 1792, while the French were destroying their aristocracy and monarchy, Pitt predicted fifteen additional years of peace for Europe. In April, however, Europe's kings declared war

Map 10.3—France in 1789

on the French Revolution, and in January 1793 the revolutionaries executed Louis XVI. England's great peacetime minister had no other choice
than to plunge his country into a conflict that was to last twenty years,
exceeding in scope and violence anything that had preceded it.

THE COLLAPSE OF THE ANCIEN RÉGIME IN FRANCE

Winners and Losers: 1763–1774

Between 1763 and 1774, France enjoyed good harvests and a modest commercial expansion based on the judicious use of credit. Wholesale wheat and
meat prices rose steadily, and large-scale agriculture became extremely profitable. As short-term rents skyrocketed, prospering absentee landlords invested in sumptuous town residences, shipbuilding, and overseas trade.
Aping the cultural lifestyles of the English country gentry, French nobles
and wealthy bourgeois alike purchased rural properties. Some were caught
up in the passion for "improvement," though never to the extent of their
contemporaries across the Channel. Of course, prosperity was relative and
there were losers too. Unable to keep up with inflation, French agricultural
tenants and urban workers were the chief victims. Entrapped by a rent
squeeze and unable to maintain their scattered plots before the onrushing
domain of landlords, peasants sold out to them and headed for towns. Their
sense of community lost, they became helpless atoms, floating about in an
unpoliced world of vagrants, prostitutes, and thieves.
    Private prosperity did not benefit the French state. During the
Seven Years' War military expenditures skyrocketed, and thereafter the costs
of building a navy gobbled state income. In 1763 the state debt doubled from
what it had been ten years earlier. Although finance ministers tried ingenious
means of raising fiscal revenue, direct taxpaying in France remained a mark
of social inferiority. Great churchmen and the entire nobility, shipbuilders,
holders of government trading monopolies, and most officeholders were exempt from paying the *taille,* the regime's chief revenue source. A 5 percent
emergency tax on land and offices, the *vingtième,* had been instituted in
1749, was doubled in 1756, and temporarily increased again several years
later. However, honest assessments were difficult to come by and exemptions
were purchased; so the *vingtièmes* failed to alleviate the government's fiscal
plight. Moreover, once money brought them a degree of status, tradesmen
preferred land purchase and other safe, dignified investments with tax breaks
to risky capitalist schemes. Therefore, peasants and urban workers, victims of
prosperity in the first place, were the chief source of the state's income, and
their contributions alone were insufficient for the state's needs. After 1770
it was clear that France no longer could sustain traditional forms of fiscal

privilege, but neither the Church nor favored individuals and groups would yield an inch. Mindful of its long night of dependence under Louis XIV, the French aristocracy did not find the idea of a dependent, financially strapped monarchy to be unpleasant at all.

France's thirty-four parlements and taxation courts particularly appreciated the image of royal ministers coming to them, hat in hand, desperately searching for funds. Seeking political concessions, the magistrates would bargain hard, and the financial desperation of the government helps explain why enlightened despotism failed in France. Another reason for its failure was royal indifference. Until 1770, Louis XV depended upon the duke de Choiseul, a brilliant soldier-diplomat who had guided France through the military disaster of the Seven Years' War. At the Peace of Paris in 1763, Choiseul's skills saved France's Caribbean sugar islands. In 1766 he managed the acquisition of Lorraine, and in 1768 he purchased Corsica from Genoa. Choiseul's abilities, however, lay in diplomacy, not domestic reform. By ridding France of the Jesuits in 1767, he hoped to ingratiate himself with the 2,300 influential magistrates sitting in the Parlement of Paris and other regional law and tax courts. He tried to convince these *robe* nobles of the need for increased and equitably distributed taxation.

By virtue of its extended judicial powers, especially its claimed right to debate and register royal orders before they became law, the Parlement of Paris stood out as France's major institutional opponent of uninhibited absolutism. Along with the regional parlements, it claimed vaguely defined authority over religion, law enforcement, corporations, public assistance, censorship, road building, taxes, and education. The regional parlements controlled the politics of many provincial cities and subsidized culture by establishing academies and funding both literary and scientific contests. Despite its flirtation with the Enlightenment, parlementary culture was essentially conservative, suspicious of most philosophes, skeptical of fiscal and administrative reform, and intensely patriotic. Because they considered the Jesuits to represent a fifth-column agency of the pope, *parlementaires* hated the religious order. Most importantly, by virtue of their landed and moneyed wealth, they were tied to the worlds of the military aristocracy and of finance. Although coordination of specific programs among the parlements may easily be exaggerated, the sovereign courts did form an influential social element in France. Politically, they were a dangerous source of opposition to the wills of the king and his ministers.

The Brittany affair illustrated the renewed strength of the parlements and contributed to Choiseul's downfall. Brittany was an isolated region whose parlement, provincial Estates, and rural nobility had always resisted the interference of Versailles in local matters. Early in the 1760s, the king's military commander in the province, the young duke d'Aiguillon, insisted that Brittany's fiscal charges were too light. Brittany's parlement told d'Aiguillon to mind his own business and then opposed the government's demand that the province pay for a series of military roads linking

Breton ports to the interior. The parlement at Rennes even challenged d'Aiguillon's contention that the government was authorized to build roads in the province. Choiseul supported d'Aiguillon, and in 1765 Brittany's parlement dissolved itself in protest. Its procurer-general Louis-René La Chalotais, his son, and four other *parlementaires* were arrested; but no judge could be found in Brittany to try the state's case. The Parlement of Paris backed La Chalotais, and at this point, on March 3, 1766, Louis XV reminded the magistrates of the absolute nature of the French monarchy (see pp. 215–216).

Characteristically, the king failed to follow through. The parlement in Brittany sat again and brought charges against d'Aiguillon, who was recalled. Other parlements converted the matter into a confrontation with the royal government. They corresponded with each other, challenged nearly every prerogative Louis had claimed in his Seance of Flagellation of 1766, declared themselves the genuine institutional representatives of the nation, and helped force Choiseul's fall from office. The king was advised to be firm. He now depended upon his chancellor, an able, ambitious lawyer, René-Nicolas Maupeou (1714–1792), and his controller-general of finance, an iron-willed priest, Joseph-Marie Terray (1715–1778). Maupeou knew the magistrates well. Before casting his lot with the royal administration, he himself had served in the Parlement of Paris. He believed that behind the Brittany affair lay a basic political and constitutional question: Who was to rule France—the king and his ministers or the parlementary magistrates?

As director of the treasury, Terray demanded a reform of the tax structure. He predicted a long bitter fight with the parlements. One way of averting such a struggle, however, was to reduce their powers drastically. Although it risked civil war, in January 1771 Louis permitted Maupeou to maneuver the Paris *parlementaires* into another rejection of royal authority. Then the king exiled them to the provinces and deprived them of their offices. Royal courts were established to assume most of the judicial functions of the old Parlement of Paris, and the tenure of newly chosen magistrates was revocable. Although the parlementary committee which had registered royal orders was retained and Louis delayed dissolving the provincial parlements, a beginning had been made. Maupeou believed that now the laws of France might be codified and unified, and Terray attacked the fiscal problem from several sides. He repudiated part of the national debt, suspended high interest payments on state loans, and forced new loans on financiers. He reassessed the *vingtième* on noble and clerical properties so that the tax might become a meaningful revenue source, and he renegotiated with the Farmers General their contract for indirect tax collection according to terms favorable to the government. Although Terray never attacked the fiscal exemptions enjoyed by socially privileged groups, his retrenchment policies were even less popular with the aristocracy than Maupeou's political coup d'état against the parlements had been. Still there was no violence. Becoming less interested than ever in public affairs, Louis allowed his reforming ministers free rein. They had three years. On April 29, 1774, court physicians observed an outbreak of small sores on the king's body. Two weeks later, he was dead of smallpox, leaving as successor a thoroughly unprepared twenty-year-old grandson.

Financial Crisis, Political Paralysis: 1774–1788

As dauphin, Louis XVI had spent nearly all his life in suburban palaces outside Paris. He did not know the capital and was totally ignorant of the country. Governmental affairs had been kept from him. His queen, the Austrian princess Marie Antoinette, sister of Joseph II, was an irresponsible, spoiled young woman chiefly interested in court intrigues. Her marriage to Louis in 1770 had been a consequence of the rapprochement between Bourbons and Hapsburgs; however, it never was well received in France, particularly among the *robe* aristocracy. The death of Louis XV had come at a critical moment. Maupeou and Terray were in midprogram; France had done nothing about the recent partition of Poland; an Austro-Russian alliance was poised to destroy the Ottoman Empire; and Britain's North American colonies were at the edge of rebellion.

Inexperienced, well intentioned, and stupid, the new king disliked the tyrannical ways of Maupeou and Terray. An aged courtier, the count de Maurepas, advised reconciliation with the aristocracy. Maupeou and Terray were dropped and the Parlement of Paris restored. The magistrates proclaimed victory over tyrants and looked forward to rebuilding their influence. Maurepas gave Louis a gifted new ministry. The intendant of Limoges, A.-R.-J. Turgot (1727–1781), became controller-general of finances. A disciple of the physiocrats and friend of the philosophes, Turgot had abolished the *corvée,* compulsory and nonremunerative road building by peasants, in his poor, remote intendancy. He also had improved canals and schools. Arriving at Versailles with many ideas, he reduced court expenses and removed collection of some indirect taxes from control of the Farmers General. In September 1774 he organized free export of grain from one province to another, a necessity if one was to prevent regional famine from degenerating into catastrophe. He suppressed the *corvée* throughout the kingdom and recommended a special landholder's tax to pay for road upkeep. Considering the right to work to be dictated by the laws of supply and demand, Turgot abolished most of the merchant and craft guilds. Whenever he could, he removed monopolies from private contractors and foresaw wide landowner participation in both local and national affairs. He also showed himself firm in moments of crisis. Following a poor harvest in spring 1775, Parisians feared that provisions intended for the capital might be sent to other hard-pressed regions. There was rioting. Turgot ringed the capital with 30,000 troops and hanged the riot leaders.

Other talented reformers entered Louis's first ministry: Malesherbes and Sartine, who as directors of the book trade earlier had tolerated circulation of the philosophes' works in France; the count de Vergennes, supporter of the American Revolution; the count de St. Germain, desirous of abolishing favoritism and unmerited officerships in the military. As usual, court and parlementary opposition challenged innovation. By May 1776 the queen and even Maurepas urged Louis to retreat. Turgot, Malesherbes, and St. Germain were dismissed. Saddened by the turn of events, the young king wrote, "Only Monsieur Turgot and I truly love our people." However, Louis XVI lacked courage to resist the pressures.

During the next eleven years financial crisis deepened. Searching for a solution, the government stumbled from ministry to ministry. Once the crisis cojoined with a series of poor harvests, new revolts by the parlements, and a general administrative paralysis, the ancien régime in France simply crumbled. Accelerating the financial catastrophe were the costs of the new war against Britain, which included the grant of supplies, loans, and troops to the American revolutionaries. In October 1776, Louis XVI restored the *corvée* and the guilds. Then he gave responsibility over state finances to a Geneva banker, Jacques Necker (1732–1804), who had made a fortune speculating in East India stocks. A technician rather than social reformer, Necker did not believe in strict economies or extended taxation. In order to lighten the state's burden of debt he resorted to credit. Necker's banking connections loaned the government huge sums at 8 to 10 percent interest, and half a billion livres enriched the treasury. Considering the intendants to have had too much power in the countryside, Necker proposed representative provincial assemblies which would assume some of the responsibilities held by the royal appointees. To test the scheme, Louis agreed to the assemblies in two provinces; but he was reluctant about extending the experiment to all of France.

For a while Necker's wizardry amazed all observers. France was financing a war without tax increases and without economies. By 1781, however, the loans began drying up and Necker's critics predicted that the bubble soon would burst. The clergy and parlements rankled that the nation's fortunes lay in the hands of a Swiss Protestant, and the American war bill stood at 2 billion livres. Furthermore, an economic recession had settled in. Wishing to justify his policies by appealing to public opinion, Necker published an accounting of his actions. He listed a 4 percent surplus of receipts over expenses and exposed the fact that one-tenth of government expenditures was being devoured by the pensions of aristocrats at court. However, in challenging his critics, Necker was less than candid. As his successor illustrated, his figures covered up the greatest expense of all, the American war. Church, court and parlementary attacks on him continued, and in May 1781 he resigned in a huff.

Most of Necker's successors were intelligent men saddled with the task of reestablishing the state's financial respectability within the framework of a fiscal system built on widespread privilege. As controller-general of finance from 1783 to 1787, Charles-Alexandre Calonne (1734–1802) first resorted to borrowing. The debt rose accordingly and expenses exceeded income by 20 percent. Once the sources of loans dried up, Calonne turned reformer. To increase revenue and halt mounting deficits, he proposed a new tax on land, called the territorial subvention, without the customary loopholes, and he urged the establishment of regional assemblies elected by prosperous landowners, the purpose of which would be supervising collection and administering public works projects.

Calonne knew that the parlements and provincial Estates would resist his reform and accuse him of reinstituting the despotism of the Maupeou-Terray years. Therefore, the controller-general tried a dangerous gamble. He asked the king to summon an Assembly of Notables, including great clerics, nobles, magistrates, and civic dignitaries. If the Assembly of Notables accepted his reforms, perhaps the parlements and Estates might be neutralized. Courageous as it was, the move failed. Handpicked by Calonne himself, the Assembly of Notables met in February 1787 and refused to adopt the controller-general's program. Angered, Calonne abandoned secrecy, published the text of his proposed reforms, and circulated a denunciation of what he considered to be the notables' self-serving delaying tactics. This crass appeal to public opinion infuriated the distinguished aristocrats in the assembly, and the notables attacked Calonne personally with cries of "ministerial despotism." Reform through the assembly now was impossible and Calonne was disgraced. In April 1787 Louis dismissed him and he left for England.

His successor, Étienne-Charles Loménie de Brienne, archbishop of Toulouse (1727–1794), was a political rival of Calonne's in the Assembly of Notables. Brienne now asked the notables to propose their own solution to the financial crisis; however, they resisted, declaring that only the "authentic representatives of the nation" had the right to grant a new tax. By authentic representatives the notables clearly did not mean the king's ministers. A royal tax decree would invite a new parlementary revolt, and the parlements themselves were not authorized to initiate legislation. The Assembly of Notables therefore asked for the convocation of an elected Estates-General, composed of representatives from the three social orders: clergy, nobility, and bourgeoisie. Such a body had met on occasion in the sixteenth century, but the hardening absolutism of the French monarchy had kept it out of political life for the past 170 years. Neither Louis nor his ministers desired to revive it. Thanking the Assembly of Notables for its suggestion, on May 25, 1787, the king dismissed the body.

Even if the Assembly of Notables had sanctioned Calonne's reforms, it is doubtful whether the French Revolution would have been avoided. In fact, the reforms themselves—abandonment of fiscal privilege and establishment of representative local administrations—were revolutionary, acknowledging abandonment of the traditional distinctions among the three Estates for more subtle variations based on property and wealth. Moreover, the economic condition of France in 1787 was grave. For the past ten years the post-1763 boom had given way to a prolonged recession. The production of wheat and wine was low. Except for poor harvest years, when they skyrocketed, prices generally lagged behind, thus contributing to hard times. Absolute famine and widescale mortality, supposedly relegated to the nightmarish seventeenth century, again seemed possible. There were other ominous signs: food shortages, rural unemployment, lack of demand for textiles, layoffs in urban industry, and social unrest in the form of roaming bands of the hungry. Moreover, landlords sought compensation for declining production and sales, hiring lawyers to hunt down abandoned feudal dues and increase those in existence.

Working a plot too small to support his family and saddled with rents already increased during the boom of the 1760s, the tenant farmer viewed this seigneurial reaction with immense bitterness. Taken by themselves, the feudal dues were more an inconvenience than a crushing burden. In difficult times, however, the petty payments to use the lord's mill, oven, wine press, and bull, as well as the services the peasant rendered to maintain manorial roads and manorial security, not only symbolized the regime of authority and subjection but also contributed to genuine economic hardship. The tenant still had to pay the *taille* to the state, the tithe to the Church, and rents which had doubled over the past half century. In the late 1770s free tenants were falling behind in their payments. Increasingly, farmers slipped into sharecropping or became migrant laborers. They blamed their misery on the seigneurial aristocracy, which controlled half of the country's rural property.

The Assembly of Notables dissolved, Brienne requested the Parlement of Paris to register as law most of Calonne's reform projects, including the territorial subvention and a stamp tax. The magistrates refused, declaring that only an Estates-General could legally sanction any new fiscal imposition. Promoting its self-declared role as protector of the people's liberties, the Parlement agreed to the ministry's Edict of Toleration, granting civil liberties to Protestants. However, such self-interested cooperation did not hide the fact that, as in the early 1770s, a constitutional crisis was erupting. *Parlementaires* in the provinces supported their Paris colleagues in opposing Brienne's tax measures. Tracts proliferated, and royal ministers once more were denounced as tyrants. Although the magistrates were defending privilege, they covered their position behind a shield of constitutional doctrine, and persuaded public opinion that they were saving France from despotism.

Exasperated, the government resorted to desperate acts. In August 1787 it declared as royal law both the territorial subvention and stamp tax. Louis exiled the Parlement of Paris to the city of Troyes. All political clubs in Paris were ordered closed. Meanwhile Prussian troops were putting down the Dutch Patriot revolt, and France was unable to come to the aid of the Patriots. As the exiled *parlementaires* still resisted the Crown, Brienne offered an olive branch: He would rescind the new taxes and simply extend the *vingtièmes* for four more years. The Parlement of Paris returned to the capital.

However, the compromise broke down in November, when Louis refused to permit parlementary discussion of fiscal matters, forced through registration of new government loans, and ordered the arrest of two magistrates.

For the next five months parlements renewed their opposition to Brienne's ministry. The Parlement of Paris condemned arbitrary government including royal *lettres de cachet,* declared that any new taxation had to be approved by an Estates-General, and published what the magistrates considered to be the "fundamental laws" of the kingdom. These included civil rights for all individuals and freedom of the press. Louis responded by accusing the *parlementaires* of wishing to turn France into an "aristocracy of magistrates." On May 8, 1788 the royal ministry issued six edicts, largely the work of Chrétien de Lamoignon, a former *parlementaire* now serving Louis XVI as keeper of the seals. With royal troops ringing the Palais de Justice, home of the Parlement of Paris, the government compelled the magistrates to accept a newly constituted supreme court composed of carefully selected *parlementaires,* princes, and ministers of state. The court was intended to assume parlementary political functions, including registration of royal orders. Already established local courts would assume parlementary judicial functions. The so-called May edicts also sought to replace seigneurial justice with royal jurisdiction and transferred some prerogatives of the provincial Estates to royal courts. Two intransigent *parlementaires* were arrested. However, the government underestimated the explosive consequences of the May edicts. From courtiers at Versailles to the petty rural nobility, most of aristocratic France stood with the Parlement of Paris. The Assembly of the Clergy and the Orléans branch of the house of Bourbon protested formally. Publicists dependent on the aristocracy for their livelihood printed tracts depicting the clergy and nobility as struggling to save the people's liberties from rapacious ministers.

Throughout the summer of 1788 indignation over the May edicts swept over France and public order seemed to be breaking down. In Rennes, capital of Brittany, the intendant was beaten up and had to flee. In Grenoble, rioting resulted in four deaths. In Pau, townspeople and mountaineers restored the parlement there to its customary functions while troops stood by idly. The country nobility was at the brink of revolt, and the king's army seemed untrustworthy. Royal absolutism was equated with Oriental despotism; petitions, remonstrances, and pamphlets called for a new constitutional arrangement for the country. Brienne retreated. On July 5, he invited written proposals on how an Estates-General might be convened. Early in August he learned that the treasury was empty, and by the middle of the month the government suspended payments on loans which had fallen due. Contemporaries equated the situation to admission of national bankruptcy. Brienne then suspended the May edicts, agreed to convene an Estates-General for May 1, 1789, and restored the parlements. He then resigned.

The Estates-General of 1789

Convinced that public opinion was behind them, *parlementaires* savored their triumph over the royal will. If tax reform was to come, they intended that an Estates-General controlled by the high clergy and nobility would wrench compensation from the government in the form of major political concessions. Breaking with the trends of enlightened despotism elsewhere in Europe, France then would become an aristocratized monarchy. However, the struggle between the parlements and royal ministry during the summer of 1788 had an unforeseen political consequence and became the prelude to wider and deeper unrest. For two centuries rival aristocratic elites—one ministerial, the other parlementary—had controlled the uneasy balance of political power in France. On one occasion, from 1648 to 1653, the balance was upset and the elites provoked a civil war. Under Louis XIV the ministerial aristocracy appeared to have gotten the upper hand, directing taxation, running the military, and distributing favors. However, even Louis knew that absolute government was based on reconciliation with elites, and the king courted their approval of his policies in municipal councils, provincial Estates, and parlements dominated by the *robe* aristocracy.

This political arrangement itself outlived Louis XIV and gave France a relatively stable government until the 1740s. Then an unprecedented growth of military expenditure, accompanied by France's waning prestige in Europe, created a new wave of antiministerial sentiment that was orchestrated by the Parlement of Paris. Although the new sentiment was expressed in the dignified language of constitutional principle, words were deceiving. The rules of the game were changing. By the 1770s and 1780s, at stake no longer was where the balance of aristocratic-royal government belonged, but rather the very *source* of political legitimacy in France. Apologists for the royal ministry and for the parlements alike appealed to history and natural law in order to determine what kind of country France properly should be. All previous certainties were abandoned. Whatever constitutional language the conflicting sides chose to use, the issue at hand was nothing less than the arrogation of political power.

Why this occurred at the time it did historians only now are beginning to ask. The skepticism of late Enlightenment thought, revived Jansenism, the state's financial crisis, France's loss of international prestige, flip-flops of royal weakness and aggressiveness—all may help to explain the growing tensions that converted late eighteenth-century politics into a life-and-death struggle between competing elites. The climax occurred in mid-1788 with the apparent parlementary victory. Dizzy with their triumph, however, *parlementaires* failed to see how the conflicts of a generation had offered the country an unprecedented political education. Both the parlementary and ministerial sides had used petitions, pamphlets, and tracts not merely to promote their causes, but more important, to court public opinion. By so doing the two sides unwittingly sharpened the political consciousness of nonelites, those heretofore denied a voice in the country's political life. The language of politics simply slipped from the hands of those who had controlled it for the past two hundred years.

In 1788 there were clear signals that politics no longer were limited to differing interpretations of elitist ideology. For example, in July 1788 a gathering of nearly five hundred nobles, clergy, and commoners from the province of Dauphiné protested the May edicts and demanded both the restoration of the parlements and convocation of the province's Estates, defunct since the early seventeenth century. This accomplished, Dauphiné's nonaristocrats went further, proposing that the Estates be freely elected, that bourgeois members have as many seats as the clergy and nobles combined, and that voting inside the Estates be by head rather than by order. Elsewhere in France programs to revive provincial Estates followed Dauphiné's procedural example, and shortly thereafter pamphleteers were demanding a doubled Third Estate and vote by head in the impending Estates-General. This contradicted traditionally accepted systems of representation and balloting, by which the combined wills of clergy and nobility generally prevailed over that of the outvoted, underrepresented bourgeoisie.

In retrospect, it is a wonder that antiaristocratic political consciousness had remained dormant for so long. For an entire generation, urban professionals, shopkeepers, physicians, law clerks, merchants, artists, writers, low-rank military officers, and skilled artisans had been receptive to the Enlightenment and had followed with excitement the course of unrest in Great Britain and revolution in North America. All the while, France's warring political elites were appealing to public opinion in order to justify rival claims to political power. In 1771 Maupeou had hired hack writers to champion his reforms, and his enemies used the presses of the Parlement of Paris to resist him. Turgot prefaced his edicts with preambles that sought to convince readers, and Necker's published *Compte rendu* of 1781 was clearly intended to revive his sagging popularity. Louis XV hesitated abolishing the provincial parlements in toto in 1771 because he did not want to appear to be a despot, and Louis XVI restored them to full power three years later because he believed that it was the public's desire.

By the 1770s public opinion very definitely had become a factor in French politics. Ten years later this opinion was calling for action. As the nonaristocrats in Dauphiné made their revolutionary proposals in July 1788, political clubs revived throughout the country. The clubs adopted specific programs which went beyond grievances and questions aimed at the government. They challenged France's political and social leadership directly, asking such questions as: Why had a bankrupt regime tolerated fiscal privilege for so long? When would corporate "liberties" be translated into civil equality? What was to be done about the abuses inherent in officeholding and arbitrary justice? What was to be done about corruption in the clergy? Why were landed seigneurs permitted to squeeze dry their tenants? Why were parlements, provincial Estates, and guilds allowed to strangle the political life of the country's regions? Pamphlets circulated anew, awakening bourgeois political consciousness over the issue of the Estates-General. They called for a doubling of the Third Estate, vote by head, and overhaul of the tax structure. A hard-edged underground literature accompanied the tolerated pamphlets. It discussed political issues in irreverent, pornographic, and violent ways. Not even the royal family was spared. Politics had turned wholly public. Government censorship controls collapsed.

Necker replaced Brienne. Given a second chance, the Swiss banker tried to pacify the aristocracy by recognizing the parlements and reconvening the Assembly of Notables. He let it be known that he favored an Estates-General with increased representation for the Third Estate. Agreeing that the Estates-General should propose the needed tax reforms, he would not commit himself on the crucial procedural question of vote by order or head. However, the Parlement of Paris and Assembly of Notables insisted that the forthcoming Estates-General should imitate as closely as possible the procedures dominating the previous one, which had met in 1614–1615. Each of the three orders should have an equal number of delegates, and the vote should be by order.

Bitterly disappointed by these positions, the bourgeoisie ceased to be taken in by aristocratic propaganda. It was clear that the only liberties which interested the magistrates and notables were their own. They knew that some form of constitutional government and an end to fiscal privilege were in the offing, and they were determined to keep reform from degenerating into a democratization of political and social life. Above all, they wished to gain control over the king, protect seigneurial rights, and maintain officeholding. The strategy of the Parlement of Paris backfired badly. By year's end the public support it had enjoyed in May 1788 totally disintegrated. During the last three months of the year, pamphlets inundated France at a rate of five dozen per week. Most of them denounced the privileged orders and called for vote by head in a freely elected Estates-General dominated by the bourgeoisie. Recognizing the new course that events had taken, in January 1789 the Swiss journalist Mallet Du Pan wrote, "The debate has changed aspect. The issue of the king, ministerial despotism, and the constitution have become secondary. Now it's war between the Third Estate and the other two Orders."

Mallet was prophetic. The Royal Council tried compromise. In the forthcoming Estates-General, it declared, the number of bourgeois delegates might equal the number of clerics and nobles combined; however, it was assumed that voting would be by order. In early spring 1789 adult males in France went to the polls and voted for delegates to the Estates-General. Elections took place in open meetings—40,000 in all—at which time memoranda of grievances called *cahiers de doléances* were drawn up. Nobles and clergy elected their delegates more or less directly. For the

Third Estate, however, male taxpayers twenty-five years and older gathered together to choose electors, two representing every hundred households. These electors then chose the district's representative to the Estates-General. As a result of the elimination process, men of speaking ability and with knowledge of public affairs were the ones ultimately elected to represent the Third Estate. Not a single peasant, not a single town laborer, went to the great conclave at Versailles. In all, more than 1,100 delegates were chosen: 303 for the clergy, of whom nearly two-thirds were parish priests; 282 for the nobility, of whom one-third had expressed public sympathy for nonaristocrats; and 578 for the Third Estate, nearly half of whom were lawyers.

The delegates brought with them the distillations of the 40,000 *cahiers de doléances,* grievances that revealed a country in deep trouble. *Cahiers* from peasant villages denounced the universe of seigneurial privilege and exaction superimposed on the burden of high rents, insufficient land, and the state's tax demands. The *cahiers* of townspeople reflected the conflicting aspirations of workers and employers, artisans and merchants. The *cahiers* of the nobility called for constitutional government and accepted the end to tax privilege, but they also demanded maintenance of the prevailing social hierarchy. Practically no *cahier* questioned the monarchical conception of the state, and there was large agreement for the need to enlarge civil liberties and establish representative political assemblies in all the provinces. There was widespread agreement that ministerial tyranny was intolerable, that France should have a written constitution, and that the Estates-General should vote on taxes. The country seethed with anticipation and excitement. The harvest of 1788–1789 had been the worst in years, and scarcities resulted in very high grain and bread prices. In good times the French town worker paid half his income for bread. Now 80 to 90 percent was required. Textile sales dropped sharply; the building trades braked to a halt. By April 1789 half the urban labor force was idle, and in the countryside bands of human misery clogged roads. Manor houses were sacked. Urban riots erupted, including two serious ones in Paris which brought the army into the streets.

In such a volatile atmosphere the Estates-General gathered at Versailles on May 4, and the king opened the assembly the next day. Although everyone expected the Estates-General to bring change, rigid seventeenth-century forms of procedure were in force. Members of the Third Estate had to dress in black, keep their heads bare in deference to the clergy and nobility, and even enter the meeting hall through a side door. Louis XVI, Marie Antoinette, and the court attended the opening ceremonies, but the royal speech greatly disappointed Third Estaters, who had hoped that the king would make a dramatic recommendation for the vote by head. Instead, Louis warned against excessive reforms, and the government speeches that followed were silent about both voting procedure and redistribution of the tax burden. By the next day it was clear that the regime had no program.

At this point the Third Estate initiated its parliamentary revolution. The commoners would do nothing until the three orders met in a single assembly and delegates voted by head. Invitations were sent to the clergy and nobles to verify credentials in common. In their separate meeting halls, the delegates of the Church voted against joining the commoners by 133 to 114; the nobles did the same, by 188 to 46. Attempts at concilation proved fruitless, and for the next six weeks the great convocation was stalemated. Meanwhile the Third Estaters organized their leadership. On June 10 they sent another invitation to the two privileged Estates to join them in the verification of credentials. Three priests arrived. Seven days later, verification of its membership complete, the Third Estate assumed the title of National Assembly, formally declared the universe of orders to be null and void, and announced that it alone stood for the French nation. This was not meant to be the nation in the traditional sense, composed of hierarchical corporate fragments, each with distinctive liberties, privileges, rights, and obligations. It was meant to be a community of citizens.

Revolution in France

The declaration of June 17 was a seizure of power. Once again, clergy and nobles were invited to join the commoners. Sixteen priests came, and on June 19 a majority in the clerical Estate voted to enter the National Assembly. Assembly delegates affirmed their right to authorize taxation. The gauntlet had been thrown down. By their own will, the commoners had just invalidated a constituted representative body, and now they were assuming powers over taxation. Deeply concerned, the king decided to address a joint session of the three orders and hurriedly scheduled it for the commoners' meeting hall. Carpenters were set to work to refurbish the room. Somehow, however, word failed to reach the commoners, and as they assembled on June 20, they found themselves locked out of their customary meeting place. While the carpenters worked within, troops guarded the building. Suspecting a plot, the delegates were drenched by a sudden downpour. Nearby was an unused indoor tennis court. In a state of anxiety, anger, and determination, they rushed for the arena to hear some impassioned speeches. Next they swore an oath "never to separate and to gather wherever circumstances dictated until a constitution was written and solidified upon firm foundations."

The royal session took place on June 23. It was a stormy occasion. Inspired by the court and goaded by a Parlement suddenly committed to the cause of royal authority, Louis unequivocally declared that any program for change must emanate from the throne. Self-constituted political groups like the so-called National Assembly were illegal. The royal position was that seigneurial dues and all forms of privilege represented inviolable rights of property. The king promised decisions on taxation and constitutional reform. The government would introduce a system of provincial assemblies.

Louis scolded the delegates for having accomplished nothing, reminded them that his explicit approval alone gave legal sanction to their recommendations, and commanded that they return to their different chambers to resume their sessions. Louis then left the hall, followed by his royal officials, most of the noble delegates, and a few of the clerical ones. All the other deputies remained in the chamber.

The event would not be forgotten. Faced with the choice, the king had forsaken the commoners for the aristocracy. He had insisted that the old orders must be preserved. Disappointed but not cowed, the deputies remaining in the chamber cheered wildly as a repentant aristocrat, the marquis de Mirabeau, declared that bayonets alone would drive the National Assembly from its appointed task. On June 25 the assembly met again. More clergy joined. So did nearly fifty noble delegates, including the king's cousin, the duke d'Orléans. On June 27, Louis made a sudden about-face. Exhausted, grieving over the recent death of his eldest son, and hearing of renewed violence in the countryside, he agreed to the transformation of the Estates-General into the Constituent National Assembly. He ordered all the delegates to gather together at once. Observers considered the crisis surmounted. An Englishman in France at the time, the agrarian innovator Arthur Young, called the revolution "complete."

Of course, Young was wrong. It was only the beginning. One-third of the deputies to the National Assembly were there simply because their exasperated king had ordered them to attend, and they sullenly refused to participate in assembly deliberations. From this nucleus of aristocrats and clerics who believed that the constitutional legitimacy of the French monarchy was being torn asunder, the counterrevolution would emerge and influence the course of France's history for the next quarter century. Already in the late spring of 1789, however, those wishing to preserve the old order of things were clearly on the defensive. The monarchy's inability to cope with economic crisis, social injustice, and political mismanagement had ignited a desire for fundamental change, and the recent boldness of the Third Estate gave direction. The essential problem facing the National Assembly in June 1789 was not the consolidation of past victories, but how far the revolution would go.

It went very far, destroying the very alliance of monarchy, Church, and aristocracy on which the ancien régime had been built. Although the most radical changes would occur in France, where the old alliance had been perfected and served as an example to the other states of Europe, the revolution itself became an international phenomenon. Within a few years the Northern and Southern Netherlands, Italy, Germany, Spain, the Caribbean, and Latin America would feel its shock waves. Subsequently, for millions the French Revolution came to represent history's most inspiring political dream. During the summer of 1789 the urban and rural poor of France would themselves become revolutionaries, preventing royal countermeasures, pressing their prosperous and reluctant leaders into radical actions, and eventually bearing the ideology of change far beyond France's borders.

This book, however, is not about the revolution. It is about the long-term political, social, and cultural conditions in Europe that gave way to a revolution. Curiously enough, revolts introduced our period. They illustrated that even in the mid-seventeenth century, people could respond passionately to political mismanagement, social injustice, and economic crisis. For the century that followed, however, the elites who directed the ancien régime tried patching up difficulties with administrative, ideological, and symbolic solutions that brought relative sense and order to Western civilization. Absolutism and Enlightenment coexisted in a tense kind of harmony, while economic improvement and growing literacy helped create a more articulate populace than had been the case in previous centuries. Increased political, cultural, and social awareness yielded heightened hope and expectations. Once the elites of the ancien régime revealed the limits to fulfilling popular aspirations and engaged in a renewed series of internal conflicts, old Europe was endangered. In 1789 its destruction began. Some would say that a new, chilling, and even more exploitative order succeeded the ancien régime. But that is another story.

BIBLIOGRAPHY

With a few exceptions, what follows is a bibliography of books in English published since the first edition of *Crisis, Absolutism, Revolution* (1977). While the bibliography does not pretend to be comprehensive, it can serve as a working guide to further research.

CHAPTER 1

Addy, John. *Sin and Society in the Seventeenth Century*. 1989.
Alexander, John T. *Bubonic Plague in Early Modern Russia: Public Health and Urban Disaster*. 1980.
Amelang, James S. *Honored Citizens of Barcelona: Patrician Culture and Class Relations, 1490–1714*. 1986.
Anderson, Bonnie S., and Judith P. Zinsser, eds. *A History of Their Own: Women in Europe from Pre-History to the Present*, vol. 2, 1988.
Anderson, M. S. *War and Society in Europe of the Old Regime, 1618–1789*. 1988.
Avrich, Paul. *Russian Rebels, 1600–1800*. 1972.
Barry, Jonathan, ed. *The Tudor and Stuart Town*. 1990.
Beatty, J. M. *Crime and the Courts in England, 1660–1800*. 1986.
Beier, Lucinda McCray. *Sufferers and Healers: The Experience of Illness in Seventeenth-Century England*. 1987.
Bertrand, Marc, ed. *Popular Traditions and Learned Culture in France: From the Sixteenth to the Twentieth Century*. 1985.
Borsay, Peter, ed. *The Eighteenth-Century Town*. 1990.
———. *The English Urban Renaissance: Culture and Society in the Provincial Town, 1660–1770*. 1989.
Boxer, Marilyn J., and Jean H. Quataert, eds. *Connecting Spheres: Women in the Western World, 1500 to the Present*. 1987.
Braudel, Fernand. *Civilization and Capitalism: 15th–18th Century*. 3 vols. 1982–1984.
Breidenthal, Renate, and Claudia Koonz, eds. *Becoming Visible: Women in European History*. 1977.
Bromley, J. S., ed. *The Rise of Great Britain and Russia, 1644–1715/25*. Vol. 6 of *The New Cambridge Modern History*. 1970.
Carsten, F. L., ed. *The Ascendancy of France, 1648–1688*. Vol. 5 of *The New Cambridge Modern History*. 1961.
Chandler, David G. *The Art of Warfare in the Age of Marlborough*. 1976.
Chartres, John, and David Hey, eds. *English Rural Society, 1500–1800. Essays in Honour of Joan Thirsk*. 1990.

Chaunu, Pierre. *La Civilisation de l'Europe classique.* 1966.

Childs, John. *Armies and Warfare in Europe, 1648–1789.* 1982.

———. *The Army of Charles II.* 1976.

Clark, Alice. *Working Life of Women in the Seventeenth Century.* 1982. [Original edition, 1919.]

Clark, J. C. D. *English Society, 1688–1832: Ideology, Social Structure and Political Practice During the Ancien Régime.* 1982.

———. *Revolution and Rebellion: State and Society in England in the Seventeenth and Eighteenth Century.* 1986.

Cockburn, J. S., ed. *Crime in England, 1550–1800.* 1977.

Corvisier, André. *Armies and Societies in Europe, 1494–1789.* 1979.

Cragg, Gerald R. *The Church and the Age of Reason, 1648–1789.* 1966.

Cressy, David. *Literacy and the Social Order: Reading and Writing in Tudor and Stuart England.* 1980.

Deyon, Pierre, et al. *Les Hésitations de la croissance, 1580–1740.* Vol. 2 of Pierre Léon, ed. *Histoire économique et sociale du monde.* 1978.

Doyle, William. *The Old European Order, 1660–1800.* 1978.

Duby, Georges, and Armand Wallon, eds. *Histoire de la France rurale,* vol. 2. 1975.

Duffy, M., ed. *The Military Revolution and the State.* 1980.

Durston, Christopher George. *The Family in the English Revolution.* 1989.

Edwards, John. *The Jews in Christian Europe.* 1988.

Fairchilds, Cissie C. *Poverty and Charity in Aix-en-Provence, 1640–1789.* 1976.

Flandrin, Jean-Louis. *Families in Former Times: Kinship, Household, and Sexuality.* 1979.

Flinn, M. W. *The European Demographic System, 1500–1820.* 1980.

Forster, Robert, and Orest Ranum, eds. *Deviants and the Abandoned in French Society: Selections from the "Annales."* 1978.

George, Margaret. *Women in the First Capitalist Society: Experiences in Seventeenth-Century England.* 1988.

Goody, Jack et al., ed. *Family and Inheritance: Rural Society in Western Europe, 1200–1800.* 1976.

Goubert, Pierre. *The Ancien Régime: French Society 1600–1750.* 1972.

———. *The French Peasantry in the Seventeenth Century.* 1986.

Grigg, David. *Population Growth and Agricultural Change: An Historical Perspective.* 1980.

Hanson, Carl A. *Economy and Society in Baroque Portugal, 1668–1703.* 1981.

Hellie, Richard. *Slavery in Russia, 1450–1725.* 1982.

Herrup, Cynthia B. *The Common Peace: Participation and the Criminal Law in Seventeenth-Century England.* 1987.

Hittle, J. Michael. *The Service City: State and Townsmen in Russia, 1600–1800.* 1979.

Hoffer, Peter C., and N. E. H. Hull. *Murdering Mothers: Infanticide in England and New England, 1558–1803.* 1981.

Hoffman, Philip T. *Church and Community in the Diocese of Lyon, 1500–1789.* 1984.

Israel, Jonathan. *European Jewry in the Age of Mercantilism, 1550–1750.* 1985.

Kagan, Richard L. *Lawsuits and Litigants in Castile, 1500–1700.* 1981.

Kann, Robert A., and David V. Zdenck. *The Peoples of the Eastern Habsburg Lands, 1526–1918.* 1984.

Kaplan, Steven L., ed. *Understanding Popular Culture: Europe from the Middle Ages to the Nineteenth Century.* 1984.

Katz, David S. *Philo-Semitism and the Readmission of the Jews to England, 1603–1655.* 1982.

———. *Sabbath and Sectarianism in Seventeenth-Century England.* 1988.

Keep, John H. L. *Soldiers of the Tsar: Army and Society in Russia, 1462–1874.* 1985.

Klaits, Joseph. *Servants of Satan: The Age of Witch Hunts.* 1985.

Konvitz, Josef W. *Cities and the Sea: Port Planning in Early Modern Europe.* 1978.

Labrousse, Ernest, ed. *Des derniers temps de l'âge seigneurial aux préludes de l'âge industriel (1660–1789).* Vol. 2 of Fernand Braudel and Ernest Labrousse, eds. *Histoire économique et sociale de la France.* 1970.

Laslett, Peter. *The World We Have Lost.* 1966.

Levack, Brian P. *The Witch-Hunt in Early Modern Europe.* 1987.

MacDonald, Michael. *Mystical Bedlam: Madness, Anxiety, and Healing in Seventeenth-Century England.* 1981.

Macfarlane, Alan. *The Origins of English Individualism: The Family, Property, and Social Transition.* 1978.

———. *Marriage and Love in England: Modes of Reproduction, 1300–1840.* 1986.

Mennell, Stephen. *All Manners of Food: Eating and Taste in England and France from the Middle Ages to the Present.* 1985.

Mitterauer, Michael, and Reinhard Sieder. *The European Family: Patriarchy to Partnership from the Middle Ages to the Present.* 1982.

Motley, Mark E. *Becoming a French Aristocrat: The Education of the Court Nobility, 1500–1715.* 1990.

Muchembled, Robert. *Popular Culture and Elite Culture in France, 1400–1750.* 1985.

Muller, Sheila D. *Charity in the Dutch Republic: Pictures of Rich and Poor for Charitable Institutions.* 1985.

Munsche, P. B. *Gentlemen and Poachers: The English Game Laws, 1671–1831.* 1981.

Norberg, Kathryn. *Rich and Poor in Grenoble, 1600–1814.* 1985.

Nutton, Vivian, ed. *Medicine at the Courts of Europe, 1500–1837.* 1990.

Parker, Geoffrey. *The Geopolitics of Domination: Territorial Supremacy in Europe.* 1988.

———. *The Military Revolution: Military Innovation and the Rise of the West, 1500–1800.* 1989.

Perry, Ruth. *The Celebrated Mary Astell: An Early English Feminist.* 1986.

Pike, Ruth. *Penal Servitude in Early Modern Spain.* 1983.

Pollock, Linda A. *Forgotten Children: Parent-Child Relations from 1500 to 1900.* 1983.

Reinhard, Marcel et al., eds. *Histoire générale de la population mondiale,* 3rd ed. 1968.

Roebuck, Peter. *Yorkshire Baronets: Families, Estates, and Fortunes.* 1980.

Sabean, David Warren. *Power in the Blood: Popular Culture and Village Discourse in Early Modern Germany.* 1984.

Spufford, Margaret. *Small Books and Pleasant Memories: Popular Fiction and Its Readers in Seventeenth-Century England.* 1981.

Stone, Lawrence. *Family, Sex and Marriage in England, 1500–1800.* 1977.

Thomas, Keith. *Man and the Natural World: A History of Modern Sensibility.* 1983.

Treasure, Geoffrey. *The Making of Modern Europe, 1648–1780,* 2nd ed. 1985.

Walter, John, and Roger Schofield, eds. *Famine, Disease, and the Social Order in Early Modern Society.* 1989.

Wolf, Eric R. *Europe and the People Without History.* 1982.

Wrigley, E. A. *Population and History.* 1969.

————, and R. S. Schofield. *The Population History of England, 1541–1871.* 1981.
Yelling, J. A. *Common Field and Enclosure in England, 1450–1850.* 1977.

CHAPTER 2

Boxer, C. R. *The Dutch Seaborne Empire: 1600–1800.* 1965.
Cameron, Rondo E. *A Concise Economic History of the World.* 1989.
Chambers, J. D. *Population, Economy, and Society in Pre-Industrial England.* 1972.
Clark, John G. *La Rochelle and the Atlantic Economy During the Eighteenth Century.* 1981.
Clarkson, L. A. *The Pre-Industrial Economy in England, 1500–1750.* 1974.
Coleman, D. C. *The Economy of England, 1450–1750.* 1977.
————, ed. *Revisions in Mercantilism.* 1969.
DeVries, Jan. *The Economy of Europe in an Age of Crisis.* 1976.
————. *European Urbanization, 1500–1800.* 1984.
Ekelund, Robert B., and Robert B. Tollison. *Mercantilism as a Rent-Seeking Society.* 1981.
Furber, Holden. *Rival Empires of Trade in the Orient: 1600–1800.* 1976.
Gutmann, Myron P. *Toward the Modern Economy: Early Industry in Europe, 1500–1800.* 1988.
Israel, Jonathan I. *Dutch Primacy in World Trade, 1585–1740.* 1989.
————. *Empires and Entrepots: The Dutch, the Spanish Monarchy, and the Jews, 1585–1713.* 1989.
Jones, D. W. *War and Economy in the Age of William III and Marlborough.* 1988.
Kammen, Michael. *Empire and Interest: The American Colonies and the Politics of Mercantilism.* 1970.
Kriedte, Peter. *Peasants, Landlords, and Merchant Capitalists: Europe and the World Economy, 1500–1800.* 1983.
Kussmaul, Ann. *A General View of the Rural Economy of England, 1538–1840.* 1990.
Lampe, John R., and Marvin R. Jackson. *Balkan Economic History, 1550–1950: From Imperial Borderlands to Developing Nations.* 1982.
Landes, David S. *Revolution in Time: Clocks and the Making of the Modern World.* 1983.
Lis, Catharina, and Hugo Soly. *Poverty and Capitalism in Pre-Industrial Europe.* 1979.
MacLeod, Christine. *Inventing the Industrial Revolution: The English Patent System, 1660–1800.* 1989.
Mayr, Otto. *Authority, Liberty, and Automatic Machinery in Early Modern Europe.* 1986.
Mintz, Sidney W. *Sweetness and Power: The Place of Sugar in Modern History.* 1986.
Rapp, Richard Tilden. *Industry and Economic Decline in Seventeenth-Century Venice.* 1976.
Rich, E. E., and C. H. Wilson, eds. *The Cambridge Economic History of Europe.* Vol. 4, *The Economy of Expanding Europe in the Sixteenth and Seventeenth Centuries.* 1967. Vol. 5, *The Economic Organization of Early Modern Europe.* 1977.
Ringrose, David R. *Madrid and the Spanish Economy, 1560–1850.* 1983.
Schaeper, Thomas J. *The French Council of Commerce, 1700–1715.* 1983.
Thirsk, Joan. *Economic Policy and Projects: The Development of a Consumer Society in Early Modern England.* 1978.
Tracy, James D. *The Rise of Merchant Empires: Long-Distance Trade in the Early Modern World, 1350–1750.* 1990.

Wallerstein, Immanuel. *The Modern World System.* Vol. 2, *Mercantilism and Consolidation of the European World Economy.* New York, 1980.
Weatherill, Lorna. *Consumer Behaviour and Material Culture in Britain, 1660–1760.* 1988.
Wilson, Charles. *The Dutch Republic and the Civilization of the Seventeenth Century.* 1968.
———. *England's Apprenticeship, 1603–1763.* 1965.
———, and G. Parker, eds. *An Introduction to the Sources of European Economic History, 1500–1800.* 1977.

CHAPTER 3

Aylmer, G. E. *Rebellion or Revolution? England, 1640–1660.* 1986.
Barker, Nancy Nichols. *Brother to the Sun King: Philippe, Duke of Orléans.* 1989.
Baxter, Douglas Clark. *Servants of the Sword: French Intendants of the Army, 1630–1670.* 1976.
Baxter, Stephen B., ed. *England's Rise to Greatness, 1660–1763.* 1983.
Beik, William. *Absolutism and Society in Seventeenth-Century France: State Power and Provincial Aristocracy in Languedoc.* 1985.
Black, Jeremy, ed. *Knights Errant and True Englishmen: British Foreign Policy, 1660–1800.* 1989.
———. *The Rise of the European Powers, 1679–1793.* 1990.
Bonney, Richard. *Political Change in France Under Richelieu and Mazarin, 1624–1661.* 1978.
———. *Society and Government in France Under Richelieu and Mazarin, 1624–1661.* 1988.
Carswell, John. *From Revolution to Revolution: England 1688–1776.* 1973.
Casey, James. *The Kingdom of Valencia in the Seventeenth Century.* 1979.
Childs, John. *The Army, James II, and the Glorious Revolution.* 1980.
Clifton, Robin. *The Last Popular Rebellion: The Western Risings of 1685.* 1984.
Coward, Barry. *The Stuart Age: A History of England, 1603–1714.* 1980.
Davis, J. C. *Fear, Myth, and History: The Ranters and the Historians.* 1986.
Dow, F. D. *Cromwellian Scotland, 1651–1660.* 1979.
Dyrvik, Stale et al., eds. *The Satellite State in the Seventeenth and Eighteenth Centuries.* 1979.
Ekberg, Carl J. *The Failure of Louis XIV's Dutch War.* 1979.
Elliott, J. H. *Imperial Spain 1469–1716.* 1963.
Finlayson, Michael G. *Historians, Puritanism, and the English Revolution: The Religious Factor in English Politics Before and After the Interregnum.* 1983.
Fletcher, Anthony. *Reform in the Provinces: The Government of Stuart England.* 1986.
Forster, Robert, and Jack P. Greene, eds. *Preconditions of Revolution in Early Modern Europe.* 1970.
Golden, Richard M., ed. *Church, State, and Society Under the Bourbon Kings of France.* 1982.
———. *The Godly Rebellion: Parisian Curés and the Religious Fronde, 1652–1662.* 1981.
———, ed. *The Huguenot Connection: The Edict of Nantes, Its Revocation, and Early French Migration to South Carolina.* 1988.

Greaves, Richard. *Deliver Us from Evil: The Radical Underground in Britain, 1660–1663.* 1986.

Haley, K. H. D. *The Dutch in the Seventeenth Century.* 1972.

Harris, R. W. *Clarendon and the English Revolution.* 1983.

Hatton, Ragnhild, ed. *Louis XIV and Absolutism.* 1976.

———, ed. *Louis XIV and Europe.* 1976.

Hill, Christopher. *Change and Continuity in Seventeenth-Century England.* 1975.

———. *A Nation of Change and Novelty: Politics, Religion, and Literature in Seventeenth-Century England.* 1991.

Hirst, Derek. *Authority and Conflict: England 1603–1658.* 1986.

Holmes, Geoffrey. *Politics, Religion, and Society in England, 1689–1742.* 1987.

Horwitz, Henry. *Parliament, Policy, and Politics in the Reign of William III.* 1977.

Howard, Michael. *War in European History.* 1976.

Hutton, Ronald. *Charles the Second, King of England, Scotland, and Ireland.* 1990.

———. *The Restoration: A Political and Religious History of England and Wales, 1658–1667.* 1985.

James, Francis. *Ireland in the Empire, 1688–1770. A History of Ireland from the Williamite Wars to the Eve of the American Revolution.* 1973.

Jones, Clyve, ed. *Britain in the First Age of Party, 1680–1750.* 1987.

———, ed. *Party Management and Parliament, 1660–1784.* 1984.

———, ed. *A Pillar of the Constitution: The House of Lords in British Politics, 1640–1784.* 1989.

Jones, J. R. *Country and Court: England 1658–1714.* 1978.

———. *Charles II: Royal Politician.* 1987.

Kamen, Henry. *Spain in the Later Seventeenth Century, 1665–1700.* 1980.

Kenyon, J. P. *Revolution Principles—The Politics of Party, 1689–1720.* 1977.

Kettering, Sharon. *Patrons, Brokers, and Clients in Seventeenth-Century France.* 1986.

Kishlansky, Mark A. *Parliamentary Selection: Social and Political Choice in Early Modern England.* 1986.

———. *The Rise of the New Model Army.* 1979.

Klaits, Joseph. *Printed Propaganda Under Louis XIV: Absolute Monarchy and Public Opinion.* 1976.

Livermore, Harold V. *A New History of Portugal.* 1976.

Lynch, John. *Spain Under the Habsburgs.* Vol. 2, *Spain and America, 1598–1700.* 1981.

Manning, Brian. *The English People and the English Revolution, 1640–1649.* 1976.

Marin, Louis. *Portrait of the King.* 1988.

McKay, Derek. *Prince Eugene of Savoy.* 1977.

———, and H. M. Scott. *The Rise of the Great Powers, 1648–1815.* 1983.

Mettam, Roger. *Power and Faction in Louis XIV's France.* 1988.

Miller, John. *The Glorious Revolution.* 1983.

Monod, Paul Kleber. *Jacobitism and the English People, 1688–1788.* 1989.

Mousnier, Roland. *The Institutions of France Under the Absolute Monarchy, 1598–1789.* 2 vols. 1979, 1984.

Nader, Helen. *Liberty in Absolutist Spain: The Habsburg Sale of Towns, 1516–1700.* 1990.

Pennington, D. H. *Europe in the Seventeenth Century.* 2nd ed. 1989.

Plumb, J. H. *The Origins of Political Stability: England 1675–1725.* 1967.

Pocock, J. G. A., ed. *Three British Revolutions: 1641, 1688, 1776.* 1980.

Pruett, John H. *The Parish Clergy Under the Later Stuarts: The Leicestershire Experience.* 1978.

Richardson, R. C. *The Debate on the English Revolution.* 1977.

———. *The Debate on the English Revolution Revisited.* 1988.

Roberts, Clayton. *Schemes and Undertakings: A Study of English Politics in the Seventeenth Century.* 1985.

Roots, Ivan. *Commonwealth and Protectorate: The English Civil War and Its Aftermath.* 1966.

Rowen, Herbert H. *John de Witt, Grand Pensionary of Holland: 1625–1672.* 1978.

———. *The Princes of Orange: The Stadholders in the Dutch Republic.* 1988.

Sahlins, Peter. *Boundaries: The Making of France and Spain in the Pyrenees.* 1989.

Schama, Simon. *The Embarrassment of Riches: An Interpretation of Dutch Culture in the Golden Age.* 1988.

Schwoerer, Lois G. *The Declaration of Rights, 1689.* 1981.

Seaward, Paul. *The Cavalier Parliament and the Reconstruction of the Old Regime, 1661–1667.* 1989.

Sedgwick, Alexander. *Jansenism in Seventeenth-Century France.* 1977.

Sonnino, Paul. *Louis XIV and the Origins of the Dutch War.* 1988.

——— et al., eds. *The Reign of Louis XIV.* 1990.

Speck, W. A. *Reluctant Revolutionaries: Englishmen and the Revolution of 1688.* 1988.

Stradling, R. A. *Europe and the Decline of Spain: A Study of the Spanish System, 1580–1720.* 1981.

———. *Philip IV and the Government of Spain, 1621–1665.* 1988.

Symcox, Geoffrey. *Victor Amadeus II: Absolutism in the Savoyard State, 1675–1730.* 1983.

Woolrych, Austin H. *Commonwealth to Protectorate.* 1982.

Zagorin, Perez, ed. *Culture and Politics from Puritanism to the Enlightenment.* 1980.

CHAPTER 4

Anderson, M. S. *Peter the Great.* 1978.

Barker, Thomas M. *Army, Aristocracy, and Monarchy: Essays on War, Society, and Government in Austria, 1618–1780.* 1982.

Carsten, F. L. *A History of the Prussian Junkers.* 1989.

Crummey, Robert D. *Aristocrats and Servitors: The Boyar Elite in Russia, 1613–1689.* 1983.

Davies, Norman. *God's Playground: A History of Poland,* vol. 1, 1982.

Derry, T. K. *A History of Scandinavia: Norway, Sweden, Denmark, Finland, and Iceland.* 1979.

Dukes, David. *The Making of Russian Absolutism, 1613–1801.* 1982.

Evans, R. J. W. *The Making of the Habsburg Monarchy, 1550–1700. An Interpretation.* 1979.

Fedorowicz, J. K. et al., eds. *A Republic of Nobles: Studies in Polish History to 1864.* 1982.

Friedrichs, Christopher. *Urban Society in an Age of War: Nörlingen, 1580–1720.* 1979.

Furhmann, Joseph T. *Tsar Alexis, His Reign and His Russia.* 1981.

Hellmuth, Eckhart, ed. *The Transformation of Political Culture: England and Germany in the Late-Eighteenth Century.* 1990.

Ingrao, Charles W. *In Quest and Crisis: Emperor Joseph I and the Habsburg Monarchy*. 1979.

Kann, Robert A. *A History of the Habsburg Empire, 1526–1918*. 1974.

Koch, H. W. *A History of Prussia*. 1978.

Lauring, Palle. *A History of Denmark*, 7th ed. 1986.

Lukowski, Jerzy Tadeusz. *Liberty's Folly: The Polish-Lithuanian Commonwealth, 1697–1795*. 1990.

Massie, Robert K. *Peter the Great: His Life and World*. 1980.

Metcalf, Michael, ed. *The Riksdag: A History of the Swedish Parliament*. 1987.

Mitchell, Otis C. *A Concise History of Brandenburg Prussia to 1786*. 1980.

Peterson, Claes. *Peter the Great's Administration and Judicial Reforms: Swedish Antecedents and the Process of Reception*. 1979.

Raeff, Marc. *Imperial Russia: The Coming of Age of Modern Russia*. 1971.

———. *Understanding Imperial Russia: State and Society in the Old Regime*. 1984.

———. *The Well-Ordered Police State: Social and Institutional Change Through Law in the Germanies and Russia, 1600–1800*. 1983.

Riasanovsky, Nicholas V. *The Image of Peter the Great in Russian History and Thought*. 1985.

Roberts, Michael. *The Swedish Imperial Experience, 1560–1718*. 1979.

Rosenberg, Hans. *Bureaucracy, Aristocracy, and Autocracy: The Prussian Experience, 1660–1815*. 1958.

Rystad, Göran. *Europe and Scandinavia: Aspects of the Process of Integration in the Seventeenth Century*. 1983.

Spielman, John P. *Leopold I of Austria*. 1976.

Sysyn, Frank E. *Between Poland and the Ukraine: The Dilemma of Adam Kysil, 1600–53*. 1985.

Thadden, Rudolf von. *Prussia: The History of a Lost State*. 1987.

Vann, James A. *The Making of a State—Württemberg 1593–1793*. 1984.

———. *The Swabian Kreis: Institutional Growth in the Holy Roman Empire*. 1977.

———, and S. W. Brown, eds. *The Old Reich: Essays on German Political Institutions, 1496–1806*. 1974.

Vierhaus, Rudolf. *Germany in the Age of Absolutism*. 1989.

Whaley, Joachim. *Religious Toleration and Social Change in Hamburg, 1529–1819*. 1985.

Wittram, R. *Peter I, Czar und Kaiser*. 2 vols. 1964.

Zamoyski, Adam. *The Polish Way: A Thousand Year History of the Poles and Their Culture*. 1987.

CHAPTER 5

Abrahams, Roger, and John F. Szmed. *After Africa*. 1983.

Axtell, James. *The Invasion Within: The Contest of Cultures in Colonial North America*. 1985.

Bennett, Norman R. *Africa and Europe: From Roman Times to National Independence*. 1984.

Bethell, Leslie, ed. *Colonial Spanish America*. 1987.

Boxer, C. R. *The Church Militant and Iberian Expansion, 1440–1770*. 1978.

Bridenbaugh, Carl, and Roberta Bridenbaugh. *No Peace Beyond This Line: The English in the Caribbean, 1624–1690*. 1972.

Burkholder, Mark A., and Lyman L. Johnson, eds. *Colonial Latin America.* 1990.

Canny, Nicholas. *Kingdom and Colony: Ireland in the Atlantic World, 1560–1800.* 1988.

————, and Anthony Pagden, eds. *Colonial Identity in the Atlantic World, 1500–1800.* 1987.

Chapin, Bradley. *Early America.* 1968.

Claypole, William, and John Robottom. *Caribbean Story.* Vol. 1, *Foundations.* 1990.

Cohen, William B. *The French Encounter with Africans: White Responses to Blacks, 1530–1880.* 1980.

Cole, Jeffrey A. *The Potosí Mita, 1573–1700: Compulsory Indian Labor in the Andes.* 1985.

Cressy, David. *Coming Over: Migration and Communication Between England and New England in the Seventeenth Century.* 1987.

Crosby, Alfred W. *Ecological Imperialism: The Biological Expansion of Europe, 900–1900.* 1986.

Cushner, Nicholas P. *Spain in the Philippines, from Conquest to Revolution.* 1971.

Davies, Kenneth. G. *The North-Atlantic World in the Seventeenth Century.* 1974.

Davis, Ralph. *The Rise of the Atlantic Economies.* 1973.

Djait, Hïchem. *Europe and Islam.* 1989.

Eccles, W. J. *France in America.* 1972.

Dunn, Richard S. *Sugar and Slaves: The Rise of the Planter Class in the English West Indies, 1624–1713.* 1972.

Gernet, Jacques. *China and the Christian Impact: A Conflict of Cultures.* 1985.

Gibson, Charles. *Spain in America.* 1966.

Goslinga, Cornelius Ch. *The Dutch in the Caribbean and on the Wild Coast.* 1985.

Greene, Jack P. *Peripheries and Center: Constitutional Development in the Extended Polities of the British Empire and the United States.* 1986.

————, and J. R. Pole. *Colonial British America: Essays in the New History of the Early Modern Era.* 1984.

Hallett, Robert Robin. *Africa to 1875: A Modern History.* 1970.

Henretta, James A. *Evolution and Revolution: American Society, 1600–1820.* 1987.

Honour, Hugh. *The European Vision of America.* 1975.

Hsu, Immanuel C. Y. *The Rise of Modern China.* 1975.

Huang, Ray. *China: A Macrohistory.* 1988.

Kessell, John L. *Kiva, Cross, and Crown: The Pecos Indians and New Mexico, 1540–1840.* 1987.

Klein, Herbert S. *African Slavery in Latin America and the Caribbean.* 1986.

Lang, James. *Portuguese Brazil: The King's Plantation.* 1979.

Lewis, Bernard. *The Muslim Discovery of Europe.* 1982.

Lloyd, Trevor O. *The British Empire, 1558–1983.* 1984.

Lockhart, James, and Stuart B. Schwartz. *Early Latin America: A History of Colonial Spanish America and Brazil.* 1983.

Majumdar, R. C., ed. *The Maratha Supremacy.* Vol. 8 of *The History and Culture of the Indian People.* 1977.

McAllister, Lyle. *Spain and Portugal in the New World, 1492–1750.* 1985.

McCusker, John J., and Russell R. Menard. *The Economy of British America, 1607–1789.* 1985.

McGowan, Bruce. *Economic Life in the Ottoman Empire: Taxation, Trade, and the Struggle for Land, 1600–1800.* 1981.

McNeill, John Robert. *Atlantic Empires of France and Spain: Louisbourg and Havana, 1700–1763.* 1985.

Meinig, D. W. *The Shaping of America: A Geographical Perspective on Five Hundred Years of History.* 1986.

Merwick, Donna. *Possessing Albany, 1630–1710: The Dutch and English Experiences.* 1990.

Naquin, Susan, and Evelyn S. Rawski. *Chinese Society in the Eighteenth Century.* 1986.

Pak, Hyobom. *China and the West: Myths and Realities in History.* 1974.

Palmer, Colin A. *Human Cargoes: The British Slave Trade to Spanish America, 1700–1739.* 1981.

Postma, Johannes M. *The Dutch in the Atlantic Slave Trade, 1600–1815.* 1989.

Rafael, Vincente L. *Contracting Colonialism: Translation and Christian Conversion in Tagalog Society Under Early Spanish Rule.* 1988.

Rawley, James A. *The Transatlantic Slave Trade: A History.* 1981.

Rediker, Marcus. *Between the Devil and the Deep Blue Sea: Merchant Seamen, Pirates, and the Anglo-American Maritime World, 1700–1750.* 1987.

Reid, Anthony. *Southeast Asia in the Age of Commerce, 1450–1680.* 1988.

Sansom, George B. *A History of Japan.* 3 vols. 1958–1963.

Setton, Kenneth M. *Venice, Austria, and the Turks in the Seventeenth Century.* 1990.

Shaw, Stanford Jay. *History of the Ottoman Empire and Modern Turkey.* 2 vols. 1976–1977.

Sheridan, Richard B. *Sugar and Slavery: An Economic History of the British West Indies, 1623–1775.* 1974.

Silver, Timothy H. *A New Face on the Countryside: Indians, Colonists, and Slaves in South Atlantic Forests, 1500–1800.* 1990.

Spence, Jonathan D. *Emperor of China: A Self-Portrait of K'ang-hsi.* 1974.

——. *The Search for Modern China.* 1990.

Steele, Ian K. *The English Atlantic, 1675–1740: An Exploration of Communication and Community.* 1986.

Sugar, Peter F. *Southeastern Europe Under Ottoman Rule, 1354–1804.* 1977.

Thompson, Leonard M. *A History of South Africa to 1870.* 1990.

Thompson, Roger. *Women in Stuart England and America: A Comparative Study.* 1974.

Wolpert, Stanley A. *A New History of India.* 1982.

Worden, Nigel. *Slavery in Dutch South Africa.* 1985.

Wortman, Miles L. *Government and Society in Central America, 1680–1840.* 1982.

CHAPTER 6

Alpers, Svetlana. *The Art of Describing: Dutch Art in the Seventeenth Century.* 1983.

Appleby, Joyce Oldham. *Economic Thought and Ideology in Seventeenth-Century England.* 1978.

Ashcraft, Richard. *Revolutionary Politics and Locke's "Two Treatises of Government."* 1986.

Brockliss, L. W. B. *French Higher Education in the Seventeenth and Eighteenth Centuries: A Cultural History.* 1987.

Burke, Peter. *Popular Culture in Early Modern Europe.* 1978.

Eisenach, Eldon J. *Two Worlds of Liberalism: Religion and Politics in Hobbes, Locke, and Mill.* 1981.

Eisenstein, Elizabeth L. *The Printing Press as an Agent of Change: Communications and Cultural Transformations in Early-Modern Europe.* 2 vols. 1979.

Franklin, Julian A. *John Locke and the Theory of Sovereignty: Mixed Monarchy and the Right of Resistance in the Political Thought of the English Revolution.* 1978.

French, Roger, and Andrew Wear, eds. *The Medical Revolution in the Seventeenth Century.* 1989.

Grafton, Anthony, and Ann Blair, eds. *The Transmission of Culture in Early Modern Europe.* 1990.

Grant, Ruth W. *John Locke's Liberalism.* 1987.

Greyerz, Kaspar von, ed. *Religion and Society in Early Modern Europe, 1500–1800.* 1984.

Hahn, Roger. *The Anatomy of a Scientific Institution: The Paris Academy of Sciences, 1666–1803.* 1971.

Hall, A. Rupert. *Philosophers at War: The Quarrel Between Newton and Leibniz.* 1980.

Hall, David D. *Worlds of Wonder, Days of Judgment: Popular Religious Belief in Early New England.* 1989.

Harth, Erica. *Ideology and Culture in Seventeenth-Century France.* 1983.

Hill, Christopher. *The Experience of Defeat: Milton and Some Contemporaries.* 1984.

Houston, R. A. *Literacy in Early Modern Europe: Culture and Education, 1500–1800.* 1988.

Hunter, Michael. *Science and Society in Restoration England.* 1981.

Jacob, James R. *Robert Boyle and the English Revolution.* 1977.

Jacob, Margaret C. *The Cultural Meaning of the Scientific Revolution.* 1988.

———. *The Newtonians and the English Revolution, 1689–1720.* 1976.

———. *The Radical Enlightenment: Pantheists, Freemasons, and Republicans.* 1981.

Keeble, N. H. *The Literary Centers of Non-Conformity in Later Seventeenth-Century England.* 1987.

Keohane, Nannerl O. *Philosophy and the State in France: The Renaissance to the Enlightenment.* 1980.

Kors, Alan Charles. *Atheism in France, 1650–1729.* Vol. 1, *The Orthodox Sources of Disbelief.* 1990.

Macpherson, C. B. *The Political Theory of Possessive Individualism: Hobbes to Locke.* 1962.

Pagden, Anthony, ed. *The Languages of Political Theory in Early Modern Europe.* 1987.

Ranum, Orest. *Artisans of Glory: Writers and Historical Thought in Seventeenth-Century France.* 1980.

Rapaczynski, Andrzej. *Nature and Politics: Liberalism in the Philosophies of Hobbes, Locke, and Rousseau.* 1987.

Speck, W. A. *Society and Literature in England, 1700–1760.* 1983.

Sullivan, Robert E. *John Toland and the Deist Controversy: A Study in Adaptations.* 1982.

Tarcov, Nathan. *Locke's Education for Liberty.* 1984.

Walton, Gary. *Louis XIV's Versailles.* 1986.

Wood, Neal. *The Politics of Locke's Philosophy: A Social Study of "An Essay Concerning Human Understanding."* 1983.

CHAPTER 7

Adams, Thomas M. *Bureaucrats and Beggars: French Social Policy in the Age of Enlightenment.* 1990.

Anderson, M. S. *Europe in the Eighteenth Century: 1713–1783,* 3rd ed. 1987.

Andrew, Donna T. *Philanthropy and Police: London Charity in the Eighteenth Century.* 1989.

Bamford, Paul W. *Privilege and Profit: A Business Family in Eighteenth-Century France.* 1988.

Berg, Maxine. *The Age of Manufactures: Industry, Innovation, and Work in Britain, 1700–1820.* 1985.

Bergeron, Louis. *Inerties et Révolutions, 1730–1840.* Vol. 3 of Pierre Léon, ed. *Histoire économique et sociale du monde.* 1978.

Black, Jeremy. *Eighteenth-Century Europe, 1700–1789.* 1990.

Blum, Jerome. *The End of the Old Order in Rural Europe.* 1978.

Bonac, Ivo, and Paul Bushkovitch, eds. *The Nobility in Russia and Eastern Europe.* 1983.

Borsay, Peter, ed. *The Eighteenth-Century Town.* 1990.

Brennan, Thomas Edward. *Public Drinking and Popular Culture in Eighteenth-Century Paris.* 1988.

Callahan, William J., and David Higgs, eds. *Church and Society in Catholic Europe of the Eighteenth Century.* 1979.

Cameron, Ian A. *Crime and Repression in the Auvergne and the Guyenne, 1720–1790.* 1981.

Cameron, John. *Aristocratic Century: The Peerage of Eighteenth-Century England.* 1984.

Chambers, J. D., and G. E. Mingay. *The Agricultural Revolution, 1750–1880.* 1966.

Chaunu, Pierre. *La Civilisation de l'Europe des lumières.* 1970.

Corfield, P. J. *The Impact of English Towns, 1700–1800.* 1982.

Curtin, Philip. *The Atlantic Slave Trade: A Census.* 1969.

———— et al., eds. *Africans in Bondage: Studies in Slavery and the Slave Trade.* 1986.

Darmon, Pierre. *Damning the Innocent: A History of the Persecution of the Impotent in Pre-Revolutionary France.* 1986.

Davis, David Brion. *The Problem of Slavery in the Age of Revolution, 1770–1823.* 1975.

DeLacy, Margaret. *Prison Reform in Lancashire, 1700–1850: A Study in Local Administration.* 1986.

Etlin, Richard A. *The Architecture of Death: The Transformation of the Cemetery in Eighteenth-Century Paris.* 1984.

Fairchilds, Cissie C. *Domestic Enemies: Servants and Their Masters in Old Regime France.* 1984.

Fox-Genovese, Elizabeth. *The Origins of Physiocracy: Economic Revolution and Social Order in Eighteenth-Century France.* 1976.

Freeze, Gregory L. *The Russian Levites: Parish Clergy in the Eighteenth Century.* 1977.

Frey, Linda, and Marsha Frey. *Societies in Upheaval: Insurrections in France, Hungary, and Spain in the Early Eighteenth Century.* 1987.

Garrioch, David. *Neighbourhood and Community in Paris, 1740–1790*. 1986.

Gelfand, Toby. *Professionalizing Modern Medicine: Paris Surgeons and Medical Science and Institutions in the Eighteenth Century*. 1980.

Georgelin, J. *Venise au siècle des lumières*. 1978.

Hartwell, R. M., ed. *The Causes of the Industrial Revolution in England*. 1967.

Hay, Douglas et al. *Albion's Fatal Tree: Crime and Society in Eighteenth-Century England*. 1975.

Hertz, Deborah Sadie. *Jewish High Society in Old-Regime Berlin*. 1988.

Hill, Bridget. *Women, Work, and Sexual Politics in Eighteenth-Century England*. 1989.

Hoppit, Julian. *Risk and Failure in English Business, 1700–1800*. 1987.

Hufton, Olwen H. *Europe: Privilege and Protest, 1730–1789*. 1980.

———. *The Poor of Eighteenth-Century France, 1750–1789*. 1974.

Isherwood, Robert M. *Farce and Fantasy: Popular Entertainment in Eighteenth-Century Paris*. 1986.

Jones, Colin. *Charity and "Bienfaisance": The Treatment of the Poor in the Montpellier Region, 1740–1815*. 1982.

Kaplan, Steven Laurence. *Bread, Politics, and Political Economy in the Reign of Louis XV*. 2 vols. 1976.

———. *Provisioning Paris: Merchants and Millers in the Grain and Flour Trade During the Eighteenth Century*. 1984.

———, and Cynthia J. Koop, eds. *Work in France: Representations, Meaning, Organization, and Practice*. 1986.

Komlos, John. *Nutrition and Economic Development in the Eighteenth-Century Habsburg Monarchy*. 1989.

Kosáry, Domokos. *Culture and Society in Eighteenth-Century Hungary*. 1987.

Langbein, John. H. *Torture and the Law of Proof: Europe and England in the Ancien Régime*. 1977.

LaVopa, Anthony J. *Grace, Talent, and Merit: Poor Students, Clerical Careers, and Professional Ideology in Eighteenth-Century Germany*. 1988.

LeGoff, T. J. A. *Vannes and Its Region: A Study of Town and Country in Eighteenth-Century France*. 1981.

Maccubin, Robert Purks, ed. *'Tis Nature's Fault: Unauthorized Sexuality During the Enlightenment*. 1987.

Malcomson, Robert W. *Life and Labour in England, 1700–1780*. 1981.

Mathias, Peter. *The Transformation of England: Essays on the Economic and Social History of England in the Eighteenth Century*. 1979.

Maza, Sarah. *Servants and Their Masters in Eighteenth-Century France: The Uses of Loyalty*. 1983.

McClynn, Frank. *Science and Punishment in Eighteenth-Century England*. 1989.

McKendrick, Neil, John Brewer, and J. H. Plumb. *The Birth of a Consumer Society: The Commercialization of Eighteenth-Century England*. 1982.

Miller, Joseph C. *Way of Death: Merchant Capitalism and the Angolan Slave Trade, 1730–1830*. 1988.

Porter, Roy. *English Society in the Eighteenth Century*. 1982.

Post, John D. *Food Shortage, Climatic Variability, and Epidemic Disease in Preindustrial Europe: The Mortality Peak in the Early 1740s*. 1985.

Raeff, Marc. *Origins of the Russian Intelligentsia: The Eighteenth-Century Nobility*. 1966.

Ransel, David, ed. *The Family in Imperial Russia: New Lines of Historical Research.* 1978.

Riley, James C. *The Eighteenth-Century Campaign to Avoid Disease.* 1987.

———. *International Government Finance and the Amsterdam Capital Market, 1740–1815.* 1980.

———. *Population Thought in the Age of Demographic Revolution.* 1985.

Roche, Daniel. *The People of Paris.* 1986.

Rousseau, G. S., and Roy Porter, eds. *Sexual Underworlds of the Enlightenment.* 1988.

Rudé, George. *Paris and London in the Eighteenth Century.* 1971.

Schwartz, Robert M. *Policing the Poor in Eighteenth-Century France.* 1988.

Sherwood, Joan. *Poverty in Eighteenth-Century Spain: The Women and Children of the Inclusa.* 1988.

Sonenscher, Michael. *The Hatters of Eighteenth-Century France.* 1987.

———. *Work and Wages: Natural Law, Politics, and the Eighteenth-Century French Trades.* 1989.

Spencer, Samia I., ed. *French Women and the Age of Enlightenment.* 1984.

Stein, Robert Louis. *The French Slave Trade in the Eighteenth Century: An Old Regime Business.* 1979.

Tackett, Timothy. *Priest and Parish in Eighteenth-Century France: A Social and Political Study of the Curés in a Diocese of Dauphiné, 1750–1791.* 1977.

Traer, James F. *Marriage and the Family in Eighteenth-Century France.* 1980.

Troyansky, David G. *Old Age in the Old Regime: Image and Experience in Eighteenth-Century France.* 1989.

Williams, Alan. *The Police of Paris, 1718–1789.* 1979.

Woloch, Isser. *Eighteenth-Century Europe: Tradition and Progress, 1715–1789.* 1982.

CHAPTER 8

Anderson, Wilda C. *Between the Library and the Laboratory: The Language of Chemistry in Eighteenth-Century France.* 1984.

Bailey, Charles. *French Secondary Education, 1763–1790: The Secularization of Ex-Jesuit Colleges.* 1978.

Baker, Keith Michael. *Condorcet: From Natural Philosophy to Social Mathematics.* 1974.

Bender, John. *Imagining the Penitentiary: Fiction and the Architecture of Mind in Eighteenth-Century England.* 1987.

Berlin, Isaiah. *Vico and Herder: Two Studies in the History of Ideas.* 1976.

Betts, C. J. *Early Deism in France.* 1984.

Birn, Raymond, ed. "The Printed Word in the Eighteenth Century," in *Eighteenth-Century Studies*, 17(4). 1984.

Black, Jeremy. *The English Press in the Eighteenth Century.* 1987.

Blum, Carol. *Rousseau and the Republic of Virtue: The Language of Politics in the French Revolution.* 1986.

Braham, Allan. *The Architecture of the French Enlightenment.* 1980.

Browne, Alice. *The Eighteenth-Century Feminist Mind.* 1987.

Bryson, Norman. *Word and Image: French Painting of the Ancien Régime.* 1981.

Burke, Peter. *Vico.* 1985.

Camic, Charles. *Experience and Enlightenment: Socialization for Cultural Change in Eighteenth-Century Scotland.* 1983.

Carnochan, W. B. *Gibbon's Solitude: The Inward World of the Historian.* 1987.

Carpenter, Kenneth, ed. *Books and Society in History.* 1983.

Censer, Jack, and Jeremy D. Popkin, eds. *Press and Politics in Pre-Revolutionary France.* 1987.

Chartier, Roger. *The Cultural Uses of Print in Early Modern France.* 1987.

———. *Cultural History: Between Practices and Representations.* 1988.

———. *The Cultural Origins of the French Revolution.* 1991.

Chisick, Harvey. *The Limits of Reform in the Enlightenment: Attitudes Toward the Education of the Lower Classes in Eighteenth-Century France.* 1981.

Cranston, Maurice W. *Philosophers and Pamphleteers: Political Theorists of the Enlightenment.* 1986.

Crow, Thomas. *Painters and Public Life in Eighteenth-Century Paris.* 1985.

Cunningham, Andrew, and Roger French, eds. *The Medical Enlightenment of the Eighteenth Century.* 1990.

Darnton, Robert. *The Business of Enlightenment: A Publishing History of the Encyclopédie, 1775–1800.* 1979.

———. *The Great Cat Massacre and Other Episodes in French Cultural History.* 1984.

———. *The Literary Underground of the Old Regime.* 1982.

Donakowski, Conrad L. *A Muse for the Masses: Ritual and Music in an Age of Democratic Revolution, 1770–1870.* 1977.

Donnert, Erich. *Russia in the Age of Enlightenment.* 1986.

Ellenburg, Stephen. *Rousseau's Political Philosophy: An Interpretation from Within.* 1976.

Foucault, Michel. *Discipline and Punish: The Birth of the Prison.* 1978.

Frängsmyr, Tore, ed. *Linnaeus: The Man and His Work.* 1983.

——— et al. *The Quantifying Spirit in the Eighteenth Century.* 1990.

Fried, Michael. *Absorption and Theatricality: Painting and the Beholder in the Age of Diderot.* 1980.

Gascoigne, John. *Cambridge in the Age of Enlightenment: Science, Religion, and Politics from the Restoration to the French Revolution.* 1989.

Gay, Peter. *The Enlightenment: An Interpretation.* 2 vols. 1966, 1969.

Gelbart, Nina Rattner. *Feminine and Opposition Journalism in Old Regime France: "Le Journal des Dames."* 1987.

Gillispie, Charles Coulston. *The Montgolfier Brothers and the Invention of Aviation, 1783–1784.* 1983.

———. *Science and Polity in France at the End of the Old Regime.* 1980.

Goodman, Dena. *Criticism in Action: Enlightenment Experiments in Political Writing.* 1988.

Graff, Harvey J. *The Legacies of Literacy: Continuities and Contradictions in Western Culture and Society.* 1987.

Gunn, J. A. W. *Beyond Liberty and Property: The Process of Self-Recognition in Eighteenth-Century Political Thought.* 1983.

Hampson, Norman. *A Cultural History of the Enlightenment.* 1968.

———. *Will and Circumstance: Montesquieu, Rousseau, and the French Revolution.* 1983.

Hankins, Thomas L. *Science and the Enlightenment.* 1985.

Harari, Josué. *Scenarios of the Imaginary: Theorizing the French Enlightenment.* 1987.

Hertzberg, Arthur. *The French Enlightenment and the Jews.* 1968.

Hildesheimer, Wolfgang. *Mozart.* 1982.

Hont, Istvan, and Michael Ignatieff, eds. *Wealth and Virtue: The Shaping of Political Economy in the Scottish Enlightenment.* 1984.

Jacob, James R. *Henry Stubbe, Radical Protestantism and the Early Enlightenment.* 1983.

Jacob, Margaret, and James R. Jacob, eds. *The Origins of Anglo-American Radicalism.* 1984.

Joyce, William L. et al., eds. *Printing and Society in Early America.* 1983.

Kernan, Alvin. *Printing Technology, Letters, and Samuel Johnson.* 1987.

Kors, Alan Charles. *D'Holbach's Coterie: An Enlightenment in Paris.* 1976.

Koselleck, Reinhard. *Critique and Crisis: Enlightenment and the Parthogenesis of Modern Society.* 1988.

Kramnick, Isaac. *The Rage of Edmund Burke: Portrait of an Ambivalent Conservative.* 1977.

Levine, Joseph M. *Dr. Woodward's Shield: History, Science, and Satire in Augustan England.* 1977.

Maestro, Marcello. *Cesare Beccaria and the Origins of Penal Reform.* 1973.

Marker, Gary. *Publishing, Printing, and the Origins of Intellectual Life in Russia, 1700–1800.* 1985.

Marshall, P. J., and Glyndwr Williams. *The Great Map of Mankind: Perceptions of New Worlds in the Age of Enlightenment.* 1982.

McClellan III, James E. *Science Reorganized: Scientific Societies in the Eighteenth Century.* 1985.

McClelland, Charles. *State, Society, and University in Germany: 1700–1914.* 1980.

McManners, John. *Death and the Enlightenment: Changing Attitudes to Death Among Christians and Unbelievers in Eighteenth-Century France.* 1981.

Miller, James. *Rousseau: Dreamer of Democracy.* 1984.

Paulson, Ronald. *Hogarth: His Life, Times, and Art.* 1974.

Payne, Harry C. *The Philosophes and the People.* 1976.

Pocock, J. G. A. *Virtue, Commerce, and History: Essays on Political Thought and History, Chiefly in the Eighteenth Century.* 1985.

Popkin, Jeremy D. *News and Politics in the Age of Revolution: Jean Luzac's "Gazette de Leyde."* 1989.

Porter, Roy. *Gibbon: Making History.* 1988.

———. *Mind Forg'd Manacles: A History of Madness in England from the Restoration to the Regency.* 1987.

———, and Dorothy Porter. *Doctors and Doctoring in Eighteenth-Century England.* 1989.

———, and G. S. Rousseau, eds. *Exoticism in the Enlightenment.* 1989.

———, and Mikulás Teich, eds. *The Enlightenment in National Context.* 1981.

Reill, Peter H. *The German Enlightenment and the Rise of Historicism.* 1975.

Richter, Melvin. *The Political Theory of Montesquieu.* 1977.

Rivers, Isabel, ed. *Books and Their Readers in Eighteenth-Century England.* 1982.

Root-Bernstein, Michele. *Boulevard Theater and Revolution in Eighteenth-Century Paris.* 1984.

Rosen, Charles. *The Classical Style: Haydn, Mozart, Beethoven.* 1971.

Schwartz, Joel. *The Sexual Politics of Jean-Jacques Rousseau.* 1984.
Sher, Richard B. *Church and University in the Scottish Enlightenment: The Modern Literati of Edinburgh.* 1985.
―――, and Jeffrey R. Smitten, eds. *Scotland and America in the Age of Enlightenment.* 1990.
Shklar, Judith N. *Montesquieu.* 1987.
Spanafora, David. *The Idea of Progress in Eighteenth-Century Britain.* 1990.
Starobinski, Jean. *Jean-Jacques Rousseau: Transparency and Obstruction.* 1988.
―――. *1789: The Emblems of Reason.* 1982.
Teichgraeber III, Richard F. *"Free Trade" and Moral Philosophy: Rethinking the Sources of Adam Smith's "Wealth of Nations."* 1986.
Venturi, Franco. *Italy and the Enlightenment: Studies in a Cosmopolitan Century.* 1972.
Verene, Donald Phillip. *Vico's Science of Imagination.* 1981.
Wade, Ira O. *The Intellectual Origins of the French Enlightenment.* 1971.
―――. *The Structure and Form of the French Enlightenment.* 1977.
Walker, Mack. *Johann Jacob Moser and the Holy Roman Empire of the German Nation.* 1981.
Ward, A. *Book Production, Fiction, and the German Reading Public, 1740–1790.* 1974.
Wilson, Arthur. *Diderot.* 1972.
Wuthnow, Robert. *Communities of Discourse: Ideology and Social Structure in the Reformation, the Enlightenment, and European Socialism.* 1989.

CHAPTER 9

Anderson, M. S. *Historians and Eighteenth-Century Europe, 1715–1789.* 1979.
Behrens, C. B. A. *Society, Government, and the Enlightenment: The Experiences of Eighteenth-Century France and Prussia.* 1985.
Black, Jeremy, ed. *Britain in the Age of Walpole.* 1985.
―――. *British Foreign Policy in the Age of Walpole.* 1985.
―――. *Natural and Necessary Enemies: Anglo-French Relations in the Eighteenth Century.* 1986.
Bosher, J. F. *The Canada Merchants, 1713–1763.* 1987.
Brewer, John. *The Sinews of Power: War, Money, and the English State, 1688–1783.* 1989.
Campbell, Peter. *The Ancien Régime in France.* 1989.
Carey, John A. *Judicial Reform in France Before the Revolution of 1789.* 1981.
Clark, J. C. D. *The Dynamics of Change: The Crisis of the 1750s and English Party Systems.* 1982.
Dickinson, H. T. *Liberty and Property: Political Ideology in Eighteenth-Century Britain.* 1978.
Doyle, William. *The Ancien Régime.* 1986.
Duffy, Christopher. *The Army of Maria Theresa: The Armed Forces of Imperial Austria, 1740–1780.* 1977.
―――. *Frederick the Great: A Military Life.* 1988.
Ekirch, A. Roger. *Bound for America: The Transportation of British Convicts to the Colonies, 1718–1775.* 1987.

Ellis, Harold A. *Boulainvilliers and the French Monarchy: Aristocratic Politics in Early Eighteenth-Century France.* 1988.

Göçek, Fatma Müge. *East Encounters West: France and the Ottoman Empire in the Eighteenth Century.* 1987.

Gross, Hans. *Rome in the Age of Enlightenment.* 1990.

Hargreaves-Mawdsley, W. N. *Eighteenth-Century Spain, 1700–1788: A Political, Diplomatic, and Institutional History.* 1979.

Hatton, Ragnhild. *George I: Elector and King.* 1978.

Holmes, Geoffrey. *Augustan England: Professions, State, and Society.* 1982.

Johnson, D. et al., eds. *Britain and France.* 1980.

Klang, Daniel. *Tax Reform in Eighteenth-Century Lombardy.* 1977.

Kreiser, B. Robert. *Miracles, Convulsions, and Ecclesiastical Politics in Early Eighteenth-Century Paris.* 1978.

Langford, P. *A Polite and Commercial People: England, 1727–1783.* 1989.

Lenman, B. *Integration, Enlightenment, and Industrialization: Scotland, 1746–1832.* 1981.

Lieberman, David. *The Province of Legislation Determined: Legal Theory in Eighteenth-Century Britain.* 1989.

Lindsay, J. O., ed. *The Old Regime, 1713–1763.* Vol. 7 of *The New Cambridge Modern History.* 1963.

Liss, Peggy K. *Atlantic Empires: The Network of Trade and Revolution, 1713–1826.* 1983.

Lynch, John. *Bourbon Spain, 1700–1808.* 1990.

Marshall, P. J. *India and Indonesia During the Ancien Régime: Essays.* 1989.

Meehan-Waters, Brenda. *Autocracy and Aristocracy: The Russian Service Elite of 1730.* 1982.

Mendelsohn, Ezra, and Marshall S. Shatz. *Imperial Russia, 1700–1917: State, Society, Opposition.* 1988.

Merrick, Jeffrey. *The Desacralization of the French Monarchy in the Eighteenth Century.* 1990.

Newman, Gerald. *The Rise of English Nationalism: A Cultural History, 1740–1830.* 1987.

Owen, John B. *The Eighteenth Century, 1714–1815.* 1975.

Parry, J. H. *Trade and Dominion: The European Overseas Empires in the Eighteenth Century.* 1971.

Pritchard, James. *Louis XV's Navy.* 1987.

Riley, James C. *The Seven Years' War and the Old Regime in France: The Economic and Financial Toll.* 1986.

Roberts, Michael. *British Diplomacy and Swedish Politics, 1758–1773.* 1980.

Roider, Karl A. *Austria's Eastern Frontier, 1700–1790.* 1982.

Shennan, J. H. *Liberty and Order in Early Modern Europe: The Subject and the State.* 1986.

———. *Philippe, Duke of Orléans: Regent of France, 1715–1723.* London, 1979.

Speck, W. A. *The Butcher: The Duke of Cumberland and the Suppression of the Forty-Five.* 1981.

———. *Stability and Strife: England, 1714–1760.* 1977.

Stein, Robert Louis. *The French Sugar Business in the Eighteenth Century.* 1988.

Stroup, John. *The Struggle for Identity in the Clerical Estate: Northwest German Protestant Opposition to Absolutist Policy in the Eighteenth Century.* 1984.

Sutton, John L. *The King's Honor and the King's Cardinal: The War of the Polish Succession*. 1980.

Thomson, Ann. *Barbary and Enlightenment: European Attitudes Towards the Maghreb in the Eighteenth Century*. 1987.

Van Kley, Dale K. *The Damiens Affair and the Unraveling of the Ancien Régime, 1750–1770*. 1984.

Venturi, Franco. *Settecento riformatore*. 4 vols. 1969–1984.

Walker, Geoffrey J. *Spanish Politics and Imperial Trade, 1700–1789*. 1979.

Woolf, S. J. *A History of Italy, 1700–1860: The Social Constraints of Political Change*. 1979.

CHAPTER 10

Alexander, John T. *Catherine the Great: Life and Legend*. 1989.

Baker, Keith Michael, ed. *The French Revolution and the Creation of Modern Political Culture*. Vol. 1, *The Political Culture of the Old Regime*. 1987.

———. *Inventing the French Revolution: Essays on French Political Culture in the Eighteenth Century*. 1990.

Barbier, Jacques A., and Allan K. Kuethe, eds. *The North American Role in the Spanish Imperial Economy, 1760–1819*. 1984.

Barton, H. Arnold. *Scandinavia in the Revolutionary Era*. 1986.

Beales, Derek. *Joseph II*. Vol. 1, *In the Shadow of Maria Theresa*. 1987.

Blanning, T. C. W. *Joseph II and Enlightened Despotism*. 1970.

Bonwick, Colin. *English Radicals and the American Revolution*. 1977.

Bradley, James E. *Popular Politics and the American Revolution in England: Petitions, the Crown, and Public Opinion*. 1986.

Christie, Ian. *Wars and Revolutions: Britain, 1760–1815*. 1982.

Doyle, William. *The Origins of the French Revolution*, 2nd ed. 1988.

Dull, Jonathan. *The French Navy and American Independence*. 1975.

Echeverria, Durand. *The Maupeou Revolution: A Study in the History of Libertarianism in France, 1770–1774*. 1985.

Egret, Jean. *The French Pre-Revolution, 1787–1788*. 1977.

Ehrman, John. *The Younger Pitt*. 2 vols. 1969, 1983.

Gagliardo, John G. *Reich and Nation: The Holy Roman Empire as Idea and Reality, 1763–1806*. 1980.

Goodwin, A., ed. *The American and French Revolutions, 1763–1793*. Vol. 8 of *The New Cambridge Modern History*. 1965.

Harris, Robert D. *Necker, Reform Statesman of the Ancien Régime*. 1979.

———. *Necker and the Revolution of 1789*. 1986.

Herr, Richard. *Rural Change and Royal Finances in Spain at the End of the Old Regime*. 1987.

Hill, Peter P. *French Perceptions of the Early American Republic*. 1988.

Hubatsch, Walther. *Frederick the Great of Prussia: Absolutism and Administration*. 1975.

Hull, Anthony H. *Charles III and the Revival of Spain*. 1981.

Hunt, Lynn Avery. *Revolution and Urban Politics in Provincial France: Troyes and Reims, 1786–1790*. 1978.

Ingrao, Charles W. *The Hessian Mercenary State: Ideas, Institutions, and Reform Under Frederick II, 1760–1785.* 1987.

Jones, Robert E. *The Emancipation of the Russian Nobility.* 1973.

————. *Provincial Development in Russia: Catherine II and Jacob Sievers.* 1984.

LeDonne, John P. *Ruling Russia: Politics and Administration in the Age of Absolutism, 1762–1796.* 1984.

Levy, Darline Gay. *The Ideas and Careers of Simon-Nicolas-Henri Linguet: A Study in Eighteenth-Century French Politics.* 1980.

Mandariaga, Isabel de. *Russia in the Age of Catherine the Great.* 1981.

Melton, James Van Horn. *Absolutism and the Eighteenth-Century Origins of Compulsory Schooling in Prussia and Austria.* 1988.

Morgan, Edmund S. *Inventing the People: The Rise of Popular Sovereignty in England and America.* 1988.

Murphy, Orville T. *Charles Gravier, Comte de Vergennes: French Diplomacy in the Age of Revolution, 1719–1787.* 1982.

Palmer, Robert R. *The Age of the Democratic Revolutions: A Political History of Europe and America, 1760–1800.* 2 vols. 1959, 1964.

Parker, Harold T. *The Bureau of Commerce in 1781 and Its Policies with Respect to French Industry.* 1979.

Sainsbury, John. *Disaffected Patriots: London Supporters of Revolutionary America, 1769–1782.* 1987.

Schama, Simon. *Patriots and Liberators: Revolution in the Netherlands, 1780–1813.* 1977.

Scott, H. M., ed. *Enlightened Absolutism: Reform and Reformers in Later Eighteenth-Century Europe.* 1990.

Sutherland, Donald. *The Chouans: The Social Origins of Popular Counter-Revolution in Upper Brittany, 1770–1796.* 1982.

Stone, Bailey F. *The French Parlements and the Crisis of the Old Regime.* 1986.

————. *The Parlement of Paris, 1774–1789.* 1981.

Stone, Daniel. *Polish Politics and National Reform, 1775–1788.* 1976.

Tracy, Nicholas. *Navies, Deterrence, and American Independence: Britain and Seapower in the 1760s and 1770s.* 1988.

Tucker, Robert W., and D. C. Hendrickson. *The Fall of the First British Empire: Origins of the War of American Independence.* 1982.

Venturi, Franco. *The End of the Old Regime in Europe.* 2 vols. 1990.

Vovelle, Michel. *The Fall of the French Monarchy, 1787–1792.* 1984.

INDEX